Violence, Inequality, and Human Freedom

Violence, Inequality, and Human Freedom

Second Edition

Peter Iadicola and Anson Shupe

ROWMAN & LITTLEFIELD PUBLISHERS, INC.
Lanham • Boulder • New York • Toronto • Oxford

Dedicated to Petrea, Kirstin, Joey, Oliver, Abigail, and Andrew. May they grow up and live in a world with greater peace and freedom.

ROWMAN & LITTLEFIELD PUBLISHERS, INC.

Published in the United States of America
by Rowman & Littlefield Publishers, Inc.
4501 Forbes Boulevard, Suite 200, Lanham, Maryland 20706
www.rowmanlittlefield.com

PO Box 317, Oxford OX2 9RU, United Kingdom

British Library Cataloguing in Publication Information Available

Library of Congress Cataloging-in-Publication Data

Iadicola, Peter.
  Violence, inequality, and human freedom / Peter Iadicola and Anson Shupe.— 2nd ed.
    p. cm.
  Includes bibliographical references and index.
  ISBN 0-7425-1923-6 (cloth : alk. paper) — ISBN 0-7425-1924-4 (pbk. : alk. paper)
  1. Violence. 2. Civil rights. I. Shupe, Anson D. II. Title.
  HM886 .I18 2003
  303.6—dc21

                                                        2002151629

Printed in the United States of America

∞™ The paper used in this publication meets the minimum requirements of American National Standard for Information Sciences—Permanence of Paper for Printed Library Materials, ANSI/NISO Z39.48-1992.

Contents

Preface   vii

1   The Domain of Violence   1

2   The Cultural Roots of Violence   48

3   Interpersonal Violence: Murder and Rape   98

4   Family Violence   148

5   Religious Violence   174

6   Economic Violence   206

7   State Violence   260

8   Structural Violence   315

9   Conclusion: Violence, Inequality, and Human Freedom   371

Index   393

About the Authors   405

Preface

Since writing the first edition of this book, the levels of violence in wars, terrorist attacks, and the general deprivation of peoples throughout the Southern Hemisphere of the world has increased. On September 11, 2001, we all watched in horror as a commercial aircraft commandeered by terrorists crashed into the World Trade Center, killing thousands of people. After the initial shock, for a brief moment there began a discussion as to why this happened. How could people be willing to kill themselves to kill others? This was the first attack on the United States since World War II and it was from an enemy of whose identity we were uncertain. Unfortunately, questions of why were soon dismissed and replaced with a sense of righteous indignation and calls for revenge. Those who began to ask questions about why this happened were viewed with suspicion and were often targeted for public attack. The American public never was able to have a conversation as to how people could be so desperate to attack us that they would intentionally kill themselves in the process. In Israel, similar events are occurring on a weekly basis. A young Palestinian girl blows herself up in a marketplace in the hope of killing Israeli citizens. We learn of slaughters of hundreds of thousands of people in Rwanda and East Timor and there is little discussion as to why this could have occurred. And the remedy that we choose to stem this violence is more violence, which leads to an escalation of violence around the world. Every day in our newspapers, on our evening news broadcasts on radio and television, that story of violence is told. But the story is incomplete. We only hear of the violence occurring, but we are offered little analysis as to why. Instead, we hear simplistic explanations that only a child would appreciate. The president of the United States talks of evil people and evil in the world. We are told to pray to God for his help in defeating this evil and our chosen weapon is more violence. Now, more than any other time in our history, we need to ask the question why, and we need to go beyond the simplistic childish responses of bad people and evil in the world. We need to look at how we have structured human existence throughout the world and how this has resulted in such horror as killing the most innocent among us, our children.

In our studies of violence in the past, it has become compartmentalized and fragmented. The vast majority of research focuses on the interpersonal violence of criminals. In general, only a small category of violence is studied. However, what we learned in our own study of violence is that violence is pervasive in human existence. The scope of the phenomenon goes way beyond the criminal violence that the mass media and public officials have focused on. It exists in virtually every institutional setting and has been a feature of all societies throughout human existence. The first goal that we had as authors was to tell a more complete story of violence, to educate the reader to the many different forms of violence that lead to the death or injury of millions of people in a given year.

This book tells the story of the violence that harms people throughout the world. It tells the story of the violence that most people think of when they hear the words murder and rape. But it also tells the story of the forms of violence that most people do not think of when they hear the word violence. In these categories of violence, we discuss the violence that is the product of institutional actions (family, economy, state, and religious organizations) and violence that is the product of the very organization of societies (structural violence). Most writings about violence focus on interpersonal violence. This book is unique because the focus is principally on those other more devastating forms of violence. This book examines a greater range of violence from the interpersonal to institutional to structural forms.

Another story that this book tells is how the forms of violence are linked together. We have learned in the course of our study that there is an important linkage between the many different forms of violence that occur throughout a society and the world. Although we can think of a form of violence in isolation, in reality the forms of violence that exist in the society and the world are linked together. We discuss the idea of a chain of violence that links the interpersonal forms of violence with the institutional and structural violence. The more we understand the nature of this linkage, the greater our ability becomes to address the problem of violence.

The book also tells the story of how violence is related to inequality. At the most fundamental level, what allows us to violate another is our ability to define those others as separate and less than ourselves. The structures that we have created and act to maintain and extend create this ability and teach it to the next generation. The story of violence is a story of inequality. We have learned that inequality is both a cause and an outcome of violence. How we respond to the structures of inequality in the society and world will determine the nature of violence within these systems.

Last, this book tells the story of how violence is related to freedom—a value that we in the United States celebrate and in our public messages to the world promote. However, freedom is linked to violence. We discuss how violence is fundamentally about control and the control over freedom of action. Violence is ultimately a form of power that at the same time extends and denies freedom to the actors involved. The more violence that occurs in the world, the less freedom exists for us all.

We view this book as an introduction to the subject of violence. It is not intended to be a theoretical treatise on the topic. Instead, our goals are more modest. It is to provide the reader with a new way of looking at the phenomenon and to gain an appreciation for the scope and complexity of the topic. The book is written to begin a conversation about why violence in its many forms occurs, a conversation beyond the psychology or presumed evil of those who commit such acts. This book is rooted in the sociological disciplinary perspective. For those who are not familiar with this perspective, we hope that the introductory chapter will provide the reader with the necessary disciplinary lens to gain a better understanding of the phenomenon of violence.

Several people have provided us with resources and insight into the subject of violence and have contributed their labor for the completion of this project. Many of them are cited throughout the text. However, there are those who are not and yet who provided us with valuable critiques, insights, and encouragement. Specifically, we thank Larry Tift, Harold Pepinsky, Alan Sandstrom, and Lawrence Kuznar for their theoretical and substantive critiques and sources. Laura Nagy and Irene Glynn provided suggestions for clarifying points and improving the style of presentation. None of those mentioned, of course, is responsible for what we have thought out and written, but they are to be credited for having improved the book beyond what it would have been without their contributions.

Chapter One

The Domain of Violence

White youths shoot an African American teenager who accidentally ventures into the "wrong" neighborhood of New York City.

A mob of teenagers go "wilding" in Central Park and gang rapes a female jogger, punching and kicking her even as she is repeatedly violated.

In Jasper, Texas, three white men chained a black man to the back of a pickup truck and dragged him until the body was torn apart.

Islamic terrorists kidnap a Marine officer serving on a U.N. peacekeeping force in Lebanon, then execute him by hanging and send the whole grotesque episode into America's living rooms via videotapes provided to the nightly news.

It is learned that industrial factories that produce radioactive elements for nuclear weapons have been systematically and knowingly polluting their surrounding communities for years, with no one punished.

Unarmed Chinese university students are ruthlessly gunned down by government troops in Tiananmen Square because they dare to demonstrate for democracy.

A coordinated attack by terrorists from a Middle Eastern terrorist group sends four planeloads of passengers to their fiery deaths. Two of the planes crash into the World Trade Center in New York City killing almost 3,000 people, another crashes into a section of the Pentagon killing another 288 people.

Violence against individuals, against minorities, against nations, against even our home planet is the overarching problem of our age. It is no exaggeration to say that every conceivable social problem interfaces with this destructive phenomenon. Violence's myriad forms consume the attention of news media reports and cost us dearly as citizens as we try to cope with or prevent their destructive effects. Many other social problems—drug addiction, the breakup of the American family, deteriorating city schools, corporate corruption, terrorism, religious intolerance—are interwoven with violence. Violence is not simply linked to such obvious controversies as building larger prisons, tightening criminal sentences, or passing gun control laws. It is also linked to problems of famine, pollution, and overpopulation. Moreover, the advanced technology of nuclear destruction in the hands of increasing numbers of countries has made it a fundamental element of twentieth-century social, cultural, political, and economic life, and an inevitable element of twenty-first-century reality.

The various behavioral sciences, from anthropology and psychology to economics and political science, have developed theories about the causes of destructive actions. Considerable research has accumulated, especially during the past thirty years. Most importantly, a rich scholarly legacy of testing and refining concepts has made it abundantly clear that the sum of violence in any society must be understood as multiply determined. No single viewpoint, no solitary theoretical "slant," will suffice.

For example, psychology is better able to address questions about imitation and the learning of actions, innate drives, and personality as these relate to interpersonal violence than about the economic, social, political, and historical circumstances most conducive to political revolution. Anthropology tempers our Western understandings of violence with analyses of the roles and function violence and conflict play in cross-cultural settings. Political science casts violence in the rational, decision-making mold of being a conscious policy alternative used by statespersons, instead of simply serving as a physiological release of frustration, anger, or sadism.

Ball-Rokeach (1980) notes that because "the phenomenon of violence cuts across many disciplines and fields of inquiry, it tends toward a fragmented inquiry into this or that form of violence." There is a need for a more unitary approach, discussing violence as a phenomenon in and of itself. The sociological perspective, which we believe permits the most comprehensive understanding of violence, is the likely place for such a unitary approach to develop.

Sociology examines the phenomenon as a pattern of behavior that emanates fundamentally from the very organization of society. For sociologists, the pattern of violence in a given society is unique to that social system. It emanates from structural and institutional sources that are suprapersonal but, to most persons, are manifest at the interpersonal level. Nevertheless, sociologists seek to discuss the common features of societies that produce a particular pattern of violence. Sociology takes the most general perspective in trying to uncover the social forces that produce violence.

There are several reasons why the sociological perspective lends itself to the development of this unitary approach. First, sociology facilitates the viewing of action from the position of an outsider or an objective position by providing us with a lens to see *what is strange in what is familiar to us*. All of our behavior can be viewed as unusual or strange when taken out of the cultural context in which we are immersed. The foods we eat, the dwellings we reside in, and the style of fashion—all can be seen as unusual. What we define and consider to be violent or nonviolent also can be seen as strange. In fact, what is violent may often not be defined as violence by those socialized to accept it as natural or justifiable. For example, the spanking, slapping, or even belt lashing of children by their parents when they are deemed to be unruly is not viewed as violent unless it exceeds some established norm. Yet, in Sweden the spanking of children is an act of violence and is criminal. In many societies, and in our own in a not-so-distant past, husbands striking their wives was not considered violence. During the 1950s and 1960s, the beating of one's wife was the subject of jokes or situation comedies as in the case of *The Honeymooners*, a comedy produced during the 1950s. At moments of comedic frustration, Ralph Kramden would physically threaten his wife Alice. Shaking his fist he would say, "Oh Alice someday," and then he would wave his arms to simulate how Alice would fly through the air, bouncing off walls—"bing, bong, zing." The audience laughter was heard at this moment signaling to the viewers at home to see the humor in this. Yet in colonial America, wife beating brought severe corporal punishment by the community on the abusing male. Today, courts and the police are compelled by social pressure to treat spousal abuse as a serious case of assault that requires criminal justice intervention. Yet in other parts of the world wife beating is seen quite differently. Harris notes that among the Yanomamo, no "woman escapes the brutal tutelage of the typical hot-tempered, drug-taking Yanomamo warrior-husband. All Yanomamo men physically abuse their wives. Kind husbands merely bruise and mutilate them; the fierce ones wound and kill" (Harris, 1974, 74).

The denial of medical care to those in need because of their economic status is not considered violent. Infant mortality rates for African American infants that are twice that of white infants are not considered violent. Neither is paddling children in school for their misbehavior, nor the dumping of industrial waste into the nation's waterways. Often we do not even think of capital punishment as violent. Yet from another perspective, all these acts can be considered forms of violence. Sociology helps one to view the "social reality" from the position of a stranger, inviting the viewer to step back and "out" of the social situation so that what was first viewed as nonviolent and even commonplace comes to be viewed in a different light.

Alternately, not only does sociology allow us to view the world from the vantage point of a stranger but it also helps the viewer to be cognizant of the different positions that the actors occupy in the violence. It furthermore allows one to assume the subjective positions of the actors themselves in order to understand the social reality from the position of the victims and perpetrators of violence in the performance of roles in the violent interaction. How is an act of violence defined differently because of the different statuses and roles of the actors participating in the interaction? How is the form of violence understood by the actors involved? What social processes and contexts allow actors to see some forms of violence and not others, or to judge violence differently as a result of the different roles they are performing in the violent interaction? How is the role of victim and offender defined in each form of violence?

If one individual were struck by another as a result of an altercation, we would define this as an assault. If the perpetrator were a mugger using violence as a way to get money from an elderly woman, this would be clearly understood. The victim and perpetrator would experience the violence as violence. In contrast, if the perpetrator was an adult women, a mother, and the victim was a small child, her son, we would think of the violence another way, and the victim and perpetrator would experience the violence differently. Or say that the perpetrator was a police officer and was using violence to apprehend a suspect who was resisting arrest. What about the case of a soldier assaulting a soldier of an opposing army during the time of war: do we consider this violence? Again, the objective violent act of striking another is the same; however, in viewing the subjective phenomenon from the vantage point of the different actors, we understand the violence differently.

A second characteristic of this unique disciplinary perspective is that sociology searches through various instances of action for patterns. In short, sociology looks for the *general in the particular.* What are the patterns of violence in our society? Who is more likely to participate in violence? What kinds of people are more likely to be offenders or victims of a particular form of violence? Under what social circumstances or contexts are people more likely to be violent or to be victimized by violence?

Although we hear about the random act of violence, this is a rarity. Violence is patterned. Some people are more likely to be victims of violence than others because of social, temporal, and geographic positioning. Today the leading cause of death among African Americans aged fifteen to thirty-four is homicide. Blacks were six times more likely than whites to be murdered in 1999 (Fox and Zawitz, 2001). Almost half of homicide victims are African American. The National Center for Health Statistics found that in 1994 the risk of victimization for violent crime in general was almost four times greater for individuals whose family income was under $7,500 compared to those whose family income was $50,000 and over (National Center for Health Statistics, 1997). According to the Uniform Crime Reports in 1999, 63 percent of persons murdered were under age thirty-five, and about 12 percent were under age eighteen. Last, more than three-quarters of the victims of violence are men. Thus, violence is hardly random. It is patterned. The more we know about the patterns of violence, the greater insight we have as to the causes.

Sociology also looks for the interrelationship among the patterns. How may one pattern of violence be related to another? Are the patterns of violence noted above related? Is the violence within the minority population related to income? Are there relationships between types of violence? For example, are the patterns of violence between parents and children at all related to the patterns of violence between husbands and wives? Does the violence that children experience today with their parents prepare them to be violent with their own children in the future? Does it prepare them to be violent with their spouse? At a more macro level, are the patterns of violence we see between nations related to the patterns of violence experienced within nations? In short, how are patterns of violence related within a society and between societies? Sociology as a discipline directs us to look for the relationship between the patterns of violence.

Last, sociology facilitates our understanding of individual behavior as it is the product of the way society is organized and functions. In the language of sociology the discipline *depersonalizes the personal*. Sociology helps us see how our individual behavior is the product of the nature of the society. This does not mean that social forces are deterministic. As individuals, we choose our behavior, yet social forces limit the range of choices available to us and influence us to choose one option over another. Every day we make individual decisions as to which actions to choose. We decide what time to wake, what and when to eat, whether and how to clothe ourselves, and what to do once we have awakened, eaten, and dressed. Nevertheless, there are forces that make us choose to get up at a certain time, to eat one food as opposed to another, to wear a particular article of clothing, and so forth. Some of these forces are a product of cultural expectations as they define diet and style of dress; others are a result of the statuses we occupy and the role expectations that stem from these positions. These are some of the social forces that limit the range of choices of our action and direct us to choose from a more limited range of alternatives that we may have available to us. In all our actions, including violence, these are seen as personal decisions, but what choices we have available to us and what choices we are likely to choose are products of the social forces that compose the society.

Sociology asks, How are the patterns of violence that exist in our society the product of the social forces rooted in how our society is organized? How is the pattern of violence in a society related to how families, schools, the economy, the religious and political systems, and the like are organized and function? How is it that the way the family, school, the economy, and the religious and political systems are organized and function to limit the range of choices of people and direct some to choose acts of violence as opposed to other routes to accomplish their goals? Moreover, not only is the pattern of violence in a society a product of how that society is organized, but also the people's cultural understandings of violence is the product of the nature of that society's system of shared meanings and knowledge. Culture provides a lens in which we define or not define acts as violent. In short, sociology facilitates our understanding of violence as a societal phenomenon with particular attention to how violence is linked at all levels within the society, and how it is fundamentally a product of how society is organized and functions. Furthermore, sociology teaches us that how we understand violence is conditioned by the forces of the society of which we are products.

In addition to the general sociological perspective, the basic assumptions that underlie the disciplinary viewpoint facilitate the conceptualization of violence as a unitary phenomenon. For example, sociologists assume that *individuals are by*

their nature social beings. Children enter the world totally dependent on others
for their survival. They have a longer period of dependency than any other animal. Our need for an association with a "group" is an essential element of human
nature. Human beings can survive only in social groups of one kind or another.
The importance of group affiliation is most clearly evident in primitive societies,
where the most severe punishment was banishment from the group.

A second disciplinary assumption is that *individuals are, for the most part, so-*
cially determined. During infancy, the child is at the mercy of adults, especially
parents. These persons shape the infant in an infinite variety of ways, depending
on their proclivities and those of their society. Parents will have a profound impact on the child's way of thinking about him or herself and about others. Parents will transmit religious views, political attitudes, and attitudes toward other
groups. Most significantly, parents act as cultural agents, transferring the ways of
the society to their children. These processes continue beyond the primary group
level to all the groups of which we are a part. Thus, how we define ourselves and
the world we are part of are products of the society in which we are members.

According to sociologists, we are the products of the groups of which we are
members. The groups we are members of provide the most fundamental social
forces that direct our behavior. Whether we are talking about the family, the
nation-state or country, the ethnic group, or a school class, they all provide the
social forces in constraining our actions. It makes little sense to conceive of us
apart from such group affiliations. For example, today many babies born in
poorer countries to parents of little means are taken from birth and adopted by
parents of higher status in wealthier countries. Babies born to poor parents in
Guatemala, Romania, Bolivia, or the Philippines and then adopted by people
in upper-class positions in advanced capitalist countries experience a dramatic
change in who they are and who they are likely to become. This affects not only
what language they will speak but also how long they are likely to live, how
healthy they will be in their lives, how they are likely to live in terms of quality
of life, how they will be educated, what occupation they will choose, who they
will marry, how large their family will be, and so on. Who they are and what
they think of themselves change because of the change in the social groups of
which they are a part. In this way, we are socially determined.

A third disciplinary assumption is that *individuals create, sustain, and*
change the social structures within which they conduct their lives. Social
groups of all sizes and types are human creations. The social world that we
are immersed in is a human creation. All the structures, beliefs, norms, and institutions we are a part of are a social creation, a creation of the groups we are
participating in or that were participated in by previous generations of members of the society. We are born into a society that is a product of the social
creation efforts of previous generations. The social world we are born in becomes the context in which we interact with others. As we interact in the context of groups within the society, we act on structures that frame our social
interaction. We act to change, sustain, and create new structures, beliefs,
norms, institutions, and the like that then set the social context for interaction

for ourselves and other new members of the society. This is a continuous on-going phenomenon of creating, maintaining, and changing the social structures in which we live our lives. Thus, as social beings, we are products of the society we are born in, and we are the principal force in changing those structures that define the initial social context of our existence.

It is important to qualify this last statement by noting that we all do not have the same power or ability to create, maintain, and change the social structures within the society. One's position via systems of stratification provides us with differences in the amount of power we have to create, maintain, and change social structures. Nevertheless, it is important for the reader to recognize that the social reality that they experience is human made.

The significance of these assumptions as they relate to the issue of violence is that, first, violence is a problem because it fundamentally weakens the social web that is the basis of human life. Violence that reaches a critical level threatens the interconnectedness of people that is necessary for human survival. Second, violence in a society is ultimately a product of social organization. All social or antisocial behaviors can ultimately be understood only as products of the nature of the society. Thus, we may discuss acts of interpersonal violence that appear on the surface to be a clear expression of individual behavior, but this level views a phenomenon out of its societal context. Sociology provides the viewer with this context. Last, since the social world is a human creation, so are the patterns of violence that permeate it. Thus, as humans act to create, sustain, and change the social world, they also create, maintain, and change the patterns of violence within it.

ORDER AND CONFLICT APPROACHES WITHIN SOCIOLOGY

It is important to recognize two orientations within the field that provide differences in emphasis in viewing social reality in general and violence in particular. The order and conflict approaches are these two paradigmatic approaches. Each approach establishes a framework for us to view a phenomenon, and in many ways their implications for addressing violence problems are radically different.

Table 1.1 presents a comparison of these two approaches to the study of society. The order approach views the society as normally stable. All members of the society have, relatively speaking, the same values, interests, and cultural orientation. The primary social process in the society is cooperation. All individuals are performing roles within the formal institutions contributing to the ongoing maintenance of the social order. The organismic analogy best describes how the order approach defines how a society functions. It refers to the idea of viewing the social system in the same way one views a biological system. For example, the human body is made up of organs. Each organ carries out a specific physiological function. The heart functions as a pump to move or circulate the blood throughout the system. The lungs function to transfer gases, removing carbon dioxide from the blood and replacing it with oxygen. Processes link the organs to one another; respiratory processes, digestive processes, circulatory processes, and so forth. When all organs are appropriately carrying out their function, working in coordination with one another, linked via processes, we say that the organism is in a state of health.

Table 1.1.   Order and Conflict Approaches to the Study of Society

	Order	Conflict
Conception of the Social Order	Homogeneity, stability and in balance. Organismic analogy is applied. Primary social process is cooperation.	Heterogeneity, instability, and imbalance. Primary social process is conflict/competition.
Foundation of Social Systems	Cultural system/knowledge system (idealism). Cultural values/ideals/traditions are the foundation of the order.	Structural divisions rooted in system of material and human reproduction; class, and gender systems (materialism) are the foundation of the order.
Position of Divisions	Natural, necessary, and functional to the social system.	Product of historical development. Dynamic foundation of the social order. Ultimately maintained by means of oppression and social control.
Position of Institutions	Structural reflections of cultural/knowledge systems. Stress on linkages and functional efficiency. Also stress on their integrative/boundary maintaining function.	Mechanisms to maintain and reproduce the order, including the structural divisions that are its foundation. Institutions seen as mechanisms of coercion or social control.
Origins/Method of Change	Evolutionary/natural progression. Originates from the top down to the masses. It is a product of innovation of the elites (intellectual, political, economic, etc.).	Product of conflict between the divisions within the order that develops because of the clash of forces of (re)production with relations of (re)production. Change comes from the bottom up, product of social movements.
Political Orientation	Conservative/liberal (within the ideological parameters of the system).	Radical (outside of ideological parameters of the system).
Central Questions	What is the nature of the social bond? What holds society together? How is stability and development maintained?	What conditions provoke the conflicts between the structural divisions? What conditions promote structural position consciousness?

The society is composed of institutions that are analogous to organs. Each institution carries out a specific social function. The education institution functions to enculturate and provides the skills necessary for neophytes to assume statuses or positions within social institutions. The economic institution functions to distribute the scarce resources in the society in order to reproduce the population. As in the case of organs, institutions are linked via processes (i.e., socialization processes, exchange processes, governing processes, etc.). As with the organism, when all the organs are working appropriately and in coordination, the society is normatively in a state of balance. All parts of the system are carrying out their designed function, linked via processes, all working to the maintenance or reproduction of the whole.

To continue our description of the order approach, the foundation of the society is the cultural system, the system of ideas, beliefs, knowledge, attitudes that unify the population. The divisions that exist in the society along class, race, and gender lines are viewed as either basically natural to people in the society and/or necessary or functional to the nature of the society (Parsons et al., 1955; Jensen, 1969; Hernstein, 1973; Davis and Moore, 1945).

For the order approach, the functioning and organization of institutions are manifestations of the cultural system. For example, the structure and the processes within education systems in this country emphasize individual achievement, as it is a product of competition in the classroom and self-interested/rational action by the student. These are all central cultural values of our society. Furthermore, the order approach focuses on how the institutions are linked via processes. It asks, is the nature of the linkages efficient given the functioning of the institutions in fulfilling the needs of the larger social order? For example, do the methods we use to socialize our children in the home and their outcomes, complement the methods used in the schools and the outcomes expected? Or do they conflict? Last, the order approach emphasizes how institutions serve to create and maintain boundaries that separate members of this society from other societies and give members of the society a sense of unity or cohesiveness.

The order approach emphasizes and views social change as part of a natural, evolutionary progression of the society. Change principally comes from the top down, a product of the innovation of elites who govern the basic institutions of the society. In any particular case, elites may be responding to social pressure. However, they, through their power and actions, are the engine of change. The political orientation of the order approach is within the ideological parameters of the system it is describing; therefore, it is either conservative or liberal. The order is seen as good; problems within the society are a result of dramatic changes to the system that disrupt the functioning of institutions. Both the content and speed of change are defined as the primary sources of social problems.

The central questions for the order approach are: What is the nature of the social bond? What holds society together? How do we maintain the social order? More precisely, for developmental or modernization theorists (order theorists that focus on the nature of societal development), how is stability and development maintained by a society?

In sociology there are two general conflict orientations: pluralist conflict and structuralist conflict. The difference between these two orientations is principally in the identification of the dimensions of conflict. For the pluralist conflict approach, the conflict of values and interests stems from the diversity of the population. Because the population is diverse along a series of dimensions—age, gender, occupation, lifestyle, religion, locality, ethnicity—members of the society are likely to come into conflict over issues and interests. The specific dimensions of the diversity of the population are not as important as the amount of dimensions or diversity of the population. Thus, one dimension is not necessarily more important than another as it relates to the organization of society and the nature of the conflict within it. What is important in accounting for the occurrence of conflict is the amount of diversity of the population. In contrast, structuralist conflict analysis argues that although diversity of the population is important, the major dimensions of conflict are along the structural divisions or systems of stratification that form the basis of the society: class, gender, and race or ethnicity.

In the following description we discuss a structuralist conflict approach. The conflict approach conceptualizes the social order in a very different manner. As opposed to homogeneity of interests and values, the conflict theorist sees heterogeneity of interests, values, and cultural orientation. Or, more precisely put, the conflict theorist sees conflicting values, interests, and cultural orientations, especially along the divisions within systems of stratification within a society. The primary social process here is conflict or competition.

We can extend the order approach's organismic analogy to the conflict approach. The institutions function like organs of an organism, linked via processes, functioning to maintain the whole system. For the conflict approach, however, the question is, Whose values or interests dominate the functioning of the institutions of the society? The structuralist conflict approach focuses on the divisions as they are rooted in the systems of material and human reproduction as the basis of the society. The conflict approaches rooted in a Marxist theoretical orientation are fundamentally materialist.

For a materialist, understanding any system begins with describing what that system needs to exist and how it goes about meeting its needs. All societies need to organize themselves to reproduce their populations. Human reproduction has two fundamental components or modes to accomplish—physical reproduction and material reproduction. That is, society must organize itself for procreation and socialization (mode of reproduction) and for the production of the necessities of survival for the population (mode of production). These modes constitute the foundation of the society. (See figure 1.1.)

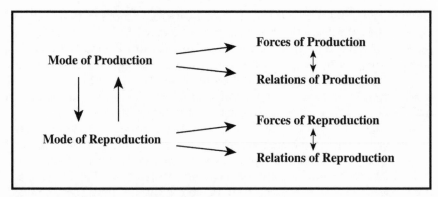

Figure 1.1. Substructure or Societal Base.

Each of the modes has two components: relations and forces of production and reproduction. The forces refer to the technology, the skill level of the actors, the energy and material resources necessary for the production of things and the reproduction of people. The relations refer to how the population is organized to produce things and reproduce people. For the relations of production, the fundamental organizing principle is social class. The social-class system in any society specifies the relations that people have to production. Social class simply refers to a category of people who have a common relationship to production. A social-class system is a hierarchy of positions defined in terms of one's relationship to production.

For example, in describing the class structure of the United States as a capitalist society, we can identify two essential class positions. The first class position, the one that is in the dominant power position, is the capitalist or owning class. The capitalist or owning class refers to a category of people who own and control production and receive their income or wealth through a right of expropriation of the surplus produced by others. The ability to expropriate surplus produced by those who work the property held by the capitalist is fundamental to the right to hold private property. This is the basis of the profit that is the driving force for capitalists to accumulate private property. Marxist conflict theories refer to this process of expropriation of surplus by owners from those who produce it as exploitation. Although the surplus is produced at the site of production, the realization of this surplus takes place in the marketplace. This is why a free market, one without interference of the right of expropriation by government or any other collectivity, is crucial to the functioning of capitalism.

Those who produce the surplus are in the second essential class position, the working class. The working class refers to a category of people who do not own or control production, but sell their capacity to labor to those who do or their representatives. Although workers are free in capitalist society, as opposed to slaves and serfs under two previous modes of production, workers are fundamentally coerced to work. Since capitalists control the means of production, the only means by which workers are able to survive is by selling their capacity to work to a capitalist. The two class positions are fundamentally in conflict. The goal of the capitalist is to generate increasing amounts of surplus (the basis of profits) by means of increasing control over work in order to increase levels of efficiency. The goal of workers is to have more control over their labor and to get an increasing share of the surplus they produce.

Two other class positions are managers and independent producers (petty bourgeoisie or, more commonly, the self-employed). Although not essential class positions, they add stability to capitalist systems as they develop. For managers, their specific relationship to production is that they do not own but they do control production for those who do own. Because managers do not own production, like workers they sell their labor to those who do or their representatives via a labor market. Independent producers are like capitalists in that they own and control production. Unlike capitalist, however, they do not receive their income principally from the expropriation of surplus produced by the labor of others; instead, the surplus is for the most part produced by their own labor.

In terms of the relations of reproduction, the fundamental organizing principle is gender. Gender refers to the social transformation of the biological category of sex. It refers to the role and behavioral expectations associated with one who is a member of one gender or the other. Generally speaking, in all societies of the world there is the institutionalization of dominance of one gender over the other. This institutionalized pattern is called patriarchy. Patriarchy refers to the pattern whereby men have more power than women in the functioning of the family and schools, two spheres of physical and cultural reproduction of the population, as well as all other institutional spheres (economy, polity, and religious institutions). Conflict theorists define our own society as patriarchal capitalist. This refers to a specific level of development and organization of the forces of production and reproduction and relations of production and reproduction. For the conflict approach, the relations of production and reproduction, the divisions along class and gender lines, are at the foundation of the social order. The character of these divisions (numbers of positions within the divisions and distances between them) is a product of the historical development of the forces of production and reproduction and the struggles and conflict between and within the divisions in the society.

Ethnic or "racial" designation is also an important organizing principle of the population and cuts across class and gender divisions. In the United States and many other capitalist nations, labor markets have been organized in terms of ethnic/racial categories. In the most overt cases, laws have been passed to establish discriminatory treatment of categories of people who occupy a particular ethnic/racial group. The legal discriminatory treatment of Native Americans, African Americans, Hispanics, and Asians through the system of apartheid or legal segregation in the United States was outlawed with the *Brown v. Board of Education* Supreme Court decision in 1954. This system of institutionalized discrimination continued to be eroded with the Civil Rights Acts of 1964 and 1968 and the Voting Rights Act of 1965. The system of apartheid in South Africa is still in the process of being dismantled. These are all examples of overt cases of organizing labor markets for subordination along ethnic/racial lines. Today, legal forms of discrimination have given way to patterns of subordination that are a product of this historical experience, cultural traditions, and institutional practices that are racist in outcome, but not necessarily by intent. When we look at patterns regarding the distribution of power, they fall along these divisions of class, gender, and race/ethnic stratification. The intersection of these divisions defines specific positions along a power hierarchy. Those at the top are capitalist, in most cases male, and of white European ancestry; those at the bottom are working class, usually female, and of minority ethnic status (Native American, African American, Latin American in the United States).

From the conflict perspective, the institutions of the society are mechanisms to maintain and reproduce the social order. In particular, the institutions function to reproduce the divisions that are at the foundation of the society (i.e., relations of production and reproduction). In this way, institutions are seen as mechanisms of coercion and social control. For example, whether we are discussing education or the criminal justice system, both function to maintain and reproduce the order either through the promotion of ideas or ideologies that legitimate the order, as in the case of schools, or through threats of violence directed at those whose actions threaten the order, as in the case of the police, courts, and the prison system. In this way, both institutional spheres are principally fulfilling a social-control function.

Furthermore, the institutions of the society function systematically to benefit those with the most power in the society based on their position, and function to the disadvantage of those with the least power in the society based on their position. Thus the economy is structured as in the functioning of a market, to be more responsive to those with more power (money) to participate and least responsive to those with the least power (money) to participate. The political system in the United States, although based on a system of universal suffrage for adult citizens, is intimately connected to the distribution of economic power. We know that the amount of money individuals have to contribute to candidates influences election outcomes. Furthermore, those who are in the highest offices in local, state, and federal governments are disproportionately drawn from the economic elite positions of those respective jurisdictions. Last, Miliband (1983) notes that aside from the economic power of the capitalist class and the importance of the shared culture among the elite, there is the power that capitalists have in influencing the state as a result of their control of production. Economic activity is the tax base of government funding. Furthermore, if the state acts in ways that are counter to the interest of capital, capital has the ultimate power of reducing its investment in production or shifting it to sites outside of the jurisdiction of specific governmental bodies. This will have serious impact on the economic well-being of the populace and the political careers of those in control of the state (Miliband, 1983).

In terms of the educational institution, we know that all citizens have a right to an education in the United States, but we also know that the quality of schooling in the United States is very much tied to school resources and the income and wealth of the school population it serves. Kozol's *Savage Inequalities* documented the tremendous disparities in resource distribution across public schools throughout the nation. The inequities between public schools that are best funded and the elite private schools are even greater (Kozol, 1991).

Change is caused by the conflict between the divisions within the society. This conflict is stimulated because of what is referred to as contradictions that develop within and between modes of production and reproduction. In regard to the contradictions that develop within the mode of production, as the forces of production develop they come into conflict with the relations of production. There is constant pressure for capitalists to develop the forces of production. Capitalists are in competition with other capitalists for the sale of their products in the marketplace. Only through the sale of products in the marketplace can capitalists realize the surplus produced in the production process through the exploitation of labor.

To garner a larger and larger share of the market to maximize the realization of surplus, the capitalist attempts to produce in a more efficient manner. This efficiency may refer to the introduction of increasing mechanization of production to streamline and speed up the production process. With increasing mechanization, workers working at the same time intervals can produce a larger amount of products than workers who are producing without the machinery. This refers to increasing the relative surplus of production. Efficiency also can be achieved by paying workers less for the same labor. This can result directly by redefining the nature of work from skilled to semiskilled or machine operator status. It can also be caused indirectly as a result of the increasing levels of unemployment as workers are increasingly displaced by machines in the production process, thus lowering wages. These latter methods are referred to as increasing the level of absolute surplus. For the capitalist, the fundamental rule of the market is that you grow or you die. What this means is that if you, as a capitalist, do not continue to garner a larger and larger share of the market at greater and greater levels of surplus produced and realized, you risk being beaten in the market by capitalists who have more capital to expand and improve the efficiency of production. These forces push the further development of the forces of production. Thus, capitalists are pushed to produce increasing amounts of surplus in order to continue to expand their capital. If they do not, they risk losing it. This is the nature of the capital accumulation processes that is at the heart of capitalist systems. This further development of the forces of production has consequences on the relations of production or, as Marxist conflict theorists describe them, the forces of production come into contradiction with the relations of production.

An example of a contradiction that can develop as a result of this fundamental dynamic of capitalist society results from the fact that as production develops it requires less and less human labor. Machines are increasingly taking over work that humans used to perform. On the one hand this is progress; less human labor is required for the material reproduction of the society, and humans will have more leisure time to develop their talents and interests. On the other hand, this poses a serious problem for our society and is the basis for the stimulation of conflict that has the potential of leading to fundamental changes in the society. If less labor is required in the society, how will the increasingly large segment of the society without work be able to acquire the necessities of survival? This is a fundamental contradiction that develops because of the nature of the mode of production in our society. Other examples of these contradictions inherent to our mode of production take us beyond the scope of our discussion at this time. These contradictions all serve to stimulate conflicts between the divisions in the society that, for the conflict approach, are the basis of change in the society.

Regarding contradictions that develop within the mode of reproduction, the same dynamic is present. As the forces of reproduction develop they come into contradiction with the relations of reproduction or gender relations. For example, the impact of changes in the technology of birth control affects the power relations between men and women. Many sociologists have pointed to the development of the birth control pill as a factor that led to the women's movement during the late 1960s that created changes in the nature of the relations between men and women in our society (Mauss, 1975; Tallman, 1976). As women gain more control over their reproduction, their power increases relative to men in the society. They have the ability to choose not to have children, to seek employment, and thus be less dependent on men in their role as breadwinner. This reduces the power disparity between women and men and thus has the potential of changing the nature of gender relations in the society. Thus, as the forces of reproduction develop, they come into conflict with how we have organized the population in terms of gender to physically and culturally reproduce the population.

Contradictions may develop between the modes of production and reproduction. Both systems are linked as part of a whole system. As one system changes in response to the conflicts stimulated by contradictions within, it reverberates back to the other system. For example, as women have increasingly entered the workforce in part because of changes in birth control technology, this has had an effect on gender relations. Women, who were once entirely dependent economically on men, are no longer as dependent. This independence has affected the distribution of power between men and women in the home. Divorce rates have climbed dramatically in this country from the 1950s until the early 1980s. Furthermore, as capitalists have mechanized and automated production and have increased in size and holdings (tendency toward monopolization), they have been able to shift production continually to cheaper labor areas, increasingly outside of the United States to poorer developing countries. This has resulted in an increasing displacement of workers, especially male workers, as a result of dein-dustrialization. The resultant fall in the standard of living of the working popula-tion resulting from deindustrialization and the increasing internationalization of the labor market have pushed women into the labor market in order for families to maintain their economic position or slow down their decline. This increased entry of women workers as a result of both forces affects not only gender rela-tions but the relations of production; as more women enter the workforce, in-creasing the pool of available workers, it affects the price of labor and the nature of work conditions. Thus, as one mode changes in response to contradictions that develop between forces and relations and the resultant conflict that devel-ops, so does the potential for change in the other mode.

The political orientation of the conflict approach is radical, that is, outside the ideological parameters of the system. Problems within the society are endemic, a product of the organization of the society, not incidental to the society. They fundamentally occur because of the class, gender, and ethnic divisions within the population. The central questions for the conflict approach are: What are the conditions that provoke conflicts between the structural divisions? What are the conditions that provoke a class, ethnic group, or gender's awareness or con-sciousness of their interest and action that attempts to realize their interests? The focus is on the forces for change in the society.

How does each of these two approaches view violence? Table 1.2 contrasts the two approaches on the concept of violence. First, regarding the concep-tualization of violence, the order approach sees violence as principally the re-sult of actions of people acting alone or within small groups. Violence as a product of institutional action or the structural organization of society is not usually considered violence under the order conceptualization. In this way, vi-olence exists only when it threatens order.

Also, the intent of the action is crucial to understanding the behavior. The actors must intend violence for it to be violent behavior. Action that is willful but not intended as violence is not considered a violent act. Thus, actions by corporations that are not intended to be violent but have violent conse-quences, such as knowingly selling unsafe products to unsuspecting con-sumers, would not be considered violence. Violence is also generally under-stood as a product of deficits of individuals. Acts of violence by individuals are more likely to be seen, not as a part of a pattern of violence that is a product of larger societal forces, but as a problem of a syndrome of illness or mal-adaptation of individuals or groups (e.g., minority youth). Moreover, defini-tions of violence are system specific. What is defined as violence in one soci-ety may not apply to another. Violence is defined in terms of the cultural system, often in terms of a violation of law. Thus, from the order approach, the study of criminal violence and violence are one in the same. Generally, vi-olence not defined as criminal is not considered an object of study.

The conflict approach, in contrast, sees violence as principally the result of the organization of society. Here, the principle causes of violence in a society

Table 1.2. Order and Conflict Approaches to the Study of Violence

	Order	Conflict
Conceptualization of Violence	Individual and collective action. Intent of action is of primary importance.	Individual, institutional, and structural action. Outcome is of primary importance.
	Stress is on cultural relative definitions of violence. A certain level of violence is innate to humans.	Stress is on universal definitions of violence tied to human rights. Violence is not innate but learned.
Cause of Violence	Incidental to the social order. Violence is principally seen as a deficit of the individual. Deviant forms of violence are seen as a product of physical, psychological, and/or socially adaptive deficits together with natural tendencies.	Social forms in which we live our lives are the causes. Hierarchies and exploitative relationships are the fundamental causes of violence.
Role of Violence in the Society	Focus is principally on its disruptive role. Violence that is used to maintain the order is seen as legitimate and necessary and not defined as an area of study.	Constructive, adaptive, and disruptive to the social order. Violence is seen as playing a role in reproducing hierarchical/ exploitative relations within the order and as a form of adaptation to or rebellion from those relations.

are systems of stratification that are the basis of the organization of that society. Also, the violence of individuals is only one source of violence. More important to the conflict theorist are institutional and structural forms or levels of violence. Thus, violence by the state or economic institutional actors in the pursuit of profit is recognized to be more destructive than acts of interpersonal violence. Furthermore, these higher levels of violence are ultimately the causes of interpersonal violence.

For conflict theorists, the intent of action is secondary to the outcome. Although violence may not be intended by the actors, their actions are willful, and the violent outcomes are the same. For example, businesses that knowingly engage in selling unsafe products to unsuspecting consumers would still be violent, regardless of whether or not the intent of the sale was to cause violence to consumers.

For the conflict approach, the stress is on seeing the forms of violence as interdependent or interrelated. Violence of an interpersonal nature is linked to institutional and structural levels of violence. Additionally, violence is defined in terms of universal criteria. For example, conflict theorists conceptualize violence as actions or conditions that are threatening to the well-being of individuals or groups and as actions that are a violation of fundamental human rights. The distinction between normative and deviant forms of violence is not central to the definition of violence for the conflict approach as it is for the order approach. Therefore, an act of female infanticide among the Yanomamo would be defined as an act of violence by those using a conflict approach, as well as the denial of needed medical services to the poor and uninsured that leads to premature death. Or the violence that results from the dumping of toxic wastes unsafely near residential areas is defined as violence by the conflict theorist, whereas in societies where these acts occur, they would not be defined as violence and are thus not violent by the conceptualization of order theorists.

Pepinsky notes that "if indeed crime and punishment are arbitrary distinctions for forms of violence, and if indeed the distinctions are politically partisan, then it is morally and epistemologically unacceptable for criminologists to accept any of these distinctions; instead, nonpartisan criminologists ought to develop a theory of violence which presupposes that the only way to reduce the level of crime or punishment in any person or any group is to reduce violence generally" (1991, 17). This is ultimately the goal of a conflict analysis of violence.

Regarding illegitimate violence, the order approach views violence as fundamentally a problem of an actor's lack of adaptation or maladaptation to the social order. Usually this is a result of individual deficiencies or the individual's immediate environment. The root of this maladjustment may be biological. For example, acts of violence have been attributed to genetic defects as in the case of Klinefelters syndrome (XYY chromosome), hormonal or dietary imbalances, or as a result of a physiological illness (e.g., linking epilepsy and violent behavior) (Fishbein, 1990). Or the root cause may be psychological. A plethora of research focuses on the psychopathic personality and acts of violence, and other research focuses on deficiencies in maternal or paternal relationships and violence. Last, order theorists may see the root cause as sociological. Violence may be seen as caused by a disorganized social environment, anomie, the learning of violence from intimates, or from the absence of social control as a result of inadequate bonds to the social order. In all these cases, however, the basic organization of the society is not seen as the central problem, but the focus is on a deviation from normality either in the individual or the immediate social environment of the violent individual, or both. All of these deviations are correctable within the parameters of the social system.

Ball-Rokeach (1980) lists the most common deficit theoretical approaches as biogenetic deficits, ecosystem malfunction (i.e., crowding, hampered territoriality), deficits of person (psyche, insufficient internal controls), source of socialization or learning, and social system malfunction (breakdown of control or the authority system). In general, violence is understood as incidental to the way society is organized. It is not because society is organized in a certain way that we have violence; it is because of individuals' adaptation to the way in which society is organized.

For the conflict approach, the pattern of violence in a society is endemic to the way society is organized or ordered. Violence is a mechanism to protect and extend the social relations that are at its foundation. It is either a product of the way society functions to reproduce itself or a product of an individual's adaptation or rebellion to the way society is organized. In the first case, both institutional and structural acts of violence are mechanisms that reproduce the society. The violence over protecting property here and abroad serves to maintain property relations that are at the foundation of class systems. Violence committed by the police and military are in the vast majority of cases ultimately a defense of property rights. The police use violence to apprehend a thief or stop illegal markets in drugs. The violence is used to defend property rights or the distribution of income that results from this right. The use of violence by the military to redress the threat to national interests is usually translated to mean property rights of U.S. citizens or corporations or the functioning of the market, whereby the surplus controlled by capitalists is realized.

In the second case, violence is understood as a product of individual adaptation to or rebellion against the way society is organized. Violence is a form of striking back at society and how society reduces the range of choices of action for individuals to reach their goals, as well as defining appropriate goals. In many cases, violence can provide a sense of power that has been stripped away by the functioning of institutions in the society as they reproduce the structural divisions within the social order. In either case, the violence can be instrumental or expressive as an adaptive or rebellious response to the social context in which one lives.

Remember, as noted earlier, conflict theorists view institutions as fundamentally acting to reproduce the divisions that are at the foundation of the social order. For example, conflict theorists, in viewing the nature of the education system in our society, focus on how it functions to reward and enrich those who enter schools with the most educational resources and punish and impoverish those who enter with the least, through mechanisms of individual competition, "ability" grouping, and norm reference testing. Another example of the reproductive function of institutional processes is how the political system responds to different interests in the society as a result of the influence of money in elections. Political rulers follow their self-interest by responding favorably to the interests of those who have the greatest wealth and thus will preserve and reproduce the order that produces this wealth distribution. These reproductive processes reduce the range of choices for those who are seeking economic opportunity through education and those who are seeking political empowerment through democracy in a capitalist society.

Although order theorists in some cases have viewed deviance as functional to the social order (Durkheim, 1938; Dentler and Erickson, 1959), order theorists principally view violence as disruptive to the social order. Solutions to the problems of violence are defined in terms of improving the efficiency of agencies of social control, improving the integration or connection between institutions (connections between schools and family, schools and the economy, etc.), and reducing the problems of maladjustment to the social order.

Although conflict theorists see violence in society as personally disruptive, they view violence as either constructive to reproducing the social order, as a vehicle for social change, or as a destructive adaptation to the system. In the first instance, violence is an important tool for social control and the maintenance and defense of the social order. Violence and the threat of violence is also a tool by which those with little power are able to disrupt the system and potentially change it. Social welfare reform has often come about in the aftermath of riots. A report by the National Advisory Commission on Civil Disorders (1968), a commission appointed by Lyndon Johnson, identified more than 150 riots or major disorders between 1965 and 1968. In 1967 alone, eighty-three people were killed (most of them black), 1,800 were injured, and property valued at more than $100 million was destroyed. These riots preceded a significant expansion of the welfare sector during the late 1960s and early 1970s.

Last, violence can be destructive to the life chances of those who commit it, furthering the oppression and exploitation of the system. The use of violence by relatively powerless males to exert the rights of patriarchy (i.e., rape) is an example where violence is a learned response to exploit those who have less power than oneself. The legitimation of the use or exploitation of another is learned from a system based on contractual relationships of exploitation; the violence is used to enforce a right that stems from capitalist and patriarchal relations. Ultimately, conflict theorists see the solution to violence in terms of changing the nature of the social order as defined in terms of the social divisions that form the foundation of the order and the functioning of institutions in reproducing these divisions.

This book takes a conflict approach to the study of violence. Beginning with the development of a definition of violence, the conflict approach guides us in our investigation of the phenomenon. Although we could have developed both approaches throughout the book, we found this to be too cumbersome and awkward. Furthermore, the order approach limits the study of violence by defining violence only within the definitional parameters of the society it is studying. In this way, the most severe forms of violence are excluded from study.

IMPORTANCE OF CROSS-CULTURAL ANALYSIS IN SOCIOLOGY

Cross-cultural analysis is an important tool of the sociological perspective in general and conflict analysis in particular. It facilitates our ability to see the strange in the familiar. In looking at patterns of violence in different societies, cross-cultural comparisons allow us to make the transition in viewing the violence in our own society as an outsider to our own society.

Furthermore, cross-cultural analysis facilitates our ability to see the general in the particular. In viewing the violence in another society, it is much easier to see patterns of behavior. We are less likely to get lost in the trees and not see the forest. In viewing patterns of violence in other societies, we are more able to make this transition to gain a better understanding of the patterned violence in our own society, whether the subject be suicide, rape, or state violence.

Last, cross-cultural analysis makes it easier to depersonalize the personal. It is much easier to view the patterns of violence in another society as the product of that society than it is to see the patterns of violence in our own society as the product of our own society. In discussing how violence, say, in South Africa, is part of the legacy of their system of apartheid, we may see some parallels in our own society and how violence may relate to the racial divisions within our society. Without the benefit of cross-cultural analysis we are more likely to engage in reductionism, seeing the violence of African Americans as a product of choices of individuals. Comparative approaches are crucial to the conflict approach. Again, the conflict approach sees the pattern of violence in a society as an artifact of that society. In particular, we start this analysis by looking at the organizational structure, and more specifically, the hierarchical arrangements that are at the foundation of the society under study. Only by means of cross-cultural analysis do we see how these structures vary and have different consequences for patterns of violence. Unfortunately, since most of the research on violence is conducted from an order approach, there is little comparative research. Nevertheless, we integrate some of the research that has been conducted into our discussions of violence to highlight the importance of social system variables in understanding violence.

WHAT IS VIOLENCE?

Violence is a phenomenon that is often taken for granted—"I-know-it-when-I-see-it." Such commonsense understandings can be both time and culture bound. For example, in 1934, when Adolf Hitler and the Nazi Party assumed control of Germany, the *Encyclopedia of the Social Sciences* defined violence as "the illegal employment of methods of physical coercion for personal or group ends" (Hook, 1934, 264). The explicit understanding was that a sovereign state, by definition, could not commit violence, whether in its own defense or in an effort to "control" its citizenry to maintain the order. "State violence" was assumed to be a matter of expediency, not a subject for social ethics. Violence committed by the state, in other words, was in the minds of sociologists at that time an oxymoron, a contradictory pairing of two terms. Incredibly, by that 1934 definition, the Nazi genocides of Jews and other ethnic and sexual minorities would not have met with the then current "social scientific" criteria to have been labeled violence.

Even today, most social science definitions of violence as they are rooted in the order paradigm are conservative and biased in favor of the status quo. Only deviant forms of violence are considered violent. Violence is largely conceived in social psychological or interpersonal terms, with individuals the primary perpetrators. As a result, neither state (i.e., governmental) nor corporate-based actions are subject to discussion in studies of violence. Violence is seen basically as a breakdown in individual self-control or in the social control mechanism external to the individual. In this view, violence is problematic only when it is directed against the social order and "law-abiding" citizens. As Archer and Gartner note:

> The term violence conjures up the image of dangerous individuals. We tend to think of violent acts and violent actors in concrete, personalized form. This individualistic bias obscures the very real violence committed by authorities in the pursuit of domestic social control, or by governments in the pursuit of foreign war. Serious violence, including homicide, is produced routinely in the course of law enforcement, criminal punishment and executions, crowd and riot control, political subversion and assassination and, of course, war (Archer and Gartner, 1984, 63).

With the development of the conflict approach to the study of crime, in part, stemming out of the development of labeling theory in the 1960s and the expansion and further development of the critical school of criminology during the 1970s and 1980s, the political nature of the definition of crime has been a central focus of discussion. A central tenet of conflict theory is that those with the most power in a hierarchically ordered society have the most power to define crime, and those acts that threaten their interests ultimately become defined as criminal. Furthermore, acts that are in the interests of those who have power, even though they may cause harm to others (especially those with least power), are less likely to be defined as criminal. As conflict or critical theorists have moved beyond the critique of what is crime, they have struggled with developing a definition of crime that is inclusive of all the harms to people in a society or in the world as a whole. Thus there has been an increasing focus on defining crime in terms of acts that are a violation of universal standards or rights (Michalowski, 1985; Beirne and Messerschmidt, 1991). Nevertheless, the definition of crime implies a legal foundation, and thus a legislative body that defines law. Critical theorists have increasingly focused on international bodies that create laws or conventions as the basis of this definition. As in the case of a law within a society, however, if it is not enforced, acts violating it are not considered crime in terms of the consequential reaction to offenders.

There has been less attention by critical theorists to the phenomenon of violence as an area of study. Yet by focusing on violence instead of crime, critical criminologists may avoid some of the problems of definition that plague them in defining crime. Ball-Rokeach in 1980 presented a conflict analysis of violence. She focused on how violence was a product of the hierarchical arrangements of society. She defined violence as "a struggle to maintain, change, or protest asymmetric social relations governing the distribution of scarce resources, by the threat or exertion of physical force" (46). Although her work was very significant in initiating a study of violence from the conflict analysis, her definition focused on the fundamental cause of violence as opposed to defining the concept itself.

Another definition of violence offers a broader, more inclusive view. Criminologists Weiner, Zahn, and Sagi (1990), in an anthology entitled *Violence: Patterns, Causes, Public Policy*, define violence as "the threat, attempt, or use of physical force by one or more persons that results in physical or nonphysical harm to one or more other persons" (xiii). This definition, because it considers action completed or attempted and psychological as well as physical effects, broadens the domain of violence. The authors omit the issue of a person's intent, claiming that being concerned about motives (i.e., whether the harm done is or is not violence if he or she did not *mean* to do it) renders violence a subjective concept depending on the actor's viewpoint, instead of permitting it to be a behavior that can be identified by independent observers. The definition, nevertheless, is limited in that the focus is principally on interpersonal forms of violence. Institutional and structural violence are not excluded by the definition; however, they are not explicitly included.

Weiner, Zahn, and Sagi view their definition as a useful heuristic device for expanding the classification, analysis and discussion of violence. We agree. They deal, in one way or another, with those elements that need to be considered in any definition of violence: the degree and type of injury, the intentionality of violent participants, the object of the attack, and whether the harm occurring is the result of acts committed or omitted (i.e., failed to be performed). Although we agree with the basic thrust of this definition, we see a need for modification in expanding the definition of actors beyond that of individuals and groups to include institutions and the structural foundations of societies. Regarding the latter category, violence that is an outcome of social structure, systems of stratification, is not necessarily a result of actions by individuals or groups but more a result of lack of access to requirements for health and safety because of an individual's position in the society that results in death or injury. For example, infant mortality rates in the United States that are higher for African American infants than for white infants are a product not as much of individual action as of the structural arrangements based on class and race that limit or deny access to prenatal and postnatal medical care. Differences in the rate of AIDS between countries in the northern and southern hemispheres of the world would be another example of structural violence.

Given this problem with Weiner, Zahn, and Sagi's definition, we propose the following general definition with the necessary specifications: *Violence is any action or structural arrangement that results in physical or nonphysical harm to one or more persons.* Incorporated in its simplicity are six important points of elaboration.

First, actions or social relationships based on structural arrangements that result in harmful outcomes must be willfully or deliberately committed or condoned by an actor or agent of the actor. Harmful effects need not be the primary goal of an actor, but the action or social relationship must be within the sphere of control of the actor. Otherwise, it would have to be thought of as an accident. To be sure, accidental patterns can be regarded as social problems; that status alone does not qualify them to be included within the domain of violence.

Thus a traffic accident that occurs because the brakes in a driver's car suddenly fail on a curve, causing the car to veer off the road into a group of children waiting at a bus stop, does not meet the willful criteria of our definition, however harmful the effects might be. The same automobile accident caused by a driver who was intoxicated would be considered violence. Or another instance would be a traffic accident that occurs because a manufacturer-known defect in the design of the car makes it difficult to control when making a curve at high speed, causing the driver to veer off the road into a group of children waiting at a bus stop. Furthermore, the denying of food by a shopkeeper to poor children because they do not have the money to pay for it is violent because of the structural position that these children are in relation to the shopkeeper (a product of the class structure of the society). The action is willful and has violent outcomes, the premature illness or death of the children as a result of malnutrition. Another example would be a hospital's denial of medical services to indigent patients. Again, the status of indigency is based on a structural relationship (a product of the class structure of the society), the action of denial of medical services is willful and has violent outcomes rooted in the class structure of the society. To see how this action is violence, consider the same action outside the institutional context or in another society where the structural divisions are not present. For example, let's say you are walking down the street when you come across an individual lying on the sidewalk seriously injured and in need of help. If you choose to ignore the individual and keep on walking, your action has a violent outcome, an outcome of harm to the individual in need of help. But, would it be defined as violence? Now place yourself in the context of a community of the San of the Kalahari. The San are a people of southern Africa who traditionally have lived as hunters and gathers. They are grouped in small bands of thirty to 100. The effective organizational unit in traditional San society is the band, the members of which are linked by elaborate kin networks. You are a member of this community and are injured and asking for help. It would be considered very wrong and an act of violence if other members of the band ignored your request for help. Questions about whether you had enough resources to pay for the help would not enter the mind of members of the band (Lee, 1979).

Second, as a corollary to the first point, *violence can be intended or not intended by the actor.* Here we are addressing intent, not consciousness and deliberation, as in the previous point. For example, in instances of rape or homicide, where violence is intended we would have little problem in regarding these acts as violent. But what of the act that was never intended to produce violence? Take the example of the automobile company who manufactures a product it knows to be unsafe. It produces the product to increase profits, and the product causes damage to those who consume the product. Two examples would be the Ford Pinto with its faulty design of a gasoline tank that could turn the vehicle into an incendiary bomb in a collision, and the Dalkon Shield birth control device that produced deadly infections in the women who used them. Both are instances where the fatal consequences were never intended by corporate decision makers, yet were nevertheless the results of the willed action of producing a product that they knew had violent consequences. Similarly, in the examples of structural violence, the actors who deny food or medical services do not intend violence, they are merely following the rules of the structural relationships that have violent consequences. The action is willed, nonaccidental action; however, the violence is not the intent of the action.

Third, the violence may be justified or unjustified. Sociology has long maintained the importance of any viewer's possible positions in age, gender, educational, economic, and power hierarchies, as well as the influence of the vested interests caused by such positions on his or her interpretations of social action. Often, there is widespread agreement that a violent action is justified, such as when a person defends himself or herself against assaults by muggers, rapists, or burglars. Likewise, government's use of violence as a mechanism to maintain social order can be perceived as justified, for example in response to looters who rampage through the streets after a hurricane or earthquake. Capital punishment would be an example of this. Thus, the execution of more than 4,000 persons in the United States since 1930 would be considered 4,000 acts of state violence.

Usually, judgments that actions are unjustifiably or justifiably violent depend on whose interests are at stake or who stands to lose or gain by the violence. "Justifiability" is undoubtedly the most negotiable of meanings for violent actions. For example, the eighteenth-century revolution by the North American colonies began as an illegal insurrection from the British point of view. Likewise, the 1989 Tiananmen Square student demonstrations in the People's Republic of China were sternly but, from the Chinese government's standpoint, necessarily suppressed in the interest of civil order. The deaths of thousands of Afghani citizens who were killed as a result of the United States attack and overthrow of the government of Afghanistan in the wake of the September 11, 2001, terrorist attack on the United States would be another example in which the violence was defined as justified by the Government of the United States.

As a result of the subjective nature of social life that underlies our everyday "taken for granted" social reality, any definition of violence must not allow for a shifting, never-final yardstick of the "justifiability" dimension—because that yardstick will vary depending on the power and interests of the interpreters of violence. Thus violence is violence whether it is justified or unjustified as defined by either the actors or the audience to the action.

Fourth, violence and its harmful effects address both physical and psychological well-being. What unites these two forms of well-being is that the safety and security of the person is damaged or threatened to the point of impairment. Obviously a physical attack by a man pummeling his wife or, after a series of such beatings, threatening to do so again, can injure her body, not to mention her sense of personal security. Likewise, persistently demeaning her with insults that question her self-worth has serious consequences in regard to her well-being and whether she acts to further the development of herself or sublimates her interests and will to that of another. As often noted by sociologists and psychologists researching family violence, the long-term traumas and injuries from forcible rapes and domestic violence are often psychological, not physical. Thus, both physically and psychologically oriented actions (though, practically speaking, it is not always easy to separate the two) can unquestionably damage well-being. Well-being also refers to thriving and progressing. Thus, when we refer to violence, it is not only damage to one's current state of existence, but also damage to one's ability to progress and develop one's human potential. Here violence may be action that denies a minority group's access to education, health care, housing, an adequate diet, and other necessities of survival and human development.

Fifth, there is the issue of perception or awareness. Violence may be recognized or not recognized by either the recipient of the action, the actor, or both. Certain forms of violence may be so integral to the structure of society and the functioning of its institutions that they may not be recognized as violence per se, just as the more important racial/ethnic forms of discrimination in the post-1960s United States have been almost invisibly *institutional* compared to more obvious forms of bigotry and prejudice on an interpersonal level. Thus, practices of redlining by banks and insurance companies have serious detrimental effects on the ability of residents of an area to maintain the quality of their housing and prevent neighborhood deterioration. Often, the long-range effect is an increase in the risk of violence to residents as a result of the social disorganization that accompanies the physical deterioration of neighborhoods. The dramatic increase in homeless populations throughout the country is in part related to government decisions to reduce funding for low-income housing and the impact of deinstitutionalization of the mentally ill. In both cases, the actions of institutions result in violent outcomes. It is a sociological truism that ideologies or interest-based perspectives of social groups often create blinders that prevent individual members from seeing violence that is a result of the system(s) of hierarchy, or inequity, and associated rationalizations that affect them. These ideologies often are supportive of institutional actions and the structural arrangements that have violent consequences for people.

For example, however surprising it might seem to students of the late twentieth century, wife beating has had a mixed history of being defined as violence, both by the men who committed it and by the women who endured it. Fifty years ago, kicking and punching/slapping a woman was not legally defined as assault. It was most likely to be regarded as "necessary, if regrettable, discipline." Yet, during colonial times and even during the nineteenth century, women battering was viewed as a serious social problem (viewed, that is, by men, no less, who ran the legal establishments), and punishments (in terms of fines, prison terms, and even public whippings) were also much harsher than today. Marital rape and the phenomenon of "honor killings of women" in countries in the Middle East, Asia, and South America is another form of violence that is in transition as it relates to its perception.

Anthropologist Paul Heelas (1982) argues that we cannot define violence outside its cultural context. Heelas contends that there are two perspectives on violence, that of the perpetrator and that of the victim. Problems occur when these two perspectives are not in agreement as to whether the violence existed or not. A larger problem occurs when neither victim nor perpetrator defines the act as violent, yet by universalistic standards it is violence. For example, in the Amazonian Yanomamo tribe, the husband, the wife, or the community as a whole would not define wife beating as violence. Nevertheless, these actions would be considered acts of violence under our proposed definition. Another example would be the outcomes of a system of institutionalized racism, such as that which until recently existed in South Africa. This system of institutionalized racism resulted in an infant mortality rate for black South Africans that was and still is many times higher than it is for white South Africans. Under our proposed definition this would be considered violence. In all these cases, the term violence may not be used by either the victimized, the perpetrators, or benefactors of the relationship, however, the action is violent. In the same way, raping one's wife in a large portion of the world is not considered violence; by the definition proposed, it is a form of violence. Also, the widespread occurrence of young girls forced into prostitution to help pay off the debt of poor peasant families in Thailand would be considered violence.

This is not to say that the perceptions of perpetrators or victims of violence are not relevant to the study of violence. How violence becomes defined in a society is indicative of how a society is organized. Nevertheless, a definition of violence must be fundamentally separable from the perceptions of the actors involved. Thus, in principle, some acts may be perceived as violent by the perpetrators *and* the recipient, some acts by the recipient but *not* the perpetrators, and some acts by neither.

In our conceptualization of violence we do not intend to limit the domain of violence to instances where all actors, recipients, or perpetrators agree that violence has occurred. Indeed, we suspect that because of how ideology may alter perceptions, actors or recipients do not recognize most of the violence in a society. The effort to flesh out the existence and social consequences of violence is part of what the late C. Wright Mills termed the "sociological imagination," sometimes as much an art as a science but nevertheless using the humanistically informed scientific method (Mills, 1959, 4). As such a method, the goals in the case of violence are to define violence in such a way as to encompass all actions and structures that damage current and future well-being.

Sixth, the proposed definition of violence is a universal as opposed to a relative definition of violence. Following from the above point regarding the recognition of violence, violence must be defined as a culturally universal phenomenon as opposed to one that is defined specifically in terms of the particularistic culture of the society in which it occurs. Although this clearly violates the cultural relativistic value premise of anthropology, it is consistent with the movement of international bodies (International Labor Organization, World Court, and Human Development Program of the United Nations) attempting to develop international standards of rights, trade, and law to judge and influence the development of social systems throughout the world to promote the greatest human development. In short, our position is that we can and must define violence by focusing on voluntary actions or social arrangements that injure human well-being regardless of (1) the intent of the actor, (2) whether it is recognized as violence by any of the actors involved, (3) whether it is defined as legitimate or illegitimate, or (4) whether it is justified or unjustified.

CONTEXTS OR SPHERES OF VIOLENCE

Now that we have defined violence, let's discuss the social contexts in which violence occurs. These contexts can be understood as representing different interactional spheres. We can talk about the interpersonal context or sphere, the institutional context or sphere, and the structural context or sphere. By the context or sphere of violence we are *not* specifically addressing the *cause* of the violence. However, in the sense that the context describes the rules of behavior of actors, it is accordingly part of an explanation of the cause of violence. So the institutional context of a soldier or law enforcement officer committing an act of violence against a defined enemy or criminal may in part explain the cause of the action. Similarly, in the institutional context of a corporate officer who decides to authorize a product that he or she knows to be unsafe, the context describes the rules of behavior of actors that are part of an explanation of the cause of violence. All violence takes place in social contexts. The social contexts of our interaction, including violent interaction, are a part of the organization of the whole social system.

Furthermore, although we discuss violence in separate contexts, many forms of violence overlap two or even three contexts. Thus, at separate points in this book we examine family violence within the institutional context of the family and later consider family violence as a manifestation of gender violence at the structural context or level. Let's first discuss each sphere of violence. Figure 1.2 depicts the three contexts or interactional spheres of violence.

Interpersonal violence is violence that occurs between people acting *outside* the role of agent or representative of a social institution. The aggravated assault between strangers at a bar, a gang fight between rival gangs, the rape by a stranger in the parking lot of a shopping mall, the lovers' quarrel that leads to homicide—all are examples of interpersonal violence.

Institutional violence is violence that occurs by the action of societal institutions and their agents. Institutional violence is violence by individuals whose actions are governed by the roles that they are playing in an institutional context. Institu-

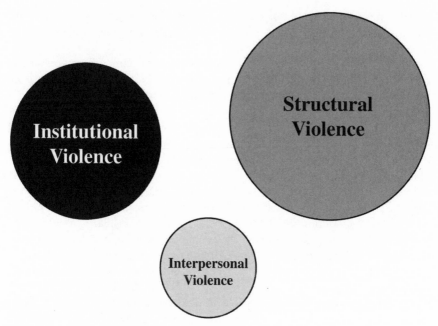

Figure 1.2.   Spheres of Violence.

tions represent a collective response to common problems in the society. They are organizational mechanisms to solve problems that all members of the society confront. Sociologists recognize five important institutions in society: economy, polity, family, education, and religion. Within the broad categories of institutions there are organizations that are carrying out an institutional role. For example, within the category of the educational institution there are schools of various levels. It is the school that sets the specific context for individual action. In this way institutional violence is always violence by an organization. However, not all organizations are institutional actors. Each one of these listed institutions, the organizations within them and their agents, may be actors in enacting violence.

Violence in the *economic institution* would include violent acts by agents of corporations, such as producing a product that the manufacturer knows to be defective and not informing the consumer of the defect or forcing workers to work under conditions that may result in their harm and not informing them of the dangers of their employment.

Violence in the *political institution* or by the state includes violent acts by government, such as conducting assassinations, executions, torture, wars against foreign nations, genocide, drug or chemical warfare experiments conducted by the government without the knowledge of the victims, and harm resulting from police riots that occur during civil unrest.

Violence in the *religious institution* includes acts by religious organizations, such as intersect violence, witch hunts, heresy persecutions, religious ritualistic suicides, and cult violence, forced religious conversions, rape and molestations, and patriarchal religious systems that encourage violence in the home under the guise of discipline.

Violence in the *family institution* includes acts by family members acting within the contexts of their familial institutional role, such as child abuse by parents, spousal abuse, elder abuse, and marital rape.

The least obvious forms of institutional violence are in the *educational institution*. Educational violence would include violence enacted by agents of schools directed principally at students in these institutions. The most obvious example is the use of corporal punishment by schoolteachers and administrators. The vast majority of states allow for corporal punishment of students in public schools. Another area of violence within schools that is of growing concern is the violence by students directed at students or school personnel. The recent rash of school shootings during the 1990s in the United States in places like Littleton, Colorado; Pearl, Mississippi; West Paducah, Kentucky; Jonesboro, Arkansas; Edinboro, Pennsylvania; and Springfield, Oregon, raised public concern about this type of violence. But despite the most recent heightened media attention, this form of violence is relatively rare (Donohue, Schiraldi, and Zeidenberg, 1998). Furthermore, both these types of violence occurs less frequently than other forms of educational violence that manifest themselves as institutional practices (methods of school funding, tracking, competitive processes, and norm reference testing) that deny educational resources to students who have the greatest need for them, thus resulting in violent outcomes as defined in terms of stunting the intellectual development of these students.

The concept of educational violence also includes what is referred to as "symbolic violence" (Bourdieu and Passeron, 1977). Symbolic violence refers to defining the dominant group's culture as universal knowledge and therefore denying the culture of dominated groups. The establishment of Indian schools by the Canadian and U.S. governments is a good example of symbolic violence on young children taken from their families and enrolled in boarding schools far away from their homes. In these schools they were not allowed to speak their native language, dress in native clothes, or exhibit any rituals or practices of their native culture. They were taught the inferiority of their cultural heritage and the superiority of the dominant white European culture. Historically, Hispanic and Asian students experienced similar practices within segregated schools throughout California and the southwestern United States as did African Americans throughout the country.

Symbolic violence has significant consequences to the well-being of culturally distinct indigenous populations. The systematic denigration of a people has a heavy impact on their social development. This together with other racist practices results in a devastating pattern of violence. One has only to look at the condition of Native Americans in our society to see the results. The median family income of Native Americans is 60 percent that of whites. Life expectancy is two-thirds the national average. Seventy-four percent of this population use contaminated water and live in crowded conditions. Native Americans have a lower educational attainment than any other minority group, and the illiteracy rate of the population is one-third (Dinnerstein et al., 1990; U.S. Bureau of the Census, 1991).

Structural violence is violence that occurs in the context of establishing, maintaining, extending or reducing the hierarchical ordering of categories of people in a society. For example, violence directed at a racial minority that establishes, maintains, or extends the system of hierarchy is structural violence. The 1989 episode in Bensonhurst, New York, where Yusuf Hawkins was gunned down because he was an African American male in a "white neighborhood" is an example of structural violence ("Death," 1989). There were 4,742 recorded lynchings in America between 1882 and 1968. All but 10 percent of the victims were black (Allen, 2000). Although, this is clearly interpersonal violence, the roots of the violence are in a system of racism that legitimates and maintains the racial divisions in this country.

The active subjugation and enslavement of native populations on contact by Christopher Columbus and his soldiers is an example of structural violence. Zinn notes that in 1495 Columbus went on a great slave raid, rounding up 1,500 Arawak men, women, and children. He placed them in pens and then selected the 500 best and sent them back to Spain to sell to pay off his creditors. Two years after this initial raid, half the estimated 250,000 Indians on Haiti were dead. Less than 100 years later, no Indians remained on the island (Koning, 1976; Zinn, 1980). Here violence was used to establish a hierarchy between European and native or indigenous populations in the Western Hemisphere. Many other instances of this active subjugation and creation of structural divisions as defined in terms of ethnicity occurred on every continent of the world.

Structural violence is also violence when the harmful action is an outcome of the hierarchical ordering of categories of people. Here structural violence takes less obvious forms. For example, the different infant mortality rates and differences in life expectancy between African Americans, Native Americans, Hispanics, and those of European ancestry in this country are examples of violence that manifests itself because of the class and ethnic stratification systems that exist in this country. The same pattern of poverty is found throughout the Southern Hemisphere of the world. In Central Australia, 40 percent of Aboriginal children are hospitalized with acute respiratory illness in the first two years of their lives. The rate of infant mortality in Australian indigenous communities is about three times the national average. In Guatemala 87 percent of indigenous people are below the poverty line and 61 percent are below the line of extreme poverty. In Peru 79 percent of the indigenous people are poor. In Mexico 80 percent of the indigenous population are poor (United Nations Department of Public Information, 1997).

Structural violence also can be directed at women, youth, and workers. The systematic abortion of female fetuses in India because of male child preference is another case of structural violence. The act of rape, although clearly a case of interpersonal violence, systematically furthers the hierarchy between men and women in this society. Rape threatens principally women, not men (with the exception of male prison inmates); as an act of violence and an act of domination by males, it serves to inhibit the social freedom of women in the public sphere of life and thus maintains and extends the hierarchy between men and women. The violence directed at children to "discipline" them for behavior that offends adults who are defined as having control and responsibility for them is another example. The violence directed at strikers by company agents and the violence directed at scab laborers by strikers are all products of the class system in capitalist societies and thus structural violence.

INTERSECTION OF THE SPHERES OF VIOLENCE

Although we can think of spheres of violence as conceptually distinct, in reality there is a great deal of overlap between them. Figure 1.3 illustrates the overlap between sectors or contexts. In speaking of *institutional structural violence*, we are talking about violence by institutions and their agents as they function to maintain, extend, or reduce the hierarchical ordering of categories of people within the society. One example of this is hospitals refusing to treat individuals who cannot afford their services. The action of the institution damages the well-being and extends or maintains the differences in life expectancy of individuals that stem from their position in systems of stratification. Another example would entail worker safety violations that result in hazards in the workplace that lead to the death or injury of workers. Again this is a case of violence where institutional agents, typically owners or managers of a private business, act to extend or maintain the differences in life expectancy of individuals that stem from their position in systems of stratification. A third and more obvious case is where the military, as in many Central and South American countries today and the United States in the not-too-distant past, acted in the interest of landowners to remove Indian populations, peasants, or both from land they had worked for generations. Death squads in many Central American countries, in many cases sponsored and supported by the police and military, also perform the same function to intimidate and evict indigenous peasant populations throughout countries in Central and South America. There is ample evidence that death squads operating in Guatemala, Chile, Argentina, and El Salvador are unofficial extensions of the military. Sometimes, however, they may not be linked to official state organs and therefore may fall into the next category, interpersonal structural violence.

Another area of overlap is *interpersonal structural violence*. Here, individuals or groups acting outside the roles of institutional agents commit violent acts to maintain, extend, or reduce hierarchical structures in the society. A typical example of this type of violence is a race riot. Race riots have occurred often in U.S. history and have functioned in most cases to further the hierarchy, as did the riots in St. Louis in the first part of the twentieth century where white

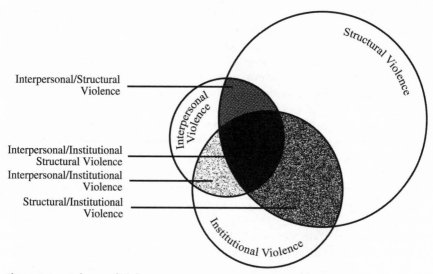

Interpersonal/Structural Violence

Interpersonal/Institutional Structural Violence

Interpersonal/Institutional Violence

Structural/Institutional Violence

Figure 1.3. Spheres of Violence.

workers attacked blacks because they were used as strike breakers by local capitalists. The New York City draft riots of 1863, when Irish immigrant laborers refused to be drafted into the Union Army to fight for the freeing of black slaves whom they saw as potential competitors for their jobs, is another similar example. More than 1,000 persons died during these riots. The peak of race rioting in the United States occurred in the summer of 1919 when riots erupted in twenty-five cities. In all these riots, African Americans were the principle target of white working-class wrath.

Violence by members of the Ku Klux Klan and other hate groups is another example. Silberman (1978) notes that between 1882 and 1903, no fewer than 1,985 blacks were killed by southern lynch mobs. Today, hate crimes are directed at ethnic and religious minorities, women, and gays and are an example of interpersonal structural violence.

Riots have also been instigated by minorities against the majority. The riots in Harlem (1964), Watts (1965), Chicago (1966), and Detroit (1967), and the more recent riots in Liberty City (1980) and Overtown (1986) in Florida, Los Angeles (1992), and Cincinnati (2001) are examples where minorities attempted to strike out against the establishment (usually precipitated by police force actions) and the system of stratification as it manifested itself to the disadvantage of categories of people. The violence of groups of black South Africans rebelling against the old system of apartheid is another example of interpersonal structural violence.

A third area of overlap is *interpersonal institutional violence,* where the interpersonal dimension overlaps with institutional violence. Here we are talking about violence by individuals or groups acting outside institutional roles directed at institutions and their agents. The deranged assassin, for example

John Hinckley, who shot President Reagan and Press Secretary James Brady, would be an example of this. The intent was not to strike out at the institution or its agent to extend, maintain, or change a system of stratification. For John Hinkley, the goal was to achieve notoriety to win the affection of movie actress Jodie Foster. Another example is the murder of Salvo Lima, the sixty-four-year-old mayor of Palermo, Italy. Two Mafia gunmen gunned the mayor down March 12, 1992, as he drove through a beachside suburb in Palermo. There were allegations that Mayor Lima had worked with the Mafia. Similar murders of public officials have occurred in Colombia regarding the government's drug war with the Medellín cartel.

Interpersonal, institutional, structural violence refers to violence by individuals or groups outside institutional roles, whose actions are directed at institutions or their agents for the purpose of maintaining, extending, or reducing hierarchical arrangements of people in society. The assassinations of Abraham Lincoln, Tsar Nicholas II, Indira Gandhi, and Anwar Sadat illustrate cases of interpersonal institutional structural violence. Here interpersonal violence directed at an institutional agent, or government, is attacked to change or stop the changes in the social structure. Terrorist activities of the African National Congress and South African neo-Nazi groups that resulted in death or injury of institutional agents are another example. The coordinated terrorist attack by Al Qaeda that destroyed the World Trade Center and damaged the Pentagon, killing more than 3,000 people, is a more recent example.

In general, interpersonal violence is more likely to be defined as violent in the society and is viewed as more threatening by elites in the system. Institutional and structural violence is less likely to be defined as violent in the society and is viewed as least threatening by elites in the system. Yet acts of institutional and structural violence are more destructive as measured by the amount and extent of violent injury. Interpersonal violence directed at institutions and/or the social structure as in the cases of interpersonal institutional violence, interpersonal structural violence, and interpersonal institutional structural violence is generally viewed as more threatening than interpersonal violence alone, and punishments for these acts are more severe than acts of interpersonal violence alone. Also the attempted killing of a government official by a lone assassin is deemed to be more serious than the killing of ordinary civilians by means of unsafe production or products, during times of warfare or through the actions of Death Squads, or by means of starvation or lack of access to medical care.

PRINCIPLES OF VIOLENCE

Ten principles of violence form the basis of our conflict analysis. These principles outline a framework by which we can analyze violence. They are not propositions in the strict sense but are axioms that describe an understanding of violence rooted in the conflict paradigm within sociology.

The first principle of violence is that *violence and the threat of violence are ultimately forms of power* used to control people's behavior. They are used by parents in controlling their children, by an abusive husband to control his wife, by a rapist to control a woman he wishes to take advantage of, by a robber who wishes to acquire money, and by the state to control behavior that threatens the social order. Violence is a form of coercive power based on the threat or enactment of physical harm. The central question for conflict sociologists is, Under what social conditions will this form of power be used?

The second principle is that *violence takes place within the context of the social structures in which we live our lives.* Violence is a form of power that is an instrument for the maintenance of social structures in the society. In this sense, violence occurs in the enforcement of the social structures. Those who most benefit from these structures and have sufficient power will act to maintain the structures, ultimately by violence. In this way, violence occurs when there is violation or threatened violation of those structures. Thus, parents may use violence to force compliance to the order they define as normative. The state may use violence to enforce the rules regarding the distribution of power that define the social order. In capitalist societies, this distribution is fundamentally rooted in property relations. Most crimes in capitalist societies generally threaten property relations or rules regarding the distribution of property. Thus the state often uses violence to enforce these rules. In these cases, those with the greatest amounts of power—parents, governing elites, and owners of property—have a vested interest in the use of violence to maintain these structures.

Violence also occurs as an act of conscious rebellion or as an instrumental or expressive response to the structures. The responses may be an act of violence to challenge or change the structures. Examples of this include terrorist actions by the Palestinian Liberation Army, Nicaraguan Contras or Sandinistas, Irish Republican Army, Italian Red Brigades, as well as the violence enacted by the American revolutionaries against the British colonial governors.

The responses may also be an act of violence to achieve an end that the structural arrangement may create blockages to achieving. Organized crime is an example of this. Organized crime syndicates use violence to maintain, expand, or create black markets as a means to gain economic and political power in the society. Many organized crime syndicates are ethnically based, so they represent a path for social mobility for ethnic minority populations (Ianni, 1973). But it does not have to be an organized crime syndicate. The lone bank robber also uses violence as an instrumental response to the structures of the larger society as it relates to the distribution of income and wealth. In these ways, violence is an instrumental adaptive response to the structures.

The responses may be an act of violence as an emotional expression of frustration in response to social conditions stemming from the structures. The violence of gangs of economically and socially displaced youth in our society is one example of this. Violence often result from insults stemming from a lack of respect or recognition by another that connects to a sense of powerlessness as a result of the positions they occupy in systems of stratification. Even acts of violence by those who have power within an institutional context (the family) may stem from frustration in response to social conditions that the individuals have little control over. For example, child and spousal abuse are often connected to acts of frustration and a sense of powerlessness derived from economic displacement, poverty, and unemployment.

The third principle is that *violence is more likely to occur in the context of hierarchical social structures.* This is a further specification of the second principle. Not only do acts of violence occur in the enforcement of, rebellion toward, or adaptation to social structures, but they are more likely to occur when the structures are hierarchically arranged.

A hierarchical social structure refers to a ranking of people in terms of specific identifiable attributes that allow one category of people to possess more power in social interaction than another category of people. Systems of stratification of all kinds are by definition hierarchical social structures. In hierarchical structures, violence occurs because hierarchical structures are fundamentally based on relationships of exploitation. An exploitative relationship by definition creates differential benefits and commitments for the actors involved. As a result of this inequality of benefits, there is ultimately a need for coercion to maintain them. This coercion may be latent—often times exercised through the use of symbols, as in the role of ideologies that help those who are disadvantaged in the relationship to accept the structures as natural, necessary, or just. Or the coercion may be manifest or overt, as in the use of physical force by the military and the police to maintain order and the hierarchical relationships that form its foundation.

Hierarchical structures also can be more generally understood as rules that allow for the unequal distribution of a scarcity or power either based on chance, family position, a specific skill, or a specific attribute. Because differential benefits accrue from the rule, violence is more likely to occur. In foraging societies, which generally have much less developed systems of stratification, violence often occurs because of conflict over the rules of distribution of the scarcities. This is the same case as in more complex industrial societies. Although the rules may be more formally institutionalized in economic relations, there is a level of violence in maintaining and resisting them.

This third principle is consistent with the first five assumptions of the conflict analysis applied to violence as noted by Ball-Rokeach (1980).

1. An unequal distribution of societal resources produce asymmetric social relations.
2. Asymmetric social relations produce conflict between constituent parts.
3. The asymmetric social relations that constitute a society's social structure generate and shape the unequal distribution of resources that produce asymmetric social relations between interacting subunits.
4. Therefore, conflict between strata in the social structure generates and shapes conflict between interacting subunits.

5. The transition from latent to manifest conflict is conditional upon: (a) legitimacy of asymmetric social relations; (b) perceived threat to established asymmetric social relations; (c) dissatisfaction with established asymmetric social relations; and (d) capacity to manifest conflict (50).

A corollary to this third principle is that the more hierarchical structures exist within a society (race, class, gender, age, etc.), the more intricate the structures and the greater the distance between positions within the hierarchical structures, the more violence will exist in that society as a means of preserving, adapting, or rebelling against these structures. Thus, in a society such as India, with complex systems of stratification, more violence will exist than in societies such as Iceland or Japan.

The fourth principle is that *violence as a form of power is learned.* It is learned first by the imitation of those who use violence to maintain power and control. In these instances we principally learn that power can be instrumental. As those with power use violence to maintain and extend their control and domination, we learn the appropriateness of violence for maintaining hierarchies or, more likely put, maintaining order and the control of the social relations that stem from these hierarchies. Thus, violence that is structural and institutional spreads to the interpersonal level as we learn to use violence to maintain the order in our own life that stems from these structures of domination. The violence directed at children is violence fundamentally committed by men or women, often directed by men, to maintain control. This violence is then learned by children as a means to control others with whom they engage in social interaction.

Violence also can be learned as an imitation of those who are dominated or controlled. In this instance, we learn that violence can be expressive in that it is defined as an "appropriate" response to anger or frustration. Our ability to enact violence allows us to experience the illusion that we have power, when usually it is because of the absence of power that we enact violence.

Learning provides the linkages between levels of violence noted earlier. Violence that we are accustomed to at the structural level becomes a matter of policy or practice at the institutional level and becomes a mode of personal behavior at the interpersonal level. As we learn the cultural and ideological justifications for the structural violence, and learn the legitimacy of the violent policy actions at the institutional level, the violence we enact in our personal life becomes "natural" or "normal." Straus's research on child discipline patterns and their relationship to delinquency suggests a pattern where violence by parents is used as a means of controlling order in the home and violence as a form of power is learned by their children as an appropriate method of exerting control in social interaction (Straus and Gelles, 1991a).

The fourth principle does not necessarily preclude the assumption that humans are innately aggressive, although this is an untestable assumption and is best relegated to the realm of ideology. Nevertheless, whether we are innately aggressive or not, we must learn when and how to be violent. Learning is the channel in which our biological inclinations or potentials manifest themselves into social action. We learn to be violent, we learn to exercise this form of power in social interaction. Ultimately, the culture of a society contains the curriculum of violence that we learn through the socialization processes and the structures that are legitimated by the systems of ideas that are part of this larger system of shared understandings. In the next chapter we discuss the role of culture in creating the lessons of violence.

We contend that an act of violence is not in the vast majority of cases a product of a physiological or psychological defect. Given the pervasiveness of violence at all societal levels, it would be difficult to argue that it is a product of individual pathology. Unless one assumes that the vast majority of the population, including those in the highest positions within institutions (presidents and other government officials, and corporate and religious leaders), are infected with physiological or psychological diseases that cause violence. Generally, all biological and psychological approaches suffer from the problem of not being able to draw connections between the defective gene or syndrome and the actual behavior. Furthermore, for biological and psychological approaches not to examine the pathological roots of legitimate or normative violence reveals its principal ideological bias and function of displacing attention from the nature of the social system and placing attention (and blame) for violence on those who are least powerful in the system. For example, if we are to use a biological or psychological argument to account for the actions of a violent gang member, why do we not apply the same model to account for the heroism of a soldier who is very effective in killing the enemy? Both individuals may see themselves as acting for the benefit of the group and acting to defend geographic or market position or territory, social status or position, or honor.

The fifth principle is that *violence is defined as legitimate or illegitimate as it relates to whether it furthers or threatens the social structures in the society*. Robbery is defined as an illegitimate act of violence because it threatens property relations. Assault is violent because it exerts control or power over another (not necessarily defined as assault if it is directed at women and children) outside of legitimate, institutional channels. Illegitimate rape threatens patriarchy. "Legitimate" rape, marital and date rape, that reinforces patriarchy is less likely to be defined as an act of violence. For example in Pakistan, rape is used as a means of punishment carried out by tribal leaders. On June 22, 2002, in the Pakistani province of Punjab, a tribal council convened to determine the fate of an eleven-year old boy seen walking in the fields with a girl of the higher-caste Matsoi tribe. "In a village like Meerwala, such an act is considered a great dishonor to the entire tribe. The boy's father tried to convince the council that his son had done no wrong. He even volunteered for his son to marry the girl in question and wed his own daughter to one of the Matsoi men. The council, however, could not allow a Matsoi girl to marry a lower caste male. After two hours of deliberation, the council ordered a ruthless punishment. Four Matsoi tribesmen, also members of the judicial council, were told to inflict dishonor on the family by raping Mukhtaran [the boy's sister]. Recounting that day, Mukhtaran says she fell to her knees, crying and weeping. She said she appealed to the council members' morality, reminding them that she taught their daughters to read the Koran. "But they tore my clothes and raped me, one by one" (Masood, 2002). According to a recent human rights report in Punjab alone, a woman is raped every six hours and a woman is gang-raped every four days, yet only 321 rape cases were reported to the police last year (Masood, 2002).

Another example is that of state violence which is often defined as legitimate and is often not defined as violent but rather as a defensive or police or peacekeeping action. Military interventions by the United States are all defined this way including the recent military actions taken in Panama, Grenada, Iraq, Libya, and Afghanistan, as well as the secret or covert wars in Nicaragua, El Salvador, or Colombia. The military now brands wars to define their purpose (Desert Storm, Enduring Freedom) and claims the use of smart weapons that have minimal impact on innocent citizens as a means to cover the violent nature of the warfare. Furthermore, enemy and civilian casualty counts are not reported because of concerns about public support for the violence.

A corollary to this last principle is that those who are more powerful in the society have a greater ability to commit violence and the violence they commit is more likely to be defined as legitimate, and thus not problematic. State violence is a large category of legitimate violence used by those who are most powerful. Conversely, those who are least powerful in the society have less ability to commit violence, and the violence they commit is more likely to be defined as illegitimate and thus problematic. This is consistent with the seventh assumption of Ball-Rokeach (1980). She notes that the

> conflict behaviors of subordinates against superordinates are more likely to be defined as violent than conflict behaviors of superordinates against subordinates. . . . Control of the semantic politics of violence is a resource that usually resides with occupants of superordinate positions. While violence typically plays a role in the construction, maintenance, and change of asymmetric social relations, maintenance violence is likely to be labeled as something else. If superordinates relative to subordinates, have a greater capacity to define the violence out of their violent acts, then they would experience less psychological, social, and behavioral cost or be freer from social control forces when they engage in violence. Superordinates, especially those actively maintaining high positions in the social structure, should thus exhibit more violence than subordinates (51).

A sixth principle of violence is that *violence takes place in the context of levels: interpersonal, institutional, and structural*. All levels are a part of the general system of violence in a particular society. As we move from the interpersonal to institutional and to structural violence the scale and scope of violence increase. At the same time, the higher levels of violence are less likely to be recognized as violence and thus are not seen as problematic. One qualification to the above principle is where interpersonal violence intersects with institutional and/or structural violence. In this case, as mentioned previously, the violence is seen as more problematic and threatening than just interpersonal violence. Thus the individual who attacks representatives of authority of institutions is seen as more violent than the individual attacking his neighbor or a stranger. A race or class riot is more violent than a 'just' war.

The seventh principle refers to the *chain of violence. Most violence that occurs in a society is linked to other levels of violence.* Violence begins at the structural level. What allows us to victimize others is our ability to think less of those we victimize, our ability to separate ourselves from those we victimize. Pepinsky notes in his description of violence as unresponsiveness: "Violence entails a willful disregard for one's effect on others. . . . Violence or disregard for others may be direct and personal or indirect and structural, as when the plight of impoverished classes remains unaddressed by privileged classes in a shared economic order" (1991, 17). Fundamentally, in the act of violence we think of our victim as less because we are conditioned to view others in our society differently, based on our perception of human differences of value or quality. This difference in perception in the evaluation of others is rooted in the structural divisions that form the basis of the social order. Inequalities of all kinds are social constructions. Differences exist between people on a whole range of attributes. The transformation of these differences into inequalities is a social transformation based on systems of stratification within the society. Thus men and women are different, those of African American ancestry and those of white European ancestry are different, individuals have different talents and abilities rooted in intellectual, physical, and psychological differences. What transforms these differences into a system of access to greater or lesser privileges and rights is a social construction.

The violence that begins at the structural level (i.e., differential illness rates, differences in infant mortality rates, differences in life expectancy rates, differences in life chances to develop one's human potentials) as illustrated in Figure 1.4 is the first link in the chain of violence in the society. This violence is then linked to institutional violence. Those victimized at the structural level, at birth, are more likely to be victimized at the institutional level in families, schools, religious institutions, in the economy, and in the political system. Last, the violence manifests itself at the interpersonal level, sometimes directed at those perceived as victimizers at the higher levels, in most cases at those who experience similar or greater levels of victimization.

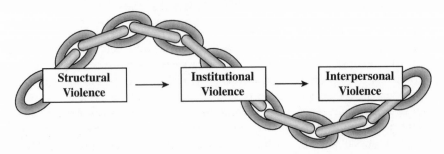

Figure 1.4.   Chain of Violence.

The dominant pattern of interpersonal violence, whether we are talking about murder, assault, or rape, is that those who are participants in violence at this level were likely previously victimized at higher levels. Thus, the causal chain of violence in any society begins with structural violence and ends with interpersonal violence. At this point in the chain the violence is officially recognized and defined as violence. The earlier links are made invisible as defined in terms of violence. Thus, in searching for the causes of violence in a society, it is crucial to begin by assessing the society in terms of patterns of structural violence and institutional violence and then to look at the patterns of interpersonal violence and how they are linked to the other two. Unfortunately, because we have traditionally been blinded from understanding violence as anything but interpersonal, we often look only at the causes of violence at the interpersonal level. Thus our focus ends in a classic blaming-the-victim posture in explaining the violence in our midst.

A corollary to this principle is that societies with high levels of structural violence also have high levels of institutional and interpersonal violence. Conversely, societies that have low levels of structural violence have low levels of institutional and interpersonal violence. Thus to assess the level of violence in a society it is crucial that we begin by measuring the levels of violence at the highest levels.

The eighth principle of violence refers to the *internationalization of violence*. Although we can talk of violence as a societal phenomenon, it is crucial that we understand the phenomenon as a force that links societies throughout the world. Though these international linkages of violence occur at all three levels, the major links are at the structural level, followed by the institutional levels, and finally, the least important linkages, at the interpersonal levels. Structural violence at the international level refers to how the hierarchical divisions along major systems of stratification manifest themselves internationally in the positioning of nation-states and people within them and how these structures manifest themselves in differences in life chances. Life expectancies, morbidity and mortality differentials are much greater internationally, say, comparing Namibia or Afghanistan to the United States, than what you would find in any one society. Institutional violence internationally can be understood not only in terms of military violence between states but more pervasive is the violence in the economic arena: toxic dumping and the dumping of unsafe products and production overseas are examples of this. Another area not often discussed as international violence is the violent consequences of religious missionary work that has occurred throughout history and continues today. This is the often genocidal violence that results from the forced assimilation and destruction of indigenous cultures that is widespread throughout the Southern Hemisphere of the world.

Like interpersonal violence in general, interpersonal violence internationally is most likely of the three types to be defined as violence and has received the most attention. As in all cases regarding levels of violence, enforcement networks have been well established for interpersonal violence. This is also true for international, interpersonal violence, and international, interpersonal, institutional, structural violence, (international terrorist activities). Similarly, as with institutional violence, enforcement is weak or nonexistent. This is also true for international institutional violence. Enforcement for international institutional violence is usually relegated to U.N. agencies such as the International Labor Organization (ILO) and the World Health Organization (WHO), both of which have extremely limited power to enforce the regulations to prevent international institutional violence. For structural violence at both national and international levels, enforcement is generally weak. Some noted cases would be the case of the Nazis and the Holocaust, the more recent case of South Africa and the system of apartheid, and the World Court's decision in 1986 that found the United States in violation of international law in its support of a mercenary army to overthrow the Nicaraguan government. In all these cases, there has been international response either in the form of a trial or tribunal or some organized international pressure or sanctioning. Most recent attempts to establish an International Criminal Court to address crimes of genocide are being hampered by the United States which seeks exception to the powers of the court in matters relating to the operations of the U.S. military and allies of the United States (Shelton, 2000; Ambros, 1998).

The ninth principle is that *violence at the international level is defined as legitimate or illegitimate as it relates to whether it furthers or threatens the divisions between and within societies.* Thus the invasion of Kuwait by Iraq was defined as illegitimate violence, but the more violent attack by the United States and its allies on Iraq that has continued for more than ten years thereafter is defined as legitimate and necessary. As with violence at the societal level, international violence defined as legitimate is often not defined as violent but rather as a defensive or peacekeeping action. It is curious that after the Gulf War, there were a good many charges of rape, torture, and killings of Kuwaiti nationals and attacks on the Kurdish minority by Iraqi forces, however, there was little information regarding the level of destruction in Iraq and on its civilian population.

A corollary to this last principle is that nations and alliances among nations that are more powerful internationally have a greater ability to commit violence and that the violence they commit is more likely to be defined as legitimate and thus nonproblematic. Conversely, those who are least powerful in the international community have less ability to commit violence and the violence they commit is more likely to be defined as illegitimate and thus problematic. Thus, the potential for and occurrence of violence by the weakest states are systematically exaggerated relative to the potential for and occurrence of violence by the more powerful states.

Herman (1987) makes this point in his discussion of the use of the term terrorism. He notes that the most powerful states define terrorism to exclude their acts and those of their friends and clients. He notes several ways that this is done. Two ways, in particular, are to confine the use of the term to non-state actors and to distinguish between terrorism and retaliation. Thus, terrorists are understood to be principally small groups from the developing world who cross nation-state boundaries to inflict violence. The violence sponsored by the economically and militarily dominated states or by countries in alliances with these states, the violence of death squads composed of military and police, overt and covert military actions, legal and extra-legal executions, torture of prisoners, and so on are not defined as terrorism. Who is more likely to be defined as a terrorist group: the Palestinian Liberation Organization or the Contras during the war in Nicaragua, the Libyan government or the governments of Argentina and Guatemala? In all cases, it is the groups or governments that are defined as our enemies and not those who may be responsible for the greater numbers of civilian deaths as a technique of terror. The U.S. State Department currently designates seven countries, Iran, Iraq, Syria, Libya, Cuba, North Korea, and Sudan as state sponsors of international terrorism (U.S. State Department, 2001). Countries such as Colombia and Israel whose militaries recently have been linked to death squad, torture, and assassinations are missing from the list (Human Rights Watch, 2001; Smyth, 1998; CNN.Com/world, 2001; Lewis, 2001). Furthermore, by the criteria used by the United States government to determine which states would be terrorist states (for example harboring groups that have committed terrorist acts), the United States itself would be considered a terrorist state. This does not even consider U.S. assassination plots and attempts, funding, training, and directing mercenary armies to overthrow governments, possessing and distributing weapons of mass destruction, training and participation in torture of political prisoners, etc. (Blum, 2000).

The tenth and last principle refers to *the international chain of violence. Although, violence principally has a societally specific causal chain, it is important to understand the international causal chain.* In order to comprehend the pattern of interpersonal violence in our own society, we must first recognize how it is a part of an international chain. This chain of violence begins at the highest levels of international systems of stratification within a world political economic system (international structural violence). It leads to international institutional violence that reproduces, maintains, and extends the hierarchy in social relations between nation-states and sectors of the world system. This then leads to the pattern of structural violence within a given social system stemming from the patterns of stratification that are in part a product of world structural position as well as part of that system's history. This structural violence leads to the institutional violence that reproduces, maintains, and extends the hierarchy within nation-states. Finally, we arrive at the interpersonal violence between those who are acting in response to the social conditions and social relations that are a product of positions within social systems. (See figure 1.5.)

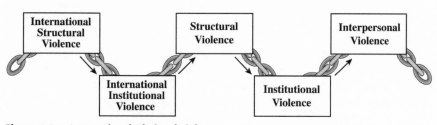

Figure 1.5. International Chain of Violence.

The impoverishment of nations and their people because of their structural position in the world economy and the enforcement of the maintenance of this position by imperialist relations between advanced industrialized societies and countries on the periphery is the beginning of this chain. The international structural violence of disease, famine, and lower life expectancies resulting from the impoverishment of people in Africa, South and Central America, and Asia begins the chain. This international structural violence may also manifest itself in the displacement of working-class populations in dominant countries of the world as a result of the superexploitative relationships that multinational corporations are able to create with workers in poorer, less developed countries because of their victimization. This leads to international institutional violence as military forces from dominant nations, mercernary armies hired by these nation-states, or the military of the client states enact violence to maintain the hierarchical ordering between people and nation-states. Last, the interpersonal violence throughout the world by those who are most displaced is a product of the structural and institutional violence that they have experienced. This occurs both within the poorest nations, where most of the world's population reside, and among those who are most displaced in the ghettos of the wealthiest nations.

If we focus only on the lowest levels, we see the trees but miss the forest of which they are a part. In so doing, we fail to understand the forces beyond the individual actors who are in their personal drama of violence. This is how we generally view the violence in our own society as we look for the defects in the individual actors or their immediate social situation. We fail to understand and see how the violence that is committed at the highest levels by those with the greatest power manifests itself in the violence of those with least power in the society and the world. These ten principles form the basis of our analysis of violence. They provide the lens we use to understand the disparate forms of violence that exists in the society and the world.

CONCLUSION

Violence, as we have seen in this introductory chapter, can be perceived from different vantage points. It can be approached at increasingly abstract levels of conceptualization (interpersonal, institutional, or structural) that lend important insights into the contextual dynamics of how violence occurs and even point to forms not previously recognized. It also can be interpreted through separate disciplinary perspectives. A limitation of much previous treatment of the violence phenomenon, however, is that often it is considered only at one level (most frequently the interpersonal) within an order paradigm. Moreover, assumptions of the "abnormality" of violence are often implicit (usually from a pro-status quo orientation that views the sources of violence as located in aberrant individuals), and the official working data of violence is likely to be narrowly grounded in one culture or society.

Sociology offers a disciplinary perspective that follows the scientific method in describing the patterns of violence in societies and investigating the social forces that create these specific patterns. The goal of a sociology of violence is to sensitize us to ultimately recognizing that violence is fundamentally a product of the organization of the society. This perspective challenges us to assess critically the nature of the social order for its contribution to creating the violence that threatens human existence.

Some of the instances of violence discussed in the following chapters are apparent, even familiar, to readers. Others, however, may be less obvious and perhaps never considered. To the extent that we can contribute a sense of connectedness to both the familiar and unfamiliar types of violence, movement toward a better theoretical realization of violence's pervasive and extensive sociological grounding will have been achieved, and consequently a better understanding of the nature of violence in this society and throughout the world will have been accomplished.

REFERENCES

Allen, James, editor. 2000. *Without Sanctuary: Lynching Photography in America.* Santa Fe, NM: Twin Palms.

Ambros, Kai, editor. 1998. Special issue of *European Journal of Crime, Criminal Law, and Criminal Justice* 6, no. 4

Archer, Dane, and Rosemary Gartner. 1984. *Violence and Crime in Cross-National Perspective.* New Haven, Conn.: Yale University Press.

Ball-Rokeach, S. J. 1980. "Normative and Deviant Violence from a Conflict Perspective." *Social Problems* 28: 45–62.

Beirne, Piers, and James Messerschmidt. 1991. *Criminology.* New York: Harcourt Brace Jovanovich.

Blum, William. 2000. *Rogue State.* Monroe, Maine: Common Courage Press.

Bourdieu, Pierre, and Jean-Claude Passeron. 1977. *Reproduction in Education, Society and Culture.* Beverly Hills, Calif.: Sage.

CNN. 2001, July 5. "Annan condemns 'targeted assassinations' by Israel." Atlanta: Cable News Network. www.cnn.com/2001/WORLD/meast/07/05/un.mideast/.

Davis, Kingsley, and Wilbert Moore. 1945. "Some Principles of Social Stratification." *American Sociological Review* 10: 242–44.

"Death on a Mean Street." 1989, September 11. *Time,* 28.

Dentler, Robert, and Kai T. Erickson. 1959. "The Functions of Deviance in Groups." *Social Problems* 7: 98–107.

Dinnerstein, Leonard, Roger L. Nichols, and David M. Reimers. 1990. *Natives and Strangers.* New York: Oxford University Press.

Donohue, Elizabeth, Vincent Schiraldi, and Jason Zeidenberg. 1998. *School House Hype: The School Shootings, and the Real Risks Kids Face in America.* Washington, D.C.: The Justice Policy Institute.

Durkheim, Emile. 1938. *The Rules of the Sociological Method.* New York: Free Press.

Fishbein, Diana H. 1990. "Biological Perspectives in Criminology." *Criminology* 28, no. 1: 27–57.

Fox, James Alan, and Marianne W. Zawitz. 2001. *Homicide Trends in the United States.* Washington, D.C.: Bureau of Justice Statistics, U.S. Department of Justice. www.ojp.usdoj.gov/bjs/homicide/homtrnd.htm#contents.

Harris, Marvin. 1974. *Cows, Pigs, Wars and Witches.* New York: Vintage Books.

Heelas, Paul. 1982. "Anthropology, Violence and Catharsis." In *Aggression and Violence,* edited by Peter Marsh and Anne Campbell. New York: St. Martin's Press.

Herman, Edward S. 1987. "U.S. Sponsorship of International Terrorism: An Overview." *Crime and Social Justice* 27–28: 1–29.

Hernstein, Richard. 1973. *I.Q. in the Meritocracy.* Boston: Little, Brown.

Hook, Sidney. 1934. "Violence." In *Encyclopedia of Social Sciences,* edited by R. A. Seligman and Alvin Johnson. Vol. 15, 264–67. New York: Macmillan.

Human Rights Watch. 2001. *The "Sixth Division" Military-paramilitary Ties and U.S. Policy in Colombia.* New York: Human Rights Watch. www.hrw.org/reports/2001/colombia/.

Ianni, Francis A. J. 1973. *Ethnic Succession in Organized Crime.* National Institute of Law Enforcement and Criminal Justice. Washington, D.C.: Government Printing Office.

Jensen, Arthur R. 1969. "How Much Can We Boost IQ and Scholastic Achievement?" *Harvard Educational Review* 39: 1–123.

Koning, Hans. 1976. *Columbus: His Enterprise.* New York: Monthly Review.

Kozol, Jonathan. 1991. *Savage Inequalities: Children in America's Schools.* New York: Crown.

Lee, Richard B. 1979. *The !Kung San: Men, Women and Work in a Foraging Society.* New York: Cambridge University Press.

Lewis, Flora. 2001, January 12. "Israel Defiles Itself with These Assassinations of Palestinians." *International Herald Tribune.* www.iht.com/frontpage.html.

Masood, Naveen Naqvi. 2002, July 7. "A brutal rape case riles Pakistan." MSNBC. www.msnbc.com/news/776838.asp.

Michalowski, Raymond. 1985. *Order, Law, and Crime: An Introduction to Criminology.* New York: Random House.

Miliband, Ralph. 1983. *Class Power and State Power.* London: Verso.

Mills, C. Wright. 1959. *Sociological Imagination.* New York: Oxford University Press.

Nader, Ralph. 1972. *Unsafe at Any Speed: The Designed-In Dangers of the American Automobile.* New York: Bantam.

National Center for Health Statistics. *Health United States 1996–1997 and Injury Chartbook.* Washington, D.C.: U.S. Department of Health and Human Services. www.cdc.gov/nchs/data/hus/hus96_97.pdf.

Parsons, Talcott, Robert Bales, et al. 1955. *Family Socialization and Interaction Process.* New York: Free Press.

Pepinsky, Harold. 1991. *The Geometry of Violence and Democracy.* Bloomington: Indiana University Press.

Report of the National Advisory Commission on Civil Disorders. 1968. New York: Times Books.

Shelton, Dinah. 2000. *International Crimes, Peace, and Human Rights: The Role of the International Criminal Court.* Ardsley, N.Y.: Transnational Publishers.

Silberman, Charles E. 1978. *Criminal Violence, Criminal Justice.* New York: Random House.

Straus, Murray A. 1991. "Physical Violence in American Families: Incidence Rates, Causes, and Trends." In *Abused and Battered,* edited by JoAnn L. Miller and Dean D. Knudson. New York: Aldine de Gruyter.

United Nations Department of Public Information. 1997, December. "Indigenous people: Challenges facing the international community." DPI/1937/B— December. Prepared for posting by the Information Technology Section (ITS) of the Department of Public Information. www.un.org/rights/50/people.

U.S. Bureau of the Census. 1991. *Statistical Abstract of the United States: 1991*. Washington, D.C.: Government Printing Office.

U.S. State Department. 2001, April 30. *Overview of State-Sponsored Terrorism: Patterns of Global Terrorism—2000*. Released by the Office of the Coordinator for Counterterrorism. www.state.gov/s/ct/rls/pgtrpt/2000/2441.htm.

Weiner, Neil Alan, Margaret A. Zahn, and Rita J. Sagi. 1990. *Violence: Patterns, Causes, and Public Policy*. New York: Harcourt Brace Jovanovich.

Zinn, Howard. 1980. *A People's History of the United States*. New York: Harper & Row.

Chapter Two

The Cultural Roots of Violence

In 1971 a band of twenty-four people calling themselves the Tasaday was discovered living in a remote rain forest on the Philippine island of Mindanao. Believed never to have been exposed to the "outside world," the Tasaday remarkably possessed no weapons (nor even words to describe them) and had no history of war or conflict. They were living a primitive existence as simple hunter-gatherers, sleeping in caves, digging wild yams, foraging for nuts, and storing water in bamboo stalks.

After two *National Geographic* articles and a book entitled *The Gentle Tasaday* made the tribe a worldwide sensation, journalists and other observers flocked to Mindanao to investigate these nonviolent people. The Tasaday, it seemed, cut off from and uncontaminated by modern civilization, had found a way to survive successfully from some earlier, more harmonious age. Representatives of the New Age loved the Tasaday. So did those who argued, in the face of then-popular bioanthropological theories claiming human beings to be inherently aggressive, that the Tasaday demonstrated how the dynamics of social forces, not people's biological inheritance, lead them to do violent things. The Tasaday offered hope to a world grown weary of terrorism, dictatorial repression, civil war, and the Vietnam conflict.

But in 1986 a Swiss journalist named Oswald Iten pricked this euphoric balloon. He revealed that the Tasaday were impostors, part of a hoax concocted by the politically ambitious head of the Philippine government agency in charge of that country's "indigenous peoples." When Iten encountered the Tasaday they were wearing jeans and T-shirts, growing crops, and living in huts elevated above the ground just like other Philippine natives. He learned that the government official had paid the villagers of two Westernized tribes to smear themselves with dirt, clad themselves in the briefest of loincloths, and conduct themselves like classic Stone Agers. In actuality, the Tasaday as some kind of "lost tribe" did not exist.

The short-lived notoriety of the Tasaday illustrates the nostalgic value that such a pristine, if hypothetical, people possesses. These "savage innocents" seemed to confirm the myth of a basically nonaggressive human nature. They also lent support to countercultural critics who rejected modern materialism and its assumed relationship to crime and violence. As one popular news magazine, in revealing the Tasaday fraud, put it: "the Tasaday served as model 'paleohippies' by living communally, by shunning materialism and leadership and by eating natural foods" (Brownlee, 1990).

This was not the first time that Western observers (professional or otherwise) had idealized a tribal people as virtually free of violence when it later turned out that there was really considerable turmoil there all along (see, e.g., Barnouw, 1963, 39–58, 83–91). Indeed, the ubiquitous presence of conflict in virtually all societies seems to make the imaginative exception of a violence-free case a tantalizing possibility. It is no wonder that many persons *want to believe* that somewhere, somehow, such an idyllic nonviolent culture has survived or evolved.

Sociologically, such a utopia is strictly wishful thinking. Even in the simplest societies studied by anthropologists there exist scarce resources, hierarchies along gender lines and family status, and (consequently) struggles that involve power and coercion. Yet we would contend that none are of the same magnitude of the more hierarchically organized and structured societies of today. And the documented conflicts even among so-called nonviolent people include interpersonal aggression, gender disagreements, corporal punishment of children, emotional and violent ostracization of deviants, and occasionally homicides (Montagu, 1978). These are patterns of social disturbance familiar to us all.

Yet at the same time cross-cultural analyses show that societies manifest a wide variation in the prevalence, acceptance, and even valuation of violence. Anthropologist Ashley Montagu (1978), in surveying over two dozen relatively nonviolent, non-Western societies, asked, "How can one account for the marked differences in the expression of violence?"(6). He concluded that the answer lay in "the environmental stimulation" (or culture) of a social group rather than in its members' genes. No one starts out life developing his or her own language without reference to other people, and likewise, no one adopts aggression and violence as social tactics without the influence of others in the context of performing roles or outside institutional role performance.

Recall the importance of roles in the definition of interpersonal and institutional violence. Culture, in its symbols, values, and traditions, sets the definitions and contexts of appropriate roles within social institutions. It also demarcates the appropriateness of violence in those roles and the inappropriateness of violence outside those roles. Thus, culture and its learning are important areas to investigate for an analysis of violence, particularly for conceptualizing the forms that violence takes.

CULTURAL ROOTS

The Symbols of Violence

Human beings are symbol-creating, symbol-manipulating creatures. It is a truism held by sociologists that we do not live merely in a world of physical reality but, more important, in a world of *social reality*. In every society members attach a myriad of negotiated or constructed meanings to all facets of their interpersonal relationships, and they use symbols to represent those meanings, whether the latter are the presumed intentions of others as they act or the shifting power and statuses of various social actors. Given the cognitive and speech capabilities of human beings, symbols can stand for nearly anything, such as concrete objects (e.g., a swastika or a cross representing a political and religious creed), and, conversely, nearly anything can become a symbol. Voice tone, facial gestures, body posture, skin color, numerous insignias, flags, uniforms, car models, clothing brand names, colors, lights, occupational titles, hairstyles—all can serve as symbolic guideposts affecting persons' treatment of each other and the flow of their interactions.

Consideration of symbols is important in the study of violence because so much aggression occurs between persons involving stimuli in the physical environment that have broader symbolic meanings within their shared social reality. Take, as a simple example, insulting gestures. The meanings of derogatory body gestures to insult people are not universal but particular to specific cultures (as symbol systems). The various individual physical movements involved would be inconsequential minus their symbolic power to arouse emotions.

Thus, the familiar North American hand gesture of touching the tips of the index finger and thumb to form a circle while extending the other three fingers together, an innocuous way to signal "OK" or approval/understanding, represents something altogether different and possibly offensive in some South American countries. There it may stand for *la sena* (mark or sign) *del burro*, meaning the anus of the animal. Likewise, raising a rigid middle finger while simultaneously curving the others, unquestionably North Americans' favorite obscene gesture meaning "Fuck you!" referring to male power in the context of patriarchy, elicits virtually no reaction from non-Westernized Japanese. Nevertheless, in that Far Eastern culture, muttering *yotsu* (the number four, referring to the number of legs on a nonhuman animal) implies that the person spoken about is a despised member of the former medieval outcast *burakumin* stratum of society. Worse, curling the thumb and two middle fingers inward while extending the index and little fingers symbolizes horns (also a sign for the allegedly subhuman outcast minority) and can provoke a literal riot in a crowded Tokyo subway car (Devos and Wagatsuma, 1972). In France, a driver responding to another angry motorist's horn or vocalizations will stick his arm out the window and straight up. By patting the roof of the car directly over him, he signals: "Put your testicles up here for me to smash!" As is well known, Italians, Spaniards, and East Europeans, among many others, have their own special gestures to express rejection, disagreement, and contempt that often establish provocation for aggression. Possibly spitting is the only candidate for a universal motion of contempt. Admitting that one exception, obviously none of the other physical movements described is inherently threatening or insulting. Instead, over time they have come to serve as symbolic "short-hand" ways for expressing aggressive emotions.

Another case in point is art. Recently two European scholars examined ancient (mid-ninth to seventh century B.C.E) Assyrian art and concluded that the Assyrians' artistic renditions of themselves in war and victory parades as well as on the hunt were symbolic statements of power and violence deliberately communicating those themes. Commenting on bas-reliefs at King Ashurbanipal's excavated palace at Nineveh, they wrote:

> The celebratory nature of the reliefs, the obvious relish with which the defeat, humiliation, and slaughter of Assyria's enemies are portrayed, and the profusely gory detail of the battle and hunting scenes, would seem to confirm the historians' view of the Assyrians as an intensely nationalistic, imperialistic, and violent people (Bersani and Dutoit, 1985, 3).

Likewise, Nazi propaganda extolled so-called Aryan virtues in posters that displayed robust men and women in heroic poses suggesting determination, strength and even belligerence. Interestingly, the above pair of authors compared the 2,800-year-old Assyrian bas-reliefs to the German filmmaker Leni Riefenstahl's classic *Triumph of the Will*, a propaganda movie that Hitler commissioned to record and glorify the 1934 Nazi Party Congress meeting in Nuremberg. Both ancient Assyrian sculptors and Nazi propagandists, they concluded, understood the manipulation of violence and aggression in symbolic ways to promote fear and awe of the regime.

The important point here is that a symbol can become a proxy for intended or implied violence. The closer such a proxy resembles the act or potential effects of violent acts, the greater is its salience and its power to elicit an equally violent reaction. A fist shaken in another's face, a knife pulled in anger during a bar disagreement, or the North American middle-finger gesture (which could be used literally to penetrate someone either vaginally or anally) are all common examples. The range of possible violence proxies, and their deep integration into our daily physical and vocal expressions as well as our literature and popular entertainment, is considerable indeed.

Values and Definitions of Violence

The Yanomamo are a primitive polygynous tribe of approximately 15,000 Indians who inhabit the rain forests straddling the borders of Venezuela and Brazil. They have the unparalleled distinction in anthropological research of being the meanest, fiercest, and most relentlessly violent people ever studied (Chagnon, 1968; Shapiro, 1971). The men are habitual users of a hallucinogenic powder that they blow through tubes into each others' noses, a drug that serves as an analgesic (dulling pain) and induces a stupor that leaves the users draining long trails of green mucus from their nostrils. When not raiding the villages of their fellow tribesmen, Yanomamo males constantly pick fights with each other. They challenge each other to physically punishing duels over the slightest matters: first trading hard punches into each other's pectoral muscles, sometimes escalating to taking turns delivering blows with heavy poles to an unresisting adversary's bowed head, and then occasionally culminating in fights with six-foot-long spears. Constantly eager to demonstrate their aggressiveness, Yanomamo males are proud of their scars, even shaving the crowns of their heads and rubbing red pigments into the skin to make the lesions stand out. Writes anthropologist Marvin Harris (1974) of this incredibly violent segment of humanity:

> By the time a typical Yanomamo male reaches maturity, he is covered with wounds and scars of innumerable quarrels, duels, and military raids. Although they hold women in great contempt, Yanomamo men are always brawling over real or imagined acts of adultery and broken promises to provide wives. Yanomamo women are also covered with scars and bruises, mostly the result of violent encounters with seducers, rapists, and husbands. No Yanomamo woman escapes the brutal tutelage of the typical hot-tempered drug-taking Yanomamo warrior-husband. All Yanomamo physically abuse their wives. Kind husbands merely bruise and mutilate them; the fierce ones wound and kill. Perversely, Yanomamo women not only expect some amount of such abuse as normal but even measure their own self-worth and social status by the beatings and scars they receive. (74–5)

Various theories contend among anthropologists as to what lessons we can learn from this "laboratory of human conflict," as one journalist described the Yanomamo (Allman, 1988). Some take a sociobiological view, that is that the "real" (if unconscious) motive for such aggressive competition is reproductive success (gaining more women by conquest, thus ensuring more offspring). Others say the real struggle is sociological, that is, over resources (as defined in terms of material possessions as well as women), pure and simple.

For our purposes, the Yanomamo illustrate one extreme on a continuum of culturally approved interpersonal violence, the opposite, say, of Quakers or Australia's famously cooperative hunter-gathering aborigines. It is unlikely that any social group of any size is totally violence free. The members of societies have always had to accommodate themselves to some certain level of violence perceived as "necessary." As anthropologist Catherine H. Bernadt (1978) notes, "The problem . . . is not whether there is some modicum of aggression in any given society, or whether there are expressions of what could be called aggression. It is whether there are checks and balances that restrain or contain these, how successful or otherwise they seem to be, and how they are transmitted" (158).

Clearly social institutions prescribe rather broad roles of sanctioned violence and even may promote violence as entertainment. In Elizabethan England, for example, "bear baiting" (placing a defenseless bear in a deep pit and gradually stabbing it to death with long poles) was a popular form of amusement alongside Shakespeare's plays. The gladiatorial extravaganzas of Imperial Rome, sometimes pointed to as simply a more brutal and fatal extension of the aggressive drama in modern professional football or hockey, served up a considerable amount of gore for mass amusement.

Human sacrifice is another extreme of institutional violence that has been shown by scholars to have been a truly global phenomenon, although it is probably true that no one surpassed the Aztecs of pre-Columbian Mexico in the scale on which it was practiced. The most common Aztec ritual sacrifice was carving out the living victim's heart while he or she was stretched across an altar. Flaying (skinning alive) was another favorite form. Sacrifices of men, women, and children were offered to various gods to ensure fertility for crops, dedicate new public buildings, celebrate military victories, coronate emperors, and perform funerals for elites. When Ahuitzotle, a powerful fifteenth-century leader and warrior, died, 200 slaves accompanied him into the afterlife. Ahuitzotle, once dedicating a temple to the War God, himself participated in innumerable removals of hearts until, wading in blood, he finally became exhausted and passed his dagger to a replacement. Countless more unfortunate individuals were sacrificed during the four-day celebration when the last Mexican emperor, Moctezuma II, was crowned (Davies, 1981, 216).

The Aztecs and their Meso-American neighbors understandably conducted war for conquest and tribute, but they also institutionalized human sacrifice to the point that the capture of prisoners to receive cardioectomies became in itself the main purpose of many military actions. The ritual combat called the "War of the Flowers" was really more like a medieval European jousting tournament, a mock battle staged by armies using weapons more likely to wound than kill. A warrior's status and rank resulted from the number of prisoners for sacrifice that he captured, not slew (Davies, 1981, 216–17).

Human sacrifice, in fact, has been a culturally respectable and "normal" phenomenon within prescribed institutional roles in societies from India to Africa to Polynesia to East Asia to Europe to the New World. The famous Hindu ritual of *suttee*, in which a man's living widow was burned on a funeral pyre along with her husband's corpse, was in no way unique. The bodies of Indian rajahs were frequently accompanied into the fires by a host of wives and concubines. Human sacrifices have also been regarded in many societies as desperate but mandatory ways to cope with military emergencies, droughts and natural disasters, and epidemics. Anthropologist Nigel Davies reports that the ancient Phoenicians and Carthaginians believed that the gods would improve their chances in war through sacrificial appeasement. Thus, at one point during the Punic Wars with Rome, noble Carthaginian families offered up 200 of their sons for sacrifice to the god Baal out of altruistic patriotism. Pre-Christian Scandinavians buried children alive to stop plagues, while small children in Peru's pre-Columbian empire were sacrificed both to "cure" the emperor if he became ill and otherwise to preserve him in good health. Likewise, the rite of interring both children and adults within the foundations of new buildings, under city gates, and in the supports of bridges was common in pre-Christian Europe, the Far East, and is even reported practiced by the Israelites in the Old Testament (Davies, 1981, 61ff).

Not to be outdone by the past, there have been horrendous instances of mass slaughter in modern times. Some cases, like the two atomic bomb attacks on the civilian populations of Hiroshima and Nagasaki or the fire bombings of Dresden and Tokyo, have been defined as within the normative bounds of institutionalized warfare. Other instances, such as Adolf Hitler's Nazi depredations on "non-Aryan" Europeans (including his genocidal holocaust that exterminated 6 million Jews) or Stalin's murder of millions of Soviet minorities and political prisoners, have been internationally condemned as violence falling outside the pale of any institutional legitimacy, hence branded "crimes against humanity" or "war crimes." Meanwhile, technological sophistication of the instruments of violence has grown exponentially since even these recent examples.

Yet, at the same time, as we've entered the third Christian millennium, the case could be made that the citizens of most industrialized nations are increasingly becoming sensitized to, and concerned about, violence. Indeed, there may be movement in narrowing the boundaries of its acceptability even into the areas of institutional violence. As sociologists Jack D. Douglas and Frances C. Waksler (1982) observe,

> The most striking change (in American violence) has been the rapid increase in social disapproval of violence, particularly in its illegal forms, and in repressive social reactions toward it. Social definitions of deviant behavior have been expanding to include more and more forms of action, while definitions of nondeviant violence have been contracting; this development has led many people to believe that there has been a great upsurge in violence (230–1).

The twin problems of spousal and child abuse, which we will take up in greater detail in chapter 3, are evidence of this new awareness. Woman battering, for example, has at various times in American history been considered a serious social offense requiring harsh corporal punishment and imprisonment, or, alternately, a man's prerogative, that is, for "necessary disciplining" of a woman. The women's movement, among other factors, has been effective in changing the definition of domestic interpersonal violence as illegitimate (Stacey and Shupe, 1983).

At the same time, the rash of school shootings during the last ten years, including Colorado's Columbine High School rampage of random, wanton murders of students by an indisputably disturbed pair of students, has alarmed educators and parents. Whether similar events occurred independently inspired or following a copycat pattern, they are equally alarming, To a time traveler forwarded from the 1960s, the extent of "security" consciousness now part of public life, whether in our schools or courthouses or even in our airports following the 2001 bombings of New York's World Trade Center towers, would be astonishing and, given the taken-for-granted assumptions of safety of several decades earlier, would appear paranoid. Yet to twenty-first-century Americans, routine metal detection screenings before entering a school or boarding an aircraft have become acceptable, even desirable.

A further example is the growing concern over media violence, particularly as filmmakers have increasingly perfected special effects that glorify explicit, even exaggerated, portrayals of aggression and its grisly, splattering aftermath in shootings, slashings, explosions, and crashes. Since the 1960s several federal commissions and numerous independent studies (see, e.g., Goldstein, 1986; Rowland, 1983; Cater and Strickland, 1975), including one conducted by the American Academy of Pediatrics (Jubera, 1991), have confirmed that a constant diet of violent entertainment can have deleterious effects on audiences, particularly children. At best, this stylized violence desensitizes many members of any audience and prevents them from fully empathizing with characters in dramas. But this change, in turn, is generalizable to real life when these persons are then blocked from being emotionally affected by real occurrences. At worst, such violence has been found to offer role models for antisocial behavior and can lead to increased aggressive behavior during teenage and adult years (for a readable review of such findings, see Goldstein, 1986, 35–51, 170–5). Given studies that claim the typical American child watches more than twenty-seven hours of television each week and by age sixteen will have been exposed to 50,000 attempted murders as well as approximately 200,000 acts of violence (simulated and real), there has been great concern voiced by behavioral scientists, family advocates, and governmental representatives. Virtually all research by the end of the twentieth century confirmed these findings.

Various women's advocates have voiced additional justifiable concern, arising out of this "new sensitivity" to violent themes in modern Western culture, over violent pornography. Research on adults demonstrates, among other things, that such aggressive erotica provides subtle (and sometimes not so subtle) images to males depicting females masochistically enjoying and inviting rough treatment during sexual intimacy. Moreover, experimental research has found disturbing evidence that repeated exposure desensitizes *both* men and women, leading them to consider such violence as forcible rape a less serious criminal offense than they would otherwise have felt (see, e.g., Gubar and Hoff, 1989; Malamuth and Donnerstein, 1984). When one major publishing house, Alfred A. Knopf, was arranging to publish *American Psycho*, a novel in which women are kidnapped and dismembered, cannibalized, and sexually tortured (one victim has a starving rat inserted into her vagina, which then eats its way out of her body; another is literally nailed into captivity on the floor.), one magazine columnist wrote in disgust:

> The real issue is our increasingly degraded and brutal popular culture. The fact that our rape and murder rates are triple those of other Western nations has a lot to do with the violent images and fantasies flooding our culture. . . . Why is Knopf dealing in violent junk? Because pots of money can be made by brutalizing the culture (Leo 1990c, 62).

Popular music has come under fire. Although critics assailing rock lyrics is nothing new, in 1990 controversy flamed over 2 Live Crew, a black (male) rap group that sang about (among other things) damaging a girl's vagina during intercourse, anally raping her, and forcing her to lick human excrement. The group was banned in various communities and arrested in Florida for obscenity. "Why should our daughters have to grow up in a culture in which musical advice on the domination and abuse of women is accepted as entertainment?" one commentator lamented (Leo 1990b, 32). Simultaneously, stand-up comedian Andrew Dice Clay, who demeans women and minorities in his monologues, has attracted large, predominantly white male audiences but also has been ostracized by parts of the entertainment industry as a hatemonger.

Even violence in children's video games became controversial in the 1990s. Two games in particular, Night Trap and Mortal Kombat, raised concern. In Night Trap, three men in black masks charge into the bedroom of a woman dressed in a flimsy negligee. The player's challenge is to prevent the men from dragging her off and holding her down while a companion drives an electric drill into her neck. In Mortal Kombat, a gruesome extension of martial arts street fighting videos, opponents splatter blood with their blows and winners can triumphantly rip out the spinal columns of the defeated. One newspaper columnist wrote, "Profit, of course, is the only motivation that matters. That's why companies are in business, right? They have no obligation to be socially responsible" (Kolson, 1993).

And sports violence among athletes, once controversial but contained to the playing fields or in arenas, has spilled over into the audiences. So-called little league or peewee baseball/football/soccer parents' emotions have, of course, long been a staple of children's amateur sports. Adults who exhort their children and even become heated and profane are considered part of the sports ritual. Such adults are as much or more so driven for victory than their children. Americans were shocked, however, in early 2002 when Thomas Junta, a forty-four-year-old father, came out of the bleachers and attacked the hockey coach. Junta, weighting 270 pounds, literally pummeled 156-pound Michael Costin to death in front of numerous witnesses, including children. The issue was over roughness in both their sons' hockey practice that day. Junta reportedly punched Costin a number of times and slammed his head against the floor between locker rooms, rupturing an artery in Costin's neck. Americans could even witness the criminal trial live on the CNN cable network (Associated Press, 2002).

Junta's violent behavior was extreme but by no means abnormal. Syndicated newspaper columnist Bonnie Erbe wrote:

> They say adult violence surrounding kids' sports is on the rise. . . . Parents who attend children's practice or games have become inured to other pushy parents yelling at the coach or chastising children in public for poor performance. Kids, in turn, seem to have become more violent as well. [Sympathizing with Junta's conviction for involuntary manslaughter, she added:] Those parents who cannot control themselves at kids' sports events should stay away or face official retribution (Erbe, 2002).

These examples demonstrate an increasing willingness on the part of many Americans to hold a more inclusive definition of violence, a definition that on the popular level closely resembles our sociological one and that devalues violence in interpersonal and institutional role relationships. We are not suggesting that Americans should expect the cultural pendulum to swing away anytime soon from an entertainment industry often steeped in sensationalist violent imagery. As sociologist Michael Parenti has observed about American mass media, in general, private profitability instead of social need or responsibility is the driving fact in capital investment. And thus far, there is considerable profit in providing the novelty, titillation, and vicarious thrills associated with media violence. This is an ongoing economic fact of modern North American culture (Parenti, 1986).

But it is also true that new conflicts are arising as interest groups, sometimes aligned, are protesting violence merchants in modern American culture. Indeed, this reaction against profit-driven violent entertainment may prove to be one of the most powerful emerging social movements of the late twentieth and early twenty-first century.

The Heritage of Violence

In a sense all of us living in modern industrialized societies, regardless of our language or specific nationality, are inheritors of a violent tradition. This tradition began when humankind made the transition from hunting-gathering bands to a more settled agrarian existence, creating a more complex division of labor and specialized "agencies" of coercion (warriors) and learning/legitimation (priests) apart from resource producers (farmers). This major agricultural revolution occurred during the Neolithic Age (9000–6000 B.C.E. in the Middle East and around 6000 B.C.E. and 2000 B.C.E. in South America and North America, respectively). It irrevocably set in motion many issues new to human groups that have never left us since, such as how to deal with crop surpluses, storage, wealth, and class hierarchy. As historian Ernest Gellner (1988) writes in *Plough, Sword and Book: The Structure of Human History*:

> Agrarian society is doomed to violence. It stores valuable concentrations of wealth, which must be defended, and the distribution of which has to be enforced . . . during the agrarian age, most of mankind was not free and on the edge of starvation. It was oppressed and half-starving. It starved in accordance with rank (154–5).

Yet even with the similar archaic economic origins of inequality and coercion, historical traditions of violence do not necessarily lead to common contemporary outcomes. A case in point is the United States, where serious problems of urban gang- and drug-related violence, interpersonal assault, occasional "spree" shootings, race riots, and widespread gun possession are commonly accounted for by referring to the nation's "frontier tradition." The latter includes Indian (and other) wars, slavery, untamed mining and cattle towns and outlaw raids, frequent absence of law enforcement officials, and lynch mob and vigilante actions. During the 1960s, in particular, when the U.S. government enlisted historians and social scientists to help make sense of violent student and minority demonstrations, antiwar protests, and assassinations, the interpretation in vogue was that America had a very violent heritage that still pervades the many forms of interpersonal aggression in modern times (see, e.g., Pierce, 1970; Brown, 1969a, 1969b; Frantz, 1969; Elliot, 1944). For example, the historian Nigel Davis (1970, 56), after analyzing violence in American literature, wrote that it has always been difficult to conceal the fact that the nation was conceived in violence, that its birth was accompanied by mobs and confiscations, and that a burden remained on the people collectively to validate their rebellion against lawful authority. The same author perceived the telltale effects of this nation's violent birth running rampant in its literary history: "Critics who interpret violence in contemporary literature as a symptom of a sick society may be reassured to know that American writers have always been preoccupied with murder, rape, and deadly combat" (66).

Sociologist William A. Gamson (1975) reviewed a broad sample of American social movements and concluded that, however uncomfortable it might make advocates of nonviolence feel, "unruly" interest groups that employed tactics such as strikes, property destruction, and violent confrontation had a better-than-average success rate in surviving and achieving their goals. Some regions of the United States have even been singled out as particularly steeped in violent traditions. One such region, in addition to the frontier West, has been the Old South, with its cavalier codes of defending one's honor, dueling, vendettas, vigilante night-riders, and racial conflict both pre– and post–Civil War ((Newman, 1979, 42–3; Hofstadter and Wallace, 1971,12; Hackney, 1969; Franklin, 1956).

But other scholars have rejected some deterministic link between current (admittedly severe) patterns of American violence and the nation's alleged past. McGrath, in *Gunfighters, Highwaymen and Vigilantes: Violence on the Frontier* has observed that while there were many assaults and homicides between armed, inebriated men in mining town saloons, nevertheless rape, robbery, burglary, and what we moderns would call "muggings" were rare, chiefly because women were often few in number and men were frequently armed (1984). Even stagecoach robberies were usually aimed at the stage's commercial freight, not at the possessions of the passengers themselves. Calculating crime rates for two Trans-Sierra mining towns (using categories of the FBI Uniform Crime Reports) and comparing them to similar statistics for such modern urban metroplexes as Miami, Atlanta, Chicago, and San Francisco, McGrath found the frontier towns unstereotypically low in many offenses we usually think of as violent. In addition, vigilante actions, as others have noted (Burrows, 1976, 19ff; Hofstadter and Wallace, 1971, 22; Brown, 1969a, 1969b), were disciplined, involved many of a community's elite members, and hardly resembled the rough "mob justice" caricatures of popular imagery. Contrary to conventional wisdom, frontier communities actually saw more violence overall as they became more "civilized" and urbanized (McGrath, 1984, 256ff). McGrath blames our popular fixation about frontier violence on fictional television and film portrayals of such flamboyant deviants as Billy the Kid, Wyatt Earp, Bat Masterson, and Wild Bill Hickok.

Other scholars agree that claiming a causal connection between modern American violence and an alleged frontier tradition is overblown. Hofstadter and Wallace (1971) warn:

> The conventional attribution of American violence to our long history should not be given too much credence. It is true, of course, that frontier conditions somewhat enhanced the American disposition to violence, as they did, for example, in the history of Indian warfare and the attitudes it engendered. Yet it is worth emphasizing that over the whole course of our history only a small portion of the total American population—and always a decreasing portion—has ever seen or been on a frontier (11–12).

These authors attribute American culture's heavy emphasis on violence in its entertainment and literature to a popular legacy of "acceptance" of violence's purported widespread existence. Likewise, Lynn (1969) has acknowledged the "pleasures of hyperbolic exaggeration" that American audiences have persistently craved in their fiction and fantasy, be these the famous "dime novels" of the late nineteenth century that romanticized such characters as Kit Carson, William F. Cody, and Wyatt Earp or the twentieth century's glamorization of martial arts movie stars such as Bruce Lee, Chuck Norris, Steven Seagal, and Jean Claude Van Damme. Criminologist Graeme Newman (1979, 39) has even bluntly accused historians of the 1960s of fabricating a culture of violence somehow integral to North American society in order to explain the waves of riots and civil disorder they were witnessing rather than consider class warfare or institutional discrimination.

It is instructive to contrast America's indisputably high rates of interpersonal violence and its contested history of violent actions with those of Japan, an equally industrialized urban society that has a much longer history of civil disturbances, peasant uprisings, dynastic wars, and the famous samurai warrior ethic but also much lower rates of nearly all forms of interpersonal violence. Despite its legacy of bloodshed, Japanese society's interpersonal "style" of relating involves individual self-effacement and personal control in the face of authority, emotion, and egocentric desire. This does not mean that the Japanese do not joke or become angry, jealous, or ambitious. Nor do they lack individual desires, competitiveness, or even aggressiveness. They are simply more thoroughly conditioned, and constantly reinforced, to live within a culture that values restraint, self-sacrifice for the greater good of the larger group, and a public "face" of courtesy, as they have for centuries (Nakane, 1970; Benedict, 1946). Thus, there exists the irony that grueling martial arts, such as judo, karate, and kendo (broadsword fencing) are taught almost everywhere in the country in junior and senior high schools (often to females as well as males), yet Japan's levels of officially documented interpersonal violence are modest. In a classic comparative analysis of crime and police work in the United States and Japan, Bayley (1976, 5) noted that in 1973 there were four-and-a-half times as many murders per 100,000 persons in the United States as in Japan (population-wise, half the size of the latter country). In fact, the New York metropolitan area alone during the early 1970s had three-fourths as many murders as all of Japan.

One important factor in explaining such differences is the heritage from medieval Japan of only elites (the aristocracy and samurai warrior castes) being entitled to carry weapons, whereas not only America's frontier tradition but also our hallowed Bill of Rights guarantees *every* adult not convicted of a felony the right to own almost every imaginable weapon. In Japan only police officers, soldiers in the self-defense forces, and a few hunters and Olympic shooters possess firearms. Swords and even knives beyond a certain length must be registered with the government.

Perhaps just as important a factor in Japan's low levels of interpersonal violence is its cultural emphasis on loyalty to a larger group, such as the family and by extension one's employer or company, which exercises much greater and more thorough social control on emotional outbursts and actions than most Americans understand or would tolerate. For example, Bayley (1976, 71) observes about males' connection to their occupational world:

> Responsible behavior is secured in Japan by developing the allegiance of the individual to the work group in such a way as to legitimate its disciplinary claims on him and to intensify his feeling of obligation not to offend against it. The work group in Japan dominates personal life. It has the emotional overtones of a family— a word policemen use frequently to describe the kind of emotional fulfillment they want to achieve in the group.

This illustrative comparison between the United States and Japan has not been made to suggest that generalizations about the social sources and circumstances of interpersonal violence among societies, or even within a single society's culture over time, are impossible to make. The point is that they require our explanations to be more complex. Culture and history clearly prepare, but do not completely determine, how each generation of a society interprets its collective experience of violence. The range of popular acceptance of violence being quite varied over time and place, any social science analysis must recognize the role of culture in prompting a society's members to receive instances of violence as either normative, i.e., acceptable, or deviant, i.e., nonacceptable. Before moving to specific examples of violence, therefore, we briefly turn to the general phenomenon of learning such normative boundaries.

SOCIALIZATION TO VIOLENCE

Most social scientists have abandoned the nature versus nurture, or instincts versus learning debate over the source of human violence. Attempts by such ethologists as Konrad Lorenz and some sociobiologists as Edward O. Wilson to demonstrate a strong continuity of biologically determined aggression from lower animals through primates to *homo sapiens* have proved largely fruitless because, in the words of psychologist Jeffrey H. Goldstein (1986, 6), "to argue that because we *can* behave like lower organisms, we *must* behave like them is preposterous. While human beings possess diffuse innate biological urges, they also have extremely malleable psychological potentials. The same human mind can devise a fishing pole or a throwing spear, a telephone or a ballistic missile, a hypodermic needle or a flame-thrower. There is no question that even if individuals were born with some genetic predisposition to be aggressive, and we are not suggesting they are, it would be well within their rational, cognitive capabilities to learn to restrain, suppress, or creatively divert such urges. Thus the key to understanding how individuals deal with aggressive feelings as well as "make sense" out of the violence they see and in which they may even become involved is socialization, or learning.

In particular, much of this socialization occurs through what social psychologists term *social learning*. That is, persons do not have to be directly involved in violence to learn that it can be effective, rewarding, and even satisfying. Alternately, they can come to regard it as destructive, painful, and horrifying. Unlike classical conditioning, where learners are passive, or direct *operant* conditioning, where learners are given positive or negative reinforcement immediately after performing a response, social learning is vicarious or indirect. Essentially one watches another who is a perpetrator or victim, sees the consequences of the violent action, and then internalizes a reaction to the outcome as well as, in many cases, the techniques of committing the violence. This modeling process is akin to imitation in everyday parlance, and a good deal of social psychological research has been amassed to explain its dynamics.

Learning the Role of Perpetrator

Laboratory experiments have conclusively demonstrated that children, after being exposed to an adult acting out aggression and not being punished, will imitate that aggression. The most famous type of such experiments was developed by psychologist Albert Bandura (1963, 1965, 1973, 1977) and several colleagues in the early 1960s. For example, in one typical experiment (Bandura, 1965), sixty-six children of nursery school age were shown one of three five-minute films. All children witnessed an adult attacking a plastic Bobo doll (a tall rubber inflated clown figure with sand in its base as weight to keep it upright) and yelling specific words like "Pow!" and "Socko!" In one condition of the experiment the adult model received rewards of candy and soft drinks following the repeated striking of the doll. In a second condition the adult was verbally punished and even spanked after the doll attacks. In a third condition children saw no rewarding or punishing of the model after aggression against the doll. All children then were permitted ten minutes of "free play" in a room in which had been placed a variety of toys, including a Bobo doll. After experimenters observed each child, they said that he or she would receive a drink and colorful picture booklets after imitating the behavior acted out in the film. The findings showed that: (1) the "spontaneous" behavior during the ten minute free-play period was significantly aggressive *both* among children in the first model-rewarded condition *and* among children in the model-neither-rewarded-nor-punished condition; (2) the least aggression was seen by experimenters in the model-punished condition; (3) yet when promised rewards for imitating the film's aggression *all* children, regardless of their experimental condition, were equally able to replicate the model's aggression, even down to the details of incorporating specific expressions uttered by the model while striking the doll.

The findings of Bandura and his colleagues, as well as those of many other social psychologists, demonstrate that children's learning to imitate aggressive acts can take place regardless of whether there is some immediate reward or punishment to the violent actor or the viewer. If there is either a rewarding outcome to the violence or at least no punishment, however, the probability of the aggression being repeated is significantly enhanced.

While this type of laboratory experiment using nursery schoolchildren may seem artificially simplistic, its basic logic has been repeated successfully on adults as well (see, e.g., Eron et al., 1972; Cater and Strickland, 1975). Clinical studies of violent men, for example, found that adult men who responded violently to their wives or girlfriends during domestic quarrels often experienced "generational transfer," or social learning, of physical and verbal abuse in their families as a way of settling arguments. In a study of more than 200 men who had beaten their female significant others, the authors wrote that:

> most of these men had witnessed violence between their parents during arguments. They saw violence used as a strategy by the father to win those arguments with the mother, or at least to get his way. They saw it portrayed as manly, as the man's right, and associated it with a male parent figure whom they naturally wanted to imitate. Thus as boys many of these men learned (indirectly or vicariously) the appropriateness of men's using violence against women as well as its effectiveness. Little in what they were to learn from American culture, either in how power and resources are distributed by gender or through the mass media with its macho heroes and docile female stereotypes, contradicted those impressions (Shupe, Stacey, and Hazelwood, 1987, 38).

And, as we mentioned earlier when examining public sensitivity to violence, even if the tendency to engage in a specific act of violence such as rape is not immediately enhanced, repeated exposure to similar acts can at least desensitize our emotional reaction to it.

The famous Milgram experiments may also provide some insights into other acts of institutional violence. Milgram (1974) was examining the extent of obedience to authority among people who were led to believe their own obedience would harm another person. Milgram told volunteer subjects that they were to be involved in an experiment in learning. The subjects (the teacher role) were told to give electric shocks to another subject, the learner, who was part of the experimental team, when he failed to provide the correct answer to a word-association test. The learner in reality received no shocks and merely faked the response when a shock was supposedly emitted. On a desk in front of the subject teacher was a series of switches labeled 15–450 volts (thirty switches altogether) with the last six marked danger: severe shock. The subject teacher was called on by an experimenter dressed in a white lab coat to pull a progressively higher voltage switch each time the learner provided an incorrect answer. There was also a prearranged response that the learner gave out in the next room, where he could not be seen. The responses began with a simple "Ouch." At 150 volts the learner would plead, "Experimenter! That's all. Get me out of here. I told you I had heart trouble. My heart's starting to bother me now." This type of prearranged response continued until the subject reached the 330-volt switch. After this point, all succeeding shocks at higher levels received no response on the part of the learner. After the initial cries of protest from the learner at 150 volts, virtually none of the teacher participants wanted to continue applying the shocks. But the experimenter (the person in authority) told them to continue. Over 60 percent of the teacher subjects continued applying the shocks through to the 450-volt level.

The Milgram experiments provide insight into how individuals acting in the context of institutional roles such as soldier, executioner, or police officer can commit acts of violence because they were told to do so by someone in authority. One can still hear the testimony of war criminals at Nuremberg testifying about their role in the atrocities in the Holocaust, stating that they were just following orders. More recently, in the My Lai massacre, one of the grimmest episodes of the U.S. involvement in the Vietnam war, more than 300 unarmed Vietnamese civilians were massacred by an American infantry company. The Americans, under the command of Capt. Ernest L. Medina and Lt. William L. Calley, Jr., entered the village of Son My, and in the hamlet they called My Lai 4 they lashed out at whomever they found, mostly women, children, and old men. Some villagers were herded into ditches where they were shot. After Calley was court-martialed, a significant segment of the American public felt that he was unjustly prosecuted because he was just following orders (Bilton, 1992). More recently, after Colonel Oliver North was convicted in May 1989 of three of the twelve criminal counts involving his role in the Iran Contra scandal, a large segment of the American public contended that he should not be prosecuted because he was just following orders ("Partial," 1989).

An extreme example of learning the role of perpetrator of institutional violence is discussed by Browning in his work on the Order Police of Nazi Germany, who were assigned the task of rounding up Jewish populations in Poland and Russia and killing them or transporting them to death camps. Browning details the killings of Jews by a number of battalions of the Order Police. He cites the case of Police Battalion 309, which undertook the slaughter of between 2,000 and 3,000 Jews in the city of Bialystok. Jews collected at the marketplace were taken to a park, lined up against a wall, and shot. The killing lasted until dark. At the synagogue, where at least 700 Jews had been collected, gasoline was poured at the entryways. A grenade was tossed into the building, igniting a fire. Police shot anyone trying to escape. The fire spread to nearby houses in which Jews were hiding, and they too were burned alive. The next day, thirty wagonloads of corpses were taken to a mass grave (Browning 1992, 12). In another case, two battalions of Order Police murdered more than 33,000 Jews in the ravine of Babi Yar in Kiev.

Browning focuses his research on one particular battalion, Battalion 101. His research discussed the difficulties encountered by these working class and middle class older men, many of whom had joined the Order Police to avoid military service, in carrying out their orders of conducting a mass murder of Jews. He discusses the first major massacre the battalion participated in, the killing of 1,800 Jews in Jozefow, Poland. The commander of the battalion would not witness the killings, but stayed in his headquarters and wept openly. Older men were initially given the option of not participating. About a dozen asked for reassignment to other duties. As the slaughter began, many others sought permission to be reassigned. The soldiers were specifically instructed as to how to execute the Jews. Each was to place his bayonet on his rifle, place it at the base of the head of the victim, and fire. However, many of the police missed their target, intentionally in many cases. This resulted in the back of the heads of the prisoners exploding, spraying the soldiers around them with skull fragments and pieces of brain tissue. The soldiers were also instructed to kill infants, young children, and the elderly in their homes as opposed to bringing them to the market square. Browning reports that this order was rarely followed as in the case of infants and the children who were later brought to the market square where they were murdered along with their mothers. The men were sent into the woods where they were told to lie down on the ground and then shot in the back of the head. Browning notes that as darkness came the task was not finished and it became increasingly difficult for the squads of police to find a spot where Jews were not lying about dead. Officers supplied the executioners with alcohol to ease the process. Browning notes that after the killings in Jozefow, the men were despondent. The commanding officer and his superiors in Lublin had to deal with the broad demoralization of the battalion as a result of the reaction to the horror of the killing process. The battalion was reassigned for a time to ghetto clearing and deportation, instead of carrying out the executions. After a time the battalion was again participating in executions. Browning observes that in the end, the 500 men of Battalion 101 had directly participated in the deaths of 38,000 Jews and the deportation of 45,000 Jews to death camps.

What can account for the behavior of these 500 men? According to Browning, like the rest of German society, the men of Battalion 101 were immersed in a deluge of racist and anti-Semitic propaganda. Browning notes that Order Police were provided with additional indoctrination as part of their training and as an ongoing practice within the units. Browning contends that such incessant propagandizing must have had a considerable effect in reinforcing general notions of Germanic racial superiority and a certain aversion toward the Jews (184). This is consistent with what was discussed in the previous chapter regarding the importance of defining the victim as less, as deserving of violence. Browning also notes that conformity to authority (as discussed in the Milgram experiments) was a factor. The battalion had orders to kill Jews, but each individual did not. Yet 80–90 percent of the men proceeded to kill, though almost all of them, at least initially, were horrified and disgusted by what they were doing. To break ranks and step out, to adopt overly nonconformist behavior, was simply beyond most of the men. It was easier for them to shoot (Browning, 1992, 184).

In later chapters, when we discuss institutional violence, it will be important to recall the importance of the systems of thought that allow us to define victims as less and think about the power of the group within the institutional agency to promote conformity to the role expectations. Whether we are discussing the violence of police or military or priests or ministers or corporate executives, the dynamic is similar. The lesson of Battalion 101 is that perpetrators of violence must be able to separate themselves from their victims. Ideologies that teach us to accept and perpetuate through our actions inequalities and separateness between people are crucial in this regard. Furthermore, when engaged in repetitive forms of violence, as in the case of many forms of institutional violence, social supports of the group or agency may be crucial to reinforce the mandates of the roles they are performing.

Social learning research tells us that aggressive attitudes and violent techniques are learned, just like other behaviors. Relatives, friends, media personalities, actors, political leaders and others in authority all can be role models. Given our culture's heavy saturation with values, symbols, and instances of violence (real or fictionally glorified), together with the pervasiveness of systems of thought that divide people along hierarchical dimensions, perhaps we should ask why more do not commit acts of violence given the overwhelming opportunities for learning violence. Violence, after all, can serve as a satisfying, even cathartic, shortcut that bypasses many frustrating problems and social responsibilities. Perhaps nonviolence more urgently requires an explanation.

Learning the Role of the Victim

It might seem commonsensical to say that no one consciously prepares to become the victim of violence. A family that has had its possessions stolen during a burglary, a man mugged on a subway platform, or a woman raped—none of these persons deliberately invited their own victimization. To suggest otherwise might seem like engaging in a not-so-subtle game of "blaming the victim," placing at least some causal blame for the event on the victim rather than on the perpetrator. The women's movement has been particularly insistent on this point in countering the (predominantly male) conventional wisdom that rape victims often somehow "ask for it" by their dress or presence in a given location. As the movement's spokespersons have stressed, susceptibility and vulnerability do not equal culpability.

Likewise, despite early speculation in the 1970s about little girls learning that being the victim of domestic violence is part of an adult woman's role (just as little boys learn that violence toward women is a man's prerogative), in fact research shows just the opposite. Many adult women who are victims of batterings by husbands or boyfriends were raised in nonviolent homes, and many who fled to women's shelters or sought help elsewhere manifest no signs that they somehow thought the abuse they received was "normal," appropriate, or part of a woman's role (Pagelow, 1981; Stacey and Shupe, 1983, 41–6). Why they remain in violent relationships, as we discuss in the next chapter, is more a matter of economics than psychology.

On the other hand, we have cross-cultural and historical instances of persons being deliberately indoctrinated to accept their own victimization. The practice of human sacrifice was an important part of the religious rituals of the Aztecs and Incas prior to the sixteenth century (Davies, 1981). It is estimated that for the Aztecs alone, more than 20,000 humans were sacrificed annually, the vast majority of them children. For the Incas such violence occurred twice a year at the solstice celebrations in June and December. Then the empire's best crops, most prized livestock, most precious artwork, and finest clothes, along with the most beautiful children of the empire, were gathered together at Cuzco, the Incas' 11,000-foot-high capital. Everything, including children, was herded into a corral to be inspected. The children were examined for deformities and signs of disease. Those who were not in excellent shape were weeded out. The remaining children listened to speeches from the Inca high priest about the benefits of their upcoming sacrifice to the empire. During this time they learned the role of victim. There were then ten days of festivities in the capital during which the children were celebrated as semidivine. The children were then sacrificed at the highest altars as payment for the Inca rulers' sins.

There are also some situations when the repeated experience of interpersonal violence, or the expectation of such violence, can become a real factor in the social roles one acts out on a regular basis. Fear of muggings, for example, leads many residents of such metropolises as New York City to adopt abrupt, defensive interpersonal styles, like refusing to talk to strangers or avoiding certain public places. Likewise, clinicians who have studied violent marriages have noted a sort of symbiotic relationship that develops between abuser and victim. It is not that the woman enjoys being slapped or hit by the stronger male during an argument but that the violence comes to be part of an overall role (e.g., wife) that she is unwilling to give up.

Perhaps more significant is how all of us learn the cultural distinctions between persons who are "legitimate" or innocent victims of violence (they did nothing to deserve, thus we can hold empathy for their plight as "true victims") as opposed to those who are technically victims but who fall outside the limits of "legitimacy" (thus they do not deserve our sympathy). In the latter case, victimization is actually regarded as a well-deserved punishment. For example, in 1990 and 1991, the citizens of Kuwait who were shot, tortured, and raped by invading Iraqi troops were portrayed as victims by the American media and became recognized as victims in most Americans' eyes. Hardly so the starving Iraqi soldiers in the trenches abandoned and in some cases buried alive by the allied forces equipped with bulldozers and tanks, or the civilian casualties that occurred during and after the war as a result of the intense allied bombing runs over Baghdad. The semantics of victimization is the propagandist's art: invaders and aggressors (i.e., those outside our own politically drawn "circle") rarely produce martyrs or heroes in our eyes. Defenders do that.

The role of the victim is a culturally defined one, and vested interests may seek to restrict the definition for their own purposes. Americans trapped in exploding Ford Pintos struck from behind, for example, were not initially regarded as legitimate "victims" of any corporate violence due to a faulty gas tank design. They simply had the bad luck to be in traffic accidents. Their identity as victims emerged when it was revealed that the Ford Motor Company knew ahead of time that the design was dangerous and finally discontinued production of Pintos (Dowie, 1977). Similarly, the major manufacturing scandal of the late 1990s involving Bridgestone/Firestone tires that spontaneously lost their tread and caused accidents at first appeared as "driver error" for dozens of deceased drivers until National Highway Traffic Administration investigators found that the tires were defective. Recall of the tires cost the firm hundreds of millions of dollars, not to mention the loss of sales to the Ford Motor Company whose Explorer line came equipped with those tires (Wood, 2001).

In a sense, more and more North Americans are coming to appreciate learning the role of victim. Indeed, it portends to be a trend in our increasingly litigious society. Alvin Toffler, in a futurism analysis entitled *Powershift*, claims that violence for millions of Americans has been sublimated, or redirected, into law. Instead of settling civil disputes by feuds, shootouts, or even fistfights, Americans, more than any other people on earth, are turning to attorneys as "hired guns" to take their stylized combat into the arena of the courtroom. Toffler (1990) notes than in the United States more than 1,000 *new* lawsuits are processed every working day. And the United States now possesses *5 percent* of the world's population yet *70 percent* of the planet's lawyers. Complained one American observer of his litigation-happy fellow citizens: "No other industrialized nation permits such arrant nonsense. The United States has thirty times more lawsuits per person than Japan. . . . In Japan there are more than twenty engineers for each lawyer. We have a ratio of 2.5 to 1, and it is falling fast" (Gergen, 1989, 43). What angered him, among other things was the case of a burglar, who, in the process of looting a California high school, fell through a skylight and sued the local school board for personal damages. Shockingly, he won $260,000 in damages *plus* a $1,200 per month stipend!

There is another twist on learning the role of the victim and that occurs when the individual has not been a victim. In several cases prosecuting attorneys have led children into believing that they were the victims of child molestation. In the McMartin Case, the longest, one of the most expensive trials in U.S. history, after two of the defendants spent two and five years in jail respectively, they were acquitted. There has been a similar problem of therapists convincing clients in the process of therapy that they were victims of child abuse. Shupe (1991) reports of one particular episode among the Mormons in Utah, the Lehi case, where a therapist's coaching of her child clients into making false charges of sexual abuse against their parents resulted in the state of Utah passing legislation making it a crime for persons to raise false accusations of child abuse or to induce children to make false accusations thereof. Thus, learning the role of the victim may no longer be the straightforward social psychological phenomenon it was once thought to be.

Learning the Role of the Audience

The audience to violence is not merely a passive group of witnesses but has become an integral part of the definition, discovery, and interpretation of violence. And an audience possibly desensitized or sensitized regarding specific forms of violence by a steady stream of disclosures about street crime and glorified entertainment violence is not the only audience issue. There is also fear arousal.

During the past two decades sociologists have substantially documented the role of journalistic and entertainment mass media, both newspapers and television, in inadvertently socializing audiences to accept a particular image of violence in American society that leaves them anxious and concerned. Dominick (1978) found in one study that murder, assault and armed robbery were the most frequently portrayed crimes, accounting for 60 percent of 119 crimes counted during one prime-time segment. And studying newspaper coverage of crime, he discovered that major metropolitan newspapers devoted 5–10 percent of all available space to individual violent crime. Alternately, less than 5 percent of the crime news was devoted to the causes and remedies of crime that social science has investigated. Ironically, individual violent crimes, always the more sensational and easiest for readers to identify with, were emphasized at the expense of more widespread and costly property, white-collar, and corporate crimes.

Sanford Sherizen (1978), in a similar analysis of media reports of crime, has written of the "unreality" of their portrayal. Crime reporters, he concludes, are often mere conduits for official views of crime (relying as they do on police sources for crime news). Researchers have also generally agreed that the unreality that is constructed has two aspects: first, blacks, young people, and lower socioeconomic "types" are stereotypically overrepresented (compared to FBI statistics); and second, particularly in the television "world" of criminal justice, the legal process is unrealistically pictured as ending, for all intents and purposes, with police capture of suspects that the audience already "knows" are guilty. Sherizen (1978) has commented on the "scare" effect much non–supermarket tabloid newspaper coverage of crime has:

> Crimes are that which occurs outside of the potential for the police to prevent, especially homicides found in the newspapers were presented as being "caused" by

passions and insanities. For an individual reader who absorbs this imagery, crime appears to be violent, probably rampant, out of control, and likely to strike physically at any moment (215).

Barak (1994, 34) notes that the news discourse surrounds itself with very subtle "explanations" that appear in enclosed forms that do not enhance causal understanding. Barak describes the common portrayal of crime in the news: "serious crime has been 'diagnosed' as having little or no relationship to political economy. Not only is the presentation of crime and crime control severed from its underlying socioeconomic conditions; it is also disconnected from its own historical development" (Barak, 1994, 249). Erickson notes that when an explanation can be read into the news, it "is more likely to be tacitly evoked by cues in the text or by the powerful master labels such as 'violent' and 'criminal' which carry unambiguous connotations and meld together disparate phenomena and their meanings. . . . They are deployed stereotypically. The stereotypes are blended with imputations of motives, whether noble or blameworthy. The imputations of motives, in turn, carry excuses and justifications for behavior" (Erickson et. al., 1991, 269). In general, the violence that is represented to us focuses on interpersonal violence that is defined to be most illegitimate by those who write and voice "official" opinions. The violence at the institutional and structural levels and the violence that is deemed to be legitimate are not represented to us as violence.

Images and stories about crime and, especially violence dominate the news and entertainment industry. Studies that have been done over the years in the United Sates have documented the frequency of violent images in the media. According to an American Psychological Association task force report on television and American society (Huston et al., 1992), by the time the average child (i.e., one who watches two to four hours of television daily) leaves elementary school, he or she will have witnessed at least 8,000 murders and more than 100,000 other assorted acts of violence on television.

For the entertainment industry, television reality shows on crime do not appear to diverge much from the news programming in terms of frames or explanations. Fishman and Cavender (1998) note that television crime programs are informed by conservative ideologies that support current crime policies. The messages in these shows reinforce the idea that criminal violence is a serious problem, and longer prison sentences are offered as the solution. Criminals are presented as different from their victims. They are presented as stereotypical caricatures such as Satanists, drug dealers, and crazed, cold-blooded murderers. Victims are seen in equally stereotypical images—respectable and physically attractive. The final message of these shows is that what stands between order and chaos is the thin blue line of the police.

What is the social psychological effect on individual audience members and the ultimate social roles they fill as witnesses, internalizers, and evaluators of the violence in media? In the opinion of psychologist Jeffrey Goldstein (1986) the end result is a *mechanistic* view of violent behavior:

> there is a consistent theme that (1) the causes of human violence exist within the individual, (2) that if only psychiatrists, psychologists, and biologists were clever enough, they could identify the genetic or personality factors that give rise to violent behavior, and (3) given the "fact" that the causes of violence reside within the individual's skin, it is assumed to be at least theoretically possible to identify potential offenders before they ever commit an offence by using some sort of early childhood screening procedure (215).

Viewers/readers, in other words, come away with the impression that "those who commit crimes or acts of violence are different in tangible and predictable ways from those who do not (Goldstein, 1986, 15).

The upshot is that ordinary citizens are being slowly conditioned by the mass media to (1) expect more interpersonal violence potentially in their lives than will likely occur, (2) overestimate rates of interpersonal violence in their communities, (3) think only in terms of lurid interpersonal violence when the overall subject is brought up, and (4) isolate violence as a phenomenon within the realm of the bizarre and pathological rather than a product of the nature of our society. That, essentially, is what has happened in creating the "new sensitivity" of America to much interpersonal violence.

Michalowski (1985) adds to this discussion regarding what our cultural understandings of crime are and what forces create them. Although he is discussing the imagery of crime, the same forces are responsible for creating our image of violence. He notes that the systematic generation and dissemination of crime statistics is culture work. For Michalowski, culture work refers to activity that serves to create or maintain widely accepted perceptions of the nature of reality. Insofar as our cultural understanding of crime is shaped by the institutional mechanisms for gathering and disseminating crime data, those institutional mechanisms play an important role in shaping what we perceive to be the "reality" of crime. The same logic applies to our understanding of violence. As various levels of government disseminate reports about the problem of violence in our society, and as this information is presented in the media through news items and television documentaries, it becomes part of our cultural understanding of what violence is. We are the audience for the orchestration of a particular image or cultural reality of violence.

Michalowski goes on to note that the production and distribution of crime data reflect distinctions between common crimes and crimes of capital or corporate crime. Only those institutions charged with controlling common crimes actively produce and publicly disseminate data about the offenses under their jurisdiction. It becomes a self-fulfilling prophecy of sorts. This selective generation and dissemination of data on social harms in American society serves to shape our awareness of crime in such a way that the category of "crime" in American culture generally includes only those harms most often committed by the poorer segments of American society. Excluded from such a definition of the reality of "crime" are harms more often committed by the elite in America in pursuit of profit and power. In regard to violence the same pattern would apply; only forms of violence (interpersonal violence) that are disproportionately committed by the poorer segments of the society are part of the social reality of violence created by the agencies who create and disseminate the statistics. Institutional violence and structural violence are not part of this social construction and therefore are outside our understanding of the reality of violence. For example, there are no statistics regularly collected and disseminated on economic violence (death resulting from production, death resulting from defect in design of products, death resulting from ill disposal or chemical wastes from production, etc.). Therefore, when we think of the problem of violence, this type of violence is excluded from our conceptualization.

Another example is the lack of information on killings by the police in this country. The U.S. government has just recently begun to collect information on the number of people killed each year by law enforcement officers. However, reporting of this information is not required of police departments. What about violence resulting from government military or military sponsored by the government? Again, if these types of violence were systematically reported, indicating trends, who are most vulnerable, and so forth, how would this change our understanding of violence? Why do we have this selective generation of images, and how does this relate to the structure of power relations of the society? How are cultural understandings that allow us to be a perpetrator, victim and audience influenced by the power relations of the larger society? Do those who have more power in the society have more power to create and promote understandings of reality that better serve their interests and possibly not our own?

IDEOLOGY: THE BRIDGE BETWEEN CULTURE AND SOCIAL STRUCTURE

A major focus of this book is the connection between how a society is organized in terms of social structure (i.e., its systems of stratification) and how this is related to patterns of violence. Our understanding of the structure of the society, our acceptance and support of it, and our understanding of violence (that is, what it is and what we believe causes it) are products of the ideologies we are taught as part of the socialization we experience in the society and are reinforced by the dominant media in the country. A society's dominant ideology is the cultural mechanism that defends, preserves and legitimates the structural arrangements or, more specifically, the systems of stratification that form the foundation of the society and the normative systems that support and preserve them. We accept the differences we see in our society as they relate to living conditions, levels of power, and social status because we feel that the mechanisms that create these differences are legitimate. Hunt (1981, 3) refers to an ideology as "the ideas and beliefs that tend to justify morally a society's social and economic relationships". He notes that most members of a society internalize the ideology that is dominant in the society and thus believe that their functional role, as well as the role of others, is morally correct and that the method by which society divides its produce is fair.

Another way of defining an ideology is as a viewpoint based on one's vantage point in the social order. The vantage point of an individual in the society is based on the position that one occupies relative to the systems of stratification in the society. In this sense, there are as many ideologies as there are unique structural positions in social space. Thus, in our own country we can identify three major systems of stratification: class, gender, and ethnicity. The intersection of these systems of stratification creates unique vantage points or positions in that the life experiences of people who occupy these positions will be different because of these systems of stratification. For example, the life experience of a male capitalist of European ancestry, such as Henry Ford II or one of the male heirs to the Campbell Soup Company, will be different from the life experience of a black woman or male worker, a male or female worker of European ancestry, or a male or female worker of Mexican ancestry. They will experience social institutions and processes differently because of the different positions they occupy.

For example, an increase in unemployment in a society will affect the people who occupy these positions differently. The male capitalist of European ancestry benefits, in the short term at least, from an increase in the rate of unemployment. When unemployment is high there is less demand for higher wages and better working conditions. The male and female workers and managers will experience unemployment differently because gender, ethnicity, and occupational position influence their different locations in the labor market.

The cost of health care is another phenomenon that people experience differently because of the differences in the positions they occupy. The same applies to all other areas of social life, education, housing, crime, the welfare system, and war. In short, society as a whole is experienced differently because of the positions we occupy, positions determined by the intersection of the systems of stratification in the society. Thus the fact that we experience our society differently because of the differences in the positions we occupy provides the basis for an understanding of our society or, more specifically, provides the basis of an ideology.

Each stratified society during periods of stability will have a dominant ideology. This dominant ideology will reflect, first, the mode of production and reproduction that is dominant in the society and, correspondingly, the interests of the dominant structural position as defined in terms of class, gender, and ethnicity (i.e., in this case white European ethnicity, male, capitalist class). The dominant ideology will also reflect the historical experience of the social system as experienced by the dominant class and gender, the history of conflict and compromise between the structural divisions within the society, and the history of conquest and colonization within the world system. The dominant ideology will also be colored by the cultural and religious heritage of the country. Thus, in looking at different patriarchal capitalist societies throughout the world one sees a great deal of commonality in the dominant ideologies, despite the presence of differences in history, religious traditions, and culture.

Just as there are dominant ideologies, so there are competing ideologies. The dominant ideology fundamentally reflects the interests of the dominant structural positions as defined in terms of class, gender, ethnicity, and age. Competing ideologies reflect the interests (or viewpoint of the society from the vantage points) of the dominated structural positions. The majority of the population during periods of stability will view their world through this dominant ideology or from the vantage point of this dominant stratum. Assuming a perspective that does not reflect ones structural position in the social system is false consciousness. That is, people are viewing social reality from the vantage point of a structural position that is not their own and that actually may be counter to their interests.

As mentioned, the institutions that play a role in integrating and socializing neophytes into the social order (educational, familial, religious, political, and economic via the mass media) serve to reinforce and perpetuate the dominant ideology and thus promote false consciousness for dominated groups. The dominant ideology will be taught to the members of the society as they are socialized in the family, schools, religious institutions, and through the mass media. One's experience in the social system based on the social relations one enters, which in turn are rooted in structural divisions that form the basis of the social system, will also serve to reinforce the dominant ideology. For example, in a capitalist society we experience and define people's basic nature as fundamentally selfish, individualistic, rational, and competitive. This nature is reflective of the social relations that are rooted in a capitalist mode of production. People are taught, and it is demonstrated to them by those who have most power, that in order to be successful in our society one must act this way. Furthermore, we are taught that this way of behavior is part of our basic nature.

In contrast, Inuit (Eskimos) or American Indians prior to contact with white European people, and still today to some extent, would describe people's basic nature in a different light. Their experiences in that society promotes behavior that would be very different from our own. They are taught that to be successful in their society one needs to be concerned with the welfare of others, to be cooperative, and to be spiritually conscious. They would have a dominant consciousness or ideology that reflects what anthropologists would term a more ascephelous, or consciously interdependent, society on which their social relations are based.

As people who are products of other societies as defined in terms of the systems of stratification that form their foundations become members of our society, they are socialized to this different dominant ideology, and their own experience reinforces this new understanding. Historically, an early fear of immigrants spreading foreign ideologies was important in the establishment of universal public education. Employers in particular were very concerned about the ideologies of working people in Europe, where socialist ideologies were more popular among the working class than in the United States. The concern was that these ideas might create problems of worker unrest in our own country (Billington, 1974; Olson, 1979; Handlin, 1957). The forced civilizing by missionaries of indigenous populations who reside on lands that are being conquered is another example of the threat of different systems of understandings and assumptions about the nature of humans and the appropriate ordering of society.

FOUR CURRENT IDEOLOGIES IN U.S. PUBLIC POLICY DEBATES

Let us examine briefly some of the different ideologies that are current in public policy debates in the United States and discuss how we would understand the nature of violence from viewing this social reality from these different sets of lenses (Greenberg, 1985; Hunt, 1981; Williamson et al., 1985). Table 2.1 provides a summary description of the first two of these ideologies: *organic conservative* and *individualist conservative*. Table 2.2 (p. 84) summarizes the last two ideologies: *reform corporate liberal/feminist,* and *socialist/feminist*. It is important for the reader to understand that these are only four of the many different ideologies that exist in this society. Black nationalist, anarchist, and radical feminist are some of the others represented by groups and organizations and their publications. We focus on these four because of how well represented they are in public policy debate.

These particular ideologies principally represent perspectives derived from the class and gender positions within the society. Also, recognize that these are general descriptions and that within each ideology there is a diversity of more specific viewpoints that represents the interests of a specific group or faction. In describing these four ideologies, we mention some of the variants within each; however our major focus is on providing a general description of the ideology that glosses over the differences within. These ideologies are briefly discussed with regard to their views of human nature, their central values, the nature of the social order, the role of the state orientation toward change, ideal system, cause and solution to social problems in the society, and finally their view of the problem of violence.

Table 2.1.   Organic and Individualist Conservative Ideologies in the United States

	Organic Conservative	Individual Conservative
Human Nature	Humans are inherently aggressive, selfish, hierarchical, and motivated principally by biological needs. Men and women have different natures. Women are more temperate in their qualities and also have nurturing, caretaker qualities. Men are more aggressive, rational, and dominant.	Humans are inherently selfish, competitive, rational, individualistic, and basically lazy or inert. Humans are motivated by a rational calculation of self-interest. Inequality is inherent to differences in humans. Inequality between men and women is seen in terms of different choices that men make relative to women. Differences are not inherent to gender.
Central Values	Authority and tradition as rooted in terms of class and gender relations. Freedom *within* prescribed bounds.	Individual liberty and private property (laissez-faire). Liberty is not possible without the right of private property. Freedom *from* restraint.

Nature of the Social Order	Humans need society to protect themselves from other humans, especially men. Gender and class structure/hierarchy is necessary for society and humans to exist. Society is founded on basic human principles that are reflected in customs and traditions.	Free market and private property are the foundation of the economic and political order. Government is a coercive force. The invisible hand of competition is the just allocator. Gender and class hierarchies are the outcomes of individual differences and choices. Society is no more than the sum of the individuals who make it up; it is a social contract.
Role of the State	Elites should guide the state according to basic human principles, in Judeo-Christian societies, as they are stated in either the Bible or Natural law. *Anti-democratic traditions.*	State should abstain from interfering with the free market and restrict activities to national defense and safeguarding private property rights, criminal justice/system of courts, and maintaining monetary system. *Limited democratic traditions.*
Orientation Toward Change	Change is disruptive. It should be gradual, from the top down, guided by institutional elites, and consistent with principles that form the foundation of the society.	Change occurs in a naturally slow and incremental way as a result of individuals acting in competition with each other, trying to realize their self-interest in the marketplace. Social change is cyclical, like the market.
Ideal System	Patriarchal capitalist—stability through class and gender elite—directed development.	Free-market capitalism. Increase production through individual decisions stimulated by competition in the marketplace that benefits everyone in the society.
Cause of Social Problems	Sudden changes that are in violation of the basic principles and resultant breakdown in social control mechanisms of the society.	Government coercion and disruption of the free market (the natural regulator of the social order). As government interferes with the system, misallocation of goods and services disrupts human incentives to produce, leading to social problems.
Solution to Social Problems	Found in past traditions that reflect basic human principles.	Found in the basic principles of capitalist society (neoclassical economics); found in private property and unfettered free market.

The Organic Conservative Perspective

The historical root of the *organic conservative* ideology is the Christian paternalism of feudal society as exhibited in the writings of Thomas Aquinas and Edmund Burke (Hunt, 1981). Traces of the ideology are also found in the writings and speeches of American royalists in the colonies and southern aristocrats prior to the Civil War. The *organic conservative* ideology fundamentally legitimates a socioeconomic system that is primarily agriculturally based on landed wealth and precapitalist relations of production (slave, serf, and/or indentured labor systems). Gender relations are based on the traditional patriarchal gender division of labor that would be found among the elite in agrarian societies. In general, this perspective represents the worldview of a landed gentry.

Although the United States never experienced a period of feudalism, the period in the history of the United States that most closely coincides with the dominance of this ideology includes the colonial period up to the early part of the nineteenth century, the Civil War representing a transition in class dominance and dominant ideology. During the colonial period and until the early part of the nineteenth century, bonded labor systems (slavery and indentured) dominated social relations in the southern part of the country. The economy was principally based on agriculture, while the manufacturing sector was at an early stage of development. Production was small-scale, with individualized workshops and simple technology. The class structure consisted of a large, independent producer class of small farmers, a small landowning gentry class that was dominant, a class of indentured or slave laborers, a growing merchant class, and small but growing classes of factory owners and free workers. In general, class development in the southern part of the country lagged behind the northern in terms of the dominance of more classical capitalist relations of production. *Organic conservatism* was dominant in the southern region because of this difference in class structure. In the North during the first part of the nineteenth century, classical liberalism or what we referred to as *individualist conservatism* provided the legitimation for the emerging merchant and manufacturing classes. In general, the *organic conservative* ideology is more developed in Europe and in many Latin American and Middle Eastern societies where a landed oligarchy once clearly dominated these societies.

The religious fundamentalism of today is tied to an organic conservative ideology that looks to past wisdom and social formation for direction. Swift (1990) notes that Christian (largely Protestant) fundamentalism grew up in the U.S. at the turn of the century. The Judaic version has only surfaced in the last fifty years while Islamic fundamentalism dates from just before World War II and has only grown in the last twenty years. Swift contends that fundamentalism is principally a reactionary movement. He notes that "cultural and economic confusion provide fertile ground for the growth of fundamentalism. Who would not want a return to certainty in an uncertain world (Swift, 1990, 2)?"

Today in the United States there are three divergent variants of the *organic conservative* ideology: (1) religious moral conservative (Concerned Women For America, Christian Coalition, American Coalition for Traditional Values, Christian Voice, and Eagle Forum), (2) populist conservative (Ku Klux Klan and John

Birch Society), and (3) traditionalist (a variant of Classical Conservatism—Neo-Conservatism would be a more recent example of this variant—William F. Buckley and popular talk show host Rush Limbaugh would be well known representatives as well as think tanks such as the Heritage Foundation). The first two variants have been most popular among segments of the working class population and independent producers who reside in more economically depressed and politically conservative regions of the nation (southern states and the Bible Belt especially). Although these variants are quite different, and the adherents of each would not recognize their common philosophical grounding, the points of commonality center on the central values and conception of human nature. Publications in the United States that generally represent these variants are represented by the following: moral conservatives *Plain Truth, Saturday Evening Post,* and *Readers Digest;* populist conservative, *The Spotlight, Washington Times,* and *American Opinion;* and traditionalist or classical conservative, *National Review, American Spectator, and Conservative Digest.*

The *organic conservatives* contend that humans are naturally prone to anarchy, evil, and mutual destruction. Humans are seen as inherently aggressive, selfish, and hierarchical by nature. Humans, in this view, are motivated primarily by their base biological urges. The moral/religious organic conservative will focus on humans as being motivated by the propensity to sin which in turn may be motivated by biological urges.

Following from this cynical and negative view of human nature, *organic conservatives* see the social order as the only thing that stands between civilization and anarchy. The social order is an organic entity that is greater than the sum of its individual members. For the *organic conservative,* the social order takes primacy over the rights of its individual members. It represents the embodiment of the customs and traditions that reflect basic principles of human life.

For the *moral/religious organic conservative,* these basic principles are reflected in the Bible as the foundation of the Judeo-Christian heritage. For the traditionalist/classical conservative, they are found in the U.S. Constitution as they define the founding principles of the nation and in Greek and Roman natural law as it provides the philosophical basis of Western civilization. The customs, traditions, and basic institutions of the society are rooted in these basic principles that are the founding principles of the social order and should guide its development. Social policy and the behavior of individual members of the society are evaluated in the light of these standards. Interpretations of these principles and documents are prescribed narrowly. *Organic conservatives* are generally strict constructionists of the principles that are embodied in these documents. Williamson, Evans, and Munley (1985) note that the *organic conservative* values past wisdom in dealing with the social problems of the day and that this past wisdom is reflected in the customs, laws, and religion of the society.

Inequality and hierarchy in the society are natural and necessary for the proper functioning of the social order. Class, gender, and ethnic hierarchies are legitimated as a product of natural differences between people who occupy these positions. These hierarchies are also understood to be functional to the society. Following from this, organic conservatives argue that the elite has a greater responsibility to others in the society as leaders and benefactors of those who are unable to take care of themselves. They are to serve as a patriarch taking care of the poor and disabled as a husband and father takes care of his wife and children.

Hunt also suggests that the Christian paternalist ethic that is an element of the organic conservative perspective can be understood by comparing society to a family. "Those with positions of power and wealth can be likened to the father or keeper of the family. They have strong paternalistic obligations toward the common people the poor or, in our analogy, the children. The common person, however, is expected to accept his or her place in society and to be willingly subordinate to the leadership of the wealthy and the powerful in much the same way that a child accepts the authority of his or her father" (Hunt, 1981, 5). The paternalistic analogy of the husband taking care of his wife and children was often used to describe the role of the lord in caring for the serfs during feudalism or a master caring for his slaves during ancient times or periods of slavery during the pre–Civil war United States. The same analogy would apply in describing how the organic conservative would see the role of a corporate elite in taking care of the poor through the establishment of charitable foundations.

The elite is defined in terms of class, but also in terms of gender and ethnicity. Owners of production, men, and the ethnic or cultural elite have an obligation to lead and care for those who serve them in factories, homes, and in service to the state. Hunt notes that this hierarchy is rationalized in the will of God, the order of nature, or in terms of the congenital and ineradicable differences between people, or in some combination of these explanations.

The *organic conservative* ideology is also referred to as the law and order approach. Primacy is the maintenance of the social order, to conserve the past. Individual freedom is possible only when there is social order. People are free only when they choose to act in socially prescribed ways, that is, consistent with the basic principles that underlie the society. Freedom is discussed in terms of freedom *within* prescribed bounds established by the system of customs and traditions, as they are reflective of the basic principles that underlie the social order.

The central values of the *organic conservative* perspective are authority, order, and tradition. Authority is essential to the social order and is defined as legitimate coercion derived from the hierarchical positions within the society. Nisbet (1962) notes that, like power, authority is a form of constraint, but, unlike power, it is based on the consent of those under it. This consent is ultimately given as a result of the moral obligations of citizens to preserve the order and to be respectful and obedient to those who are in positions of power. Order refers to the institutionalized hierarchy of statuses and roles within the society. This hierarchy is understood as natural and necessary for human survival and is legitimated by the traditions reflecting those basic human principles firmly rooted in the cultural heritage.

The state is to be ruled by elites who guide it in the interests of all in terms of the time-honored traditions and customs of the society. Democratic processes are not consistent with the logic of this perspective. For the *organic conservative*, democracy often translates into mob rule, whereby those with the least abilities to govern have the ability to do so. *Organic conservatives* promote non-democratic mechanisms (electoral colleges, appointed commissions, and so forth) to limit the potential harm to the social order from popular rule.

Social change is viewed with suspicion from this perspective, for it is seen as essentially disruptive to the social order. Change that is unavoidable or deemed necessary should be slow, within the institutional framework of the social order, and guided by elites. Historically, the ideal system for the *organic conservative* is reflected in the social relations of feudal society with its notions of reciprocal responsibility, fixed duty, and noblesse oblige. Nevertheless, *organic conservatives* today accept the historical ascension of capitalism as the dominant mode of production while desiring to retain some characteristics of past feudal social relations. The ideal for the *organic conservative* is paternalistic capitalism: a basic stability in the social order brought about by adherence to traditional values that reflect the basic principles embedded in the Judeo-Christian heritage or the philosophical precepts of Western civilization and through elite-managed growth. In countries where military rule is aligned with a landed oligarchy, the *organic conservative* ideology will be dominant in public policy. Many countries in Latin America, Africa, and the Middle East follow this pattern.

Organic conservatives understand violent behavior to be endemic to humans. Violence stems from our aggressive nature that is part of our connection to the animal world or our proneness to sin resulting from our falling from grace, according to the Judeo-Christian heritage. In either case, the potential for violence is normal and inherent to our nature. The occurrence of violence is checked by the social order, which restrains and structures our behavior. The problem of violence occurs when the social order and the controls of the larger society have weakened or broken down. This can occur because of social changes that have been inconsistent or counter to the basic principles of the society as noted in the sacred texts or traditions. Grassroots movements are particularly viewed with suspicion as they represent change without the wisdom of the elites within the system. Furthermore, change itself is seen as disruptive in that it creates disruptions of institutional mechanism to control the natural, potentially violent, impulses of humans.

The focus is on interpersonal violence. Most violence conducted by elites is deemed to be incidental and/or necessary for the maintenance of the order, although some elite violence is recognized to be a result of moral failings. This is the case for interpersonal violence conducted by the elite and state, and for economic violence deemed to be excessive or immoral, that is, not justifiable in terms of preserving the social order.

The solutions to the problem of violence are to reinforce the order, to strengthen the bonds to the order, and to improve the efficiency of the mechanisms of social control that keep sin or animal impulses in check. The *organic conservative* looks to the basic principles that underlie the order as providing insight as to how to control violence. Stress is placed on promoting steps to educate or inculcate morals and traditional values among the masses. Often this is done by increasing the role of religion in public life. Another strategy is to increase the level of external restraints by promoting more criminalization and the use of the criminal justice system in controlling disruptive behavior. Last, by promoting the obligations of individuals to the needs of the community (usually defined in terms of the state), *organic conservatives* hope to reduce violence and preserve the order. In short, solutions are ultimately defined in terms of strengthening institutional controls, applying further restrictions on behavior, and increasing the levels of punishment to control behavior that is threatening to the status quo. In criminology, the theory of crime control that is most rooted in the *organic conservative* ideology is control theory. The assumptions regarding the propensity to crime and the strategies to reduce crime by strengthening ones bond to the social order (Hirschi, 1969) and the strengthening of containment mechanisms (Reckless, 1962) follow from this ideology.

The Individualist Conservative Perspective

Individualist conservatism, or classical liberalism, was the dominant perspective of capitalism during the eighteenth and nineteenth centuries. Although much of this perspective took root and gained wide acceptance during the mercantilist period, it was in the nineteenth century that classical liberalism dominated social, political, and economic thought in England. The perspective reflects a temper of mind that found the essence of society to lie in the individual autonomous, self-sufficing, and rational action and the essence of history to lie in the progressive emancipation of the individual from the tyranny of the past feudal order. Competition, individualization, dislocation of status and custom, impersonality, and moral anonymity were hailed by the rationalist because through them the natural stable and rational individual would be given an environment in which he would develop without constraint his inherent potentialities.

The *individualist conservative* legitimates the dominance of capitalist social relations in the stage of competitive industrial capitalism and the interests of the dominant class of entrepreneurs. In the United States, this stage occurred between the early nineteenth and early twentieth centuries, though the ideology of classical liberalism had been a powerful influence on the founding fathers during the eighteenth century. The craft sector declined during the nineteenth century, and the scale, mechanization, and integration of coordinated manufacturing production increased rapidly. There arose simultaneously a small but powerful factory-owning class and a large industrial working class made up of immigrants, displaced farmers, and artisans. The ranks of the independent producers were shrinking in the wake of increasing periods of economic concentration. These changes left in their wake the destruction of the *Gemeinschaft* of the previous colonial order where the remnants of feudal structures were legitimated by organic conservatism.

Today, the *individualist conservative* ideology is most representative of the viewpoint of owners of businesses in competitive sectors of the economy and the petty bourgeoisie (i.e., independent producers, small farmers, and shopkeepers). This viewpoint is represented in the positions of the National Association of Manufacturers, Rotary clubs, and the U.S. Chamber of Commerce. Libertarians present a rather extreme version of the *individualist conservative* ideology. Although they represent a relatively small number of American followers, their numbers have been growing since the 1980s. Publications that present a *individualist conservative* ideology are *Human Events, Commentary, The Economist, The Public Interest, U.S. News and World Report, Business Week, Forbes,* and the editorial pages of the *Wall Street Journal.*

The *individualist conservative* ideology possesses a view of human nature that, in some respects, overlaps with the organic conservative ideology: humans are basically aggressive (*individualist conservatives* would define this as competitive) and selfish. There is, however, this crucial difference: *individualist conservatives* see humans as highly rational, individualistic, and basically inert or lazy. The utilitarianism of Thomas Hobbes and Jeremy Bentham is an important element of *individualist conservatism.* Individuals in this view are assumed to be motivated by their own self-interest and to engage in a completely rational calculation of the cost and benefits of alternatives before they engage in any action.

The free market and private property are the foundations of the social order and the basis of political freedom, according to this perspective. The free market, the competitive arena where individual producers are competing to sell their products at the best possible price, and where workers are competing to sell their labor power at the best possible price, provides for the channeling of the individual's egoistic drives for the ultimate good of the social order. As Adam Smith observed:

> Each producer intends only his own security; and by directing that industry in such a manner as its produce may be of the greatest value, he intends only his own gain, and he is in this, and in many other cases, led by an invisible hand to promote an end which was no part of his intention. Nor is it always the worse for the society that it was not a part of it. By pursuing his own interest he frequently promotes that of society more effectually than when he really intends to promote it. I have never known much good done by those who affected to trade for the public good. It is an affection, indeed, not very common among merchants, and very few words need be employed in dissuading them from it (Smith, 1937, 423).

In this view, the free market untampered with allows for a just allocation of goods and services, an allocation that serves the needs of the individual actors within the market and thus the social order as a whole. The primary coercive force within the society, according to *individualist conservatives,* is the state. The state, under both the previous policies of mercantilism and contemporary liberal policies, disrupts the market. For example, by establishing a minimum wage and regulating the marketing of goods and services, the state essentially coerces individuals to act in opposition to their interests, which, in their view, results in inflationary prices and depressed market conditions. This leads to further problems in the society as the rational behavior of individuals within the society become increasingly disruptive as they respond to the irrational outcomes of a disrupted market. The state is to serve three essential functions: (1) protect the country from external threats; (2) protect citizens against injustices committed by other citizens, such as violation of contracts and property rights; and (3) erect and maintain public institutions and public works that are in the public interest, such as currency, standards of weights and measures, and physical means necessary to conduct business.

Society for the *individualist conservative* is defined as no more than the sum of its parts (i.e., the individuals composing it). The social contract as described by Jean Jacques Rousseau is the foundation of the social order. The ideal is "to find a form of association that may defend and protect with the whole force of the community, the person and property of every associate, and by means of which each, coalescing with all, may nevertheless obey only himself, and remain as free as before" (Rousseau, 1967, 17).

According to the *individualist conservative*, inequality and hierarchy in the society are natural insofar as the market determines them. Each individual competes with others to nurture and develop the talents they were born with and each is assessed by the market as to their worth. Those with the greatest talent and greatest initiative compete for the highest income, their talents being in short supply and high demand. Those with the least talent and the least initiative receive the lowest income, their talents being ordinary, in great supply, and with little demand. Just as supply and demand determine the price of a product, so also do they determine the price of labor and thus one's income. Gender, class, and ethnic stratification are understood only as they are the products of individual choices in the marketplace. They are not understood as systems outside the context of the individual choices and actions that created them. The only exception to this is in describing forms and levels of inequality resulting from irrational discrimination that has occurred as a result of government actions that have blocked the market force and rational decision making.

Individual liberty and private property are the two central values of the *individualist conservative* ideology. In order for the social order to exist and progress each individual must be free to realize his or her own interests, and by each individual having the ability to possess property, the means of production, he or she is less likely to be coerced by others. Individual liberty through ownership of private property can be realized only by the presence of a free market. It is in the marketplace where the benefits of one's free entrepreneurial action can be realized. Freedom is understood in terms of freedom *from* restraint. The primary agency of restraint is government.

For the *individualist conservative* change occurs in a naturally slow and incremental way as a result of individual actions. Social change is cyclical, like the cycles of the market. Change results from individuals acting as individuals in the pursuit of their own interests.

The ideal system for the *individualist conservative* is free market or laissez-faire capitalism, a social order that allows individuals to manifest their egoistic drive for material accumulation (profit) through the market, which results in benefits to all members of the society.

How do *individualist conservatives* understand the problem of violence? Again, like the organic conservatives, the focus is interpersonal violence. Institutional violence and certainly structural violence is generally not recognized to be violence by *individual conservatives*. Unlike organic conservatives, they see violence as less a result of an unchecked natural inclination than a conscious decision. Violence is an action perceived to be rational by the actor, rational in the context of the relative value of the costs and benefits of action. The armed robber who kills a victim, the rapist, the contract killer, even the spouse abuser, evaluates the costs and benefits of the action and rationally chooses violence. For the *individualist conservative,* the key to the problem of violence is found in understanding how the costs and benefits of violence have been created. In most cases, *individualist conservatives* will charge actions by the state interfering with natural forces (market forces) as the cause of the distortion in the rational calculus.

The solution to the problem of violence is then understood in the context of changing the costs and benefits of violent behavior for the individual offender. The principle focus in public policy from the *individualist conservative* approach has been changing the costs of the violent behavior, rather than in providing alternatives ways to achieve the benefits that is the goal of the action. Thus the criminal justice system is the principle agency to address the problem of violence. Increasing the penalties and the certainty that punishment will result from the action are ways promoted by *individualist conservatives* to control violence.

In regard to the issue of alternative means to achieve the benefits, *individualist conservatives* understand the problem of limited means to achieve the benefits as a problem of government interference with the marketplace. For *individualist conservatives*, government has limited the legitimate, appropriate means to achieve the good in the society. Government has limited employment opportunities by welfare and market regulation; it has discouraged individual initiative and drive by providing for people in a way that rewards their idleness, has destroyed families by making individuals increasingly dependent on the state for their well-being and not their own initiative and enterprise. All of these increase the likelihood that violence will be chosen by the individual in the exercise of illegitimate, disruptive alternatives to achieving wealth, status, and power.

Solutions to addressing the benefits side of the equation would focus on reducing the role of government in the marketplace in order to encourage further enterprise and initiative that would have the result of providing more alternatives to achieve the benefits that result from violent action. Even forms of violence that are a result of frustration and interpersonal conflict are understood as a result of the disruptive influence of government in the society, and again, with the reduced role of government in the marketplace, the level of conflict and frustration will be reduced as more opportunities for self-fulfillment are created through unrestrained individual initiative in the marketplace.

In criminological theory, the classical school of thought, or what is more commonly referred to as deterrence theory, is based on the ideological assumptions of *individual conservatism*. The focus is on individual choice based on the calculation of costs and benefits of action. The policy implications of deterrence theory focus on changing the severity and certainty of punishment in response to the occurrence of criminal behavior. (See table 2.2.)

Table 2.2.   Reform Corporate Liberal/Feminist and Socialist/Feminist Ideologies in the United States

	Reform Corporate/Liberal Feminist	Socialist/Feminist
Human Nature	Same as individualist conservatives with the exception that humans can be motivated by altruism under certain circumstances. Inequality is inherent to differences in humans. Inequality between men and women is the result of socialization differences, patterns of institutional discrimination, and differences in choices made. Gender and racial differences are not rooted in biology.	Human nature defined in terms of needs and how they are realized through interaction with nature. Humans have projective consciousness (species need)— need to think, to imagine, to create. The essence of human nature is the capacity and realization of these needs. Humans have the same needs, differences that exist are a product of the gender, class, and racial divisions in patriarchal, capitalist society.
Central Values	Individual liberty (civil rights), private property, and equal opportunity. Freedom *of* opportunity.	Equality and community. Freedom to develop capacities and potentials.
Nature of the Social Order	Free market and private property are the foundations of the economic and political order. However, capitalism has tendencies toward instability and concentrations of wealth and power. The result is social injustices in the meritocratic structure of the society that require government fine-tuning to keep the system expanding and beneficial to all.	Modes of production and reproduction and their articulation are the basis of social order. Patriarchal, capitalist society is based on inequality, coercion, exploitation, and alienation, whereby those in dominant position determined by their relationship to production (class) and reproduction (gender) benefit at the expense of those in dominated positions.
Role of the State	By means of pluralistic democracy, the state serves everyone's interests. The state must act as a regulator of the system to make sure there is equal opportunity and stable growth. *Open contest democratic system.*	Politics and the state are dominated by the interest of the ruling class as defined in terms of class and gender. *Economic democracy*— class and gender position does not influence outcomes of democratic decision making.
Orientation Toward Change	Collective action on the part of citizens, in many cases mediated by government action, is necessary to keep the system progressing. Social change is evolutionary, a result of government directed capitalist growth and development.	Fundamental social change occurs as a result of conflict between the divisions within the society. This conflict of divisions is stimulated by contradictions within and between modes of production and reproduction. *Change is dialectical.*

Ideal System	Welfare state capitalism—capitalist society with an open meritocracy (open educational, economic, and political contests) and welfare safety net necessary to insure stability and development.	Democratic—nonpatriarchal socialism—elimination of class, gender, and all other forms of oppression. Society organized and functions to promote the collective fulfillment of natural and species needs of all humanity.
Cause of Social Problems	Uncontrolled economy and lack of equal opportunity in the meritocracy.	Structured inequality and inherent contradictions create problems and have the potential to stimulate conflict within the society that may be a force for change.
Solution to Social Problems	Government monitoring of the economy and the meritocracy and regulation to maintain fairness.	Elimination of hierarchical structures and exploitative social relations.

The Reform Corporate Liberal/Feminist Ideology

The *reform corporate liberal* position developed primarily in response to increasing problems of economic instability and, secondarily to public outcry over increasing concentration of wealth and monopolization in the marketplace as industrial capitalism developed. The historical context for the development of the *reform corporate liberal* ideology is the monopoly stage of capitalist development. The ideology reflects the interests of large-scale monopoly capital that looks to the state to stabilize the system and provide increasing amounts of subsidies to maintain its monopoly positions. The disruptiveness of the economic cycle that goes boom to bust takes on more gravity as the economy grows in size. With each recession the costs to employers and employees grows, and it becomes increasingly more difficult to resolve the crisis in order to begin the next boom period. Rapid acceleration of fixed capital costs as there is increasing mechanization of production, together with the normal operation of the business cycle, result in increasing concentration and centralization. Work becomes increasingly routinized with the introduction of mechanization and the transition from technical to bureaucratic control of the workplace.

New conflicts develop as a result of the division of the economy into monopoly and competitive sectors, and as a result of the internationalization of capital, that is, center-dominant capitalist societies versus periphery-dominated, dependent-capitalist societies. There are not only increasing divisions within the owning class (nationally and internationally) but also increasing divisions within the working class. There is also at this stage the increasingly rapid growth of a relative surplus population and the need for the state to respond to this economic and political problem. John Maynard Keynes's work *The General Theory of Employment, Interest, and Money*, which was written during a time of worldwide crisis for the capitalist system in the 1930s, is one of the centerpieces of this perspective (Keynes, 1964). This work legitimates the role of the state to resolve this crisis by means of increasing intervention in the marketplace.

This *reform corporate liberal* perspective was the dominant perspective in the United States from the Great Depression up through the 1960s with President Lyndon Johnson's War on Poverty and the civil rights initiatives of that period. In recent times, beginning in the mid-1970s, the *reform corporate liberal* perspective has suffered a serious setback in terms of its dominance in public policy. Greenberg (1988) notes that this fall of the *reform corporate liberal* policy regime resulted from the combination of a sputtering economy, international retreat (Vietnam and Iran, reversal of the Bretton Woods agreement), and stagnant living standards (inflation and stagnation). Attempts have been made to dress up the perspective in new clothes or to make some fundamental changes in the economic tenets of the perspective. (Neo-Liberalism, the combination of fiscal conservatism and liberal social consciousness when it comes to civil rights and the environment would be an example of the latter.) Some political scientists have already declared the perspective dead. Traditional liberal periodicals are *Newsweek, Time Magazine, The Atlantic Monthly,* and *Harpers.*

The liberal/feminist component is rooted in the first women's movement in the United States with the co-optation of the radical wing of the movement (represented by the thinking of Stanton and Anthony) into the National American Women's Suffrage Association (NAWSA) and the definition of the problem of women's rights as principally the right of suffrage. Today, in the wake of the second women's movement, the National Organization for Women (NOW), has succeeded the NAWSA as the paramount liberal/feminist political organization. Although today's liberal feminism embraces the radical agenda of the first women's movement (Equal Rights Amendment), this no longer appears to be central to its agenda. The focus of NOW, like its predecessor, is to work through the established institutional mechanisms within the state and corporate structure to achieve incremental gains for women as defined in terms of extending opportunities for women to be equal participants in the institutions of the larger society. Changing institutional structures are only promoted when they serve to block women's opportunities for participation. A critique of patriarchy as it manifests itself in the functioning of all institutions in our society is not part of liberal feminism. Inclusion, not revolution is the goal.

Reflecting their common roots in classical liberalism, the *reform corporate liberal/feminists'* view of human nature is similar to that of *individualist conservatives*; it is not, however, as cynical. While *reform corporate liberal/feminism* accepts the *individualist conservatives* position that humans are fundamentally selfish, they believe that individuals can, *under certain limited circumstances,* be motivated by altruism, through an appeal to their "better nature." In regard to gender, differences between men and women are the result of socialization differences, patterns of institutional discrimination, and differences in choices made. Differences are not rooted in biological differences. Equality and sameness are stressed in viewing men and women.

In terms of their conception of the social order, *reform corporate liberal/ feminists* believe, like *individualist conservatives*, that the capitalist system provides a foundation for its central value, individual freedom. Unlike the *individualist conservative* ideology, which promotes laissez-faire, free-market capitalism, the *reform corporate liberal/feminist* ideology supports a role for government to fine-tune the economic system in order to maintain freedom and opportunity for individual development. Liberals contend that because the economic system has tendencies toward economic instability and concentration of ownership and wealth, they see the role of the state as one of monitoring or fine-tuning the system to maintain steady or stable economic growth and safeguarding the competitive nature of the free market through slowing down the problem of concentration. Both liberal and conservative policymakers encourage promotion of trade and the strategic lifting of trade barriers in areas to create national economic advantage. The establishment of welfare (government subsidies for workers who are displaced), wealthfare (government subsidies for owners to support capital accumulation), and adjusting the money supply to control the pace of economic activity are all liberal methods used to control the economic cycle. Antitrust actions and redistributive tax systems have been used (although less vigorously) by liberal policymakers to slow down the pace of concentration in the marketplace in terms of distribution of wealth and income.

This monitoring of the system is not restricted to the economic sphere. *Reform corporate liberal/feminists* also express concern as to the fairness of the meritocracy, the system of contests (education, work, and politics) that ensures the proper placement of individuals in the social order on the basis of their abilities and efforts. Liberals are concerned to ensure that the outcomes of these contests are fair in that all participants (men, women, and ethnic minorities) have an "equal opportunity" to succeed. If the contests of the meritocracy are not fair, not only do individuals suffer in terms of their lack of opportunity but also the social order as a whole suffers, for human talent is not being used efficiently by the system.

Reform corporate liberal/feminists assume that inequality is natural to the human condition; however, they hope that the outcomes of the meritocracy follow a model of distributive justice. Legal strategies disallowing forms of illegitimate discriminating practices (against racial and gender minorities) and social expenditures to assure equal opportunity in each of the contests are central elements of their strategy. Liberals are confident that their program can be implemented, despite the inconvenience to some individuals, by an appeal to the altruism inherent in human nature. However, liberals underestimate the competition between groups formed along class, ethnic, and gender dimensions that often undermines these efforts.

Pluralism best describes the nature of the political process from the *reform corporate liberal/feminist* point of view. An open arena of competition in the policy sector with different interest groups, each representing the interests of their membership to the best of their ability, ensures that the state will serve everyone's interests. The state is the neutral arbiter of conflicting interests in a pluralistic society. *Reform corporate liberal/feminists* conceptualize social change in terms of an evolutionary model. The social system is inherently rational (or can be made so) and will progress as humans increase their knowledge and intervene (collectively by means of the state pressured by interest groups) to make appropriate modifications in the system. The two central values of the *reform corporate liberal/feminist* ideology are individual civil liberties and equal opportunity. Freedom is discussed in terms of freedom of opportunity.

The ideal system for *Reform corporate liberal/feminism* is the corporate welfare state. Government works with business in a partnership with other interests in the society to maintain a pattern of stable growth and an increasing standard of living for working people, and increasing profits for owners and investors.

Violence from the *reform corporate liberal/feminist* ideology is understood as principally a result of a lack of equal opportunity in the meritocracy. Like the previous two ideologies, interpersonal violence is the principle focus. *Reform corporate liberal/feminists* will also recognize institutional violence by economic actors (corporate violence), by the state, and by men dominating women in the family. Violence is not seen as endemic to human nature, but a result of an uncontrolled economic system that leads to distortions in the meritocracy. Violence, principally committed by men, is understood as a response (not necessarily rational) to the blocked opportunities resulting from the undirected, unfettered market force. Specific focus of these blocked opportunities is in the area of employment and educational opportunities. Violence among the young is particularly understood in terms of lack of opportunities in these areas, which leads to frustration and violence as a means to seek alternatives, or more likely, as a means to strike out at the system that denies these opportunities.

The solution to the problem of violence in the society is the maintenance of fairness in the meritocracy through the regulating of market relations and enforcing laws that prohibit individual and institutional discrimination that denies opportunities for participation by women and ethnic minorities. Furthermore, general economic progression resulting from government actions to direct and subsidize investment in promising growth areas (high tech) is also seen as important. As the economic pie expands, there is more for everyone, reducing the societal pressures rooted in unequal distribution of income and wealth.

In criminological theory liberalism has been represented in the positivist school of thought. The stress is in identifying the defect in the individual or the immediate environment that leads to the individual not having access to equal opportunity for participation in the meritocracy. Biological and psychological positivist theories have been the more conservative approaches within this paradigm in that they see that the problem of violence is more fixed within the individual as a result of his or her deficiencies. There is little need to change the social environment to accommodate the individual's pathology. The implications of these theories are that there are biological and psychological interventions that will reduce levels of violence in individuals. The violence of the individual will be controlled directly by the therapeutic intervention or indirectly by providing access to opportunities once the physical or personality defect is corrected.

Sociological positivist theories have located the cause of violence in problems of the opportunity structure resulting from problems of the immediate environment or the individual's adaptation to it. Strain or opportunity theory is a good example of this latter approach. In strain or opportunity theory the problems of crime are rooted in lack of access to opportunities to achieve the goals of the society. This frustration can lead to adaptations, violence being one. Versions of strain theories of the violent delinquent focus on how aggression stems from the frustration resulting from blocked opportunities (Cohen, 1955; Cloward and Ohlin, 1960). Solutions are defined in terms of expanding opportunities in the meritocracy to reduce levels of crime and violence and correcting the deficits in the individual's adaptation to the environment.

In all three of the preceding ideologies, the problem of violence and the solutions are addressed within the context of the society. In none of the ideologies discussed thus far is the problem of violence understood as endemic to how the society is organized. Violence is ultimately seen as incidental to the fundamental organizational-political-economic structure as defined in terms of systems of stratification. Even the *reform corporate liberal/feminist* analysis views the solution to the problems of the society, violence as well, in fine-tuning the system, making sure that women and ethnic minorities have access to participation in the system, not fundamentally changing the nature of class or gender relations or the rights of property or market relations that allow for the power of private property. The last ideology defines the problems of the society, violence specifically, as endemic to how we have organized the society. This ideology is outside the ideological parameters of the system, and thus these ideas pose the greatest threat to the system. The preceding ideologies are well represented on the editorial pages of local and national media and in public commentary heard on television and radio programs. This is not the case with this last ideology.

The Socialist/Feminist Ideology

It is important to recognize that the *socialist/feminist ideology* represents a merging of elements of radical feminism with a socialist ideology. The socialist ideology has a long tradition rooted in the utopian socialists going back as early as the fifth century. More well-known utopian socialists of the eighteenth and nineteenth centuries include Babeuf, Proudhon, Saint-Simon, and Fourier. The socialist ideology today is still dominated by a variant of scientific socialism based on the writings of Karl Marx.

Early Marxist feminists include Clara Zetkin and Rosa Luxemburg. The weakness of this perspective was in the theoretical primacy of the class dimension of stratification over the gender dimension. The institutionalization of private property was understood as the basis of all other forms of oppression and stratification, including the subjugation of women. A similar perceived weakness was seen in the radical feminist analysis, which contends that gender oppression and stratification is the basis of all other forms of oppression and stratification, including social class. However, *socialist/feminist* ideology circumvented the weaknesses of both analyses by integrating the centrality of the radical feminist agenda with the socialist agenda. This perspective represents a materialist analysis grounded principally in Marxist political economy and an incorporation of the radical feminist emphasis of patriarchy as a separate structure within a social system (Hartman, 1981; Vogel, 1981). In this ideology, both patriarchy and class oppression are seen as separate but interlocked systems of stratification that form the basis of patriarchal capitalist societies today.

Socialists, in general, proceed from the premise that human nature is rooted in human needs. Although the topic of human needs is one that has been a focus of great philosophical and psychological debates, from the socialist ideology we can simply identify two general areas of needs: physical or natural needs that are similar to the needs of all animals, and species needs, that is, needs that are unique to humans (McMurtry, 1978).

Humans' physical needs are reflected in their needs to fulfill their physical being. Humans' physical needs include sustenance and protection from the elements. Humans' species needs are reflected in the unique qualities of the species. Species needs are defined in terms of the drive for members of the species to realize their species potentials. Species needs are based on the human abilities to think, create, and imagine. McMurtry refers to this species need as *projective consciousness*, the ability to imagine something that does not exist in nature and to project it into reality through the creative powers of humans. Both human physical or natural and species needs are fulfilled through human interaction with nature. Humans objectify and re-create themselves through interaction with nature, developing themselves and developing nature simultaneously. Other human beings are a crucial component of nature. Humans need other human beings in order to exist, to fulfill their physical and species needs. This is sometimes referred to the *social nature of human beings* (Azizah, 1981). For the *socialist/feminist*, that is all that there is of human nature. It is a *tabula rosa* that is based on needs that reflect the essence of humanity and the need to be social, to interact with nature and, especially other humans, to realize these needs. That humans are selfish, individualistic, rational, competitive, and hierarchical in society today is not a result of human nature but the reflection of the nature of humans as they are a product of capitalist society.

The concept of alienation is at the core of a socialist conception of human nature (Ollman, 1972). Alienation essentially refers to the separation of humans from nature and thus from their ability to reproduce and fully actualize their needs and potentials through interaction with nature. All systems of stratification in societies, especially those based on class and gender, create problems of alienation in that they inhibit a segment of the population from reaching its potential as human beings through their interaction with nature. In all cases of alienation, the dominated interactions with nature are controlled for the benefit of those who dominate.

The inequality between men and women is not a reflection of differences in their natures per se but is a product of the gender stratification system rooted in patriarchy. Thus, as social systems change in terms of the nature of gender oppression (i.e., patriarchy), so does the nature of the inequality between men and women and the presumed differences in nature that are used to legitimate this inequality. The same is true for class inequality.

Both the modes of production and reproduction form the foundation of the social system. The specific nature of these modes of production and reproduction as defined in terms of forces and relations of production/reproduction define the social system, thus American society is a capitalist patriarchy. Furthermore, although these systems can be described as independent of each other, they are articulated as part of a whole system. Today the vast majority of the world's societies are patriarchal capitalist systems, although the specific nature of these systems and their articulation are not the same from society to society. Nevertheless, one's position in the social order in patriarchal capitalist societies is characterized in terms of one's structural position in relation to each of the modes of production/reproduction: male worker, female worker, male capitalist, and so forth. Ethnic/racial and age stratification systems are significant as they intersect with these fundamental structural divisions. Racism and nationalism have been used by the capitalist class historically to maintain control over the workforce by maintaining a divided opposition and by furthering imperialist goals of domination of other social systems to meet the needs for expanding markets and access to resources.

Patriarchy for *socialist/feminists* is defined both ideologically and more importantly, materially. Patriarchy is a set of social relations that has a material base and in which there are hierarchical relations between men. These hierarchical relations are institutionalized in the customs, norms, and structure of social relations in all arenas of human interaction. This hierarchy is also maintained through solidarity among men. The material base of patriarchy is men's control over women's labor power. Control over women is maintained by restricting women's access to necessary economically productive resources and restricting and controlling women's sexuality.

For any social system to survive, there must be an articulation, a fitting together, of the modes of production and reproduction. This does not mean that the two systems do not come into conflict or contradiction with each other. Change in one ordinarily creates movement, tension, or contradiction in the other (Hartman, 1981). The gender and class system change as a result of struggle between the dominant and dominated groups within each sphere that is stimulated by the contradictions that develop out of each respective mode, and as a result of the conflict that may develop as the aims of those who dominate in each sphere conflict (Dworkin, 1976). (For a further discussion on the concept of contradiction, the reader is referred back to the discussion in chapter 1).

The major factor perpetuating gender inequality is that the modes of production and reproduction and the nature of the articulation of these two modes form the foundation of the social order. Institutional processes maintain the stability of the social order because those who dominate each system as defined in terms of the relations of production and reproduction benefit from the continuation of the domination and from the specific nature of the articulation of the two systems. For example, capitalists benefit from patriarchy because of a defined pool of workers who are excluded or discriminated against in gaining access to production (a reserve army of unemployed). The divisions between men and women serve to divide the workforce, making it easier to control. For example, the superexploitation in women's wages and the unpaid labor by women in home maintenance serve to hold wages down and maximize profits for capitalists. Men benefit from the free labor at home, a psychology of domination, control over sexuality, and the production of their progeny. The articulation of the two systems benefits all men in that the superexploitation of women in the workforce serves to maintain their dependence and powerlessness for the continued maintenance of patriarchy.

As each of the two modes change, so does the nature of the articulation between the two modes. Contradictions between the two modes develop and increase conflict between the opposing classes/genders within and between the modes of production and reproduction. Depending on the nature of the power differences between these opposing classes/genders, these contradictions have the potential to bring about fundamental changes in the overall social system.

The ideal system for the *socialist/feminist* is nonpatriarchal democratic socialism. This implies a society that has eliminated class, gender, and all other systems of stratification. Society is organized and functions to promote the collective fulfillment of natural and species needs of all humanity.

What is the cause and solution to the problem of violence in our society? For the *socialist/feminist*, that violence which is larger in scope and severity is structural and institutional. Violence is not inherent in humans, but is a product of the social organization of humans. In particular, it is a product of the hierarchical organization of the society whereby humans are valued and devalued relative to each other as they occupy positions within this hierarchy. Violence is fundamentally the means by which the hierarchies are established, maintained, extended, and ultimately challenged and changed. Thus at the highest level, violence (structural) is a direct outcome of this hierarchical organization in that the development of some is sacrificed for the development of those who are dominant. The violent consequences of this arrangement as it manifests itself in mortality and morbidity differences, and differences in human development of those who occupy differing positions in the hierarchy, are recognized to be central to defining the problem of violence. At another level, violence takes the form of institutional practices that maintain and extend the systems of stratification. In this sense, violence is the use of force to acquire wealth, status, and power legitimately as they are defined in terms of the rules of the systems of stratification that underlie the social order. These rules of ownership, control, and power establish the parameters for the functioning of institutions of the larger society. This institutional violence is crucial for the maintenance and reproduction of systems of stratification. Last, violence is the illegitimate use of force to acquire wealth, status, power and control over women through the violation of the rules of systems of stratification that underlie the social order. This is the problem of interpersonal violence. Although not seen to be as large in scope and severity as institutional or structural, it is nevertheless violence that threatens human life and is a product of hierarchical relations of the larger society.

Solutions to the problems of violence focus on empowering those who are dominated to make change in the systems of stratification that are the basis of their oppression. Class and gender oppression is ultimately the basis of violence. As those who are dominated are empowered to change these structures and allow all members of the society to realize their species and physical needs, levels of violence will be reduced.

The critical school of criminology (Michalowski, 1985) and the emerging *socialist/feminist* criminological theories (Messerschmidt, 1986) are rooted in this ideology. The problem of crime is rooted in systems of stratification. Nonreformist reforms, those that fundamentally change systems of stratification, are seen as appropriate strategies to reducing crime. For example, reforms such as full employment would change the distribution of power between owners and workers so that it would have an impact on the pattern of crime in the society. The comparable worth reform, whereby wage differentials are determined on the basis of the amount of work required to attain the skill and not by means of the market alone, would have an impact on the economic position of men relative to women and thus be a nonreformist reform and would have an impact on patterns of violence in the society.

CONCLUSION

In conclusion, how we perceive and understand violence and the roles we play in relation to the violence we experience in our lives as actors, victims, and observers takes place through a cultural prism. This cultural prism is a social creation, like the violence we are observing. This cultural prism is constructed in part by the ideologies that are dominant in our society. These ideologies allow us to see some forms of violence and not others. To understand what violence is and how we experience it, it is first necessary for us to understand the nature of the prism and how it may restrict our recognition and understanding of violence.

In this book we are attempting to extend the reader's understanding of violence by first developing a definition of violence based on universalistic criteria. We are also attempting to allow the reader to go beyond the limitations of understanding created by the cultural and ideological lenses that one has acquired as products and actors within a particularly society. As we discuss and describe different kinds of violence based on the definition of violence developed within the first chapter, the reader will sense the pull of the culture and more specifically the ideologies that are dominant in the society. We hope we have begun to provide the tools to be able to step back and look at this phenomenon from different ideological frameworks or vantage points to allow for a more complete understanding of what violence is.

REFERENCES

Allman, William F. 1988. "A Laboratory of Human Conflict." *U.S. News and World Report* 104: 57–9.

Associated Press. 2002, January 11. "Jury Deliberating Hockey Dad's Fate." *The Fort Wayne (Ind.) Journal Gazette.*

Azizah, Al-Hibri. 1981. "Capitalism Is an Advanced Stage of Patriarchy: But Marxism Is Not Feminism." In *Women and Revolution: A Discussion of the Unhappy Marriage of Marxism and Feminism,* edited by L. Sargent. Boston: South End Press.

Bandura, Albert. 1965. "Influence of Model's Reinforcement Contingencies on the Acquisition of Imitative Responses." *Journal of Personality and Social Psychology* 1: 589–95.

———. 1973. *Aggression: A Social Learning Analysis.* Englewood Cliffs, N.J.: Prentice Hall.

———. 1977. *Social Learning Theory.* Englewood Cliffs, N.J.: Prentice Hall.

Bandura, Albert, D. Ross, and S. S. Ross. 1963. "Imitation of Film-Mediated Aggressive Models." *Journal of Abnormal and Social Psychology* 66: 3–11.

Bandura, Albert, and Richard H. Walters. 1963. *Social Learning and Personality Development.* New York: Henry Holt.

Barak, Gregg. 1994. *Media, Process, and the Social Construction of Crime.* New York: Garland Publishing.

Barnouw, Victor. 1963. *Culture and Personality.* Homewood, Ill.: Dorsey Press.

Bayley, David H. 1976. *Forces of Order: Police Behavior in Japan and the United States.* Berkeley: University of California Press.

Benedict, Ruth. 1946. *The Chrysanthemum and the Sword.* New York: Houghton Mifflin.

Berndt, Catherine H. 1978. "In Aboriginal Australia." In *Learning Non-Aggression: The Experience of Non-Literate Societies,* edited by A. Montagu, 144–60. New York: Oxford University Press.

Bersani, Leo, and Ulysse Dutoit. 1985. *The Forms of Violence.* New York: Schocken Books.

Billington, Ray. 1974. *The Origins of Nativism in the United States, 1800–1844.* New York: Arnor Press.

Bilton, Michael. 1992. *Four Hours in My Lai.* New York: Viking Press.

Brown, Richard Maxell. 1969. "The American Vigilante Tradition." In *The History of Violence in America*, edited by Hugh D. Graham and Ted R. Gurr, 154–226. New York: Bantam Books.

Browning, Christopher R. 1992. *Ordinary Men: Reserve Police Battalion 101 and the Final Solution in Poland*. New York: Harper Collins.

Brownlee, Shannon. 1990, February 17. "If Only Life Were So Simple." *U.S. News and World Report*, 54–6.

Burrows, William E. 1976. *Vigilante!* New York: Harcourt Brace Jovanovich.

Cater, Douglass, and Stephen Strickland. 1975. *TV Violence and the Child*. New York: Russell Sage Foundation.

Chagnon, Napoleon. 1968. *Yanomamo: The Fierce People*. New York: Holt, Rinehart and Winston.

Cloward, Richard, and Lloyd E. Ohlin. 1960. *Delinquency and Opportunity*. New York: Free Press.

Cohen, Albert. 1955. *Delinquent Boys*. New York: Free Press.

Davies, Nigel. 1981. *Human Sacrifice in History and Today*. New York: Dorsett Press.

Davis, David Brion. 1970. "Violence in American Literature." In *Violence: Causes and Solutions*, edited by Renatus Hartogs and Eric Artzt, 54–66. New York: Dell Books.

Devos, George, and Hiroshi Wagatsuma. 1972. *Japan's Invisible Race*. Rev. ed. Berkeley: University of California Press.

Dominick, Joseph R. 1978. "Crime and Law Enforcement in the Mass Media." In *Deviance and Mass Media*, edited by C. Winick, 105–208. Beverly Hills, Calif.: Sage.

Douglas, Jack D., and Frances C. Waksler. 1982. *The Sociology of Deviance*. Boston: Little, Brown.

Dowie, Mark. 1977, September/October. "Pinto Madness." *Mother Jones*, 18–32.

Dworkin, Andrea. 1976. *Our Blood*. New York: Harper & Row.

Elliot, Mabel A. 1944. "Crime and the Frontier Mores." *American Sociological Review* 9: 185–92.

Erbe, Bonnie. 2002, January 21. "Make an Example of Violent Parent at Youth Sports." *Fort Wayne (Ind.) Journal Gazette*.

Erickson, R. V., P. M. Baranek, and J.B.L. Chan. 1991. *Representing Order: Crime, Law, and Justice in the News Media*. Toronto: University of Toronto Press.

Eron, L. D., L. R. Huesmann, M. M. Lefkowitz, and L. O. Walder. 1972. "Does Television Violence Cause Aggression?" *American Psychologist* 27: 253–63.

Fishman, Mark, and Gray Cavender. 1998. *Entertaining Crime: Television Reality Programs*. New York: Aldine de Gruyter.

Franklin, John Hope. 1956. *The Militant South*. Cambridge, Mass.: Harvard University Press.

Frantz, Joe B. 1969. "The Frontier Tradition: an Invitation to Violence." In *History of Violence in America*, edited by H. D. Graham and T. R. Gurr, 127–54. New York: Bantam Books:

Gamson, William A. 1975. *The Strategy of Social Protest*. Homewood, Ill.: Dorsey Press.

Gellner, Ernest. 1988. *Plough, Sword and Book: The Structure of Human History*. Chicago: University of Chicago Press.

Gergen, David. 1989, May 8. "Secrets behind the Gun Lobby's Staying Power." *U.S. News and World Report*, 26.

Goldstein, Jeffrey H. 1986. *Aggression and Crimes of Violence*. New York: Oxford University Press.

Greenberg, Edward S. 1985. *Capitalism and the American Political Ideal*. Armonk, N.Y.: M. E. Sharpe.

Gubar, Susan, and Joan Hoff. 1989. *For Adult Users Only*. Bloomington: Indiana University Press.

Hackney, Sheldon. 1969. "Southern Violence." In *Violence in America: Historical and Comparative Perspectives*, edited by H. D. Graham and T. R. Gurr, 505–27. New York: Bantam Books.

Handlin, Oscar. 1957. *Race and Nationality in American Life*. Boston: Little, Brown.

Harris, Marvin. 1974. *Cows, Pigs, Wars and Witches*. New York: Vintage Books.

Hartman, Heidi. 1981. "The Unhappy Marriage of Marxism and Feminism: Towards a More Progressive Union." In *Women and Revolution: A Discussion of the Unhappy Marriage of Marxism and Feminism*, edited by L. Sargent. Boston: South End Press.

Hirschi, Travis. 1969. *Causes of Delinquency*. Berkeley: University of California Press.

Hofstadter, Richard, and Michael Wallace. 1971. "Reflections on Violence in the United States." In *American Violence: A Documentary History*, edited by Richard Hofstadter and Michael Wallace. New York: Vintage Books.

Hunt, E. K. 1981. *Property and Prophets: The Evolution of Economic Institutions and Ideologies*. 4th ed. New York: Harper & Row.

Huston, A. C., E. Donnerstein, H. Fairchild, N. D. Fashbach, P. A. Katz, J. P. Murray, E. A. Rubinstein, B. L. Wilcox, and D. Zuckerman. 1992. *Big World, Small Screen: The Role Of Television In American Society*. Lincoln, Nebr.: University of Nebraska.

Jubera, Drew. 1991, August 17. "Tied to the Tube: is Television Hazardous to Our Children?" *Fort Wayne (Ind.) Journal-Gazette*.

Keynes, John Maynard. 1964. *The General Theory of Employment, Interest, and Money*. New York: Harcourt Brace Jovanovich.

Kolson, Sally. 1993, December 17. "Put Boss' Kids Faces on Video Games." *Fort Wayne (Ind.) Journal-Gazette*, 1D.

Leo, John. 1990a, July 2. "Polluting Our Popular Culture." *U.S. News and World Report*, 15.

———. 1990b, December 3. "Marketing Cynicism and Vulgarity." *U.S. News and World Report*, 23.

Lynn, Kenneth. 1969. "Violence in American Literature and Folklore." In *Violence in America: Historical and Comparative Perspectives*, edited by H. D. Graham and T. R. Gurr, 226–242. New York: Bantam Books.

Malamuth, N. M., and E. Donnerstein. 1984. *Pornography and Sexual Aggression*. New York: Academic Press.

McGrath, Roger D. 1984. *Gunfighters, Highwaymen and Vigilantes: Violence on the Frontier*. Berkeley: University of California Press.

McMurtry, John. 1978. *The Structure of Marx's World-View*. Princeton, N.J.: Princeton University Press.

Messerschmidt, James W. 1986. *Capitalism, Patriarchy, and Crime*. Totowa, N.J.: Rowman and Littlefield.

Michalowski, Raymond. 1985. *Order, Law, and Crime: An Introduction to Criminology*. New York: Random House.

Milgram, Stanley. 1974. *Obedience to Authority*. New York: Harper Colophon.

Montagu, Ashley. 1978. *Learning Non-Aggression: The Experience of Non-Literate Societies*. New York: Oxford University Press.

Nakane, Chie. 1970. *Japanese Society*. Berkeley: University of California Press.

Newman, Graeme. 1979. *Understanding Violence*. Philadelphia: Lippincott.

Nisbet, Robert. l962. *Community and Power.* London: Oxford University Press.

Ollman, Bertell. 1972. *Alienation: Marx's Conception of Man in Capitalist Society.* Cambridge: Cambridge University Press.

Olson, James Stuart. 1979. *The Ethnic Dimension in American History.* New York: St. Martin's Press.

Pagelow, Mildred Daley. 1981. *Woman Battering: Victims and Their Experiences.* Beverly Hills, Calif.: Sage.

Parenti, Michael. 1986. *Inventing Reality: The Politics of the Mass Media.* New York: St. Martin's Press.

"A Partial Vindication." 1989, March 15. *Time,* 34.

Pierce, Chester M. 1970. "Violence and the National Character." In *Violence: Causes and Solutions,* edited by R. Hartogs and E. Artzt, 119–26. New York: Dell Books.

Reckless, Walter C. 1962, March/April. "A Non-Causal Explanation: Containment Theory." *Excerpta Criminologica.*

Rousseau, Jean-Jacques. l967. *The Social Contract and Discourse on the Origin and Foundation of Inequality among Mankind.* New York: Washington Square Press.

Rowland, Willard D. Jr. 1983. *The Politics of TV Violence.* Beverly Hills, Calif.: Sage.

Shapiro, Judith. 1971. *Sex Roles and Social Structure among the Yanomamo Indians in North Brazil.* Ph.D. diss., Columbia University.

Sherizen, Sanford. 1978. "Social Creation of Crime News: All the News Fitted to Print." In *Deviance and Mass Media,* edited by C. Winick, 203–24. Beverly Hills, Calif.: Sage.

Shupe, Anson. 1991. *The Darker Side of Virtue.* Buffalo, N.Y.: Prometheus Books.

Shupe, Anson, William A. Stacey, and Lonnie R. Hazlewood. 1987. *Violent Men, Violent Couples: The Dynamics of Domestic Violence.* Lexington, Mass.: Lexington Books.

Smith, Adam. 1937. *The Wealth of Nations.* New York: Modern Library.

Stacey, William A., and Anson Shupe. 1983. *The Family Secret: Domestic Violence in America.* Boston: Beacon Press.

Swift, Richard. 1990, August. "Fundamentalism: Reaching for Certainty." *New Internationalist,* no. 210.

Toffler, Alvin. 1990. *Powershift.* New York: Bantam Books.

Vogel, Lisa. 1981. "Marxism and Feminism: Unhappy Marriage, Trial Separation or Something Else?" In *Women and Revolution: A Discussion of the Unhappy Marriage of Marxism and Feminism,* edited by L. Sargent. Boston: South End Press.

Williamson, John B., Linda Evans, and Anne Munley. 1985. *Social Problems: The Contemporary Debates.* Boston: Little, Brown.

Wood, Owen. 2001, May. "The Firestone Tire Recall." *CBC News Online.* http://cbc.ca/news/indepth/background/tirerecall_timeline.html.

Chapter Three

Interpersonal Violence: Murder and Rape

Contractor Carey Kovacs was just a guy having a good time at a Saturday-night bachelor party in a strip joint on Detroit's Eight Mile Road. The twenty-five-year-old Kovacs was to have been the best man at his friend's wedding the next week. Then a fight broke out between Kovacs' friends and another group of men. Kovacs was knocked to the ground and repeatedly kicked in the head by Benny Jovanovic. Kovacs died of head injuries on Sunday morning (Adler, 1994, 41).

Last September a fifteen-year-old Houston boy raped and murdered a sixty-six-year-old woman, then burglarized her home. In May a fifteen-year-old Detroit boy was charged with killing another teenager with a sawed-off shotgun, apparently in a dispute over a stolen bicycle. Ten months ago, a sixteen-year-old boy drove 150 miles from his home in Princeton, Kentucky, and shot to death a woman he did not know. The boy, who came to be known as "Little Rambo" to his schoolmates, told police that he "just wanted to get away and kill somebody" (Toufexis, 1989, 52).

In Watsonville, California, Ignacio Vasquez Segura on Tuesday walked into a packing shed on a mushroom farm where a former girlfriend worked. She was not there, so he asked for one of her friends, Raquel Gutierrez, age twenty-four, shot her dead, and blasted away with a semiautomatic rifle, wounding two coworkers. Segura fled in a sports car and shot himself in the head as police were closing in (Church, 1989, 20).

Violence between two gangs in Fort Wayne, Indiana, during a two-and-one-half-year period has resulted in five deaths and twelve shootings (Eaton et al., 2002).

Nineteen girls were killed and seventy-one raped by male schoolmates on July 14th, 1991, at the St. Kizito Mixed Secondary School in Kenya. Twenty-nine boys faced manslaughter charges, and two were also charged with rape (Chua-Eoan, 1991).

George Hennard crashed his blue pickup truck into a Luby's cafeteria and in less than a ten-minute period randomly shot and killed twenty-two patrons before taking his own life (Woodbury, 1991).

These are some true instances of interpersonal violence, stories of human tragedy that occur regularly in the world today. How often do they occur? When are they likely to occur? Who is likely to be the offender(s) and the victim(s)? Why does it happen? In short, what are the patterns of interpersonal violence in this country and in the world today? In this chapter we explore the patterns of interpersonal violence, focusing on murder and rape. Although distinct acts in themselves, we argue that both phenomena represent similar expressions of power. In general, those who are victims of rape and/or murder tend to be the least powerful as defined in terms of structural relations, and where rates of murder and assault are high, usually rates of rape are high as well (Kutchinkski, 1988). Thus, in our discussion of interpersonal violence it is first important to focus on these two severe forms of interpersonal violence: who, when, and where murder and rape occur. We look at these patterns historically and cross-societally in order to uncover the social forces that influence the formation of these patterns.

MURDER

We begin by defining what we mean by murder. Legally, murder and non-negligent manslaughter are both defined as the intentional and unlawful killing of a person or persons. This excludes what is considered to be justifiable homicide, whether it is committed in the act of duty, as in the case of a police officer or soldier, or as an act of self-defense by a private citizen. Nevertheless, whether justified or unjustified, this is an act of interpersonal violence. By the classification system suggested in chapter 1, murder as an area of interpersonal violence would focus on the killing that occurs outside the institutional roles the actors are performing. Thus the acts of violence committed by a police office or a soldier would be considered appropriate institutional violence and would not be included in homicide statistics. On the other hand, other areas of institutional violence would be defined as illegal homicides yet are also institutional violence. One example is that of a husband or wife killing each other or killing one of their children during a domestic quarrel; family violence or violence among intimates composes a significant proportion of homicides. In most of these cases we are talking about institutional violence that maintains, extends, or challenges asymmetric gender/age/power relations. In these latter cases of violence, they are included in the statistics on homicide yet they are cases of individuals acting in the context of roles within a social institution. Why one type of institutional violence (killings by police and military), as opposed to another type of institutional violence (murders by husbands or wives), would not be counted as homicide may say more about which dimension of stratification is more threatened by these crimes and whether those who are dominant are threatened by the violence than about the actions themselves. Despite these problems of the data available, let us look at the patterns of homicide as indicated by government statistics.

Gender

Who are identified as murderers? We find that those who are arrested for murder and nonnegligent manslaughter are principally men. In 1999, males were nine times more likely to commit murder than females were (Fox and Zawitz, 2001). This is a pattern that will be repeated over and over again in all forms of violence. Overall, men commit most of the violence in a society (Maguire, Pastore, and Flanagan, 1993).

For victims of murder, we find similar patterns. Most (76 percent) of the victims of homicide are males (Fox and Zawitz, 2001). Both male and female offenders are more likely to target male victims than female victims. However, 90.8 percent of female victims of homicide were murdered by males (Federal Bureau of Investigation, 2001). Males are more likely to be victims of homicides when the relationship between victim and offender is more distant (Zahn and Sagi, 1987), such as outside the home. Females are more likely to be the victim when the relationship between victim and offender is characterized as intimate (Fox and Zawitz, 2001). Women are more likely to be murdered by men whom they know than by men who are strangers. About one third of female murder victims were killed by an intimate, for males it is about 4 percent of male murder victims were killed by an intimate. Of all female murder victims, the proportion killed by an intimate has been relatively stable between 1976 and 1999, while for male murder victims, the proportion killed by an intimate has dropped significantly during this period. What is also most interesting is that the rate of intimate murders by spouses has dropped dramatically. This is especially the case for males, and especially black males, who have seen the greatest drop in being victims of intimate murders for all types of intimate relationships (spouse, boyfriend, and ex-spouse) (Fox and Zawitz, 2001).

In regard to same sex killings, Barlow notes that males kill males more than ten times the frequency that women kill women (Barlow, 1990, 159). On one offender/one victim incidents, both victim and offender were male in 88.5 percent of the cases in 2000 (Federal Bureau of Investigation, 2001). In general, Daly and Wilson point out that there is no known society in which the level of violence among women begins to approach that among men (Daly and Wilson, 1988, 146). Even though men are more likely to be victims of murder, it is important to note that the rate of death by homicide and legal intervention (death by police and other legal authorities) for women doubled between 1950 and 1989 (Reiss and Roth, 1993). Since 1989 the rates for both males and females have generally declined. Fox and Zawitz analyze the most recent trend in homicide from 1976 to 1999. In 1999, the homicide rate for males was 11.7/100,000.

This rate was almost half the rate for men during the peak for this period in 1991, 20.7. For women the rate is considerably lower at 1.3/100,000 in 1999. Their rate peaked earlier in this period in 1980, 3.1/100,000.

Age

American criminologists unanimously agree that younger persons are most likely to be the perpetrators of murder and lethal assault. The majority of offenders in this country are under thirty-five years of age. According to the 2000 Uniform Crime Reports, 69 percent of arrests for murder and nonnegligent manslaughter were of suspects 17–34 years old (Federal Bureau of Investigation, 2001). Fox and Zawitz (2001) note that highest rates for homicide offenders were in the 17–24 age group. According to the Uniform Crime Report for 2000, this group was arrested for 29 percent of homicides. Since 1986, the offending rates for this age group have been higher than the next highest age group, 25–34. For the younger age group arrest rates peaked in 1993 (24.4/100,000) and have fallen since (15.5/100,000 for 1999). The 25–34 age group rose and fell during the same period (16.1/100,000 in 1993), and those rates have also fallen to 10.0/100,000 for 1999.

For 14- to 17-year-olds, the rate went from 11 per 100,000 in 1976, increasing to 13 per 100,000 in 1980. Fox and Zawitz note that from 1981 to 1984 the rate decreased, reaching 9 per 100,000 in 1984. Then after 1984 it increased dramatically, reaching 30 per 100,000 in 1993. Like the previous age groups discussed, this rate decreases to 11 per 100,000 in 1999. For persons ages 35–49, the rate of offending begin at 11 per 100,000 in 1976 and increases to 13 per 100,000 in 1980. After 1981 it gradually decreases to 5 per 100,000 in 1999. For persons age 50 and older, the pattern of decline is more gradual and even, beginning at 4 per 100,000 in 1976 declining to 1.5 per 100,000 in 1999.

The pattern of victimization parallels those of the pattern of offending. Fox and Zawitz (2001) note that 18- to 24-year-olds experienced the highest homicide victimization rates. They indicate that this is a change from the late 1970's when 25- to 34-year-olds had the highest rates. Like the pattern of offending, the rate of victimization peaks in 1993 at 24.4/100,000 and then declines steadily to 15.5/100,000. This is still higher than the rate for this age group that occurred in 1976, 13.8/100,000. The victimization rates have generally declined for adults ages 25–34, 35–49, and 50 and over and are lower in 1999 than for the 18–24 age category. The homicide victimization rate for 14-17 year-olds was stable for the period 1976 to 1985 at approximately 5/100,000, the rates then increased almost 150 percent from 1985 to 1993, then declined steadily to 5.9/100,000 which is the rate of victimization for 35- to 49-year-olds. For those under 14, the rates have been steady throughout the period. In the age patterns of homicide victimization, we find that young persons are disproportionately victims of murder. The problem of homicide victimization among young persons has increased dramatically in recent years, especially among minority males. Recent statistics indicate that the declining age trend is continuing. The end result is that today homicide is the second-leading cause of death among American children 1–18 years of age (National Center for Health Statistics, 1998). This offense and victim trend parallels the changes in poverty for this group.

In general, the offender is usually younger than the victim. Wolfgang (1958) uncovered this pattern in his classic work on homicide in Philadelphia. This pattern has been replicated in more recent research. O'Carroll and Mercy (1970) found in their research that the majority of those convicted of murder were between 20 and 30 years old, whereas their victims were approximately five years older. Fox and Zawitz (2001) note that a four year difference between victim and offender persists during the 24-year period that they are analyzing; however, the ages decline for both victim and offender, 35–31 years of age for the victim and 31–27 years old for the offender.

In addition to this general age pattern, Zahn and Sagi (1987) found differences in this age pattern for type of murder. The greatest disparity in age between victim and offender was in the case of felony murder between strangers (robbery, murder) where the average age of the victim was 40 and the average age of the offender was 26, and the smallest distance was between acquaintances aged 31 and 30, respectively. There is a difference in the average age of homicide offenders. In stranger homicides, the ages of perpetrators are generally younger than in family homicides and the victims are older. Furthermore, Fox and Zawitz note that where there are multiple offenders as in the case of gang related violence, over 25 percent of the victims were less than 18 years of age. Young people are also disproportionately represented as victims in homicides that occur in the home and the younger the age the more likely their victimization is to be at the hands of a parent.

This declining age of victimization is a pattern of developing capitalist societies. In earlier stages of capitalist development and in pre-capitalist societies, peak ages of victimization for murder was higher (Greenberg, 1985). In all acts of interpersonal violence, those who are in the most marginal positions in the society have the highest rates of involvement. As youth have become more displaced and marginalized economically in a society as it develops along a capitalist path of industrialization, they are more likely to be involved in crime and delinquency, including acts of interpersonal violence.

Race or Ethnic Minority Status

There are clear racial patterns in homicide statistics. In Wolfgang's 1958 study of homicide in Philadelphia he notes that the arrest rate for African Americans is approximately eight times the rate for whites. Bensing and Schroeder (1960) and Pokorny (1965) discovered similar patterns in Cleveland and Houston. In 2000, African Americans accounted for 51.4 percent of offenders where ethnicity of offender was known. In sum, the overall pattern is that ethnic minority populations (disproportionately represented at the bottom of the income hierarchy) are overrepresented as homicide offenders.

Although African Americans made up the majority of those arrested for murder in 2000, they constituted almost one-half (48.4 percent) of the victims of murder. In general we find that murder, like rape and assault, is principally an intraracial crime. In 2000, of the offenders known to police, 93.7 percent of African American homicide victims were murdered by a African American assailant and 86 percent of white homicide victims were murdered by a white assailant (Federal Bureau of Investigation, 2000). Zahn and Sagi (1987) point to differences in racial characteristics of victims and offenders for different types of homicides. The authors point out that where the victim and offender know each other the homicide is most likely to be intraracial (95 percent of homicides in the family and 92 percent of homicides among acquaintances); in the case of stranger homicides for white victims, 74 percent were interracial (black and Hispanic offenders), while for African Americans 89 percent were intraracial. Felony homicides generally had the highest rates of interracial homicides for both African Americans and whites. But, when you combine all forms of homicide, about 80 percent of interpersonal violence occur between persons of the same race or ethnic minority status. Today, the leading cause of death for African American males between 15 and 34 years of age is homicide (National Center for Injury Prevention and Control, 1998).

The U.S. Department of Justice noted that from 1987 to 1992 the average annual rate of handgun victimization per 1,000 young African American males was 3–4 times higher than the rate of victimization for young white males. Younger African American males (12–24 years old) were fourteen times as likely to be a homicide victim than members of the general population in 1992. For older African American males, they were eight times more likely than the general population (Bastian and Taylor, 1994). In 1999, African Americans were six times more likely to be murdered than whites (Fox and Zawitz, 2001). An earlier calculation by the U.S. Justice Department (1988) calculated the following alarming lifetime odds of being murdered: white female, 1 in 495; white male, 1 in 179; African American female, 1 in 132; and African American male, 1 in 30. Messner and Rosenfeld (1994) report that 40 percent of all deaths of 15- to 24-year-old African Americans was attributable to homicide. It is important to note that the rates of homicide have declined dramatically since 1993. In 1999 the rates for African Americans declined 47 percent, from 38.7/100,000 in 1993 to 20.6/100,000 in 1999. For those of European ancestry (white), the rates declined 34 percent, from 5.3/100,000 in 1993 to 3.5/100,000 in 1999.

Prior to this most recent period, rates of homicide for African Americans have increased dramatically, whereas the rates for white European ancestry have declined. Gurr (1990) concludes that "the long-term trend in homicide rates among whites has been generally downward until recently, whereas homicide rates among African Americans not only have been higher and more variable but have moved generally upward since the beginning of the twentieth century, perhaps earlier" (21). Gurr attributes these increases in part to the increasing problems of dislocation of minority youth in the inner cities. Again, the most recent decline in poverty among minorities parallels this decline in homicide.

Social Class

When we discuss the research on the relationship between social class and both homicide and rape, the data available are based on either income or occupational status. Little research analyzes crime patterns and social class as classically defined categories discussed previously: capitalist, worker, independent producer, and manager. Generally, income and status differences are rather poor proxies for social-class differences. There is overlap in that capitalists generally make more than workers do, capitalists receive more income than managers and independent producers, and managers and independent producers generally receive more income than workers. Nevertheless, we can all list examples of workers who make more than managers and independent producers and in some exceptional cases receive more than capitalists do. Recognizing this weakness in the data, we discuss the patterns of homicide and rape in terms of income and socioeconomic status differences.

Research shows that most people involved in homicide in this country, as either victim or offender, are poor. Wolfgang (1958) estimated that 90–95 percent of the offenders came from the lower end of the occupational scale. More recent studies showed that 92 percent of those convicted of murder were semiskilled workers, unskilled laborers, or welfare recipients (Parker, 1989; Swigert and Farrell, 1976). According to the National Crime Victimization Survey for the year 2000, the rate of violent crime victimization for those who earned less than $7,500 was 60.3/1000, while the rate declines for each higher income grouping to a rate of almost 2/3 less or 22.3/1,000 for those whose household income is $75,000 or more (U.S. Department of Justice, 2001). Hawkins (1983) concluded after reviewing the literature that homicide victims and offenders are both more likely to be African American, poor, uneducated, and residing in the South. From all recent statistics, this overall pattern has not changed in the interim years.

Victim/Offender Relationship

Thus far, we have seen that homicides are not simply random acts. Some of us, because of the position we occupy in society, as defined by age, class, gender, and ethnic position, are more likely to use interpersonal violence to exert power and are more likely to be victims of violence. Another important factor in accounting for differences in the risk of victimization is the nature of the relationships we have with others. The majority of homicides in which we know the nature of victim/offender relationship involve people who know each other; often they are intimates. Homicide as a form of power is likely to be exerted over people who are at least acquainted. Stranger relationships of victim and offender are consistently found to occur less frequently than relationships where the victim and offender are known to each other. This pattern is found in research on larger cities (Wolfgang, 1958; Pokorny, 1965; Block, 1981; Zimring, Mukhergee, and Van Winkle, 1983) and research on smaller cities as well (Hewitt, 1988). Fox and Zawitz found that for homicides that occurred in the years 1976 to 1999, 7.1 percent were between husbands and wives, 7.8 percent were between other family members, 4.3 percent between boyfriend and girlfriend, 33.2 percent other acquaintance, 14 percent strangers, and 33.5 percent where the relationship is unknown. The research of Daly and Wilson (1988) following up homicides that occurred in Detroit in 1972 gives further support to this finding. They found that by 1980, of cases that were solved, 370, or 72.8 percent were between acquaintances or relatives, whereas 138 or 27.2 percent, were between strangers.

Research by Riedel (1987) contends that government statistics systematically underestimate the rate of stranger homicides. He has noted that there is a problem of lag in the reporting of stranger homicides and that there are problems in the accuracy of the robbery/murder classification. Riedel reviewed case studies of several large cities and found that the rate of stranger homicide was significantly higher (as high as 29.6 percent in Chicago) and that the trend in recent years is that the rate of stranger homicides is increasing.

Zahn and Sagi (1987), however, observe that the category of stranger homicide is too heterogeneous to be useful to gain an understanding of this type of homicide. They suggest dividing the category into stranger felony-associated homicide (homicides that occur in the context of committing a felony crime such as robbery) and stranger nonfelony-associated homicide. Zahn and Sagi offer the following example. "The victim and three companions were riding down the street when they became involved in an argument with the occupants of another car. When the car pulled over, the victim, a twenty-two-year-old white male, got out, as did the person in the other car. The latter killed the victim with a shotgun." Many gang-related killings (so-called drive-by shootings) would also fall into this type. The authors find that approximately 42.7 percent of stranger homicides are nonfelony-associated, while 57.3 percent are felony-associated stranger homicides. The overall breakdown in relationships between victims and offenders in Zahn and Sagi's nine-city survey followed the familiar pattern: acquaintance homicide, 54 percent; family homicide, 18 percent; stranger felony homicide, 16 percent; and stranger nonfelony homicide, 12 percent. As noted earlier, the majority of victims and offenders in all homicides were male, especially in cases of stranger homicide. In general, although the majority of homicides occur between those who know each other, stranger homicides are increasing. Part of this increase is certainly a result over conflicts of control over the black market in drugs.

Most recently Fox and Zawitz (2001) find that the rates of violence by intimates have declined significantly over the period of 1976 and 1998. They note that on average for this period, the number of murders by intimates decreased by 4 percent per year for male victims and 1 percent per year for female victims. They note that the sharpest decrease in number of intimate murder has been for black male victims. There was a 74 percent decrease in the number of black men murdered between 1976 and 1998. The authors note however that intimate violence is primarily a crime against women—in 1998, females were the victims in 72 percent of intimate murders and the victims of about 85 percent of non-lethal intimate violence. In general about one third of female murder victims were killed by an intimate, whereas only 4 percent of male murder victims were killed by an intimate. Women age 16–24 experienced the highest per capita rates of intimate violence (19.6 victimizations per 1,000 women).

THE ROLE OF ALCOHOL AND FIREARMS IN HOMICIDE

The Handgun and Homicide

Alcohol and firearms are indisputably and precipitously associated with homicide. Approximately 60 percent of homicides are committed with a firearm, most likely a handgun (Flanagan and Jamieson, 1988). The risk of death from a firearm is not uniformly distributed throughout the population. The Panel on the Understanding and Control of Violent Behavior found that the risk of homicide by a gun is highly elevated for adolescents in general, and black male adolescents in particular (Reiss and Roth, 1993). They report that in 1988, the gun homicide rate was 8 per 100,000 for 15- to 19-year-olds and less than 6 for the population as a whole. Among 15–19 year olds, the rate was 83.4 per 100,000 for black males and 7.5 per 100,000 for white males, an 11 times greater risk of homicide by firearms. The council notes that the highest fraction of homicides committed with firearms peaks for 15–19-year-olds, at 81 percent of homicides, and consistently declines relative to other weapons used as the victims age increases. Fox and Zawitz (2001) found that murders with the use of a handgun peaked in the early 1990s for all age groups and have declined although levels for 14–17 and 18–24 are still slightly higher than they were in 1976, for those under 14 and over 24 the rates returned to these previous levels.

Handguns are also most common in homicides between strangers (Riedel, 1987). Regardless of the political controversy in the United States regarding gun ownership, what is clear is that the presence of handguns increases the likelihood that an assault will turn into a homicide. The Panel on the Understanding and Control of Violent Behavior concluded that in most circumstances those who use a firearm did not choose the weapon with the intent to kill but rather chose a weapon that was available and because of the power of the weapon ended up killing (Reiss and Roth, 1993). Whether in domestic disturbances or felony murders, there are indications that the availability of the type of weapon used was most important in determining whether a homicide took place. Wright and Rossi's (1985) survey of incarcerated convicted felons found that only 36 percent reported firing a weapon with the intent to kill the victim.

The type of gun is also important in discussing the incidence of homicide. Two thirds of guns owned in the United States are long guns, yet handguns are three times more likely to be used in a homicide than long guns. Generally, more than 80 percent of the time when the weapon is known, the handgun is the weapon used (Zawitz and Strom, 2000).

How does the availability of handguns relate to the incidence of homicide? One particular study comparing homicide and assault rates in Seattle and Vancouver, two cities of comparable size and demographic characteristics yet with very different regulations regarding handgun ownership, gives some insight into this question. The risk of being murdered in Seattle, where there is a significantly higher rate of handgun ownership, is approximately five times higher than in Vancouver (Sloan, Kellerman, and Reay, 1988).

Other studies have substantiated that gun ownership facilitates occurrences of murder. The region of the country with the highest level of firearm ownership—the South—has the highest murder rate, and the region of the country with the lowest level of firearm ownership—the Northeast—has the lowest rate of murder (FBI, 1988). Furthermore, research has indicated that, over time, increases in murder rates are positively correlated with increases in firearm ownership (Farley, 1980). Gun ownership has increased dramatically in the United States during the past forty years. According to government statistics, the number of guns increased from 54 million in 1950 to 201 million in 1990 (Bureau of Alcohol, Tobacco, and Firearms, 1991). The percentage of households who have a gun in their home has fluctuated between 35 to 50 percent of households. The percentage reporting having a gun in the household for 2000 is 42 percent, which is up from the previous year when only 36 percent reported (Maguire and Pastore, 2000).

Another piece of evidence supporting the impact of availability of handguns as it relates to the occurrence of violence is an evaluation of the 1977 District of Columbia Firearms Control Act. This act prohibited handgun ownership among civilians, with the exception of previously licensed gun owners. During periods of vigorous enforcement of this act, gun homicides, robbery, and assault were significantly reduced (Jones, 1981; Loftin, McDowall, Wierseman, and Cottey, 1991). In the Loftin et al. research, homicides declined during the period of this law until an increase in homicides resulting from the cocaine black market. It is important to state that we are not suggesting a causal relationship between the presence of handguns or guns in general and violence. We are suggesting that their presence increases the likelihood that existing violence will be escalated with the lethal force, thus serving as a catalyst or facilitator.

Alcohol Abuse and Homicide

Alcohol, too, can serve as a catalytic factor in violence. In Wolfgang's classic study of homicide, he found that more than 63 percent of the cases involved alcohol consumption. This pattern has been replicated in study after study of homicide (Greenberg, 1981). Most recently Dawson and Langan (1994) found that alcohol was present in 47 percent of the victims and 64 percent of the defendants. Barlow (1990) describes the significance of alcohol in the following way: To the extent that alcohol lowers social inhibitions and reduces anxiety and guilt, people who have been drinking may act more aggressively than otherwise would have been the case. The underlying dispute may have erupted anyway, and the individuals concerned may well have been tempted to seek a violent solution. With the situational influence of alcohol missing, fear, anxiety, guilt, and social inhibitions are there to serve as constraints (166). On the other hand, Kantor and Straus (1987) note that being drunk may indirectly help prepare an individual to commit an act of violence by providing a later rationalization for the act.

In sum, the overall pattern regarding the occurrence of homicide is that those who are in more marginal positions in the society in terms of income, age, and ethnicity are more likely to be both victims and offenders of homicide. This pattern is exemplified by the fact that the leading cause of death among young African American males is homicide. Furthermore, homicide is most often used to address interpersonal problems that stem from problems that may be institutional or structural in nature. Thus, what society officially defines as homicide is a phenomenon of power pursued by those who have less access to other forms of power (institutional). Homicide also is more likely to be exercised to exert one's influence over those with whom he or she has personal relationships. Finally, the presence of alcohol and handguns often serve as accelerators or catalytic factors to transform acts of violence into homicide.

HISTORICAL TRENDS IN MURDERS

What have been the historical trends in homicide? Are societies today more or less violent in terms of rates of homicide? As a generalization, most scholars contend that the earliest civilized societies were more violent than modern societies. Political scientist Ted R. Gurr states that

> homicide rates were three times higher in the thirteenth century than the seventeenth, three times higher in the seventeenth century than the nineteenth, and in London they were twice as high in the early nineteenth century as they are now. The decline in homicide has been particularly great in the towns and rural areas. And though Londoners today are more murderous than in the recent past, the metropolis remains a far safer place than it was in earlier centuries (Gurr, 1979, 414).

Gurr (1990) further indicates that there were waves within this general trend, noting that high levels were reached during the fourteenth century after the Hundred Years War and partly as a result of the turmoil connected to the Black Death, later during Elizabethan times, and again in early-nineteenth-century London.

With regard to the United States, Gurr (1979) contends that violent crime in nineteenth-century America indicated a stable or declining trend for the first half of the century, and a shift upward shortly before the Civil War that persisted into the 1870s. However, violent crime was not unheard of during the colonial era. In 1776, Benjamin Franklin petitioned the British Parliament to stop solving its crime problem by shipping convicted felons to the American colonies. He complained that transported felons were corrupting the morals of the poor and terrorizing the rest of the population (Silberman, 1978). Later, in the early 1800s, the problems of violent crime were still being noted in public speeches of politicians. In a speech that made Abraham Lincoln known in political circles, delivered in Springfield, Illinois, in January 1838, he argued that internal violence was the nation's major domestic problem (Silberman, 1978). Indeed, just before the Civil War, a U.S. Senate committee investigating crime in Washington, D.C., reported that "riot and bloodshed are of daily occurrence, innocent and unoffending persons are shot, stabbed, and otherwise shamefully maltreated and not infrequently the offender is not even arrested" (Silberman, 1978, 29).

While it is important to note that most of the data available for these earlier periods of U.S. history are from urban areas and principally eastern cities, there is nevertheless some indication that murder rates may have been higher in smaller cities and noneastern areas. Silberman notes that in a fifteen-month period in the 1850s, forty-four murders were recorded in Los Angeles, then a town of only 8,000 inhabitants. This is about forty or fifty times as high as rates in the city today.

After the Civil War, there was a dramatic increase in violent crime. Silberman (1978) reports that in the twenty years after the Civil War, the murder rate quadrupled, far outstripping the growth in population. Family blood feuds kindled by hatreds generated during the war and refueled by political and economic conflicts became increasingly frequent. This rate continued to climb during a period of a high level of violence connected to labor unrest in the late nineteenth century through to the early twentieth century. The rate declined during the Great Depression in the 1930s until the 1960s and then the rate began to climb again. Research generally indicates that rates are higher today in the United States than previously recorded during this century, as shown in figure 3.1.

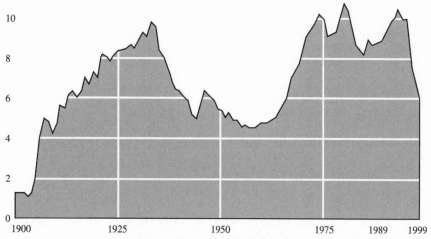

Figure 3.1.   U.S. Homicide Rate Trends per 100,000 population, 1900–1999.
Source: Vital Statistics of the United States, National Center for Health Statistics.

War is an important factor in stimulating high levels of violence in all societies (Archer and Gartner, 1984; Gurr, 1990). Archer and Gartner (1984) found that most combatant nations, compared to a control group of noncombatant nations, experienced substantial postwar increases in rates of homicide. Furthermore, they found that the increases were pervasive and occurred regardless of the size of the conflict. Homicide rates increased in both victorious and defeated nations; in nations with either improved or worsened postwar economies; among both men and women offenders, and across several age groups. Finally, postwar increases were most frequent among nations with large numbers of combat deaths. Archer and Gartner (1984) conclude that their findings regarding the effect of war on homicide rates is consistent with the legitimization of violence model. Wars provide concrete evidence that homicide under some conditions is acceptable in the eyes of a nation's leaders. This wartime reversal of the customary peacetime prohibition against killing may somehow influence the threshold for using homicide as a means of settling conflict in everyday life (79). In looking at the increasing involvement of the United States in wars both covert and overt since World War II, one may suspect that promotion of this war mentality may have contributed to the increasing levels of violence in the society throughout this same period.

Barlow (1990) sees three recent trends in homicides in the United States: (1) the typical homicide offender is getting younger, the proportion of offenses committed by persons under age twenty-five has been rising; (2) interracial homicides seem to be on the increase, though the increases are small; and (3) the proportion of homicides involving strangers has been increasing, though it remains low relative to homicides involving friends and acquaintances.

Trends indicate that although rates of homicide may have been significantly higher during the Middle Ages, rates of homicide during 1980 reached the highest that they have been throughout the twentieth century at 10.7/100,000. These rates then declined throughout the 1980s, increased again at the beginning of the 1990s, then have declined recently to a rate of the mid 1960s at 6.2/100,000 (Bureau of Justice Statistics, 2001). In general, in the United States since the Civil War, rates of homicide have been increasing with the exception of the period of the Great Depression and the 1950s and the most recent decline in the latter half of the 1990s. What explains these increases in homicide? The conflict perspective we employ suggests that as the structures of inequality increase so also will increasing levels of interpersonal violence in either rebellion, adaptation, or enforcement of these structures. Furthermore, as violence is increasingly used by the state to repress and control populations that threaten these structures, nationally and internationally, violence is learned as an appropriate means to address interpersonal problems. Given the recent trends in increases in levels of inequality as a result of the changes in the economic structure (Eitzen and Zinn, 1989; Philips, 1990) and during the same period the increases in the use of the military to address international political problems (the United States has been involved in more than a dozen wars since 1980, five of which required overt

U.S. military action—Grenada, Panama, Libya, Iraq, and Afghanistan), these facts, together with an increase in the use of domestic military-style policing to crack down on the drug trade, would all contribute to an escalation in interpersonal violence in the United States. Let's further investigate the connection between the occurrence of homicide and structures of inequality.

HOMICIDE AND INEQUALITY

It is important to reiterate that the relationship between homicide and inequality can be viewed in two ways: how inequality causes homicide, and how homicide causes inequality. If members of a particular group are more likely to be victims of homicide than members of another group, this creates a disadvantage in terms of power and over access and control of scarcities. An example would be young African American male teens. It is, in part, because they experience a higher rate of homicide victimization that this group is disadvantaged relative to other racial and gender groups in terms of access to life chances and power. As African American males are increasingly victimized by violence, they are less capable of achieving a quality education as well as economic and political opportunities for advancement. The violence serves to inhibit their development relative to groups that do not experience the same levels of violence, leading to further levels of inequality.

Similarly, in terms of gender stratification, as females are victimized or are more likely to fear victimization relative to males, this disadvantages them in the pursuit of human development. As we discuss later in this chapter, this is most evident in the case of rape. However, it is also present when we look at who women are murdered by and under what circumstances. A woman's murderer is more likely to be a man she is at least acquainted with and, in most of these cases when they were at least acquainted, they were involved intimately. Fear of victimization inhibits women's ability to pursue careers and in general work outside the home and is a factor in the control of women by men in the home. In these ways, the differential homicide victimization by a category of people serves to create further inequity for that category and for those who are dependent on them in primary social relationships.

Inequality can also lead to higher levels of homicide victimization. Both poverty and inequality have been found to be related to rates of homicide across different states and different countries. Avison and Loring (1986) found that both ethnic heterogeneity and income inequality were important in accounting for variations in rates of homicide across nations. They note that "structural conditions such as inequality appear to be cleavages that increase the probability of social conflict. When cultural differentiation is also present, that probability is further increased substantially. In one sense, then, structure and cultural factors have more than just additive effects on cross-national homicide rates. It appears that cultural differences within societies tend to magnify the effects of inequality on homicide" (748). Krahn, Hartnagel, and Gartrell (1986), in their study on income inequality and homicide, find that income inequality has a moderate effect on levels of homicide. Furthermore, the authors find that the effect of income inequality on homicide rates is strongest in wealthier countries and countries with larger law enforcement systems.

Table 3.1 lists the different age standardized rates of homicide for various societies. The data is taken from the World Health Organizations annual statistics on homicides. The statistics selected are age adjusted so that age differences in populations do not affect the rates. We classified the data into three categories: high, medium, and low homicide rates. Those countries with the highest rates were principally countries in the former Soviet Union that are undergoing the greatest economic and social dislocations as a result of the transformation of their political economic system from state socialist to capitalist. The only exception to the rule is the southern, southeastern, and midwestern areas of Brazil that are also undergoing significant social and economic transformation. The medium homicide rate countries were either from the former Soviet Union or from countries representing South and Central American, and Caribbean countries. The only exception to this is the United States. This is using the most recent data listed in the report. If rates for the early 1990s were used, the United States would have been listed in the high homicide grouping. The low rate of homicide group is principally the more advanced countries of the world. As can clearly be seen, the United States has one of the highest rates of homicide in the modern world. Rates in the United States are generally 3–5 times higher than any other advanced industrialized country. The Krug, Powell, and Dahlberg (1998) analysis of countries from the same data set but from the early 1990s concluded that the United States had the highest rate of homicide of the twenty six high income countries that reported rates. Countries that have significantly higher homicide rates are ones that have experienced large-scale popular unrest as a result of guerrilla warfare, death squads, or military activities connected to increasing levels of inequality and economic displacement. For example, Chile, Guatemala, and the Philippines during the 1970s had significantly higher rates of murder, ranging from 45.7 per 100,000 for Chile to 20.8 per 100,000 for Guatemala. International data summarized by Foster, Siegel, Plesser, and Jacobs (1987) indicate that for 1987, other than Northern Ireland, no country has a rate that comes close to that of the United States.

Baron and Straus (1988) concluded in their research that legitimate violence, poverty, and economic inequality are significantly associated with state-by-state differences in rates of homicide. They found that the more urbanized states, and states with higher levels of poverty and inequality, had higher rates of homicide.

There is at this time an unresolved controversy as to whether it is absolute or relative deprivation that is important in effecting levels of homicide. For example, Blau and Blau (1982) note that socioeconomic inequalities between races and within them were positively related to higher rates of violent crime in SMSAs, and when these factors are controlled, the rate of poverty is not related to levels of vi-

Table 3.1. Age-standardized Homicide Rates for Selected Countries

Country	Year	Rate/ 100,000	Country	Year	Rate/ 100,000
High Homicide Rates (rate >9/100,000)			Czech Republic	1998	1.5
Belarus	1998	11.5	Denmark	1996	1.1
Brazil			Finland	1996	3.3
(South, SE, Mid-West)	1995	25.8	France	1996	1.0
Estonia	1998	16.4	The FYR of Macedonia	1997	2.2
Latvia	1998	11.9	Germany	1997	0.9
Republic of Moldova	1996	13.6	Greece	1997	1.4
Russian Federation	1997	22.2	Hungary	1998	3.0
Ukraine	1998	11.3	Iceland	1995	0.0
			Ireland	1996	0.9
Medium Homicide Rates			Israel	1996	1.0
(rate <9 and >4/100,000)			Italy	1995	1.4
			Japan	1997	0.6
Azerbaijan	1997	6.3	Luxembourg	1997	0.5
Argentina	1996	4.6	Malta	1997	0.4
Costa Rica	1995	5.2	Mauritius	1997	1.7
Cuba	1996	6.1	Netherlands	1997	1.3
Kyrgyzstan	1998	8.9	New Zealand	1996	1.8
Lithuania	1997	8.6	Norway	1995	1.0
United States of America	1997	7.6	Poland	1996	2.5
			Portugal	1998	1.2
Low Homicide Rates (rate <5/100,000)			Romania	1998	3.1
Armenia	1997	2.5	Slovak Republic	1995	2.0
Australia	1995	1.6	Slovenia	1997	2.0
Austria	1998	1.1	Spain	1995	0.8
Belgium	1994	1.7	Sweden	1996	1.2
Bulgaria	1998	3.5	United Kingdom	1997	0.7
Canada	1997	1.4			
Cayman Islands	1994	3.3			
Croatia	1997	2.5			

Source: Data from World Health Statistics Annual 1997–1999 (online edition) http://www3.who.int/whosis/menu. cfm?path=whosis,whsa&language=english.

olent crime. "Thus, aggressive acts of violence seem to result not so much from lack of advantages as from being taken advantage of, not from absolute but from relative deprivation. Southern cities have higher rates of criminal violence not as the result of the historical experience of the South that produced a tradition of violence but owing to the greater economic inequality there" (126).

Loftin and Hill (1974) and Messner and Tardiff (1986) find that poverty, not inequality, is the major determinant of homicide. Loftin and Parker (1985) and Parker (1989) find that the relationship between poverty and homicide depends on the type of homicide. Parker finds that in looking at homicides between family intimates, acquaintances, and nonrobbery felony homicide, rates of poverty are very significantly related. Only in the case of homicides committed in the occurrence of a robbery is poverty not significantly related. In general, what the research seems to confirm is that as segments of the population become increasingly powerless (relatively or absolutely), homicide is increasingly likely to occur.

Brenner's research (1978, 1979, 1983, and 1984) gives further support to this pattern of homicide. His research points to the impact of economic recessions on homicide rates over the years 1900 to 1980. In a more recent work, Petras and Davenport (1991) examine the impact of economic transformation on crime in general. The authors find that as deindustrialization occurred in the five large cities they studied over a twenty-six-year period, homicide increased threefold.

An interesting example of how economic inequality and gender inequality manifest themselves in homicide is the case of dowry deaths in India. McCoid has found that higher and higher dowry demands constitute one attempt by middle-class men to become upwardly mobile in India. Conflicts over the amount of the dowry can result in the murder of the wife. Women who are most economically dependent on their husband are most likely to be victims of homicide by their husbands or other members of the husband's family (McCoid, 1989).

Research on the relationship between gender inequality and homicide is sparse. Our contention would be that gender inequality is related to violence in such a way that the lower the rates of gender inequality, the lower the rates of violence. This is suggested by the family violence research discussed in the next chapter. Since a large portion of homicides in particular center on men's attempts to control women, as women become more powerful this is a less viable means available to men. Unfortunately, there is little research specifically on the relationship between gender inequality and homicide. But a simple analysis comparing rates of homicide and a measure of gender inequality (labor force participation rates) indicates a strong relationship between the two (see table 3.2).

We selected countries where United Nations data were available on homicide rates and labor force participation rates. We found thirty-seven countries where recent data were available on both measures. The analysis indicated that the variables were inversely correlated, minus .50. Thus countries with higher female labor force participation rates generally had lower levels of homicide. This is not a conclusive analysis, since we are using a convenience sample and are not controlling for other variables related to the level of development of the society. Nevertheless, the relationship holds for the thirty-seven countries included in our sample. This finding is also consistent with research on tribal societies that shows that the status of women is lower in more violent societies (Divale and Harris, 1976; Reiss, 1986).

What about band or tribal societies where levels of inequality would be much lower? How are their rates of homicide? What has the anthropological literature found as it relates to patterns of homicide? There have been investigations that attempt to calculate rates of homicide in non-Western, nonindustrialized societies (Bohannan, 1960; Knauft, 1987; Lee, 1979). Overall, the problems of calculating rates of crime in general and homicide in particular in

Table 3.2. Comparison of Homicide Rates per 100,000 and Labor Force Participation Rates for Women

Country	Homicide Rate 1986–1988	Women in Labor Force 1988	Country	Homicide Rate 1986–1988	Women in LaborForce 1988
Czech	1.1	53.2	China	1.4	43.2
Poland	1.8	51.4	Korea (Rep)	1.0	42.1
U.S.S.R.	6.0	51.2	Belgium	2.1	41.6
Sweden	1.2	51.4	Netherlands	0.7	41.2
Finland	2.7	51.1	Italy	1.6	40.4
Canada	1.9	50.3	Kuwait	0.5	39.8
Japan	0.7	50.0	Mauritius	2.1	39.0
Norway	1.4	50.0	Israel	1.8	38.9
Bulgaria	2.6	49.8	Uruguay	2.9	38.9
Hungary	2.7	49.6	Brazil	14.8	36.6
USA	8.5	48.9	Chile	2.7	35.8
Germany (FR)	1.1	48.3	Panama	6.9	35.6
Singapore	1.3	48.0	Zimbabwe	6.9	35.0
Austria	1.2	47.3	Costa Rica	4.0	34.1
Australia	2.4	47.2	Mexico	19.9	33.8
Portugal	1.4	45.6	Paraguay	4.0	33.0
Yugoslavia	1.8	45.5	Ecuador	10.1	30.4
France	1.0	45.0	Dom. Rep.	4.8	14.5
Greece	0.8	38.2			

these societies are complex. One major obstacle is the problem of definition. Often, what the community defines as an execution of a sorcerer is defined as a murder by anthropologists. This is well illustrated by the work on the Gebusi by Knauft (1987). A second problem is the reliability of the data. Most data in these societies are based on recollection of the past by informants or re-creation of rates based on the occurrence of murder during the time the society was being studied. For example, Gibson notes of the Buid, "I am aware of only one homicide occurring within a Buid population of one thousand in a ten year period, and that was carried out by a man with a fearsome reputation as a sorcerer" (Gibson, 1990, 131). Despite the limits of such research, the circumstances of murders can give us further insight into their cause.

For example, The !Kung, once described as the harmless people (Thomas, 1959), are in fact noted as having a rate of homicide of 29.3 per 100,000, almost three times the U.S. rate (Lee, 1979, 1984). This rate is based on twenty-two murders occurring between 1920 and 1955. All the killers were male and seventeen out of the twenty-two acted alone. Most of the killers were between the ages of twenty and fifty. A poison arrow was the primary weapon. Fifteen of the killings were part of feuds, seven were isolated killings. Likewise, Lee notes that most of the victims of homicide were not part of the conflict but were innocent bystanders struck by spears. Of the eighteen cases reviewed by

Lee, eight were principles in an argument and ten were struck more or less at random in the process of observing the conflict, acting as peacemakers, or coming to the aid of someone. He says that of the eight homicides involving a principle in a prior dispute, the circumstances include the following: a man attacked and killed a non-San who had been sleeping with his wife, a man killed another man and ran away with the victim's wife, a man who had slept with another's wife was attacked by the husband but killed the husband, and a man killed his wife in an argument over her adultery (Lee, 1979, 392).

Another example is the Gebusi, a society of approximately 450 persons living in the lowland rain forest of south central New Guinea (Knauft, 1987). Subsistence is based on hunting and foraging, nonintensive agriculture, and small-scale husbandry of pigs. The population resides in a long-house arrangement, with each long house holding approximately twenty-six persons. There are two to six long houses to a settlement. Settlements are made up principally of kin as defined in terms of affinal or matrilineal. The political and economic life of the Gebusi is highly decentralized. Knauft (1987) observes that the Gebusi recognize no indigenous positions of secular male leadership. Men are highly self-effacing in social interaction and avoid taking a public stance which could be perceived as either ordering or pressuring other men in the community to conform to their point of view (460). The men of the settlement usually attempt to build consensus among themselves to solve problems.

Knauft also notes that the Gebusi are unusual for practicing no competitive exchanges and having no custom of material compensation to resolve disputes or to transact marriages (460). Furthermore, males among the Gebusi generally do not engage in status competition or rivalry. Males of a settlement generally have strong bonds of friendship. Furthermore, according to Knauft, hostility and aggressive behavior is seen to be individualistic and antisocial, which conflicts with the central cultural values of communal sociality. Along with this, fear and withdrawal in the face of violence are strongly approved and encouraged.

Despite social patterns that are conducive to a relatively low level of violence, Knauft calculates that the rate of homicide among the Gebusi prior to Western contact to be 683 per 100,000 per year, after contact, the rate drops to 419 per 100,000. Overall, Knauft estimates the rate of homicide among this New Guinea tribe to be forty times the rate of U.S. lethal violence including wars and executions for the same period. Why?

First, it is important to note that Knauft used a very broad definition of homicide. Of the total 129 homicides discovered by Knauft, 84, or 65 percent were called sorcerer killings. Sorcerers are individuals accused of causing the death by sickness of another Gebusi. They are believed to be bad people motivated to kill their victim through illness because of general maliciousness or spite. Most of the killings recorded by Knauft were executions of sorcerers by members of the community. Can we define the killings of sorcerers as interpersonal violence, or are they more accurately classified as a form of institutional violence within this lesser developed society? Let us look more closely at these killings.

The identity of sorcerers is determined by an inquest that begins with a seance that lasts an entire evening. Mediums conduct seances. The body of the medium is inhabited during the seance by spirits who know of details of the sickness unknown by humans and know the identity of the sorcerer. The medium is believed to be unbiased and in particular not allowed to be a relative of the primary kin of the sickness victim. To assure this, given the kinship basis of this society, mediums often come from other settlements or communities. Mediums are not paid; seership is considered to be a civic duty. The position of medium is not given a special status within the community.

Indictment by the medium begins the process of divination. Knauft reports that this spiritual evidence must be validated by public divinations undertaken by the suspect, often done by the cooking of a large divination packet with meat or fish inside. The failure of a suspect to perform this part of the ritual properly may be regarded as a sign of his or her guilt. Public torture for the guilty is not unknown. Some have been killed on the spot.

> When a suspect is indicted for having caused the sickness death of a member of his or her own patriline, close kinsmen perpetrate the killing. In many instances, however, the closest kin of the alleged sorcerer are ambivalent about the suspects guilt. Especially if the outcome of the public divination is not definitive, the potential of armed support for the suspect by these people precludes an immediate killing. In these cases, the accusers typically wait until the initial tensions of the situation wanes—perhaps for several weeks or months—and then organize a consensual plan in the community to ambush the suspect when he or she is in the forest, unsuspecting, with few supporters. . . . The kin of the alleged sorcerer, while often not completely convinced that the suspect is guilty, rarely risk their lives to resist or avenge a killing that has the consensual approval of the many different clans in the community at large. In the great majority of cases, then, the killing of the suspect is accepted and goes unavenged. Indeed, there is a general feeling of relief in the community that a lethal sickness sender in the group has been expunged (Knauft, 1987, 465).

Knauft reports that only four homicides out of the 129 resulted from revenge deaths.

The remaining homicides were either battle deaths (9 percent) or deaths resulting from individual conflict (26 percent). This latter group would be considered homicide for comparative purposes. The other two categories, which compose 74 percent of homicides, would be considered acts of institutional violence. They are either executions by members of the community or killings resulting from warfare.

Whether we are talking about homicides, executions, or warfare, what unites them is the cause of the violence. Knauft (1987) observes that lack of marital reciprocity in sister exchange is a condition that is likely to lead to homicide via sorcerer inquest. Knauft finds that sorcery homicide is ultimately about male control of marriageable women. Similar patterns of homicide as they stem from

male control over women are found in other societies that are essentially class-
less societies. Research on the Eskimo finds similar patterns whereby most of
the violence is a result of conflict over issues of adultery, and then most of the
murders occur as a result of retaliation for the killing (Hoebel, 1964;
Rasmussen, 1932). Similar patterns are found among the Mbuti (Turnbull, 1961),
the Semai (Dentan, 1978), and the Hadza (Woodburn, 1979).

As property relations become more developed, homicide stems from not
only controlling women but also disputes over property. The assertion of
witchcraft or sorcery is again a common mechanism to rid the individual or
community of the threat to the distribution of power established by the class
or gender relations. Among the Swazi, the Batsakatsi are the witches and sorcerers (Kuper, 1963). Kuper notes that the propensity for witchcraft is passed
on through the female to her children. Ritual murders occur as sacrifices to enhance agricultural fertility or for personal aggrandizement. Kuper claims that
where the murder occurs for medicine to doctor the crops, capital punishment
is prescribed for the principles while others involved receive long prison
terms. Where the crime is committed for personal aggrandizement, capital
punishment is invariably imposed. Witchcraft and sorcery can be directed at
anyone, but there are patterns. Conflict over the hierarchy established by class
or gender relations often result in violence.

> First, because they emanate from hatred, fear, jealousy and thwarted ambition they
> are usually aimed at persons who are already connected by social bonds. . . . In the
> polygynous homestead, the *unsatkatsi* (victim) is usually a jealous co-wife or an un-
> scrupulous half-brother who is ambitious of the inheritance; outside the homestead,
> suspected evil doers are blatantly successful and aggressive peers. Important men do
> not need to use sorcery against insignificant inferiors, nor are they suspected of do-
> ing so. Sorcery is an indication of status and of the ambitions for improvement of sta-
> tus that operate within the limits of the stratified traditional society (Kuper, 1963, 66).

Daly and Wilson describe research on the Bison-Horn Maria of India. Citing
Verrier Elwin's 1950s research account, 107 cases of murder occurred between
1920 and 1941. Verrier Elwin estimated that the rate of homicide among the
Bison-Horn Maria were sixty-nine homicides per million per year. This would
be a rate that is slightly higher than the rate for New Zealand and Northern Ireland. Among these were very high proportions of family homicides. Out of
107 murder victims, only one was killed by a stranger. The rest were done in
by spouses, stepparents, in-laws, cousins, and other blood kin. Most of the violence was precipitated by conflicts over land. The killing of Marvi Buti by his
paternal half-brother, Marvi Chule, is a typical case:

> Upon their father's death, the elder Buti had inherited the family farm. Like many a
> disenfranchised younger brother through human history, Chule left home to seek
> his fortune. He did not find it, and so, after several years, the prodigal Chule re-
> turned to his father's land, there to rent a plot from his brother and farm it. So he
> did, but only for one year. When the lease came up for renewal, Buti at first dou-
> bled the rent, and then reneged on the agreement altogether, in order to bestow the

land on a third brother. Defeated, Chule again moved away, but on a return visit to collect his possessions, he was confronted by Buti brandishing a knife. To be thus run off his natal farm was too much for the propertyless Chule, whose resentment at last exploded. Close at hand was an ax (Daly and Wilson, 1988, 28).

Taylor (1979) described some similar patterns of homicide in colonial Mexico. First, among the Indians of central and southern Mexico in the 1700s, males were generally the offenders in homicide. In both regions, no more than 4 percent of offenders were female, while approximately 18 percent of the victims were female. Furthermore, the age of offenders was significantly above what would be expected given today's patterns. For Indian offenders in the central Mexico region, the average age was thirty-three, while in the southern region it was twenty-nine. Seldom were victims and perpetrators strangers. A significant proportion were wives, sex partners, and sex rivals. Taylor notes that adultery and the jealousies of villagers caught up in sexual affairs—situations intimately related to the position of women in these village societies—appear to be the fundamental sources of violent conflict in both of our rural areas (85).

Furthermore, Taylor notes that the violence was more likely to be within the community and more specifically within the nuclear family. In general, for the two Indian regions of Mexico studied by Taylor, the conjugal unit was the principal site of conflict.

Conflict over property also existed within these communities. Taylor reports that there was a difference between the two Indian communities as to whether such conflict spilled over into acts of violence. For the central region, property disputes rarely resulted in violence, whereas in the southern region violence occurred more frequently. Comparing the two regions of colonial Mexico overall, he found that violence was precipitated by sex-related and conjugal disputes, property disputes, insults to honor, and excessive consumption of alcohol (Taylor, 1979). This is a pattern that is not dissimilar from what would be found in Mexico and other societies around the world today.

Likewise, writing about the incidence of homicide in more recent times in rural Mexico, Greenberg (1989) describes a very high rate of homicide in the Juquila District. Between 1973 and 1977 he discovered a homicide rate in the village of Yaitepec of 511 per 100,000. Although this was the most severe rate for a village within the district, unexpectedly high rates were also found in Ixtapan (408 per 100,000) and Panixtlahuaca (450 per 100,000). In general, the average rate in seven villages in the district was 300 per 100,000.

Greenberg's analysis lends further credence to the importance of hierarchies and their effect on increasing levels of violence. In particular, Greenberg sees the transition to capitalist relations as the major impetus for these increasing rates of homicide. There are increasing conflicts between classes over land and increasing conflicts within classes due to economic displacement, which result in acts of violence. He points out that in the late 1940s and early 1950s, when peasants in the region began to specialize in coffee as a cash crop, the inequalities created by changing land tenure violated village norms of sharing, cooperation, and reciprocity. Instead of casting these conflicts in class terms, people personalized them. They blamed their misfortunes on the greed, envy, and jealousy of evil people. They explained these changes as caused by witchcraft and saw them as personal attacks. Villagers began to suspect one another of witchcraft, and, as Fortino notes, started killing witches in great numbers (Greenberg, 1989, 202).

Greenberg (1989) believes that capitalist relations of production and exchange cause conflicts that corrode the social bonds within classes. As capitalist forms have expanded and have rationalized systems of production and concentrated wealth in fewer and fewer hands, households and families in Juquila have come under growing pressure (214). Economic pressures are often at the root of domestic difficulties. These pressures can result in conflicts over the division of labor within the home and perceived unfulfillment of role expectations and disputes over the distribution of power along gender lines. Similar patterns can be found throughout the world.

Other conflicts within the family often result because of disputes over inheritance and issues of courtship. As the position of peasants becomes increasingly marginalized, the scarce resources they possess can become objects of intense competition. Regarding courtship, arranged marriages are still common, and families in general have a considerable stake in marriage alliances. Parents attempt to control female children's relations with males in order to maintain or increase family economic position. Greenberg notes that courtship involves delicate negotiations between families, and this can often result in conflict. Because of the obstacles parents place on couples, elopement is not uncommon, although, it is considered equivalent to rape. The crime involves not just stealing a women but also depriving her family of the compensation for the loss of a daughter that are ordinarily part of marriage arrangements. Because the family sees elopement as a form of theft, even where the woman is a willing partner, this act of "rape" can be a dangerous, even violent, enterprise (Greenberg, 1989, 216).

In addition to conflicts within family relations, Greenberg claims that increasing conflicts with friends and *compadres* are also a product of the transformations present with capitalist development. These relationships are based on a delicate balanced set of reciprocity that becomes altered. According to Greenberg (1989), the rationality of market relations intrudes on friendship relations, forcing individuals to choose between the former or economic self-interest. "Despite egalitarian attempts to mask inequalities and disjunctions of interest, money is often put ahead of friendship. Misunderstandings and conflicts among friends are common. This is especially true among men, because they are more prone to use friendship as an instrument to achieve economic and political ends" (217).

Two other major areas of conflict are politics and community disputes over common lands. Beyond family and friends, an array of institutions are found in the district. . . . The principal complaint about such institutions is that authorities abuse their power and position. Few problems can be solved unless one has connections or cash, or can repay favors in some way. Without these, unless one has a patron who can intercede, little help can be expected from institutions. Not only do individuals become entangled in conflicts with them, but conflicts frequently pit organizations against one another (Greenberg, 1989, 218). Mafia-style organizations develop based principally on client-patron relationships that function to control resources of institutions. Conflicts, in turn, develop between Mafias for control over these resources.

Last, Greenberg notes that conflicts develop between communities over control of communal land. These conflicts can often lead to a scale that is best defined as warfare. But such conflicts do not occur exclusively between communities. As the process of capitalist development accelerated, conflicts developed over ambiguities about land tenure. Communal land that was available to villages for subsistence purposes began to be used by villages to plant coffee for the market. This led to conflicts within the community regarding the use of the land.

Greenberg (1989) mentions in the afterward of his book that since completing his fieldwork significant changes in the incidence of violence has occurred. Rates of murder have dropped dramatically. He attributes these changes to three forces: (1) land reform which gave peasants access to the communal lands that were a source of conflict; (2) an emerging women's movement with political clout that resulted in a ban on alcohol in the region and increased the power of women in the home; and (3) the increasing empowerment of the villagers through their struggles for land reform. All these factors are again related to changes in the pattern of inequality in the communities.

The importance of anthropological research on homicide is in the analysis of the precipitating cause of the act and how the experience and transformation of these societies to more hierarchical patterns is connected to increasing levels of violence. Generally speaking, when we review patterns of homicide in lesser developed and developed societies, we find that the precipitating conflict focuses on (1) disputes over sexual access or privilege—in most cases conflicts are over control of women by males; (2) disputes over access to property—control of material; and (3) disputes over access to power and status—control of position. Inequities as they relate to gender, class, and power/status are the fertile soil for violence to grow. The conflicts that stem from the exploitation and assault on one's dignity can lead to death. Homicide is an ultimate outcome of conflict, conflict over control of material or power, where the resources to resolve the conflict in nonviolent ways are not present. In general, murder as a type of interpersonal violence is a technique used by those who do not have access to legitimized or institutional forms of power and violence to exert their will. Thus it is most frequent among poorer and more marginal segments of the society.

WHY PEOPLE KILL: A QUESTION OF MOTIVES

Another way of looking at the relationship between structures of inequality and violence is to examine the problem at a micro level by investigating the motives noted by the offender. Under what circumstances will lethal violence be used to assert one's will? By looking at the goals for the action, we may be better able to understand these circumstances. Wolfgang (1958) in his analysis of homicide in Philadelphia analyzed the motives of both the victim and the offender. Table 3.3 focuses on the motivations of the offender in the act of homicide. The first striking fact is that the largest single category of motives is to resolve a relatively trivial dispute. There is often a verbal insult which leads to violence. The issue here is a threat to status or position. Daly and Wilson (1988) also conclude in their analysis that the most common type of homicide involves two acquainted, unrelated males in a dispute over status or face. Rutherford and Chapman note that such altercations are directly or indirectly tests of masculinity in a society where the accepted masculine man must adopt the values of male superiority (Rutherford and Chapman, 1988, 24).

This follows directly to the next homicidal motives. Both Wolfgang's categories of domestic quarrel and jealousy, 13.4 percent and 11.1 percent respectively, can be understood in terms of conflicts over controlling sexuality. This is what is found to be dominant in several of the ascephelous societies we discussed earlier. Last, conflicts over property (combining altercations over money, 10.3 percent, and robbery, 7.9) would follow in frequency. Thus if we combine all homicides that are directly connected to conflict over status, property, and control of women, at least 80 percent are attributed to either creating, maintaining, or extending structures of inequality.

Polk and Ranson's (1991) analysis of homicides in Victoria, Australia, find a somewhat similar pattern, although their analysis is more refined in the specification of the typology. The authors find that most homicides in Victoria are between intimates. Slightly over one-half of the homicides occur where the victim and the offender are in a close personal relationship. Polk and Ranson further break down this category into three subtypes: (1) homicide originated in an intimate relationship that was sexual in nature (62 percent of intimate homicides or 32 percent of all homicides), (2) those who were linked together by family ties, mostly children (20 percent of intimate homicides or 10 percent of all homicides), and (3) persons who had been at some earlier point bound together by friendship (17 percent of intimate homicides, or 9 percent of all homicides).

Regarding the first subtype, the majority of victims were women, most of whom experienced intimate murder. In all cases, the conflict was over pos-

Table 3.3.   Offender's Motives in Homicide, Philadelphia, 1948–1952

Altercation of relatively trivial nature	36.6	Self-defense	1.3
Domestic quarrel	13.4	Halting a felon	1.1
Jealousy	11.1	Escaping arrest	1.0
Altercation over money	10.3	Robbery	7.9
Concealing birth	0.8	Other	4.2
Revenge	4.8	Unknown	3.1
Accidental	4.5		

Source: M. Wolfgang, *Patterns in Criminal Homocide* (Philadelphia: University of Pennsylvania, 1958).

sessiveness, usually the male attempting to control the female in the relationship or in general defining the female as an object of possession. One unusual example cited by the authors is where an older man, experiencing extreme depression, decided to take his wife's life at the same time he took his own. Here the wife was viewed as a possession to be taken as a partner in death. Most homicides in this category are where the husband kills his wife because of sexual infidelity. Within this category of violence developing from sexual intimacy, the authors identify a minority of cases where a female is the victim of another female (two cases), where a male is the victim of the female (six cases), and where a male is the victim of another male (two cases)

In the second subtype of intimate homicide, family killings (excluding the husband and wife relationship) were entirely homicides between adults and children. The third subtype refers to murder among friends where the homicide can best be understood as stemming from the relationship. The dominant example was where violence resulted from debts that were not resolved. The authors note that all these cases occurred between those who were on the margins of the society as a result of criminality, prison, drug use or unemployment.

The second major pattern of homicide is referred to as confrontational homicide. In this type, the conflict itself defines the relationship that brings the victim and offender together. In other words, no personal relationship existed between the victim and offender. This is homicide that occurs as a result of an affront to position or honor. In all cases males are either the victim or the offender. Polk and Ranson (1991) describe the homicide as occurring in the following general manner: in its simplest form, the parties come together, a challenge is laid down, and a fight ensues (92).

The authors apply Luckenbill's analysis of the situated transaction of a confrontation. Luckenbill (1977) identifies the following six stages that apply to confrontational homicide. The first stage is referred to as the opening move. This consists of one of the parties performing some act that the other party interprets as an affront or threat to his position, such as insults. The second stage occurs when the offended party recognizes that the affront was directed at him or her. Stage three is when a decision is made as to how to respond to the affront. If the offended party is not able to rationalize or excuse the other person's behavior, he or she will have to retaliate or retreat. If retreat is not the option taken, then retaliation takes place in stage four. In this stage the original offender may continue or escalate the insulting behavior, perhaps using violence. It is at the point of the fifth stage that it is difficult for both parties to break out of the confrontation without losing status or face. Weapons are likely to be produced during stage five, if they have not appeared earlier. In the sixth stage police enter the situation influencing the behavior of the remaining actors. Using this six-step model, Luckenbill nicely describes the nature of the interaction over a conflict of position or status. He observes that murder is the outcome of a dynamic interchange between an offender, victim, and in many cases bystanders (185). Overall, Polk and Ranson (1991) point out that the Luckenbill description accurately describes the pattern of confrontational homicide over a concern for masculine honor, face, or status. The authors furthermore note that those involved in confrontational homicide are more likely to be males in marginal positions in the society. Again, this is consistent with the observation that murder as a type of interpersonal violence is a technique used by those who do not have access to legitimized or institutional forms of power and violence to exert their will.

The third major pattern of homicide stems from another crime. Eighteen percent were connected to another crime. Most of these homicides were cases of felony homicide. A typical example would be one in which the victim of a robbery is murdered. Other murders within this type were those in which (1) the initial offender was killed by the police, security guard, or victim; (2) professional killings; and (3) police officers slain off-duty.

In concluding our discussion of homicide, there is a repeatedly seen pattern whereby violence occurs over conflict that stems from gender, status (position), and class relations. Homicide is seen as a solution to the conflict over maintaining, extending, or resisting interpersonal relations rooted in the power relations of the larger society as defined in terms of systems of stratification. These solutions may be seen as legitimate or illegitimate depending in part on the relative power of the victim and offender and whether the action serves to maintain or change the institutionalized power relations of the larger society. Brazil provides a good example of the legitimacy of homicide as it pertains to gender relations (Neier, 1992). A suitable defense for homicide in Brazil has traditionally been an affront to honor. Men dishonored by the adulterous behavior of their wives were legally justified in seeking revenge through violence. This situation is changing in Brazil as a result of women becoming increasingly powerful. In a recent case, after a husband stabbed to death his wife and her lover, the highest court in Brazil overturned the acquittal based on the defense of honor. Nevertheless, when the case was retried in the lower court, the killer again was acquitted.

RAPE: THE VICTIMS AND THE OFFENDERS

Let us now turn to the question of rape, another area of interpersonal violence. What are the patterns of rape? Who are the victims? Who are the offenders? And how do systems of inequality relate to these patterns? Within a four-day period in July, three rapes and one attempted rape occurred in Fort Wayne, Indiana, a moderately sized community that proudly defines itself as All-American City. Yet local police were relatively optimistic that the number of rapes reported so far during that month indicated that the number would not be as high as the previous July, during which 21 rapes were reported (Hebel, 1992). Meanwhile, the recent rapes stirred interest in the community for more self-defense classes offered by the Women's Bureau, a local women's self-help agency.

During the 1990s, the problems of rape and the sexual harassment of women in general increasingly appeared in the news. Trials involving two well-known males accused of rape, Willliam Kennedy Smith and Michael Tyson, received daily newspaper and television coverage. The confirmation hearings of Supreme Court Justice nominee Clarence Thomas became subject to much controversy when Anita Hill testified to being a victim of sexual harassment by the candidate.

The sexual control of women through acts of physical and/or verbal abuse is increasingly recognized as a very common form of violence in our society. Nevertheless, arrest rates for rape decreased dramatically through the 1990s (U.S. Department of Justice, 2001). The U. S. Justice Department reports that rape rates fluctuated from 1973 to 2000, however the general trend was downward. Rates of rape for 2000 were significantly lower than the adjusted rates for 1973.

It is important to recognize that rape, like homicide, is not only a manifestation of interpersonal violence but also a form of institutional and structural violence. In traditional societies such as the Yanomamo, rape and abduction of women are frequent practices accompanying warfare (Chagnon, 1968). This is also the case in modern societies. For example, throughout history, rape has accompanied war, and in many cases has been part of the war policy of a nation. Brownmiller (1975) notes that rape has been an inevitable accompaniment of religious crusades, revolutions, liberations, and wars of imperial conquest. The systematic rape by soldiers of innocent women in towns and villages in the United States during the American Revolution; during the conquest and attempted genocide of native people on the North American continent; during the American Civil War; during World Wars I and II in Belgium, France, China, and Germany; and during the most recent wars of our time in Korea, Vietnam, Bangladesh, Nicaragua, El Salvador, Russia, and the former Yugoslavia are just a few examples. Rape has been used to punish the enemy and as a reward for the victors.

At times, the military has organized brothels of captured young women to service the soldiers, as occurred in Poland during World War II. The Germans organized in Warsaw a wholesale and official abduction of young girls from the Solec district and the streets of the suburb of Czerniakov. An estimated 80 percent of the young women were arrested in and outside their houses and sent to the hospital of Saint Lazare, where they were examined by military doctors. After the examination for venereal diseases, healthy girls were placed in brothels to service the German soldiers (Creel, 1944, 31). Similar accounts are reported for the Japanese in their abduction of young Korean women, who were then forced to perform the role of "comfort women" for Japanese troops in Korea and China. In December 2001, The Women's International War Crimes Tribunal at the Hague made its final judgment and found that Japan is responsible under international law for the internationally wrongful acts—the rapes and sexual slavery—committed by the Japanese army against Korean women and seeks restitution and reparation for the women victimized by these crimes. A leading Bosnian women's group claimed that 10,000 Bosnian women were being held in Serbian detention camps where their captors raped them repeatedly (Guttman, 1992). Amnesty International (1993) has reported that abuses against women, including rape, have been widespread in the conflict and that Muslim women in particular have been the victims. In one instance, Amnesty International reported the raping of forty women between the ages of 15 and 30; they were held in a furniture warehouse by Serbian soldiers and were raped repeatedly. Rape was also employed by Hutu troops against Tutsi women in the genocidal campaign that Hutu leaders conducted in Rwanda in 1994.

In some extreme cases, rape can also be a business strategy of the husbands or fathers of the women victims. The economic plight of a population can often lead to women being coerced into prostitution, as was the case during destitute conditions among Italians in Palermo, Italy, after World War II. The American troops set up their camps in public parks. Husbands brought their wives to victorious troops and took the money. Soldiers queued in front of hastily erected tents. As soon as one man came out, another went in. Park keepers even provided the mattresses so that the Yanks would be comfortable (Brownmiller, 1975, 75).

Recently, there has been growing concern about the spread of AIDS among young women abducted in the countryside and placed in brothels in Thailand and Cambodia. Robinson (1993) reports that one study estimates that 50 percent of the child prostitutes in Thailand are HIV positive. She notes that sex workers are typically recruited from rural families, the sum given to the parents representing several months' advance salary, with the rest to be remitted after a ten-month or one-year term. The lump-sum payments provide subsistence for a family with few other resources and may even finance a new house, cultivation of the family land, or schooling for young siblings. This form of contract binds the sex worker to her job, the sense of family obligation overwhelming negative feelings about the work itself (493). A similar pattern of selling female children is present in Cambodia. A survey of 399 prostitutes in Cambodia by a local women's rights group reported that nearly half had been taken to brothels and were unable to leave. The epidemic is spreading rapidly in Southeast Asia as a result of expansion of the prostitution trade. We address these forms of rape when we discuss institutional and structural violence. For now, we concentrate on the discussion of rape as interpersonal violence.

What is rape? Who are those who rape? Who are those who are victims of rape? Why does rape occur? These are all crucial questions to take up in describing this form of interpersonal violence. Rape is defined in criminal law as the carnal knowledge of a female forcibly and against her will (FBI, 1988, 13). Bierne and Messerschmidt (1991) suggest that because the criminal law concentrates on the "against her will" threat component, the use of violence must be present for the charge of rape to be made. Thus the criminal law labels rape principally in terms of forcible rape. This is distinct from statutory rape, which refers to acts of sexual intercourse with a minor, that is, someone who is not legally able to give consent.

The history of the development of rape laws reflects the power context of this form of violence and how that has changed over time as women have gained power to question the male privileges derived from patriarchy. From Old Testament Jewish codes to medieval Europe, rape was treated as a property offense committed against men who "owned" the woman who was raped (Porter, 1986). Usually the "owners" were fathers or husbands. In the case of a maiden, rape destroyed her property value on the marriage market and brought shame to her family. Financial compensation was usually awarded to address the compensation warranted by the damage done to the father or husband. Furthermore, most legal traditions, from Hamurabi's code to ancient Jewish law to British common law, exempted husbands from raping their wives, since a husband could not be held liable for stealing or damaging his own property

Today, the definition of rape is still a highly charged political and moral issue. Battles are fought over whether married women can be raped by their husbands, the degree and type of force (physical and/or economic) that is necessary in establishing rape (Box, 1983; Hite, 1976; Bourgue, 1989; Finkelhor and Yllo, 1985), the relevance of the victim's sexual histories in court proceedings (Bourgue, 1989), the sexual versus nonsexual definition of the act (Bourgue, 1989), the inclusion of males as victims (Bourgue, 1989), and whether sexual acts that are pressured and forced in the context of a date is considered rape (Koss, Gidycz, and Wisniewski, 1987). Consider the following incident:

> It was late in the evening, Melanie was doing the laundry when it happened. Her husband had come home and flopped down on the bed—passed out. He had been out drinking most of the evening. She went to the next building where the laundry room was to put in another load. As she walked back into the apartment, a man jumped out of the closet, grabbed her from behind, and began to rip off her clothes. At first, she did not even realize that it was her husband. Though she screamed and struggled to get away, he used his superior strength and size to overpower her, tear her clothes off, and rape her anally (Finkelhor and Yllo, 1985, 51).

Marital rape is a crime in all states; however, in thirty-three states, there are exemptions given to husbands from rape prosecutions. When his wife is most vulnerable (e.g., she is mentally or physically impaired, unconscious, or asleep) and is legally unable to consent, a husband may be exempt from prosecution in many of these thirty-three states (Bergen, 1996; Russell, 1990). Bergen (1999) notes that because of the existence of some spousal exemptions in the majority of states, this indicates that rape in marriage is still treated as a lesser crime than other forms of rape. Still, the women's movement worldwide has made a significant impact in redefining the legal concept of rape. But the enforcement of the definition is limited within our own society and even more so internationally. Additional legal views in the United States are changing in the following areas: (1) sex of offender and victim: new laws are gender neutral; (2) nature of penetration: new laws include any intrusion however slight and by any object at all, of genital or anal openings (including oral sex); (3) force: new laws focus on the behavior of the offender, including threats of violence and use of superior strength to restrain or confine a victim; and (4) resistance: victims no longer have to prove that they resisted and in some states the notion of "reasonable" resistance, which takes into account the age, strength, and other factors, is considered (Barlow, 1990).

Nevertheless, popular definitions lag, possibly reflecting more the true nature of gender stratification in the society. Koss (1989), in a survey of 6,000 students on thirty-two American college and university campuses, found that nearly 90 percent of males who admitted to using force to obtain sexual intercourse were adamant that their behavior was definitely not rape. Men were not alone in possessing more traditional definitions of rape. Koss found that only 27 percent of the women whose experience met legal definitions of rape labeled themselves as rape victims, and only 5 percent reported their victimization to the police. In a more recent study of undergraduates at thirty colleges in the United States, Koss and Cook (1998) found that in a twelve-month period 8 percent of college, women experienced one or more attempted or completed rape. In 80 percent of the rapes they were committed by a nonstranger and more than half of the rapes or attempted rapes occurred on a date. The research also indicated that one out of every four college men reported that they had used some form of sexual coercion since the age of fourteen.

The problems of definition are magnified when we look at rape in less complex societies. Levine notes that among the Gusii, legitimate sexual encounters may be considered rape within our own society. The following passage describing the institutionalized sexual practices during the wedding night illustrates the definitional problem.

> The bride usually refuses to get onto the bed. If she did not resist the groom's advances, she would be thought sexually promiscuous. At this point, some of the young men may forcibly disrobe her and put her on the bed. The groom examines the bride's mouth for pods or other magical devices designed to render him impotent. As he proceeds toward sexual intercourse she continues to resist and he must force her into position. Ordinarily she performs the practice known as *ogotega*, allowing him between her thighs but keeping her vaginal muscles so tense that penetration is impossible. If the groom is young, the young men intervene, reprimand the bride and hold her in position so that penetration can be achieved on the first night. . . . Once penetration has been achieved, the young men sing jubilation and retire from the house to allow the groom to complete the nuptial sexual relations. They are keenly interested in how many times he will be able to perform coitus on the first night, as this is a matter of prestige and invidious comparison. . . . Six is considered a minimally respectable number and twelve is the maximum of which informants had heard. . . . The explicit object of such prodigious feats is to hurt the bride. If the bride is unable to walk on the day following the wedding night, the young men consider the groom a real man and he is able to boast of his exploits, particularly the fact that he made her cry (Levine, 1977, 194–95).

Levine notes that the use of force in the context of a resistant woman and the causing of pain during coitus is not limited to the wedding night. It continues to be an important part of marital sexual relations. Furthermore, Levine notes that young husbands claim to desire coitus twice a night. When a wife stubbornly resists, husbands are eventually moved to beat them and possibly send them back to their parents and demand return of the bridewealth. Levine points out that, in addition to this marital rape, the rate of recognized rape in Gusii society is almost four times the rate of rape in urban areas in the United States.

Thus, this problem of definition plagues the interpretation of the data on rape. If we confine ourselves to official statistics on rape, we of course underestimate the violence because of reluctance to report rape, especially marital and date rape. Unlike with murder, where the vast majority of murders are reported and the clearance rate is the highest of all crimes (usually 65 to 70 percent), only 20 percent of rapes are reported to the police, and the rate of clearance is significantly lower (47 percent in 2000) (Federal Bureau of Investigation 2001; Tjaden and Thoennes, 2000). As a result, victimization surveys are particularly important in providing additional information to validate and supplement the data collected via arrest reports, though we still overlook large areas of rape that are not always recognized as rape by the law enforcers or by victim or offender, such as marital rape, or by the victims in cases of rape recognized by the law, such as date rape. Nevertheless, it is worth examining the patterns indicated in official statistics as to who are officially defined as the offenders and who are officially defined as victims of rape.

Gender

Obviously, the dominant pattern is that males are offenders and females are victims. Of those arrested for rape, 98.8 percent are male. Rape is clearly an act whereby men victimize women in an act of violence. But it is important to note that rape does not fit this pattern exclusively. Male and female homosexual rape is a problem in prison and jail settings. Here again, males are more likely to be the victimized and the victimizers. Cahill (1985) estimates that one in five male inmates has been raped, and that with increasing problems of prison overcrowding, longer sentences, and budget cutbacks leading to staff cuts, the rates are likely to increase. Younger males in jails and prisons are particularly vulnerable to sexual assault (Scacco, 1982; Groth and Birnbaum, 1979). It is in the prison setting where rape as an issue of power and control is unquestionable. Rape is a very important mechanism in establishing and maintaining the inmate hierarchy within prisons as well as in the larger society, where women are the victims. Instances where women rape men or other women are quite rare (Groth and Birnbaum, 1979). In 1989, 366 women were arrested for rape, compared to 30,178 men. When women are charged with rape, the vast majority of cases are of statutory rape. Tjaden and Thoennes (2000) found that approximately 23 percent of the men who had lived with a man as a couple reported being raped, physically assaulted, and/or stalked by a male cohabitant, while 7.4 percent of the men who had married or lived with a woman as a couple reported such violence by a wife or female cohabitant.

Age

According to official statistics, rape offenders and victims tend to be young, usually under age 25. Teenagers 16–19 were more than twice as likely as any other age group to be victims of rape or sexual assault. People age 12–15 and 20–24 are also in high-risk groups; after age 24, the rate of attacks steadily declines (Rennison, 2001). In terms of arrests, 45 percent of those arrested are under 25 years of age and 62 percent are under 30 years of age. The peak ages of arrest is for those 18 to 24 years of age, followed by the 25–29 age group (Federal Bureau of Investigation, 2001).

A similar pattern is found when we look at marital rape. Finkelhor and Yllo (1985), in their review of cases of marital rape in the first two years after the California statute went into effect in 1980, found that two-thirds of the offenders were under 30 years of age. Likewise, Russell (1983) found that approximately two-thirds of the sample of the husbands in the marital rape cases studied were under age 30.

Race or Ethnic Minority Status

African Americans are overrepresented in rape arrest statistics. In 2000 almost 34 percent of those arrested were African American (almost three times their representation in the population), while 63 percent were white or of European ancestry (Federal Bureau of Investigation, 2000). During the last ten years, there has been a significant decline in rape and sexual assault for the African American population. Eleven years earlier, 53 percent arrested were African American, while 46 percent were white (Federal Bureau of Investigation, 1990), Rape, like homicide, is predominantly an intraracial act. African American women have a slightly higher rate of reported rape than white women. The rape and sexual assault victimization rate for whites in 2000 was 1.1/1,000; for blacks, the rate is 1.2/1,000 (Rennison, 2001). Some research that is restricted to adolescent and more educated women finds that there are no differences in rates of victimization for white and African American women (Ageton, 1983; Hall and Flannery, 1984). This suggests that the racial victimization pattern may be a result of income and class differences between the two populations. In one case the opposite pattern is found. Russell's research on college women found that white women had the highest victimization rates (Koss et al., 1987; Russell, 1984; Sorenson et al., 1987).

There is also a difference in rates of reporting of rape by ethnicity. In a victimization study surveying twenty-six of the largest cities, the Department of Justice found that minority victims were more likely to report rape to the police than white victims (76 percent versus 62 percent) (McDermott, 1979). In the case of marital rape, Finkelhor and Yllo (1985) found in a state-by-state analysis that the racial breakdown of husbands arrested mirrored respective states racial distributions. Russell (1982), on the other hand, found that white husbands were overrepresented in her study of husbands who had raped their wives. There are a number of issues, including differences in definition, law enforcement, and willingness of victims to report rape cloud the statistical picture.

Social Class

As with homicide, the most likely victims who report rape and offenders caught in rape incidents, regardless of race or ethnicity, come from relatively low socioeconomic neighborhoods in the nation's larger cities. Justice Department statistics indicate that the relationship is linear and direct (Rennison, 2001). As family income increases, the rate of rape victimization declines. The sexual assault/rape rate for those with a family income less than $7,500 is 5.2 per 1,000, while for the next highest income, $7,500 to $14,999, it is 1.7 per 1,000. The lowest rate of victimization is among women whose family income is $75,000 or more, 0.2 per 1,000.

As to the social-class background of the offender, a classic study on rape in Philadelphia for the years 1958 and 1960 found that more than 90 percent of offenders of both races belonged to the lower end of the occupational scale (Camir, 1971). In particular, 92 percent of African American offenders were unemployed. The obvious problems with generalizing from this data to the current era is the high level of unreported rape during this period and how this nonreporting may be, in part, class and racially biased. Rates of reported rape increased dramatically beginning in the middle 1960s through the early 1980s, principally as a result of changes in perception of rape and rape victims and increased sensitivity to the problem of rape. Yet there is little research that replicates the earlier research on rape as it relates to social class. We would suspect, however, that given the potential discretionary power of the police and prosecuting attorney, middle- and upper-class offenders would be systematically underrepresented. Some research suggests that there is bias in the judicial process whereby men of middle-class backgrounds are less likely to be successfully tried and convicted than men from traditional working-class backgrounds (Davis, 1979; Clark and Lewis, 1977).

Research on marital and date rape does not consistently reflect this same class pattern. Here social class is either irrelevant or relates only to the nature of the coercion in rape. For example, Russell (1982) finds that 45 percent of wife rape victims were upper middle class, 35 percent were middle class, and 21 percent were lower class. On the other hand, Finkelhor and Yllo's research on marital rape in Boston (1985) found that 24 percent of the sample with incomes of less than $10,000 reported forced sex, whereas only 2 percent of families with more than $35,000 in income did. In reviewing cases where sexual assault occurred, only 5 percent of those who reported that forced sex and battering took place had business or professional jobs, whereas 46 percent of those who reported force only without battering had business/professional jobs.

Victim/Offender Relationships

According to Department of Justice statistics on victimizations, 62 percent of rapes (both attempted and completed) were committed by nonstrangers (Rennison, 2001). Because of the problem of the nonreportage of rape as a result of official and unofficial perceptions as to whether or not the rape occurred in cases of marital and date rapes, there may be a significant underrepresentation of nonstranger rapes. Recalling the Koss et al. (1987) survey of college students, most of the victims of rape who know their offender do not define what happened to them as rape. Generally, only one in four rape victims defines what they experienced as rape, despite the fact that such violence fulfills the legal requirements of rape. Koss also found that over half the women sampled had been victims of attempted or completed rape since the age of fourteen, and 84 percent of these rape victims knew their assailants.

Most victimization studies have indicated that the majority of rapes are among persons who are romantically involved (Tjaden and Thoennes, 2000). These types of rapes have the lowest probability of being reported to police (Ellis, 1989). On anonymous questionnaires, 20 to 25 percent of sampled college males admit to having used some degree of physical force at least once to make sexual advances beyond their dates' wishes; 10–15 percent have reported having actually forced a date to have sex against her will. Additional support for this comes from a *Ms. Magazine* nationwide survey of more than 700 college students on 35 campuses that found that 13 percent of women had been raped and that 52 percent had experienced some form of sexual assault (Sweet, 1985). The research of Check and Malamuth (1985) follows this same pattern: between 40 and 50 percent of all high school boys in Los Angeles expressed the view that it would be acceptable to force a girl to have sex if she repeatedly sexually teased her date or if she agreed to have sex but changed her mind at the last minute.

The most recent victimization studies found that intimate partner violence is pervasive in U.S. society. The results of the survey found that nearly 25 percent of surveyed women and 7.5 percent of men said they were raped and/or physically assaulted by a current or former spouse, cohabiting partner, or date at some time in their lifetime (Tjaden and Thoennes, 2000). Approximately, 1.5 million women and 834,732 men are raped and/or physically assaulted by an intimate partner annually in the United States. Whether the victim is a female or male, the survey found that intimate partner violence is perpetrated primarily by men. The incidence of marital rape is more underestimated because most states still provide for a marital exemption in their rape statutes (Bergen, 1999), and law enforcement agencies haven't been as vigilant in publicizing the problem of marital rape.

As noted earlier, most countries throughout the world do not recognize marital rape legally or in practice. The following countries were noted in a UNICEF report (2000) on domestic violence as having legislated against marital rape: Australia, Austria, Barbados, Canada, Cyprus, Denmark, the Dominican Republic, Ecuador, Finland, France, Germany, Ireland, Mexico, Namibia, New Zealand,

Norway, the Philippines, Poland, Russia, South Africa, Spain, Sweden, Trinidad and Tobago, the United Kingdom, and the United States of America. However, Russell (1982) notes that in both Norway and Denmark husbands who rape their wives are subject to milder penalties. This is similar to the pattern in the United States given the presence of the exemptions provided for married men under certain conditions of the rape. However, in countries like Kenya rape is widespread. In a recent report issued by Amnesty International, rapes reported to police have increased more than 300 percent since 1990. These statistics do not include marital rape in Kenya, which is not illegal (Amnesty International, 2002).

Even though the law has changed in many states in this country enforcement is lagging behind. This does not mean that few cases occur since research on marital rape indicates that it is a quite frequent occurrence. Russell (1982) reports that one in seven women who were or had been married were victims of at least one completed or attempted rape by a husband or ex-husband. 84 percent of these rape incidents involved some physical force. Finkelhor and Yllo (1985) in their survey of 323 Boston-area women conducted in 1980 and 1981 found that 10 percent of married or previously married women said that their husband had used physical force or threat to try to have sex with them (6–7). In addition to this figure on marital rape, the authors report that 10 percent of the women in the sample reported that they had experienced date rape. The authors conclude that sexual assault by intimates is the most common form of rape. Angela Browne's (1987) study on battered women who kill their husbands found that many had also been raped often and violently, indicating how rape and murder are intimately connected.

In sum, because the occurrence of date and marital rape is significantly underestimated and often undefined by both victim and offender, we would expect the true incidence of nonstranger rape to be much higher. Furthermore, as opposed to seeing rape as an isolated, unusual occurrence, rape and coercive sexual relations may be more accurately understood as normative in the context of patriarchal relations.

HISTORICAL TRENDS

Because of the differences in rates of reporting and the changes in perception and definition of crime, it is extremely difficult to measure the incidence of rape over time. Today, according to official police records, there were 90,186 rapes reported to police according to the Uniform Crime Reports (Federal Bureau of Investigation, 2001). This is translated into a rate of 62.7/100,000 for female victims. The rate of rapes reported to police has declined about 15 percent over the last ten years. This is up substantially from about 25 per 100,000 women reported in the 1950s and almost three times the rate reported in the 1940s. The rate of reportage to police increased steadily from 1965 at a rate of 4.9/100,000 males and females reaching a peak in 1992 at 42.8/100,000 males and females. Recently, the rate of re-portage has declined approximately 20 percent from this peak (Maguire and Pastore, 2001). The rate of rapes reported in the U.S national victimization survey has declined at an even greater level, 60 percent between 1993 and 2000 (Rennison, 2001). Nevertheless, the level of unreported rape is almost twice that of reported rape.

CROSS-NATIONAL CULTURAL PATTERNS

What is the pattern of rape cross-nationally? Is the U.S. unique or typical in its patterns of rape? First, the problem of comparing statistics from different societies with different definitions of rape is almost insurmountable This is especially true for marital rape because, as noted earlier, relatively few countries recognize the social and legal existence of rape between marriage partners. Yet, despite these difficulties, we can form some conclusions. In looking at industrial societies with similar legal statutes pertaining to rape, we find considerable variability. The comparative research that has been done consistently shows that as in the case of homicide, the United States has a much higher rate of rape than any other industrialized country (Ellis, 1989).

Anthropological research on rape is quite scarce. Some anthropological re-search has focused on whether rape is a biological propensity (innate to the human species) (Shields and Shields, 1983; Thornhill and Thornhill, 1987) or learned and a product of nurture (Baron, 1985; Sanday, 1981; Sunday and To-bach, 1985). Anthropological research on rape in general suffers from two problems: little data on rape and problems of accuracy of the data that are available (Palmer, 1989). As Palmer notes, despite the problems with the re-search, it appears that rape is present in all societies to some degree. There are no societies that can claim to be rape-free.

WHY PEOPLE RAPE: A QUESTION OF MOTIVES

Research that attempts to classify rapes and rapists in terms of a typology fo-cuses on the issue of motives. Groth identifies three major types of rape: (1) power rape, where sexual aggression is an assertion of control and domina-tion; (2) anger rape, where coercive sex vents anger and frustration; and (3) sadistic rape, where violent sex satisfies a pathological need to inflict suffer-ing (Groth and Birnbaum, 1979). Groth contends that power rape is the most common type. He furthermore notes that rape is always a symptom of some psychological dysfunction. But this view of rape as psychopathology has come under increasing attack. Barlow (1990) contends that there is little impressive evidence that rapists are in general psychologically abnormal and that the most promising approach is one that links structural and cultural factors with situational inducements, as was the case with explanations of violence in general (204). Barlow cites Russell's description of the "patriarch" as a common mental attitude of rapists.

> [Patriarchs] see themselves as superior to their wives because they are men; they believe their wives are their property and that it is the duty of their wives to accommodate them sexually whenever they want; they believe they should be the boss in the marriage, and that wives who behave in an insubordinate fashion deserve punishment. . . . They subscribe to a sexual double standard in which it is acceptable for husbands to have other sexual attractions or affairs, but it is totally unacceptable for their wives to do the same (Russell, 1983, 123).

Scully and Marolla (1985) also critique the presumption of psychopathology of rape research. Citing Abel, they note that fewer than 5 percent of men were psychotic when they raped (Abel, Becker, and Skinner, 1980). Scully and Marolla (1985) identify a number of motives for rape. The first motive they describe is revenge and punishment. In most cases, the rape victim was a substitute for the women on whom they wanted to enact revenge. The authors note an upsetting event, involving a woman, preceded a significant number of rapes. When they raped, these men were angry because of a perceived indiscretion typically related to a rigid, moralistic standard of sexual conduct, which they required from their woman but, in most cases, did not abide by themselves (255). The authors add that sometimes the target of the revenge is the rape victim's husband.

A second motive was sexual access. Here males felt that they were entitled to the sex withheld from them or that rape was the only means of getting sex from a particular woman. In many cases of date and marital rape, because they are lost in their own ideologies of dominance, men cannot see that rape could even exist in the context of marital or dating relationships. It is a product of an obligation that extends from the marriage contract or the exchange that occurs in a dating relationship.

Impersonal sex and power was another motive noted by Scully and Marolla. For the rape offender, rape required no concern for the victim in the act of sex. Said one rapist: "Rape gave me the power to do what I wanted to do without feeling I had to please a partner or respond to a partner. I felt in control, dominant. Rape was the ability to have sex without caring about the women's response. I was totally dominant" (Scully and Marolla, 1985, 259). A third motive noted was recreation and adventure. This occurs most frequently in gang rape. Here rape offenders noted that it was exciting or a challenge.

Overall, when we review the motives of men who rape and consider the frequent occurrence of marital and date rape, it is increasingly evident that we are not dealing with abnormal behavior but what has been defined as normal behavior that stems from acceptable ideas and beliefs that guide gender relations in this society. As Barlow (1990) notes,

> in virtually all areas of American life—family, work, politics, sports, education, and so on—males have traditionally found themselves in positions of power, domination, independence, and self-determination. Women, on the other hand, are expected to take subordinate positions and to acquiesce to the decisions and demands made by men. The world of sexuality is no different. The prevailing cultural image of maleness supports the idea of men as being dominating, powerful, and active and as the instigators of sexual interaction; the female as weak, passive, and submissive (200).

Thus rape is a form of violence that stems from the nature of gender relations, that is, it is not a deviation from normal gender relations, as would be explained by the focus on the psychologically pathological causes of rape. Women in the context of patriarchy are defined as commodities to be acquired by men and to be owned in the context of marriage. Historically speaking, rape has been defined as deviant principally when it occurs in violation of these rights of ownership and control. This results in defining rape principally from a man's perspective. Rape is problematic not because it reduces the rights of males who control women but because it is a technique of control by men in general in patriarchal society. For women are ultimately controlled by the occurrence of rape.

The women's movement has attempted to redefine rape in the context of egalitarian gender relations, defining rape from the victim's perspective. Broadening the definition of rape to include women's understanding, will provide women with greater freedom in the society. It is in the issue of control over a resource, here women and sexuality, that links rape to murder and as we discuss in later chapters, other forms of violence as well. Both rape and murder represent forms of power to have access and control over a resource. In patriarchal class societies men attempt to dominate each other through the control of the production of what is valued in the society and through the control of women, who produce their progeny and serve as an outlet for their sexual drive. This leads us to the discussion of rape and inequality.

RAPE AND INEQUALITY

The relationship between rape and inequality is complex. First, rape is a tactic that maintains inequality because one gender is predominantly victimized by another. In effect, the crime itself places one group at a disadvantage relative to the other. Women experience a loss of freedom and opportunity to develop because of the occurrence of rape or the threat of it.

Riger and Gordon (1981) have found that women's fear of violence sometimes results in their not taking certain jobs, not visiting friends, and not venturing out at night for walks or entertainment. They found that 22 percent of men and 68 percent of women avoid doing necessary errands (such as shopping) because of the fear of criminal violence. In terms of recreational activities, 25 percent of men and 70 percent of women avoid them because of fear for their safety. Thus rape specifically limits the freedom of women to engage in social interaction and limits opportunities for women's advancement in our society. In general, it is women's time and space freedom that is limited by rape. Furthermore, the occurrence of rape serves to reinforce women's dependency on men to protect them from other males, thus reinforcing patriarchy. Thus, rape maintains or increases the level of inequality between men and women in a society.

On the other hand, rape may be regarded as a consequence of gender inequality. In this context, if women were not seen as the property of men, then rape in all social relations, including marriage and dating, would be unacceptable. Kokopeli and Lakey (1994) argue that masculine sexuality as it is defined by patriarchy involves the oppression of women, competition between men, and homophobia. The authors note that patriarchy shapes men's sexuality in terms of the importance of domination in sexual relations. Patriarchy tells men that their need for love and respect can only be met by being masculine, powerful, and ultimately violent. As men come to accept this, their sexuality begins to reflect it. Violence and sexuality combine to support masculinity as a character ideal. To love a women is to have power over her and to treat her violently if need be (451). According to Kokopeli and Lakey, rape is the logical end of masculine sexuality.

Most of the research appears to give support to the link between patriarchy and rape. Baron and Straus's (1989) research is one of the more comprehensive studies testing the relationship. The authors compared rates of rape across the fifty states for 1980 to 1982. The authors found that social disorganization (measured by, among others things, level of geographic mobility, divorce, lack or religious affiliation, households headed by males with no females present, female-headed households with children, and the ratio of tourists to residents in each state) is positively related to rape. Other independent variables influencing the rate of rape were sex-magazine circulation (positively related), gender equality (inversely related), level of income inequality as percentage of population in SMSA (positively related), and percentage of the population unemployed (positively related).

Furthermore, the authors noted that the less economic inequality, the greater the gender equality and thus the lower the rate of rape. The authors concluded that the greater the disparity between men's and women's statuses, the higher the rape rate (a finding consistent with feminist theory). They suggested that gender inequality contributes to a social climate that is conducive to violence against women (Baron and Straus, 1989, 185). They called for equal rights with men in all spheres of life, including the passage of an equal rights amendment and the elimination of the income gender gap as a way to reduce the incidence of rape.

Peterson and Bailey (1992) examined the relationship between rape rates and various measures of general, racial, and gender socioeconomic inequality for U.S. metropolitan areas for the year 1980. These authors concluded that the greater the income gap between males and females in metropolitan areas, the higher the rate of rape. They observed that if income equality between men and women were achieved, the rape rate would be reduced by 16.24 persons per 100,000 female population. In addition, both the general levels of economic inequality and racial inequality were strongly and positively related to levels of rape in metropolitan areas.

Baron and Straus (1989) note that societies with the highest levels of violence have the highest levels of gender inequality. This is consistent with the analysis we conducted which indicated a strong relationship between female labor force participation rates and rates of homicide in thirty-seven countries. Rape may fit in here as well. Problems of reportage and definition make it very difficult to test this relationship; however, given that there is a strong relationship between rape and other forms of violence, in those areas of violence where the data are available, the relationship with gender inequality is supported. Given that most research is based principally on nonmarital rape, one might ask if the same patterns would apply to marital rape. The answer appears to be yes. Research indicates that egalitarian marriages, as opposed to male-dominant marriages, have the lowest incidence of violence (Coleman and Straus, 1986; Straus, Gelles, and Steinmetz, 1980).

Another indication of how rape is related to gender inequality is to look at how the definition of rape is related to women's relationship to men. For example, when women are in a relationship with men (either in a marriage or dating relationship), the definition of rape becomes problematic. In marriage it generally is not defined as rape, and in dating it legally can be defined as rape but in most cases is not recognized as rape in the context of law enforcement. When there is no relationship between men and women, then rape is clear. Thus, the nature of the relationship, a power relationship, either in marriage or dating, limits the definition of rape. It is as if women have less rights when they are in a relationship with men. The male defines her rights, and as noted earlier, has the greater power in defining rape. This is classically patriarchal. In the same way that the salutation for a woman (Miss and Mrs.) is important in defining women's relationship to men, so is the nature of the relationship important to understanding the nature of rape.

In regard to both date and marital rape, these are also more often considered areas of victim-precipitated rape. Here it is the women's fault for not acting in a way that is appropriate as defined in terms of gender relations that lead to rape. How is the appropriateness of ones behavior defined in terms of patriarchy? What are appropriate women's role responsibilities in terms of a dating relationship? Who is responsible when sexual petting goes too far? What are women's obligations in marriage as it relates to sexual relations? Even in stranger rape, the victim precipitation argument is present. It is how she was dressed, where she was at what time, or how she led the male on that is considered in defining responsibility and whether the offender is truly guilty. Nevertheless, in general, the more distant the relationship, the less likely these role obligations are present and thus the victim is defined as truly a victim within patriarchal society.

Another way gender inequality is related to rape is how the law and law enforcement changed as a result of women's empowerment. Much of the increased concern regarding rape and the treatment of victims of rape is in part related to the increase in the political power of women in this society and their increasing entry into such professions as law and criminal justice. Another way of looking at how law changes in response to women's empowerment is to look at how the history of rape laws reflect the central importance of gender inequality, as discussed earlier.

Rape may also be related to how patriarchy is connected to other forms of stratification. How are class and racial inequality related to rape? Men who are dominated by the nature of their class and ethnic position can still dominate women, and this may be important as they experience class and racial oppression as a way to assert power and control over their lives. This pattern was supported by the research of Peterson and Bailey (1992) noted earlier. Cross-culturally, one study on rape in South Africa highlights the dynamics of race and class inequality and rape. Vogelman's (1989) analysis of rape in South Africa found that in 1988 there were officially 19,368 rape cases. Official annual figures for rape in the 1980s record between 15,000 and 16,000 cases, 9,000 prosecutions, and 5,000 convictions. He notes that unofficially 399,000 rapes are committed annually in South Africa, meaning on the average that over 1,000 women are raped daily in South Africa—almost one every one and a half minutes. He furthermore notes that the figures for rape from 1986 to 1987 showed an increase of 14.7 percent. Vogelman concludes that the high incidence of rape in South Africa is attributed to the powerlessness of women that stems from patriarchy. This, together with the oppressive class and racial systems of stratification, makes women vulnerable to being victimized by black South African working-class men who are seeking to exert power over women to compensate psychologically for the powerlessness they experience as a result of class and racial oppression.

This interconnection of class, race or ethnicity, and gender stratification as it relates to violence directed at women is highlighted in critical criminology. In all social classes men learn to see themselves as privileged, yet society prohibits marginalized men a privileged economic position. Marginalized male youth experience disproportionately severe economic problems arising from the inherent mechanisms of capitalism. Given these conditions, for some males, the importance of manipulating and controlling women, by violence, if necessary, is elevated (Messerschmidt, 1986, 139). Also, the fact that women are more likely to be lower in class position (as defined in terms of income and occupational status) than men (two-thirds of the adult poor in the U.S. are women) does have an impact on their level of victimization (McDermott, 1979). Ethnic minority, working-class women are more likely to be victimized than white, upper class women. Messerschmidt (1986) states that in a racist and sexist society, African American women, because they are viewed as less worthy of respect than other women, become rape victims in very high numbers (139).

Smith and Bennett (1985) conclude in their study on the relationship between rape and poverty that greater degrees of poverty are part of a community environment that is conducive to high rates of violence. They agree with the Schwendingers (1983) that conditions of poverty in general serve to promote contempt for others and that this contempt is likely to be directed at those who are less powerful, women in particular. Smith and Bennett further note that the percentage divorced is a powerful correlate of rates of rape in a community. They contend that divorce is a measure of interpersonal conflict between men and women, and that this conflict may manifest itself in rape.

CONCLUSION

In conclusion, rape, like homicide, is a learned strategy to exert power over another in interpersonal relations. Inequality contributes to the use of violence because it makes the victim vulnerable and because dominance of another is a normative characteristic of the society and the social relations that are endemic to it. Furthermore, as structured systems of inequality are legitimated through belief systems that define those who are dominated as less than those who are dominant—less in quality, less in talent, less in intelligence, and so forth—they contribute to the occurrence of violence by creating a disassociation between victim and offender and a legitimization for the use of force in controlling those who are less and may be in need of control because of their lower abilities.

Furthermore, we have discussed how this pattern of victimization increases levels of inequality, as those at the lower ends of the economic spectrum are in general more seriously affected. This is true for both homicide and rape. Last, we see how the structures of inequality may contribute to increasing use of violence, as those with the least power rely upon increasingly desperate and violent means to gain some measure of control for themselves and power over others, which is defined as a value in hierarchically structured societies. We learn the value of dominance as we are dominated by others. We learn that through the dominance of others, we gain control over our lives. We learn that power over others is a good and necessary feature of social relations in our society. Whether this is defined in terms of control over women, children, racial and ethnic minorities, or those with little status or property, violence may be more often chosen as a mechanism to exert power in situations of limited access to wealth, status, or control over one's life.

How do these patterns of victimization as they are a product of inequality carry over to the next level of violence, institutional violence? Who are the victims and who are the offenders of this type of violence? What are the patterns and how do they vary across different social systems? These are the questions we address in succeeding chapters.

REFERENCES

Abel, Gene, Judith Becker, and Linda Skinner. 1980. "Aggressive Behavior and Sex." *Psychiatric Clinics of North America* 3: 133–51.

Adler, Jerry. 1994, August 15. "A Week in the Death of America." *Newsweek*, 41.

Ageton, S. S. 1983. *Sexual Assault among Adolescents*. Lexington, Mass.: D.C. Heath.

Amir, Menachem. 1971. Patterns in Forcible Rape. Chicago: University of Chicago Press.

Amnesty International. 1993, January. *Bosnia-Herzegovina: Rape and Sexual Abuse by Armed Forces*. AI Index: EUR 63/01/93. New York: Amnesty International.

———. 2002. *Kenya: Rape the Invisible Crime*. Amnesty International. http://www .amnestyusa.org/stoptorture/women/kenya_invisible.pdf.

Archer, Dane, and Rosemary Gartner. 1984. *Violence and Crime in Cross-National Perspective*. New Haven, Conn.: Yale University Press.

Avison, William R., and Pamela L. Lorin. 1986. "Population Diversity and Cross-National Homicide: The Effects of Inequality and Heterogeneity." *Criminology* 24: 733–49.

Barlow, Hugh D. 1990. *Introduction to Criminology*. Glenview, Ill.: Scott, Foresman/ Little, Brown Higher Education.

Baron, L. 1985. "Does Rape Contribute to Reproductive Success: Evaluations of Sociobiological Views of Rape." *International Journal of Women's Studies* 8: 266–77.

———. 1989. *Four Theories of Rape in American Society*. New Haven, Conn.: Yale University Press.

Baron, L., and Murray Straus. 1988. "Cultural and Economic Sources of Homicide in the United States." *Sociological Quarterly* 29, no. 3: 371–390.

Bastian, Lisa D., and Bruce M. Taylor. 1994. *Young Black Males*. Bureau of Justice Statistics Crime Data Brief. Washington, D.C.: Government Printing Office.

Beirne, Piers, and James Messerschmidt. 1991. *Criminology*. New York: Harcourt Brace Jovanovich.

Bensing, Robert, Jr., and Oliver Schroeder. 1960. *Homicide in an Urban Community*. Springfield, Ill.: Charles C. Thomas.

Bergen, R. K. 1996. *Wife rape: Understanding the response of survivors and service providers*. Thousand Oaks, Calif.: Sage.

———. 1999. "Marital Rape." *Applied Research Forum: National Electronic Network on Violence Against Women*. www.vaw.umn.edu/Vawnet/mrape.pdf.

Blau, Judith R., and Peter M. Blau. 1982, February. "The Cost of Inequality: Metropolitan Structure and Violent Crime." *American Sociological Review* 47: 114–29.

Block, R. 1981. "Victim-Offender Dynamics in Violent Crime." *Journal of Criminal Law* 72: 743–61.

Bohannan, Paul. 1960. *African Homicide and Suicide*. Princeton, N.J.: Princeton University Press.

Bourgue, Linda Brookover. 1989. *Defining Rape*. Durham, N.C.: Duke University Press.

Box, Steven. 1983. *Power, Crime, and Mystification*. New York: Tavistock.

Brenner, Harvey. 1978. "Impact of Economic Indicators on Crime Indices." *Proceedings of the Hearings before the Subcommittee on Crime of the Committee on the Judiciary*, Washington, D.C.

Browne, Angela. 1987. *When Battered Women Kill*. New York: Macmillan.

Brownmiller, Susan. 1975. *Against Our Will*. New York: Simon and Schuster.

Bureau of Alcohol, Tobacco, and Firearms. 1991, May 22. "How many guns?" Press release.

Cahill, Tom A. 1985. "Rape behind Bars." *The Progressive* 49: 12–21.

"Cambodian Girls Forced into Prostitution." 1994, April 2. *News Sentinel*, 2.

Chagnon, Napoleon. 1968. *Yanomamo: The Fierce People*. New York: Holt, Rinehart and Winston.

Chua-Eoan, Howard G. 1991, August 19. "The Uses of Monsters." *Time*, 66.

Church, George. 1989, February 6. "The Other Arms Race." *Time*, 20.

Clark, L., and D. Lewis. 1977. *Rape: The Price of Coercive Sexuality*. Toronto: Women's Press.

Coleman, Diane H., and Murray A. Straus. 1986. "Marital Power, Conflict, and Violence in a Nationally Representative Sample of American Couples." *Violence and Victims* 1: 141–57.

Creel, George. 1944. *War Criminals and Punishment*. New York: R. McBride.

Daly, Martin, and Margo Wilson. 1988. *Homicide*. New York: Aldine de Gruyter.

Davis, A. Y. 1979. "Rape, Racism and the Capitalist Setting." In *The Women Say, the Men Say*, edited by E. Shapiro and B. M. Shapiro. New York: Dell.

Dawson, John M., and Patrick A. Langan. 1994. *Murder in Families*. Washington, D.C.: U.S. Department of Justice.

Dentan, Robert K. 1978. "Notes on Childhood in a Nonviolent Context: The Semai Case." In *Learning Non-Aggression*, edited by A. Montagu. New York: Oxford University Press.

Divale, William, and Marvin Harris. 1976. "Population, Warfare, and the Male Supremacist Complex." *American Anthropologist* 78: 521–38.

Eaton, Sara, Laura Emerson, and Mike Gruss. 2002, December 15. "Feuding City Gangs Caught in Cross Fire." The Journal Gazette.

Eitzen, Stanley D., and Maxine Baca Zinn. 1989. "Structural Transformation and Systems of Inequality." In *The Reshaping of America: Social Consequences of the Changing Economy*, 131–43, edited by Stanley D. Eitzen and Maxine Baca Zinn. Englewood Cliffs, N.J.: Prentice Hall.

Ellis, Lee. 1989. *Theories of Rape: Inquiries into the Causes of Sexual Aggression*. New York: Hemisphere Publishing.

Farley, Reynolds. 1980. "Homicide Trends in the United States." *Demography* 17: 177–88.

Federal Bureau of Investigation. 1988. *Crime in the United States. Uniform Crime Reports*. Washington, D.C.: Government Printing Office.

———. 2000. *Crime in the United States. Uniform Crime Reports*. Washington, D.C.: Government Printing Office.

———. 2001. *Crime in the United States. Uniform Crime Reports*. Washington, D.C.: Government Printing Office.

Finkelhor, David, and Kersti Yllo. 1985. *License to Rape: Sexual Abuse of Wives*. New York: Free Press.

Flanagan, Timothy J., and Katherine M. Jamieson. 1988. *Sourcebook of Criminal Justice Statistics.* Washington, D.C.: Government Printing Office.

Foster, C. D., M. A. Siegel, D. R. Plesser, and N. R. Jacobs. 1987. *Gun Control.* Plano, Tex.: Information Aids Inc.

Fox, James Alan, and Marianne W. Zawitz. 2001. *Homicide Trends in the United States.* Washington, D.C.: Bureau of Justice Statistics, U.S. Department of Justice. www.ojp.usdoj.gov/bjs/homicide/homtrnd.htm#contents.

Gibson, Thomas. 1990. "Raiding, Trading, and Tribal Autonomy in Insular Southeast Asia." In *The Anthropology of War*, edited by J. Haas. Cambridge: Cambridge University Press.

Greenberg, D. F. 1981. "Methodological Issues in Survey Research on the Inhibition of Crime." *Journal of Criminal Law and Criminology* 72: 1094–1108.

———. 1985. "Age, Crime, and Social Explanation." *American Journal of Sociology.* 91: 1–21.

Greenberg, James B. 1989. *Blood Ties.* Tucson: University of Arizona Press.

Groth, A. Nicholas, and Jean Birnbaum. 1979. *Men Who Rape.* New York: Plenum.

Gurr, Ted. 1979. "On the History of Violent Crime in Europe and America." In *Criminology Review Yearbook*, edited by Egon Bittnerr and Sheldon I. Messinger, 411–32. Beverly Hills, Calif.: Sage.

———. 1990. "Historical Trends in Violent Crime: A Critical Review of the Evidence." In *Violence: Patterns, Causes, and Public Policy*, edited by N. A. Weiner, M. A. Zahn and R. J. Sagi. New York: Harcourt Brace Jovanovich.

Guttman, Roy. 1992, August 23. "Victims Say Serbs Rape as War Tactic." *Journal Gazette*, 5A.

Hall, E. R., and P. J. Flannery. 1984. "Prevalence and Correlates of Sexual Assault Experiences in Adolescents." *Victimology: An International Journal* 9: 398–406.

Hawkins, D. F. 1983. "Black and White Homicide Differentials." *Criminal Justice Bulletin* 10: 407–40.

Hebel, Sara. 1992, July 23. "12th July Rape Reported; Defense Classes Added." *Journal Gazette*, 1.

Hewitt, John D. 1988. "The Victim-Offender Relationship in Convicted Homicide Cases: 1960–1984." *Journal of Criminal Justice* 16: 25–33.

Hite, Shere. 1976. *The Hite Report on Female Sexuality.* New York: Knopf.

Hoebel, E. Adamson. 1964. *The Law of Primitive Man: A Study in Comparative Legal Dynamics.* Cambridge, Mass.: Harvard University Press.

Jones, E. D., III. 1981. "The District of Columbia's Firearms Control Regulations Act of 1975: The Toughest Handgun Control Law in the United States—Or Is It?" *Annals of the American Academy of Political and Social Sciences* 455: 138–49.

Kantor, Glenda Kaufman, and Murray A. Straus. 1987. "The 'Drunken Bum' Theory of Wife Beating." *Social Problems* 34: 214–30.

Knauft, Bruce M. 1987. "Reconsidering Violence in Simple Human Societies." *Current Anthropology* 28: 457–500.

Kokopeli, Bruce, and George Lakey. 1994. "More Power Than We Want." In *Race, Class, and Gender: An Anthology*, edited by Margaret L. Andersen and Patricia Hill Collins. New York: Wadsworth.

Koss, Mary P. 1989. "Hidden Rape: Sexual Aggression and Victimization in a National Sample of Students in Higher Education." In *Violence in Dating Relationships*, edited by M. A. Pirog-Good and F. E. Stets. New York: Praeger.

Koss, Mary P., and Sarah L. Cook. 1998. "Facing the Facts: Date and Acquaintance Rape are Significant Problems for Women." In *Issues in Intimate Violence*, edited by Racquel Kennedy Bergen, 147–156. Thousand Oaks, Calif.: Sage.

Koss, Mary P., C. A. Gidycz, and N. Wisniewski. 1987. "The Scope of Rape: Incidence and Prevalence of Sexual Aggression and Victimization in a National Sample of Higher Education Students." *Journal of Consulting and Clinical Psychology* 55: 162–70.

Krahn, Harvey, Timothy F. Hartnagel, and John W. Gatrell. 1986. "Income Inequality and Homicide Rates: Cross-National Data and Criminological Theories." *Criminology* 24: 269–95.

Krug, E. G., K. E. Powell, and L. L. Dahlberg. 1998. "Firearm-related deaths in the United States and 35 other high- and upper-middle-income countries." *International Journal of Epidemiology* 27: 214–221.

Kuper, Hilda. 1963. *The Swazi*, edited by George and Louise Spindler. New York: Holt, Rinehart and Winston.

Kutchinkski, B. 1988, June 16. "Pornography and Sexual Violence: The Criminological Evidence from Aggregated Data in Several Countries." Paper presented at the 14th International Congress on Law and Mental Health in Montreal, Canada.

Lee, Richard B. 1979. *The !Kung San: Men, Women and Work in a Foraging Society*. New York: Cambridge University Press.

———. 1984. *The Dobe !Kung*. Chicago: Holt, Rinehart, and Winston.

Levine, Robert A. 1977. "Gusii Sex Offenses: A Study in Social Control." In *Forcible Rape: The Crime, the Victim, and the Offender*, edited by Duncan Chappell, Robley Geis, and Gilbert Geis, 189–226. New York: Columbia University Press.

Loftin, Colin, and Robert H. Hill. 1974. "Regional Subculture and Homicide." *American Sociological Review* 39: 714–24.

Loftin, Colin, and Robert Nash Parker. 1985. "The Effect of Poverty on Urban Homicide Rates: An Error in Variable Mode." *Criminology* 23: 269–87.

Loftin, Colin, D. McDowall, B. Wierseman, and T. J. Cottey. 1991, December 5. "Effects of Restrictive Licensing of Handguns on Homicide and Suicide in the District of Columbia." *New England Journal of Medicine* 325: 1615–20.

Luckenbill, D. F. 1977. "Criminal Homicide as a Situated Transaction." *Social Problems* 26: 176–86.

McCoid, Catherine Hodge. 1989. *Dowry Deaths in India: A Materialist Analysis*. Working papers, Women in International Development, Michigan State University.

McDermott, Joan M. 1979. *Rape Victimization in 26 American Cities*. Washington, D.C.: U.S. Department of Justice.

Maguire, Kathleen and Timothy J. Flanagan. 1991. *Sourcebook of Criminal Justice Statistics—1990*. Washington, D.C.: U.S. Department of Justice.

Maguire, Kathleen, and Ann L. Pastore, eds. 2001. *Sourcebook of Criminal Justice Statistics*. www.albany.edu/sourcebook/.

Maguire, Kathleen, Ann L. Pastore, and Timothy J. Flanagan. 1993. *Bureau of Justice Statistics Sourcebook of Criminal Justice Statistics—1992*. Washington, D.C.: U. S. Department of Justice.

Malamuth, N. M., and J.V.P. Check. 1985. "The Effects of Aggressive Pornography on Beliefs in Rape Myths: Individual Differences." *Journal of Research in Personality* 19: 299–320.

Messerschmidt, James W. 1986. *Capitalism, Patriarchy, and Crime*. Totowa, N.J.: Rowman and Littlefield.

Messner, Steven, and Richard Rosenfeld. 1994. *Crime and the American Dream*. Belmont, Calif.: Wadsworth.

Messner, Steven, and Kenneth Tardiff. 1986. "Economic Inequality and Levels of Homicide: An Analysis of Urban Neighborhoods." *Criminology* 88: 997–1007.

Mishel, Lawrence, Jared Bernstein, and John Schmitt. 2001. *The State of Working America*. Ithaca: Cornell University Press.

National Center for Health Statistics. 1991. *Vital Statistics of the United States 1988. II: Mortality*. Washington, D.C.: Government Printing Office.

National Center for Health Statistics. 1998. *Health United States 1996–1997 and Injury Chartbook*. Washington, D.C.: U.S. Department of Health and Human Service. www.cdc.gov/nchs/data/hus/hus96_97.pdf.

Neier, Aryeh. 1992, November 9. "Watching Rights." *The Nation*, 533.

Palmer, Craig. 1989. "Is Rape a Cultural Universal? A Re-examination of the Ethnographic Data." *Ethnology* 28: 1–16.

Parker, Robert Nash. 1989. "Poverty, Subculture of Violence, and Types of Homicide." *Social Forces* 67: 983–1005.

Peterson, Ruth D., and William C. Bailey. 1992. "Rape and Dimensions of Gender Socioeconomic Inequality in U.S. Metropolitan Areas." *Journal of Research in Crime and Delinquency* 29: 162–177.

Petras, James, and Christian Davenport. 1991. "Crime and the Transformation of Capitalism." *Crime, Law and Social Change* 16:155—75.

Philips, Kevin. 1990. *The Politics of Rich and Poor*. New York: HarperCollins.

Pokorny, A. D. 1965. "A Comparison of Homicides in Two Cities." *Journal of Criminal Law* 56: 479–87.

Polk, Kenneth, and David Ranson. 1991. "Homicide in Victoria." In *Australian Violence: Contemporary Perspectives*, edited by D. Chappell, P. Grabosky, and H. Strang. Canberra: Australian Institute of Criminology.

Porter, Roy. 1986. "Rape—Does It Have a Historical Meaning?" In *Rape*, edited by S. Tomaselli and R. Porter. New York: Basil Blackwell.

Rasmussen, Knud. 1932. *Intellectual Culture of the Copper Eskimo*. Gyldendalske, Boghandel: Nordisk Forlag.

Reiss, Albert J., and Jefferey A. Roth. 1993. *Understanding and Preventing Violence*. Washington, D.C.: National Academy Press.

Rennison, Callie Marie. 2001. *Criminal Victimization 2000 Changes 1999–2000 with Trends 1993–2000*. Washington, D.C.: U.S. Department of Justice Office of Justice Programs, Bureau of Justice Statistics.

Riedel, Marc. 1987. "Stranger Violence: Perspectives, Issues, and Problems." *Journal of Criminal Law and Criminology* 78: 223–58.

Riedel, Marc, and M. A. Zahn. 1985. *The Nature and Pattern of American Homicide*. Washington, D.C.: Government Printing Office.

Riger, S., and M. Gordon. 1981. "The Fear of Rape: A Study in Social Control." *Journal of Social Issues* 37: 4.

Robinson, Lillian S. 1993, November 1. "Touring Thailand's Sex Industry." *The Nation*, 492–97.

Russell, D.E.H. 1982, 1990. *Rape in Marriage*. New York: Macmillan.

———. 1984. *Sexual Exploitation: Rape, Child Sexual Abuse, and Workplace Harassment*. Beverly Hills, Calif.: Sage.

Rutherford, J., and R. Chapman. 1988. *Male Order: Unwrapping Masculinity*. London: Lawrence and Wishart.

Sanday, P. 1981. "The Socio-Cultural Context of Rape: A Cross-Cultural Study." *Journal of Social Issues* 37: 5–27.

Scacco, Anthony M. 1982. *Male Rape: A Casebook of Sexual Aggressions.* New York: AMS Press.

Schwendinger, Julia R., and Herman Schwendinger. 1983. *Rape and Inequality.* Beverly Hills, Calif.: Sage.

Scully, Diana, and Joseph Marolla. 1985. "'Riding the Bull at Gilleys': Convicted Rapists Describe the Rewards of Rape." *Social Problems* 32: 251–263.

Shields, W. M., and L. M. Shields. 1983. "Forcible Rape: An Evolutionary Perspective." *Ethnology and Sociobiology* 4: 115–36.

Silberman, Charles E. 1978. *Criminal Violence, Criminal Justice.* New York: Random House.

Sloan, John Henry, Arthur L. Kellerman, and Donald T. Reay. 1988. "Handgun Regulations, Crime, Assaults, and Homicides." *New England Journal of Medicine* 319: 1256–262.

Smith, M. Dwayne, and Nathan Bennett. 1985. "Poverty, Inequality, and Theories of Forcible Rape." *Crime and Delinquency* 31: 295–305.

Sorenson, S. B., J. A. Stein, J. M. Siegel, J. M. Golding, and M. A. Burnam. 1987. "The Prevalence of Adult Sexual Assault: The Los Angeles Epidemiologic Catchment Area Project." *American Journal of Epidemiology* 126: 1154–64.

Straus, Murray A., Richard J. Gelles, and Suzanne K. Steinmetz. 1980. *Behind Closed Doors: Violence in the American Family.* New York: Doubleday/Anchor.

Sunday, S. R., and E. Tobach. 1985. *Violence against Women: A Critique of the Sociobiology of Rape.* New York: Gordian Press.

Sweet, Ellen. 1985, October. "Date Rape: the Story of an Epidemic and Those Who Deny It." *Ms. Magazine.*

Swigert, Victoria Lynn, and Ronald A. Farrell. 1976. *Murder, Inequality, and the Law.* Lexington, Mass.: Heath.

Taylor, William B. 1979. *Drinking, Homicide, and Rebellion in Colonial Mexican Villages.* Stanford, Calif.: Stanford University Press.

Thomas, Elizabeth Marshall. 1959. *The Harmless People.* New York: Knopf.

Thornhill, Randy, and Nancy Wilmsen Thornhill. 1987. "Human Rape: The Strengths of the Evolutionary Perspective." In *Sociobiology and Psychology: Ideas, Issues, and Applications,* edited by C. Crawford, M. Smith, and D. Krebs, 269–91. Hillsdale, N.J.: Lawrence Erlbaum Associates.

Toufexis, Anastasia. 1989, June 12. "Our Violent Kids." *Time.* 52.

Turnbull, Colin M. 1961. *The Forest People.* Garden City, N.J.: Natural History Press.

U.S. Department of Justice. 1988. *Report to the Nation on Crime and Justice.* Washington, D.C.: U.S. Department of Justice.

U.S. Department of Justice, Bureau of Justice Statistics. 2001, June 13. "Rape rates declined slightly between 1999 and 2000." www.ojp.usdoj.gov/bjs/glance/rape.htm.

UNICEF. 2000. "Domestic Violence against Women and Girls." *Innocenti Digests* Volume 6. Florence: UNICEF Innocenti Research Centre. www.unicef.org/lac/ingles/urgente/deten5.htm.

Vogelman, Lloyd. 1989. *The Sexual Face of Violence.* Johannesburg, South Africa: Ravan Press.

Wolfgang, Marvin. 1958. *Patterns in Criminal Homicide.* Philadelphia: University of Pennsylvania Press.

Woodburn, James C. 1979. "Minimal politics: The Political Organization of the Hadza of North Tanzania." In *Politics in Leadership: A Comparative Perspective*, edited by W. A. Shack and P. S. Cohen, 244–66. Oxford: Clarendon Press.

Woodbury, Richard. 1991, October 28. "Ten Minutes in Hell." *Time*, 31.

World Health Statistics Annual. 1997–1999. www3.who.int/whosis/menu.cfm?path= whosis,whsa&language=english.

Wright, J. D., and P. H. Rossi. 1985. *The Armed Criminal in America: A Survey of Incarcerated Felons*. Washington, D.C.: National Institute of Justice.

Zahn, Margaret A., and Philip C. Sagi. 1987. "Stranger Homicides in Nine American Cites." *Journal of Criminal Law and Criminology* 78: 377–97.

Zawitz, Marianne, and Kevin J. Strom. 2000. *Firearm Injury and Death from Crime, 1993–1997*. NCJ 182993. Washington, D.C.: U.S. Department of Justice.

Zimring, F. E., S. K. Mukhergee, and B. Van Winkle. 1983. "Intimate Violence: A Study of Intersexual Homicide in Chicago." *University of Chicago Law Review* 50: 910–30.

Chapter Four

Family Violence

Lee was always armed because he worked as a correctional officer at the Kankakee Jail, and he always carried handcuffs. He frequently tied Caroline up or handcuffed her before he beat her. The handcuffs, in fact, became such an integral part of his torture routine that he had only to give a signal—tapping his left wrist with his right hand and pointing to where they were kept—to tell her to get the cuffs and bring them to him so he could shackle her and begin the beating (Gillespie, 1981, 2).

Although she had been beaten so severely that she had been hospitalized on at least two occasions, had lost an eye and part of an ear, her assailant was released each time on his promise to the judge that he would not repeat the offense. The victim, I am told, finally solved the situation herself. She committed suicide (U.S. Commission on Civil Rights, 1982, 47).

William and Carrie present a clear case of mutual abuse, jealousy, and insecurity. He is a product of two alcoholic, verbally abusive parents. She was raised in a home in which her father had fistfights with her older brothers. William now has strong needs to control her behavior, afraid she will leave him for another man. She has a history of sexual promiscuity, knows his fears, and by acting flirtatiously in public plays to them. Within a year of their last violent incident she told him she had a lesbian lover to test his reaction. . . . Once, to punish her for her "waywardness" (his term), William dumped "goop" on her head, smearing a combination of "piss, tuna, and anything else I could get my hands on" into her hair (Stacey, Hazlewood, and Shupe, 1994, 108, 111).

Abigail Abbot Bailey wrote the first autobiographical account of family violence published in the United States. Born in 1746 and a deeply religious woman, Abigail married Asa Bailey at the age of twenty-two. Within one month of their marriage, Asa began physically abusing her. Over time he was to have an affair with a hired woman and attempt to rape another female servant. After Abigail had been married to Asa for twenty-one years and had born fourteen children (all of whom the father regularly bullied), he began to abuse physically and sexually one sixteen-year-old daughter. Abigail described one such violent incident that she witnessed:

> In great rage, and with a voice of terror, he asked why she did not come to him, when he first called her? She respectfully told him that he called her to get up, which she immediately did, and went to her work. But she said she did not hear him call her to come to him. He seized his horsewhip, and said in a rage, he would make her know that when he called her, she should come to him. He then fell to whipping her without mercy. She cried, and begged, and repeated her assertion that she did not know he called her to come to him. . . . But he was not in the least appeased. He continued to whip her, as though he were dealing with an ungovernable brute; striking over her head, hands, and back; nor did he spare her face and eyes; while the poor girl appeared as though she must die (Taves, 1989, 75–76).

Finally, in August 1793 Abigail obtained a divorce from Asa. While divorce was permissible in late eighteenth-century New England, it was not casually obtained. One of the marriage partners had to have broken the understood "covenant" established between them. This marital covenant clearly assumed that one partner (the woman) was subordinate to the other (the male), though within this two-tiered hierarchy both partners were recognized as having rights and responsibilities. Adultery, cruelty (wifebeating), and desertion were all considered examples of breeches of these "rights and responsibilities." Interestingly, the primary grounds on which Abigail eventually secured a divorce from her abusive husband were *not* his violence towards her *nor* because of what we moderns would regard as his incest or his child abuse, but rather his adultery regarding his wife and daughter: that is, by engaging in incestuous relations with his own daughter, Abigail's husband had posed a threat to her, the marriage, and the larger social order. In this view, however curious it may seem to modern family advocates, the wife, not the child, was assumed to be the primary victim of the father-daughter incest (Taves, 1989, 26).

The experiences of Abigail Abbot Bailey 200 years ago demonstrate a fundamental fact about the perception of family violence as a social problem:

> Historically, the greater the level of intimacy associated with partnerships in which violence was observed, the less likely the institutional response was to characterize the behavior as criminal. . . . [T]he labeling of intimate violence as "domestic" not only creates the perception that it falls within the private realm of the family, but, further, that it is better treated outside the jurisdiction of the criminal justice system" (Cardarelli, 1997, 2).

Its definition as a social problem has differed tremendously throughout history and, as we show, continues to change.

FAMILY VIOLENCE IN HISTORICAL PERSPECTIVE

Only within the past century or so has violence within the family been regarded as a serious, widespread problem and then largely in Western societies. Yet the phenomenon has existed probably as long as the domestic institution itself. Consider child abuse. Commenting on biblical history, Naomi
Chase (Chase, 1975, 12–13) observes:

> Although denounced by the prophets, the sacrifice of first-born sons was ordinary
> enough in ancient Palestine. The Book of Chronicles specifically names the Moabite
> King Mesha, who burned his eldest son for the god Chemosh; the Ammonites, who
> offered their sons to the Moloch; the Arameans, who sacrificed their children; and
> Ahazand Manasseh (as killers of their children). The practice of child immolation
> was so common in ancient Israel that some scholars think Hell was the name orig-
> inally given to Gehenna or Ge-Hinnom, the valley near Jerusalem where children
> were sacrificed. The valley, which was later turned into a garbage dump that
> burned continuously, has ever since been a literary image for the fires of Hell.

As David Bakan (1971) chronicles in grisly detail in *Slaughter of the Innocents*,
systematic exploitation and abuse of children is interwoven with the very history of civilization. The movement to establish children's rights to be safe from
physical and sexual abuse is relatively young. In the United States it began just
after the Civil War. Interestingly, the case that helped the movement gain vis-
ibility and momentum involved the Society for the Prevention of Cruelty to
Animals. A little girl named Mary Ellen had to be taken from her family because in addition to being frequently beaten, she had been seriously neglected and had become malnourished. There were no social service agencies
for children that could argue in court on her behalf, so the Society for the Prevention of Cruelty to Animals maintained that as a member of the animal kingdom she should be removed from her abusive parents, as was an animal's
right by law. The Society won its case. The obvious need for an entirely separate advocate to safeguard children led to the formation of the Society for the
Prevention of Cruelty to Children in 1871 in New York City (Radbill, 1974).

But it was not until 1962 that the term "battered child syndrome" came into
our lexicon when it was introduced at a symposium for the American Academy of Pediatricians by Dr. C. Henry Kempe. Likewise, only in the past few
centuries has woman battering been viewed as a problem at all, much less a
serious problem. In fact, for much of history violence in the home was viewed
as obligatory on the part of the husband to maintain control and chastise his
wife with physical force (Dobash and Dobash, 1977).

The "right" of husbands to beat their wives has its roots in Roman law, which
originally permitted a husband to kill his wife if she committed a variety of offenses, particularly adultery. This common law tradition was modified in medieval Europe, limiting male-directed punishment to beating women rather than
taking their lives. For many centuries, during the Dark and Middles Ages as well

as the Renaissance, women were routinely subjugated by physical violence. The physical punishment that accompanied their taken-for-granted inferior status, justified by the so-called laws of chastisement, went unquestioned. Such violence was simply regarded as part of the divinely ordained order of things:

> Accompanying these moral imperatives (of the Church) were the many laws of chastisement. During the Middle Ages women throughout Spain, Italy, France and England could be flogged through the city streets, exiled for years or killed if they committed adultery or numerous "lesser" offenses. In France a man could beat his wife "when she contradicts or abuses him, or when she refuses, like a decent woman, to obey his reasonable commands." . . . Even the French code of chivalry specified that the husband of a scolding wife could knock her to the earth, strike her in the face with his fist and break her nose so that she would always be blemished and shamed. Thus, "the wife ought to suffer and let the husband have the word, and be the master" (Dobash and Dobash, 1977, 429).

In his history of divorce in Western society, Roderick Phillips (1988, 525) describes a seventeenth-century English commentary on the law relating to women. The commentator states that just as a man might beat an outlaw, a pagan, or a traitor with impunity, so a husband might legitimately beat his wife, but only as long as he did not do "any bodily damage, otherwise than appertains to the office of a Husband for lawful and reasonable correction." And Phillips (1988, 328) quotes from a book published in London in 1612, entitled *A Godlie Forme of Householde Government*, that admonished (male) readers: "If she be of a gentle spirit, he may use gentle means which will then doe the most good, but if she be of a more hard nature, rougher means must be used and she must be dealt withal after a more round manner." He goes on to cite an old French proverb that said: "Don't expect any good from an ass, a nut or a woman unless you have a stick in your hand."

In the New England colonies, only Massachusetts considered wife abuse a criminal offense. In general, North American legislators followed their British counterparts in shaping laws concerning woman battering. An example was the now-infamous "rule of thumb," an expression that has become a part of everyday speech. British common law during the nineteenth century, in a reform effort to put limits on how harshly a husband could legally chastise his wife, stipulated that the "reasonable instrument" to be used by a husband in a beating could be "a rod not thicker than his thumb."

Gradually during the nineteenth century legislatures on both sides of the Atlantic began to remove males' "automatic entitlement" to use violence against their spouses. A series of marital laws appeared in England, such as the 1853 Act for the Prevention and Punishment of Aggravated Assaults on Women and the 1882 Wife Beaters Act, mandated fines and imprisonment for woman-abusers. Likewise, various states in this country enacted quite severe statutes regarding husbands' assaults on wives. For example, a Maryland law passed in 1882 prescribed forty lashes or one year in prison for wifebeaters. In Delaware an abusive man could be punished with five to thirty lashes at the whipping post, while in New Mexico he could be given a fine of $255 to $1000 or one to five years in prison. By 1910 only eleven states still did not permit divorce by reasons of cruelty by one spouse toward the other (Pleck, 1979, 61).

FAMILY VIOLENCE AND INEQUALITY

For most of the history of Western civilization the family unit has resembled an asymmetric power hierarchy. It has been what Australian sociologist Robert W. Connell has termed a "domestic patriarchy" or a "gender regime" in which stratification is determined by both age and gender: adult males at the top of the pyramid, all children at the bottom (though they can be stratified also by age), and women somewhere in between. There may have been exceptions in individual households where strong-willed women "ruled the roost" and basically made the key decisions instead of men, and it is true that modern families are witnessing more egalitarian relations between the sexes. Nevertheless, as a system patriarchy (i.e., men holding maximum power and autonomy) has held sway as opposed to matriarchy (where women enjoy such resources and men are subjugated). Indeed, writing about the status of women in preindustrial societies, anthropologist Martin King Whyte (1978, 6) concludes that there is no known society where women have ever been generally dominant over men in civil and political life. Matriarchy is a concept; patriarchy is far and away most often the reality.

It is also important to remember that domestic patriarchy is dependent for support from the larger society of which the family is merely one unit (Connell, 1987, 123–24). Inequality of power in marriage is a reflection of gender inequality in the larger society. This means that the culture's gender roles, its procedures for (and contents of) the socialization of children, its traditional patterns of educating and employing persons, and even its literary/folklore/mass media portrayals reinforce for both men and women what they "should" expect of one another when they form families.

A related debate has been how universally dispersed across all socioeconomic levels is family violence. All surveys find, for example, that spousal violence appears to occur more frequently at the lower socioeconomic levels. Writes one author: "The theories that relate family violence to inequalities assume that life as an underdog is more stressful and frustrating" (Little, 1995, 257). Some have argued that the poorer elements of society versus the more affluent elements are more reluctant to report violent incidences to law enforcement officials out of traditional suspicion or pessimism, or vice-versa those more affluent families fear the stigma of police involvement and thus underreport. The best that can be said at this time is that if there is a relationship between patriarchy and socioeconomic class and the use of violence in the family, then patriarchy is related to levels of violence, and those levels of spousal violence mirror inequality in the larger society.

As a consequence, no specific interpersonal act of family violence is unrelated to the larger institutional and cultural context. Dobash and Dobash (1979, 24) write: "men who assault their wives are actually living up to cultural prescriptions that are cherished in Western society—aggressiveness, male dominance, and female subordination—and they are using physical force as a means to enforce that dominance." One has only to interview a cross-section of battered women who have become clients of a safe haven or shelter to appreciate how fundamentally the various sociocultural dimensions of family violence are interwoven into the pain and tragedy of an individual family. In any hypothetical case of woman battering in North America, for example, these would include:

- His enculturated macho ideal of male supremacy and control (accompanied by secondary predilections for violence, sexual aggression, and alcohol/drug consumption *versus* her enculturated ideal of passivity, deference, tolerance, and reservation
- His inability to communicate openly and constructively about his male needs and feelings *versus* her mirror inability to communicate openly and constructively about her female needs and feelings
- His likelihood of earning all or most of the income (hence possessing greater resources, from checking accounts and income to employability to the mobility of an automobile) *versus* her likelihood of not having her own independent access to financial (and resultant) resources or having lesser resources
- His likelihood of being less involved in the daily responsibilities of feeding, cleansing, and caring for children *versus* her likelihood of being the primary caregiver for their children

This list is certainly not exhaustive. Also to be considered are the factors that intimate relationships allow a freer flow of emotions (including anger), there are minimal "inhibitors" of emotions, and man-woman living relationships inevitably bring to the front such issues as the division of labor in household chores and sexual access. But the point is that each of the previous comparisons can be linked sociologically to the institutional context of the modern family. At the interpersonal level they constitute the issues of stress, strain, anger, and hostility that fuel violence in an intimate situation. They are the stuff of police blotters, divorce courts, and files in women's shelters. But they are, in the larger picture, specific manifestations of macrothemes that exist in a hierarchical system of power.

How this asymmetric arrangement originated has generated a running debate among sociologists and anthropologists since the two disciplines began. The biological reductionists point to basic qualitative differences between the two sexes. Men are physically stronger and bigger than women (Collins, 1971); have an evolutionary tendency to band together, whether in hunting parties or at taverns (Tiger, 1970); and cannot become pregnant; and thus women raise boys who must ultimately reject femininity and seek masculine identity (Chordorow, 1974). Men's advantage that results in their predominant asymmetric power, in other words, is fundamentally physiological (and therefore somehow "natural"). The historicists, on the other hand, take a more materialist, or Neo-Marxist, point of view. What is produced in a society, how it is produced, who produces it, and who controls it after production are all factors that determine a lot about women's and men's statuses in any society.

Resolving this issue is beyond the scope of this chapter. At this time it appears that a recognition of both cultural-economic and biological factors provides the best working explanation for the persistence of patriarchy, particularly in modern industrial societies where women are not "inexorably" destined to be full-time "child producers" for most of their adult years. Anthropologist Alice Schlegel (1977, 27), in developing a theory of sexual stratification using both Western and non-Western case studies, comes to just such a conclusion. She writes of the "modern" situation: "In the industrial society the status of the women is increasingly dependent on her roles in the public sector and depends very little on her procreative activities in the domestic." The result, as feminists have pointed out, is a conflict between the demands of the full-time workplace and the full-time home. Schlegel concludes that the hierarchy that subjugates women, or at best subtly limits their horizons beyond homemaking, is not based on their childbearing monopoly but rather on a male-oriented legacy of leaving an overwhelming proportion of the childcare/primary socialization to women. As long as women are given such tasks, by default the "glass ceiling" of limited advancement and opportunity will confront them. Schlegel (1977, 27) observes that "the time, energy, and freedom of movement required to attain positions of importance in an achievement-oriented society are simply not available to women with children to the degree they are to men." With this view of the modern Western family as a hierarchy of asymmetrical power, many of the patterns found by family violence researchers become more easily understood.

SPOUSAL VIOLENCE

Assault between married partners or cohabiting adults has not readily been accepted by authorities as the same type of serious crime as assault between two strangers. Indeed, during the early 1980's, while Stacey and Shupe (1983) were researching a book on domestic violence, an incident occurred in Fort Worth, Texas, that illustrates this point. A man repeatedly struck and knocked down a woman in an alley off a city street. When citizens, both male and female, were attracted by her cries and stopped to see if they could help, the man reassured them with the statement, "It's okay. She's my wife." And they moved on without interfering.

And this has been as true of public officials as of the average citizen. In one study of 1,323 felony arrest bail decisions collected during 1983–1984, for example, the courts clearly discriminated in assault cases in ways that showed family violence to be considered less "serious" than other types of violence. The authors concluded:

> Violent crimes against a family member are handled differently at the bail-setting stage than the same crimes against unrelated victims. Although related and unrelated offenders are equally likely to obtain release from pretrial detention, suspects who are related to their victims and are charged with a violent offense are treated more leniently. Related suspects tend to be released on recognizance more often than unrelated ones and, if required to post a bond, are required to post a lesser amount (Herzeberger and Channels, 1991, 70–71).

But times are changing. The Attorney General's Task Force on Family Violence (1984, 4) stated: "The legal response to family violence must be guided primarily by the nature of the abusive act, not the relationship between the victim and the abuser." There is now considerably more concern generated and attention paid to violence against women (generally) and violence between spouses/cohabiting partners (in particular). Domestic violence as a social problem no longer runs up against the believability problem it faced in the 1970s. Advocates of victims in the antifamily violence movement no longer have to adopt a defensive stance in pressing their case for abused constituents.

Still, the passage to a greater sensitivity about spousal violence has not been without controversy and argumentation.

Patterns

One often encounters in books and magazine articles dealing with family violence, "official" statistics that state a women in the United States is beaten every so many seconds or somber pronouncements that one out of every two (sometimes three, sometimes four) females in this country will at some time in their adult lives become the victim of a man's violence in a relationship. Are such figures accurate, and where do they originate?

The fact is that such statistics are "guesstimates" put out by well-intentioned, concerned "experts" who want to impress on readers that spousal violence (and here we include cohabiting partners and same-sex partners [see, e.g., Renzetti, 1992, 1997; Island and Letellier, 1991] as well as married couples) is no trivial problem. No one really knows for sure how many battered women there are at any given moment or within any time frame. No official agency in the federal government acts as a clearinghouse for such information or comprehensively monitors the numbers on family violence. There is no Uniform Crime Report category for these kinds of assaults similar to the ones that the Federal Bureau of Investigation compiles annually on robbery, murder, and so forth.

Instead, our ability to generalize about the patterns and dynamics of spousal violence comes primarily from two sources: victimization surveys and studies of women's shelter residents. Relying solely on either source can be misleading. Sociologist Murray A. Straus (1991) has warned of both the representative sample fallacy and the clinical fallacy. In the first case the survey methods employing representative sampling will probably miss some of the more violent cases because respondents can be embarrassed and reluctant to talk about their experiences with total strangers, either face to face or by telephone. On the other hand, persons receiving treatment or assistance for a problem like violence to the point they have to flee their homes and take up residence elsewhere are often not representative of the entire population (as is true with most persons who turn to public agencies for assistance). Based on what we know from in-depth studies of battered women in shelters and from what women and men in national surveys have recounted about violence they experienced, it is apparent that many shelter residents display the more severe cases of violence, certainly many times worse than what a random sample survey would pick up. For example, in a 1985 survey Straus found that only 13 percent of the 644 assaulted women among the thousands of respondents he sampled had ever gone to a shelter.

Thus, it is best to use both types of data on family violence, but with caution. Surveys give us a good picture of how widespread this violence is within the general population, while clinical studies help us understand the dynamics involved between family members. Unquestionably the most comprehensive and reliable survey research has been conducted by sociologists at the Family Research Laboratory at the University of New Hampshire. Over the past two decades Murray A. Straus, Richard J. Gelles, Suzanne K. Steinmetz, and many of their colleagues have given us a detailed analysis of incidents (acts committed within a specific period of time, such as a year) and prevalence (acts committed over the entire span of a relationship) of spousal violence in American families. What they have revealed are patterns that confirm the existence of what Stacey and Shupe (1983, 195–203) term a "cult of violence" in American society: an environment of patriarchy and cultural glorification of violence that serves as fertile soil for violence's cultivation. In both 1975 and 1985 Straus and his colleagues conducted extensive national surveys of American households, drawing on representative samples. Altogether they analyzed responses from 8,145 families. The results show a considerable amount of violence in the home. For example, one in six (or 16 percent) of American couples experienced at least one physically violent episode during 1985. Since there are approximately 64 million couples in the United States, that means (by extrapolation) an estimated 8.7 million couples had at least one violent act committed in their home in one year. Most of the violence was "minor": pushing, shoving, slapping, and throwing or smashing household objects. But 3.4 million households had "high risk" violence, such as kicking, punching, biting, and choking (Straus and Gelles, 1991b, 96–97). Almost one out of every eight North American husbands carried out one or more violent acts in 1985, and three out of every 100 women in their study that year (which translates into 1.8 million women nationally) were severely assaulted by their male partners. In fact, the 12 percent of the women interviewed who reported being beaten by husbands or partners during the year of the survey had been assaulted an average of six times.

Another pattern in the 1985 survey was consistent with results from the 1975 survey (Straus, Gelles, and Steinmetz, 1980). Women committed roughly an equal amount of violence against men as men did against women. Straus and Gelles (1991b, 98) point out that many of the assaults by women against their husbands or partners were acts of retaliation or self-defense:

> One of the fundamental reasons why women are violent within the family (but rarely outside the family) is that for a typical American women [sic], her home is the location where there is the most serious risk of assault. . . . Since women are so often the victims of murderous assault within the family, it is not surprising that women, who commit only about a tenth of the non-spouse murders in the United States, commit nearly half (48 percent) of the murders of spouses.

This pattern of female-initiated violence is controversial but not unique to Straus et al.'s surveys. Well over a decade ago Steinmetz (1977) wrote of a "battered husband syndrome" in which men, not women, were the primary victims of physical abuse. Shupe, Stacey and Hazlewood (1987) devoted an entire chapter in their book on family violence to the dynamics producing violent women who ended up in counseling. Indeed, they later devoted an entire book, entitled *The Violent Couple*, to the study of a sample of 100 male/female partnerships in which both men and women were violent towards one another, often aggressively so (Stacey, Hazlewood, and Shupe, 1994). Several other researchers have documented female violence that is not always purely in self-defense (e.g., Dutton, 1988; McLeod, 1984; Nisonoff and Bitman, 1979; Wolfgang, 1978; Blum and Fisher, 1978; Scanzoni, 1978). Such mounting findings suggest, as two social workers concluded in the journal *Social Work*, that the domestic violence problem is "a falsely framed issue" if we cling to the popular assumption that men "exclusively or nearly exclusively perpetrate domestic assaults" (McNeely and Robinson-Simpson, 1987). These authors also demonstrate how clinical studies of battered women (as Straus warned) can miss part of the overall picture: victimized women entering a shelter are rarely-to-never asked about their possible violence toward men.

This view has been criticized (falsely) as claiming that acknowledging women's violence against men also claims that there is a "symmetry" or equality of harm and danger to men and women from each other's violence (e.g., Dobash et al., 1992). Actually no one has made such an improbable assertion. As criminologist Browne (1997, 51) reminds us,

> As adults, men are at greater risk of violence from acquaintances and strangers than from their wives or girlfriends, with the majority of their assailants being

other males. Compared to the danger men face from the violence of other men, the risk of severe physical injury or death from their wives is quite low.

And as two social scientists (Miller and Wellford, 1997, 17) have noted:

In a society characterized by high rates of violent crime, women experience the majority of the violence directed at them by those with whom they have ongoing relationships. In effect, intimate violence—violence committed by those individuals one is more likely to trust and have continuing social relations with—represents the type of violence most likely to be increasing for women.

But the idea that women are (not just could be) contributing aggressively to violence in the home is anathema to feminists. It has been described as a "backlash against the challenge to male privilege mounted by the battered women's movement" (Gondolf, 1988, 5). For years most researchers in the area of family violence (who were also usually feminists) maintained that a marriage license is in reality a "hitting license" for husbands and that it is almost always women who are the victims of violence. They have resisted using terms like "mutual combat" in describing spousal violence, characterizing women's violence as a myth (Berk, Berk, Loseke, and Rauma, 1983). When Straus first presented his findings on female violence in the late 1970s, booing, shouting, and picketing protesters interrupted his presentations. Suzanne K. Steinmetz, who first coined the term "battered husband syndrome," received threatening phone calls, had a bomb threat called in to a conference where she was to speak, and had to face a negative letter-writing campaign to her university when she was being considered for promotion (Straus and Gelles, 1991c, 11).

But the indisputable fact is that Straus et al. show that women are violent, and not always in self-defense. In the 1985 survey the researchers asked who hit first in any violent episodes that year. According to husbands interviewed, they were the ones who struck first in 44 percent of the episodes, the wives struck first in 45 percent of the episodes, and the men were unsure in the remaining 11 percent of the episodes. According to wives interviewed, husbands struck first in 53 percent of the cases, the wives struck first 42 percent of the time, and the women were unsure in the remaining 5 percent of the episodes (Straus and Gelles, 1991b, 104–5). Regardless of men and women's different perspectives, it is clear that women's violence against men is not a negligible factor in spousal violence. All of this is not to say that men are at greater or equal risk compared to women. In fact, men are less likely to be seriously injured than women are when the former are assaulted in the home (Stacey, Hazlewood, and Shupe, 1994; Stets and Straus, 1991).

Yet there is one further interesting pattern that changed from the 1975 to 1985 studies. While Straus and his colleagues found a 22 percent decrease in wifebeating over a decade's time, overall wife-to-husband violence increased slightly (Straus and Gelles, 1991a, 118–19). Straus and Gelles (1991b, 105) conclude:

Violence by women is a critically important issue for the safety and well-being of women. . . . ([The] danger to a woman of such behavior is that it sets the stage for the husband to assault her. . . . Unless women also forsake violence in their relationships with male partners and children, they cannot expect to be free of assault. Women must insist as much on non-violence by their sisters as they rightfully insist on it by men.

And as Okun (1986, 107) observes about some feminist resistance to acknowledging the widespread existence of women's violence: "By analogy, historians are able to discuss instances of unprovoked violence by Native Americans, without obviating the overall portrait of genocide by whites against Native Americans."

The ugly truth is that an individual in the United States of America is far more likely to be murdered by a member of his or her own family than by anyone else (Straus, 1991, 20). For men, the likelihood of being assaulted by a family member is twenty times greater than being assaulted by a stranger; for women, that risk of being assaulted in the home rather than by a stranger jumps to more than 200 times greater. Worse, based on his studies, Straus (1991, 21) considers the statistics from both 1975 and 1985 surveys to be *underestimates*. Incidences vary between one in six and one in eight families each year experiencing violence at least once but often more. The prevalence of such violence occurring at least once in a relationship is likely for approximately 60 percent of American families. Domestic violence in American homes is a reliably documented fact. With a phenomenon so prevalent, therefore, we must ask, what is generating it?

Dynamics

Three levels of social life contribute to spousal violence. (Notice we do not say "cause" because some levels provide more of a context than specific determinants of violence.) The *social structural level* is the system of patriarchy endemic in this country as well as in virtually every modern society. It is about inequitable distributions of power and access to opportunity within and outside the family unit. The *cultural level* is made up of stereotypical and normative ideas about gender-appropriate behavior. The *social psychological* level is concerned with the interaction between individuals' differences and their sociocultural influences in socialization, personality, and anger-management/communication skills. What is important to emphasize is that specific experiences of violence are embedded in a structural-hierarchical context reinforced by cultural definitions of what is "normal." In other words, family violence incidences are not isolated, unrelated phenomena.

For example, Shupe, Stacey and Hazlewood (1987) studied in-depth and over a period of several years 241 known violent men (supplemented with information about 542 other violent men taken from interviews with their wives and girlfriends) who had entered counseling either because a court mandated rehabilitation or because of family pressure (such as a partner threatening to leave). They found that the economic backgrounds of violent men covered the gamut: from homeless to the financially comfortable. The same range was true for education and occupation. While the unemployment rate among violent men, whether being counseled or not, was almost double that of the national level and more than double the state's rate, white-collar professionals as well as regularly employed blue-collar workers were also solidly represented in the non-random sample.

Most importantly for the social psychological level, Shupe, Stacey, and Hazlewood (1987, 33–44) identified four critical foundations for men's spousal violence:

1. Physiological factors
2. Trauma from abuse as a child
3. Childhood learning
4. Lack of communication skills and impulse control

Physiological factors included a high rate of alcohol/substance use (true for both men and women in violent households as well as in nonviolent families) with the drugs proving to be depressants and/or disinhibitors. Nevertheless, the authors concluded that in terms of actual causation "such factors played a minor role in influencing any of the family violence we encountered" (Shupe, Stacey, and Hazlewood, 1987, 35).

Trauma from abuse as a child was a more significant issue. It gave rise to an emotional dependence of adult men on women who, however inadequately, try to express their needs and codependency with maltreatment and violence. Write the authors:

> The love/hurt/rage reactions that helpless young boys felt toward their abusive, powerful parents (for whom the boys nevertheless felt attraction) were replayed by these men in their own marriages. . . . Because many of these men found their fathers to be cold, unresponsive, or indifferent, they turned to their mothers for warmth and the protective side of parental strength. Only the mothers would give the boys positive feelings of self-worth and genuine comfort. . . . These men typically had very little to do with their own children, particularly infants and young children, as if they were aloof from or uninterested in their offspring. Actually they lacked the ability to relate fully and effectively, just as their own fathers had (Shupe, Stacey, and Hazlewood, 1987, 35).

Early childhood learning as well as lack of communication skills and poor impulse control constituted an even more important cluster of social psychological factors. For example, *the intergenerational transfer hypothesis* was a proposition initially taken for granted by many professionals in the family violence field during the mid-to-late 1970s and only empirically tested by the early 1980s. This hypothesis assumed that little boys learn to be adult batterers from watching their fathers successfully use violence in the home to settle husband-wife disputes (what social psychologists term "modeling") while little girls learn that beatings are part of the adult woman's lot in life from watching their mother-victims, a normal (however unpleasant) part of the female role as wife and homemaker. But social service providers who worked with spousal violence victims who did not have personal histories of domestic violence came to question this "conventional wisdom" (Jayaratne, 1977, 18). Indeed, interviews with large numbers of women's shelter residents have shown just the opposite trend: they report relatively low rates of having experienced or witnessed interparental or childhood violence in their homes when growing up.

Thus, generational transfer of violence must become a modified concept: it only works for learning violence as an acceptable strategy of conflict resolution, not for learning victimization. The earlier, simplistic version of the intergenerational transfer hypothesis has been criticized by others (e.g., Cappell and Heiner, 1990; Herzberger, 1983). And, interestingly, in its most recent form appears to work in the same social learning way for women as well as men. In examining past research literature as well as their own clinical research findings on 100 couples, Shupe, Stacey and Hazlewood (1987, 45–62) found that, other than instances of women's violence committed in self-defense against men's violence, the dynamics of women's violence in general were similar to those of men. Violent women, in other words, struck out in jealousy, because of limitations in anger management, because of a lack of communication skills, or with histories of past childhood trauma and abuse. In these violent couples, both partners had witnessed and internalized the pragmatic lessons of male/female violence in the home. Correspondingly, they both had been raised within a surfeit of genuine, useful, constructive strategies for effectively communicating with the opposite sex. They had, in essence, learned hitting as a mechanism for gaining attention and (however dysfunctionally) resolving disputes.

But the spousal violence issue is more than a problem of poor communications. There are, more importantly, structural issues of patriarchy and inequality in the modern family. The two most common characteristics of violent spouses, reported in numerous published testimonies, studies, and interviews, are "the need to control" and "the need to dominate." Whether out of sexist *macho* ideals of male superiority in the home or from dysfunctional male feelings of overdependence on women, there is little question that male power to direct women is the central issue in most research on spousal violence. This fact emerges in both explicitly feminist (Schechter, 1982; Okun, 1986) and sympathetic (though not necessarily feminist—see Stacey and Shupe, 1983) writings, and as in most cases of spousal violence, it crosses class and race/ethnic boundaries (Cazenave and Straus, 1991; Straus, 1991; Stark and McEvoy, 1970).

Sociological research provides insight into how these hierarchical issues have an impact on spousal abuse of women. Coleman and Straus (1991) found that when conflict (such as arguments) occurred in couples with "asymmetrical power structures" (i.e., either male-dominant or female-dominant) there was a much greater risk of violence than when conflict occurred in couples with "egalitarian" or symmetrical power structures. The latter power arrangement, they concluded, can tolerate a much greater amount of tension, conflict, and aggravation without the disagreements turning into physical violence. On the other hand, Coleman and Straus observed that the amount of agreement between both partners if an asymmetrical couple concurs as to the "legitimacy" or "appropriateness" of the power inequity was a key factor in predicting the level of conflict over family responsibilities and, ultimately, subsequent violence. For example, if the man and woman both agreed that a given arrangement such as patriarchy was desirable or acceptable, then there was less violence than when the partners in a patriarchal relationship did not agree. (However, the patriarchal relationships overall still tended to be more violent than the egalitarian ones.) The authors concluded that "the results provide one more indication of the importance of including the power structure of intimate relationships as part of an analysis of marital violence" (Coleman and Straus, 1991, 301).

In another study on a wife's marital dependency and possible abuse, Kalmuss and Straus (1991) examined the relationship between the resources a woman might or might not have (e.g., separate income, a job, presence of dependent children, and so forth) and physical abuse. Their findings confirmed the key role resources play in why women stay and endure physical violence in the home when they know it is not right or "normal." The likelihood of leaving the abusive situation is directly tied to the availability of resources "to go it alone." Earlier (Stacey and Shupe, 1983, 53ff) rejected the psychologically oriented theory of Lenore Walker (1979) that battered women stay in abusive relationships because they have become conditioned into states of "learned helplessness." Instead, they argued, look in her purse for cash, car keys, credit cards, and other signs of independent means. Likewise, Kalmuss and Straus (1991) determined that women with a high dependency on their marriages experience more physical abuse from their husbands than less dependent women.

Support for the role of patriarchy in increasing physical violence against women in homes came from a study by Yllo and Straus (1991). They found in a state-by-state analysis, examining factors such as educational levels, employment/unemployment, and women's legal rights, that where women's economic-educational-political-legal statuses were lower, female victimization rates in spousal violence were higher. In fact, "the rate declines steadily as the status of women increases" (Yllo, 1991, 394). States with the most male-dominant, traditional norms, as measured by a sophisticated set of scales, had double the rates of wifebeating as did states with the more egalitarian cultures.

Thus, the relationship between spousal violence and the hierarchical structure of many American families has been empirically established. Next we consider the other aspect of violence in this hierarchy: the victimization of children.

CHILD ABUSE AND MALTREATMENT

Two sociologists who set out to study battered women in shelters in 1979 found themselves also having to examine child abuse (since most of the women in their sample brought at least two young children with them to safe havens). They recalled the visceral reactions to child maltreatment from a wide range of persons whom they encountered in their research:

> Excluding professionals working daily with child abuse cases, no one we talked to during our research reacted dispassionately to the problem. Indeed, it aroused extraordinary vindictive anger in otherwise respectable citizens whose backgrounds ranged across a broad spectrum, such as school teachers, police officers, college presidents, ministers, university students, auto mechanics, and landlords. This anger was vehement and unrelenting. Many acquaintances and colleagues suggested without so much as batting an eye that child abusers deserved castration, execution, or worse. These abusers were even condemned as subhumans. In short, no one seemed able to separate personal emotional outrage from objective attempts to understand the phenomenon (Stacey and Shupe, 1983, 61).

Such reactions manifest a sensitized viewpoint of children's special vulnerability by modern Western standards. But it was not always so. A variety of scholars have traced the sad historical and cross-cultural patterns of child maltreatment (Boswell, 1989; Chase, 1975; Radbill, 1974). Two experts in human development relate: "When we examine the history of mankind, whether from paleontological evidence, documentary accounts such as the Bible, or culture-specific myths and fairy tales, we see evidence of children being mistreated, abandoned, sacrificed, or eaten to go along with evidence of their being cuddled, nurtured, and encouraged" (Burgess and Garbarino, 1983, 88). Many historians even argue that the very concept of childhood as we moderns understand it did not exist before the seventeenth century.

The source of much of this abuse can be located in the taken-for-granted perspective that has existed for millennia that children (particularly females) are the property of their families—patriarchal, hierarchical families (Tower, 1989). In Roman society, for example, the father's rights under the law included killing or maiming a son or daughter, sacrificing him or her to the gods, or even selling children as slaves. This ownership principle has receded slowly in Western civilization. The later European feudal system continued much of the Roman hierarchical principle giving adult men power over women and putting children, particularly poor children, at the bottom. It was not until the Renaissance that some recognition of children's special needs emerged. For example, only in 1548 and 1576, respectively, did England pass laws to provide some shielding of children (as we now define children) from sexual abuse. In the first instance a law was created protecting boys from forced sodomy; in the second instance a law was enacted prohibiting forcible rape of girls under the age of ten. And in 1601 the Elizabethan poor laws recognized orphaned or abandoned children as a class or group entitled to special relief (Tower, 1989: 2–5).

Yet maltreatment legally unacceptable today in the United States continued. In the nineteenth century it was still common for parents to indenture (or apprentice) their children from an early age into their teenage years under working conditions that were often appalling. One only has to read Charles Dickens's *Oliver Twist* to catch a flavor of such exploitation. Sociologist Dean Knudsen (1992, 6–10), summarizing the literature on this subject, observes that it was only during the period of high industrialization in North America during the 1880s and 1890s that the vulnerability and exploitation of children became issues. The rise of unions, Victorian perspectives that women belonged in the home rather than in the workplace, and the rising tide of immigrants from Europe all played roles in forging this new concern for children (recall the case of Mary Ellen mentioned earlier in this chapter). It is also not coincidental that both psychology and sociology—both disciplines that began to examine the dynamics of socialization and childhood development—arose during this era. Indeed, many of the early behavioral scientists were activists in "progressive" movements such as child labor reform.

But the problem of child labor, as just one form of child abuse or maltreatment, is still endemic on a global level. For years the United Nations International Labor Organization has reported that children continue to be at risk, not just from disease and malnutrition (see our chapter on structural violence) but also from systematic murder (see our later chapter on state violence).

Unfortunately, on the global level the problem will persist for the indefinite future. Poverty is too great a reality in many countries to spare families the necessity of their children working. And the United States, once a leader in pressing for laws ending the exploitation of child labor, is not helping. President George Bush Sr. refused to sign the 1989 UN Convention on the Rights of the Child that argued against such exploitation (curiously on the grounds that the UN law might not agree with U.S. laws). Likewise, U.S. Representative Dan J. Pease of Ohio introduced a bill forbidding importation of goods made by foreign exploited child labor, but the U.S. Congress stalled action on it.

So exploitation of child labor and physical and sexual abuse are still rampant worldwide. Mpondah (1990), citing a recent report published by the International Labor Organization, notes that at least 100 million young boys and girls around the world are working. The report points out that most of these children are poor recent migrants from rural areas and that they are most likely employed in unsafe conditions for long hours at a time. Most children are still helplessly at the bottom of an often-unkind hierarchy, with the youngest the farthest down. In this country child labor has some controls on it, but violence against children has not ended by any means.

Patterns

Given the extensive financial costs and personal care and attention that raising a healthy child usually entails, and considering the known amounts of abuse and neglect that many of our fellow citizens heap on the young children they have created, Kenneth Kenniston in 1975 (at that time chairman and executive director of the Carnegie Council on Children) asked in the title of an article, "Do Americans Really Like Children?" His point concerned the love-hate ambivalence that so many parents display toward their children. (In that sense, child maltreatment mirrors the emotional ambivalence many abusive spouses show toward each other.) The child's dependence on the more powerful parent is both a source of affection and of frustration for many adults. Scholars and child advocates typically define child abuse as the deliberate and willful injury of a child by a caretaker adult, most often by hitting, binding, burning, cutting, or pushing (including sexual abuse). Neglect can be more passive and even subtle: treatment of the child that does not adequately (by pediatric and legal standards) care for emotional and physical needs or provide a healthy chance to pass into adulthood. It is a lack of basic nurturance, in other words, and as one might expect, legal definitions and opinions about what constitutes neglect are more variable from state to state and community to community than are ones for physical abuse (Chase, 1975, 1).

As with the case of woman battering, the figures on the extent of child maltreatment are often rough estimates, for most child abuse and neglect is never reported or is covered up by the abusers. Many times the victims are too young to tell anyone outside the home or to leave home. The child may have been socialized by parents to believe that he or she deserved "appropriate" punishment for some mistake. There are also, to be sure, as with the case of men's traditional "right" to discipline women in the patriarchal home, cultural norms of the "spare the rod and spoil the child" variety that instruct fathers and mothers to incorporate corporal punishment into childrearing. And in reporting violence against the child there is also the problem that both parents can conspire to hide any maltreatment for what they perceive as the good of their overall family relationship, even if only one of them is directly abusing the young person.

Knudsen (1992, 40–47) points out that we basically have four sources of information on child maltreatment: self-reports of victims and perpetrators (sometimes retrospectively obtained), studies done of professionals/agents/clients that deal with the problem, official reports, and "evaluated reports" (that is, cases in which a thorough substantiation of each incident is made). What do all these sources tell us?

Sociologist David Gil is one of the premier researchers on the subject of child abuse. He estimated in 1965 that there was anywhere from 2.5 million to 4 million abused children in the United States (1975, 1970). (There are approximately 63 million children aged 0–17 years in this country.) Critics quickly charged that he had greatly exaggerated the problem, but an official study published by the U.S. Department of Health and Human Services pushed the figures of known abuse incidents back toward Gil's original levels. The National Center on Child Abuse and Neglect reported that their estimate of 652,000 instances every year in this country was a bare minimum number. And in a footnote the report followed this figure with another estimate: "Very likely, the actual number of children abused and neglected annually in the U.S. is at least

1,000,000" (U.S. Department of Health and Human Services, 1988, 3). A recent report by UNICEF (Grant, 1994) noted that reported child abuse cases had tripled during the 1980s. James Grant, executive director of UNICEF, claims that today three children die each day from maltreatment in the United States.

Sociologists Murray A. Straus and Richard J. Gelles looked for evidence of violence against children in both their 1975 and 1985 surveys. They found that young children (0–3 years) were almost all struck (even if only spanked) during both 1975 and 1985. In 1985 (extrapolating to the general population) 6.9 million children 0–17 years experienced what the researchers rated as severe violence, and 1.5 million experienced what was termed very severe violence. And this the researchers learned in spite of the fact that all the acts of violence were self-reported by the parents!

Curiously, Straus and Gelles report a drop of 47 percent in reports of severely violent incidents against children from 1975 to 1985, but they consider such a drop to represent differences in the ways questions were worded in the two studies and to many adult Americans' greater sensitivity to the child abuse issue, hence their reluctance to admit it (Straus and Gelles, 1991a). Nevertheless, despite the fact that there are now compulsory child abuse reporting laws in all fifty states, comparisons of the Straus-Gelles 1985 National Resurvey rates for child abuse with the rates of cases known to the Child Protective Services agencies of each state reveal that the incident rates found by the former are about three and one-half times greater than the number of abuse cases known to the CPS agencies. Straus and Gelles (1991b, 111) report: "If child abuse is defined to include hitting a child with an object, then the survey rate is about sixteen times greater than the number of cases reported to protective service agencies in 1985.

Official rates of violence against children have risen dramatically in recent years. For instance, a 1988 national study sponsored by the U.S. Department of Health and Human Services, the National Center and Child Abuse and Neglect, and other federal agencies discovered that since the last major federally sponsored national survey in 1986 there have been significant increases in reporting various kinds of child abuse. To take one illustration: the number of reports of sexual abuse tripled in just two years (xiii–7.5). But many experts, such as Knudsen (1992, 26–37), do not see the United States suddenly undergoing any "epidemic" of adult violence against children. It is simply being recognized and reported more frequently. Douglas J. Besharov, former director of the National Center on Child Abuse and Neglect, has observed that "years of public awareness campaigns and professional education have had their intended effect. Americans are much more sensitive to the plight of maltreated children, and are more willing than ever to report suspected cases" (Besharov, 1988). In fact, some critics have charged that some overzealous "child-savers" are going overboard, creating a child abuse "industry" (Best, 1990, Pride, 1986), reading satanic ritual abuse into situations where violence against children may not even have occurred (Richardson et al., 1991, Shupe, 1991), and creating a hysteria that, for innocent persons falsely accused by "child-savers," has become akin to the seventeenth-century Salem witch hunt (Gardner, 1991). At any rate, several million children are at risk of serious violence every year, and unlike spousal violence, most of the perpetration is flowing in one direction.

Dynamics

All family members are capable of emotional maltreatment of one another, and most will have engaged in such psychological abuse at one time or another. Emotional abuse and neglect of children occur most often in families possessing the fewest resources, be these financial, interactive skill-related, or psychological (Knudsen, 1992, 95). The same is true of physical abuse of children. But precisely what causes adult violence toward children in some homes rather than others is a matter of debate. Actually the debate is not so much over what factors are involved as much as over which ones are the most important determiners. Confounding matters is the fact that the dynamics of violence are often not the same in different families. Here is a classic case of the interface of sociological (contextual) parameters within which psychological (individual) differences can operate. Furthermore, the twin notions of patriarchy/hierarchy play an important role in producing the violence.

In recent years there has been a move away from individualistic psychodynamic (i.e., personality) explanations toward more social psychological models that incorporate dimensions of the social environment (Tower, 1989). A recent review (Knudsen, 1992, 63–5) surveying dozens of clinical studies of psychological factors of batterers turned up the following characteristics: (1) low self-esteem of the violent adult and poor self-concept that fosters feelings that one needs constantly to reinforce or "prove" one's control over the members of the family unit; (2) poorly developed perceptual/attentive/decision-making skills; (3) unrealistic expectations of children's abilities and self-control as well as of the rewards of child-rearing in general; and (4) relatively low levels of adult emotional status and competence.

As Shupe, Stacey and Hazlewood (1987, 33) observe, violence in the home is often "over-determined." This means that one spouse's violence against another, or against a child, "is likely to be a product of more than one cause of influence working simultaneously." Thus, in any single instance of child abuse it is statistically impossible to portion out precisely how much of any of the four factors above contributed to the violence.

Likewise, there have been investigations of victimization, that is, what characteristics of the young victims render them to become more likely targets of violence. These include (1) being born out of wedlock, hence resented by both father and mother; (2) being born prematurely, hence presenting special needs that require greater cost and attention; (3) being born with a congenital infirmity (i.e., deformed and retarded), hence less immediately attractive; and (4) becoming a stepchild (Tower, 1989, 62–3).

Finally, sociological factors in the adult violence-against-children problem include environmental stress, socioeconomic status, gender, and cultural reinforcers. *Environmental stress* works social psychologically through the phenomenon of *excitation (arousal) transfer* which leads an adult already hassled or angered from some other source to take out (or displace) his or her frustration on a child who may simply be boisterous or in some other way behaving perfectly normally for his or her age. *Socioeconomic status* can be a stressor, particularly where one parent is unemployed, hospitalized, or imprisoned. For example, Stacey and Shupe (1983: 86) found in a study of battered women and their children (many of whom were also abused) that unemployment among abusive men was more than double the highest unemployment rate in their metropolitan area over a two-year period. Likewise, Straus and Smith (1991a, 249–51) found that while official reports show that child advocacy agencies process greater numbers of low-income persons, representative surveys also reveal that lower-income families experience greater rates of such violence. Some of the higher rate for violence against children in these families may be due to an authoritarian style of child-rearing, greater acceptance of physical punishment, and less understanding of child psychology that sociologists have long documented (Kohn, 1969), but as Straus and Smith point out, low-income areas also have high rates of violence outside the home as well.

Gender is also an issue (however controversial): patriarchal family structure has traditionally placed women in a role primarily responsible for child-rearing. In modern North America, where the family is often a mixture of patriarchal authority and egalitarian economics (i.e., both spouses work), stressors are even greater for women who find themselves in the role-conflictive position of being nurturer/bread-winner/social controller of children's behavior. Straus and Smith (1991) found in the 1985 Straus-Gelles National Resurvey that women are essentially as abusive of their own children as are men. Such a finding emphasizes the significance of social (as opposed to psychodynamic) factors in making sense of child abuse. Women, it has long been established, are much less unlikely to be violent outside the home than men. Thus, Straus and Smith conclude, the reasons why women are violent in the home are better explained by their social roles than by any personality characteristics that would otherwise be expected to show up across various social situations within and outside the home.

As feminists have argued over the past two decades, *cultural reinforcers* (i.e., norms and values) play a critical contextual role in approving or excusing forms of family violence. The same logic that "permits" a man to beat his wife in the quest for domestic harmony and order also "forgives" him for exercising physical, even painful control over recalcitrant children. By extension of patriarchal logic, the woman (as an agent of the man's authority) then is also justified in exercising such control.

FAMILY VIOLENCE IN A GLOBAL HIERARCHICAL PERSPECTIVE

The family violence problem in the United States is widespread, and, from a researcher's perspective, somewhat intimidating in its enormity. There are so many aspects that we cannot even touch on here, such as abuse of the elderly ("granny bashing") by their adult children. But out of all the rich data collected by the Family Research Laboratory at the University of New Hampshire, Straus (1983) stresses that one fact emerges: violence begets violence, so children in violent homes are more likely to be violent towards their siblings and later in their adult relationships with partners as well as with their own children.

We indicated earlier that child maltreatment occurs worldwide. In some ways the United States sees less of the worst cases than many other countries. We have, for example, no teenage or preteen girls sold to legalized brothels by their parents. But there is evidence that men's violence against women in the United States may be closely equivalent to that of other Western countries as varied as England, New Zealand, Canada, Scotland (Dobash and Dobash, 1979; Burgess and Garbarino, 1983), France, and even Papua New Guinea (Neal, 1992). Likewise, studies have been done of Afro-Caribbean women (Morrow, 1992) and in South Asian families in the United States (Abraham, 1992). Meanwhile, Denmark now even has its first "halfway house" for battered men ("Help for husbands," 1991).

Violence against women is worse in non-Western societies where traditions of patriarchy are even more ingrained and concepts of equal rights for both sexes are less developed. Mary Daly (1978) catalogues in gruesome detail how men have subordinated women through the centuries by binding their feet (Manchu-dynasty China), mutilating (i.e., circumcising) their genitals, immolating them as "dutiful wives" in ritual funeral fires with the bodies of their deceased husbands (the Hindu ritual of *suttee*), and torturing them (along with males) in Nazi pseudo-scientific experiments. In modern India dowry deaths, in which a woman who has contributed a dowry to her husband's family upon marriage is killed by her husband or in-laws, are becoming more common as women are becoming emancipated, increasingly involved in the labor force and exposed to nontraditional lifestyle options, and resistant to patriarchy (Rao, 1992; Kumari, 1989).

Thus, violence in the home, within a place usually thought of as a safe haven from an often unfeeling and even brutal world, can ironically feed on the properties of intimacy that most of us consider normal for a family. A major reason that such violence is so widespread and so systematic is that most families are hierarchies, with unequal distribution of power and decision-making authority. Perceived threats to that authority can be dealt with in a variety of ways, but obviously one strategy is the violence option. To that extent the relationships among power, conflict and violence in the home resemble those in the large asymmetric hierarchy of society.

REFERENCES

Abraham, Margaret. 1992. "Marital Violence among South Asians in the United States." Unpublished paper presented at the annual meeting of the *American Sociological Association*, Pittsburgh.

Attorney General, 1984. *Attorney General's Task Force on Family Violence.* Washington, D.C.: Government Printing Office.

Bakan, David. 1971. *Slaughter of the Innocents: A Study of the Battered Child Phenomenon.* Boston: Beacon Press.

Berk, Richard A., Sarah Fenstermaker Berk, Donileen R. Loseke, and David Rauma. 1983. "Mutual Combat and Other Family Violence Myths." In *The Dark Side of Families*, ed. R.J.G. David Finkelhor, Gerald T. Hataling, and Murray A. Straus, 197–212. Newbury Park, Calif.: Sage.

Besharov, Douglas J. 1988, August 4. "The Child Abuse Numbers Game." *Wall Street Journal.*

Best, Joel. 1990. *Threatened Children: Rhetoric and Concern about Child-Victims.* Chicago: University of Chicago Press.

Blum, Alan, and Gary Fisher. 1978. "Women Who Kill." In *Violence: Perspectives on Murder and Aggression*, ed. Irwin L. Kutash, Samuel B. Kutash, Louis B. Schlesinger, and Associates, 187–91. San Francisco: Jossey-Bass.

Boswell, John. 1989. *The Kindness of Strangers.* New York: Random House

Burgess, Robert L., and James Garbarino. 1983. "Doing What Comes Naturally?" In *The Dark Side of Families*, ed. by David Finkelhor, Richard J. Gelles, Gerald T. Hotaling, and Murray A. Straus, 88–100. Newbury Park, Calif.: Sage.

Cardarelli, Albert P. 1997. "Violence and Intimacy: An Overview." In *Violence between Intimate Partners*, ed. Albert P. Cardarelli, 1–9. Needham Heights, Mass.: Allyn & Bacon.

Cappell, Charles and Robert Heiner. 1990. "The Intergenerational Transmission of Family Aggression." *Journal of Family Violence* 5 (2): 135–52.

Cazenave, Noel A., and Murray A. Straus. 1991. "Race, class, network embeddedness and family violence: a search for potent support systems." In *Physical Violence in American Families*, ed. Murray A. Straus and Richard J. Gelles, 321–39. New Brunswick, N.J.: Transaction Books.

Chase, Naomi. 1975. *A Child Is Being Beaten.* New York: McGraw-Hill.

Coleman, Diane H., and Murray A. Straus. 1991. "Marital Power, Conflict, and Violence in a Nationally Representative Sample of American Couples." In *Physical Violence in American Families*, ed. Murray A. Straus and Richard J. Gelles, 287–304. New Brunswick, N.J.: Transaction Books.

Collins, Randall, 1971. "A Conflict Theory of Sexual Stratification." *Social Problems* 19: 3–20.

Connell, R. W. 1987. *Gender and Power.* Stanford, Calif.: Stanford University Press.

Daly, Mary. 1978. *Gyn/Ecology: The Metaethics of Radical Feminism.* Boston: Beacon Press.

Dobash, R. Emerson, and Russell P. Dobash. 1977. "Wives: the 'Appropriate' Victims of Marital Violence." *Victimology: An International Journal* 2: 426–42.

———. 1979. *Violence against Wives: A Case Against Patriarchy.* New York: The Free Press.

Dobash, Russell P., E. Emerson Dobash, M. Wilson, and M. Daly, 1992. "The Myth of Sexual Symmetry in Marital Violence." *Social Problems* 39: 71–91.

Dutton, A. 1988. *The Domestic Assault of Women: Psychological and Criminal Justice Perspectives.* New York: Allyn and Bacon.

Gardner, Richard A. 1991. *Sex Abuse Hysteria: Salem Witch Trials Revisited.* Cresskill: Creative Therapeutics.

Gil, David. 1970. *Violence against Children.* Cambridge, Mass.: Harvard University Press.

———. 1975. "Child Abuse: Levels of Manifestation, Causal Dimensions, and Primary Prevention." *Victimology: An International Journal* 2: 186–94.

Gillespie, Cynthia. 1981. *Justifiable Homicide: Battered Women, Self-Defense, and the Law.* Columbus: Ohio State University Press.

Gondolf, Edward W. 1988. "The State of the Debate: Review Essay on Woman Battering." *Response* 11: 3–8.

Grant, James. 1994, February 3. *The State of the World's Children.* Oxford: Oxford University Press. "Help for Husbands." *Parade,* 1.

Herzberger, Sharon, 1983. "Social Cognition and the Transmission of Abuse." In *The Dark Side of Families: Current Family Violence Research,* ed. David Finkelhor, Richard Gelles, G. Hotaling, and Murray Strauss, 317–29. Beverly Hills, Calif.: Sage.

Herzeberger, Sharon D., and Noreen L. Channels. 1991. "Criminal justice processing of violent and nonviolent offenders: the effects of familial relationship to the victim." In *Abused and Battered,* ed. by Dean. D. Knudsen and J. L. Miller, 63–78. New York: Aldine de Gruyter.

Island, David, and Patrick Letellier. 1991. *Men Who Beat the Men Who Love Them: Battered Gay Men and Domestic Violence.* New York: Harrington Park Press.

Jayaratne, Srinika. 1977. "Child Abusers as Parents and Children: A Review." *Social Work* 22 (January): 17–29.

Kalmuss, Ebra S., and Murray A. Straus. 1991. "Wife's marital dependency and wife abuse." In *Physical Violence in American Families,* ed. Murray A. Straus and Richard J. Gelles, 369–82. New Brunswick, N.J.: Transaction Publishers.

Keniston, Kenneth. 1975. "Do Americans Really Like Children?" *Today's Education* 64: 16–21.

Knudsen, Dean D. 1992. *Child Maltreatment: Emerging Perspectives.* Dix Hills: General Hall.

Kohn, Melvin L. 1969. *Class and Conformity: A Study in Values.* Homewood, Ill.: Dorsey Press.

Kumari, Ranjana. 1989. *Brides Are Not for Burning: Dowry Victims in India.* New Delhi, India: Radiant Publishers.

Little, Craig B., 1995. *Deviance and Control.* 3rd ed. Itasca, Ill.: F. E. Peacock Publishers.

McLeod, M. 1984. "Women against Men: An Examination of Domestic Violence Based on an Analysis of Official Data and National Victimization Data." *Justice Quarterly* 1: 171–93.

McNeely, R. L., and Gloria Robinson-Simpson. 1987, November-December. "The Truth about Domestic Violence: A Falsely Framed Issue." *Social Work* 485–90.

Miller, Susan L. and Charles F. Wellford. 1997. "Patterns and Correlates of Interpersonal Violence." In *Violence between Intimate Partners,* ed. Albert P. Cardarelli, 16–28. Needham Heights, Mass.: Allen & Bacon.

Moore, Angela M., 1997. "Intimate Violence: Does Socioeconomic Status Matter." In *Violence between Intimate Partners,* ed. Albert P. Cardarelli, 90–100. Needham Heights, Mass.: Allen & Bacon.

Morrow, Betty Hearn. 1992. "Afro-Caribbean Women and Domestic Violence." Unpublished paper presented at the annual meeting of the American Sociological Association, Pittsburgh.

Mpondah, Dingaan. 1990. "Million Youngsters." In *Third World Guide 91/92*, ed. R. R. Bissio, 38–39. Montevideo, Uruguay: Garamond Press.

Neal, Andrea. 1992, June 20. "My generation." *Indianapolis Star*.

Nisonoff, L., and I. Bitman. 1979. "Spouse Abuse: Incidence and Relationship to Selected Demographic Variables." *Victimology: An International Journal* 4: 131–40.

Okun, Lewis. 1986. *Woman Abuse: Facts Replacing Myths*. Albany: SUNY Press.

Phillips, Roderick. 1988. *Putting Asunder: A History of Divorce in Western Society*. New York: Cambridge University Press.

Pride, Mary. 1986. *The Child Abuse Industry*. Westchester, Ill.: Crossway Books.

Radbill, S. X. 1974. "A History of Child Abuse and Infanticide." In *The Battered Child*, ed. Ray E. Helfer and C. Henry Kempe, 3–24. Chicago: University of Chicago Press.

Rao, Neeraja. 1992. "Dowry Deaths in India." Unpublished paper presented at the annual meeting of the North Central Sociological Association, Fort Wayne, Ind.

Renzetti, Claire M. 1992. *Violent Betrayal: Partner Abuse in Lesbian Relationships*. Newbury Park, Calif.: Sage.

Renzetti, Claire M. 1997. "Violence and Abuse among Same-Sex Couples." In Albert P. Cardarelli, ed., *Violence between Intimate Partners*. Needham Heights, MA: Allyn & Bacon, 70–89. Richardson, James T., Joel Best, and David G. Bromley. 1991. *The Satanism Scare*. New York: Aldine de Gruyter.

Scanzoni, John. 1978. *Sex Roles, Women's Work, and Marital Conflict*. Lexington, Mass.: Lexington Books.

Schechter, Susan. 1982. *Women and Male Violence*. Boston: South End Press.

Schlegel, Alice. 1977. "Toward a Theory of Sexual Stratification." In *Sexual Stratification: A Cross-Cultural View*. ed. A. Schlegel, 1–40. New York: Columbia University Press.

Shupe, Anson. 1991. *The Darker Side of Virtue*. Buffalo, N.Y.: Prometheus Books.

Shupe, Anson, William A. Stacey, and Lonnie R. Hazlewood. 1987. *Violent Men, Violent Couples: The Dynamics of Domestic Violence*. Lexington, Mass.: Lexington Books.

Stacey, William A., Lonnie R. Hazlewood, and Anson Shupe. 1994. *The Violent Couple*. Westport, Conn.: Praeger Publishers.

Stacey, William A., and Anson Shupe. 1983. *The Family Secret: Domestic Violence in America*. Boston: Beacon Press.

Stark, Rodney, and James McEvoy III. 1970. "Middle Class Violence." *Psychology Today* 4: 52–65.

Steinmetz, Suzanne K. 1977. "The Battered Husband Syndrome." *Victimology: An International Journal* 2: 499–509.

Stets, Jane E., and Murray A. Straus. 1991. "Gender Differences in Reporting Marital Violence and its Medical and Psychological Consequences." In *Physical Violence in American Families*, ed. Murray A. Straus and Richard J. Gelles, 151–65. New Brunswick, N.J.: Transaction Books.

Straus, Murray A. 1983. "Ordinary Violence, Child Abuse, and Wife-Beating: What Do they have in Common?" In *The Dark Side of Families*, ed. Richard J. Gelles, Daniel Finkelhor, Gerald T. Hotaling, and Murray A. Straus, 213–34. Newbury Park, Calif.: Sage.

———. 1991. "Physical Violence in American Families: Incidence Rates, Causes, and Trends." In *Abused and Battered*, ed. Dean D. Knudsen and J. Miller, 17–34. New York: Aldine de Gruyter.

Straus, Murray A., Richard J. Gelles, and Suzanne K. Steinmetz. 1980. *Behind Closed Doors: Violence in the American Family*. New York: Doubleday/Anchor.

Straus, Murray A., and Christine Smith. 1991a. "Family Patterns and Child Abuse." In *Physical Violence in American Families*, ed. Murray A. Straus and Richard J. Gelles, 245–61. New Brunswick, N.J.: Transaction Books.

Straus, Murray A., and Christine Smith. 1991b. "Violence in Hispanic Families in the United States: Incidence Rates and Structural Interpretations." In *Physical Violence in American Families*, ed. Murray A. Straus and Richard J. Gelles, 341–67. New Brunswick, N.J.: Transaction Books.

Straus, Murray A., and Richard J. Gelles. 1991a. "Societal Change and Change in Family Violence from 1975 to 1985 as Revealed by Two National Surveys." In *Physical Violence in American Families*, ed. Murray A. Straus and Richard J. Gelles, 113–31. New Brunswick, N.J.: Transaction Books.

Straus, Murray A., and Richard J. Gelles. 1991b. "How Violent Are American families? Estimates from the National Family Violence Resurvey and other studies." In *Physical Violence in American Families*, ed. Murray A. Straus and Richard J. Gelles, 95–112. New Brunswick, N.J.: Transaction Books.

Straus, Murray A., and Richard J. Gelles, eds. 1991c. *Physical Violence in American Families*. New Brunswick, N.J.: Transaction Books.

Taves, Ann. 1989. *Religion and Domestic Violence: The Memoirs of Abigail Abbot Bailey*. Bloomington: Indiana University Press.

Tiger, Lionel. 1970. *Men in Groups*. New York: Vintage Books.

Tower, Cynthia Crossan. 1989. *Understanding Child Abuse and Neglect*. Boston: Allyn and Bacon.

U.S. Commission on Civil Rights. 1982. "Under the Rule of Thumb: Battered Women and the Administration of Justice." Washington, D.C.: U.S. Commission on Civil Rights.

U. S. Department of Health and Human Services. 1988. *Study of National Incidence and Prevalence of Child Abuse and Neglect: 1988*. Washington, D.C.: Government Printing Office.

Walker, Lenore. 1979. *The Battered Woman*. New York: Harper and Row.

Whyte, Martin White. 1978. *The Status of Women in Preindustrial Societies*. Princeton, N.J.: Princeton University Press.

Wolfgang, Marvin. 1978. "Violence in the Family." In *Violence: Perspectives on Murder and Aggression*, edited by S. B. Irwin, L. Kutash, Louis B. Schlesinger, and Associates, 58–69. San Francisco: Jossey-Bass.

Yllo, Kersti A., and Murray A. Straus. 1991. "Patriarchy and violence against wives: the impact of structural and normative factors." In *Physical Violence in American Families*, ed. Murray A. Straus and Richard J. Gelles, 383–99. New Brunswick, N.J.: Transaction Books.

Chapter Five

Religious Violence

The question of how many people at Jonestown willingly took the poison always will be open to debate. Certainly young children could not have evaluated very well what their actions would mean. The presence of armed guards shows at least implicit coercion, though the guards themselves reported their intentions to visitors in glorious terms and then took the poison. No one rushed up to tip over the vat of Fla-Vor-Aid. Wittingly, unknowingly, or reluctantly, they took the poison (Hall, 1989, xii).

Joshua continued his wars of conquest until a total of thirty-one kings and thirty-one cities were overthrown and all of the inhabitants put to death. Assuming the cities averaged 10,000 people, Joshua slaughtered about 310,000 people inhabiting that part of Palestine which was reduced to his command (Scott, 1979, 66).

In 1171 at Blois, France, thirty-eight Jewish leaders were sentenced to death because the mayor's servant thought he saw a Jew throw a child's body into the river—even though no body was found and no child was missing. The thirty-eight were given a chance to save their lives by converting to Christianity, but they refused. They were locked in a wooden shed, which was burned (Haught, 1990, 44).

Religion is usually regarded as a force for goodwill and nonviolence among human beings, a positive set of beliefs and values undergirding social order, law, and harmony. This conventional wisdom holds that the greater the consensus among people about the fundamentals of religious truths, the greater the reduction in misunderstandings, discrimination, violence, and other social problems that have a moral dimension.

In reality, the truth-claims of various religions often inspire invidiousness, hostility, and intolerance. Religion can inflame passions of outrage and fear that motivate not just individual believers but also, on occasion, entire soci-

174

eties to repress or eliminate "non-believers." Violence thereby becomes an ironic servant to the ultimate goal of ushering in, or enforcing, utopian schemes thought to be divinely ordained.

Thus, starting in 1979, a virtual reign of terror existed in Iran. It was in large part initiated by fundamentalist Muslim mullah (holy leader) the Ayatollah Ruhollah Khomeini in an attempt to turn his nation away from "Satanic" Western influence toward a "pure" revolutionary Islam. Meanwhile, a group of virtually harmless non-Islamics called Baha'is literally became an endangered species in that country. The religion of Baha'ism originated in mid-nineteenth-century Persia. It is a faith that recognizes Moses, Jesus of Nazareth, and Mohammed as successive prophets of God, to be joined by a Persian mystic named Baha'ullah who felt called to spread a Quaker-like message of peace, love, and universal spiritual unity. The Ayatollah decided that the 300,000 Baha'is living in Iran presented a subversive presence to the Islamic revolution and began a systematic campaign of persecution. Tens of thousands of Baha'is fled the country. Thousands of those remaining were rounded up for summary kangaroo court trials, torture, imprisonment, and given a choice of either conversion to Islam or execution. By the late 1980s over 400 had been hung or shot, and in some instances the government even coerced the families of victims to pay for the firing squads' bullets before letting them claim their loved ones bodies (Wright, 1989, 106, 181). Since traditional Islamic law prohibits capital punishment for female virgins, some Baha'i women and girls were reportedly first raped in the prison cells by Iranian soldiers before being executed (Haught, 1990, 202).

A more recent example would be the Taliban regime, extremist Muslims in Afghanistan, which enacted a series of social taboos (that movies and music be banned, that women follow severe restrictions on their dress and public appearances, that all men grow beards, and so forth) and destroyed artistic expressions of all non-Islamic religions. They appeared to have been sponsored by and harbored terrorists, particularly the al-Qaida network and Saudi Arabian Osama bin Laden who was one of the instigators of the September 11, 2001, horrific attacks on New York's World Trade Center towers and the Pentagon. Another series of examples would be the Palestinian suicide bombers and shooters who have indiscriminately killed Israeli citizens in public places such as markets, cafes, and shopping malls. They have been revered by their co-nationalists as heroes and martyrs. It is unknown as to whether the deaths of these Palestinians will ever hasten their goal of statehood, but such violence has indisputably achieved destructive reprisals by the Israeli army and many more resulting deaths among Palestinians than Israelis.

The French philosopher Blaise Pascal pessimistically observed about violence and religion: "Men never do evil so completely and cheerfully as when they do it from religious conviction" (cited in Evans, 1968, 210). Likewise,

Thomas Jefferson (1954, 160), commenting on Christianity's tendency over the past 2,000 years to enforce religion at the point of a sword, concluded:

> Millions of innocent men, women, and children, since the introduction of Christianity, have been burned, tortured, fined, and imprisoned, yet we have not advanced one inch toward conformity. What has been the effect of coercion? To make one half of the world fools and the other half hypocrites. To support roguery and error all over the earth.

A conflict perspective on the spiritual aspect of the violence phenomenon points to the fact that a human symbolic creation, religion, over the past five known millennia has produced a myriad of cases wherein religionists have dehumanized, slain, and tortured countless millions of their fellow human beings. Such massacres are in no way abnormal. Religion is, in the end, about power: power not just to ensure one's salvation and immortality, or to be healed, or to find succor in times of grief, but also power to control, enslave, thwart, and destroy. Religion buttresses the social realities of believers and justifies that all-too-human tendency to create walls between in-groups and out-groups, between the "saved" and the "damned," between true believers and infidels. Religion also legitimizes regimes and systems of inequality and is often seized upon by elites, from the brutal empires of antiquity to such modern nation-states as pre–World War II Imperial Japan, Nazi Germany, and Khomeini-era Iran.

In this chapter we consider several general categories of religious violence. These cases are illustrative but in no sense comprehensive, since it would require many volumes to handle the topic in full detail.

RELIGIOUS WARS AND CRUSADES

Wars between the defenders of separate religions and crusades (which really amount to the same thing) are the violent outcomes of collisions among competing sacred symbol systems. To take one recent example: modern Lebanon, a once-beautiful, thriving urban center, is now largely in ruins, scarred with acres of crumbling bombed-out buildings and left with a shattered economy. There various Muslim and Christian sectarians (Sunnis, Shiites, Druzes, Marionites, Alawites, and Jews) who previously lived in peaceful tolerance now arm themselves in shifting, violent alliances for and against each other as well as with Syrians, Palestinians, Israelis, and numerous terrorist organizations. Over 130,000 Lebanese citizens have died in the civil war thus far, not to mention 241 U.S. Marines killed in 1983 while sleeping in their barracks near the Beirut Airport when a terrorist on a suicide mission drove a truckload of explosives into the building (Martin, 1988, 125–45).

Religious wars also serve to legitimate imperialistic conquest of other nations under the guise of the need to save those who are to be dominated by means of religious enlightenment. In reality they are conquests for territory, resources, and markets. Probably the most spectacular series of such religious conflicts were the nine separate Christian Crusades that took place between the eleventh and thirteen centuries. The First Crusade began in 1095 when Pope Urban II preached spiritual revival and a call to arms following the capture of Jerusalem by Turkish forces (and an appeal to the West for military assistance by Alexius, Emperor of Constantinople). Under the Truce of God the Church had for a half century previously attempted to limit feudal warfare. Now, at the Council of Trent, Urban II was attempting to recruit knights for his crusade. Urban offered to all "knights who with pious intent took the Cross would earn a remission from temporal penalties for all his sins; if he died in battle he would earn remission of his sins" (Cohn, 1971, 61). Urban also recognized that there would be material gains and that knights who were in constant battle over the shortage of land would reap new lands as an outcome of the Crusade. At the time the Christian Church, as well as Europe in general, was in an expansionist mood. Agricultural improvements, swelling populations, developing urban areas, and religious passions for reform and conversion were all pressuring Western Europeans to look Eastward. Moreover, the church was concerned with channeling the growing power of the military estate into an extended enterprise that did not threaten the church's own authority at home (Rowling 1979, 106ff) while steering knights away from innumerable petty wars and violent exploitation of the peasantry (Gies, 1984, 17ff).

The typical Crusader, while often sincere in his idealistic quest to reclaim Jerusalem and free the Holy Land from the Saracens, was also in it for the adventure and the spoils to be won. He was also ethnocentric to the extreme, a fact that no doubt contributed to the merciless behavior of crusading armies. Writes historian Robert Payne (1984, 352) of these soldiers for Christ:

> They despised the Saracens, knew very little about them, believed that God was on their side, and were quite certain that their civilization was far superior to the civilization of the Arabs at a time when it would have been clear to a visitor from another planet that in the sciences, philosophy, theology, medicine, and poetry, the Arabs were far more advanced than the West.

The Crusaders (whether French, German, English, Flemish, or Spanish) lustily raped, looted, and massacred both Muslim and unlucky Christian populations on their paths through the Middle East and perceived the gore and destruction they caused as part of a divine strategy. Raymond of Aquilers, a contemporary chronicler and eyewitness to the slaughter of Muslims in Jerusalem, recorded the violence with a relish for religiously inspired violence that compares well to the Ayatollah Khomeini's:

> Wonderful things were to be seen. Numbers of the Saracens were beheaded. . . . Others were shot with arrows, or forced to jump from the towers; others were tortured for several days, then burned in flames. In the streets were seen piles of heads and hands and feet.

One rode about everywhere amid the corpses of men and horses. . . . In the temple of Solomon the horses waded in blood up to their knees, nay, up to the bridles. It was a just and marvelous judgment of God, that this place should be filled with the blood of the unbelievers (Haught, 1990, 25–26).

Atrocities by modern standards were commonplace on both sides and simply expected parts of the campaigns. When Richard the Lion-Hearted of England captured the city of Acre in 1191 he ordered that 3,000 prisoners (the majority of them women and children) be slain, then their bodies slit open to see if they had concealed jewels by swallowing them (Haught 1990). There have actually been many more localized wars of religious liberation and struggles for hegemony that are less well-known or recognized outside scholarly circles. Many have involved what anthropologists refer to as "revitalization movements" (Wallace, 1966). Such phenomena arise typically when a less technologically advanced people confront a more sophisticated industrial civilization. In the process of the former being subdued and colonized, prophets arise who speak a common message: a day of apocalypse is coming when the old gods (or ancestors) will join with the living in overthrowing the foreign oppressors. The victors will then have their sovereignty restored and enjoy the fruits of the advanced civilization minus the foreigners. Sometimes, as in Melanesian "cargo cults," the ghostly ancestors are to arrive on the same ships that bring colonial overlords and carry off raw materials, with the rebellious natives set to take possession of the desirable manufactured goods (i.e., the cargo) in the ship's holds (see Adas, 1979; Lanternari, 1963). Such prophecies resonate well with popular frustrations and discontent among groups of displaced and alienated persons.

In the North American case the Ghost Dance movement among Native Americans predicted that their ancestors would arrive on trains (rather than ships) prior to purging their lands of whites in warfare. The familiar Hollywood stereotype of painted Indians chanting and whooping as they shuffle around a fire or totem pole is actually a caricature of the Ghost Dance ritual that included a prolonged dance that induced trances and mobilized Native Americans for battle. The Ghost Dance cult spread across North America as it became increasingly apparent to Native Americans that they were losing out to the hoards of whites inexorably pushing westward. Many of the so-called Indian Wars, such as the Great Sioux Uprising during the 1870s, were, from Native Americans' perspective, religious wars as much as political struggles over territory. Sitting Bull, the Sioux chief whose warriors wiped out General George Armstrong Custer's Seventh U.S. Calvary at the Little Big Horn River, was as much a religious prophet as military leader to his people (Lanternari, 1963, 63–122).

The Ayatollah Khomeini, Iran's late leader, exhorted literally hundreds of thousands of young Iranian men, including adolescents used as human minesweepers, to be slaughtered in human-wave assaults against better-armed Iraqi troops during the 1980s. The carnage was reminiscent of the bloody (and equally futile) trench warfare in Europe during World War I. An entire generation of Iranian males was subsequently decimated in the name of a nationalistic Muslim holy war.

Khomeini elevated death in battle to religious martyrdom. It did not matter if the enemy was the Great Satan of the Christian West (the United States) or other Muslim believers who opposed his uncompromising Islamic Revolution. In 1984 Khomeini proclaimed in a speech:

> War is a blessing for the world and for all nations. It is God who incites men to fight and kill. The Koran says, 'Fight until all corruptions and all rebellion have ceased.' The wars the Prophet led against the infidels were a blessing for all humanity. . . . Thanks to God, our young people are now, to the limits of their means, putting God's commandments into action. They know that to kill the unbelievers is one of man's greatest missions (quoted in Haught, 1990, 203).

To this end, Iranian leaders have sponsored and harbored a variety of terrorist organizations that kidnap, bomb, assassinate, and sabotage their Western enemies. But Khomeini was not adverse to spreading Islamic *jihad* (holy war) to other Muslim societies, such as Saudi Arabia, where leaders did not share his single-minded vision. In 1979, at Khomeini's instigation, over 200 Iranian "pilgrims" to the annual *hajj* (return) to the Grand Mosque in Mecca smuggled in automatic weapons, fired on a crowd of 40,000 worshippers, briefly occupied the mosque, and only after nine days of intense house-to-house fighting with police were all killed or captured. (The Saudis ordered sixty-three of the Iranian terrorists beheaded.)

In South Asia religiously inspired violence between Hindus and Muslims has been repeated again and again in India/Pakistan and between Hindus and Sikhs in the southern part of the Indian subcontinent. In 1984 alone, mobs of each faith near the Bombay region, inspired by a Hindu speaker's anti-Islamic barbs and returned Islamic insults, killed 216 persons, injured 256, left 13,000 homeless, and resulted in 4,100 arrests. That same year, an armed contingent of Sikh extremists (Sikhism is a mixture of Islam and Hinduism.) barricaded themselves in Amritsar's Golden Temple, a Sikh shrine, in a demonstration aimed at gathering support for a separate Sikh theocracy to be called Khalistan. India's then Prime Minister, Indira Gandhi, ordered 1,000 troops to retake the temple; then Sikhs among Gandhi's own personal guard assassinated her. In an enraged response that lasted over three days, Hindu mobs killed 5,000 persons. According to eyewitnesses, mobs dragged Sikhs from homes, stores, buses, and trains, slashing and pounding them to death. Some were doused with kerosene and burned alive. Sikh boys were castrated (Haught, 1990, 172).

The violence repeated itself in India early in 2002. Hindu extremists in Gujarat state, for example, killed more than 600 people in a week-long riot, most of the victims Muslim but some Christian. In the city of Ahmadabad hundreds of Hindu militants broke into a mosque where Muslims had gathered for daily prayers. Wielding sledgehammers, metal rods, and shovels, they smashed walls and minarets. During the previous week Hindu mob behavior killed hundreds of Muslims and drove thousands more out of the city. Muslim gravestones were desecrated and whole neighborhoods were burned.

The ethnic/racial/religious hatred behind such violence is complex and long-standing. It in many respects resembles Israeli-Palestinian violence: everyone is fighting for revenge against their last depredation in a seemingly endless (and hopeless) cycle. Part of the Indian violence is due to Hindu revitalization sentiment; part of it is also grounded in the brutal poverty undoubtedly surrounding the rioters' lives. Many have nothing left to lose by immersing themselves in what to many outsiders seems transparently a self-destructive campaign. Thus the nonviolent alternatives offer little, if anything, better (Chandrasekaran, 2002; Mahapatra, 2002).

VIOLENCE AS AN INTEGRAL PART OF RELIGIOUS TRADITION AND THEOLOGY

Some religions explicitly incorporate violence into their theologies, making aggression a virtue. Two classic cases are the Assassins and the Thugs. These terms today commonly refer to hired murderers and violent thieves, respectively, yet both are derived from the name of past religious groups.

The Assassins were an extremist branch of Islam made up of professional cutthroats enlisted and trained to murder politicians and rulers. They were formed during the Christian-Muslim conflict of the First Crusade. They derived their name *assassins* from the Arabic *hashishiyan*, or "users of hashish." They apparently used the drug deliberately to accentuate their violent tendencies, that is, "to become wired" for their violence. The Assassin's founder, Sheikh Sinan, was known as the Old Man of the Mountain and was believed during his lifetime to have commanded a force of 1,000 men to contract out as Ninja-like killers (Payne, 1984, 184ff, 252). One writer (Annan, 1967) has compared the Assassins to the modern Mafia in the way that the former's agents systematically employed violence and harassment, creating an extensive twelfth- to thirteenth-century extortion racket that gathered protection payments through Middle Eastern towns, villages, and along caravan routes. At times they even "cut deals" with Christian crusaders if the politics were right and profits were high enough (Daraul, 1969, 1–33; Heckethorn, 1965, 116–22, 243). Their agents' modus operandi was to deliver death by way of a ceremonial dagger.

Similarly, the cult of *Thuggee* was a sect of polytheistic Hindu religion in India. The focus of its followers' devotion was the "Black" goddess Kali, deity of death. In Hindu theology Kali required human sacrifices and at the same time empowered her followers with spiritual merit when they robbed and murdered victims, particularly travelers on the highways. Thugs were part of an intergenerational/multifamily cartel, professional bandits/murderers who used sacred strangling scarves and ritually anointed pickaxes to kill, rob, and bury their victims (Heckethorn, 1965, 245–51). During the late eighteenth century, British colonial administrators began to investigate and prosecute this homicidal religious network. In 1810 alone magistrates discovered the bodies of thirty travelers ritually disemboweled and dumped down public wells (Annan, 1976b, 53). This secretive cult is believed to have murdered 20,000 victims a year since it began in the thirteenth century, perhaps dispatching as many as several million victims altogether before it was finally broken up by British officials (Haught, 1990, 34).

Some authors (Sutherland, 1987; Scott, 1979) have argued that major world religions such as Judaism, Christianity, and Islam graphically glorify and legitimize violence in their scriptures: from homicide to rape to genocide. It is undeniably true that the scriptures of these religions are replete with incidents of warfare, slaughter, and interpersonal aggression. For example, in the Bible the writer of 2 Kings 19:35 states that in one night alone an angel of Jehovah slew 185,000 Assyrians for the purpose of defending Jerusalem. The Book of Numbers (25:4, 9) details the beheading of 24,000 Israelites who married or cohabited with Moabite women and worshiped the pagan god Baal. 2 Chronicles 28 says that 120,000 Judaens were massacred by Israel's King Pekah for religious apostasy, to name only a few biblical references to bloody mayhem.

Nevertheless, to enumerate such cases out of context, and ignore the ethical/theological purposes for including them in religious writings apart from the original authors' standpoints, is to commit an obvious distortion. For example, an outraged Jesus of Nazareth taking a whip to drive the moneychangers out of the Jerusalem temple cannot logically be used to develop a Christian theory of aggression or retribution. Likewise, the Prophet Mohammed, who led his earliest followers repeatedly into battles, "hated the idea of fighting even in self defense and had to be inured to it" (Pickthall, 1961, xvii).

Those who wish to read into Islamic theology some inherent justification for terrorism, violence, and fanaticism will just as surely find it as have those who have "proof-texted" from the Bible to legitimize crusades, pogroms, slavery, or the arms race. Despite the visceral pro-violence statements that some religionists, such as Iran's Ayatollah Khomeini, have made, they speak no more for Islam's ultimate position toward violence or peace than did Richard the Lion-Hearted for Christianity when he butchered thousands of helpless Muslim prisoners.

Pathological, or "deviant," religions have incorporated violence into their principle tenets. For example, there is now substantial reason to regard Adolf Hitler's Nazi movement as more than just a fascist political phenomenon. It was also an ongoing religious concern of the first magnitude. Hitler did more than dabble in magic and the paranormal: he was obsessed with astrology, the Arthurian Holy Grail legends, German/Nordic mythology, racial mysticism, and other aspects of the occult (Sklar, 1977; Angebert, 1974; Brennan, 1974). Hitler also regarded his role in the growth of the Third Reich as a messianic one:

At a Christmas celebration in 1926 he thought it appropriate to compare his own historical importance favorably with that of Jesus. Christ had changed the dating of history; so would Hitler, for his final victory over the Jews would mark the beginning of a new age in the history of the world. 'What Christ began," he observed, he, Hitler would complete. . . . In a speech on 10 February 1933 he parodied the Lord's Prayer in promising that under him a new kingdom would come on earth, and that his would be 'the power and the glory, Amen' (Waite, 1974, 30).

As historian Robert G. L. Waite (1974, 32) has observed about Hitler, "He did not view the (Nazi) Party and the Reich merely as secular organizations." Such a messianic view may in part explain the otherwise sociopathic zeal with which Hitler dispatched millions of Jews, gypsies, Slavs, and other ethnic minorities to concentration camps and gas chambers. Worse, it probably reveals his complete detachment in approving so-called scientific experiments where many unfortunate persons were sterilized and operated upon to discover, for example, how fast injected gangrene would spread in a patient's body, what the product of a female human inseminated with ape sperm would be like, and other aberrant investigations (Muller-Hill, 1988; Bernadac, 1967).

On a micro level, various racist tax-protesting/right-wing/survivalist groups in the Mountain West, including Christian Constitutionalists, The Order, The Aryan Nations, American Israelites, and the Posse Comitatus, have incorporated religious justifications for violence in their ideologies of militant resistance (Aho, 1990; Corcoran, 1990), and in recent decades there have been several sensational cases of groups integrating violence with theology. One was the Reverend Jim Jones (an ordained Disciples of Christ minister) and his People's Temple. There is no question that Jones, who claimed to be a reincarnation of both Karl Marx and Jesus Christ, systematically introduced abuse and intimidation of adults and children into his cultic congregation (Hall, 1989; Moore and McGhee, 1989; Levi, 1982), even to the point of having followers engage in macabre mock communions that he told them might or might not include poison instead of wine.

Eventually, when Jones perceived that his movement (the headquarters of which he had moved from San Francisco to a remote jungle compound called Jonestown in Guyana, South America) was about to be seriously investigated by the U.S. federal government, he ordered his followers to undergo suicide by drinking grape Fla-Vor-Aid (similar to Kool-Aid) mixed with cyanide. Not all followers eagerly or willingly drank it. A third of the group were, after all, infants and small children panicked by the screams and moans of those already dying. (Cyanide does not provide an instantaneous or painless death.) Even a dog had a pipe inserted down his throat to get the deadly drink down it. But whether passively or at rifle-point, over 900 persons died of the poison, except Jones, who died mysteriously from a gunshot to his head.

Such suicidal tendencies are by no means unique. There were repeated outbursts of religious zealots known as "Old Believers" in eighteenth- and nineteenth-century Russia. The Old Believers mutilated, castrated, and even immolated (burned alive) themselves out of religious fervor and political protest long before Jim Jones ever chose to make a fatal statement of defiance with his followers' suicides in the jungles of Guyana. The Old Believers protested reforms in the Russian Orthodox Church regarding liturgy and hymns, attracting many peasants who also were unhappy with political centralization efforts of the czars. The Russian *Skopzi*, both males and females, believed strict, irrevocable celibacy was the spiritual ideal and mutilated their genitals with red-hot irons, knives, razors, hatchets, and glass (Heckethorn, 1965, 292–300; Robbins, 1986). Thousands died during these cultic revolts.

One of the most recent examples of violence and religion combined occurred during the spring of 1993 just outside the town of Waco, Texas. On a remote ranch known as the Mount Carmel compound, an apocalyptic Christian sect called the Branch Davidians followed a charismatic prophet named David Koresh (originally known as Vernon Wayne Howell). Koresh, a rock musician from California who had not passed the ninth grade in school, regarded himself as the person who could finally decipher the seven seals or mysteries in the Bible's final Book of Revelations, thereby bringing about the End of Time or Final Conflagration of Earth which he believed was prophesied in various places in the Bible.

The Branch Davidians began in conflict and violence. In 1918 Victor Houteff, a Bulgarian immigrant, joined the Seventh-Day Adventist sect, but by 1934 he had disagreed with leaders over interpretations of last days prophecies in the Book of Revelations. He formed his own group, consisting of several dozen former Adventist members, and moved them to a location outside the small town of Waco, Texas.

In 1942 the group officially adopted the name Branch Seventh-Day Adventists. When Houteff died in 1955, his wife, Florence, took charge and publicized her own prophecy that the Kingdom of King David would be recreated on April 28, 1959 (tantamount to predicting the return of Jesus Christ to earth). About 1,400 persons responded with hope and flocked to her. With their property and assets all handed over to Florence, she bought the Mount Carmel compound about ten miles east of Waco. After her prophecy failed, there was a split, the largest group going with Florence's rival leader, Ben Roden. Roden gave his faction the name with which most Americans are familiar: the Branch Davidians.

When Ben Roden died in 1978, there was further conflict as his son, George, and Vernon Wayne Howell (not yet Koresh) vied for leadership. Eventually the hostilities culminated in a shoot-out that drove Roden off the Mount Carmel property, charges of attempted murder filed against Howell and seven followers, and a trial in which those followers were found innocent, the charges against Howell eventually dropped, and Roden committed to a mental asylum for murdering another Texas man by reason of insanity (Wright, 1995).

Koresh had a fascination with guns and armaments that became an integral part of his doomsday theology. That is why the U.S. Bureau of Alcohol, Tobacco, and Firearms (BATF) initially came into contact with him. That was also the primary pretext behind a disastrous raid on the Mount Carmel compound on February 28, 1993 by 130 BATF agents. According to the search warrant issued by a federal judge (and ironically never served), Koresh had acquired grenade and flare launchers, numerous handguns, rifles, and semiautomatic weapons (evidence of almost 300 were found in the later wreckage), explosives, and the necessary parts to convert the weapons so as to make them fully automatic (BATF, 1993, 193ff).

It is still debated who fired first, the Davidians who knew the federal agents were coming or the BATF agents. It is still contested as to whether either the fifty-one-day siege of the compound by a small army of Federal Bureau of Investigation agents or the final assault on compound buildings with armored vehicles was justified (Lewis, 1994). And we will likely never know the true extent to which Koresh and his followers posed any serious danger to citizens outside their doomsday group.

Inside the group, allegations by disillusioned ex-members that Koresh physically and sexually abused children were never verified by state social workers who visited the compound, yet President Bill Clinton and newly appointed Attorney General Janet Reno steadfastly maintained that the final assault on the compound had to be undertaken for the children. (One wonders, then, why all utilities and water had been cut off to the families inside for weeks, and why a form of tear gas, outlawed by the Geneva Convention for use in warfare, was pumped into the compound buildings hour after hour.)

After becoming frustrated with Koresh's seemingly unlimited stalling tactics, their own inability to deal with an erratic religious leader, and the embarrassing negative publicity growing nationally day by day, on April 19 the FBI decided to end the stand-off. Some eighty-six Davidians died in the fiery holocaust that resulted. Seventeen of the dead were children.

This chapter is not the place to determine whether events in Waco were interpersonal violence, institutional violence, or state violence (though the violence had aspects of all three). Moreover, what most American citizens know of the events at Waco is based on information, some of it deliberately disinformational and provided by government sources for their own purposes, filtered through a noncritical mass media that had little access to independent data (Shupe and Hadden, 1995). What can be said is that not all religions manifest a clear potential for violence but that violence, as manifested in stored armaments, in theology, and in the everyday expectations of committed followers was a clear theme running throughout the affairs of the Branch Davidians.

Likewise, there have been several other spectacular examples of cult violence at the end of the twentieth century. The Order of the Solar Temple was an Euro-American group associated with drugs and suicide; the Japanese-based group Aum Shinrikyo purposefully spread sarin nerve gas in Tokyo's subway system, killing twelve persons and injuring 6,000; and the Heaven's Gate UFO cult, believing a spaceship was coming to transport them to another planet and that males should have themselves castrated to be "purer," tried to recruit believers on the Internet and ended up committing suicide (all in uniforms, wearing Nike athletic shoes and covered in purple sheets). It is as if people destroying themselves as well as others is an episodic but continuing phenomenon through religion in virtually every culture (see, e.g., Hoffman and Burke, 1997; Kaplan and Marshall, 1996; and Boyle, 1996, for popular but reliable accounts of these groups).

In a previous chapter we also examined martyrdom as a time-honored cultural role in various religious traditions. It is a role both the Ayatollah Khomeini and the Reverend Jim Jones chose to offer up to their followers with grisly consequences. Human sacrifice as well was mentioned earlier. Given its widespread practice throughout history and on virtually every continent, there is absolutely no way to be sure how many victims altogether have perished at the hands of priests, Crusaders, and ecclesiastical executioners. Undoubtedly the numbers would run into many millions. One generalization, however, can be made with certainty about any "officially" sanctioned religious violence: the symbol-manipulating potential of human beings presents a capability to rationalize and justify virtually any activity, no matter how heinous, in the name of faith in the supernatural, and to regard it as consistent with the loftiest ideals.

PERSECUTION OF HERETICS AND NON-BELIEVERS

Journalist James A. Haught (1990, 14) observes: "A grim pattern is visible in history: when religion is the ruling force in a society, it produces horror. The stronger the supernatural beliefs, the worse the inhumanity. A culture dominated by intense faith invariably is cruel to people who don't share the faith—and sometimes to many that do."

One need look no further than the Iranian theocracy of the 1980s for evidence to support Haught's assertion. Closer to home the religiously minded colonists of seventeenth- and eighteenth-century North America also exercised their share of intolerance (Morgan, 1968). Despite the image of America as a land of religious freedom, it is just as accurate to say that this country has always been a cauldron of religious tension. The Calvinist Puritans, who fled England seeking religious freedom, in turn felt quite comfortable in denying it to others. In seventeenth-century New England, pacifistic Quakers who refused to pay taxes, serve in the military, or take oaths were hanged, flogged, deported, tortured, and sold into bondage by Puritan councils (Hill, 1980, 58). Between 1659 and 1661 the city fathers of Boston hung four Quakers on Boston Common as public menaces.

During the eighteenth century the Shakers (a pentecostal-style sect promoting strict celibacy and monastic-like piety) were accused of disturbing the peace, disloyalty and treason, heresy, and witchcraft (Foster, 1981, 30–5; Andrews, 1963, 58). Their refusal to fight in the American Revolution brought charges that they were really British spies (Holloway, 1966, 58–59). As a result, mobs broke into their dormitory-style homes and roughed up Shaker men or attacked them in the streets. Shakers were imprisoned for refusing to take oaths of loyalty and fined repeatedly.

The experiences of many Irish Catholic immigrants from the 1820s to the 1860s were no less tranquil. Accused of being the advance guard for a Vatican plot to take over the United States, the Irish confronted blatant discrimination and hostility from the dominant Protestant culture. Throughout the 1830s and 1840s there were numerous instances of anti-Catholic mobs destroying homes, churches, and convents. In 1834 an Ursuline convent in Charleston, Massachusetts, was looted and burned to the ground by a Protestant mob. The latter riot was incited by rumors that a young woman was being held inside against her will. Undoubtedly one of the worst riots occurred in Kensington, a suburb of Philadelphia, in 1844. There, a series of rumors inspired a mob to swarm into a predominantly Catholic neighborhood. Two churches and a convent were torched, and thirteen people died in the violence. The riot was halted only after the militia was called out and finally forced to fire point-blank into the crowd to quell it. Religious tensions continued. As late as 1871 a riot broke out in New York City between Protestant and Irish Catholic immigrants (Gilje, 1987; Marty, 1984; Wittke, 1970; Shannon, 1966).

Likewise, members of the Church of Jesus Christ of Latter-Day Saints, as is well known, experienced constant persecution from non-Mormons ("Gentiles") in mid-nineteenth-century America (Hill, 1989; Arrington and Haupt, 1988; Arrington and Bitton, 1980). Things became so bad for them in Missouri and Illinois, including the mob murder of founder Joseph Smith and his brother Hyrum, that most of the Mormons finally packed up and trekked to Utah, at that time one of the most desolate and inhospitable regions of North America.

The most systematically ruthless persecution of "heretics" was unquestionably the Spanish Inquisition, with the name of its most famous inquisitor general, Tomas de Torquemada, now a synonym for cruelty and religious fanaticism. The Inquisition functioned at a time when Spanish kings were retaking their kingdoms league by league from the Moors, who had ruled the greater part of Spain for eight centuries. At the same time, Christian intolerance of Jews was increasing.

The Inquisition began in the twelfth century in response to various pre-Protestant Reformation sects that arose and after Pope Innocent III urged secular and ecclesiastical officials to persecute such heretics. In Spain the tribunals of the Inquisition achieved a prominence unlike anywhere else. Calling it a "hideous monster," one historian observes:

> There must have been many—Jews and Moslems—who fervently wished that Jesus Christ had never made His appearance on Earth, when contemplating all the misery which would have been spared them, their families and friends, but for this, to them a calamitous event. . . . Thousands were submitted to the cruelest torture these (Inquisitors) could devise; the flesh of the victims was torn with red hot pincers, and molten lead poured into the wounds; many suffered the agonies of the hoist and the water torture; some were racked to death; some were burned at the stake; every means of dealing pain and indignity to the human body was explored, and all this was done in the name of One who had commanded his followers to love one another (Plaidy, 1969, 16).

Christians, particularly political dissidents, were also among the victims. The Inquisition coincided with political events in Spanish history from the fifteenth to nineteenth centuries. (The last Inquisitor General died in 1834.) But inquisitions and torture/executions of alleged heretics were well under way elsewhere in Europe earlier. As Norman Cohn (1975) chronicles so well in *Europe's Inner Demons*, the obsession to ferret out heretics was premised on the assumption that society and the church were under attack by a subversive conspiracy of Satanists. This "subversion fantasy" maintained "that there existed, somewhere in the midst of the great society, another society, small and clandestine, which not only threatened the existence of the great society but was also dedicated to practices which were felt to be wholly abominable, in the literal sense of anti-human" (Cohn, 1975, xi).

We can go back even earlier in the history of Christianity during the first century when its institutional structure was less secure and messiahs who were supported by the most marginal elements of feudal society posed a serious threat to the social order. Cohn mentions a number of cases of messiahs who were killed because of the threat they posed to the church and the established order.

> Under the year 591 Gregory (St. Gregory, Bishop of Tours) tells of a freelance preacher who set himself up as a messiah. A man of Bourges, having gone into a forest, found himself suddenly surrounded by a swarm of flies; as a result of which he went out of his mind for two years. Later he made his way to the province of Arles, where he became a hermit, clad in animal skins and wholly dedicated to prayer. When he emerged from this ascetic training he claimed to possess supernatural gifts of healing and prophecy. . . . People flocked to him with their sick, who were cured by his touch. He also foretold future events, prophesizing sickness or other misfortunes for most of those who visited him, but salvation for a few. . . . It was at Le Puy that the messiah met his doom. When he arrived at this important episcopal city he quartered his "army" as Gregory calls it—in the neighboring basilicas, as though he were about to wage war against the bishop, Aurelius. Then he sent messengers ahead to proclaim his coming; they presented themselves to the bishop stark naked, leaping and somersaulting. The bishop in his turn sent a party of his men to meet the messiah on the way. The leader of the party, pretending to bow, grabbed the man around the knees; after which he was quickly secured and cut to pieces (Cohn, 1971, 41–42).

Cohn traces the growth of folklore about black masses, Satanic covens, and witchcraft as church leaders, in their attempt to consolidate power over diversifying medieval society, used it as a pretext for imprisonment, torture, and execution. In related fashion, Phillip the Fair, king of mid-thirteenth-century France, used the mythology of witchcraft to break up the Knights Templar. The Templars were members of a military religious order of the church that not only fielded its own warrior-monk armies but also created an extensive, lucrative, influential banking system throughout Europe. Envious of the Templars' wealth and claiming that they actually constituted an underground cult of Satan-worshippers and heretics, Phillip attacked the order, driving its leaders into exile or torturing and burning them at the stake (Partner, 1987; Burman, 1986).

This concern to weed out heretics gradually focused on persons accused of being witches, the supposed tools of Satan and the real scapegoats for strains and fears of the power establishment in a Europe shifting from feudal to capitalist economies. Anthropologists (e.g., Marwick, 1968) and sociologists (Mac-Farlane, 1970; Bednarski, 1968) regard "outbreaks" of witchcraft as well as its alleged ongoing existence as indications, or "gauges," of social strain in societies, occurring particularly in times of widespread economic change. Discontent with social structural changes becomes focused on suspicions of interpersonal wrongdoing, in particular on alleged usages of antisocial means to get ahead or deal revenge. Old norms and vested interests, meanwhile, are threatened, while new ones compete for ascendance.

Thus witch-hunts occurred throughout Europe during the sixteenth and seventeenth centuries, most victims of which were women who were also the most powerless, "convenient" scapegoats (MacFarlane, 1970, 160–61). Likewise, Karlsen (1987, 20, 47–49) relates how, between 1620 and 1725, 344 North American colonists were formally accused of being witches, 78 percent of them women. Women accounted for many more of the executions (usually by hanging) than men.

Massachusetts, with its staunch Puritan heritage, saw disproportionately more witch hunting hysteria than other colonies. Most famous was the witch hunt that occurred at Salem in 1692. It is a classic example of the "strain-gauge" hypothesis. By the late seventeenth century, New England was witnessing a breakdown in its theocratic political structure, caused in large part by British trade policies and an influx of non-Puritan immigrants. There was an unmistakable clash between the strict values of the Massachusetts Bay Colony's original settlers and emerging religious pluralism. The colony was diversifying and urbanizing. As a consequence, the homogeneous "small town" quality of life among Puritan believers and neighbors was rapidly, and stressfully, disappearing. Amid these profound changes came charges of witchcraft that transformed much of Massachusetts, in the words of one sociologist (Bednarski, 1968, 156) into "a society gone mad—a society blind to rationality and reason, driven by fear and distrust."

According to the horrifying testimonies of a handful of adolescent and teenage girls, a network of demonically inspired witches was systematically hexing and possessing people as well as attempting to wreck the social order. It is generally agreed among modern scholars that there was no real outbreak of witchcraft, only a case of public panic. (The girls also later recanted their testimonies and apologized.) The witch-finding prosecutors at Salem nevertheless sent nineteen persons to the gallows. Two more died in jail awaiting hanging, and one man was crushed to death by heavy rocks piled on him during interrogation. Meanwhile, in response to public clamor for the Satanic conspirators to be apprehended, more than 150 suspected witches were held in custody and an additional 200 had been accused. Only gradually, as the girls' accusations became more indiscriminate and incredible, did the scare collapse (Bednarski, 1968; Hansen, 1969; Starkey, 1969).

Recent fears of a rising Satanist network of pornographers, ritual child abusers, cattle mutilators, and murderers (Raschke, 1990; Johnston, 1989; Kahaner, 1988) have caused alarm in communities across the United States as well as abroad, expanding on the demonological motifs of medieval witchcraft folklore. Reliable social science, law enforcement, and journalistic research (Richardson et al., 1991; Victor, 1993; Hicks, 1991), however, find that claims of Satanic violence, like those of the alleged abducted "milk carton" children (the vast majority of which are abducted by parents) or the rumors of poison and razor blades hidden in Halloween trick-or-treaters' candy, are largely "urban legends," plausible because they feed off our worst fears of impersonal/potentially dangerous society but nevertheless empirically disconfirmed (Best, 1990). The FBI, for example, has yet to find a single case of a person murdered by an organized Satanistic conspiracy, even though promoters of a satanic scare loudly proclaim (with absolutely no substantiation) that 50,000 persons are ritually sacrificed (i.e., murdered) every year in the United States.

CLERGY VIOLENCE

A serious form of religious violence first came to light during the mid-1980s, involving clergymen (though a few women were likewise accused) who physically and sexually abused prepubescent boys and girls, teenagers, and women. The molestations included oral and anal sex, rape, and outright seduction, all in unequal power situations within an otherwise trusted institution, the church. Much of the media attention, whether in the press, on investigative television magazines like *20-20* and *Prime Time Live* or on talk shows like *Montel Williams* or *Oprah Winfrey* has focused on Roman Catholic priests and children (Burkett and Bruni, 1993; Berry, 1992; Rossetti, 1990), though there are plenty of comparable cases of Protestant sexual abuse of laypersons (Enroth, 1992; Poling, 1991; Cooper-White, 1991; Brock and Lukens, 1988). In fact, several scholars have examined this sort of violence occurring across a broad array of religious traditions (see Shupe, 1995; Cartwright and Kent, 1992; Jacobs, 1989).

For example, in 1991 the Reverend John Blume, once a priest at St. John the Baptist Catholic Church in New Haven, Indiana, was sued along with his diocese by a woman who alleged he had repeatedly and sexually assaulted her when she was an elementary parochial school student. A later suit against the diocese alleged misconduct by church leaders who, she said, told her not to speak out about the incidents. Within a month's time, a Fort Wayne, Indiana, man sued the Fort Wayne–South Bend diocese and Blume for clergy malpractice, claiming that he also had been the victim of repeated sexual abuse while a teenager (French, 1993).

Meanwhile, the Villa Louis Martin, a sprawling 2,000-acre Roman Catholic retreat operated by an obscure order called the Servants of the Paraclete at Jemez Springs, New Mexico, has catered to over 600 sexual deviants (mostly pedophiles), all active Catholic clergy, since 1975. Many have backslid after leaving the ranch and continued their sexual abuse in new parishes. Father James Porter may have established the record for recidivism, with close to 200 known victims, but other clients of the retreat have left and gone on to injure additional trusting victims. In November 1993 the courts decided a judgment of $8 million in favor of twenty-five persons who sued the Servants when they had been victimized after Porter had been treated there, discharged, and then reassigned to religious duties in surrounding areas (Burkett and Bruni, 1993).

In November 1993 a major scandal was revealed at St. Anthony's Seminary in Santa Barbara, California. As the Franciscan Order announced following its own investigation between 1964 and 1987 twelve priests had victimized a minimum of thirty-four boys. The sexual abuses included nude games, fondling and forced sodomy (oral and anal intercourse). One priest had a total of eighteen victims; another had at least seven victims (Rice, 1993). In 2001–2002 dioceses in both Los Angeles and Boston were rocked by scandals involving several hundred victims and a dozen pedophile priests who had done their harm over decades, and the pattern was classic: bishops knew of the priests' deviant behavior but quietly moved each priest from one parish to another, hoping the problem would disappear. The scandal eventually cost the dioceses millions of dollars from lawsuits.

To be sure, such abuse and violence is not limited to Roman Catholics. In four recent cases one writer referred to the zipper factor where Jewish congregations (including the largest in northern California) had rabbis who resigned after female members charged sexual harassment or worse (Bonavoglia, 1990). Da Love-Ananda, an eastern guru who challenged his followers to break through conventional attachments to this world, including their sexual fidelity to their spouses, used to marry various female devotees in order to shake up their husbands and lovers. Recalled one: "In front of me, my wife was being sexually prepared for the guru. I coped with my violently irrational feelings by going into emotional numbness. Happily, I did not have to witness my teacher bedding my wife (Feuerstein, 1991, 91)." In a Protestant case (Fortune, 1989), a minister sexually abused (including rape) or seduced as many as forty-five female church members in *one* congregation, and he had obtained that job after he was asked to be reassigned from his previous church where he had likewise hurt women but bargained for reassignment on the condition of hushing up the scandal.

Much of what is being studied about sexual violence among clergypersons is social psychological, concerned with the motives of both perpetrators and their victims who often remain silent (Nason-Clark, 1991). Not surprisingly, analogies have been drawn between sexual violence by clergy directed at victims in the pew or serving at the altar and violations of sexual trust by other professionals, such as teachers, counselors, psychiatrists, and physicians (Rutter, 1989).

But to focus only at the social psychological or interpersonal level is to lose sight of the larger significance of clergy violence, since (by our definition) it is a premier case of institutional violence. Any religious organization, as we intimated at the beginning of this chapter, is a hierarchy of power, a system of levels of trusted authority, wherein followers/believers/congregants/lay persons often drop their guards when dealing with leaders they assume will show benevolence, integrity, and ethical professionalism toward them. Several authors (see Fortune, 1989; Shupe, 1995) have compared a religious leader's authority in this case to one that legal experts refer to as fiduciary responsibility, that is, that the professional is not supposed to substitute what is in his or her own best interest for what is in the best interest of the client or parishioner (i.e., the fiduciary).

In fact, Shupe (1995) has developed a structural conflict theory of clergy malfeasance that bases its propositions on the organizational polity, or political structure, of individual religious groups. Polities, he maintains, recruit personnel and manage the handling of deviance (in this case, sexual violence against vulnerable church members) in different ways. He distinguishes between hierarchical groups, in which local congregations are part of larger systems or denominations to which they are accountable (such as United Presbyterians, United Methodists, Roman Catholics, Church of Jesus Christ of Latter-Day Saints, or Episcopalians) and congregational groups (such as Independent Baptist and Fundamentalist Christian churches, the Bhagwan Shree Rajneesh movement, various televangelist paraministries, and numerous sect-cult groups).

Using this hierarchical/congregational typology, Shupe has developed propositions about how hierarchical religious groups, with their accountability to authority outside the local congregation, would react to clergy deviance differently from congregational groups in terms of perpetration of abuse, official organizational response, and victims responses. He concludes that hierarchical church groups, with their relatively greater bureaucratization, shield abusers longer than do congregational groups, but the former ultimately do better in discouraging the normalization, or members acceptance, of clergy malfeasance. Shupe contends that hierarchical groups provide religious leaders with greater opportunities to rationalize or dismiss victims claims of abuse but at the same time are more likely than congregational groups to develop policies addressing clergy abuse. Lastly hierarchical groups, thanks to their layers of authority and ecclesiastical traditions, at first promote ambivalence among victims and/or fear of elite retaliation for whistle-blowing on clergy but ultimately empower them to protest more so than in congregational groups.

The recognition and analysis of clergy violence against followers is relatively new in social science. The subject has not been subjected to much study and analysis except in spectacular cases like the People's Temple or the Branch Davidians. Nevertheless, it appears to be a growing topic of concern among social scientists who study institutional violence.

MISSIONARIES, MILITARY CONQUEST, AND IMPERIALISM

Religious missionaries during the past five hundred years have played an important role in furthering the spread of empires throughout history, notably in the conquest of the Americas, Africa, and Asia by European imperial powers. Missionaries have played the role of assimilators of those who have been conquered. They function as a mechanism of social control as they establish symbolic internal mechanisms to coerce conformity to the culture of the imperial power. Unfortunately, the methods of assimilation have often had a devastating effect, often exerting violence on those who are the subject of their missionary work. Indeed, in 2001 Pope John Paul II even publicly apologized to the world for his church's role in aiding oppressors and conquerors. Missionaries serve to make the area safe for the later penetration of economic actors to secure valued resources. And they also have made areas safe for settlement of citizens from the conquering nations.

Missionaries played this role during the period of the European discovery and conquest of the Western Hemisphere and continue today on the South American and African continents. Hayford (1970) states that "it is the favorite practice with European nations to precede the Flag with the Gospel of Jesus Christ. . . . The missionary points to the cardinal lesson of truth, love and brotherhood as proclaimed by the Gospel, which are in accord with the higher impulses of the Native, and commands his ready respect and obedience. In the course of time, the Flag makes its appearance, and with it boldly emerges the merchant and tradesman, who before were merely sneaking round the corner" (232).

Tinker (1993) argues that Christian missionaries throughout North America were partners with the state in genocide of the indigenous populations. He argues that the missionaries were guilty of complicity in the destruction of Indian cultures, tribal social structures, and the devastating impoverishment and death of the people to whom they preached. Focusing on several major missionary efforts in North America (John Eliot in colonial Massachusetts, Junipero Serra in California, Pierre-Jean De Smet in Missouri, and Henry Benjamin Whipple in Minnesota), Tinker documents the role that their efforts played in the cultural, social, political, and economic destruction of the tribal groupings that they were assimilating and converting to the European and Christian way of life. He concludes that the European colonial conquest of the Americas was fought on two separate symbiotically related fronts. One front involved the political and military strategy that drove Indian peoples from their land to make room for the more civilized conqueror and worked to deprive Indian peoples of any continuing self-governance or self-determination (120).

The second front, just as decisive in the conquest of the Indian population, was the religious one pursued by missionaries of all denominations. Tinker notes that missionaries arrived first, to be followed in due course by the flag, armies, farmers, and merchants. But the missionaries for the most part have stayed on and continue to this day to exert a subtle social control over Indian communities. For Tinker, the missionaries played a crucial role in the European conquest of Indian people, a conquest that resulted in genocide.

Tinker claims that the genocidal violence directed at the indigenous populations of North America was cultural and spiritual as well as physical. These forms of genocide are linked. Destruction of a people's cultural system often resulted in their physical destruction. He defines cultural genocide as the effective destruction of a people by systematically (intentionally or unintentionally in order to achieve other goals) destroying, eroding, or undermining the integrity of the culture and system of values that defines a people and gives them life (Tinker, 1993, 5). The cultural genocide the missionaries practiced began with destroying those cultural structures of existence that gave a people a sense of holistic and communal integrity. By limiting a people's freedom to practice their culture and to live out their lives in culturally appropriate patterns, they effectively destroyed a people by eroding both their self-esteem and the interrelationships that bind them together as a community (5).

Tinker argues that missionaries utilized four interrelated vehicles of cultural genocide. The first vehicle is the political means. This is the use of political power, backed by the threat of military or police intervention, to control and subdue a weaker, culturally discrete entity. Tinker cites the "Civilization" Act passed by the U.S. Congress in 1819 that gave missionaries land grants and funding for mission schools as one example of the linkage of the missionaries with the state. This act was important in indicating the state sponsorship of the penetration of missionaries into Indian territories. He also cites the Grant Peace Policy of 1870, which delegated to the denominations the responsibility for filling the positions of Indian agent and parceling out particular nations or reservations to various denominations. Here missionaries were operating directly in their capacity as officers of the state in controlling the indigenous populations. Through these legislative actions, the government of the United States was utilizing missionaries as part of the larger strategy of territorial expansion.

In discussing the missionary work of Father Junipero Serra and how it was related to the goals of the Spanish colonial and imperial governments, he notes that Serra and other missionaries were on the payroll of the viceroy and effectively functioned as a branch of the civil service in their mission endeavors. Tinker observes that this relationship had been in existence since the sixteenth century, whereas the "state assumed responsibility for the conversion of the natives in return for papal support for the Crown's colonial expansion and concessions permitting royal intervention in ecclesiastical affairs of the colonies" (Tinker, 1993, 43). Tinker does not doubt that the Franciscans, Dominicans, and Jesuit missionaries came to their task with pious intentions, while the government in New Spain saw their evangelistic outreach as serving the purpose of conquest in terms of pacification of the countryside. Tinker views the development of the California mission system from its beginning as an integral part of Spain's strategy of colonization and conquest. He concludes that Serra was a mere religious-political agent for imperial Spain, helping Spain achieve its colonial goals in the late eighteenth century" (Tinker, 1993, 46).

Tinker also discusses the link between the state and the missionary efforts of John Eliot in Massachusetts. The Puritan government in Massachusetts was under attack in England for not fulfilling its missionary obligations to their faith. This was one factor in forcing the Winthrop government to act to sponsor Eliot's work. The other important factor was that the government wanted to bring the Indians under their control, and the establishment of a mission would accomplish this.

Not only were missionaries acting as an extension of the states that sponsored them by destroying the political independence of the people they were converting, through the assimilation process they destroyed the native forms of self-governance. The *reducción* system which was based on the creation of separate Indian communities controlled by the missionaries for the purpose of assimilation and conversion presupposed both the inability of the native people to govern themselves as civilized people and the need for authoritarian governance by the missionary in each locale. Tinker (1993) notes that the indigenous political leadership was recognized only to the extent that it could be exploited by either the colonial government or the missions themselves.

Tinker views the missionaries as acting as an arm of the state in furthering the national interest of acquiring more territory and controlling populations that might pose a threat to this expansionism. In all of the cases of missionaries in North America that Tinker discusses, he finds them playing this same role and linked closely to the functioning of the state.

The second vehicle of cultural genocide is economic. Here Tinker is referring to the forced transformation of the indigenous population, removing them from their cultural roots and establishing relationships of domination between missionaries and Indians. "The economic aspects of genocide involve using or allowing the economic system, always with political or even military support, to manipulate and exploit another culturally discrete entity that is both politically and economically weaker. The results can range from enslavement and the direct exploitation of labor to the pillaging of natural resources that leaves a people unable to sustain themselves (7).

In general these forced economic changes resulted in the transformation of a people who were economically self-sufficient to those who were dominated and dependent as they produced for their colonial overlords, the missionaries and the colonial state. Tinker discusses the economic plight and role of these isolated communities, praying towns, which were located on the frontier of white settlements to serve as a military buffer. The economic aspect of the missionary work of John Eliot in the Massachusetts colony (for example, the imposed changes to European-style agriculture and fencing) resulted in the destruction of the general cohesion of the population and destruction of the social organization of the tribes.

Tinker also notes how the economies of these praying towns were subservient and dependent in their development on the white colonial settlements. "Essentially limited in their ability to compete, the praying towns became suppliers for the more substantial and stable Puritan economy. Allowed to produce goods and services for Puritan trade, the praying towns became a dependent, client economy. The resulting economic codependency is a phenomenon that continues to this day. Indian tribes in the United States today function largely around a carefully conceived and federally controlled *comprador* system that rewards an educated class of tribal members for maintaining the well-behaved client status of their tribes" (Tinker, 1993, 33).

With regard to Serra in California, Tinker notes that the *reducción* system he established and the resultant economic transformation of the indigenous population resulted in problems of famine that were unheard of previously among those populations. Work on the missions was geared to the production of surplus that was controlled by the missionaries. The Indian producers received the bare minimum as daily sustenance. According to Tinker,

> profit motives then were nurtured by teaching natives to sell surpluses, and by using profits to enhance the mission's capital by purchasing more livestock and tools from European markets. An appetite for luxury was also instilled with the purchase of blankets, cloth, and apparel from Mexico City. Moreover, these economic lessons were accompanied by the imposition of a new hierarchical valuing of labor that gave priority to certain types of work and taught specialization: the hierarchy was implicit in the superiority of the European priest, and was made explicit in the special gifts given, for instance, to those who did the more physical labor of tilling (1993, 49).

It is not only nation-states that utilized missionaries to fulfill their own economic interests. Tinker notes the self-interest of the fur trading companies which was evident as they made substantial contributions to both Protestant and Catholic missionaries for their pacification efforts, which according to Tinker aided and abetted the companies' exploitation of Indians, Indian lands, and Indian resources.

In regard to the religious vehicle of cultural genocide, Tinker states that this involves the overt attempt to destroy the spiritual solidarity of a people. One of the ways this was done was to outlaw native ceremonial forms of worship. For example, the performance of the Sun Dance of the Plains Indians and Hopi Snake Dance were defined as punishable crimes, and the performance of the Ghost Dance resulted in the massacre of 350 people at Wounded Knee on December 29, 1890. Another way religion was used was as a vehicle of cultural genocide was through the forced participation of native populations in the conqueror's religious ceremonials by means of the threat of physical punishment. Tinker notes that Serra in his missionary work in the Sierra Gorda region of central Mexico used the power of the military to force attendance at religious services for Indian converts and nonconverts alike. In describing the efforts of Eliot in Massachusetts, Tinker cites "the imposition of Puritan theology and theological language across the cultural chasm that separated Indian and English certainly generated a sense of low self-worth on the part of Indian converts from which Indian people have not yet recovered" (Tinker, 1993, 40).

This pattern of forced conversion has been going on for centuries in the history of Christendom. In 1531, Pizarro invited the Inca ruler, Atahualpa, to visit him. Atahualpa arrived along with thousands of unarmed Inca soldiers. The priest that accompanied Pizarro on his mission, Vicente de Valverde, was sent out to meet the ruler and to inform the Incan ruler that he must accept Christianity and Spanish rule. The Incan ruler rejected the offer, throwing the Bible that was handed to him down onto the ground. This was a signal the armed Spanish soldiers were waiting for as they swooped in on their horses killing more than 7,000 unarmed Incan soldiers and their attendants (Gage, 1991). For the Spanish it was a precondition of conquest to require that those who they were about to conquer be given the opportunity to voluntarily accept conversion and their rule. If they chose not to accept, they would be slaughtered.

After conquest, the Spanish clergy throughout the Americas forbid the native population from practicing their religion. In 1614 the Archbishop of Lima announced to the native people of Peru that they were no longer allowed to perform their traditional songs or dances. Native instruments were burned and severe punishments were levied upon those who violated the rule (Gage, 1991).

Tinker notes that the social aspects of cultural genocide involved a wide variety of social changes imposed on Indian people with destructive consequences. He observes that these changes included seemingly minor changes of impersonal behavior as well as fundamental changes relating to the social organization of the community. One major area of these latter changes was the attack on the Indian family. Tinker sees attacks on extended and often polygynous family systems as particularly powerful in destroying the solidarity of the community and the self-identity of the population. He also notes that resultant displacement of wives and their children after husbands forced to convert to nuclear family structures abandoned them had a significant impact on the physical and psychological well being of these abandoned elements of the community.

Tinker does not regard the action of missionaries as a product of sinister motives designed to subjugate and dominate the Indians. This subjugation and domination resulted from their ethnocentric commitments to their own European cultures and social structures and institutions. Tinker notes that they naturally assumed the superiority of their way of life and felt it was in the interest of the native populations to accept these ways, even if they had to be forced on them.

> Thus, it was almost natural for the missionaries to participate in the political process of subjugation and to support the repressive efforts of their own government in whatever program had been devised at the time to serve that interest. It was just as natural for them to support the economic enterprises that manipulated and exploited Indian labor and resources. What finally must be realized is that the missionaries were deeply involved in symbiotic relationships with the very structures of power that crushed Indian resistance to European invasion every step of the way, as Manifest Destiny moved from California to the New York Island, from the redwood forest to the gulf stream waters (1993, 17).

A similar, subtly exploitative role by religionists has been documented for the Mormons (i.e., members of the Church of Jesus Christ of Latter-Day Saints) and their modern-day relations with Native Americans (Heinerman and Shupe, 1985, 223–7).

The cultural genocide by religious missionaries is not a thing of the past. Today, especially in South American countries such as Paraguay, Bolivia, and Brazil, Protestant missionaries have succeeded the Catholic missionaries of an earlier era in representing the dominant imperial interests of Western capitalist countries. Munzel, in discussing the missionary work in Paraguay, documents that in one particular mission run by U.S. fundamentalist missionaries the minister himself has engaged in Indian hunts where the young child captives are sold into slavery. Munzel notes that those who are not sold are herded into reservations where they are subjected to psychological degradation to break their spirit to prepare them for assimilation.

> Fundamentalist missionaries have followed the official line of the Paraguayan Indian Affairs Department with greater cruelty than their predecessors; they have attempted and continue to attempt to secure the rapid cultural integration of the Ache at almost any cost. Their technique is "civilizing with a sledgehammer," in the words of the Director of the South American section of the Hamburg Ethnographic Museum, who discusses their "racist feeling of superiority" and suggests that their disdain for Indian culture may be the reason why they were selected by the government to run the reservation. Indians are forced to give up their names, customs, traditions, and taught to think that anything connected with their own culture is shameful (Munzel cited in Chomsky and Herman, 1979, 112).

In Bolivia, Chomsky and Herman (1979) discuss the role of the Summer Institute of Linguistics and the Wycliffe Bible Translators in missionizing the Indian population. Chomsky and Herman note that the SIL, possibly the richest and most powerful of the North American religious bodies devoted to missionary work in South America, is supported by the Bolivian government under the Ministry of Culture and Education.

> The standard missionary technique when an uncontacted group is found is to leave gifts along forest paths to draw the Indians to the mission compound, where "often at the end of a long journey, far from the Indian's source of food, his fish, his game, (the trail) comes abruptly to an end." The Indians are then taught that they must work for money on local farms and they agree, "when they realize that there's no going back," according to the head of SIL, an official of the Ministry of Culture and Education (1979, 122).

According to Chomsky and Herman, North American missionaries have become the servants of such right-wing military dictatorships as that of Bolivia and their supporters to the north.

As noted, this form of violence has occurred in virtually every continent throughout history. Today it occurs in South and Central America, Africa, and Asia. Wilson and Kvale (1994) describe how in the Central African Republic the Baaka people and their way of life are under threat from both the government and Catholic missionaries. Both groups are trying to force the Baaka to move from their villages deep in the forest to organized village settlements where they can be under the control of the government and the church. Wilson and Kvale note that as part of this move they are encouraged to build wells and latrines, and to adopt domestic agricultural techniques as opposed to their traditional hunting and gathering. The authors note that the government officials and missionaries justify their actions by arguing that the Baaka need to be brought into the modern age in order to participate in the national culture and economy. Behind these supposed humanitarian concerns are economic interests. According to Wilson and Kvale, the government wants to tax the Baaka and wants a freer hand in granting timber felling concessions to foreign companies in the forest where the Baaka currently live.

There is resistance on the part of the Baaka. "We are happy in the forest because it provides everything we need," says Theresa, a spokesperson for the community of Sanguila in the forest of Haute-Sanga in the country's southern region. "We want to carry on living here. . . . I do not think that the forest will disappear; how can you think it would? People may damage the forest but this village will continue. . . . When I die my children will live here. . . . The village is expensive and there is a lot of hunger," according to Theresa. "The villagers exploit us a lot. The missionaries would like our children to go to school there but they cannot go because village children tease them. It would be better to have a school in the forest. The missionaries want to change us, but they will not change us. As for the Government, they do not give us anything—they do not know us yet (Wilson and Kvale, 1994, 17)."

CULT VIOLENCE

Sensational instances of violence between fringe religious groups in the United States give the impression that so-called cults are inherently dangerous. Media treatments of such groups are usually unsympathetic, so when cult violence is reported it is invariably given a "spin" that is unflattering to all unconventional religious groups. J. Gordon Melton, director of the Institute for the Study of American Religion in Santa Barbara, California, conducted a two-year study of reported incidences of violence concerning cult groups. He looked at three types of reported violence: violence directed against cults, violence initiated by cults, and cult-on-cult violence.

Overwhelmingly, nonconventional religious groups have been free of reported incidences of violence. Most groups in the survey were quite similar to the more familiar and established mainline church bodies; they experienced one or two scattered incidents atypical of their day-to-day life. Those few nonconventional religious groups which have suffered a history of violent interaction with society are very much the exceptions of those groups which have been labeled "cult" (Melton, 1986, 241).

His conclusion is that more violence has been aimed at unconventional religions by mainstream society than vice versa. Some reported instances of cult-related violence or public menace are overblown or just plain false. For example, it is true that the Hare Krishnas "stockpiled" weapons at their New Vrindiban temple/farm complex in West Virginia during 1978, but their entire weapons cache consisted of several .22-caliber weapons (which were never used) and were purchased only after local rowdies had threatened and shot at Krishna members as they worked. There were several other cases involving Krishnas and guns during the 1980s, but these all involved maverick members who were disciplined and/or excommunicated for violating the Hare Krishna prohibition on violence (Melton, 1986, 243–4). Likewise, rumors that members of The Way International (a controversial Christian sect) were engaging in paramilitary and guerrilla warfare training at The Way College in Emporia, Kansas, during the late 1970s proved groundless; the college, among other schools in the state, actually offered only a state-approved course in hunting safety (Melton, 1986, 244).

Nevertheless, it cannot be denied that there are real instances of cult violence. We have already mentioned the People's Temple (a congregation in the Disciples of Christ denomination that was labeled a "cult" only after the massacre at Jonestown, Guyana), the Order of the Solar Temple, the Branch Davidians, and the Heaven's Gate UFO groups (all now extinct). Within Mormonism there always have been breakaway groups and splinter sects quarreling over issues of leadership or polygamy (plural marriage). The longest running cult-on-cult violence involved the renegade Mormon LeBaron brothers: Ervil, Joel, and Verland. Joel founded the polygamous Church of the First Born of the Fullness of Time, then Ervil quit to form his own Church of the Lamb of God and demanded all other Mormon sect groups acknowledge him as God's leading prophet. When they refused, Ervil dispatched execution squads, particularly targeting his brothers. Joel and several other polygamous sect leaders were subsequently murdered. Ervil was arrested, convicted of murder, and incarcerated in Utah State Prison where he died of a massive heart attack in 1981. The bloody family saga finally ended two days after Ervil's death when his brother Verland was killed in an automobile accident (Bradlee and Atta, 1981; LaBaron, 1981).

More recently, in Kirtland, Ohio, self-proclaimed prophet Jeffrey Lundgren and his followers broke away from the Reorganized Church of Latter-Day Saints (itself a breakaway Mormon group) and formed their own cult. Then they lured five members of a Mormon family, including three little girls, one by one into a barn on Lundgren's property. There Lundgren shot them with a .45-caliber Colt Combat Elite pistol, then had the five bodies dumped in a large pit dug in the barn's dirt floor. Lundgren explained the murders as a "blood atonement," a nineteenth century Mormon notion that Mormons were justified in violence against "Gentiles" as blood atonement, or revenge, for the murder of Joseph and Hyrum Smith. Lundgren was sentenced to death five times over and to a maximum of five consecutive 10–25-year terms for kidnapping. He is currently in prison awaiting execution (Sasse and Widder, 1991).

The Nation of Islam (popularly known as the Black Muslims) was entangled in open civil war among rival factions during the 1960s. One charismatic dissenter from the leadership, Malcolm X, was machine-gunned in 1965, and various other leaders, including founder Elijah Muhammed's son-in-law, were shot or killed (Melton, 1986, 248).

One highly publicized form of violence directed at members of a wide variety of both conventional and unconventional religious groups during the 1970s and 1980s was deprogramming, a pseudo-scientific process of physical abduction, restraint, and coercive browbeating aimed at deconverting adult converts to groups such as the Hare Krishnas, the Way International, the Unification Church, the Children of God, even the Old Catholic Church. Often well-meaning parents and relatives rationalized deprogramming on the grounds that no sane person would voluntarily join such groups; thus their loved ones must have been programmed, that is, subjected to some little-understood procedures of brainwashing or mind control. Since most of the persons to be deprogrammed were legal adults, important issues of civil liberties and religious freedom were raised. (In one case, Greek Orthodox parents hired deprogrammers because their post-college daughters refused to attend church or continue to live at home and refused to allow their parents to select their husbands for them in the traditional Greek manner.)

Behavioral scientists, including sociologists who have done field work and participant observation, have found little evidence that such extreme conditioning, or programming, ever existed in cultic groups, and retaliatory legal pressures from the groups themselves as well as from angry members who outwitted and escaped their deprogrammers pretty much ended coercive deprogrammings by the late 1990s (Shupe, 1980, 1994; Bromley, 1989; Bromley and Shupe, 1981).

No one was ever killed by deprogrammers, but the tendency to go beyond gentle persuasion in matters of spiritual conviction runs like a red letter throughout American religion. This is not to make an argument against religion per se or to suggest that every group is capable of cruelty and violence and simultaneously justifying these. But, religious coercion and persecution are staples of every major society's culture and history. And because the social reality that every religion proclaims is difficult to substantiate empirically, human beings will (if they feel they have to) at times fight, repress, even murder others who accept different social realities.

CONCLUSION: THE UBIQUITY OF RELIGIOUS VIOLENCE

Religious violence is no aberration. It is normal, patterned, and to be expected along the same structural, historical, and symbolic lines that all inequality, oppression, and rationalization thereof occurs. When we look at who are the victims of religious violence, those who are least powerful appear to suffer from the highest levels of victimization. This is the case whether we are talking about the violence of crusades, missionaries, or the abuse of small children or women by religious functionaries. Religious institutions have been so interwoven with political and economic institutions that the same could hardly be otherwise. Religion is a two-edged sword: it can be a force for revolution and change (the Weberian vision) or a social influence to repress moral outrage and infuse acquiescence among those downtrodden with legitimate grievances (the Marxist vision).

The relation of religion and violence, therefore, is twofold. First, religious leaders and the beliefs they preach have led to direct violence in the name of the religious creed, and second, religion has served to facilitate or maintain some violent modes of political conquest and economic exploitation. Our point is neither to apologize for nor condemn religion per se. Instead, we want to indicate its role as a crucial human institution that is deeply involved in the otherwise political/economic/ideological matrix of violence by social groups acting against one another or against individuals.

REFERENCES

Adas, Michael. 1979. *Prophets of Rebellion: Millenarian Protest Movements against the European Colonial Order*. Chapel Hill: University of North Carolina Press.

Aho, James A. 1990. *The Politics of Righteousness: Idaho Christian Patriotism*. Seattle: University of Washington Press.

Andrews, Edward Deming. 1963. *The People Called Shakers*. Enlarged ed. New York: Dover Books.

Angebert, Jean-Michel. 1974. *The Occult and the Third Reich*. Translated by Lewis A. M. Sumberg. New York: McGraw-Hill.

Annan, David. 1967. "The Assassins and the Knights Templar." In *Secret Societies*, ed. N. McKenzie, 88–108. New York: Penguins Books.

Arrington, Leonard J., and David Bitton. 1980. *The Mormon Experience*. New York: Vintage Books.

Arrington, Leonard J., and Jon Haupt. 1988. "Intolerable Zion: The image of Mormonism in nineteenth century American literature." *Western Humanities Review* 22: 243–60.

Associated Press. 2002, March 4. "Sex Abuse Ravages Diocese Finances."

Bednarski, Joyce. 1968. "The Salem Witch-Scare Viewed Sociologically." In *Witchcraft and Sorcery*, ed. M. Marwick, 151–63. Baltimore: Penguin Books.

Berry, Jason. 1992. *Lead Us Not into Temptation: Catholic Priests and the Sexual Abuse of Children*. New York: Doubleday.

Best, Joel. 1990. *Threatened Children: Rhetoric and Concern about Child-Victims*. Chicago: University of Chicago Press.

Bonavoglia, Angela. 1990, March-April. "The Sacred Secret." *Ms.*, 4–5.

Boyle, James J., 1995. *Killer Cults*. New York: St. Martin's.

Bradlee, Ben, Jr., and Dale Van Atta. 1981. *Prophet of Blood*. New York: Putnam's.

Brennan, J. H. 1974. *The Occult Reich*. New York: Signet Books.

Brock, Raymond T. and Horace C. Lukens, Jr. 1988. "Affair Prevention in the Ministry." *Psychology and Christianity* 8: 44—55.

Bromley, David G. 1989. "Hare Krishna and the Anti-cult Movement." In *Krishna Consciousness in the West*, ed. by D. G. Bromley, and L. D. Shinn, 255—92, Lewisburg, Penn.: Bucknell University Press.

Bromley, David G., and Anson D. Shupe, Jr. 1981. *Strange Gods: The Great American Cult Scare*. Boston: Beacon Press.

Bureau of Alcohol, Tobacco, and Firearms. 1993, September. *Report of the Department of the Treasury on the Bureau of Alcohol, Tobacco, and Firearms Investigation of Vernon Wayne Howell also Known as David Koresh*. Washington, D.C.: U. S. Government, Treasury Department.

Burkett, Elinor, and Frank Bruni. 1993. *A Gospel of Shame: Children, Sexual Abuse, and the Catholic Church*. New York: Viking Press.

Burman, Edward. 1986. *The Templars: Knights of God*. Rochester: Thorsons Publishers.

Cartwright, Robert H., and Stephen A. Kent. 1992. "Social Control in Alternative Religions: A Familial Perspective." *Sociological Analysis* 53: 345–61.

Chandrasekaran, Rajiv. 2002, March 5. "Militants Raze Mosque, Install Statue of Monkey God." *Washington Post*.

Chomsky, Noam, and Edward S. Herman. 1979. *The Washington Connection and Third World Fascism*. Boston: South End Press.

Cohn, Norman. 1971. *The Pursuit of the Millennium*. New York: Oxford University Press.

———. 1975. *Europe's Inner Demons*. New York: New American Library.

Cooper-White, Pamela. 1991, February 20. "Soul Stealing: Power Relations in Pastoral Sexual abuse." *The Christian Century*: 196–99.

Cooperman, Alan. 2002, January 31. "Catholic Church Settles Suits Alleging Sex Abuse by Priest." *Washington Post*.

Corcoran, James. 1990. *Bitter Harvest*. Baltimore, Md.: Penguin Books.

Daraul, Arkon. 1969. *A History of Secret Societies*. New York: Pocket Books.

Enroth, Ronald M. 1992. *Churches That Abuse*. Grand Rapids, Mich.: Zondervan.

Evans, Bergen. 1968. *Dictionary of Quotations*. New York: Delacorte Press.

Farragher, Thomas, 2002, March 8. "Law Adds Top Specialists to Abuse Prevention Panel." *Boston Globe*.

Feuerstein, Georg. 1991. *Holy Madness: The Shock Tactics and Radical Teachings of Adepts, Crazy-wise Adepts, Holy Fools, and Rascal Gurus*. New York: Paragon House.

Fortune, Marie M. 1989. *Is Nothing Sacred?* San Francisco: Harper-Collins.

Foster, Lawrence. 1981. *Religion and Sexuality: Three American Communal Experiments of the Nineteenth Century*. New York: Oxford University Press.

French, Ron. 1993, December 12. "Shattered Trust." *Fort Wayne Journal-Gazette*, 5–6D.

Gage, Susan. 1991. *Colonialism in the Americas*. Victoria, British Columbia: Victoria International Development Education Association.

Gies, Frances. 1984. *The Knight in History*. New York: Harper & Row.

Gilje, Paul A. 1987. *The Road to Mobocracy*. Chapel Hill: University of North Carolina Press.

Hall, John R. 1989. *Gone from the Promised Land: Jonestown in American Cultural History*. New Brunswick, N.J.: Transaction Publishers.

Hansen, Chadwick. 1969. *Witchcraft at Salem*. New York: New American Library.

Haught, James A. 1990. *Holy Horrors*. Buffalo, N.Y.: Prometheus Books.

Hayford, J. E. Casely. 1970. *Gold Coast Native Institutions, with Thought upon a Healthy Imperial Policy for the Gold Coast and Ashanti*. London: Cass.

Heckethorn, Charles William. 1965. *The Secret Societies of All Ages and Countries*. New Hyde Park: University Books.

Heinerman, John, and Anson Shupe. 1985. *The Mormon Corporate Empire*. Boston: Beacon Press.

Hicks, Robert D. 1991. *In Pursuit of Satan*. Buffalo, N.Y.: Prometheus Books.

Hill, Daniel. 1980. *Study of Mind Development Groups, Sects and Cults in Ontario: Report to the Ontario Government*. Ontario, Canada: Government of Ontario.

Hill, Marvin S. 1989. *Quest for Refuge: The Mormon Flight from American Pluralism*. Salt Lake City, Utah: Signature Books.

Hoffmann, Bill, and Cathy Burke. 1997. *Heaven's Gate: Cult Suicide in San Diego*. New York: HarperPaperbacks.

Holloway, Mark. 1966. *Heavens on Earth*. 2nd ed. New York: Dover

Jacobs, Janet Liebman. 1989. *Divine Disenchantment: Deconverting from New Religions*. Bloomington: Indiana University Press.

Jefferson, Thomas. 1954. *Notes on the State of Virginia*. New York: W. W. Norton.

Johnston, Jerry. 1989. *The Edge of Evil: The Rise of Satanism in North America*. Dallas, Tex.: Word Publishing.

Kahaner, Larry. 1988. *Cults That Kill*. New York: Warner Books.

Kaplan, David E. and Andrew Marshall, 1996. *The Cult at the End of the World*. New York: Crown Publishers.

Karlsen, Carol F. 1987. *The Devil in the Shape of a Woman*. New York: Vintage Books.

LaBaron, Verland M. 1981. *The LeBaron Story*. Lubbock, Tex.: Verland M. LaBaron.

Lanternari, Vittorio. 1963. *The Religions of the Oppressed*. Translated by Lisa Sergio. New York: Knopf.

Levi, Ken, ed. 1982. *Violence and Religious Commitment*. University Park: The Pennsylvania State University Press.

Lewis, James R. 1994. *From the Ashes: Making Sense of Waco*. Lanham, Md.: Rowman and Littlefield.

MacFarlane, Alan. 1970. *Witchcraft in Tudor and Stuart England*. New York: Harper & Row.

Mahapatra, Rajesh. 2002, March 6. "Christians Were Targeted in India." *Associated Press*.

Martin, David C., and John Walcott. 1988. *Best Laid Plans: The Inside Story of America's War against Terrorism*. New York: Harper & Row.

Marty, Martin E. 1984. *Pilgrims in Their Own Land: 500 Years of Religion in America*. New York: Penguin Books.

Marwick, Max. 1968. "Witchcraft as a Social Strain Gauge." In *Witchcraft and Sorcery*, ed. M. Marwick, 280–95. Baltimore, Md.: Penguin Books.

Melton, J. Gordon. 1986. *Encyclopedic Handbook of Cults in America*. New York: Garland.

Moore, Rebecca, and Fielding McGhee, III. 1989. *New Religious Movements, Mass Suicide, and Peoples Temple*. Lewiston: Edwin Mellen Press.

Morgan, Richard E. 1968. *The Politics of Religious Conflict*. New York: Pegasus.

Muller-Hill, Benno. 1988. *Murderous Science*. Translated by George R. Fraser. New York: Oxford University Press.

Nason-Clark, Nancy. 1991. "Broken Trust: The Case of Roman Catholic Priests in Newfoundland Charged with the Sexual Abuse of Children." Unpublished paper presented at the annual meeting of the Society for the Scientific Study of Religion, Pittsburgh, Penn.

New York Times. 2002, March 5. "Los Angeles Cardinal Removes Priests Involved in Pedophilia Cases."

Partner, Peter. 1987. *The Murdered Magicians.* Rochester: Thorsons Publishers.

Payne, Robert. 1984. *The Dream and the Tomb: A History of the Crusades.* New York: Dorset Press.

Pickthall, Mohammed Marmaduke. 1961. *The Meaning of the Glorious Koran.* New York: New American Library.

Plaidy, Jean. 1969. *The Spanish Inquisition.* New York: The Citadel Press.

Poling, James Newton. 1991. *The Abuse of Power: A Theological Problem.* Nashville, Tenn.: Abington.

Raschke, Carl. 1990. *Painted Black.* New York: Harper & Row.

Rice, Andrew. 1993, December 2. "Franciscans Admit 34 Boys Were Molested at St. Anthony's." *The Independent.*

Richardson, James T., Joel Best, and David G. Bromley. 1991. *The Satanism Scare.* New York: Aldine de Gruyter.

Robbins, Thomas. 1986. "Religious Mass Suicide before Jonestown: The Russian Old Believers." *Sociological Analysis* 41: 1–20.

Rossetti, Stephen J. 1990. *Slayer of the Soul: Child Sexual Abuse and the Catholic Church.* Mystic, Conn.: Twenty-Third Publications.

Rowling, Marjorie. 1979. *Life in Medieval Times.* New York: Paragon Books.

Rutter, Peter. 1989. *Sex in the Forbidden Zone.* Los Angeles: Jeremy P. Tarcher.

Sasse, Cynthia Stalter, and Peggy Murphy Widder. 1991. *The Kirtland Massacre.* New York: Donald I. Fine.

Scott, Ralph A. 1979. *A New Look at Biblical Crime.* Chicago: Nelson-Hall.

Shannon, William V. 1966. *The American Irish.* Rev. ed. New York: Macmillan.

Shupe, Anson. 1995. *In the Name of All That's Holy: A Theory of Clergy Malfeasance.* Westport, Conn.: Praeger.

Shupe, Anson D., Jr., and David G. Bromley. 1980. *The New Vigilantes: Deprogrammers, Anti-Cultists, and the New Religions.* Beverly Hills, Calif.: Sage.

Shupe, Anson D., Jr., and David G. Bromley. 1994. *Anti-Cult Movements in Cross-Cultural Perspective.* New York: Garland Publishers.

Shupe, Anson D., Jr., and Jeffrey K. Hadden. 1995. "Cops, News Copy, and Legitimacy: The Social Construction of Evil in Waco." In *Armageddon in Waco*, ed. Stuart A. Wright, 177–202. Chicago: University of Chicago Press.

Sklar, Dusty. 1977. *Gods and Beasts: The Nazis and the Occult.* New York: Thomas Y. Crowell.

Starkey, Marion L. 1969. *The Devil in Massachusetts.* Garden City, N.Y.: Doubleday.

Sutherland, Charles W. 1987. *Disciples of Destruction.* Buffalo, N.Y.: Prometheus Books.

Tinker, George E. 1993. *Missionary Conquest.* Minneapolis, Minn.: Fortress Press.

Victor, Jeffrey S. 1993. *Satanic Panic.* Chicago: Open Court.

Waite, Robert G. L. 1974. *The Psycho-Pathic God.* New York: Signet Books.

Wallace, Anthony F. C. 1966. "Revitalization movements." *American Anthropologist* 58: 264–81.

Wittke, Carl. 1970. *The Irish in America*. New York: Russell and Russell.
Wilson, Margaret and Ingrid Kvale. 1994, June 17. "They Do Not Know Us Yet." *The New Internationalist*.
Wright, Robin. 1989. *In the Name of God*. New York: Simon and Schuster.
Wright, Stuart A. 1995. *Armageddon in Waco*. Chicago: University of Chicago Press.

Chapter Six

Economic Violence

400 Iraqis died in 1972 and 5,000 were hospitalized after consuming the by-product of 8,000 tons of wheat and barley coated with an organic mercury fungicide, whose use had been banned in the U.S. An undisclosed number of farmers and over 1,000 water buffaloes died suddenly in Egypt after being exposed to leptophos, a chemical pesticide which was never registered for domestic use by the Environmental Protection Agency (EPA) but was exported to at least thirty countries (Dowie, 1979, 24).

Seventy-six-year-old Amy Selle had gotten out of her '77 Thunderbird to help a friend get in. When she saw the car jump she grabbed for the wheel, but the door knocked her down. Onlookers, most of them elderly, watched in horror as she was run over twice, her skull fractured by the wildly circling Ford (Branan, 1980, 41).

On February 10, 1985, Stefan Golab staggered from the cyanide tank he was working over, stumbled to the adjacent locker room, and collapsed. Some of his fellow workers dragged him outside and called an ambulance. When the ambulance arrived back at the hospital, Golab was dead. An autopsy was performed to determine the cause of death. . . . The autopsy findings led to an eight month investigation, resulting in the indictment of five Film Recovery executives on charges of murder and the indictment of Film Recovery Systems, Inc., and two related corporations on charges of manslaughter (Frank, 1986).

On June 29, 1988, a young worker at Bastian Plating Company in Auburn, Indiana, was asphyxiated while cleaning out a tank. The tank had been treated with a substance that emitted lethal vapors when mixed with water— but nobody informed the worker. Four workers, aged nineteen to twenty-five, were subsequently asphyxiated one by one as they tried to save their friend (Shaffer, 1988).

On September 3, there was a fire at the Imperial Food Products chicken-processing plant in Hamlet, North Carolina. As the fire spread through the factory, workers rushed to the exits only to find that six of the nine exit doors were shut tight, most padlocked by the owners to prevent workers stealing chickens. Twenty-five workers who were locked in the building died from the fire (Kerr and Hall, 1992).

These are some of the stories of economic violence. Thousands upon thousands of people each year are injured or die as a result of actions taken by agents of businesses to further their interests, placing the accumulation of profits above the health and safety of consumers, workers, and members of communities around the world. What is economic violence? What are the major types of economic violence? Who are the victims and perpetrators? Why does it occur? These are the questions we address in this chapter.

We begin by defining economic violence. First, economic violence is a category of institutional violence. In general, institutional violence is violence that occurs by the action of societal institutions and their agents. In referring to economic violence in particular we are focusing on actors or agents of economic entities, in most cases businesses or economic entities formed to produce or market commodities. This would include actors in a large chemical corporation, a small farmer, a state-owned steel mill, an automobile manufacturer, or a retailer. In discussing economic violence we can identify three major types of violence: product violence, production violence, and environmental violence.

PRODUCT VIOLENCE

Product violence refers to producing commodities that because of a defect in design or manufacturing are known to lead to the death and injury of consumers and not informing consumers of these hazards. There is no way to know specifically how many people die from the use of faulty products. In the United States a number of agencies may receive reports of deaths or injuries to the public as a result of the use of consumer products. The one agency that is principally responsible for this type of violence is the National Commission on Product Safety. They have noted that as many as 20 million Americans are injured in the home because of incidents connected with consumer products each year. Of the 20 million, 110,000 are permanently disabled and 30,000 are killed (Simon and Eitzen, 1999). There would be no way of estimating this violence worldwide. Given the paucity of regulations on product safety for the majority of the world's population, levels of product violence may be significantly higher in many developing countries.

Product Dumping

One particular reason for suspecting this is a great problem in less developed countries is because of the practice by many large chemical and pharmaceutical companies of dumping unsafe products overseas on unsuspecting consumers.

This practice of product dumping is not illegal in the United States, which is the dominant producer in the world market. In the introduction to this chapter, we noted several examples of product dumping as they pertain to the dumping of unsafe pesticides or fungicides. There are many more examples of countries that receive pesticides and fungicides, such as chlordane, DBCP, DDT, and Hep-tachlor, which, although produced in the United States and/or by U.S. corporations, have been banned from sale in the United States because of their carcinogenic effects on consumers and farm workers. For example, Velsicol Chemical Company between 1987 and 1989 exported thousands of pounds of chlordane and Heptachlor to Argentina, Australia, Dominican Republic, India, Netherlands, Philippines, Singapore, Thailand, and many other countries (Bray, 1989).

Another example is that of DBCP a pesticide banned in the United States after workers who produced the chemical became aware of research conducted by some of the developers that exposure to the chemical caused testicular cancer and sterility. As early as 1955, Dow and Shell both knew that low doses of DBCP caused profound organ changes in animals, and in 1958 Dow knew that exposure caused testicular atrophy in laboratory rats. In the United States, the DBCP hush-up ended abruptly in 1977 when workers in California brought Dow and Shell to court. Dow temporarily stopped sales of DBCP in the United States. A nationwide ban went into effect soon after that. The product was officially banned from the U.S. market in 1985. It is not known how many workers; farm laborers, merchants, or consumers exposed to the chemical developed cancer or became sterile. There are reports of cases of sterility at a Shell Chemical plant in Mobile, Alabama, and reports of sterility among workers in an Occidental Chemical plant in California. According to a recent report issued by an Environmental Working Group (EWG) analysis of recent state data concluded that the tap water of more than 1 million Californians, mostly in the Central Valley, is contaminated with the banned pesticide. The Sacramento Bee reported that EWG's computer-assisted analysis of water utility test results found that DBCP contaminates tap water in thirty-eight water systems in nine counties. Fresno, Riverside, Clovis, Lodi and Madera are the largest communities with serious problems (Environmental Working Group, 1999).

DBCP continued to be produced after it was banned for use in the United States for shipment overseas. Latin America was a particular region where sales were high. In 1979, the Costa Rican government finally pressured Standard Fruit to stop using DBCP after hundreds of Costa Rican agricultural workers have discovered that they are sterile. Mokhiber (1994) notes that 15,000 Costa Rican workers have similar claims pending in Texas State courts. Other countries where governments are not as concerned about the health and safety of farm workers continue to be a target for the exportation of this deadly chemical. Honduras and Peru are countries that have recently imported substantial amounts of DBCP (Brown and Thrupp, 1991).

DDT is another pesticide banned in the United States that continues to be produced and exported to developing countries. Burbach and Flynn (1980) report that a U.N. study revealed that in the cotton-producing regions of Guatemala and Nicaragua the average DDT content in human blood is 520 parts per billion (compared with forty-six in Dade County, Florida). In Central America as a whole, between 1972 and 1975 there were forty reported deaths attributable to the use of pesticides, and 14,133 DDT-related illnesses. The authors note that doctors, priests, and peasants in the area say there are many additional unreported deaths attributable to pesticides (Burbach and Flynn, 1980). Mohkiber (1988) notes that DDT levels in cows milk in Guatemala is ninety times as high as that allowed in the United States. Nursing mothers in many Guatemalan and Nicaraguan villages have levels of DDT in their breast milk that is 200 times greater than levels in women's breast milk in the United States. In 1989 the World Bank approved a $99 million loan for Brazil's mosquito control program. The loan was to be matched by the Brazilian government and to be used for the purchase and application of 3,000 tons of DDT in the ecologically sensitive Amazon region (Gold, 1989).

Bissio (1990) contends that pesticides have killed, injured and poisoned more people in rural Brazil than were affected by the chemical disaster in Bhopal, India. In Brazil labor relations, especially in rural areas, are abominable. He notes that foremen will often send out the youngest workers, fourteen and fifteen years old, to apply pesticides. They are chosen as the sprayers because they'll last longer. They haven't built up chronic poisoning yet, and when they're 18 or 20, they're moved to other jobs. You see kids in their late adolescence or early twenties playing soccer, and they don't have the energy to keep running up and down the field (Bissio, 1990, 71). Bissio also cites the case of Sri Lanka, which has a population of 14 million and has twice as many individuals hospitalized for pesticide poisoning than the United States—despite the fact that the United States uses one-third of the world's pesticides.

One major problem with the use of these pesticides in developing countries that were banned in the United States because of their link to cancer is what Dowie (1979) calls the boomerang effect. The pesticides banned in this country, as well as other more advanced countries in the world, come back to these countries in the foods treated with these pesticides that are imported. Mohkiber (1988) notes that according to FDA estimates, 10 percent of our imported food is contaminated with illegal residues of banned pesticides. He also reports that this estimate has been challenged. Citing Weir and Shapiro's analysis of General Accounting Office Reports of the early 1980s, over 15 percent of the beans and 13 percent of the peppers imported from Mexico, during one recent period, were found to violate FDA pesticide residue standards. Nearly half the imported green coffee beans contain levels of pesticides that are banned from the United States, and imported beef from Central America often contains pesticide contamination (Mokhiber, 1988, 188). Mohkiber also notes that a 1986 General Accounting Office report suggests that conditions may have worsened since the FDA does not test domestically grown food for pesticide contamination and therefore does nothing to prevent the sale of pesticide contaminated food grown by domestic growers.

As a result of a recent lawsuit brought by the National Resources Defense Counsel, State of California, AFL-CIO, Public Citizen, and a California farmworker against the U.S. Environmental Protection Agency, the EPA may order the phasing out of use of an additional thirty-six cancer-causing pesticides that have been allowed as residue in juices, canned fruits and vegetables. Part of the agreement also requires that the EPA review within five years an additional forty-nine carcinogenic pesticides (Freeman, 1994). If the pattern of product dumping continues, however, more inspections must be done to safeguard the public from continued use of the carcinogenic pesticides here and abroad. In a recent article on the problems of the use of banned pesticides, the *New Internationalist* (2000) gave the following example of the problems of pesticide residue. They note that the average Westerner consumes over eleven kilograms of apples a year. Apples are exported from at least forty different countries. They are among the most contaminated fruits; 98 percent of all apples have pesticides on them. Chocolate is another example; the *New Internationalist* reports that "in 1994 75 percent of seventy-two samples of European chocolate tested contained low levels of lindane (or gamma-HCH), a pesticide that is banned in six countries and severely restricted in eighteen" (*New Internationalist* 2000, 23).

Although many agricultural pesticides that are defined as carcinogenic are banned for sale to farmers in the United States, they are still sold in this country as home insecticides. According to one report, tens of millions of homes in the U.S. are contaminated with varying levels of chlordane/heptachlor, pesticides still registered by EPA for termite treatment. In a recent study conducted by Mt. Sinai Hospital in New York, a medical team asked eighty major chemical industries whether they had done any epidemiological studies on carcinogens they were using. Most of the companies reported that they had conducted no such research (Bissio, 1990). One recent study done in Los Angeles on the hazards of these pesticides used in the home and on lawns and gardens indicated that children were four times more likely to develop lymphocytic leukemia if their parents used pesticides in the home and six times more likely if pesticides were used on lawns and gardens (Lowengart, Peters, and Cicioni, 1987). A recent review article described thirty-one studies of pesticides and childhood cancers reported during the period 1970–1996. The review concluded that results from leukemia studies suggest that no-pest strips and frequent use of pesticides in the home may be strongly associated with childhood leukemia (Daniels et. al., 1997).

Another example of product dumping includes the Dalkon Shield. In the late 1970s, A.H. Robbins Company arranged with the assistance of the U.S. Agency for International Development for the distribution of the Dalkon Shield intrauterine device in a number of developing countries. Dowie notes that this overseas market was sought after Robbins already knew that the shield was responsible for 20,000 cases of serious uterine infection. He furthermore notes that the use of the product resulted in several thousand women receiving hysterectomies (Dowie and Johnston, 1976). Mintz (1985) reports that the potential hazards because of the specific design of the shield were made known to company owners and executives seventeen days after the product was brought to market in the United States. The string connected to the IUD was a conduit for bacteria to invade the pelvic cavity. This created the problem of pelvic inflammatory disease. The Food and Drug Administration, after complaints from doctors, ordered the company to stop selling the shield in mid-1974. But there was no movement to tell women in the United States who had the shield placed inside them of the dangers until 1984.

Today there are many women around the world who still have the Dalkon Shield in their bodies. The recall that went into effect during the 1980s was for women in the United States. Federal Judge Miles W. Lord, who decided against the firm in a lawsuit brought by seven women who experienced degrees of injury from using the shield, describe their predicament as a depth charge in their wombs, ready to explode at any time. Judge Lord, in addressing E. Clairborne Robbins, Jr., president of the company and grandson of its founder; William Forrest, the company's general counsel; and Dr. Carl Lunsford, chief medical officer, stated at the time of his decision:

> Gentlemen, the results of these activities and attitudes on your part have been catastrophic. Today, as you sit here attempting once more to extricate yourselves from the legal consequence of your acts, none of you has faced up to the fact that more than 9,000 women have claims that they gave up part of their womanhood so that your company might prosper. . . . If one poor young man were by some act of his—without authority or consent—to inflict such damage upon one woman, he would be jailed for a good portion of the rest of his life. Yet your company, without warning to them, invaded women's bodies by the millions and caused them injuries by the thousands (1984, 2).

Other examples of product dumping cited by Dowie include Depo-Provera, an injectable contraceptive banned for use in the United States because of laboratory studies that indicated a link with cancerous tumors. At the time Dowie (1979) was reporting the problem of product dumping, Depo-Provera was sold by the Upjohn Company in seventy other countries and widely used in U.S-sponsored population control programs. Five manufacturers exported baby pacifiers of the type that caused choking deaths overseas. And, as an example of the boomerang effect, pajamas sprayed with a fire retardant that was carcinogenic were shipped overseas. A foreign company bought these same pajamas after the labels were changed and shipped them back for sale in the United States.

Pharmaceutical Industry

Many other cases of product violence within the pharmaceutical industry have occurred in the United States. One classic case is that of Richardson Merrell

Company and MER 29 (Ungar, 1972). MER 29 was a drug designed to lower cholesterol levels in the blood. Before it was to be marketed, the FDA routinely requested further testing to determine potential hazards and drug side effects. Merrell assured the FDA that animal tests had been completed and that the results were satisfactory. The required test results were submitted to the FDA for drug approval. In 1960 Merrell began a large-scale sales campaign praising the drug to physicians. Soon after it was introduced, physicians began to notice side effects from the drug that were not indicated in the drug literature. Some of these problems were inflammation of the skin, loss of hair, color change of hair, and loss of sex drive. Merrell instructed its sales personnel to shift the blame to other drugs the patients might be taking, a result not of the drug itself but rather due to an interaction effect.

Not until 1962 did the FDA discover that Merrell had falsified test results. In tests using monkeys and dogs, several had become ill using the drug. The researchers replaced sick animals with new animals and continued the study. In rat studies in which whole samples had died, the results were not reported. Permission was awarded to market the drug after the test results were reviewed. After physicians had reported many reports of harmful consequences, however, permission to market the drug was withdrawn by the FDA. The Health Department of the State of California later discovered that 500 people developed cataracts while using the drug. This was not the only case of corporate violence committed by Merrell and its subsidiaries. During the 1960s, Merrell was responsible for distributing Thalidomide, a drug given to pregnant women to treat morning sickness during the first three months of pregnancy. Thalidomide was never tested to determine if it caused birth defects. Unfortunately, this was the case. Later, Merrell was involved in withholding information from the FDA on the link between Bendectin and birth defects (Dowie and Marshall, 1980; Mokhiber, 1988).

There are other cases of pharmaceutical companies producing and marketing hazardous products that are not reported to the public or the medical profession that prescribes them. Eli Lilly and their products Oraflex and DES; SmithKline and Beecham and the product, Selacryn; Upjohn and the product Halcion; and the Cordis Corporation and defective heart pacemakers are all examples of this. In these cases, the manufacturers knew of the hazards they did not report, which resulted in the death and injury of consumers. (Mokhiber, 1988, 1994; Simon, 1999)

Food Industry

The selling of unwholesome or spoiled food is another area of product violence. In some cases the food processor will wash and clean spoiled meat and resell it. Simon (1999) reported the following cases.

In 1984, Nebraska Beef Processors and its Colorado subsidiary, Cattle King Packing company—the largest supplier of ground meat to school lunch programs and a major supplier of meat to the Department of Defense, supermarkets, and fast-food chains was found guilty of (1) regularly bringing dead animals into its slaughter-houses and mixing rotten meat into its hamburgers, (2) labeling old meat with phony dates, and (3) deceiving U.S. Department of Agriculture inspectors by matching dis-eased carcasses with the healthy heads from larger cows. In 1979, a New Jersey firm was convicted of making pork sausage with an unauthorized chemical that masks discoloration of spoiled meat. And in 1982, a California company used walkie-talkies to avoid inspectors while doctoring rotten sausage (134).

Another case of selling adulterated food was reported by employees of Food Lion, a grocery store chain. Employee whistleblowers charged Food Lion with adding Clorox bleach to old fish to remove the spoiled smell, then putting the repackaged fish out for sale; pouring barbecue sauce on old chicken, repackaging it and selling it; grinding dirty and spoiled beef to resell as hamburger; and sending employees into dumpsters to pick out thrown-away food to resell. (Mokhiber, Gozan, and Knaus, 1992)

A more recent case involved the death of at least twenty-one consumers of Ball Park hotdogs and other processed meat products produced by Bil Mar Company, a subsidiary of Sara Lee. The deaths resulted from a listeriosis out-break that led to the deaths of at least twenty-one consumers who ate Ball Park Franks and other meat products. Mokhiber and Weissman report that it was sus-pected that the outbreaks were caused by the replacement of an air condition-ing unit in the processing plant. This work dislodged some dangerous bacteria on the ceiling of the plant. When the plant reopened, steam from the passing hot dogs went up to the ceiling, condensed and dripped back down with the dangerous bacteria onto the hot dogs. According to a series of reports in the De-troit Free Press, plant workers were regularly testing work surfaces for the pres-ence of cold-loving bacteria, a class of bacteria that includes the deadly Listeria monocytogenes as well as some harmless bacteria. After the replacement of the old refrigeration unit, workers recorded a sharp increase in the presence of cold-loving bacteria. "Sara Lee was doing testing of the environment in the plant for cold-loving bacteria," says Caroline Smith DeWaal of the Center for Science in the Public Interest. "Then their tests started coming up positive, so they stopped testing. They knew they had a problem with bacteria in the plant. But instead of solving it, they chose to ignore it." The company paid a $200,000 fine. (Mokhiber and Weissman, 2001, 17)

Another large area of product violence in the food industry is that of food additives. More than 1,500 food additives are used in our foods. Some of these include food colorings such as Red dye number 2, Sodium nitrates and nitrates as a preservative, DES to fatten cattle, arsenic fed to hens to make them lay more eggs, and various sugar substitutes (cyclamates and aspartame). The ar-gument by industry and government is that such small amounts of the addi-tive in our foods do little harm. But in most cases these additives are stored in the fatty tissues in our bodies and may accumulate to cause cancer. We do know that the average American has increased his or her yearly consumption of food additives from three pounds in 1965 to approximately five pounds in 1977, and we suspect it is many times higher today. Rates of most types of cancer have continued to rise (Simon, 1999).

Our last example of product violence relating to food is the case of the Nestlé Corporation and the marketing of infant formula (Summa, 1988; Mokhiber, 1989). Henri Nestlé, an entrepreneur, developed an infant formula in the late 1800s as a substitute for mothers who could not breastfeed their children. Unfortunately, the company, following the dictates of capitalism, expanded the market for the formula by marketing it as superior to breast milk. This is not the case. It is not entirely clear what has been the overall impact on children of women from developed countries who substituted the formula for breast milk. However, the impact on women and their children in developing countries has been described by more than one hundred organizations in sixty countries as disastrous.

Women in poorer countries do not have access to safe water to mix with the powdered formula, resulting in infants (soon after birth) developing bacterial infections which kill them. Furthermore, these same poor women can't afford the formula and solve this problem by diluting it to the point of starving their children. Nestlé's marketing technique was deceptive to say the least. Sales personnel often dressed in white hospital garb (sometimes hiring nurses to push the formula) would provide new mothers with free samples to start the feeding. Enough free samples were given to the women in the hospital to result in the premature weaning of their infants. Once these poor mothers' own breasts had stopped producing milk as a result of the weaning, they were forced to continue the feeding of the formula. Unfortunately, many families could barely afford the price of the food required to sustain the family, and adequate amounts of the formula became a luxury many could not afford.

Nestlé also conducted a widespread marketing program promoting the use of baby formula as superior to breast milk and the modern way to feed your infant. Mokhiber notes that breast feeding declined precipitously in developing countries targeted for the marketing, and the impact on children's lives has been deadly. It has been estimated that 15 million children under the age of five die every year, partly from malnutrition, with an additional 10 million more paralyzed, made blind or deaf, or suffering from brain damage or stunted growth from disease. Most of this toll occurs in the third world, and the causes are numerous. But more and more specialists within the infant nutrition and health care community are focusing their attention on infant formula use as an important causal factor in the high levels of infant diarrhea, malnutrition, and mortality (Mokhiber, 1989, 313).

In 1981 the World Health Assembly of the World Health Organization adopted an International Code. The code, intended to be adopted as a minimum requirement by all governments, aims to protect infant health by preventing inappropriate marketing of breast milk substitutes. The United States signed the code in 1994. The code prohibits providing free samples of formula and promoting the use of formula as superior to breast milk. In a report issued by IBFAN—International Baby Food Action Network, entitled *Breaking the Rules, Stretching the Rules* (2001), evidence is presented of widespread violations in a fourteen-country survey. The monitoring results cover sixteen transnational baby food companies and thirteen manufacturers of bottles and teats (Kean and Allain, 2001).

Water quality is a problem around the world. Recently, however, consumers in the wealthiest countries in the world have been purchasing bottled water and filtering devices to obtain clean water from the water systems that have been polluted by industrial and agricultural chemical waste. But the problem of product violence has occurred here as well. In 1989 lab tests found traces of benzene, a potential carcinogen, in samples of Perrier, at the time a fashionable bottled water popular among the elite. Furthermore, Simon and Eitzen (1993) note the case of Norelco and their water-filtering system that served to contaminate the water. The authors note that between 1982 and 1986, Norelco sold water-filter machines that it knew actually contaminated water with methylene chloride, a probable carcinogen (126).

Tobacco

One of the most deadly cases of product violence is tobacco. As early as 1900, medical experts noted an increase in cancer of the lungs linked to tobacco consumption. In 1925 a British scientist established the link between tar in tobacco and skin cancer. In 1938, Dr. Raymond Pearl noted the reduced life expectancy among smokers. When *Readers Digest* in 1941 kicked off a series of articles informing the public of the potential hazards of cigarette smoking, the tobacco industry countered with an advertising campaign extolling the health virtues of smoking. Claims such as smoking cigarettes was good for digestion, that more doctors smoke Camels than any other cigarette, and that nose, throat and accessory organs are not adversely affected by smoking Chesterfields were made by the tobacco companies to counter this attack by the medical community (Mokhiber, 1988). Meanwhile, research continued to be produced illustrating the link between cancer and tobacco products. The Sloan-Kettering Institute study of 1953 found that cancer could be induced in test animals by spreading tars from cigarettes on their skin. In 1964 the U.S. Surgeon General's report concluded that cigarette smoking is a health hazard of sufficient importance that immediate action was warranted and that cigarette smoking is causally linked to lung cancer in men. Since the first report in 1900, Mokhiber (1988) notes that more than 30,000 reports have documented the link between tobacco products and pulmonary emphysema, chronic bronchitis, coronary heart disease, and cancer of the lung, mouth, esophagus, bladder, kidney, pancreas, stomach, uterus, and cervix.

By 1989, the U.S. Surgeon General declared cigarette smoking as the chief preventable cause of death in our society. Estimates at this time put the number of deaths in the United States at 1,000 a day due to cigarette smoking alone. As more evidence came in demonstrating the link, the tobacco industry increasingly got their message across, linking cigarette smoking to sex appeal, the good life, enjoyment, youth and vitality through their advertisements. In 1988 the tobacco industry spent $2.5 billion on advertising. Mokhiber (1994) reports that since 90 percent of smokers start before the age of twenty-one and 60 percent before the age of fourteen, much of the tobacco industry's marketing and promotion is geared toward children and youth (14).

As part of the 1998 multistate settlement with the tobacco industry, the tobacco companies were to eliminate advertising techniques that would appeal to teenagers. A catalyst for the tobacco companies for signing this pact was that R. J. Reynolds corporation was discovered to have specifically marketed their Camel brand cigarettes to young people with the use of a cartoon character named "Joe Camel." Company memos detailing the plan and strategies to market to the young were released by Rep. Henry Waxman (D-California), who said they provide the first detailed look at how R. J. Reynolds spurred youth sales. "These documents . . . show us that RJR's most senior executives developed and implemented a sophisticated plan to market their cigarettes to our children (CNN, 1998)." Mokhiber and Weissman (2001) recently reported that the tobacco industry continues to target young people in the United States with cigarette ads. They cite a New England Journal of Medicine study that found in the year 2000, magazine advertisements for youth brands of cigarettes (defined as cigarettes smoked by more than 5 percent of eighth, tenth, and twelfth graders) reached more than 80 percent of young people in the United States an average of seventeen times each.

Since the market of male, white, educated consumers has declined rapidly over the most recent years in the United States, the tobacco industry has also increasingly targeted minority populations and blue-collar males as important market areas in their advertising (Simon and Eitzen, 1999; Lewis, 1992; Mattera, 1992). Two new brands being developed by R. J. Reynolds that particularly target African American and working-class women are Uptown and Dakota (Mattera, 1992).

The U.S. tobacco industry has increasingly expanded overseas. Philip Morris sells more than 175 brands in 160 countries. The U.S. government has been an important ally of the tobacco companies in increasing this expansion overseas. Under authority of Section 301 of the 1974 Trade Act, the U.S. Trade Representative has threatened to impose severe trade sanctions against any country that denies U.S. tobacco companies market access. U.S. companies increasingly protest any foreign nations' attempts to protect their public with anti-tobacco health measures (Weissman, 1992b). South Korea and Taiwan were two countries that were recently unsuccessful in overcoming U.S. pressure in their attempts to block the importation of tobacco products. The U.S. General Accounting Office reported that in Korea, one year after the lifting of import restrictions on cigarettes made by U.S. based multinational corporations, the smoking rate among teenage girls rose by more than 300 percent (Mokhiber, 1994). With the passage of treaties such as the North American Free Trade Agreement (NAFTA) and the General Agreement on Trade and Tariffs (GATT) that attempt to open markets and expand trade internationally by in part removing such technical barriers to trade as consumer safety, environmental safety, and workplace safety regulations, countries have been less able to protect their citizens from the tobacco products pushed by some of the largest companies in the world.

Countries in Africa and Latin America are also being targeted by American and British tobacco companies. One marketing technique of Philip Morris was to donate streets signs to some South American cities that say Marlboro along with the name of the street. In Uganda, the British American Tobacco Company is marketing high-nicotine cigarettes with no warning label at far-reduced prices (twelve cents per pack of twenty cigarettes). The goal is obvious: addict the population with high doses of the drug and then increase the price to increase profits (Mokhiber, 1994).

More recent areas of expansion are Eastern Europe and the People's Republic of China (Weissman, 1992b). Tobacco companies in capitalist nations are not the only purveyors of this form of product violence. In Eastern Europe most of the tobacco industry were state-owned. Estimates are that more than one-third of all deaths among middle-aged East European men in 1985 were due to tobacco. Rates were highest in Poland and the Soviet Union where 40 percent of middle-aged males died because of tobacco use (Weissman, 1992b). However, there is an indication that rates of smoking may have increased with the increased advertising and sales by multinational corporations in Eastern Europe. Dr. Jiri Kozak, an adviser to the Czech Ministry of Health, noted that until the arrival of the transnational tobacco companies and the beginning of aggressive advertising, the prevalence of smoking was decreasing (Mokhiber, 1994, 14).

The largest population of smokers in the world is in the People's Republic of China. Approximately 250 to 300 million smokers live in the PRC. Richard Peto, an Oxford University epidemiologist, estimates that of all the children alive today in China under the age of twenty years, 50 million of them will eventually die from tobacco (Mackay, 1992, 9). Here again, the China National Tobacco Corporation, the government monopoly, controls 99 percent of the market. But U.S. and European tobacco companies are placing more and more attention on these potential market areas. With their increasing market penetration, it is likely the tobacco consumption will increase. Overall, the United Nations estimates that 500 million people in developing countries will die within the next decade from smoking-related illness. This together with the millions of people who die each year in the more industrialized developed world makes tobacco the largest single instance of product violence in the world today. Most recently the *New York Times* reported that a new study of schoolchildren ages 13–15 in sixty-eight countries, conducted by the W.H.O. and the Centers for Disease Control and Prevention, found that about 11 percent of the children in Latin America and the Caribbean were offered free cigarettes by a tobacco company representative in 1999 and 2000. In Russia, nearly 17 percent said they had been given free cigarettes. In Jordan, it was 25 percent (Winter, 2001).

Automobile Industry

The Ford Pinto is a classic case of product violence by the auto industry. Dowie (1977) points out in his now classic story on the case that Ford engineers discovered in preproduction crash tests that rear-end collisions at a speed exceeding twenty-five miles per hour would result in rupture of the gas tank which was positioned directly behind the rear bumper. Altogether, in more than forty crash tests, ruptured gas tanks occurred every time. Eleven of these tests occurred prior to production for sale. Despite these test results, Ford, which had made a significant investment in retooling for production, decided to go ahead with the manufacture and sale of the automobile. Later, when Ford discovered that the defective design could be corrected by minor modifications in the design of the gas tank, costing between $5.67 and $11, they conducted a cost/benefit analysis to determine whether it was cost effective to make the changes in design. In this analysis Ford executives assigned approximately $200,000 to the value of a human life and then calculated that the estimated number of deaths in fiery crashes of the Pinto and small pickup trucks that had the same design defect would be 180. They also estimated that 180 persons would be injured at an estimated cost of $67,000 per injury, and 2,100 vehicles would be damaged at an estimated cost of $700 per vehicle. The total savings in lives, injuries, and damage to vehicles if the defect was corrected was estimated to be $49.5 million. The cost of the modification in design was calculated to be $11 for each of the 11 million Pintos produced and 1.5 million light trucks, for a total cost of $137 million. Therefore, according to the analysis it was not cost effective to correct the design. But Ford made a bad decision. By the time the 1977 Dowie article was published, estimates were that between 500 and 900 people had died, and the cost to Ford Motor Company resulting from the double and triple damage lawsuits was well beyond what Ford had anticipated.

A similar case of product violence, again involving the Ford Motor Company, was a defect in the design of automatic transmissions that resulted in cars that were placed in park with the engine idling shifting into reverse unexpectedly. Ford Motor Company executives knew the defect for at least ten years before the public was made aware of the hazard. Automobiles and trucks with automatic transmissions manufactured between 1962 and 1979 had this defect. As early as 1971, office memos issued by an engineer in the Chassis Safety Systems Department to his superiors indicated that the improper position (of the transmission shift lever) appears to the customer as proper . . . that this situation has resulted in an actual high accident incidence. In November, one month before the National Highway Traffic Agency's investigation, a Ford engineer's ankle was run over after he placed the shift lever of a test vehicle into park, put the emergency brake on, and left the car in idle.

The car lurched backward, ran over Hare's ankle, barely missed four other test cars, and was headed at twenty-five miles per hour for the high-speed track when a technician corralled it with a van (Branan, 1980, 46). By the time the correction was made, seventy people had died, 1,100 were injured, and 3,700 accidents had occurred. Ford was never required to recall and correct the defect in 26 million vehicles produced between 1962 and 1979.

Another recent case of product violence in the auto industry, this time involving General Motors, was the X-car design. General Motors executives were repeatedly warned by test drivers and internal company documents of a serious braking problem and later withheld information from federal officials regarding these cars (the 1980 Chevrolet Citation, Pontiac Phoenix, Oldsmobile Omega, and Buick Skylark). Hebert, reporting in the *Denver Post*, noted that by August 1983 the government had received more than 1,700 complaints about brakes locking in the X-body cars, including accidents involving fifteen deaths when the cars went into spins (Hebert, 1983).

In a now classic case of product violence, General Motors Corvair was implicated by consumer advocate Ralph Nader. In his *Unsafe at Any Speed*, Nader focused on the problem of the car's heater which gave off carbon monoxide and the problem of vehicle instability when the car cornered.

A more recent General Motors case involves pickup trucks and the side-mounted fuel tanks outside the frame rails on all "C" and "K" style pickups manufactured between 1972 and 1987. Mokhiber (1994) notes that the Center for Auto Safety charged that GM manufactured and marketed pickup trucks with hazardous gas tanks that have led to 600 deaths. The center claims that GM covered up the exploding gas tank problem and the company's decision not to install safety liners that would have reduced crash fires in the vehicles. Secretary of the United States Department of Transportation Frederico Peña noted that of critical importance in this matter is the evidence that GM was aware, possibly as early as the mid-1970s, but certainly by the 1980s, that this design made these trucks more vulnerable and that fatalities from side-impact fires were occurring. However, GM chose not to alter the design for fifteen years (Mohkiber, 1994, 8). The design of the truck places the fuel tanks on either side of the truck. This makes the truck very vulnerable to explosions and fires on side impacts. Other manufacturers placed their pickup truck fuel tanks inside protective frame rail structures during the same model years. Mohkiber notes that GM's former president, James McDonald, rejected a 1978 company task force proposal to install an inexpensive safety liner in the fuel tanks. Installing the liners in the tanks would have reduced the fire deaths and injuries, auto safety experts charge. Had GM put the liners in the pickup, about 185 of the 248 people burned to death in side impacts of the GM vehicles could have survived, judging from death rates from such vehicles during the 1981–1986 period, says Ben Kelley, president of the Institute for Injury Reduction. GM knew about this deadly defect for twenty years and rejected a $10 fix recommended by its own top fuel tank experts, says Clarence Ditlow, of the Center for Auto Safety (Mokhiber et al., 1992, 13).

One other auto-related example involves the production of tires. Firestone Tire and Rubber Company produced and sold the defective Firestone 500 radial tire. The company was aware of the defect as early as three years after manufacture in 1975, yet continued to manufacture and market the defective tire, which was subject to blowouts, until 1978. A House of Representatives committee reported that the tire had caused thousands of accidents, hundreds of injuries, and thirty-four deaths (Mokhiber, 1988).

Most recently Ford Motor Company and Firestone Tire and Rubber Company have had to settle millions of dollars in lawsuits as a result of problems of rollover accidents and tire blowouts from the under-inflating of tires on their Ford Explorer brand SUV. Mokhiber reports that Joan Claybrook, President of Public Citizen, presented evidence before Congress in September of 2000 that "Ford internal documents show the company engineers recommended changes to the vehicle design after it rolled over in company tests prior to introduction, but other than a few minor changes, the suspension and track width were not changed. Instead, Ford, which sets the specifications for the manufacture of its tires, decided to remove air from the tires, lowering the recommended psi to 26. The Firestone-recommended psi molded into the tire for maximum load is 35 psi." Claybrook notes that within a year of introduction of the product lawsuits against Ford and Firestone were filed for tire failures that resulted in crashes and rollovers. She testified that at least five cases were filed by 1993, and many others followed in the early 1990s. Almost all were settled, and settled with gag orders prohibiting the attorneys and the families from disclosing information about the cases or their documentation to the public or Department of Transportation. She testified that there is no question the companies knew they had a problem. But they kept it secret. By 1996, state agencies in Arizona were reporting problems with Firestone tires on Explorers. By 1998, Ford and Firestone had entered into discussions over tire failures with authorities in Middle Eastern, Asian and South American countries. "Ford eventually decided to conduct its own recall without Firestone and replace the tires in the various countries in 1999 and 2000. More than ninety deaths and hundreds of injuries occurred before either company took action to notify owners of the potential defect. Company action was eventually motivated by a National Highway Traffic and Safety Administration investigation that began in 2000 (Mokhiber and Weissman, 2001).

Recently, Bridgestone/Firestone Inc. reached a $7.5 million settlement in a $1 billion lawsuit filed by a Texas family involved in a Ford Explorer rollover accident that left a thirty-nine-year-old mother paralyzed. CBS News reported that internal Firestone documents showed that executives wanted to cut costs at a Decatur, Illinois, plant that made the recalled tires. The documents also showed Firestone declined to use ninety-cent nylon strips that company research found would have reduced the risk of tread separation by three to five times. An attorney for one of the victims stated that "This tire has killed more people than Timothy McVeigh. That is the awesome nature of the tragedy" (CBS.com, 2001). At the time of this report, Firestone had settled 200 cases and there were another 300 cases pending. The family also sued Ford and settled out of court for $6 million.

Research Industry

One major case of product violence involves fraudulent product safety testing by independent testing labs. These labs contract with the companies that are to profit from positive safety tests for their product. The incentive for these companies is to provide positive test results in order for their customers to receive approval for marketing the company's products. One massive example of this type of product violence occurred in the case of Bio-Test Labs. This company was one of the major test labs determining product safety for many of the largest manufacturers in the United States. An investigation by the U.S. government determined that 80 percent of some 900 tests they reviewed were invalid. Shredding of product test results, which was against the law, was extensive. The Federal Trade Commission investigation, completed in 1980, identified 157 cases of compromised and deceptive product standards and testing lab actions, many of which led to thousands of deaths or serious injuries caused by unsafe playground equipment, toxic art materials, hazardous electrical appliances, unsafe occupational protective gear and inadequately designed vehicles, all of which had been labeled or certified safe (Dowie, Foster, Marshall, Weir, and King, 1982).

A larger problem than the fraud in testing is the industry bias in the U.S. government control systems developed to prevent unsafe and hazardous products from entering the marketplace. In the United States, the companies that produce a product are responsible to provide evidence to the government of its safety. Fagin, Lavelle, and The Center for Public Integrity in their work *Toxic Deception* (1999) analyze the cases of four dangerous chemicals that are in use throughout the United States. Two of the products, atrazine and alachlor, are herbicides widely sold to farmers and homeowners to control weeds and are listed as probable carcinogens. These herbicides are found in drinking water throughout many Midwestern states. The two other cases are perchlorethylene, which is a degreaser used by dry cleaning establishments, and formaldehyde, which is used as a preservative and binding agent for everything from cosmetics, pesticides, cleaners, and adhesives. Both products are listed as a probable carcinogenic by the International Agency for Research on Cancer.

Fagin et al. (1999) focus on the use of formaldehyde in building products such as particle board used in cabinets, flooring, and furniture. Formaldehyde was discovered to cause cancer in laboratory animals in the early 1970s. The problem according to Fagin et al. is that the companies that benefit from the marketing and sale of the products are responsible for presenting evidence to the government regarding the hazards for their use. An indication that this is not working very well is when the EPA offered an amnesty from large fines if companies turned in health studies that they should have provided to the government earlier. Manufacturers suddenly produced more than 10,000 studies showing that chemicals already on the market could pose a "substantial risk of injury to health or to the environment"—the kind of never-published data that the law says must be presented to the government immediately (Fagin, et. al., 1999, 14). Fagin notes that several of the studies not reported to the government included research on the health risk of alachlor, atrazine, formaldehyde, and percholoroethylene. The EPA is still wading through the deluge of studies to determine the safety of these products and hundreds of others that may pose significant health risks to consumers. Furthermore the authors note that these companies have an army of lobbyists and lawyers who work with legislators in crafting the regulations and the agencies that are charged with executing them. There is also a revolving door phenomenon where employees for these same agencies that police the private corporations end up working for them or worked for them previously. For example, as the authors point out "virtually half of the EPA officials who left top-level jobs in toxics and pesticides during the past 15 years went to work for chemical companies, their trade associations, or their lobbying firms" (Fagin, et. al., 1999, x).

PRODUCTION VIOLENCE

The second general category of economic violence is production violence. Here, the form of violence is a result of establishing a work environment that leads to the death and injury of workers and not informing the workers of the hazards. Estimates of the number of deaths and injuries are difficult to assess because the government does not systematically collect data nationally on this area of violence. Kinney and Mosley (1990) note that only once, in 1985, a government agency actually did try to count the number of workers who died as a result of traumatic, job-related accidents. After going through death certificates, National Institute of Occupational Safety and Health (NIOSH) put the 1985 worker death toll at 7,771. But NIOSH's count seriously underestimates the number of deaths because it counted only those deaths where the information of accidental deaths was properly recorded on the death certificate. Dr. Anthony Suruda, a physician who participated in the study, said that "the actual figure could be much higher, perhaps 50 percent higher in some states, because of improper diagnoses of the causes of deaths by coroners and physicians. NIOSH'S count further ignored at least 50,000 to 70,000 workers who die annually from workplace-related disease. . . . NIOSH also overlooked the roughly 70,000 workers who become permanently disabled from workplace accidents each year" (Kinney and Mosley, 1990, 29).

Kinney and Mosley also state that the National Safe Workplace Institute shows that the dangers of the workplace have not decreased in the past decade. The institute's analysis indicates that the shift of jobs from high-risk industries such as steel, heavy manufacturing, and construction to low-risk service jobs has diluted the fatality rates. They note that workers in high-risk jobs have an on-the-job death rate that is four times higher than that of other workers. The problem of workplace safety also appears to be higher in the United States than in other advanced industrialized societies. Using International Labor Organization (ILO) data adjusted for underreporting, the NSWI showed that the United States had a worker fatality rate at least 5.8 times higher than Sweden's and 3.5 times higher than Japan's (Kinney and Mosley, 1990, 29).

Occupational disease is one of the most underresearched, underfunded, and ignored areas of public health today. Although data are scarce, conservative estimates put the death toll from occupational diseases at 50,000 to 100,000 workers per year, with some 390,000 new cases of occupationally related diseases appearing each year. Claybrook (1984) estimates that on the job accidents cause 3.3 million injuries requiring hospital treatment annually, and exposure to toxic chemicals kills 100,000 workers annually in the United States. Furthermore, 1.7 million U.S. workers in manufacturing industries are exposed to potential carcinogens each year. These workplace exposures are believed to result in 23–38 percent of cancer deaths each year in the United States (Mokhiber, 1988). The government also estimates that 15 to 20 million U.S. jobs expose workers to chemicals that cause reproductive injury, 9 million are exposed to radio frequency/microwave radiation that causes embryonic death and impaired fertility in animals, 500,000 workers are exposed to glycol ethers known to cause testicular atrophy and birth defects in animal tests, and 200,000 hospital and industrial employees are exposed to anesthetic gases and ethylene oxides linked to miscarriages in humans (Marshall, 1987).

Rates of occupational disease and mortality from work are believed to be significantly higher in developing countries. The World Health Organization and ILO (1994) estimate that at least "120 million accidental injuries with 200,000 fatalities and 68–157 million cases of occupational disease are estimated to occur among the global workforce annually." Furthermore, they note that in high-risk occupations one-fifth of the workers may annually contract an occupational accident or disease. In their report entitled *Global Strategy on Occupational Health for All* they contend that, in principle, these deaths and injuries are preventable with the help of the modern occupational health approach. Many cases of occupational disease, however, go underdiagnosed and underreported and preventive actions are not undertaken.

The report also contends that the rates in developing countries are increasing because of the increasing use of highly toxic chemicals and machinery in agriculture and the development of heavy industry. Occupational disease figures are not included in this estimate. Also, they anticipate that the occupational accident and disease death rate should decline in developed countries as there is an increasing shift to more service-sector employment. Thus, poorer populations in the world will increasingly be exposed to hazardous working conditions either because of the increasing use of carcinogenic chemicals dumped overseas or increasingly hazardous factory employment. The new occupational health problems of industrialized countries tend to be associated with implementation of new technologies, new substances, psychosocial factors and the special needs of aging populations and vulnerable groups. The problems of newly industrialized countries stem from the more traditional occupational accidents and occupational diseases. In developing countries the problems of heavy physical work, pesticides and heat stress, as well as several vegetable and other organic dusts and biological hazards are of highest importance.

Another indication of the scope of this violence relates to workers' perceptions of the hazards of their workplace. Just as fear of violent crime is important as a feature of the crime problem and as a factor related to mental health/life satisfaction, so are perceptions of the seriousness of health hazards of one's employment. One U.S. survey of workers' perceptions of serious health and safety hazards on their jobs, conducted in 1984, indicated that almost 46 percent of male workers and 32 percent of female workers in all occupations perceive that their jobs create substantial exposure to hazardous conditions. As expected, white-collar workers had the lowest reported perceptions of hazardous exposure at almost 30 percent for male and 26 percent for female employees. But with the recent awareness of the hazards of radiation from office equipment and the effect of repetitive movements of word processors (such as carpal tunnel syndrome), these perceptions of risk may be significantly higher today, particularly for female white-collar workers. Occupational classifications that reported the highest perceived risks of exposure to hazardous conditions, ranging from 62.8 percent to 65.2 percent of male workers and 50–53.7 percent of female workers, were craft workers, laborers, and operatives (Robinson, 1991). These responses underestimate the real dangers when one considers the risk of injury from exposure to carcinogenic substances; in the vast majority of such cases, the risk is unknown to the worker. For example, Robinson found that substantially fewer than half the workers in occupations with the highest risk of cancer considered themselves at significant risk. The following case studies illustrate the type of violence we are talking about.

Asbestos

In recent years, one of the major causes of worker violence in the United States and throughout the world concerns asbestos. The link between asbestos and white lung has been known since 1900. Asbestos was implicated as a cause of cancer as early as 1935. People working with the materials, as well as those who purchased products made from asbestos, were not told of its hazards until the 1970s. Research done on asbestos workers who had worked with the material for twenty years indicated that mortality rates for the group were 50 percent higher than for average white males, and the rate of lung cancer was 700 times greater than expected. The rate for all types of cancer was four times greater (Epstein, 1978). One estimate puts the number of deaths in the U.S. each year resulting from white lung at 12,000 to 13,000 people (Mencimer, Steif, and Leventhal, 1992). This estimate is sure to be conservative since there is no way to estimate the number of cancer deaths resulting from the hundreds of millions of people who were exposed to products that contained asbestos in their home and public buildings. Up until the 1970s, asbestos was used in everything from roofing materials, insulation materials, and in hair dryers and various small and major appliances. Furthermore, in many countries around the world these products are still available and the materials are still in use in homes and public buildings.

An agency of the United Nations recently called for global trade restrictions on the sale of all forms of asbestos. On 21 February 2002, an announcement was made by the United Nations Environment Programme (UNEP). In a press release issued by the agency it stated that "all forms of asbestos should be added to an international list of chemicals subject to trade controls" (United Nations Environment Programme, 2002). This decision follows a review of asbestos which had been triggered by unilateral bans adopted by the European Union and Chile. The committee of government experts, which studied the issue, noted that the inhalation of asbestos fibers causes cancer and other illnesses and that asbestos is still used in seals, gaskets, joints, brakes, armaments, and other applications. The report noted that cost-effective substitutes are increasingly available for most applications.

Vinyl Chloride

Vinyl chloride is another illustration of production violence. As early as 1970, a study indicated that long-term intermittent exposure of rats to vinyl chloride in the air resulted in the production of several types of cancers. In 1972 research confirmed this earlier finding. Representatives of U.S. industries were given the full details of these studies in January 1973. These companies then entered into an agreement with the European consortium not to disclose the information without prior consent. The Manufacturing Chemists Association failed to disclose the dangers of vinyl chloride despite a request from a government agency for all available data on the toxic effects of vinyl chloride. The data were finally revealed to the government when three workers exposed to vinyl chloride at a B. F. Goodrich plant died of angiosarcoma of the liver. According to a special committee report of the American Association for the Advancement of Science, the Manufacturing Chemists Association had deliberately deceived the government and "because of the suppression of these data, tens of thousands of workers were exposed without warning, for perhaps some two years, to toxic concentrations of vinyl chloride" (Epstein, 1978).

In 1974, Congress passed the Safe Drinking Water Act. This law requires EPA to determine safe levels of chemicals in drinking water which do or may cause health problems. These nonenforceable levels, based solely on possible health risks and exposure, are called Maximum Contaminant Level Goals. The MCLG for vinyl chloride has been set at zero because EPA believes this level of protection would not cause any of the potential health problems described below.

Production of vinyl chloride pollution in 1993 was nearly 14 billion pounds. Its major release to the environment is as air emissions and wastewater at polyvinyl chloride (PVC) plastics manufacturing facilities. Small quantities of vinyl chloride is also released to food since it is used to make many food wrappings and containers. From 1987 to 1993, according to EPA's Toxic Release Inventory, vinyl chloride releases to water and land totaled over 38,000 pounds. These releases were primarily from plastics materials and resins industries. The largest releases occurred in Louisiana and Delaware (U.S. EPA Office of Water, 2001).

According to the National Toxicology Program of the U.S. Department of Health and Human Services ninth report on carcinogens, the primary routes of potential human exposure to vinyl chloride are inhalation and dermal contact. Potential human exposure to vinyl chloride occurs principally in the workplace, through general air and water pollution, and, to a limited extent, from the use of fabricated products (U.S. Department of Health and Human Services, 2001).

In a recent case, the Taiwan-based Formosa Plastics Corporation facility in Louisiana has been fined several times since 1987 for excessive releases of vinyl chloride. Holly Knaus reported that in 1986, a Delaware judge ordered a six-week shutdown of a Formosa plant in that state in response to a vinyl chloride monomer release so extreme that the factory's sprinkler system went off and employees were forced to wear breathing equipment. In Point Comfort, Texas, Formosa has been hit with two of the largest environmental fines in Texas history. In spring 1990, the Texas Water Commission fined the company $247,000 for seventeen violations over a three-year period, including improper storage of oil and other waste, cracked wastewater retention ponds and releases of extremely acidic wastewater into surface water. In October 1990, the five-state Region Six office of the EPA handed Formosa a proposed $8.3 million fine for illegal disposal of hazardous waste (Knaus, 2001). According to Chemical Industry Archives (2001), in 1998, Formosa Plastics Corporation in its plant in Delaware City, Delaware produced 13 percent of the total vinyl chloride emissions in the United States.

Film Recovery Systems

Rarely are cases of production violence officially defined as criminal violence. One exception concerns Stefan Golab and Film Recovery Systems, Inc. Golab, a Polish immigrant, was employed by Film Recovery. He worked with other workers in reclaiming silver from used X-ray film. The process involves the use of cyanide. Workers frequently became ill breathing in the fumes coming off the large vats of cyanide. When they became ill, they were allowed to go outside the shop, often to catch a breath of fresh air and at other times to vomit. On February 10, 1985, Stefan Golab staggered from the cyanide vat he was working over, stumbled to the adjacent locker room, and collapsed. Some of his fellow workers dragged him outside and called an ambulance. But it was too late. The cause of death: cyanide poisoning. A Cook County, Illinois, hospital study of

Golab's fellow workers, undertaken following his death, found that "at least two thirds of Film Recovery's workers suffered ten times a month or more from each of four major symptoms of cyanide intoxication; they were told to 'go outside so you can have some fresh air.'" Investigators found that many workers were not aware that they were working with cyanide (Frank, 1987).

A former bookkeeper for Film Recovery stated that illegal aliens were specifically chosen to work in the plant because they could not read English. Thus they could not read the warning labels on the drums of cyanide. Also, several employees observed skull and crossbones markings being painted or burned off the drums. Since company managers had never informed workers of the hazards of working with the chemical, workers who did see the skull and crossbones assumed that the chemical was dangerous only if it was swallowed. They did not know that it could be lethal if inhaled or absorbed through the skin. Three executives were convicted of murder and fourteen counts of reckless conduct; two corporations were convicted of involuntary manslaughter and fourteen counts of reckless conduct (Frank, 1987, 104). But the sentences were overturned on appeal, and two of the executives pleaded guilty to involuntary manslaughter (Felsenthal, 1993).

Cotton and Coal Dust

Two severe occupational diseases are black lung and brown lung. Reiman (1990) notes that about 10 percent of active coal miners have black lung disease or coal workers' pneumoconiosis. The United Mine Workers estimate that each day eleven coal miners die from black lung. They note that at least 100,000 miners have died from this malady and that 265,000 are disabled (Kerr, 1980). A U.S. Surgeon General's report in 1978 noted that 1,000 coal miners die every year in Pennsylvania from black lung. The last annual report of the number of miners who die from black lung disease in the United States was issued in 1994 and it listed 1,478 deaths for that year (Harris, 1998). A congressional report clearly placed the blame for the high incidence of the disease on the coal mining companies.

For years, the coal mining companies have worked to deny the existence of the disease; however, in recent times mine workers have been successful in having the government recognize the significant health hazard caused by breathing coal dust in mines. A congressional committee noted that "the dreadful high incidence of black lung is an immediate consequence of the coal dust created by the increased production rates of the industry. . . . [T]he incidence of this disease can be completely prevented by implementing existing technology and undertaking the research necessary to reduce the levels of respirable dust. The problem lies not in the lack of technical competence but in the lack of will to invest in health and safety" (U.S. House of Representatives, 1979, 1230).

In 1969, Congress placed strict limits on airborne dust and ordered operators to take periodic air tests inside coal mines. The law has significantly reduced black lung among the nation's 53,000 underground coal miners. But according to an investigative report that appeared in the *Courier Journal* of Louisville, Kentucky, because of cheating and lack of federal regulatory diligence, the law has fallen far short of its goal of virtually eliminating the disease (Harris, 1998). The investigative report claims that, because of widespread cheating by the mining companies in the Appalachian region of the United States, miners' lives are endangered. In a series of interviews it was revealed that two dozen mine owners or managers admitted submitting fraudulent tests. The report also notes that the government regularly ignores these obvious fraudulent reports.

Mining accidents as a result of preventable unsafe working conditions are another area of violence. Regarding the Scotia mine disaster that occurred in 1976 and killed twenty-six people, Caudill (1987) notes that the mine had been inspected hundreds of times before March 9, 1976, and 652 violations of safety laws and regulations had been cited. Of these, at least sixty infractions dealt with serious ventilation problems, including insufficient air circulating at the worker's face, line brattices out of position, inoperative methanometers, failure to follow the ventilation plan, and findings of imminent danger of explosions due to methane concentrations of 1.2 percent. Penalties amounting to $164,352 had been imposed by assessment officers, but the company had actually paid only $78,877 (98). Mokhiber (1988) notes that 100,000 miners have been killed in mining accidents in this century, and 1.5 million injuries have been reported since 1930.

Brown lung or byssinosis is another disease that has affected a large number of working people in this country and around the world. Like black lung, the disease has been known for more than a hundred years. As early as 1713, an Italian physician reported the problem among flax and hemp workers. During the nineteenth century, French, English, and Belgian doctors reported the occurrence of the disease. Despite hundreds of reports regarding the disease, textile mill owners have regularly denied its existence. According to the American Lung Association (2000) between 1979 and 1996, byssinosis caused 120 deaths; an estimated 35,000 current and former textile workers have been disabled.

Much of this problem in the United States is located in the South. Guarasci (1987) notes that there are about 400,000 textile workers in the Carolinas. Of those, 115,000 are exposed to cotton dust in their work and it is estimated that between 18,000 and 35,000 Carolinians suffer from byssinosis. Guarasci concludes in his analysis of two textile mill towns in North and South Carolina that the problem of brown lung is a result of industrial negligence, authoritarian rule in the workplace, and pernicious administration of government regulations.

Pesticides

We mentioned earlier pesticides that are carcinogenic and banned in the United States but are sold overseas to be used by farm laborers in South and Central America. But there is a very serious problem of pesticide poisoning in this country from pesticides defined by the government as suitable for agricultural production. One of the most lethal pesticides used in agriculture in the United States is parathion, a nerve gas insecticide. Moses (1993) claims that this particular poison is responsible for more occupational deaths throughout the world than any other single pesticide. The EPA notes that this pesticide causes poisoning among all categories of workers who come into direct contact with it. EPA further notes that these poisonings occur under conditions where workers are following label directions.

Moses (1993) cites epidemiological studies of workers exposed to pesticides that portend increased risks of developing a wide range of cancers. Furthermore, several studies indicate an increased risk to children exposed to pesticides. The State of California Department of Health Services (1988) found a significantly higher rate of cancer among children in agricultural communities in the San Joaquin Valley than what would be expected given the national average. There is additional research that illustrates a correlation between pesticide exposure of workers and risk for birth defects. Moses (1993) notes that this research demonstrates linkages between various pesticides and facial clefts, spina bifida, anencephaly, and neural tube defects. Also, research suggests a link between exposure to agricultural chemicals and spontaneous abortions or stillbirths. In one large U.S. study of 6,386 stillbirths, pesticide exposure of either parent increased the risk (Savitz, Whelan, and Kleckner, 1989).

There are no U.S. national statistics or worldwide statistics on the level of death and injury from pesticide poisonings. Estimates by the EPA put the figure at between 200,000 and 300,000 poisonings annually. There are no reliable death statistics. Moses (1993) notes that since the level of enforcement of OSHA and EPA standards are so low, it is likely that incidence levels are much higher. As mentioned earlier, in developing countries in South and Central America and in Africa, rates of injury and death are expected to be many times higher, not only because of the laxness of regulations and safety procedures but also because of the dumping of toxic pesticides in these countries. One study estimated that 75 percent of the pesticides applied in Central America are either banned, restricted, or unregistered in the United States (Alston and Brown, 1993). The World Health Organization estimates that there are 25 million cases of pesticide poisoning each year (Jeyaratnam, 1990). Seventy to eighty percent of all poisonings occur in developing countries where regulatory, health, and education systems are weakest (Forastieri, 1999).

Child Labor

One area where the work itself is dangerous to the person is the area of child labor. Child labor is considered violence because the nature of the work stunts the development of children. Article 32 of the United Nations Convention on the Rights of the Child states: "State Parties recognize the right of the child to be protected from economic exploitation and from performing any work that is likely to be hazardous or to interfere with the child's education, or to be harmful to the child's health or physical, mental, spiritual, moral or social development (UNICEF, 1989)." The convention has been ratified by 191 countries. Only the United States and Somalia have not ratified the convention at the time of this writing. Examples of child labor as economic violence are where children are employed to spray dangerous pesticides and fungicides on the crops controlled by the labor contractors employed by large multinational corporations. Another example is the case of young children working in the sweatshops in countries south of the equator sewing the seams on clothing and athletic shoes. And another is millions of young children who are forced into the sex trade. Regarding the latter example, in a recent article in *Time* magazine, the reporters purchased the freedom of two young girl prostitutes from a brothel for less than $1,000. The brothel owner, Mama San, says that "their mothers or the middlemen bring them to me. There are always fresh ones" (Perry and Sai, 2002, 7). The article notes that according to the International Labor Organization, at least 1 million children are working as prostitutes in Asia.

A preliminary analysis by UNICEF shows that in more than thirty countries covering 35 percent of the developing world population, 19 percent of five- to fourteen-year-olds are working. There are no significant differences between boys and girls in the proportion working. UNICEF (2002) notes that there are substantial urban-rural differences, with 21 percent of children aged 5–15 working in rural areas as compared to 13 percent in urban areas. The report also notes that two-thirds of those working do so for a family farm or business. According to UNICEF, sub-Saharan African countries show the highest proportions of children working.

The ILO estimates that 250 million children between five and fourteen work for a living, and that over 50 million children under age twelve work in hazardous circumstances. It also estimates that domestic work is the largest employment category of girls under age sixteen in the world. According to International Labor Organization statistics, some 61 percent of this total, or nearly 153 million, are found in Asia; 32 percent, or 80 million, are in Africa; and 7 percent, or 17.5 million, live in Latin America (International Labor Organization, 2002).

The ILO has begun a program to improve the knowledge base on the extent and nature of some of the worst forms of child labor through its SIMPOC program. This program has carried out thirty-eight rapid assessments in nineteen countries and one border region. The investigations explore "urgent and often sensitive" issues such as children in bondage; child domestic workers; child soldiers; child trafficking; drug trafficking; hazardous work in commercial agriculture, fishing, garbage dumps, mining and the urban environment; sexual exploitation; and working street children. For example, one of these reports assesses the problem of trafficking in Nepalese girls for prostitution. Based on their surveys of villages they estimated that 12,000 young girls have been trafficked out of Nepal to become prostitutes (KC et. al., 2001). Another study focuses on child labor in mining in Tanzania (Mwami et. al., 2002), another on the work of street children in Turkey (Aksit, Karanci, and Gunduz-Hosgor, 2001).

ENVIRONMENTAL VIOLENCE

Another major area of economic violence is environmental violence. In this category, violence occurs as a direct result of pollution of the environment. This is one area of violence that is less likely to be defined as violence, although this is more a result of who has the ability to define what is violence and who does not. Ralph Nader notes that those who define violence are those who perpetuate most of it. While the government focuses its attention on the violence that occurs from street crimes, it tends to ignore the violence that occurs from the chemical assault on the environment. More is lost in money and health through pollution than crimes of street violence, yet only the latter is defined officially as violence (Simon and Eitzen, 1993, 154).

Here we consider four categories of environmental violence. The first is knowingly disposing of wastes from production in an unsafe manner so that it kills or injures community residents. Another is knowingly emitting toxic gases into the air that result in the death or injury of residents. A third category refers to knowingly emitting toxic liquids or solids into water systems so that they result in the death or injury of residents. The last category of environmental violence we discuss is knowingly removing a resource in such a way and to such an extent that it leads to further environmental damage and to the death or injury of residents.

No official statistics are collected regarding the number of deaths resulting from environmental violence. All that is available is a series of case studies from around the globe that highlight these different categories of environmental violence.

Toxic Waste

There is an increasing crisis throughout the world connected with the disposal of hazardous waste. The problem principally originates in the richest countries in the world and then spreads to poorer countries. The United States has the greatest problems in this area. Feagin and Feagin (1990) indicate that each year the United States produces more than 160 million tons of solid waste and nearly 212 million pounds of hazardous waste each day, most of which is disposed of improperly or unsafely. Approximately 10 percent of this waste is incinerated, a process that contributes to air pollution and produces ash that must be disposed of somewhere. The largest percentage is placed in landfills throughout the United States. There is an increasing problem of finding places to dispose of the waste. Feagin observes that approximately one-third of the nation's 6,000 municipal landfills are expected to be filled and closed by the mid-1990s. Although the problem is not as severe in other advanced societies, because of greater recycling efforts, it nevertheless exists there as well.

Love Canal and Other Examples

Love Canal is an important example of environmental violence in the United States. In 1942 Hooker Chemical and Plastics Corporation negotiated an agreement to use land owned by the county power company to dispose of chemical wastes from its plant in Buffalo (Mokhiber, 1988). In 1947 Hooker bought Love Canal, drained it, lined it with clay, dumped thousands of fifty-five-gallon metal drums of waste and then covered it with dirt. Grass and weeds grew on the surface of the dump site. Mokhiber (1988) notes that in 1953, after Hooker had filled the canal with deadly chemicals (tricholorophe-nol and dioxin, two highly toxic chemicals), the company sold the land to the town of Love Canal for one dollar with the stipulation that they were not liable for any consequences resulting from use of the land. The company at the time of the sale knew that the town planned on developing an elementary school on the land. Housing developers planned on constructing homes around the school site. Mokhiber points out that the transfer deed warned that the land "had been filled, in whole or in part, to the present ground level . . . with waste products resulting from the manufacturing of chemicals [by Hooker]" and that "the [Board of Education] . . . assumes all risks and liability incident to the use thereof" (Mokhiber, 1988, 271). Hooker gave no information about the danger posed by the wastes. A school and houses were built on the perimeter of the site, and the playground for the school was located on the site.

As early as 1958, Hooker knew that some chemicals buried on the site were coming in contact with children who played on the playground. Hooker investigated the problem and found that carcinogenic chemicals were surfacing in the north and south perimeters of the site. Hooker also was aware at the time that the site was being used by children as a playground. Hooker informed the school board of the potential problem of the leakage. However, Mokhiber notes that the corporation did not warn residents of the danger. Mokhiber cites the testimony before Congress of Jerome Wilkenfeld, the Hooker Chemical executive who wrote the memo to the school board, "we did not feel that we could do this without incurring substantial liabilities for implying that the current owners of the property were [taking] . . . inadequate care [of] . . . the property" (Mokhiber, 1988, 271).

The chemicals continued to leak out of the containment system of the landfill at an increased level during the 1970s and migrate to the homes that belted around the site. There were problems in the baseball field next to the schoolyard where large holes appeared in the outfield. Eventually, the chemicals began to leach into the basements of several homes surrounding the site. A black sludge would come up through the drainage holes into the basements. Besides the effects on the homes, there were serious health effects that became apparent. Women who had lived near the site an average of 18.5 years had 3.5 times the expected number of miscarriages, as well as a disproportionate number of birth defects and spontaneous abortions.

Mrs. Timothy Schoeder, a canal resident, suffered from burning eyes and skin ailments. Her daughter, Sheri, was born with a cleft palate, a double row of bottom teeth, a deformed ear, eardrums that disintegrated, bone blockage in her left nasal passage, a hole in her heart, and slight retardation. In 1978, Sheri began to lose her hair in large clumps. . . . One woman living in the area had three successive miscarriages before giving birth to a child. The baby was born with three ears. Her second child also was born with deformed ears (Mokhiber, 1988, 273).

Mokhiber notes that Hooker denied responsibility for the damages caused by the site. They first attempted to place the blame on contractors who built houses around the site, claiming that they may have damaged the containment system in their excavation work for house construction. Hooker disowned any liability for the damages, citing the deed the Board of Education accepted when they purchased the land for a dollar in 1953. Mokhiber cites a discussion Hooker vice president John Riordan had on *The Today Show*, a popular morning news program, claiming that Hooker was not aware of the hazards of the waste when they dumped them. This claim was countered by Dr. Robert Mobbs, who had conducted research into the hazards of lindane, one of the chemicals dumped at the site. Mobbs was furious over Riordan's comments and charged that Hooker "damn well knew that the compounds it deposited in the canal were extremely dangerous to human beings. . . . I presented evidence that it was a possible cancer-causing agent in 1948." Mobbs' findings were published in the December 1948 issue of the *Journal of the American Medical Association* and had been publicized further by Washington columnist Drew Pearson. Hooker Chemical eventually settled with the 1,300 residents of Love Canal, paying close to $20 million (Mokhiber, 1988, 274). Nevertheless, as Mokhiber concludes, this hardly pays for the physical damage and death to residents in the area.

Unfortunately, the case of Love Canal is not an isolated incidence. More than 50,000 toxic waste dumps are scattered throughout the United States. In addition to these land-based dumps there are approximately 180,000 toxic pits, ponds, and lagoons throughout the states (Zastrow, 1992). Environmental experts contend that of the 50,000 land-based sites, more than 1,000 pose potential health hazards. In Anniston, Alabama, the Monsanto Company had been dumping toxic waste unsafely for almost forty years without telling residents. *The Washington Post* reported that company memos dating almost forty years ago, many with warnings such as "CONFIDENTIAL: Read and Destroy," indicated that the company knew of the danger of their dumping of PCBs into the water in creeks and open pit landfills in West Anniston, the poor minority section of the community. "In 1966, Monsanto managers discovered that fish submerged in that creek turned belly-up within 10 seconds, spurting blood and shedding skin as if dunked into boiling water." They told no one. In 1969, they found fish in another creek with 7,500 times the legal PCB levels. They decided "there is little object in going to expensive extremes in limiting discharges." In 1975, a company study found that PCBs caused tumors in rats. They ordered its conclusion changed from "slightly tumorigenic" to "does not appear to be carcinogenic" (Grunwald, 2002, A01). Grunwald notes that Monsanto enjoyed a lucrative four-decade monopoly on PCB production in the United States, and battled to protect that monopoly long after PCBs were confirmed as a global pollutant. "We can't afford to lose one dollar of business," one internal memo concluded (Grunwald, 2002, A01).

A case of toxic dumping that directly affected workers of the company that conducted the dumping was that of General Electric Company. *Multinational Monitor* reported in a June 1988 investigation that an employee parking lot had been built on a toxic dump site that had a radioactive contamination level many times higher than the New York State safety level. Though G.E. was aware of the contamination at the site, the company allowed employees to park there without any warning for over twenty years. *Multinational Monitor* reports that in March 1988, G.E. sold the parking lot to the U.S. government, effectively removing the jurisdiction of the state of New York over the property and placing the clean-up bill in the hands of U.S. taxpayers. *Multinational Monitor* reports that the G.E. weapons plant, Knolls Atomic Power Lab, is alone responsible for thirty-nine sites contaminated with radioactive waste (Mokhiber et al., 1992).

Most recently G.E. has been required to pay approximately $500 million dollars for the dredging of the Hudson River. G.E. discharged 1.3 million pounds of PCBs—whose chemical name is polychlorinated biphenyls—in the river over a forty-year period from plants in Fort Edward, New York, and Hudson Falls, New York (Shapely, 2002). Cray notes that "between the 1940s and 1976, when the U.S. Congress outlawed PCB manufacture, sale and distribution (except in 'totally enclosed' systems), G.E. discharged about 1.3 million pounds of PCBs into the Hudson River. The contamination ruined a once-thriving commercial fishing industry and devastated recreational fishing, which was only opened on a 'catch and release' basis in the 40-mile long upper Hudson in 1996, after being closed for two decades" (Cray, 2001, 11). Cray notes that the potential impact doesn't stop at the tip of Manhattan. He notes that because of PCBs' chemical stability and their ability to travel long distances, PCBs can migrate around the planet and are part of a global class of chemicals known to migrate from warmer regions to colder regions. "Inuit people living in the Arctic thousands of miles from any industrial source carry some of the highest body burdens of PCBs on the planet" (Cray, 2001, 11). G.E. has other sites for dumping of PCBs in other waterways in Massachusetts and Georgia (Cray, 2001).

In another case, the A. C. Lawrence Leather Company was convicted of violating the Clean Water Act, defrauding the U.S. government, falsifying reports to the government, and illegally disposing of hazardous waste. The company had received $1.5 million from the U.S. government to construct a demonstration effluent waste-treatment system at its plant in Winchester, New Hampshire. Company executives decided that it would be a lot cheaper to use the money to build a pipeline to dump the waste directly into the Ashuelot River. The company also had buried 600 fifty-five-gallon drums of hazardous waste on the company property (Adler, 1985). Adler notes that the illegal disposal of toxic waste is pervasive. He cites an EPA survey that estimates that one out of every seven companies that generate toxic wastes may have disposed of them illegally during the past few years.

The illegal dumping of toxic waste has become big business and according to Representative John Dingell, chairperson of the House Subcommittee on Oversight and Investigations, has connections to organized crime. On the day before Earth Day in 1980 in Elizabeth, New Jersey, Chemical Control Corporation's plant exploded sending fireballs of fifty-five-gallon drums of toxic waste hundreds of feet into the sky, spewing toxic pesticides, acids, and plasticizers over the community. The fire at the plant took firefighters ten hours to put out. Area schools were closed and residents were urged to stay indoors. For years before the fire, residents tolerated the smell of noxious chemicals that had been illegally stored at the plant. According to Miller and Miller (1985), New Jersey's Department of Environmental Protection removed 10,000 barrels of the explosive, poisonous materials prior to the explosion; 24,000 barrels remained, however, and they turned into a time bomb. A confidential federal government report found that crooked stashing of chemical wastes and pesticides at Chemical Control could have sent poisonous fumes, drifting like an angel of death, over New York City (60). A federal grand jury investigating the company found that it had links to organized crime.

The U.S. government itself is a major violator of its regulations as they relate to the disposal of radioactive waste from weapons and power plant production. Kohn (1992) contends that the problem of how governmental agencies have disposed of radioactive waste is widespread and may be greater than the toxic dumping law violation activities of private companies. He notes that billions of pounds of government-accumulated waste—containing plutonium, arsenic, cyanide, nerve gases, TNT, rocket fuels, pesticides, bacteria and other harmful substances—pose the most immediate threat to public health (Kohn, 1992, 40). The government currently has more than 14,000 dump sites that threaten the health of the public. All nuclear weapons plants (Hanford, Washington; Savannah River plant, South Carolina; Rocky Flats, Colorado; and the Fernald Plant in Ohio) have serious problems in the disposal of waste.

Kohn notes that in the Hanford plant alone it is estimated that the toxic waste would be equivalent to a forty-foot-deep lake that could cover Manhattan Island. Radioactive materials have also been found in the Columbia River, which supplies water to eastern Washington and western Oregon. At the Savannah River plant, there are increasing problems of radioactive material seeping into the regions biggest water source for the surrounding community. At the Fernald Plant, located outside Cincinnati, Ohio, it was discovered that eighty-one tons of liquid uranium had entered the Great Miami River, the major freshwater body in the metropolitan area. Last, the water supply for some of the suburbs of Denver have been contaminated by chemical and radioactive waste from Rocky Flats. Kohn notes one strategy of the U.S. Pentagon for dumping waste involves the complicity of private interests. When Pentagon officials auction used equipment by lot, they will often dump acids, solvents and other dangerous chemicals in with the valuable hardware. The toxins get pawned off on military surplus dealers, who discard them wherever they can. The Los Angeles police last year discovered 50,000 gallons of military chemicals, highly corrosive and explosive, that had been left in a vacant lot under a freeway, just a few feet from a river (Kohn, 1992, 45).

The Brookhaven National Laboratory, located on Long Island near New York City, is a serious toxic hazard in one of the most populated regions of the country (Flanders, 1994). In 1989 the Environmental Protection Agency designated Brookhaven a "superfund site." Scattered within a five-mile stretch of land adjacent to the plant are landfills that contained radioactive contaminated lab garbage, animal carcasses, and sewage sludge. The plant is located above Long Island's sole-source aquifer and well monitoring has indicated that local groundwater was contaminated with radioactive strontium-90 and tritium. The lab's own published reports stated that the lab had been a source of radioactive emissions and toxic waste for more than forty years. Flanders (1994) reports that in 1990 the Department of Energy (DOE) estimated that the contamination from the buried waste could affect 15,400 people. The DOE also estimated that it would take more than twenty years and $338 million for the cleanup. Flanders notes that a 1994 New York State Department of Health study found that women with postmenopausal breast cancer were 60 percent more likely than cancer-free women to have lived within one kilometer of a chemical plant. The state's own breast cancer statistics show elevated rates in several areas close to the lab, where there are few industrial plants.

According to *Safetyforum* (2002) research, this problem of toxic waste disposal by the United States government is not confined to our national borders, but is even a greater problem overseas. According to *Safetyforum*, the U.S. Department of Defense (DOD) is the world's biggest polluter. "DOD generates 750,000 tons of hazardous waste a year, more than the five largest U.S. chemical companies combined. The private agency in its analysis of public records claims that there are 14,401 probable 'hot spots' at 1,579 military facilities. It also notes that the U.S. military is responsible for contamination at 53 private sites—contractor-owned weapons plants and property the Department of Defense once owned or used as dumps" (Safetyforum.com, 2002). *Safetyforum* notes that in 1999, the DOD Inspector General reported "potentially significant liabilities" and pollution at U.S. bases in Canada, Germany, Great Britain, Greenland, Iceland, Italy, Japan, Panama, the Philippines, South Korea, Spain, Turkey, among other nations.

Safetyforum highlights the case of the Philippines in its report and notes that when the U.S. military operated the naval base at Subic Bay, 3.75 million gallons of raw sewage were pumped daily into the bay. They also note that toxic waste from storage and destruction of excess bombs and ammunition was either poured into a local stream or dumped in a landfill. According to workers at the site, drums of cyanide were emptied into a landfill. The federal government's estimated cost of cleaning up both Clark and Subic Bay bases: $1 billion. The U.S. government contends that its treaties with the Philippines exempt it from the clean-up costs.

Of the 4,000 people living near Subic Bay when the base was in operation, 800 have been diagnosed with asbestosis. After a political movement in the Philippines pressured the United States to abandon the site in 1992 it was used for evacuees from the 1991 Mt. Pinatubo volcano eruption. A Filipino official who monitored the evacuated population said that they experienced unusually high rates of illnesses traced to poisoned well water. The list of ailments included skin diseases, mouth, nose and throat diseases, kidney diseases, miscarriages, reproductive disorders, stillbirths, physical and mental birth defects, cancers, heart ailments, and leukemia. Surprisingly, federal agencies of the United States government are exempt from the Clean Water Act enforcement and the U.S. Environmental Protection Agency has no authority to police overseas facilities. In 1999, Congress wrote into the Department of Defense's budget language that prohibits payment of environmental fines or penalties.

The Philippines is not an isolated case. *Safetyforum* reports that raw sewage from two military bases is dumped daily into local waters in South Korea. In Germany, the estimated costs of the clean up of toxic waste improperly disposed of by the U.S. military is at least $1 billion U.S. dollars. In 1990 the U.S. Department of Defense Inspector General estimated that cleaning up U.S. bases would cost $100–$200 billion (Safetyforum.com, 2002).

Dumping on the Poor

Increasingly, advanced industrial countries have sought to dump toxic wastes in poor countries or, within the United States, in areas in the country where poor populations reside. For example, the U. S. government and waste brokers have increasingly sought to dump industrial and household waste on Native American land. Since 1990 toxic waste disposal companies have approached more than fifty U.S. indigenous groups, offering millions of dollars in exchange for the right to dump U.S. trash on Native American grounds. These waste companies seek to avoid state, county, municipal, and many federal waste-facility operating standards that do not apply to Native American reservations because of their sovereign status. They sell these disposal plans to these impoverished indigenous communities as opportunities for "economic development" and increased employment for residents of the reservations. They do not mention the serious health threats posed by the incineration and storage of hazardous and other waste (Weissman, 1992a). Weissman cites a 1989 case in which a subsidiary of Amoco named Waste Tech Incorporated approached the governing council at Dilkon, a remote Navajo community. This community had an unemployment rate of 72 percent. The company proposed taking over 100 acres of community land to build an incinerator for the burning of hazardous waste and a landfill to bury the toxic ash. For the use of the land, the company promised the creation of 175 new jobs, a new hospital, and a $100,000 signing bonus to be distributed to the residents of the community.

In another case, O&G Corporation approached the leadership of the Rosebud Lakotas in South Dakota with a proposal to build the largest landfill in the United States on the reservation. The dump would hold solid waste, incinerator ash, and sewage sludge. Weissman notes that the most significant effort of dumping waste on Native American land does not come from private corporations but from the U.S. government's Department of Energy. The DOE is responsible for securing radioactive materials and disposing of the radioactive waste from the production of nuclear weapons as well as nuclear power plants. Weissman notes that they have contacted every Native American nation with a proposal to become either an interim or permanent recipient of nuclear waste. One particular plan is for the carving out a portion of Yucca Mountain, eighty-five miles from Las Vegas, Nevada, on the Shoshone reservation, and disposing of 70,000 metric tons of high-level waste in the mountain (Weissman, 1992a). Weissman also notes that the government has been involved in issuing grants to minority businesses for the establishment of dump sites on reservations. He cites the case of the U.S. Department of Commerce awarding a $248,000 minority business grant to a promoter who arranged for a company to bring hazardous waste to an Oklahoma Kaw reservation.

The United States is not alone in trying to dump toxic waste on its indigenous population. Cohen (1995) notes that Taiwan solved its problem of disposing nuclear waste by shipping the waste to Orchid Island, off Taiwan's southeast tip. This island is the home to 3,000 Yami aborigines.

The problem of dumping waste in the United States is not isolated to reservations. Gozan (1993) notes that it is estimated that 60 percent of all hazardous waste or toxic-emitting facilities are located in or adjacent to communities of color, and that 65 percent of U.S. commercial hazardous waste is dumped in the South. In 1990, 437 of the 3,109 U.S. counties and independent cities failed to meet at least one of the EPA ambient air quality standards: 57 percent of whites, 65 percent of African Americans, and 80 percent of Hispanics live in these counties with substandard air quality. Out of the whole population, a total of 33 percent of whites, 50 percent of African Americans, and 60 percent of Hispanics live in 136 counties in which two or more air pollutants exceed standards (Wernette and Nieves, 1992, 16–17). Bullard (1993) describes places like Chicago's South Side, Louisiana's Cancer Alley (those communities along the eighty-five-mile stretch of the Mississippi River from Baton Rouge to New Orleans), and East Los Angeles as human sacrifice zones. They are characterized as having severe environmental problems because of the placement of dump sites and highly polluting industries and are attracting new polluters as a result of their relative politically powerless position. These are examples of environmental racism and classism, where those who are the poorest and the most powerless in the society experience the greatest levels of violence from environmental pollution.

Besides the dumping of waste in the United States, companies in the United States, as well as companies in other advanced countries, are dumping waste in developing countries. Feagin and Feagin (1990) note that in 1988 some 3 million tons of hazardous waste from the United States and Western Europe were transported to impoverished countries in Africa and Eastern Europe that desperately need hard currency. The Feagins refer to this as "trash imperialism," whereby the richer countries push off their problems onto poorer countries. They observe that many Third World countries lack the technical ability to deal with toxic wastes. U.S. law requires that companies shipping toxic materials abroad notify government officials who are responsible for ensuring that the receiving countries dispose of the waste properly. But Environmental Protection Agency (EPA) officials report that U.S. shippers frequently ignore this requirement. Some shippers have even tried to sell toxic ash to Third World countries as landfill, claiming the ash was nontoxic and nonhazardous.

One recent case of a company selling toxic waste as fertilizer occurred in Bangladesh (Leonard, 1993). Leonard reports that in 1991, three U.S. corporations located in South Carolina gathered what is called baghouse dust, waste captured in the smokestack filters of the metal smelting furnaces of Gaston Cooper Recycling Corporation. This dust contains toxic levels of lead and cadmium. The waste was then handled by Hy-tex Marketing Company, a hazardous waste broker. Hy-tex Marketing sold the waste to Stoller Chemical Corporation, which mixed other materials with the waste to make fertilizer. Stoller Chemical then transported the toxic waste/fertilizer mixture to Bangladesh. The toxic waste/ fertilizer mixture was then purchased with funds from the Asian Development Bank by the Bangladesh Agricultural Development Corporation, a government institution. The U.S. embassy did notify the Bangladesh government that the waste contained lead and cadmium. Samples were collected from the toxic waste/fertilizer mixture by the U.S. embassy and the Bangladesh government. The Bangladesh Agricultural Research Institute concluded that the amount of waste contained in the fertilizer did not pose a health threat. However, the U.S. test results conducted by the South Carolina Department of Health and Environmental Control indicated that the waste was a threat to human health and the environment. The results of these tests were not released to the public and the government of Bangladesh until three months after the waste had been distributed to farmers. Farms visited by Greenpeace found that children were often given the task of applying fertilizer without any protective clothing or gloves.

Leonard notes that a public outcry in Bangladesh developed over the scandal. Newspapers reported in September 1992 that the toxic fertilizer was no longer being distributed. But in November, representatives from Greenpeace were still able to purchase the fertilizer in a local market in Dinaipur and the waste was still seeping into the ground and the foodstuffs grown on the contaminated land (Leonard, 1993). In June of 1992, a U.S. federal grand jury indicted all three corporations and three individual employees who were responsible for the creation of the toxic mixture.

In another case, a hazardous waste shipping company was indicted for dumping toxic waste on a beach in Haiti. *Multinational Monitor* reports on the case of the owners of the *Khian Sea*, a ship that sailed the world's seas to find a place to dump incinerator ash from Philadelphia. The operators of the ship were indicted on July 14 in a Wilmington, Delaware, U.S. District Court for making false statements to a federal grand jury.

In 1986 Palino and Sons, a waste management company hired by the city of Philadelphia, contracted with John Dowd, of Amalgamated Shipping Corporation, and William Reilly, of the Coastal Carriers Corporation, to dispose of ash from the city's municipal garbage incinerator. The ash was carried aboard the ship *Khian Sea* for 27 months. In January 1988, the ship unloaded 4,000 tons of waste, labeled as fertilizer, on the beach of Gonaives, Haiti, in violation of Haitian law prohibiting waste imports. In May 1988, the ship sailed to the former Yugoslavia, where it docked with approximately 11,000 tons of the remaining ash in its cargo holds. In Yugoslavia, the ship's name was changed to *Felicia*. It left Yugoslavia shortly thereafter and arrived in Singapore in November 1988 with its cargo holds empty. (Gozan, 1992, 4)

Multinational Monitor notes that testimony by a member of the ship's crew led to the indictment of Dowd and Reilly on dumping the waste in the Indian Ocean. An EPA analysis revealed hazardous levels of lead, cadmium, and dioxin in the Philadelphia incinerator ash. The waste remains exposed in Gonaives, Haiti, without fencing or warning signs. It is believed that the rest of the waste was dumped in the Indian Ocean.

Mpondah (1990) notes that many companies, under pressure from environmental groups in Europe and North America, are increasingly turning to poor countries with less stringent regulations to get rid of toxic and dangerous wastes. The World Health Organization (WHO) has sharply criticized this practice. In 1989 an international treaty was introduced into the United Nations to stop this practice, but it was defeated by parliamentary maneuvers introduced by the United States and the United Kingdom that served to strip the treaty of any power to control these dumping practices (Heong, 1990). Mpondah (1990) observes that the opportunity for dumping this hazardous waste is occurring because a number of impoverished Western African countries are lured by the prospect of millions of dollars. The Nairobi-based UN Environmental Program (UNEP) reported that about twelve African countries either have "quietly" signed contracts to accept industrial wastes or are in the process of negotiations to that effect, which has placed the leaders of the Organization of African Unity in a difficult situation. Mpondah notes that African countries have increasingly been recruited because sites in the South Pacific and the Caribbean that have been used as dumps for years began to fill up in the mid-1980s. An example of this practice is Equatorial Guinea, which signed a ten-year contract with a British company based in Buckingham to bury a minimum of 5 million tons of nuclear waste a year. A down payment of £1.6 million was made.

In another case, Congolese officials agreed to accept a million tons of "heavily polluted chemical waste," as it was described, for storage or incineration over a period of eight years in return for $92.6 million. The waste was to be shipped from the Netherlands, Belgium, Luxembourg, and West Germany. Mpondah (1990) points to the profitability of this arrangement for many of these poor countries by citing the case of Guinea-Bissau, one of the poorest countries in the world. Guinea-Bissau canceled plans to import 15 million tons of toxic waste from industrialized countries. The contract would have earned the country $600 million, twice its foreign debt. Unfortunately, the wastes in many of these countries are again dumped in areas in which the poorest populations within these very poor countries are most likely to experience the deadly consequences. Feagin and Feagin (1990) refer to this practice of economic violence as toxic terrorism. Nigeria, one of Africa's most populous countries, is one of the most outspoken opponents of dumping. Incensed by reports of illegal waste dumping, Nigeria threatened to impose the death penalty on those found responsible (Mpondah, 1990).

Foster (1994) writes that since 1989, there have been more than 500 attempts to export over 200 million tons of waste from the twenty-four wealthy nations that make up the Organization for Economic Cooperation and Development (OECD) to 122 non-OECD countries (7). He notes that between 1986 and 1991 waste shipments were principally targeting Africa, the Pacific, the Caribbean, and Latin America. More recently, there has been a shift to include Eastern Europe and Asia. Each day, enough toxic waste is shipped to Asia to fill 185 forty-foot seagoing containers (Foster, 1994).

In a report issued by Greenpeace and the Basel Action Network (2000) they list a number of recent cases of toxic dumping. At the Cambodian port of Sihanoukville 3,000 tons of highly toxic mercury-tainted waste from the Formosa Plastics of Taiwan was unloaded. The toxic wastes, initially dumped on open ground fifteen kilometers outside Sihanoukville, were later packed into containers following the deaths of two workers who had direct contact with the waste. The report also notes that in December 1999, Philippine authorities seized 122 forty-foot containers carrying infectious medical wastes from Japan. The consignment was disguised as used plastic scrap for recycling purposes. The waste shipment exported by Japanese company Nisso Ltd. consisted of needles for intravenous injections, medical rubber hose and tubes, used adult and baby diapers, used sanitary napkins, discarded intravenous syringes used in blood letting and used bandages. In both these cases, the shipment was shipped back to its home country after public protest.

Eastern Europe also is being recruited for toxic dumping sites. Poland signed an agreement in the 1970s to store radioactive waste from the former West Germany (Slocock, 1992). These shipments took place until 1983 when they were finally stopped because of increasing citizen concern about pollution. Germany and other Western countries have continued to seek access to Poland's land to dump its waste. Since the capitalist transformation of Poland, more offers have been made to use land for disposal purposes, and there are increasing problems of Polish entrepreneurs bypassing the government's restrictions on dumping by importing waste as industrial materials and then dumping them once they are in the country.

Poland is one of the most polluted countries in Europe. Most of the pollution is a result of the operation of state-run industries. Environmental violence is economic in nature and is authorized by the state, which directly profits from the pollution. Poland's level of sulfur dioxide pollution is almost twice that of the United Kingdom. This level of pollution is only exceeded by that of the former Czechoslovakia (Slocock, 1992). Water pollution in Poland is in a critical condition. Slocock reports that over 68 percent of surface water is unfit for human consumption. The Vistula River, which runs through Warsaw, is so polluted by saline discharges from coal mining operations, chemical wastes, and heavy metals that it corrodes the metal barges that travel the river.

One of the most polluted regions in Poland is Katowice Province, where 55 percent of industrial waste water is discharged into the rivers. Water for human consumption has to be trucked in from outside the area. The infant mortality in Katowice is 40 percent above the national average. The Katowice environmental director states that there is an annual death rate of 878 per 1 million persons from environmentally related illnesses in the area. Another area is Upper Silesia, where an estimated 50 percent of the population live in conditions hazardous to their health. In total, more than a quarter of the population of Poland lives in areas deemed to be an immediate health hazard, according to the World Health Organization.

Besides the dumping of waste produced in advanced countries, increasingly there is the dumping of factories that are heavy polluters to poor countries that do not have the government regulations in place to protect its citizenry from the violent consequences of the pollution. Today, 850 U.S. corporations operate one or more *maquiladora* plants, foreign-owned plants operating in Mexico along the U.S. border. More than 80 percent of the *maquiladoras* are U.S. owned. There is an increasing problem of occupational disease and injury to workers at these plants. One study conducted by the Work Environment Program of the University of Massachusetts at Lowell concluded that the working conditions identified in this study are reminiscent of the nineteenth century sweatshops of the U.S. industrial towns (LaBotz, 1993, 22). This study revealed that workers were suffering from muscular-skeletal disorders and chemical poisoning resulting from their work.

But there may be even greater problems of death or injury resulting from the environmental violence due to the migration of factories to poor countries with few environmental protection regulations in place. More than eighty chemical plants, metalworking plants that use lead and zinc, and electronic assembly plants (40 percent of the *maquiladoras*) that use benzene and other toxic chemicals in the production process operate along the border (LaBotz, 1993, 22). These plants release their toxic waste in streams, open pits, the air, and dump sites close to the residential areas of workers at the plants. As a result, there are increasing problems of death or injury to people who have less ability to protect themselves from this violence.

One example is the city of Matamoros, which lies directly across the Rio Grande from Brownsville, Texas (Knaus, 1993). This community is one of many along the Mexican border of the United States that has experienced a dramatic influx of *maquiladoras*. Recently the region has suffered a dramatic rise in the birth of encephalic babies (infants born without brains). In the Brownsville/Matamoros area, confirmed cases of encephalic babies now stand at fifty in approximately a three-year period. Knauss (1993) notes that this is the largest cluster of encephalic babies ever documented, and four times the U.S. national average. She reports that physicians and health activists believe that the cause of the high incidence is the industrial chemical xylene used at the Matamoros facility of the Chicago-based Stepan Chemical. This chemical is known to cause liver and kidney damage and is linked to the birth defects. Samples taken from a drainage ditch at Stepan's Matamoros facility contained xylene at 53,000 times the allowable U.S. level. Community residents have long borne witness to the company's practice of dumping chemicals into open, unlined canals that run through the colonia. Since most of the dwellings around the plant do not contain indoor plumbing, residents will draw water from the canals for everyday purposes: bathing, cleaning, and drinking. Some residents will boil the water; however, the result is a higher concentration of the toxic chemical in the water. The residents claim that contaminated soil samples can be found just a few feet below ground level.

Another example is the impact of Texaco's drilling operations in the Amazon region of Ecuador (Jochnick, 1995). The Organization of American States began an investigation into human rights abuses by the Texaco and Maxus Oil companies. It was estimated that the oil drilling operations, 90 percent controlled by Texaco, had discharged 4.3 million gallons of toxic waste into the Orientes environment every day of operation. In this region of operation documented toxic contamination of water has reached levels that are 1,000 times the safety standards recommended by the U.S. Environmental Protection Agency. Local workers report increased health problem including birth defects, cancer, and gastrointestinal problems related to this contamination. Texaco's twenty years of operation in the region has resulted in contaminated rivers, soil, and environment, destroyed forests, fish and other wildlife. Indigenous populations in the area have been severely reduced in size as a result of the displacement and disease resulting from the encroachment of settlers participating in Texaco and related operations. Contact with outsiders and the vital loss of land has broken down traditional bonds, brought malnutrition and new diseases, and pushed indigenous communities to the bottom rung of a hostile market economy. Alcohol and prostitution, endemic to the Orientes oil towns, are among the most visible signs of the social and cultural deterioration. The World Bank has described the region's socioeconomic state as calamitous (Jochnick, 1995, 13). Jochnick notes that the government of Ecuador has discovered that several indigenous groups have been pushed to the edge of extinction. One such group, the Tetetes, has completely disappeared. There is no evidence that any people from this tribe exist today. Another group is the Cofan, whose population of 15,000 in 1950 has been reduced to 300 people. Similar examples of genocidal destruction as a result of the impact of oil exploration and drilling by Unocal and Total can be found in Thailand (Strider, 1995).

Barry Commoner (1990) summarized this pattern of environmental violence:

> The result of this division is a painful global irony: the poor countries of the south, while deprived of an equitable share of the world's wealth, suffer the environmental hazards generated by the creation of that wealth in the north. The developing countries of the south will not only experience the impact of global warming and ozone depletion, which are now chiefly due to the industrialized countries, but are also victimized by the north's toxic exports. For example, as bans have been imposed on particularly dangerous pesticides in industrialized countries, manufacturers have marketed them in developing countries instead. There, poorly regulated, they have created in the bodies of local populations the world's highest concentrations of pesticides. Similarly, as environmental concerns have limited disposal sites for trash and the toxic ash from trash burning incinerators in the United States, efforts have been made to get rid of these pollutants— not always successfully—in developing countries (142).

The United Nations Environmental Program proposed an international convention to control the dumping of wastes in developing countries. The Basel Convention on the Control of Transboundary Movements of Hazardous Wastes and their Disposal was adopted in Basel, Switzerland, on 22 March 1989. One of the guiding principles of the Basel Convention is that, in order to minimize the threat, hazardous wastes should be dealt with as close to where they are produced as possible. Under the convention, transboundary movements of hazardous wastes or other wastes can take place only upon prior written notification by the state of export to the competent authorities of the states of import and transit (if appropriate). In addition, there are outright bans on the export of these wastes to certain countries. At the Second Meeting of the Conference of the Parties (COP—2) in March 1994, parties to the agreement agreed to an immediate ban on the export from OECD (30 member Organization for Economic Co-operation and Development) to non-OECD countries of hazardous wastes intended for final disposal. They also agreed to ban the export of wastes intended for recovery and recycling (Decision II/12). As of March 2, 2002, 149 countries have ratified the convention, but the United States, Afghanistan, and Haiti have not.

Air Pollution

A second area of environmental violence results from air pollution. A survey of air quality conducted by the EPA revealed that in 1987 large U.S. companies (those producing 75,000 pounds or more of toxic substances annually) emitted a total of 2.4 billion pounds of chemicals into the air (Feagin and Feagin, 1990). The Feagins note that air pollution is a major source of cancerous diseases. In particular, polluted urban air has been linked to an increased probability of respiratory diseases, eye irritation, and asthma. Those who are already ill, children, the aged, and the poor are the most likely to be the immediate sufferers from air pollution (Feagin and Feagin, 1990). Erickson (1992) claims that in the United States today 60 percent of the population live in areas where the air does not meet the standards set by the 1970 Clean Air Act.

Kepone and Allied Chemical Company

Allied Chemical producers of Kepone, a pesticide used to kill ants, cockroaches, and pests that attack bananas, is a good example of air pollution as environmental violence. Allied Chemical initially produced the chemical in the 1960s and was aware of research that indicated that the chemical was highly toxic and that it was linked in animal studies conducted in the 1940s and 1950s to sterility, damage to nerves, and liver cancer. Here we first have a case of product violence. Allied shipped Kepone to Life Sciences Company (a company formed by former executives for Allied) in 1973. Mokhiber notes that "by contracting with Life Sciences, Allied could have its Kepone and the profits too, without the headaches involved in complying with the environmental laws" (Mokhiber, 1988, 252).

The Life Sciences plant emitted sulfur trioxide, a Kepone ingredient into the air. Mokhiber (1988) found that emissions were so bad that those who worked or resided in the area around the plant had trouble seeing the plant because of the thick white clouds emanating from it. Blood analysis of residents in the neighborhoods near the plant indicated the presence of Kepone. Not only was there a problem of air pollution, but Kepone wastes were dumped into the sewage system, which made the sewage system inoperable by the spring of 1974. "As a result, the city began pumping the Kepone-laden effluent into a nearby open field known as Kepone Lagoon. Kepone Lagoon grew enormously, eventually holding 800,000 to 1,000,000 gallons of the contaminated sludge. Traces of Kepone found their way into the city's industrial water pipeline, a pipeline that services a nearby federal reformatory and the U.S. Army's Fort Lee, as well as industrial users" (251).

Before this period, Allied directly dumped Kepone into the James River, contaminating it. Before the river was closed to fishing in late 1975, about 900,000 catfish, hundreds of thousands of pounds of shad, and 500,000 bushels of oyster were removed from the river each year for sale throughout the nation. All of the catch is believed to contain trace elements of Kepone. Hundreds of workers from both the Allied and Life Sciences companies suffer from neurological damage from exposure to Kepone (Mokhiber, 1988).

Union Carbide and Bhopal, India

A second case study, one of larger proportions, is that of Union Carbide and Bhopal, India. At 12:30 a.m. on December 3, 1984, there was an explosion in one of the storage tanks holding methyl isocyanate (MIC), a highly toxic chemical used to produce pesticides at the plant. Water had entered the tank when a maintenance worker attempted to clean out a pipe leading from the tank. The pipe leading from the storage tank had been improperly sealed, which led to the gases from the tank mixing with the water. This led to a chain reaction that created heat and pressure and an explosion that led to the release of forty tons of deadly gases into the atmosphere over Bhopal.

There were problems with the plant in Bhopal, many of which were originally anticipated by the executives in charge of the subsidiary of Union Carbide headquartered in Connecticut. In February 1985, Edward Munoz, a retired Union Carbide official and former managing director of Union Carbide of India Limited (UCIL), claimed in a sworn affidavit that in the early 1970s, Union Carbide insisted, over UCIL's objections, that large amounts of MIC be stored at the plant in Bhopal. UCIL's position was to store only token amounts in small, individual containers. But Union Carbide's corporate engineering group imposed the view that Bhopal would be the site for the construction of large bulk storage tanks patterned on similar Union Carbide facilities at Institute West Virginia (Mokhiber, 1988, 90). Union Carbide, U.S.A., owned 51 percent of Union Carbide of India Limited, in Bhopal.

Mokhiber (1988) cites several serious problems at the plant, problems that were well known to company officials. One problem was the refrigeration unit that was designed to keep the gas in the storage tank at a low enough temperature to prevent runaway chemical reactions. The refrigeration unit was not working at the time of the disaster and had been inoperable for five months before the accident. The gas was at a temperature that was higher than what was defined as safe by the plant's operating manual. Mokhiber notes that with the refrigeration unit out of commission, the instruments to measure the temperature and pressure of the gas in the tank were crucial. Workers perceived the gauges to be unreliable. The emergency scrubber system that was to function to neutralize the gas in the event of a leak was not working at the time of the disaster and had been inoperable for six weeks before the accident. The flare tower that was to be the last line of defense to burn off the escaping gas had been closed down for ten days prior to the accident because the gas line to the flare tower had corroded as a result of neglected maintenance. To make matters worse, the workers at the plant were inadequately trained because of a high turnover of personnel.

Company officials in the United States were aware of the problems at the plant as early as 1982. At that time a team of American experts, at the request of Union Carbide, pointed out major safety concerns at the plant including deficiencies in instrumentation and safety valves, lax maintenance, and high turnover of operating and maintenance staff (Mokhiber, 1988). The team of experts made several recommendations to correct the deficiencies. Soon after the report was released, Mohkiber notes that union organizers in India appealed to the U.S. management team to improve the safety conditions at the plant; however, according to spokespersons, none of the recommendations were implemented.

If the report of experts and pleas of union organizers were not enough, there was also the recent history of accidents at the plant. Between 1978 and 1984, there were six serious accidents at the plant. Each accident should have told the executives in Connecticut of the dangers at the plant. In November 1978 there was a fire at the plant that took ten hours to bring under control and resulted in $5 million in property damage. A plant operator was killed in December 1981 because of a phosgene gas leak. Another phosgene gas leak occurred in January 1982 and caused twenty-eight injuries. There were three MIC leakages reported between October 1982 and 1984. Several residents in the area surrounding the plant reported problems in breathing and burning of eyes. Four workers were seriously injured in the mishaps. Union Carbide never informed residents of the community of Bhopal of the extreme toxicity of the gas being stored at the plant. Furthermore, only a few in the medical community had been informed. When the disaster occurred at midnight on December 3, the warning siren failed to go off until two hours after the explosion. Most of the residents around the plant were asleep at the time of the leak. They woke up choking and vomiting from the fumes; many did not wake at all. Praful Bidwai, a chemical engineer and journalist, described the situation in a hospital three days after the leak:

"The scene is compelling in its display of death. There is something indescribable about the horror, the squalor, the sheer magnitude and force of death here. No one is counting numbers any longer. People are dying like flies. They are brought in, their chests heaving violently, their limbs trembling, their eyes blinking from photophobia. It will kill them in a few hours, more usually minutes" (cited in Mokhiber, 1988, 87).

Weissman (1994) quotes estimates of the death toll range from a low of 3,000 to a high of 16,000. Hundreds of thousands more suffer from blindness, permanent lung damage, gas-related cancers, posttraumatic stress disorder, and other ailments. One recent study found that 40 percent of the 865 pregnancies at the time of the disaster did not end in a live birth. This is almost four times greater than the rate in previous years.

Water Pollution

Feagin and Feagin (1990) describe the problem of water pollution resulting from the dumping of industrial and agricultural runoff in the Mississippi River.

> Beginning in Minnesota, where more than ten million pounds of toxic chemicals are dumped into its waters each year, the Mississippi River continues to be assaulted by the effluent of industries, cities, and agricultural lands along its bank as well as by

the pollutants carried by its many tributaries. Thousands of toxic waste dump sites are to be found in the river's basin; hidden dump sites are discovered each year. There are an estimated 112 toxic waste dump sites in the Memphis area alone. The Mississippi River basin, once called the "Body of the Nation," is referred to today by its residents as "Cancer Corridor" or "Chemical Alley." The basin's fertile soil and fresh water once made it one of the world's ideal habitats. Today, it is one of the most dangerous. Toxic wastes have poisoned groundwater as well as river water. Industrial toxins are released into the air from chemical manufacturers, power plants, pulp and paper mills, and hazardous waste incinerators. Areas that rely on the Mississippi River for drinking water have disease rates for certain types of cancers that are among the nation's highest. The wastes the Mississippi River pours into the Gulf of Mexico have created a seasonal "dead zone" covering nearly 2.4 million acres of prime fishing ground from the river's mouth in Louisiana to the Texas border (Feagin and Feagin, 1990, 368).

Feagin and Feagin (1990) go on to say that there has been a significant increase in cancers and other illnesses among the residents of Natchez, Mississippi. When citizens began to investigate the causes of the problem, they found that carcinogens were found in private well water. The wells had been poisoned by toxic wastes from oozing barrels in abandoned dump sites, many of which belonged to Armstrong Tire Company (368).

Unfortunately, Natchez, Mississippi, is not an isolated incident. According to Feagin and Feagin, petrochemicals are polluting a growing number of underground wells in the United States, wells that supply half of all our drinking water. Underground water pools, called aquifers, are seriously contaminated with chemical wastes in several New Jersey townships, twenty-two towns in Massachusetts, and a number of areas in Minnesota and Michigan.

In regard to some specific cases of dumping by corporations, General Electric routinely dumped water contaminated with cesium-137, strontium-90, uranium and plutonium into the Mohawk River in the early 1950s. GE claims to have stopped this dumping in 1964 but trace amounts of plutonium were detectable in the river in 1989, according to tests conducted by the state of New York (Mokhiber, Gozan, and Knaus, 1992).

In another case, Feagin and Feagin (1990) report that in 1988 residents living near Eastman Kodak's eighty-year-old Kodak Park plant in Rochester, New York, learned that highly toxic chemicals from the plant had been seeping into their groundwater for years. Although many chemical spills had occurred over the years, Kodak only noticed the problem in the fall of 1987. Still, Feagin and Feagin note that residents were not notified until March 1988. By this time, chemicals had leached into yards adjacent to the land and had eaten through carpets in the basements of some homes. Strong chemical odors were also reported by residents, and children who lived in the area were developing eye lesions and experiencing dizziness.

In another case, Chevron was fined by the California Regional Water Quality Control Board for dumping 48 million gallons of extremely toxic waste water daily into San Francisco Bay. And many people remember how medical wastes including stained bandages, containers of surgical sutures, vials of AIDS infected blood, needles, syringes, as well as miscellaneous household waste washed ashore along the beaches of Long Island during the summer of 1988 (Feagin and Feagin, 1990).

Minamata

In the 1950s in a fishing village in Japan, Minamata, the first signs of a problem were birds that fell out of the sky dead and cats that appeared to commit suicide as they staggered and then jumped into the ocean off the docks (Mokhiber, 1988). The first human case of poisoning was a five-year-old girl who developed severe symptoms of brain damage believed to be from eating the fish that were found to carry traces of mercury ethyl from the Chisso chemical plant. Mokhiber reports that the chemical plant had been dumping more than sixty poisonous chemicals directly into the bay. By the summer of 1956 the symptoms exhibited by this young girl had reached epidemic proportions. In August 1956 a research group from the local university discovered that the cause of the disease was heavy metal poisoning caused by eating fish and shellfish taken from Minamata Bay.

Mokhiber notes that the response of the company was to deny the claims of the research team and to continue dumping the chemicals into the bay and then in 1958 to begin pouring its waste into Minamata River, ignoring the warning signs of their own company doctors. The disease then spread to river residents who fished out of the river. One study, conducted by one of the company doctors, Dr. Hajim Hosokawa, clearly established the linkage between the disease and the effluent from the plant. The company's response was to remove the doctor from the research and seal the evidence.

> After receiving Hosokawa's findings, the company did not immediately halt the dumping of mercury-tainted waste into Minamata Bay, nor did it warn people not to eat the tainted fish. Chisso's first reaction was to offer the victims payments in consolation for their misfortune (in Japanese, *mimai*)—an offer many victims were in no position to refuse. Although Chisso knew about Hosokawa's findings, the affected residents did not. They only suspected that the disease was somehow contagious and that they were catching it from their neighbors. Taking advantage of the legal and scientific ignorance of their victims, Chisso negotiated one-sided contracts that limited the company's liability to the initial, minimal payment. Chisso initially accepted no legal responsibilities for the damage done and disclaimed any future monetary liability (Mokhiber 1988, 303).

Eventually, Chisso admitted wrongdoing, two company executives were convicted of involuntary manslaughter, and the corporation threatened to go bankrupt because it could not pay all the damage claims.

Reserve Mining Company

Another case study involves the Reserve Mining Company. Mohkiber (1988) notes that for more than thirty years, the Reserve Mining Company dumped thousands of tons of taconite wastes into Lake Superior on a daily basis. By the middle of the 1950s, the company was dumping 67,000 tons of waste rock into the lake every day, almost 25 million tons a year. In 1947, when the company applied for and obtained a permit to dispose of its wastes into Lake Superior, the company assured the public that the dumping would not affect the lake.

By the late 1960s, Reserve Mining's dumping of wastes into the lake came to the notice of the Department of Interior. An unofficial report written by a staff member of the department that was drafted in response to Reserve Mining Company's application for a renewal of their permit to continue the dumping suggested that a permit be granted only for another three years to give the company time to develop a land-dumping strategy. The staff member reported that Reserve Mining was polluting the lake by increasing the concentration of particulate matter. Reserve joined with Armco and Republic (the two companies that had jointly purchased Reserve Mining) to pressure the government to not release the report.

The Environmental Protection Agency picked up the fight against Reserve Mining. The company took the battle to federal court to gain permission to continue its dumping into the lake. But the evidence that came out of the court hearing showed that Reserve Mining was dumping fibers into the lake that resembled cancer-causing asbestos fibers and that the fibers were floating in the drinking water used by residents of Duluth, Minnesota, and smaller cities in the area. In July 1973 the drinking water of several of these cities was defined as unfit for human consumption. Judge Lord of the federal court ruled in April 1974 that the Reserve Mining Company must cease all discharges into Lake Superior and into the air.

Within days, Reserve had successfully appealed the order. The case was returned to Judge Lord, who was subsequently removed from the case because of the pressure by Reserve Mining and its parent corporations. The company continued to dump waste into the lake despite evidence of the health risk to residents in various cities in the area. Finally, in 1980, the federal government ordered the Reserve Mining Company to stop dumping into the lake—eleven years after the initial analysis by the Department of the Interior indicating that the dumping was polluting the lake and causing a health hazard to residents of the surrounding communities.

Resource Depletion

As companies and countries put short-term interests, profits, and the generation of surplus ahead of long-term interests, and the health and well-being of residents, there are increasing problems resulting from the irresponsible extraction of resources. Currently, 100 acres of rain forests are destroyed each minute (Population Institute, 1990). Every year the world loses an area of tropical forest-land that in size is comparable to England (Coleman and Cressey, 1990). Less than 2,000 years ago the Sahara Desert was a luxuriant rain forest. Ehrlich, Ehrlich, and

Oldren (1973) note that overgrazing by domesticated sheep and goats and clearing of the forest were major factors in destroying the area.

In the United States in the last 200 years we have lost 50 percent of our wetlands, 90 percent of northwestern old-growth forests, 99 percent of tallgrass prairies, and up to 490 species of native plants and animals (Information Please Environmental Almanac, 1993). Each year we lose 1 million acres of cropland to erosion (Pimental, 1993). In general, the people of dominant countries in the world use most of the resources. The United States population comprises 5 percent of the total world population. Yet this 5 percent consumes 30 percent of the world's resources (Hayes, 1993). To compound this damage of resource depletion is the pollution in the poorest communities around the world as a result of the overconsumption patterns in the most advanced countries. What has been the impact on the people who depended on these resources or were effected by other environmental calamities resulting from this resource depletion?

Violence in the Amazon

Currently a great deal of violence is associated with the exploitation of resources in the Amazon region. This is an old story that has been repeated on every continent of the world. Our national history of violence connected to driving indigenous populations off their land to get access to minerals, game, land for farming, timber, and so on is well known. Today, those indigenous populations that have not been eliminated are the poorest in terms of access to resources, and where these populations reside (as we have indicated) are sought after as sites for the dumping of toxic waste. The story has been repeated in Africa and, most recently, South America, Brazil in particular. In the Amazon, the violence is between the indigenous populations, which are increasingly shrinking in numbers because of disease and violence, *garimperios* (small miners, many of them sons of farmers), large ranchers and plantation owners, small farmers, rubber tappers, foreign corporations, and the military. Since 1980, more than 1,000 people have been murdered in land disputes in rural Brazil, but no more than ten people have been convicted and sent to jail (Revkin, 1990). Indigenous populations are increasingly being displaced and the government in recent years has established a reservation system to protect these populations. Missionaries are plentiful in converting and resocializing the native populations to the new order and their appropriate position in it.

Besides the murders connected with land disputes, there is environmental violence in the Amazon as a result of the method of extracting raw materials that has been even more violent to many tribal societies within the region. One example of this is gold mining. Mercury poisoning is an increasing problem among the indigenous population because of the gold mining activity. This results from the technique of gold and silver mining by which the ore is passed over mercury-coated copper plates. The gold and silver adhere to the plates and the mercury contaminated water runoff flows into streams and rivers. Fishing grounds are polluted as well as drinking water. A study by the Brazilian Department of Mines and Energy in 1988 found that Kaypo Indian children have mercury levels in their blood almost as high as the miners'. In another study, conducted by Rogerio da Silva, that analyzed the blood, urine and hair of people directly or indirectly exposed to mercury, found that 25 percent of Kaypo Indians tested had excessive amounts of mercury (Hecht and Cockburn, 1989). This pollution together with being driven from their land by more powerful groups interested in quick access to the resources that lay beneath the land is having devastating consequences for many indigenous people in the Amazon. We have previously discussed oil drilling by Texaco and its partners in the Amazon and its genocidal consequences.

Buffalo Creek

One classic case of economic violence resulting from environmental damage is the case of Buffalo Creek. Buffalo Mining Company, a subsidiary of Pittston Corporation, is one of the largest coal mining companies in the United States. In February 26, 1972, it was involved in an environmental disaster that claimed the lives of 125 persons and left between 4,000 to 5,000 residents homeless.

There are problems of disposal of waste from coal mining. Mokhiber (1988) notes that with every four tons of coal a company digs out of the ground there is one ton of slag or gob, a mixture of mine dust, shale, clay, and other impurities. Coal companies usually dispose of this waste by dumping it in a river or at the base of a mountain. Buffalo Mining Company dumped its waste in the middle of the waters of Middle Creek, one of the three streams that feed Buffalo Creek.

The dumping of waste began as early as 1957. By 1972, the company was dumping 1,000 tons of slag per day into Middle Fork, at the top of the mountain, within eyesight of 5,000 residents who resided in the valley below. The tons of waste clogged up the creek and formed a huge bank of waste, 200 feet deep, 600 feet wide, and 1,500 feet long. Mokhiber notes that the company also had a liquid waste problem. Buffalo Mining used more than half a million gallons of water per day to clean the thousands of tons of coal it mined. Before the creation of EPA, mining companies would dump the waste into nearby rivers and streams. With the new environmental awareness of the 1960s, coal companies were expected to hold on to this water until some impurities settled. Buffalo Mining dumped its waste water behind the dam created by the slag.

It rained hard for a few days before February 26, 1972. On that day in Appalachia at 8:00 in the morning, Buffalo Mining's slag dam, situated nine miles above Amherstdale, collapsed, sending a black torrent of 132 million gallons of water and a million tons of solid waste roaring through the breach. The gigantic wave caused a series of explosions as it thundered down the valley like a mass of rolling lava—a mud wave, as one engineer put it—on a roller coaster ride of destruction aimed to disturb the stillness at Amherstdale and demolish everything in its path (Mokhiber, 1988, 121). The mud wave totally demolished the town of Saunders. It took everything with it, sweeping the town clean. Saunders was only the first town in line for destruction. By the time the black wave reached the mouth of Buffalo Creek, seventeen miles down the hollow, 125 people were dead and 4,000 Buffalo Creek residents were left homeless.

The tragedy in this disaster, and what makes it a case of economic violence as opposed to an unavoidable accident, is that the corporation was well aware of the potential hazards. Mokhiber (1988) states that as early as 1926, *Coal Age*, the industry weekly, reported the dangers of dumping refuse from mining in a hollow that is the drain for a watershed in hilly or mountainous areas. The article in the magazine warned that trouble can be expected if there is no provision made to take care of potential overflows. Following the publication of this article, a West Virginia inspector checked the dam at Buffalo Creek and wrote to the company to tell them of the need for an emergency spill well. In 1966 a disaster occurred in Wales when a 300-foot coal slag mound collapsed killing 145 persons. Following this disaster, a federal investigator visited Buffalo Creek and determined that the dam was subject to a large washout on the north side from overflow of the lake (Mokhiber, 1988, 125). Pittston was finally warned in 1971, when a 150- to 200-foot section of Dam 3 gave way, spilling debris into the second dam in the chain. Despite this problem, Pittston did not build an emergency spillway to avoid a future disaster. That disaster occurred the following year.

CONCLUSION: ECONOMIC VIOLENCE AND INEQUALITY

Are there patterns of economic violence and what factors explain these patterns? It is virtually impossible to compose a representative sample of all the types of economic violence we have discussed in this chapter in order to analyze patterns. Most governments in the world do not collect statistics on the incidence of this type of violence. But from what we know and what we suspect, the incidences of this violence are not random. Indications are that they follow a pattern that is duplicated repeatedly in the story of violence. That pattern is one where those who are least powerful are more likely to experience higher levels of violence than those who are more powerful. And like the story of all other forms of institutional violence, those who are dominant within the institutional spheres enact most of the violence directed at the most powerless segments of the population. Thus it would stand to reason that as societies and the world in general are stratified, higher levels of economic violence victimization are to be found among the poor populations in a given nation state and in the world.

For production violence it is clearly the poor segments of any given society that experience the most hazardous forms of production and bear the greatest cost in occupational diseases and accidents. This is the case whether we are discussing industrial or agricultural production. For product violence, the poor segments of the population in a given country as well as the poor populations in the world are likely to be exposed to hazardous products. This is especially the case when we think of the impact of product dumping by which products banned from wealthier countries are sold in poor countries to unsuspecting consumers.

Last, for environmental violence, it is the poor segments of the population of a given society and the poor populations in the world that are likely to be exposed to hazardous air, water, and soil. Exceptions to this pattern might be a product of the population's geographic isolation. However, even in isolated areas there are serious problems of pollutions because of ocean pollution resulting from the dumping of toxic waste by developed countries and the nuclear testing programs of both the United States and the former Soviet Union. In the latter case, it is important to note that from 1945 to 1989, more than 1,800 bombs were exploded at thirty-five sites around the world. Renner (1991) notes that in virtually all cases, they were areas of colonized or subjugated native people in relatively remote areas.

Furthermore, as valuable resources are stripped away from the poorest populations of the world, not only does their impoverishment have violent consequences via interpersonal violence and other types of institutional violence, but it has a violent consequence as a result of the pollution caused by the very stripping process employed to remove the resources in the largest amounts with the least cost to owners.

More people die or are injured by economic violence than any other single category of violence that we have discussed thus far. When we look at the numbers of people who are dying or are injured because of the wanton dumping of waste, pollution of the environment to maximize economic surplus, hazardous production, and the sale of hazardous products, they are much greater than the numbers of people injured or killed in interpersonal violence or the other types of institutional violence discussed previously. In the next chapter we discuss the last form of institutional violence that we consider in this work, state violence.

REFERENCES

Adler, Bill. 1985, November/December. "Risky Business." *Sierra Magazine*, 21.

Aksit, Bahattin, Nuray Karanci, and Avse Gunduz-Hosgor. 2001. *Turkey: Working Street Children in Three Metropolitan Cities: A Rapid Assessment.* Geneva: International Labor Organization: International Programme on the Elimination of Child Labor (IPEC).

Alston, Dana, and Nicole Brown. 1993. "Global Threats to People of Color." In *Confronting Environmental Racism*, ed. R. D. Bullard, 179–194. Boston: South End Press.

American Lung Association. 2000. *Fact Sheet: Occupational Lung Disease.* http://www.lungusa.org/diseases/occupational_factsheet.html.

Bhagat, Dhiren. 1985. "A Night in Hell." In *Bhopal: Industrial Genocide?* 23. Hong Kong: Arena Press.

Bissio, Roberto Remo. 1990. "A Creeping Bhopal." In *Third World Guide 91/92*, ed. R. R. Bissio, 70. Montevideo, Uruguay: Garamond Press.

Branan, Karen. 1980, June. "Running In Reverse." *Mother Jones* 5: 40–7.

Bray, Garth. 1989. "Poison Pushers." *Multinational Monitor* 10: 10: 31

Brown, Karen, and Lori Ann Thrupp. 1991, April. "The Human Guinea Pigs of Rio Frio." *The Progressive*: 28–30.

Bullard, Robert D. 1993. *Confronting Environmental Racism*. Boston: South End Press.

Burbach, Roger, and Patricia Flynn. 1980. *Agribusiness in the Americas*. New York: Monthly Review Press.

Caudill, Harry M. 1987. "Manslaughter in a Coal Mine." In *Corporate Violence: Injury and Death for Profit*, ed. S. L. Hills, 93–102. Totowa, N.J.: Rowman and Littlefield.

CBS.Com. 2001, August 24. "Tire Giant Settles $1B Lawsuit." http://www.cbsnews.com/stories/2001/08/10/national/main305944.shtml.

Chemical Industry Archives. 2001, March 26. "The top 5 facilities accounted for over half of all vinyl chloride emissions in the country." *The Inside Story*. http://www.chemicalindustryarchives.org/dirtysecrets/vinyl/facilityrank.asp.

Claybook, Joan. 1984. *Retreat from Safety: Reagan's Attack on America's Health*. New York: Pantheon Books.

CNN Interactive. 1998. "Secret memos show cigarette-maker targeted teens. Focus Story: Tobacco Under Attack." http://www.cnn.com/HEALTH/9801/15/tobacco.kid.settlement/#memos.

Cohen, Marc. 1995, January. "Choking on Growth." *New Internationalist*, 22–23.

Coleman, James W., and Donald R. Cressey. 1990. *Social Problems*. New York: Harper & Row.

Commoner, Barry. 1990. *Making Peace with the Planet*. New York: Pantheon Books.

Cray, Charlie. 2001. "Toxics on the Hudson: The Saga of GE, PCBs and the Hudson River." *Multinational Monitor* 22, nos. 7–8: 9–17.

Daniels, Julie L., et. al. 1997, October. "Pesticides and Childhood Cancers." *Environmental Health Perspectives* 105, no. 10: 1068–1077.

Dowie, Mark. 1977, September/October. "Pinto Madness." *Mother Jones* 1: 18–32.

———. 1979, November. "The Corporate Crime of the Century." *Mother Jones* 4.

Dowie, Mark, Douglas Foster, Carolyn Marshall, David Weir, and Jonathan King. 1982, June. "The Illusion of Safety." *Mother Jones* 7: 35–49.

Dowie, Mark, and Johnston. 1976, November. "A Case of Corporate Malpractice." *Mother Jones* 2: 36–50.

Dowie, Mark, and Carolyn Marshall. 1980, November. "The Bendectin Cover-Up." *Mother Jones* 5: 43–56.

Ehrlich, Paul R., Anne H. Ehrlich, and John P. H. Oldren. 1973. *Human Ecology: Problems and Solutions*. San Francisco: W. H. Freeman.

Environmental Working Group. 1999. "Tap Water in Central Valley Tainted with Banned Pesticide Bottle-Fed Infants May Exceed 'Safe' Dose Before Age 1." Press Release Memo, *Environmental Working Group*. http://www.ewg.org/reports/dbcp/dbcpreport.html.

Epstein, Samuel S. 1978. *The Politics of Cancer*. San Francisco: Sierra Club Books.

Erickson, Jon. 1992. *World Out of Balance: Our Polluted Planet*. Blue Ridge Summit, Pa.: Tab Books.

Fagin, Dan, Marianne Lavelle, and the Center for Public Integrity. 1999. *Toxic Deception: How the Chemical Industry Manipulates Science, Bends the Law, and Endangers Your Life*. Monroe, Maine: Common Courage Press.

Feagin, Joe R., and Clairece Booher Feagin. 1990. *Social Problems: A Critical Power-Conflict Perspective*. Englewood Cliffs, N.J.: Prentice Hall.

Felsenthal, Edward. 1993, September 9. "Manslaughter Pleas: Legal Beat." *Wall Street Journal*, 12.

Flanders, Laura. 1994. "Brookhaven Lab: The Cancer Connection." Covert Action Quarterly, no. 51 (Winter).

Forastieri, Valentina. 1999. *Safework: The ILO Programme on Occupational Safety and Health in Agriculture.* Geneva: ILO. http://www.ilo.org/public/english/protection/safework/agriculture/agrivf01.htm.

Foster, John Bellamy. 1994, September/October. "Waste Away." *Dollars and Sense*, no. 195: 7.

Foundation for National Progress. 1984. "Dalkon Shield Executives Blasted by Federal Judge." *Insider* 15: 2.

Frank, Nancy. 1986. *Crimes against Worker Health and Safety.* San Francisco: Sierra Club Books.

———. 1987 "Murder in the Workplace." In *Corporate Violence: Injury and Death for Profit*, ed. S. L. Hills. Totowa, N.J.: Rowman and Littlefield.

Freeman, Aaron. 1994. "Delivering on Delaney." *Multinational Monitor* 15: 6.

Gold, Stuart. 1989, October. "The World Bank's Pesticide of Choice." *Multinational Monitor* 10: 7–9.

Gozan, Julie. 1992. "Toxic Traders Indicted." *Multinational Monitor* 13: 4.

———. 1993. "Demanding Justice." *Multinational Monitor* 14: 5.

Greenpeace and Basel Action Network. 2000, February 12–19. "Business As Usual: Case Studies of Hazardous Waste Dumping in Asia." Report prepared for the *United Nations Conference on Trade and Development* meeting held in Bangkok, Thailand. http://www.greenpeace.org/~toxics/toxfreeasia/unctad.html.

Grunwald. 2002, January 1. "Monsanto Hid Decades of Pollution: PCBs Drenched Ala. Town, But No One Was Ever Told." *Washington Post*, A01.

Guarasci, Richard. 1987. "Death by Cotton Dust." In *Corporate Violence: Injury and Death for Profit*, ed. S. L. Hills, 76–92. Totowa, N.J.: Rowman and Littlefield.

Hayes, Denis. 1993, November 10. "Eco-nomic Power." *Seattle Weekly*, 15.

Harris, Gardiner. 1998, April 19. "Dust, Deception, and Dust." *The (Louisville, Ky.) Courier-Journal.*

Hebert, H. Joseph. 1983, October 21. "Files Show GM knew X-Car Brakes Locked." *Denver Post*, sec. 1A, 12A.

Hecht, Susanna, and Alexander Cockburn. 1989. *The Fate of the Forest: Developers, Destroyers, and Defenders of the Amazon.* New York: Verso.

Heong, Yoke Chee. 1990. "Spotlight: Toxic Waste Treaty." In *Third World Guide 91/92*, ed. R. Bissio, 71. Montevideo, Uruguay: Garamond Press.

Information Please Environmental Almanac. 1993. Compiled by World Resources Institute. Boston: Houghton Mifflin.

International Labor Organization 2002. *Statistics: Revealing a hidden tragedy.* International Programme on the Elimination of Child Labour: IPEC. http://www.ilo.org/public/english/standards/ipec/simpoc/stats/4stt.htm.

Jeyaratnam, J. 1990. "Acute Pesticide Poisoning in Asia: A Major Global Health Problem." *World Health Statistics Quarterly* 43, no. 3.

Jochnick, Chris. 1995, January/February. "Amazon Oil Offensive." *Multinational Monitor* 6: 12–5.

Kean, Yeong Joo, and Annelies Allain. 2001. *Breaking the Rules, Stretching the Rules 2001.* Penang, Malaysia: International Baby Food Action Network.

Kerr, Lorin E. 1980. "Black Lung." *Journal of Public Health Policy* 1: 57.

Kerr, Mary Lee, and Bob Hall. 1992, January. "Chickens Come Home to Roost." *The Progressive* 56: 29.

Kinney, Joseph A., and William G. Mosley. 1990, April. "Death on the Job." *Multinational Monitor* 11: 29–31.

Knaus, Holly. 1991, May. "The Front." *Multinational Monitor* 12, no. 5.

———. 1993. "Stepan Chemical: Poisoning Mexican Communities." *Multinational Monitor* 14: 28–29.

Kohn, Howard. 1992. "America's Worst Polluter." In *The Rolling Stone Environmental Reader*, ed. by R. Stone, 37–50. Washington, D.C.: Island Press.

KC, Kumar, Bal Govind, Subedi Yogendra, Bahadur Gurnung, and Keshab Prasad Adhikari. 2001. *Nepal: Trafficking in Girls with Special Reference to Prostitution: A Rapid Assessment.* Geneva: Central Department on Population Studies: International Labor Organization International Programme on the Elimination of Child Labour (PEC).

LaBotz, Dan. 1993, May. "Manufacturing Poverty: The Maquiladization of Mexico." *Multinational Monitor* 14: 18–23.

Leonard, Ann. 1993, April. "Poison Fields: Dumping Toxic Fertilizer on Bangladeshi Farmers." *Multinational Monitor* 14: 14–18.

Lewis, Karen. 1992, January/February. "Addicting the Young: Tobacco Pushers and Kids." *Multinational Monitor* 13: 13–17.

Lowengart, R. A., J. M. Peters, and C. Cicioni. 1987, January. "Childhood Leukemia and parents' occupational and home exposures." *Journal of the National Cancer Institute* 79: 39–46.

Mackay, Judith. 1992, January/February. "China's Tobacco Wars." *Multinational Monitor* 13: 9–12.

Marshall, Carolyn. 1987. "An Excuse for Workplace Hazards." *The Nation*, 532.

Mattera, Philip. 1992, January/February. "RJR Nabisco: Transnational Tobacco Trafficker." *Multinational Monitor* 13: 38–41.

Mencimer, Stephanie, William Steif, and George L. Leventhal. 1992, February. "Breath Taking." *The Progressive,* 56: 14.

Miller, Judith, and Mark Miller. 1985, March. "The Midnight Dumpers." *USA Today Magazine*, 60.

Mintz, Morton. 1985. *At Any Cost: Corporate Greed, Women, and the Dalkon Shield.* New York: Pantheon Books.

Mokhiber, Russell. 1988. *Corporate Crime and Violence.* San Francisco: Sierra Club Books.

Mokhiber, Russell. 1994. "The Ten Worst Corporations of 1994." *Multinational Monitor* 15: 7–16.

Mokhiber, Russell. 2001. "Corporations Behaving Badly: The Ten Worst Corporations of 2001." *Multinational Monitor* 22:12: 8–19.

Mokhiber, Russell, Julie Gozan, and Holly Knaus. 1992. "The Corporate Rap Sheet: The 10 Worst Corporations of 1992." *Multinational Monitor* 13: 7–16.

Mokhiber, Russell, and Robert Weissman. 2001. "Enemies of the Future: The Ten Worst Corporations of 2000." *Multinational Monitor* 21:12.

Moses, Marion. 1993. "Farmworkers and Pesticides." In *Confronting Environmental Racism*, ed. R. D. Bullard, 161–78. Boston: South End Press.

Mother Jones Investigative Fund Report. 1984. *Insider*, no. 15.

Mpondah, Dingaan. 1990. "Dumping on Africa and the Third World." In *Third World Guide 91/92*, ed. R. Bissio, 72. Montevideo, Uruguay: Garamond Press.

Mwami, J. A., A. J. Sanga, and J. Nyoni. 2002. *Tanzania: Children Labour in Mining: A Rapid Assessment.* Geneva: International Labor Organization: International Programme on the Elimination of Child Labor (IPEC).

Nader, Ralph. 1972. *Unsafe at Any Speed: The Designed-In Dangers of the American Automobile.* New York: Bantam.

New Internationalist. 2000, May. "A is for Apple, P is for Pesticide." 323: 22–23.

Page, Joseph A. 1973. *Bitter wages: Ralph Nader's Study Group Report on Disease and Injury on the Job.* New York: Grossman.

Perry, Alex, and Mae Sai. 2002, March 11. "How I Bought Two Slaves, to Free Them." *Time* 159, no. 10: 7.

Pimentel, David. 1993. "United States Carrying Capacity Overview." Report presented at Carrying Capacity Network Conference, Washington, D.C.

Population Institute. 1990. *We Can Blame Billions of People for This.* Washington, D.C: Population Institute.

Reiman, Jeffrey. 1990. *The Rich Get Richer and the Poor Get Prison.* New York: Macmillan.

Renner, Michael. 1991. "Assessing the Military's War on the Environment." In *State of the World 1991,* ed. Lester R. Brown et al., 132–52. New York: Norton.

Revkin, Andrew. 1990. *The Burning Season.* Boston: Houghton Mifflin.

Robinson, James C. 1991. *Toil and Toxics: Workplace Struggles and Political Strategies for Occupational Health.* Berkeley: University of California Press.

Safetyforum. 2002. *Military Toxic Waste: Killing after the Wars are Over.* Arlington, Va.: Safetyforum.com. http://www.safetyforum.com/mtw/.

Savitz, D. A., E A. Whelan, and R. C. Kleckner. 1989. "Self-Reported Exposure to Pesticides and Radiation Related to Pregnancy Outcome-Results from National Natality and Fetal Mortality Surveys." *Public Health Report* 104: 473–77.

Shaffer, Michele. 1988, June 29. "4 Killed by Cyanide Gas in Auburn." *(Fort Wayne, Ind.) Journal Gazette,* 1A.

Shapely, Dan. 2002, February 2. "Dedging Order Signed." *Poughkeepsie (N.Y.) Journal.*

Simon, David R., and D. Stanley Eitzen. 1993. *Elite Deviance.* Boston: Allyn and Bacon.

———. 1999. *Elite Deviance.* Rev. ed. Boston: Allyn and Bacon.

Slocock, Brian. 1992. *The East European Environment Crisis: Its Extent, Impact and Solutions.* London: Economist Intelligence Unit, 2109.

State of California Department of Health Services. 1988. *Epidemiological Study of Adverse Health Effects in Children in McFarland, California.* Phase II Report. Sacramento: State Department of Health Services.

Strider, R. 1995, January/February. "Blood in the Pipeline." *Multinational Monitor* 16: 22–5.

Summa, John. 1988, November. "Killing Them Sweetly." *Multinational Monitor.* 9: 28–31.

Ungar, Sanford J. 1972. "Get Away with What You Can." *In the Name of Profit: Profiles in Corporate Irresponsibility,* ed. Robert L. Heilbroner et al. Garden City, N.Y.: Doubleday.

United Nations Environment Programme. 2002, February 17–21. "Three Deadly Pesticides and Asbestos Targeted for Action." Geneva: Press Release of Third session of the Interim Chemical Review Committee (ICRC).

UNICEF. 1989. United Nations Convention on the Rights of the Child. New York: UNICEF.

———. 2001. *Progress since the World Summit for Children—A Statistical Review.* New York: UNICEF.

U.S. Environmental Protection Agency. 2001. *National Primary Drinking Water Regulations: Consumer Factsheet on Vinyl Chloride.* http://www.epa.gov/safewater/dwh/c-voc/vinylchl.html.

U.S. Department of Health and Human Services, Public Health Service. 2001. *9th Report on Carcinogens.* Washington, D.C.: U.S. Government Printing Office. http://ehis.niehs.nih.gov/roc/ninth/known/vinylchloride.pdf.

U.S. House of Representatives Committee on Education and Labor. 1979. *Black Lung Benefits Reform Act and Black Lung Benefit Revenue Act of 1977.* Washington, D.C.: Government Printing Office.

Weissman, Robert. 1992a, January/February. "America's Killing Ground." *Multinational Monitor* 13: 5.

———. 1992b, January/February. "The Marlboro Man Goes East." *Multinational Monitor* 13: 31–34.

———. 1994, December. "Remembering Bhopal." *Multinational Monitor* 15: 5.

Wernette, D. R., and L. A. Nieves. 1992, March/April. "Breathing Polluted Air." *EPA Journal* 18: 16–17.

Winter, Gregory. 1997, August 24. "Big Tobacco Is Accused of Crossing an Age Line." *The New York Times.*

World Health Organization. 1994, October 11–14. *Global Strategy on Occupational Health for All: The Way to Health at Work.* Recommendation of the second meeting of the WHO Collaborating Centres in Occupational Health, Beijing, China. http://www.who.int/environmental_information/Occuphealth/strategy2.htm.

Zastrow, Charles. 1992. *Social Problems: Issues and Solutions.* Chicago: Nelson Hall.

Chapter Seven

State Violence

In Crescent City, California, at the Pelican Bay State Prison on the morning of April 22, 1992, guards of the facility entered Vaughn Dortsch's cell and ordered him to strip naked. The guards returned thirty minutes later shackled his legs and arms, gagged him, and carried him to the prison infirmary where one guard told him that he would receive a Klan bath. Dortsch testified that he was forced by six guards to remain in a steel tub of scalding hot water, scrubbed with a wooden brush until his skin peeled away from his body. He also testified that he was held down in the water for several minutes. Dortch collapsed after he was removed from the tub and was treated at the prison infirmary for burns before he was transferred to the burn unit of the University of California, Davis, hospital (Berma, 1994).

Thirty heavily armed men wearing army combat vests, but masked with hoods lettered death squad came to my village and seized and killed a number of campesinos. They went then to the neighboring village of Santa Helen, seized Romilia Hernandez, aged 21, raped and then decapitated her. Her relatives buried her head: the rest of her body was burned by her murderers. The head had been left in front of her relative's house. The members of the death squad were evacuated that day by a Salvadoran army helicopter.—Testimony by a Salvadoran refugee to an Amnesty International mission visiting refugee camps in Honduras, August 1981 (Amnesty International, 1983, 11).

At Kafr Kassim in October 1956, forty Arabs, including twenty-nine women and children, were massacred by Israeli police in what an Israeli judge declared to be a case of deliberate murder and which some Israeli publications called a Nazi-like atrocity. The leader of this police operation was sentenced to a token fine of two cents (Amnesty International, 1983, 31).

On September 3, 1992, Sdiq al-Karim Malallah, a twenty-three-year-old Shia Muslim and an advocate for improved civil rights in Saudi Arabia, was beheaded after he was found guilty of apostasy (renunciation of religious faith) and blasphemy (Amnesty International, 1993, 2).

In Uganda at least 100,000 people were killed during the eight-year rule of President Idi Amin (Amnesty International, 1983).

During the mid-1960s more than half a million people were killed in Indonesia after the military took over the country and began a campaign to eliminate all political opposition to their rule (Amnesty International, 1977).

Jean-Bedel Bokassa, self-proclaimed emperor of the Central African Empire, killed 50–100 school children in Ngaragba prison between the eighteenth and twentieth of April, 1979 (Amnesty International, 1977).

When officials from a township birth control office got a hold of Zhou Jiangxiong in May 1998, they hung him upside down, repeatedly whipped and beat him with wooden clubs, burned him with cigarette butts, branded him with soldering irons, and ripped his genitals off (Amnesty International, 2001a).

In Guatemala on May 29, 1978, Roman Catholic Church workers reported that 114 peasants were killed by the army in an Indian village when Indians attempted to present a petition protesting the takeover of their land by wealthy landowners (Chomsky and Herman, 1979, 282).

These are incidents of state violence. The scale of violence committed by governments is greater than interpersonal violence, yet when we think of violence what usually comes to mind is images of muggers, rapists, and teenage gangs on city streets. The state protects us from these criminals. Yet interpersonal violence makes relatively modest contributions to the overall violence phenomenon. This is consistent with the principles noted earlier regarding levels of violence. As we move from the interpersonal to institutional to structural forms of violence, the scale and scope of violence increases. Ironically, at the same time, these higher levels of violence are less likely to be defined as violence and thus are seen as nonproblematic. But before we discuss the details of state violence, we must define it.

DEFINITION

Any definition of state violence presupposes agreement on what we mean by the term "state." A working definition will equate state with government. For classic German sociologist Max Weber the modern state was characterized by three particular dimensions: territoriality, legitimacy, and violence. Weber noted that only the state has a monopoly on the legitimate use of violence (1958). But one question that is immediately raised is how we distinguish the state's legitimate use of violence from the state's illegitimate use of violence, although this is not a question particularly relevant to a definition of violence. It is violence no matter if it is defined as legitimate or illegitimate by the state. In all cases the legitimacy issue is separate from the question of the existence of violence. As Michalowski (1985) writes, "the fact that state violence is legal within any given political context . . . should not tempt us to overlook the fact that it is nonetheless violence" (279). Thus we pragmatically define state violence as referring to all forms of violence committed by government. This includes actions by police, National Guard, and military forces, or, as Michalowski observes, all forms of politically authorized violence.

Most researchers have focused on only illegitimate or illegal categories of violence. The obvious problem with this limitation from a conflict perspective is that the state is in a monopoly position of power to define the legal status of the violence. Consequently, most of the acts within the broader domain of violence that eventually become defined as violence are those acts that threaten the state. This can be seen in the use of the term "terrorism." Terrorists are usually defined in terms of individuals or groups who threaten the social order. For example, Brian Jenkins (1984), a Rand think tank specialist on terrorism, defines terrorism as the use or threatened use of force designed to cause a political change.

But what about violence used to maintain the status quo? Laqueur (1987) describes terrorism as the illegitimate use of force to achieve a political objective when innocent people are targeted. The qualifier "illegitimate" again begs the issue. Who defines legitimacy? In both of these authors' works, most of what we would call state terrorism is precluded from their definitions. If the state is unlikely to define its own acts of violence as illegitimate, then who is left to do so?

We can turn to international organizations like the United Nations or private watchdog groups such as Amnesty International, the African Human Rights Research Association, Americas Watch, Asia Watch, Cultural Survival, Helsinki Watch, and Human Rights Advocates International which have focused to a large extent on state violence or terrorism. Unfortunately, the power they have to bear on states that engage in illegitimate violence is determined by the distribution of power within the world system. Those states with the greatest amount of power in the world system have the greatest amount of power to define illegitimate state violence and terrorism. Their influence lies in their ability to inform citizens around the world of these crimes and to apply the normative pressure of world public opinion on the leaders of states that sanction such acts.

One international force that could be important in the future in controlling state violence is the International Criminal Court. This court has been formed specifically to try and convict those responsible for state violence, including genocide, crimes against humanity including rape, murder, enslavement, and various war crimes including torture, and attacking civilians. On April 11, 2002, sixty-one countries ratified the international criminal court treaty. It went into effect July 2002. The United States government has for many years attempted to block the ratification of the treaty. President Clinton signed the treaty but then never presented it to the U.S. Senate for ratification. Most recently congress passed a law entitled the "American Service Members Protection Act" that exempts all U.S. government personnel from being prosecuted by the court and also denies all military aid to non-NATO signatories of the treaty. President George W. Bush announced that the treaty will not be ratified and that the United States will not be subject to the treaty's jurisdiction.

Amnesty International has indisputably been the premier organization that monitors state violence. It defines political killings as unlawful and deliberate killings of persons by reasons of their real or imputed political beliefs or activities, religion, other conscientiously held beliefs, ethnic origin, sex, color or language, carried out by order of a government with its complicity (Amnesty International, 1983).

Violence by the state can be understood as accomplishing two general purposes. On the one hand, violence is used to maintain order, that is, the order that is in part defined in terms of particular systems of stratification that determine the distribution of resources and power and defined in terms of the particular functioning of institutions that maintain and reproduce the society from generation to generation. The state's practice of executing offenders of particular crimes is one example of state violence that we take for granted. In the exercise of capital punishment, the state is defending order by killing an individual who has threatened it and at the same time warning others that if they commit similar acts they will be dealt with in the same manner. In the United States since the 1930s there have been more than 4,000 legal executions. Between 1972 and 1976 capital punishment was outlawed by the U.S. Supreme Court and thus executions were not conducted. However, after this period executions resumed and in several states resumed with a vengeance. Between 1977 and March 1, 2002, 761 convicted murderers have been executed in the United States. Of those executed, eight were female. Although the majority of those who were executed were white with 422 (55 percent), African Americans were overrepresented with 266 (35 percent). The majority of those executed were executed by lethal injection, 599 (79 percent), including all 110 of those executed since July 6, 2000. One hundred forty-six were executed by electric chair, eleven by gas chamber, three by hanging and two by firing squad. Executions were held in thirty-two different states. However, the state of Texas had more than any other state with 261 or 34 percent.

Of these 761 executions, eighteen were of those who were under the age of eighteen at the time of their crime. The execution of juvenile offenders is rare in the world today. Amnesty International USA reports that since 1990, only seven countries in the world are known to have executed juveniles: Democratic Republic of Congo, Iran, Nigeria, Pakistan, Saudi Arabia, Yemen, and the United States (Amnesty International, 2002a). Yemen has since outlawed the practice, as did China in 1997.

The United Nations Convention on the Rights of the Child Article 37(a) states: "Neither Capital punishment nor life imprisonment without possibility of release shall be imposed for offenses committed by persons below 18 years of age." Only the U.S. and Somalia have not ratified this Convention. Amnesty International notes that twenty-four U.S. states allow for the execution of people who were sixteen or seventeen years of age at the time of the crime: Alabama (16), Arizona (16), Arkansas (16), Delaware (16), Florida (17), Georgia (17), Idaho (16), Indiana (16), Kentucky (16), Louisiana (16), Mississippi (16), Missouri (16), Nevada (16), New Hampshire (17), North Carolina (17), Oklahoma (16), Pennsylvania (16), South Carolina (16), South Dakota (16), Texas (17), Utah (16),

Virginia (16), and Wyoming (16). As of July 2001, eighty-five men on death row were sentenced as juveniles (Amnesty International USA, 2002a). Ten out of eighteen or 56 percent of the executions of juvenile offenders that have occurred between 1973 and 2001 were in the state of Texas.

In looking at the population of those executed by the United States government, the majority have been members of ethnic minorities and generally from the poorer strata of society (Bowers, 1974; U.S. Bureau of Justice, 2000). Of the 211 federal death penalty prosecutions authorized by the Attorney General since 1988, 75 percent have been against minorities. The U.S. General Accounting Office issued a report in 1990 which found that in 82 percent of the studies reviewed, race of the victim was found to influence the likelihood of being charged with capital murder or being sentenced to execution. Those who murdered whites were more likely to be charged and executed than those who murdered blacks (General Accounting Office, 1990). Amnesty International's recent report (1998) on human rights violations in the United States noted that blacks make up just 12 percent of the country's population, but 42 percent of the nation's condemned prisoners. In early 1998, of the twenty-six people under federal sentences of death (military and civilian), only five prisoners were white. The report also notes that between 1908 and 1962, all those executed for rape were black, although only 55 percent of those imprisoned for rape were black. Furthermore, blacks and whites in the U.S. are the victims of murder in almost equal numbers, yet 82 percent of prisoners executed since 1977 were convicted of the murder of a white person (Amnesty International, 1998, 109).

An argument increasingly used by abolitionists is the problem of false convictions. In recent years with the advent of DNA testing there has been the discovery of a large number of inmates awaiting execution who were found to be innocent. Most recently, Arizona prisoner Ray Krone became the hundredth person exonerated from death row in the United States since 1973.

Worldwide, Amnesty International (2002a) reports that seventy-five countries and territories have abolished the death penalty for all crimes. Another fourteen countries have abolished the death penalty for all but exceptional crimes such as wartime crimes and an additional twenty countries can be considered abolitionist in practice in that they retain the death penalty in law but have not carried out any executions for the past ten years. This would make the total number of countries that have abolished the use of death penalty in practice to a total of 109 or 56 percent of countries. Amnesty International notes that eighty-six other countries retain and use the death penalty, but the number of countries which actually execute prisoners in any one year is much smaller. During 2000, at least 1,457 prisoners were executed in twenty-seven countries and 3,058 people were sentenced to death in sixty-five countries. These figures include only cases known to Amnesty International; it is expected that the true figures are higher. Eighty-eight percent of all known executions took place in four countries: China, Iran, Saudi Arabia and the U.S. The number of executions are increasing: during 2001 Amnesty International reported that over 3,048 people were executed in thirty-one countries, more than double the previous year (Amnesty International, 2002c).

One particularly gruesome case of state violence as it relates to executions is where there is a policy by the government to remove organs for their organ transplant program before prisoners are executed or that they are executed in such a way as to keep valuable tissue undamaged for transplant. The organization Human Rights Watch/Asia reports that 3,000 executions conducted annually by the People's Republic of China have been an important source of organ transplants within the country as well as organs exported overseas. The group estimates that in 1992 alone between 1,400 and 1,700 kidneys were harvested from executed prisoners. Sometimes the executions are botched so that transplants can be conducted after the execution. In 1978 a young woman teacher, Zhong Haiyuan, accused of hiding clandestine literature, was executed in Ganzhou, Jiangxi Province. She was shot twice in the head but did not die. Instead of waiting for her death, medical personnel were allowed to take her body to a specially erected operating facility on the prison premises and to remove both kidneys while she was still living (Schmetzer, 1994, 5).

Another form of state violence is police use of deadly force. In terms of a recent government report, the police in the United States kill 400 people annually (Brown and Langan, 2001). In this report police homicides are by definition referred to as "justifiable" and to provide further justification for the police homicides the report also combines information on felons who killed police. Furthermore, the estimate provided in the report is believed to be conservative since not all police jurisdictions report to the federal government cases of killings by police. The report does note that police killed blacks in 1998 at a rate that was 4 times greater than that of whites killed by police. Young black males who made up 1 percent of the total U.S. population were 14 percent of felons "justifiably" killed by police in 1998. In 1998, the city of Detroit had the highest rate of killings by police. Recently there have been riots in several major cities in the United States as a result of police violence and homicides. In 1980 there was the Liberty City Riots in Florida, which were sparked by the police killing of an unarmed black male who ran a red light. In the decade of the 1990s in Los Angeles there were the riots in South Central Los Angeles after the acquittal of all the officers who were videotaped beating Rodney King with batons and stun weapons. In 2001, there was rioting in Cincinnati after police had shot and killed an unarmed black man. Mr. Bacre Waly Ndiaye, special rapporteur of the Commission on Human Rights, recently included the United States as one of several countries to investigate for extrajudicial executions. In his report, Ndiaye issued urgent appeals to ninety-one countries, including the United States, to end extrajudicial, summary or arbitrary executions (Ndiaye, 1996). In 1994 a U.S. law was passed requiring the federal government to collect and analyze nationwide data on police use of excessive force, but as of this date Congress has yet to provide the necessary funding.

A final form of violence we often think of in terms of the state defending it-self is the use of the military to defend the national interest. In most cases we think of governments using their military forces to defend their geographic borders. But, for states whose national interest extends beyond the territorial boundaries of the country, violence is used as a means of extending economic and political control over people of other nation-states where these interests reside. Imperialist nations or nations whose development depends upon the increasing control of resources outside of the national boundaries blur the lines between violence used to defend its internal order and violence used to extend it. Although conceptually these two general forms of violence may be distinct, analytically the distinction in the practice of state violence becomes blurred. Violence to extend the order, in other words, becomes defined as violence to defend the order. The often heard phrase in the United States by U.S. presidents and State Department officials to legitimate the use of military force to defend U.S. dominion overseas is to defend our national interest. These national interests are often in places far removed from the physical and legal boundaries of the United States. It would be more accurate to say that in defending U.S. imperial interests its leaders are utilizing military force to maintain economic domination of these regions. The rhetorical phrase "to defend our national interest" is employed to legitimize the violence, but there is also truth in this claim given the nature of imperialist societies. To maintain the socioeconomic/political and industrial system (which in part is based on military production) of the United States, it is necessary for the state to utilize violence or the threat of violence to continue its political and economic dominance over other people around the globe. The economic doomsday saying and regional complaints that occurred in the early 1990s as President Clinton began to make serious movements to cash in on the post–Cold War peace dividend are ample demonstration of the shock to a system otherwise oriented to a permanent state of war. With the recent election of President George W. Bush, military spending in response to the attack on the World Trade Center has skyrocketed and it has opened a new era of overt U.S. military interventionism in its worldwide war on terrorism.

EXTENT OF STATE VIOLENCE

Overall, there is no way of comprehensively knowing the extent of state violence in the world today. In most cases, what are counted by agencies concerned about state violence are the extralegal forms of state violence. These extralegal forms refer to the use of violence without justification or legitimization by the laws of the state that is conducting the violence. The extent of legal state violence, which includes executions by the state, police use of deadly force, and military actions, is in some respects more difficult to assess because it relies on data, if collected, that are created by the very state that is conducting the violence. One example that we have previously discussed is police use of deadly force. As

Fyfe (1988) notes, no federal agency has ever collected or published data on police use of deadly force nationwide. Some but not all of the police departments have voluntarily submitted the data that are available, while the FBI disseminates this information only on request without mentioning such statistics in its annual Uniform Crime Reports. The existence and quality of such statistics in countries around the world are even more problematic. At times there are reports that are developed by groups outside of the state concerned about the extent of police violence. For example in one recent report done by medicolegal experts in Kenya, they note that six out of every ten Kenyans who are shot dead are victims of police. According to this same report, the 2001 rate increased to nine out of every ten victims (Leyan, 2002).

From what is known about extralegal state violence, it occurs in many countries throughout the world. There is no annual census of the numbers of people who are killed by governments. According to Iain Guest (1983), at least 2 million people have been summarily executed around the world during the fifteen years prior to his writing for their opposition to governments. However, these figures may be an underestimate of the problem today. Amnesty International reported that in 1994 up to a million men, women and children were slaughtered in Rwanda in just 100 days (Amnesty International, 2001b). Ruth Leger Sivard (1982, 17) adds that among the 114 developing countries covered in the UN Human Rights Commission report, eighty-three countries—three out of four—are reported to have used violence against the public in the form of torture, brutality, disappearances, and summary executions; in these countries there appears to be frequent resort to these forms of violence; in an additional thirty-five, the practice occurs but less frequently. According to the most annual recent report of Amnesty International (2001b) extrajudicial executions were carried out in sixty-one countries and people were reportedly tortured or ill-treated by security forces, police or other state authorities in 125 countries.

In this most recent report of Amnesty International (2001b) reports of state violence are identified on all continents with the exception of Antarctica. In Africa, "confirmed or possible" extrajudicial executions were carried out in twenty-four countries. For example, "between 25 and 28 June at least 44 unarmed civilians were extrajudicially executed by soldiers in Itaba commune, Gitega province, in reprisal for military losses following clashes with the armed opposition. Most were killed with bayonets" (Amnesty International, 2001b). The report also notes that in Africa people "disappeared" or remained "disappeared" from previous years in at least nine countries. The report also cites cases in thirty-two countries where people were reportedly tortured or ill-treated by security forces, police or other state authorities. For example in the Democratic Republic of the Congo, "Kikuni Masudi, a former member of the security services, died in security service custody in Lubumbashi. He had reportedly been continuously tortured since his arrest by agents from the *Agence nationale de renseignements* (ANR), National Intelligence Agency. He had reportedly been whipped, burned and his feet had been crushed by hammer blows." There were also "confirmed or possible prisoners of conscience" in twenty-one countries.

In the Americas, "confirmed or possible" extrajudicial executions were carried out in fourteen countries in the region in 2000. For example Amnesty International reports that "in February, 200 paramilitary gunmen raided the village of El Salado, Bolívar department, killing thirty-six people, including a six-year-old child. Many victims were tied to a table in the village sports field and subjected to torture, including rape, before being stabbed or shot dead. Others were killed in the village church. During the three-day attack, military and police units stationed nearby made no effort to intervene. Instead, a Navy infantry unit reportedly set up a roadblock on the access road to El Salado, thus preventing humanitarian organizations from reaching the village."

People "disappeared" or remained "disappeared" from previous years in eleven countries in the Americas and people were reportedly tortured or ill treated by security forces, police or other state authorities in twenty-two countries in the Americas. In Venezuela, "Marco Antonio Monasterio and Oscar José Blanco Romero 'disappeared' on 21 December 1999, during the flood rescue operations. They were reportedly detained by the army in the neighborhood of Valle del Pino and transferred into the custody of the Directorate of Intelligence and Criminal Prevention Services (DISIP). By the end of the year their whereabouts had not been established." An example of a case of torture listed by Amnesty International is the case of Corcoran State Prison in California where "in June, eight prison guards were accused of staging 'gladiator style' fights among prisoners between 1989 and 1995. The guards were acquitted of criminal charges after a jury trial." However, Amnesty International notes that "although the guards were acquitted, the state had earlier been forced to change its policies after an independent panel found that 80 percent of the shootings had been unjustified. State legislative hearings in 1998 had found a pattern of brutality at the prison." Last, confirmed or possible prisoners of conscience were held in four countries in the Americas (Amnesty International, 2001b).

In Asia and the Pacific Islands, "confirmed or possible" extrajudicial executions were carried out in twelve countries in the region in 2000. "In China as a result of the crackdown on religious groups and ethnic minorities, hundreds of followers of 'heretical' religious or spiritual movements were arrested and reportedly tortured. At least 93 Falun Gong followers were believed to have died in custody." "In Myanmar, the military continued to kill ethnic minority civilians during counter-insurgency operations and seize them for forced labour duties." People "disappeared" or remained "disappeared" from previous years in six countries in Asia and the Pacific. For example, in Indonesia "repression of pro-independence movements in Aceh and Papua led to an increase in 'disappearances', torture and political killings. People were reportedly tortured or ill-treated by security forces, police or other state authorities in twenty countries in the region." Amnesty International reports that "torture was endemic in several countries including China, India, Bangladesh and Myanmar." Confirmed or possible prisoners of conscience were held in thirteen countries (Amnesty International, 2001b).

In Europe, "confirmed or possible" extrajudicial executions were carried out in six countries in the region in 2000. For example, in Russia at least sixty civilians were summarily executed in the Noviye Aldy suburb of the Chechen capital, Grozny, by Russian forces during a "cleansing operation" on 5 February. People "disappeared" or remained "disappeared" from previous years in six countries. In Yugoslavia more than 3,300 people from Kosovo were unaccounted for at the end of 2000. Most were ethnic Albanians who were believed to have "disappeared" in the custody of Serbian police or paramilitary between early 1998 and June 1999. People were reportedly tortured or ill-treated by security forces, police or other state authorities in 32 countries in the region. For example, in Turkey "in November 1996, a young Kurdish woman, Zeynep Avci, arrested during an operation against the PKK, was subjected to sexual harassment, rape and electric shocks at Izmir Police Headquarters." Confirmed or possible prisoners of conscience were held in fifteen countries including Albania, Armenia, Belarus, and Finland. People were arbitrarily arrested and detained, or in detention without charge or trial in twenty countries (Amnesty International, 2001b).

Last, in the Middle East and North Africa Amnesty International (2001b) reports "confirmed or possible" extrajudicial executions were carried out in five countries in the region in 2000. For example, in Israel and the Occupied territories Israeli security services killed at least 300 and wounded more than 10,000 Palestinians. The majority of those killed and wounded were demonstrators throwing stones or using slings; at least 100 of those killed were children under eighteen. People "disappeared" or remained "disappeared" from previous years in eight countries. Amnesty International reports that no concrete action was known to have been taken by the authorities to clarify the fate of some 4,000 men and women who had "disappeared" after arrest since 1993. For example, Habib Hamidi and Ahmed Ouadni were arrested at their homes in Reghaia in Algiers in April and August, respectively, and remained "disappeared" at the end of the year. People were reportedly tortured or ill-treated by security forces, police or other state authorities in nineteen countries in the region. In Egypt, "torture in police stations continued to be widespread. However, a decrease in arrests of alleged members of armed Islamist groups was reflected in a significant reduction in reports of systematic torture of political suspects. The most common torture methods reported were electric shocks, beatings, suspension by the wrists or ankles and various forms of psychological torture, including death threats and threats of rape or sexual abuse of the detainee or a female relative. In March, Salha Sayid Qasim was detained at Giza Police Headquarters in connection with a criminal investigation. She reported that in detention she was blindfolded, beaten, whipped, suspended by her arms and subjected to electric shocks" (Amnesty International, 2001b). Confirmed or possible prisoners of conscience were held in ten countries and people were arbitrarily arrested and detained, or in detention without charge or trial in six countries.

TARGETS OF STATE VIOLENCE

Conquered Indigenous and Ethnic Minority Populations

Who are the targets of state violence? In general, several groups are perennial prime targets of state violence. One of the largest categories of groups is made up of conquered indigenous and ethnic minority populations. Throughout the history of white conquest and colonization of lands occupied by nonwhite people, there has been a pattern of violence used to control, dominate, and exterminate these populations. Whether we are speaking about the Americas, Africa, Asia, Oceania, or Australia, the pattern is the same and it continues. In a recent report on racism and the administration of justice, Amnesty International (2001c) noted that there are 300 million indigenous people worldwide and that despite the wide range of diversity of this population, there are striking similarities of the abuse they have suffered and continue to experience. Amnesty International notes that government leaders will often incite racial or ethnic hatred against minority groups in order to stay in power. This often results in violence by state authorities against these ethnic minority populations. Violence has always been systematically used as a means to strip the indigenous populations of access to valued resources. Dee Brown (1970) begins the history of the systematic destruction of indigenous people of the Americas with a discussion of what happened to the Tainos and Arawak people after Columbus discovered America more than 500 years ago:

> The Tainos and other Arawak people did not resist conversion to the Europeans religion, but they did resist strongly when hordes of these bearded strangers began scouring their islands in search of gold and precious stones. The Spaniards looted and burned villages; they kidnapped hundreds of men, women, and children and shipped them to Europe to be sold as slaves. Arawak resistance brought on the use of guns and sabers, and whole tribes were destroyed, hundreds of thousands of people in less than a decade after Columbus set foot on the beach of San Salvador, October 12, 1492 (Brown, 1970, 2).

The violence directed at the native population in the United States has continued in recent years, as seen in the activities of the FBI, the military, and Bureau of Indian Affairs against dissident groups of Native Americans (Churchill and Vander Wall, 1990; Matthiessen, 1991). The pattern is basically the same as it was in earlier times in North American history, although it is grounded more in covert forms of violence, as opposed to the overt military actions of the past. In each case the violence is used to acquire access to valued resources held by the indigenous population. This generalization holds whether we are talking about the genocide of the Arawak and Tainos by the Spanish military beginning with Columbus's invasion or the extinction of the Powhatan in the Virginias, to the Wampanoag and Narragansett in Massachusetts, to the five nations of the Iroquois, to the deaths resulting from the forced marching of the Cherokee (referred to as the Trail of Tears), or to the violence directed at various other tribes of North America, such as Pequot, Montauk, Nanticoke, Machapuga, Catawba, Cheraws, Miami, Huron, Erie, Mohawk, Mohicans, Shawnee, Cherokees, Chickasaw, Choctaws, Creeks, Seminole, Apache, and Lakota, to name only a few. Similar stories of state violence directed at indigenous populations are repeated in Australia, Central and South America, Africa, Taiwan, and Oceania/Polynesia. Bodley has attempted to assess the level of depopulation of indigenous populations since first contacts with white Europeans. He observes:

> According to these figures, tribal populations in lowland South America (east of Andes and exclusive of the Caribbean) and North America (north of Mexico) were reduced by almost 95 percent or by nearly 18 million by 1930. . . . In Polynesia, Micronesia, and Australia, where fairly complete, although conservative, estimates have been made, the population was reduced by approximately 80 percent, or more than 1.25 million since 1980. If moderate allowances are made for further depopulation in areas not included, such as Siberia, Southern Asia, islands of southeast Asia, southern Africa, and Melanesia, and if Morels modes of estimate for the Congo is accepted, it might be conservatively estimated that during the 150 years between 1780 and 1930 world tribal populations were reduced by at least 30 million as a direct result of the spread of industrial civilization (Bodley, 1982, 39–40).

Today state violence persists in the United States where the mineral resources of the Lakota in the Black Hills constitute the prize to be acquired (Churchill and Vander Wall, 1990). We can also see a struggle in Wisconsin where the Lake Superior Chippewas have been subjected to federal and state pressure and harassment to give up their treaty rights to hunt and fish on northern Wisconsin lakes. While federal spokespersons are now suggesting that Congress may modernize the treaties first negotiated from 1834 to 1854, white protesters chant slogans like "Save a walleye. Spear a pregnant squaw." Two men were charged in 1990 with criminal conspiracy to interfere with the Chippewas civil rights after they built and exploded a pipe bomb near Chippewa spear fishers at the same time that Wisconsin officials grumbled publicly about the high cost of law enforcement to protect Native American rights (Kerr and Hall, 1992). These are just some of the many examples of conflicts between indigenous people and federal and state governments.

Mineral wealth in the Amazon and other regions of South and Central America have led to increasing amounts of violence and the displacement of indigenous populations who inhabit such lands. Chomsky and Herman (1979) cite the writings of Munzel, a German anthropologist, who notes that at the time of his research in Paraguay there was a campaign under way against the Ache Indians that included manhunts, slavery, and virtual cultural destruction:

> In manhunts with the cooperation of the military, the Indians are pursued like animals, the parents killed and the children sold. Machetes are commonly used to murder Indians to save the expense of bullets. Men not slaughtered are sold for field-workers, women as prostitutes, children as domestic servants. . . . The process of deculturation aims at the intentional destruction of Indian culture among those herded into the reservation (111).

Shelton H. Davis's research cited in Chomsky and Herman's (1979) work details a history of extermination of Brazilian Indians similar to the North American pattern, that is, genocide conducted in order to permit Western colonization.

> From 1900 to 1957, Davis estimates, the indigenous population of Brazil dropped from 1 million to less than 200,000, and by the latter day many were enduring the most precarious conditions of life in the greatest misery. Hideous atrocities came to light in 1968 when a government commission released a 5,000-page report documenting widespread corruption and sadism and the use of biological as well as conventional weapons to wipe out Indian tribes (deliberate spread of smallpox, tuberculosis, measles, etc.) (127).

The use of state violence is not restricted to indigenous minority populations. It extends to other ethnic minorities. In the experience of the United States, following the conquest and subjugation of Native American tribes, violence was directed at African populations who were brought here as slaves and at Hispanic populations who were inhabitants of conquered lands in the Southwest. Churchill and Wall (1990) describe the efforts of the federal and state government in attempting to neutralize the efforts of what was perceived to be radical wings of the civil rights movement, in particular the Black Panthers. In some cases these efforts resulted in the use of violence in the form of assassination or instigating violence by other organized groups to neutralize the efforts of targeted black civil rights groups.

The pattern of targeting ethnic minorities for state violence is not unique to the United States but can be found in other countries throughout the world. For example, in Sri Lanka the military has targeted the Tamil Sinhalese populations. Amnesty International reports that government troops have caused the disappearances or deaths of, at a minimum, thousands of civilians, including babies and elderly villagers (Amnesty International, 1993, 2). Another case is Chad, which is made up of 200 distinct ethnic groups and the country is split in terms of religion: approximately 44 percent are Muslim, 33 percent Christian, and 23 percent members of indigenous tribal religions. In Chad a commission established by President Derby concluded that approximately 40,000 people had been killed by previous regimes. But, Amnesty International (1994a) reports that since taking office, the government under Derby has carried out hundreds of extrajudicial executions and that security forces have been responsible for a number of massacres of unarmed, men, women, and children.

One term that has developed in recent years to describe the use of state violence directed at minority populations is ethnic cleansing. The term has been used to describe the state violence directed by agents of the Serbian government directed at the Muslim population in the country and countries bordering its territory. There are also reports of attacks on ethnic Albanians who resist the imposition of Serbian culture and language in the schools. The history of state violence in South Africa to control the black population (who compose more than 80 percent of the population) and the violence in Rwanda and Burundi between the Hutu and Tutsi is part of a pervasive pattern of state violence throughout the world, whereby violence is an instrument of the state employed to control ethnic minorities as they may pose a threat to the maintenance of the established order.

Dissident Political Groups, Organized Labor, and Peasants

Other categories of targets of state violence are dissident political groups and organized labor and peasants who threaten the system of property ownership in a given country. Note that these categories are not distinct. For example, dissident political groups, organized labor, and peasant populations may also be composed of ethnic minorities. The state violence in South Africa, Guatemala, Indonesia, and Burundi fits this pattern. For example, Jenny Pearce (1982) reports that with regard to the assassinations conducted by or for the state in El Salvador, 69 percent were *campesinos* (farmers and farm laborers), 14 percent were workers, and 14 percent were students. She points out that the vast majority of workers murdered by death squads or the military were trade union leaders or union members. *Campesinos* in many cases had engaged in organized protests for better wages (Pearce, 1982).

Churchill and Wall (1990) claim that a major focus of the Bureau of Investigation of the Treasury Department, the predecessor to the Federal Bureau of Investigation, was radical political movements. For example, these authors discuss the significance of the Slacker and Palmer raids as examples of this early activity by the bureau. Attorney General Thomas W. Gregory had seized upon the national war fever to act in concert with major financial supporters of the Democratic Party to make America safe for industry, crushing the radical opposition once and for all. The Slacker raids and similar broadly focused gambits were designed more than anything to intimidate the general public to a point where there was greatly diminished possibility of a popular radical resurgence after the war (20).

The United States does not illustrate the most severe cases of violence directed at dissident political groups. In Indonesia, the massive violence in the middle 1960s was targeted at members of the Indonesian Communist Party and its affiliated organizations: the trade unions, the women's organization (*Gerwani*), and the peasants association (*Barisan Tani Indonesia*). Amnesty International (1983) observed that there was no set pattern to the killings that began during those years and claimed the lives of an estimated 500,000 Indonesians over a nine-month period. Nevertheless, certain features recurred. Everywhere local officials of the PKI (the Communist Party, the largest political party in Indonesia at the time) and its affiliated organizations were rounded up and shot. Amnesty International reported that often whole families were killed to eliminate the communist menace for all time.

The army initiated the first killings in nearly every province. In some areas the army was assisted by gangs of youths belonging to *Ansor,* an affiliate of the *Nahdatul Ulama,* a fundamentalist Muslim party. Amnesty International notes that in Java, Bali, and Sumatra, night after night for months on end local army commanders loaded lorries with captured PKI members—their names checked off against lists—and drove them to isolated spots for execution, usually by bullet or knife. The international agency reports that in the town of Kediri in Central Java, a PKI stronghold, some 7,000 PKI supporters are estimated to have been killed. In Banjuwangi in East Java, 4,000 people were killed within a few days:

> As the purge accelerated in November 1965 headless bodies covered with red flags were floated down rivers aboard rafts and heads were placed upon bridges. Every day for several months riverside residents in Burabaya in East Java had to disentangle bodies that were caught on jetties. At one point so many bodies from Kediri filled the Brantas river that the downstream town of Jombang lodged a formal protest complaining that plague might break out. In the small mill town of Batu so many were executed within the narrow confines of a small police courtyard that it was decided that it would be simpler to cover the piles of bodies with layers of cement rather than bury the victims. . . . In Bali, armed with machine guns, commandos scoured villages in groups of 25, in some cases executing the entire male population. . . . In one incident alone in the city of Medan, North Sumatra, some 10,500 prisoners were reportedly killed in the space of a few days (Amnesty International, 1983).

Violence has continued throughout many of the 17,000 islands that make up Indonesia, the former Dutch colony, as they themselves seek independence.

Similar patterns of mass slaughter are found in other countries. In Kampuchea, under Khmer Rouge rule from 1975 to 1979, at least 300,000 persons were killed in a series of purges directed at counterrevolutionaries and other undesirable elements. In Guatemala the dramatic rise in political killings began with the presidency of Mendez Montenegro from 1966 to 1970. Estimates of the number of people who have been eliminated by the Guatemalan government are in the tens of thousands. In February 1981 Amnesty International issued a report stating that since President Lucas Garcia took office in July 1978 the organization had learned of the seizure without warrant and subsequent killing of some 5,000 Guatemalans. The report disputed claims by successive governments that the death squads were not under official control. It concluded that there was no evidence of pro-government clandestine groups operating independent of government support. Citing testimony from recent defectors and from survivors of disappearances, Amnesty International (1983) stated that the links between the death squads and the authorities had been particularly blatant during the presidency of Lucas Garcia.

After Garcia came to power in the late 1970s a new death squad was formed by the government, *Ejercito Secreto Anti-Communista* (Secret Anti-Communist Army). Soon after it was formed, this group issued to the press a list of people it had sentenced to death. According to Amnesty International, the list included trade unionists, student leaders, lawyers, journalists, and academics. For example, Oliverio Castaneda, president of the Student's Association of the University of San Carlos, was murdered on a busy street corner in Guatemala City by heavily armed assailants as armed security officers watched. By the end of the year, Pedro Quevedo y Quevedo, secretary general of the trade union organizing at the Coca-Cola bottling plant, was murdered. Then Manuael Lopez Balan replaced the slain leader and in turn was knifed to death in Guatemala City the following spring. In May 1980 union activist Marlon Mendizabal was killed as he waited for a bus outside the plant. In June almost the entire leadership of the Central Nacional de Trabajadores, the trade union congress (which included several labor leaders at the Coca-Cola bottling plant) were kidnapped as they met to discuss funeral plans for still another union leader. Eyewitnesses recognized some of those carrying out the abduction as members of the official security forces; vehicles used in the abduction were official issue models, and the street was closed off to traffic by uniformed National Police officers, while approximately sixty plainclothes officers raided CNT headquarters. Various officials denied that the arrests had taken place, but the late Minister of Labour, Carlos Alarcon Monsanto, informed Amnesty International (1983) that those detained had subsequently been released. The fact is that none of the trade unionists has ever been seen again.

John Booth (1991) estimates that approximately 150,000 people were killed in Guatemala between 1982 and 1985. In a recent report on state violence in Guatemala, 34,363 killings and disappearances in Guatemala were identified as committed by the State and part of a deliberate government policy of extrajudicial killing from 1960 to 1996. As noted earlier, the vast majority of these killings occurred during the Garcia regime (Bell, Kobrak, and Spirer, 1999). In December 1996 the Guatemalan Government and rebels of the National Revolutionary Unity of Guatemala (URNG) signed peace accords ending the civil war.

There is a current legal case brought by survivors of this war that centers around ten massacres in the Ixcán and Ixil regions of the Quiché and in Rabinal in Baja Verapaz. The survivors believe that Lucas Garcia and two other top military officers conspired to commit genocide against the indigenous peoples of Guatemala. The Guatemalan Truth Commission Report substantiates their claims. The report, which was an outcome of the 1996 Peace Accords, concluded that

200,000 unarmed civilians were murdered or disappeared and more than 600 Mayan villages were completely destroyed during the thirty-six-year civil war. According to the report, government agents committed 97 percent of the atrocities. The report also highlighted the role of the United States in supporting the Guatemalan military. According to the report "the United States government and U.S. private companies exercised pressure to maintain the country's unjust socioeconomic structure. In addition, the United States government, through its constituent structures, including the Central Intelligence Agency, lent direct and indirect support to some illegal state operations. On May 3, 2000, Guatemalans from around the country brought before the national court system an unprecedented case. They charged former dictator Romeo Lucas García and top officials of his 1978–1982 regime with genocide and crimes against humanity" (Guatemalan Historical Clarification Commission, 1999).

Recently, Amnesty International notes that six years after the peace accords were signed there has been an upsurge in death squad lynchings. According to the UN Human Rights Verification Mission (MINUGUA), 390 lynchings occurred between 1996 and 2001; in 97 percent of the cases, no one has been brought to justice (Amnesty International, 2002e). Similar acts of state violence have occurred in other countries in Central and South America many times with U.S. government support. In 1932, National Guard members, the army and paramilitary groups, with the collaboration of local landowners, carried out a massacre known as "La Matanza," in which they murdered at least 10,000 peasants in the western part of El Salvador in order to put down a rural insurrection (Betancur, 1993). The UN Truth Commission Report on El Salvador documents state violence and the United States Government tolerance of the activities of Salvadoran exiles living in Miami who directly financed and indirectly helped run certain death squads (Betancur, 1993). For most of the deaths by the state, the principle targets were peasant organizations, unions, and political dissidents. Similar cases of the killings have been discovered in Argentina and Chile. All these examples represent merely the tip of an immense iceberg that is state violence on an international scale.

Children

Tragically, another group that has been systematically targeted for state violence in the modern world is children. For example, in Brazil, a Parliamentary Commission of Inquiry reported that some 7,000 homeless children had been killed during the previous four years (Amnesty International, 1993). A Brazilian Parliamentary Commission report indicated that many children had been killed by death squads composed of off-duty police officers. In the first six months of 1992, 667 children and adolescents were killed in the states of São Paulo and Rio de Janeiro. Between 1988 and 1990, federal police reported that 4,611 children (82 percent of them black) had been killed. The problem is that homeless children were engaging in begging and petty thievery in several large cities in Brazil. The begging and stealing interfered with the businesses of the shopkeepers in certain areas. The solution was to remove the children through wholesale abductions and executions. The children come from peasant families and/or indigenous populations who have been economically displaced as land ownership becomes more concentrated and there is an increasing shift to cash crops for the world export market. Street children have also been killed by police officers in Guatemala City and in other countries in Central and South America.

However, Colombia may lead the world in child murders. In Bogota, there are between 5,000 and 10,000 street children. UNICEF claims there are more street children in this city than any other in South America. A recent report by Human Rights Watch/Americas noted that 2,190 children under the age of eighteen were murdered in Colombia in 1993, six children murdered per day. The report concluded that Colombia has the highest child murder rate in the world (Luft, 1995).

An interesting U.S. parallel to this is the case of merchants organizing and hiring off-duty police to rid downtown areas of the homeless. In Portland, Oregon, Seattle, Washington, and Hartford and New Haven, Connecticut, private security guards patrol the downtown areas to move vagrants out of the way of the daily commerce of the merchants. In midtown Manhattan there is a vigilante force of outreach workers commissioned by the Grand Central Partnership, Business Improvement District, an alliance of local business interests. Most of the outreach workers are homeless themselves, and are used to drive out other homeless from the area. These sidewalk mercenaries police their fellow street people for the remuneration of a shelter bed at the Partnerships St. Anthony shelter and one dollar an hour. Corporations such as Tudor Towers and several local banks have accounts with the Partnership, paying regular fees to keep their ATMs and sidewalks clear of riffraff. After roughly a year of outreach work, serious abuses, such as beatings and intimidation, have been reported. The Coalition for the Homeless was preparing a class action suit against the Grand Central Partnership (Parenti, 1994, 48).

Children are also victims of state violence because of their political activity. The killing of children by state security forces in South Africa during the turbulent times of political unrest directed at the system of apartheid is an example of this. During the latter half of the 1970s, organized school boycotts in the black townships were often responded to by violence by the state security forces. The victims of this violence were primarily school age children who were participants in the boycotts. In Guatemala, the national police in April 1992 entered two secondary schools whose students were involved in political demonstrations, and arrested 170 students; they later tortured many of those arrested. Amnesty International (1993) reports one case where a student was forced to drink bleach.

Another example of children as victims of state violence is when they are forced into the military to kill and be killed. Children as young as six are being used in combat by government and rebel forces in civil wars throughout the world (Frankel et al., 1995). International law prohibits countries from using children below the age of fifteen in military service. Despite this prohibition, estimates are between 50,000 to 200,000 children are fighting in twenty-four conflicts around the world. For example, Liberian leader Charles Taylor gave young boys their own fighting unit called Small Boy Unit (Frankel et al., 1995). Tamil rebels recruited boys as young as nine. The authors also note that young boys were also forcibly recruited in El Salvador and Nicaragua. A UNICEF worker in Liberia, Esther Guluma, states that children make more brutal fighters because they haven't developed a sense of judgment (Frankel et al., 1995, 45). The authors note that in Mozambique children fought on both sides of the civil war. Save the Children estimated that the average age for rebel leader Renamos recruits in one region was eleven. Children are often terrorized to commit acts of violence. Renamos commanders first terrorized the boys—often by hanging them upside down from trees. They forced many to shoot or slit the throats of their parents (Frankel el. al., 1995, 45). Drugs are also used to pump up the youth for battle. Before battle in Liberia children were given Valium tablets to prepare them for battle. Amphetamines and marijuana are also mentioned as drugs used to prepare children for combat. The children who are recruited are poor. They are enticed by ownership of a weapon, new clothes (uniform), three meals a day, and medical care. In Sierra Leone, both the government and the rebel forces will force children as young as seven years old into military service. A similar pattern is found in Burundi (Amnesty International, 2002d). The Coalition to Stop the Use of Child Soldiers, a group formed by various human rights organizations, estimates that half a million children are currently serving in government armed forces, paramilitaries and armed groups in eighty-five countries worldwide; more than 300,000 of these are actively participating in fighting in more than thirty-five countries (Amnesty International, 2002d).

AGENTS OF STATE VIOLENCE

Police and Military

Who commits these acts of violence on behalf of the state? In most cases it is military or government police forces. In South Africa both the police and the military were regularly involved in state violence to control the black minority population who make up approximately three-quarters of the population. A three-year study of torture under detention by the Institute of Criminology of the University of Cape Town in the middle 1970s concluded that the vast majority of people held were physically abused and that the average South African security detainee was subjected to ten different forms of coercion, both physical and psychological (Herman and O'Sullivan, 1989). D. Jonathan Gluckman, at the time South Africa's most prominent independent pathologist and a strong supporter of the de Klerk regime, contends that the police are totally out of control and are killing at least one black suspect a week. Gluck-man examined the bodies of 200 victims of police torture during a two-year period. He is convinced that the police killed 90 percent of these people. According to a 1993 Amnesty International report:

> Dr. Gluckman pointed specifically to the case of 19 year-old Simon Mthimkulu who died after police arrested him in Sebokeng Township on July 14, 1992. A friend arrested with Mthimkulu, himself beaten and then released, later stated that he saw officers viciously kick and beat Simon and drop a huge rock on his rib cage. Police had told Simon's mother that they had released the youth. However, two days later, she found her son's body at a mortuary. His face was caked in blood. Dr. Gluckman performed a post-mortem examination on the dead youth and said his own findings were entirely consistent with the witness's account. South Africa's Ministry of Law and Order denied any police responsibility for any deaths in detention, suggesting that suicide was responsible for the high number of deaths in police custody (1).

In 1988 the Independent Board of Inquiry into Informal Repression (IBIIR) corroborated the testimony of Butana Nofomela, a disaffected former police-man who claimed to have been for years part of an assassination squad. A former police captain, Dirk Coetzz, who has since fled South Africa, commanded Nofomela and others in death squads known as *Askaris*. These officially sanctioned groups targeted in particular African National Congress members and citizens suspected of being dissidents or sympathizers, both black and white. In the early 1990's, the African National Congress claimed that police had been involved in the killings of more than 11,000 people since 1990 (Associated Press, 1994).

Uganda, mentioned earlier, is another extreme case of the state's use of the military and police to kill civilians. Amnesty International has reported that systematic and deliberate killings by government forces began in the first month of President Idi Amin's military government in 1971. The practice became thereafter institutionalized as a means of eliminating those believed to be opponents of the regime.

> Those arrested were often bundled into the back or trunk of a security forces ve-hicle and taken to a military barracks, the Bureau of State Research, the Public Safety Unit, or to a secret safe house under State Research Control. Prisoners were arrested and detained without legal formalities or judicial processes, held incommunicado and often without official records. Nearly all prisoners were severely tortured; most either died under torture or were killed in other ways. Prisoners were sometimes ordered at gunpoint to kill other prisoners. In this method of execution prisoners were lined up; one was given a hammer and ordered to beat another prisoner to death with it; he in turn was then killed by another prisoner, and so on, with the last survivor of the group being shot by a prison guard. Prisoner's bodies were frequently dumped in rivers or forests. Occasionally, the bodies (usually mutilated) were returned to relatives by security officers on payment of large bribes. (38)

During the entire period of President Amin's government, no security official was ever charged, fairly tried, convicted, or punished for any act of arbitrary arrest, illegal detention, torture or murder.

The case of Argentina after the 1976 military coup is similar. Regional commanders were placed in charge of antisubversive operations throughout the country. Amnesty International reports that typically the victims were dragged from their homes in the evening by those identifying themselves as members of the police or armed forces. Between the coup in 1976 and 1979, at least 6,000 persons disappeared, often in gruesome ways. As Amnesty International found, prisoners were forced to remain in their cells in silence. Around 5:00 in the evening each Wednesday, prisoners were selected for transfer. They were each led alone to the infirmary just as they were, dressed or not, whether in hot or cold weather. At the infirmary they were given an injection, they were told, because hygiene conditions in the camps to which they were going were so poor. In reality they were given sedatives. Then they were taken by lorry to the Aeroparque (a military airfield) in Buenos Aires and put on a Fokker airplane belonging to the navy's multipurpose air squadron. From there they were flown southward out to sea to a point where the Gulf Stream would ensure the disappearance of the bodies. Then the prisoners were thrown alive out of the plane (Amnesty International, 1983, 57). These claims by Amnesty International were recently confirmed by Captain Adolfo Scilingo of the Argentine military, who stated before a federal court in Argentina that he and fellow officers threw as many as 2,000 drugged, nude prisoners into the Atlantic Ocean from naval planes (Associated Press, 1995).

Amnesty International recently expressed grave concern regarding the use of U.S. funds to fight the drug war in Colombia funding state violence. Much of this money has gone to the military and police, who have conducted an antisubversive campaign in the cities and countryside. Amnesty International contends that more than 70 percent of the 20,000 people killed in political murders since 1986 in Colombia were committed by army personnel or backed by the military. In many cases, the killings are directed at political parties deemed to be threatening to the interests of the military. According to Amnesty International more than 1,500 members and supporters of the Patriotic Union (UP) have been killed since the political party's inception in 1985. Most of the dead are peasants, who are killed in the military's attempt to neutralize guerrilla forces in the countryside. Amnesty International (1994b) cites one example of the state violence conducted by the military against peasants in the countryside.

In October, 1993 . . . there was a massacre in El Bosque, Riofrio, Valle del Cauca department. Some 25 Colombian troops appeared early in the morning and by midday had taken 13 people from their homes, tortured and killed them. They raped and killed four women; two babies and several children were orphaned (3).

Stewart (1994) estimates that in 1993 the murder rate in Colombia was 28,000 a year, more than in the United States whose population is eight times the size.

She cites the findings of the Andean Commission of Jurists that 56 percent of the political killings (excluding combat) where the killer could be identified in the first nine months of 1993 were carried out by government forces. Stewart contends that Colombia's political death toll is approximately eleven a day. She claims that each year more people die in Colombia than in the entire seventeen-year reign of General Pinochet in Chile. Colombia today has one of the worst human rights records in the world. The United States has been the major funder of the military in its war against the drug trade and the leftist rebels. Unfortunately, this often means a war against the Colombian people who pose a threat to the established rule of the elite in Colombia. More recent figures indicate that the rate of violence has continued to increase in Colombia. In 1999 the murder rate was 77.5 murders per 100,000 inhabitants, more than thirteen times higher than that of the United States. Murders in Colombia increased from 24,358 in 1999 to 26,250 in 2000. At 4.30 p.m. on the fourteenth of April 2002, Tito Libio Hernandez, a leader in the Central Union of Colombian Workers, was standing at the main entrance of the University of Nariño where he had worked for the last twenty-eight years. Two masked men sped past on a high velocity motorbike and shot him repeatedly. The United States continues to increase military spending and the use of military advisors for training and combat in Colombia (Colombia Support Network-Madison, 2002).

Military forces are also agents of state violence in the process of invading a foreign country and engaging in killing civilian and military of the enemy. The major wars of the twentieth century are examples of the tremendous levels of state violence. Since World War II, however, there is no country that has been more involved in military invasions outside its borders than the United States. The United States has been either directly or (especially more recently) indirectly involved in thirty wars since World War II. Frappier (1983) contends that in the period from 1946 to 1975 there were 215 instances in which U.S. armed forces were used as a political instrument. Two of the more recent invasions by the U.S. military, Iraq and Panama, have resulted in civilian casualty estimates of 80,000 (40,000 women and 32,000 children) in Iraq (Colhoun, 1992) and 4,000 to 10,000 in Panama (Bissio, 1990). There are no official numbers on the number of dead in the most recent war in Afghanistan. Prior to World War II the United States military activity was confined principally to the Western Hemisphere, its principle sphere of political and economic influence at the time. Frappier (1983) notes that prior to World War II for the purpose of protecting American lives and property and maintaining order the United States used armed forces in: Argentina (1833), Peru (1835–1836), Argentina (1852–1853), Nicaragua (1853–1853, 1857), Uruguay (1858), Paraguay (1859), Mexico (1859), Colombia (1860), Panama (1865), Mexico (1866), Nicaragua (1867), Uruguay (1868), Colombia (1868, 1873), Mexico (1873), Panama (1885), Haiti (1888), Argentina (1890), Haiti (1891), Chile (1891), Brazil (1894), Nicaragua (1894), Colombia (1895), Nicaragua (1896, 1898–1899), Colombia (1901–1902), Honduras (1903), Dominican Republic (1903–1904), Panama (1903–1914), Cuba (1906–1909), Honduras (1907), Nicaragua (1910), Honduras (1911–1912), Panama (1912), Cuba (1912),

Nicaragua (1912–1925), Mexico (1913–1919), Haiti (1914–1934), Dominican Republic (1914, 1916–1924), Cuba (1917–1922), Panama (1918–1921), Honduras (1919), Guatemala (1920), Honduras (1924–1925), Panama (1925), Nicaragua (1926–1933), and Cuba (1933) (4). After World War II the United States sphere of economic and political dominance expanded throughout the world where today we have more than 300 military bases that encircle the globe and a fleet of war ships in every major body of water throughout the world. In one analysis, bases were listed in sixty-one countries and territories around the world (*Monthly Review*, 2002). Most recently the pattern is that after each U.S. military engagement, new bases are established in the region of the military engagement. This is certainly the case in the Middle East where many new bases were developed during the Gulf War and the war in Afghanistan. The irony is that it is alleged that the attack on the World Trade Center that precipitated the U.S. attack on Afghanistan was in response to the increasing military occupation by the U.S. in the Middle East and by the development of airbases in Saudi Arabia that developed after the U.S. and Britain's war with Iraq that continues to this day.

At any given time, there are numerous ongoing wars occurring around the globe that annually cost thousands of civilian lives. During 1993, thirty-four major armed conflicts were waged in twenty-eight locations around the world (Stockholm International Peace Research Institute, 1994). Most recently, Project Ploughshares report of armed conflict noted that at the end of 2000, there were forty armed conflicts being fought on the territories of thirty-five countries. They noted that the total number of armed conflicts was unchanged from the previous year, although the number of countries involved was down by one. More than 70 percent of the conflicts are currently in Africa and Asia (Project Ploughshares, 2001).

National and International Secret Police

Besides the military and the domestic police force, the foreign secret police are involved in violence. Roebuck and Weeber (1978, 82) note that evidence from Senate investigating committees has shown, for example, that over a twenty-year period, one government agency—the CIA—was involved in over 900 foreign interventions, including paramilitary operations, surreptitious manipulation of foreign governments, and assassinations. A major program of assassinations orchestrated by the CIA was Operation Phoenix. William Colby, who was later to become head of that agency, directed this program. The program was formed to incarcerate and assassinate members of the Vietcong and the National Liberation Front. Members of the program engaged in massive arrests, murder and torture of thousands of Vietnamese citizens. Chomsky and Herman (1979) report that over 40,000 civilians were murdered between 1968 and 1971 as part of this program. Other secret police or spy networks, whether Libyan, Iranian, French, British, or Russian, have also been involved in assassinations overseas. However, since World War II, it is accurate to say that the scale of activity of these foreign police forces is dwarfed by the documented activities of the U.S. government through the CIA (Blum, 1988).

Savak, the secret police that operated during the rule of Reza Pahlevi, the former shah of Iran, along with the Iranian military were involved in widespread murder and torture of dissidents. After the United States engineered a coup overthrowing the Mossadegh regime in 1953, it trained Savak members at the Marine base at Quantico and CIA headquarters in Langley, Virginia, and exported over $18 billion worth of weapons to Iran over the next twenty years. Simon and Eitzen (1993) report that while the shah was in power, close to 1,500 Iranians were arrested monthly. On one day, June 5, 1963, Savak and the shah's army allegedly killed as many as 6,000 citizens. Chomsky and Herman (1979) report that political prisoners (i.e., those arrested and incarcerated because they disagreed with government policy) numbered as high as 100,000 each year in Iran. Amnesty International stated that twenty years after the CIA-Pahlevi coup Iran had the highest rate of death penalties in the world and a brutal record of torture of political prisoners. While the shah was in power, Amnesty International reported that no country in the world had a worse record in human rights than Iran. Since the overthrow of the shah, the Khomeini regime has continued a pattern of violence directed at religious minority populations and groups, which were perceived to pose a political threat to the government.

Another case in which the CIA has been implicated in assisting in state violence is Operation Condor. According to Herman (1982) in the latter half of the 1970s six South American countries—Argentina, Bolivia, Brazil, Chile, Paraguay, and Uruguay—began a joint monitoring and assassination program of dissident refugees in each other's country. The program was initially organized by Pinochet's secret police force, DINA. Hundreds of Latin Americans were abducted and murdered by these secret police organizations.

Private Groups Organized and Sponsored by the State

Another major category of actors in state violence consists of private groups organized, sponsored or sanctioned by the state to carry out violence. As mentioned earlier, death squad activity is frequently tied to the military or police in a given country and may be sponsored by foreign powers. Herman and O'-Sullivan (1989) note that the occurrence of death squad activities throughout Latin America parallels the funding and training programs made available to these governments' military and police forces by the United States for the specific purpose of civilian control:

> The death squad made its appearance in ten different Latin American countries in the 1960s and 1970s, all of them recipients of U.S. military and police aid and training, which stressed counterinsurgency and unconventional warfare against subversion from the Kennedy era onward. In a number of countries, including

Brazil, Guatemala and the Dominican Republic, death squads appeared immediately following a major U.S. intervention. Disappearances followed the same pattern of spread in the U.S. sphere of influence, with the death squad frequently the instrument of the disappearances. At a 1981 gathering of relatives of the disappeared in Latin America, it was estimated that the number of disappeared in Latin America over the prior two decades had reached 90,000 (37).

L. Fletcher Prouty is a retired U.S. Air Force colonel, a former professor of air science and tactics at Yale University, and a former chief of special operations for the Joint Chiefs of Staff during the Kennedy administration. In the latter role he was directly in charge of the global system designed to provide military support for the clandestine activities of the CIA. He concurs that most of the subcontracted state violence occurring in Third World countries following World War II has been a product of U.S. training and funding:

Foreign nations from all over the world were trained in the methods of secret operations—that is, the use of high explosives, sabotage, communications, etc.—at a military base in the United States under CIA sponsorship. The CIA developed many of its own facilities around the world, but in most cases the agency concealed its presence on military facilities in one guise or another. Many of the skilled saboteurs and terrorists of today are CIA students of yesterday. Many skilled terrorists in Iran have gone to CIA schools and other training facilities and have become experts with the weapons and tactics of the trade (Prouty, 1992, 36–7).

Likewise, Nairn (1984) contends that over the past twenty years, officials of the U.S. State Department, Central Intelligence Agency, and the U.S. armed forces conceived and organized ORDEN, the rural paramilitary and intelligence network described by Amnesty International as a movement designed to use clandestine terror against government opponents. Out of this organization grew the notorious Mano Blanco, the White Hand, which former U.S. ambassador to El Salvador, Raul H. Castro, has called nothing less than the birth of the Death Squads.

Agents of the U.S. government also conceived and organized ANSESAL, a special presidential intelligence service in El Salvador that gathered files on dissidents. The United States Government supplied ANSESAL with electronic, photographic, and personal surveillance of individuals who were later assassinated by death squads (Nairn, 1984).

One example of how the death squad ORDEN worked with the El Salvadoran and a foreign military is the massacre at Rio Sumpul on May 14, 1980. Approximately 800 peasants (mostly women, children and elderly) were relocated to Las Aradas, next to the Sumpul River, under the government's assumption that as rural citizens many of them were potential revolutionaries. Army patrols prevented them from leaving the areas. Accordingly, the peasants began to cultivate the land and carry on life as best as possible. On May 12 Honduran soldiers set up protective stone barricades along the other side of the river. At seven in the morning of Wednesday, May 14, 1980, the massacre at the Salvadoran villages of San Jacinto and Las Aradas began. Two armed helicopters, hundreds of Salvadoran National Guardsmen, army soldiers and members of ORDEN assassinated some 600 defenseless *campesinos*. The peasants who tried to cross the river seeking refuge in Honduras were returned by the Honduran soldiers to the zone of the massacre where they were killed (Herman and O'Sullivan, 1989, 240). Herman and O'Sullivan note that ORDEN has also received U.S. support in terms of training funds and weapons indirectly through programs that funded civilian security forces of friendly governments. More recently as a result of the release of more than 12,000 U.S. government documents on policy in Central America that were declassified and made available to the public in 1993, it was discovered that U.S. military officers in El Salvador trained a group of wealthy Salvadorans who called themselves *Los Patrioticos* (the Patriotic Ones). According to a New York Times article "American officers were giving weekly training to fifty to sixty wealthy Salvadorans. The American officers referred to the group as the BMW Brigade." Citing U.S. intelligence reports, the article notes that the unit "was being used as a cover for death-squad activities" (Weiner, 1993).

The United States has also been involved in organizing and funding death squads in Southeast Asia and Cuba. We have already mentioned Operation Phoenix, in which the CIA together with death squads and the secret police of South Vietnam systematically assassinated thousands of civilians believed to be involved in subversive actions. During this same period, the CIA was also organizing terrorist groups such as Alpha 66 and OMEGA 7, the Cuban terrorist groups whose goal was to destabilize the Castro regime in Cuba as well as other left-wing groups in Latin America. OMEGA 7 has been described by the FBI as the most dangerous terrorist group operating within the United States in the 1970s, and the CIA itself reported that the group was responsible for eighty-nine separate terrorist incidents within the United States and the Caribbean (Churchill and Vander Wall, 1990). Hinkle and Turner (1981) argue that Cuban exile terrorism began with assassinations and bombings in the United States, picked up tempo during the 1970s, and by the end of the decade had spun a murderous web linking Cuban exiles with elements of the American CIA, the Chilean gestapo (known as DINA), the Venezuelan secret police, the Korean CIA, and European paramilitary fascist groups.

The CIA has also been involved with organized crime in the planning and attempted assassinations of Fidel Castro. Sam Giacana, a reputed crime boss, was given a contract to kill Castro during the Kennedy administration (Church Committee, 1975; Hinckle and Turner, 1981). Before awarding this contract, the CIA had been involved in recruiting syndicate crime figures to create a criminal terror squad to force recalcitrant Marseilles dock workers to load ships with arms for use in Vietnam. For their assistance, these syndicate figures were permitted to continue to refine heroin in Marseilles for export to the United States. Bierne and Messerschmidt (1991) report a similar deal cut between the CIA and Meo tribespeople. "In return for fighting the Pathet Lao opposition forces, the Meo tribespeople of the area were compensated by the CIA's own airline—Air America—

which helped to transport opium to heroin laboratories, and ultimately into the arms of GIs in Vietnam and users in the U.S" (261).

The United States has also been frequently involved in organizing and training mercenary forces for terrorist activities. One recent example is the Contras composed of former President Somoza's National Guard and peasants forced into conscription and trained and armed by the U.S. government. The Contras were used to conduct terrorist acts in Nicaragua to destabilize the Sandinista government (Emerson, 1988). During the 1980s the United States provided nearly $300 million in overt aid and $4 to $6 billion in covert aid (Sharkey, 1990). The Nicaraguan government ruled by the Sandinista party took the United States to the International Court of Justice for its terrorist actions. The Court ruled in favor of Nicaragua, ordering reparations estimated at $17 billion. The U.S. has refused to recognize the Court's decision.

Similar examples can be found in Afghanistan in the training of the Moujahedeen or who President Reagan referred to as the Afghan freedom fighters, including the Taliban and other Islamic extremist groups who were organized and funded by the U.S. military to overthrow the government in an Afghanistan that was allied with the Soviet Union. The now infamous Osama bin Laden was running a front organization known as Maktab al-Khidamar (the MAK) that funneled money, arms and fighters from the outside world into the Afghan war. The MAK was nurtured by Pakistan's state security services, the Inter-Services Intelligence agency, which was the CIA's primary conduit for conducting the covert war against the Afghan government headed by Najibullah who was supported by the government of the Soviet Union (Moran 1998). Blum notes that throughout the 1980s, the Karmal, and then the Najibullah regimes, despite the exigencies of the war, pursued a program of modernization and broadening popular support. This included bringing electricity to villages, along with health clinics, a measure of land reform, and literacy, as well as releasing numerous prisoners unlawfully incarcerated by Amin and bringing mullahs and other nonparty people into the government. Through the U.S. funding of warlords and fundamentalist groups (referred to as the Afghan Freedom Fighters by President Reagan) they drove the Soviet backed government out of power. The fundamentalist Taliban came to power in the wake of a power struggle following the collapse of the government. Osama bin Laden and the Taliban who were previously recipients of U.S. aid in their fight against the government of Afghanistan were later charged by the U.S. government with attacking and destroying the World Trade Center on September 11, 2001.

This is an example of the problem of blowback and according to Johnson it is the cost and consequences of an American empire (Johnson, 2000). According to Johnson "the term 'blowback,' which officials of the Central Intelligence Agency first invented for their own internal use, is starting to circulate among students of international relations. It refers to the unintended consequences of policies that were kept secret from the American people. What the daily press reports as the malign acts of 'terrorists' or 'drug lords' or 'rogue states' or 'illegal arms merchants' often turn out to be blowback from earlier American operations" (Johnson, 2000, 8). Johnson cites a 1997 report to the undersecretary of defense for acquisition and technology by Members of the Defense Science Board warning of the problem of terrorist attacks. "Historical data show a strong correlation between U.S. involvement in international situations and an increase in terrorist attacks against the United States. In addition, the military asymmetry that denies nation states the ability to engage in overt attacks against the United States drives the use of transnational actors [that is, terrorists from one country attacking in another]" (9). Johnson notes that "terrorism strikes at the innocent in order to draw attention to the sins of the invulnerable. The innocent of the twenty-first century are going to harvest unexpected blowback disasters from the imperialist escapades of recent decades. Although most Americans may be largely ignorant of what was, and still is, being done in their name, all are likely to pay a steep price—individually and collectively—for their nation's continued efforts to dominate the global scene" (32).

There are many other examples of the U.S. government sponsoring terrorist or mercenary forces to overthrow governments that were not under the control of the United States. Blum (1995, 2000) outlines more than fifty interventions (overt and covert) by the United States in the overthrow of governments around the world since World War II. And the legacy of interventions and military attacks by the United States against relatively powerless foes continues into the twenty-first century.

In the United States, the CIA is not the only agency involved in utilizing private groups for violence. As we observed earlier, the Bureau of Investigation, predecessor to the FBI, had been involved in working with a vigilante group (the American Protective League) in conducting violence directed at the labor union, IWW (Churchill and Vander Wall, 1990). More recently, there has been evidence submitted to the Senate Select Committee on Intelligence that the FBI succeeded in resurrecting a previously disbanded right-wing paramilitary organization known as the Minutemen and placing an FBI informant, Howard Godfrey, in a leadership position (Coleman, 1989). Not only did the FBI pay Godfrey a regular salary, but it also provided the Secret Army Organization (the group's new name) with firearms, explosives, and other equipment, and supplied at least 75 percent of the SAOs operating expenses. A SAO cell directed by Godfrey engaged in repeated acts of violence and terrorism against the left, including the destruction of newspaper offices and bookstores, the firebombing of cars, and assaults on political activists. In one incident, Godfrey and another SAO member fired two shots into the house of a well-known leftist, seriously wounding a young woman. The following day Godfrey turned over the gun and jacket he wore during the assault to his FBI supervisor, who in turn helped conceal the evidence from San Diego police. Even after this information came to light, the FBI succeeded in protecting its operatives from prosecution (Coleman, 1989). Churchill and Vander Wall (1990) discuss other examples of the Bureau of Investigation organizing and utilizing established vigilante groups to carry out violence.

The U.S. military has since 1946 trained many members of foreign military and police in state violence. The U.S. Army School of the Americas (SOA) was established in 1946 in Panama. Since the Panama Canal Treaty, the school has moved to Fort Benning, Georgia. At the time of the move, the Panamanian newspaper *La Prensa* referred to SOA as the School of Assassins. President Jorge Illueca of Panama called it the biggest base for destabilization in Latin America (Imerman, 1994). In response to increasing public protests, the school's name was changed to the Western Hemisphere Institute for Security Cooperation.

According to Chomsky and Herman (1979), by the mid-1970s, over 200,000 Latin American military personnel had been trained in the United States, and since 1949, over 35,000 Latin American officers have trained in the School for the Americas alone. Herman (1987, 14) notes that altogether between 1950 and 1987, the United States trained over 500,000 military and more than 7,500 police personnel from eighty-five countries. He also notes that between 1950 and 1979, U.S. military aid programs transferred $107.3 billion in arms and ammunition to various U.S. client states, in addition to some $121 billion in arms sales. The vast majority of these weapons and training programs are used in internal conflicts and social control within these countries.

During 1993 alone, approximately 2,000 soldiers from Latin American and Caribbean countries were trained in low intensity conflict (LIC). According to Imerman (1994, 13), LIC aims to maintain U.S. military influence south of our borders without using (or losing) large numbers of U.S. troops. Instead, soldiers from Latin America and the Caribbean are trained in dirty little war techniques by U.S. personnel. Imerman points out that consistently those countries having the worst human rights records and those where the vast impoverished minorities have no political representation have the most graduates of this school.

An example of this is El Salvador. On March 15, 1993, the UN commission that studied human rights violations in El Salvador released its findings. In comparing the list of individuals involved in assassinations and massacres of citizens, the SOA Watch group and Witness for Peace discovered that forty-six U.S. School of Americas graduates were implicated (Imerman, 1994). SOA Watch found that often those military personnel who had received the most training at SOA had committed the worst atrocities. For example, of the three officers cited in the assassination of Archbishop Oscar Romero of San Salvador on March 24, 1980, two were SOA graduates. Of the five officers cited in the murder and rape of the three U.S. nuns and a Catholic layworker, three were SOA graduates. Of the twelve officers cited in the El Mozote Massacre, December 1991, where several hundred unarmed civilians were killed and their corpses mutilated and burned, ten were SOA graduates. SOA Watch (2002) claims that this is a pattern that is repeated throughout Latin America. SOA Watch notes that currently, Colombia, with over 10,000 troops trained at the SOA, is the school's largest customer. Not surprisingly, Colombia currently has the worst human rights record in all of Latin America.

Another interesting example of the state using private groups to conduct violence is in the case of South Africa. The South African police was secretly funding the Inkatha movement, a more conservative black South African organization, to further fragment the black population and take away support from the left-oriented African National Congress (ANC). In the following excerpt from one report, the police are implicated in organizing and assisting in a violent attack on supporters of the ANC by members of the Inkatha movement.

> Reports of the massacre of at least forty South African blacks in Boipatong and an adjacent squatter's camp on June 17 followed a familiar pattern. The attackers were Zulu-speaking supporters of the Inkatha movement from a nearby hostel. They were ferried to the scene by the South African Police, who prevented the victims from escaping and shot down some of them as they fled. If the police organized this attack, as press accounts indicate, it served a dual purpose. By further inflaming tensions between Inkatha and the African National Congress (or, in ethnic terms, between the Zulus and the Xhosas and other tribes that predominantly support the A.N.C.), it almost inevitably will lead to further violence, lending support to those who claim that a transition from apartheid to a nonracial state would produce a bloodbath (Neier, 1992,129).

TYPES OF STATE VIOLENCE

War

War is usually the single largest form of state violence. Between 1946 and 1986, there have been more than thirty-one wars worldwide. According to Sivard (1986), in the twentieth century as a whole, with less than a decade to go there have been 237 wars, each with estimated deaths of 1,000 for each year. She also points out that since the eighteenth century there has been an increase in the level of violence in terms of war deaths. Twelve times as many people died in the twentieth century compared to the nineteenth century, and twenty-two times more than the eighteenth century. In the nineteenth century there were only two wars with deaths exceeding 1 million, while in the twentieth century there have been thirteen such wars. Sivard notes that in 1986, there were twenty major ongoing wars that had at least an annual death rate of 1,000. According to Sivard, the numbers of deaths since the beginning of the twentieth century because of war is 83,642,000 (Sivard, 1986).

More recently, according to the data collected by Margareta Sollenberg and Peter Wallensteen (2001) of the Stockholm International Peace Research Institute there are on the average twenty-eight major conflicts (having at least 1,000 deaths) occurring in any given year from 1990 to 2000. Thus, since 1986 one could safely add another 200,000 to 300,000 fatalities, bringing the total to almost 84 million. Sivard (1986, 27) also notes that there is an increasing internationalization of violence in the Third World:

> Taking World War II as the turning point, there were more and bloodier regional and national wars after it than before it. Of the 120 wars recorded since World War

II, only one, Hungary, was in a developed country, while in the period pre–World War II, 28 percent of all wars took place in developed countries and, if World War I is included, 88 percent of all war deaths were in the developed world.

Sivard concludes that the rise in conflict in the Third World is associated with a complex of causal factors including rebellion rising out of intolerable deprivation, injustice, and frustration. She also observes that the superpowers play an important role in stimulating the conflicts and utilizing them for what she refers to as their own ideological crusades. Or more precisely put, utilizing them to maintain their position in the hierarchy of countries in the international political and economic system or world system. Now with only one superpower remaining the level of conflict has seemed to increase during the last decade of the twentieth century and the beginning of the twenty-first.

One important role that the superpowers played in these regional conflicts was serving as arms suppliers and providing for technical support in using the weaponry. Throughout the history of the post–World War II period, the United States has consistently led the world in arms sales and technical assistance in conducting wars in the Third World. Now being the only superpower in the world it has extended its role as arms merchant. Klare and Aronson (1981) note that under both the Military Assistance Program and the Foreign Military Sales Program, the United States is the largest single supplier of armaments in the world. According to Klare and Aronson (1981), most of the armaments sold under the Military Assistance Program were for internal repression of populations who were rebelling against the extreme conditions of poverty and inequality. Officially, U.S. arms programs are designed to strengthen the capacity of countries to defend themselves against external attack. But an examination of U.S. weapons trade data suggests that much of the equipment involved is intended for internal use, to control strikes and disorders and to suppress dissent. Thus, recent arms deliveries to these countries have included armored cars, shotguns, tear gas, riot clubs, and other weapons unsuitable for anything other than internal political warfare (5).

For example, Klare and Aronson note that U.S. arms were used by the Thai Border Patrol Police to massacre several hundred students killed during the military coup of October 6, 1976. The Iranian military used weapons purchased under military aid programs to kill thousands of unarmed demonstrators during the 1978 uprising against the shah. The Indonesian military used U.S. weapons supplied under aid programs to slaughter more than 100,000 civilians in East Timor. More recently, since 1994 the Turkish military has killed more than 13,000 people, 1,000 villages have been depopulated, and approximately 2 million civilians displaced (Wheat 1995). Most of these killings and displacements have occurred since 1993. Wheat notes that "between 1987 and 1991, 77 percent of arms delivered to Turkey came from the United States. . . . For fiscal years 1986–1995, Congress has appropriated $5.1 billion in military aid for Turkey" (Wheat, 1995, 18). And the list goes on. Klare and Aronson state that the United States stands at the supply end of a pipeline of repressive technology that extends to many of the world's most authoritarian regimes (7).

Since the dissolution of the Soviet Union, the United States is widely perceived as having won the Cold War and is no longer in competition for ideological hegemony. But supplying armaments and U.S. involvement in various Third World wars continues. Today, in the purported New World Order, the U.S. is either fighting alone or in conjunction with alliances it can construct to maintain the world political economic order and its dominant position in it. According to the *New Internationalist* (1994), the United States alone has about 48 percent of the armaments market. The *New Internationalist* furthermore comments that an estimated one-third of U.S. arms exports are paid for not by foreign governments buying arms but by U.S. taxpayers. Hidden subsidies take the form of loans for sales, forgiveness for past military debts—$7 billion to Egypt for its role as an ally in the Gulf War—and arms-related training. Wheat (1995) reports that prior to 1989 the United States delivered 11 percent of the Third World's arms; in 1994 it delivered 51 percent. Wheat claims that the U.S. taxpayers are subsidizing $4 billion a year in foreign arms purchases.

The *New Internationalist* (1994) reports that at least 20 percent of Third World debt is incurred by buying weapons. Nigeria could have immunized 2 million children with the money its government spent on eighty British battle tanks in 1992. India could have provided basic education for all the 15 million girls not in school with the money it spent on twenty Russian MiG-29 fighter aircraft, in the same year. And Iran could have provided essential machines to the whole country several times over for the cost of two submarines (*New Internationalist* 1994, 9). The report goes on to reveal that countries are encouraged to purchase additional arms with development aid, such as the British Overseas Development Agency, which was ordered to fund the unpopular and uneconomic Pergau Dam project in Malaysia in exchange for arms contracts. In general the *New Internationalist* (1994) concludes that globally, poor countries with big arms budgets get twice as much aid per person as those that spend less on military goods. They cite El Salvador, which gets five times as much aid as Bangladesh, even though the latter has twenty-four times more people and is five times poorer. Furthermore, today's world nuclear stockpile provides the equivalent of the explosive power of 1.8 tons of TNT for every child, woman, and man on earth—enough to erase the human race several times over. The Bulletin of Atomic Scientists (1998) report that current U.S. policy is to keep some 10,000 intact warheads in various states of readiness, with another 5,000 plutonium "pits" available as a reserve.

Genocide

The United Nations Genocide Convention that went into force January 12, 1951, defines genocide as any of the following acts committed with intent to destroy, in whole or in part, a national, ethnic, racial or religious group:

(a) killing members of the group; (b) causing serious bodily or mental harm to members of the group; (c) deliberately inflicting on the group conditions of life calculated to bring about its physical destruction in whole or in part; (d) imposing measures intended to prevent births within the group; and (e) forcibly transferring children of the group to another group. There have been eight persons convicted of genocide under the United Nations Convention. The first case was that of Jean Paul Akayesu, the Hutu mayor of the Rwandan town of Taba at the time of the killings. Between April 7 and June 1994, at least 2000 Tutsis were killed in Taba. In his capacity as burgomaster, Jean-Paul Akayesu was in charge of the maintenance of law and order in his commune. During this period of the massacre he did not act to prevent the massacre nor did he ask for the assistance of regional or national authorities to intervene. In a landmark ruling, a special international tribunal convicted him of genocide and crimes against humanity on 2 September 1998. Seven other Rwandans have since been convicted of genocide.

The story of the genocide in Rwanda is one of the most recent cases of genocide. Human Rights Watch (1999) has provided the most detailed account of the genocidal violence. During a thirteen week period following the mysterious assassination of the president of Rwanda on April 6, 1994, at least half a million people perished, estimated to be as many as three-quarters of the Tutsi population. Human Rights Watch notes that thousands of Hutu were also slain because they opposed the killing campaign and the forces directing it. The report discusses the cause of the genocide. "This genocide resulted from the deliberate choice of a modern elite to foster hatred and fear to keep itself in power. This small, privileged group first set the majority against the minority to counter a growing political opposition within Rwanda. Then, faced with RPF success on the battlefield and at the negotiating table, these few power holders transformed the strategy of ethnic division into genocide. They believed that the extermination campaign would restore the solidarity of the Hutu under their leadership and help them win the war, or at least improve their chances of negotiating a favorable peace. They seized control of the state and used its machinery and its authority to carry out the slaughter" (Human Rights Watch, 1999). Human Rights Watch describes how this slaughter occured through control of the hierarchical structures in the government and the organization of civilian militias who carried out the civilian defense program that was directed at the Hutu minority. Rwanda, a country that has been racked by bitter poverty as a result of a history of colonialism, was in many ways ripe for the escalation of conflict along class and ethnic groups.

Genocide has been a frequent part of the story of imperialism since Christopher Columbus's conquest of the people on the Isle of Hispaniola. In the earlier stages, genocide is product of conquest. On pre-Columbian Hispaniola in 1492 it was estimated that there was a robust population of almost 3 million; by 1542, fifty years later, approximately 200 remained. Chomsky (1993, 5) states that the conquest of the New World set off two vast demographic catastrophes, unparalleled in history: the virtual destruction of the indigenous population of the Western hemisphere, and the devastation of Africa as the slave trade rapidly expanded to serve the needs of the conquerors and the continent itself was subjugated. This was the beginning of the history of modern genocide.

This tragic story of mass extermination continued into the eighteenth and nineteenth centuries by the genocidal policies of the American colonists and U.S. military in eliminating the majority of the tribes of indigenous people in North America. Haviland (1987) describes the case of the Pequot Indians, who were exterminated in 1637 by the colonists when they burned their village in Mystic, Connecticut, and then shot all of the people, including women and children who tried to escape. Dee Brown's (1970) history of the indigenous population is a history of this genocide across the land that would become the forty-eight states of the United States. Similar patterns of genocide were repeated on virtually every continent in the world, and continue to this day.

Genocide is directed at an outgroup or minority group. Levinson (1995) notes that the term genocide was first used in this century describing the Nazi attempted extermination of Jews in Europe. The Holocaust of the Jewish population throughout Europe is the case that most people think about when they hear the word genocide. In 1933, the Jewish population of Europe stood at over nine million. By 1945, close to two out of every three European Jews had been killed as part of the "Final Solution" of the German Government. Barbara Harff (1986) defines genocide as the mass murder, premeditated by some power-wielding group linked with state power, directed against any target group within the state however defined. She points out that genocide is likely to occur when (1) a national upheaval has occurred, (2) there exists sharp internal cleavages between majority and minority populations prior to the upheaval, and (3) there is strong group identification between competing groups. Harff cites Burundi as illustrative of her preconditions. During the spring and summer of 1972, approximately 250,000 people were systematically murdered by a tribal minority government that attempted to kill every possible Hutu male of distinction over the age of fourteen.

Another example of genocidal violence in this century is the murdering of more than 1 million Armenians in Turkey in the first quarter of the century. Another million Armenians were killed in Iraq about the same time. In what was known as German South-West Africa, today Namibia, German soldiers slaughtered 100,000 Hereros for the land and livestock the tribe held. German soldiers also killed more than 100,000 Africans in what is now Tanzania when they resisted German government orders to grow cotton for export instead of food for domestic consumption.

Sybil Milton, senior historian at the United States Holocaust Memorial Museum in Washington, D.C., notes that the modern scale of violence required for genocide requires both government power and technological ability to deliver it (Levinson, 1995). According to Levinson (1995), approximately 170 million people have been killed in genocidal violence in this century.

Assassination

Assassination, the targeting of a specific individual for murder, is another form of state violence. As mentioned before, between 1960 and 1965 the CIA initiated at least eight plots to assassinate Fidel Castro. The unsuccessful and sometimes bizarre attempts included applying instantly lethal botulinium toxin to a box of Castro's cigars, hiring the Mafia to poison him, and presenting him a gift of a wetsuit treated with a fungus. The Senate Select Committee on Intelligence in 1975 found strong evidence that President Eisenhower had ordered the death of Congolese (Zaire) leader Patrice Lumumba and that CIA officials had planned the assassination. Furthermore, the United States was implicated in the assassination of Dominican dictator Rafael Trujillo, South Vietnam's President Ngo Dinh Diem, and General Rene Schneider of Chile. Simon and Eitzen (1993, 271) note that as recently as 1985, CIA Director William Casey arranged for the assassination of Sheikh Mohammed Hussein Fadlallah, a Lebanese Shiite Muslim leader, in coordination with Saudi Arabian intelligence. During the assassination attempt in Beirut eighty innocent people were killed when a car bomb exploded. Blum (2000) identifies thirty-five persons who were assassinated or who were planned to be assassinated by agents of the United States government since 1949.

Another case of planning the assassination of a world leader by the United States involved Libya's Muammar Qaddafi. Chambliss (1989) describes one plot was to lure Qaddafi into some foreign adventure of terrorist exploit that would give a growing number of Qaddafi opponents in the Libyan military a chance to seize power, or such a foreign adventure might give one of Qaddafi's neighbors, such as Algeria or Egypt, a justification for responding to Qaddafi militarily. Most recently there have been attempts and continued planning by the United States government to assassinate Saddam Hussein of Iraq. The most recent planning is in the context of the United States "war on terrorism." Iraq has the second largest known oil reserves in the Middle East. This resourse was principally controlled by Great Britain during the period between the first and second world wars (Silverfarb and Khadduri, 1997). The United States has attempted to increase its influence and control of the oil reserves in the Middle East by means of U.S. based multinational oil corporations and increasing military presence throughout the Middle East since World War II.

The United States policy regarding assassinations for most of the period since President Ford was a response to the Church Committee hearings that detailed CIA murder plots against Cuba's Fidel Castro, the Congo's Patrice Lumumba, and Dominican president Rafael Trujillo, among others. The Ford policy stated that "No employee of the United States shall engage in, or conspire to engage in, political assassinations" (Blum, 2000). Presidents Carter and Reagan issued similar orders. However Reagan canceled his executive order less than a year later. The prohibition was reinstated after a foiled plot to kill Sheikh Mohammed Hussein Fadlallah using a car bomb which killed eighty innocent persons in Beirut. However, the so-called license to kill was reinstated again. President George H. Bush issued a "memorandum of law" that would, according to Blum, allow for "accidental killings." This has provided the loophole for the U.S. bombing of Qaddafi's home that resulted in the killing of his daughter and other members of his family and the bombing of command posts in Baghdad in the attempts to kill the Iraqi head of state, Saddam Hussein. Today, under President George W. Bush, the planning to eliminate the Iraqi leader and other persons identified by the U.S. government as sponsors of terrorism is continuing. As President Bush is quoted in a recent *Newsweek* magazine article regarding Saddam Hussein, "We're taking him out" (Eisenberg, 2002).

Assassinations by the U.S. government do not occur only in foreign countries. Churchill and Wall (1990) present information indicating the FBI's involvement in the assassination of two Black Panther leaders, Fred Hampton and Mark Clark. They detail how William O'Neal, Hampton's personal bodyguard and an FBI infiltrator, gave the agency a detailed floor plan of the Chicago apartment in which the Panther leaders were staying and the information that it contained two illegal shotguns. In response to this unsubstantiated report of illegal firearms, Chicago police conducted a predawn raid on December 4, 1969, and shot Hampton and Clark to death while they were still in their beds:

Groth assembled and briefed his force at approximately 4 a.m. on the morning of December 4, using O'Neal's floorplan and other information provided by Mitchel . . . . Once there, they divided into two subteams with eight of their number deployed to the front of the apartment and six to the rear. At about 4:30, they launched an outright assault upon the Panthers, as Gloves Davis kicked open the front door and promptly shot Mark Clark point-blank in the chest with a .30 caliber M-1 carbine. Clark, who had apparently nodded off in a front room with a shotgun across his lap, barely had time to stand up before being killed more or less instantly. His reflexive response to being shot discharged the shotgun. It was the only round fired by the Panthers during the raid. David immediately proceed to pump a bullet into eighteen-year-old Brenda Harris, who was lying (unarmed) in a front room bed; Groth hit her with a second round. Groman, joined by Davis and his carbine, then began spraying automatic fire from his .45 caliber Thompson submachine gun through a wall into the bedrooms. All forty-two shots fired by the pair converged on the head of Hampton's bed, pinpointed by O'Neal's floorplan. One of the slugs fired by Davis struck Hampton in the left shoulder, seriously wounding him as he slept. While this was going on, the second subteam, firing as they came, crashed through the back door. This was followed by a brief lull in the shooting, during which Carmody and another (unidentified) raider entered Hampton's bedroom. They were heard to have the following exchange: That's Fred Hampton. . . . Is he dead? Bring him out. He's barely alive; he'll make it. Two shots were then heard, both of which were fired point-blank into Hampton's head as he lay prone, followed by Comody's voice stating, He's good and dead now. The chairman's body was then dragged by the wrist from the bed to the bedroom doorway, and left lying in a spreading pool of blood. At that point, the raiders mopped up, with Gorman directing fire from his submachine gun at the remaining Panthers who were attempting to cover themselves in the apartment's other bedroom. Doc Satchell was hit four times in this barrage, and Blair

Anderson twice. Seventeen-year-old Verlina Brewer was also hit twice. The victims were then beaten and dragged bodily to the street, where they were arrested on charges of attempting to murder the raiders and aggravated assault (Churchill and Wall, 1990, 71, 73).

Churchill and Wall note that it was not until 1983 that the victims' families won a judgment against the U.S. government. Judge John F. Grady ruled that there had been an active governmental conspiracy to deny Hampton, Clark, and the Black Panther Party plaintiffs their civil rights. The defendants were found to have been culpable, sanctions were imposed on the FBI for its cover-up activities, and an award of $1.85 million went to the survivors and families of the deceased.

Of course, the United States is not alone in conducting assassinations. The assassination of Sergei Kirov on December 1, 1934, by Leonid Nikolaev, an agent of the Stalin's government, is claimed to have set off a chain of events that culminated in the pogroms of the 1930s in the Soviet Union, which resulted in the deaths of hundreds of thousands of members of the Russian population who resisted Stalin's centralization of power (Russian Archives, 1995). Other examples of assassinations by the Soviet government are the assassination of the communist leader Leon Trotsky in Mexico City in 1940. More recently, it is alleged that the KGB tried twice to assassinate the shah of Iran, who was a key U.S. ally, and in 1979, Soviet forces killed Afghan President Hafizullah Amin during the Soviet invasion of Afghanistan (U.S. Council on Foreign Relations, 2002).

Hougan (1978) indicates that during the 1960s the French Intelligence Agency hired an international mercenary to assassinate the Moroccan leader Ben Barka. The French Intelligence Agency in 1985 bombed Greenpeace's flag ship in New Zealand, killing one member of its crew. The ship was preparing to set sail to disrupt French nuclear tests in the South Pacific. Herman and O'Sullivan (1989) list a number of assassinations conducted by the South African security forces, among these: the murder of a wounded ANC member in his hospital bed in Maseru, capital of Lesotho; a car bomb in Maputo, capital of Mozambique, maimed South African writer and lawyer Albie Sach; the assassination of an ANC representative in Paris in 1987; and a bomb in a TV set that exploded in the Harare house of a senior ANC exile, killing his Zimbabwean wife, the murder of a member of the ANC's national executive committee in Swaziland, and the murder of a teenager, Sicelo Dlomo, in South Africa a few weeks after he told CBS television of his experiences as a torture victim. Most recently, Israel has carried out a program of assassinations of Palestinians whom they have accused of being terrorists and responsible for killings in Israel. The Israeli government refers to these assassinations as "targeted attacks" (Lewis, 2001).

In Amnesty International's report entitled *Political Killings by Government* numerous other cases of assassinations by government officials are cited, including Jean-Bedel Bokassa, self-proclaimed emperor of the Central African Empire, who killed fifty to 100 school children in Ngaragba prison between April 18 and 20, 1979. Amnesty International (1983) also reports that in Guinea

President Sékou Touré's government failed to account for approximately 2,900 prisoners who disappeared after being arrested for political reasons between 1969 and 1976. In Ethiopia sixty prominent political prisoners (fifty-nine were shot without trial) were executed by firing squad. Every year Amnesty International reports hundreds of cases known to them of assassinations by governments throughout the world.

Torture

Torture is another form of state violence. Amnesty International (1977) reports that in Chile under General Pinochet the most common forms of physical torture were prolonged beating using truncheons, fists or bags of moist material, electricity to all parts of the body (especially the genitalia), and burning with cigarettes or acid. Such physical tortures were accompanied by the deprivation of food, drink, and sleep. In one Chilean case, for example, Amnesty International reported that a prisoner was found dead with his testicles burned off. He had been subjected to intensive beatings and electric shocks. One day later, another prisoner in the custody of the Chilean security police died from torture. He also showed the marks of severe burns on his genitals.

Amnesty International (1984) contends that today much of state torture is carried out by the military forces, usually elite or special units, which displace the civil police in matters of political security. The organization maintains that torture is often an institutionalized part of the state-controlled machinery to suppress dissent. It has become most often used as an integral part of a government's security strategy. When threatened by guerrillas, a government may condone torture as a way of extracting information from captured insurgents. Should the government broaden its definition of security, the number of people who appear to threaten it will naturally become larger. Under these new circumstances, many persons, such as students, trade unionists, publishers, and lawyers, may suddenly become suspect, and the rationale for torture expands. Amnesty International also claims that torture has been used to intimidate rural populations in many Latin American countries for the purpose of bringing increasing amounts of land under government control. An example is Guatemala, where government agents have displayed tortured, dying villagers to relatives and neighbors as a means of intimidation.

Torture also exists in many countries as a way of extracting confessions. In Northern Ireland, frequent use of torture by government security forces has been reported as a way to obtain confessions. Israel is the only state that has legally authorized the use of torture as a technique of interrogation. According to Amnesty International (2001b) people were reportedly tortured or ill-treated by security forces, police or other state authorities in 125 countries.

But torture is not only used as a technique of interrogation. In many countries torture has become institutionalized as a part of the legal system of punishment for crimes. Flogging, caning, and amputations or dismemberment are used in many countries as methods of punishment. Several Middle Eastern countries, such as Iran, Saudi Arabia, and Sudan, frequently apply torture as a punishment for those convicted of common crimes. In Iran in 1991 there were several known cases of common criminals being subjected to 100 lashes before being executed. In Sudan, several people in 1991 were sentenced to be hanged and then publicly crucified for armed robbery. That same year in Iran, one woman was stoned to death for being convicted of adultery, while in Saudi Arabia four Kuwaiti nationals were sentenced to prison terms ranging from fifteen to twenty years and to receive between 1,000 and 1,500 whip lashes (Amnesty International 1993).

In the United States there have been several reports of torture in prisons and police departments that have been settled out of court. In one case Gregory Banks confessed to a murder as a result of torture conducted by three officers of the Chicago police force. Banks described the nature of the interrogation:

> The sergeant kicked me out of the chair and put a nickel-plated .45 in my mouth. They was threatening to blow my head off and kicking me and hitting me across my chest with a flashlight . . . but I still persisted in denial. [Detective Peter] Dignan came back in the room . . . and said, We have something special for niggers, and he took out a plastic (garbage) bag and placed it over my head. He left it on there for about a minute. I almost suffocated. After the second time they put the plastic bag over my head, I gave them the confession. (Berma, 1994, 22)

This is not an isolated case in the Chicago Police Department. Another officer, Commander Jon Burge, was suspended for electroshocking and beating Andrew Wilson, a suspected cop killer. Berma (1994) notes that Commander Burge had also participated in or had knowledge of fifty cases of electroshock, bagging (placing a plastic bag over a suspects head to the point of near suffocation), or excessive beating during interrogations.

These cases are not isolated. Berma (1994) notes that at the Montana State Penitentiary, dozens of prisoners were allegedly stripped naked and forced to run through a gauntlet of approximately sixty guards who punched and kicked at them. In a jail in Syracuse, New York, guards have shackled inmates' feet to their bunk and cuffed their arms to the bars above their heads in such a way that they are stretched tight, hanging above the mattress. They are left suspended for hours at a time. Berma notes that after a twenty-five-year delay, the United States ratified a U.N. covenant that prohibits torture in 1992. This signing occurred only after the U.S. Congress had weakened the measure by forbidding injured parties to use the treaty's definition of torture to sue the U.S. government.

Not only has the United States been involved in acts of torture nationally, but also through its training programs of military and police the use of torture may be a part of the curriculum. Herman (1987) contends that there is a strong linkage between U.S. aid and training programs and the use of torture in many countries around the world. Of thirty-five countries using systematic torture throughout the 1970s, 75 percent of them were clients of the United States.

Herman furthermore contends that there is a great deal of evidence of U.S. training in methods of torture and the provision of torture technology. On September 20, 1996, the Pentagon released seven training manuals prepared by the U.S. military and used between 1987 and 1991 for intelligence training courses in Latin America and at the U.S. Army School of the Americas (SOA), where the U.S. trains Latin American militaries. Haugaard (1997) notes that "the manuals show how U.S. agents taught repressive techniques and promoted the violation of human rights throughout Latin America and around the globe." The manuals provide the paper trail that proves how the U.S. trained Latin American and other militaries to infiltrate and spy upon civilians and groups, including unions, political parties, and student and charitable organizations; to treat legal political opposition like armed insurgencies; and to circumvent laws on due process, arrest, and detention. In these how-to guides, the U.S. advocates tactics such as executing guerrillas, blackmail, false imprisonment, physical abuse, using truth serum to obtain information, and paying bounties for enemy dead. Counterintelligence agents are advised that one of their functions is "recommending targets for neutralization," a euphemism for execution or destruction (Haugaard, 1997, 30).

Amnesty International (2002f) also notes that the U.S. government admits that as many as 1,000 suspected torturers may have fled to the U.S. to escape justice, but has failed to prosecute a single case in the eight years since U.S. law made prosecution for acts of torture possible. Recently in the wake of the terrorist attack on the United States, the Bush Administration has considered the use of torture to extract information from those who have been detained (Pincus, 2001).

Experimentation on Populations

The most heinous case of experimentation on people was conducted by Nazi Germany. The concentration camp of Buchenwald was used for experiments by medical doctors interested in the effects of amputations, lethal germs, and poisons on the human body. More than 50,000 persons died in this camp.

In more recent times, there are cases of experimentation by other governments, including the U.S. government. One classic case is the Tuskegee Syphilis Experiment (Jones, 1987). The U.S. Public Health Service conducted a forty-year experiment in which it studied the effects of untreated syphilis on 399 black male residents of Macon County, Alabama. Those who participated in the study were paid $50 in 1932 (this sum was periodically increased over the length of the study to compensate for inflationary effects), given free medical examinations and transportation to and from the clinics, hot meals on examination days, free treatment for minor ailments, and a burial stipend to be paid to their survivors. A physician with firsthand knowledge of the early years of the experiment noted that the participants were never informed that they had syphilis. Those selected were in the third stage of the disease. Treatment was available at the time, although it was painful and not always successful.

Those in the test group did not receive treatment so that the course of the disease could be studied. Dr. J. W. Williams, who was serving his internship at Andrews Hospital at the Tuskegee Institute in 1932 and assisted in the experiments early years, stated that neither the interns nor the subjects knew what the study involved. "The people who came in were not told what was being done," Dr. Williams said. "We told them we wanted to test them. They were not told, so far as I know, what they were being treated for or what they were not being treated for." As far as he could tell, "the subjects thought they were being treated for rheumatism or bad stomachs" (Jones, 1987, 4). By 1969, Jones estimates that as many as 100 men died as a direct result of complications caused by syphilis. Others had developed serious syphilis-related heart conditions that may have contributed to their deaths.

More recently, it has been revealed that the government throughout the post–World War II period has been conducting radiation experiments on the population. As late as 1981, Rosenberg (1981) reported that doctors at an Atomic Energy Commission clinic exposed at least eighty-nine cancer patients to large doses of radiation in order to get information for NASA on levels of radiation tolerance before nausea. The House of Representatives Subcommittee on Energy Conservation and Power and the Committee on Energy and Commerce, headed by Representative Edward Markey, issued a report in 1986 detailing thirty-one experiments that took place from the 1940s to the 1970s, sponsored by the Department of Energy or its predecessors. In these experiments 695 people were exposed to radiation (Harris, 1994).

A recent release of information by the government indicates that what was previously reported was just the tip of the iceberg. Secretary of Energy O'Leary provided information to the public about experiments at major universities including MIT, University of Chicago, California, and Vanderbilt. Experimenters in this research exposed about 2,000 Americans to varying degrees of radiation (Ensign and Alcalay, 1994).

The General Accounting Office (1993) reported that government scientists deliberately released radioactive materials into populated areas so that they could study fallout patterns and the rate at which radioactivity decayed. The report describes thirteen different releases of radiation from 1948 to 1952. These releases of radioactive fallout were part of the U.S. nuclear weapons development program.

Ensign and Alcalay (1994) note that in 1949 the Green River tests at Hanford (Washington) Nuclear Reservation were conducted. The nuclear weapons plant deliberately released thousands of curies of radioactive iodine-131. This is several times the amount released from the 1979 Three Mile Island disaster. This release of radiation was done to test its recently installed radiological monitoring equipment. The authors report that a team of epidemiologists is now looking into an epidemic of late-occurring thyroid tumors and other radiogenic disorders among the downwind residents of eastern Washington State.

Between 1946 and 1958, the United States exploded sixty-seven atomic and hydrogen bombs at Bikini and Enewetok, two Marshall group atolls. The largest and dirtiest of the Marshall Islands blasts was code-named Bravo. At fifteen megatons—more than 1,000 times the size of the Hiroshima bomb—Bravo rained lethal radioactive fallout over thousands of unsuspecting islanders under circumstances that remain mysterious. The people of Rongelap atoll were especially hard-hit. They were evacuated from their home islands two days after Bravo, following the absorption of massive doses of high-level fallout (Ensign and Alcalay, 1994, 32–33). Ensign and Alcalay note that three years after the bombing, Dr. C. L. Dunham, head of the Atomic Energy Commission's Division of Biology and Medicine, expressed the commission's interest in studying the Rongelap victims to determine the long-term effects of exposure. To this day, the AEC continues to compile data on the victims of these bombings.

Additional reports of experimentation indicated a callous disregard for patients who were already suffering from terminal illnesses. In 1945 Albert Stevens, a fifty-eight-year-old California house painter suffering from a huge stomach ulcer, was injected with doses of plutonium 238 and 239 equivalent to 446 times the average lifetime exposure. Doctors recommended an operation and told his family that Mr. Stevens had only about six months to live. For the next year, scientists collected plutonium-laden urine and fecal samples from Stevens and used that data in a classified scientific report entitled *A Comparison of the Metabolism of Plutonium in Man and the Rat*. Welsome (1993) has determined that there is little doubt scientists knew of the danger. The report concluded that chronic plutonium poisoning is a matter of serious concern for those who come in contact with this material.

In another case that occurred in 1947, doctors injected plutonium into the left leg of Elmer Allen, a thirty-six-year-old African American railroad porter. After three days, the leg was amputated for an alleged preexisting bone cancer. Researchers then analyzed tissue samples to determine the physiology of plutonium dispersion. As late as 1973, scientists summoned Allen to the Argonne National Laboratory near Chicago, where he was subjected to a follow-up whole-body radiation scan, and his urine was analyzed to ascertain lingering levels of plutonium from the 1947 injection (Ensign and Alcalay, 1994, 31).

In two additional cases, the subjects of the experiments were not allegedly terminally ill. Instead, they were institutionalized and therefore unable to give free consent. In one case, young boys classified as mentally retarded were subjects in an experiment conducted by the Quaker Oats Company, the National Institutes of Health, and the Atomic Energy Commission. Beginning in 1949, the children at the Fernald School for the mentally retarded in Waltham, Massachusetts, were fed minute doses of radioactive materials in their breakfast cereal to determine if the materials prevented the body from absorbing iron and calcium. The children were told that they were joining a science club. The consent form sent to the boys' parents stated nothing about the radiation experiment (*New York Times*, 1994).

In 1963, 131 prison inmates in Oregon and Washington were given $200 each to be exposed to 600 roentgens of radiation (100 times the allowable annual dose for nuclear workers). The prisoners signed consent forms agreeing to submit to X-ray radiation of their scrotum and testes; they were not warned about the dangers of contracting testicular cancer. Doctors later performed vasectomies on the inmates to avoid the possibility of contaminating the general population with irradiation-induced mutants (*Newsweek*, 1993, 15).

Ensign and Alcalay (1994) contend that the experiments that caused the greatest number of fatalities occurred from 1960 to 1971. In this research, Dr. Eugene Saenger, a radiologist at the University of Cincinnati, exposed eighty-eight cancer patients to whole-body radiation. Many of the guinea pigs were poor African Americans at Cincinnati General Hospital with inoperable tumors. All but one of the eighty-eight patients has since died. According to Schneider (1994), there is evidence that scientists forged signatures on the consent form for the Cincinnati experiments. Gloria Nelson testified before the House that her grandmother, Amelia Jackson, had been strong and still working before she was treated by Dr. Saenger. Following exposure to 100 rads of whole-body radiation (about 7,500 chest X-rays), Amelia Jackson bled and vomited for days and became permanently disabled. Jackson testified that the signature on her grandmother's consent form was forged.

Black Jacketing, Bogus Mail, and Black Propaganda Campaigns

The last examples of state violence are less direct and tend not to involve the use of state agents in conducting acts of violence but rather promoting the use of violence by those targeted for control or destruction. One general strategy that follows this pattern is the use of false information by agents of the state to promote violence directed at someone by either members of his or her own group or by members of another group. The FBI uses several names to describe this method: black jacketing or snitch jacketing, bogus mail, and black propaganda campaigns.

The Senate Select Committee investigating the strategies used by the FBI in their COINTELPRO (counterintelligence program) operations found that the FBI used the systematic fabrication and transmittal of letters and other documents expressly intended to push ideological disagreements between party leaders Huey P. Newton and Eldridge Cleaver into the realm of open hostility. Churchill and Vander Wall (1990) report that after Los Angeles Black Panther Party leaders Jon Huggins and Alpertice Bunch Carter were killed on UCLA's campus in 1969 by gunmen from the rival United Slaves Organization (US), the FBI assigned itself a good measure of credit for having stirred up antagonism among the two groups. At least one FBI memo recommended a new round of cartoons, purportedly to be sent by US to the Panthers, designed to indicate to the Black Panther Party that the US organization felt they were ineffectual, inadequate, and riddled with graft and corruption. Churchill and Vander Wall

(1990) cited a congressional report entitled *The FBI's Covert Action Program to Destroy the Black Panther Party,* which described the specific strategy to incite violence between the two organizations.

Black jacketing or snitch jacketing is intended to create dissent and conflict within organizations. The goal is the creation of suspicion through the spreading of rumors or the manufacture of false evidence. With militant black organizations during the 1960s, the goal was to target bona fide members, usually in key positions, and to convince others within the organization that they were actually FBI/police informers or, alternately, that they were guilty of such offenses as skimming organizational funds. Churchill and Wall (1990) indicate that the purpose of such tactics was to develop suspicion of jacketed individuals and sow dissension in the ranks. They maintain that this was a very common strategy used by the FBI to disrupt dissident organizations.

Agents Provocateurs

Another indirect form of violence is the use of agents provocateurs. An agent provocateur is an agent of a law enforcement organization who is placed in a group targeted for disruption or destruction. The agent tries to persuade the leadership to engage in illegal (often violent) activity. Once this has occurred, the agent then tells the law enforcement agency the time and place of the illegal activity so that it can be there to apprehend the groups members. Andrew Karmen outlines the following steps in the agent provocateur strategy:

1. First, the FBI or local police agency selects a group, situation, or territory for infiltration.

2. Next, the agency finds an agent whose background is compatible with that of the intended victims. He or she is then sent in to join the appropriate group and begins doing minor tasks to help win acceptance.

3. After this goal is achieved, the agent seeks out militant individuals and begins urging them to commit violence. Oftentimes the agents provide guns, bombs, and other materials and even personally participate in the crimes themselves.

4. Finally, the police close in at the most compromising moment. The agent then withdraws, only to return for the trial with a carefully conceived story admitting complicity with the criminal events but denying entrapment (Karmen, 1974).

Karmen reports that thousands of infiltrators were used against the political left during the 1960s. For example, the FBI deployed 316 informers between 1960 and 1976 within the Socialist Workers Party (SWP) and its youth wing, Young Socialist Alliance (YSA). Forty-two of these FBI plants had held office within the SWP or YSA and had thus participated in shaping the very organizational policies that the bureau claimed were necessary to investigate. According to Karmen, agents provocateurs were also involved in provoking violence at the Democratic National Convention in 1968 and in instigating a violent confrontation between the Black Panthers and the Los Angeles police in 1969. Karmen also contends there is evidence that Terrence Norman, an agent of the FBI and the campus police, precipitated the volley of shots by the Ohio National Guard that killed four students at Kent State University in the spring of 1970.

Churchill and Wall (1990) mention that one of the more notorious agents provocateurs paid by the FBI was Tommy the Traveler Tongyai. Tongyai roamed from campus to campus across the Northeast in the late 1960s, agitating for the bombing of military research facilities, the burning of ROTC buildings, and similar violent actions. Marx (1974), analyzing the pattern of infiltration by informants and agents provocateurs, found that eleven involved white peace and/or economic groups, ten were directed against black and Chicano groups, and only two involved right-wing groups.

PATTERNS OF STATE VIOLENCE

Are there patterns of state violence in terms of particular features of countries that make them more or less vulnerable to its occurrence? Political scientist Ted R. Gurr (1986) has developed a series of propositions that attempts to summarize the patterns of state violence worldwide. Gurr contends that there are some necessary conditions for state violence to occur. First, the existence of a group, class, or party regarded by ruling elites as an active threat to their continued rule is necessary. In our discussion of targets of state violence, we have identified indigenous populations, ethnic minorities, unions, political opposition groups, and most recently children (in Brazil and Colombia) identified as potentially threatening or creating threatening conditions and where elites have seen violence as a means to eliminate the threat.

Gurr goes on to specify conditions that increase the likelihood of state violence. He finds that the greater the political threat posed by challengers, the greater the likelihood that a regime will respond with violence (Gurr, 1986, 53–4). The most important factor in determining the level of threat is whether the challenger's objective is to displace those in power. Another condition concerns the degree of latent popular support of those who challenge the regime. Gurr specifies that the greater the latent support within the larger population for such challengers, the greater the likelihood of state violence. On the other hand, if such groups have support among some of the elite, then the state is less likely to use violence against them. Furthermore, if the challengers of the state also rely on violence, this again increases the likelihood that the state in turn will utilize violence to counter those who threaten their rule.

Gurr maintains that the existence of a conflict situation and the presence of challengers are necessary conditions for state terrorism, but characteristics of the state and prevailing political traditions probably are more important and immediate considerations in the calculus of terror than traits of the challengers. Thus, weak regimes are more likely to use violence in response to challenges than strong regimes (Gurr, 1986, 53–4). He explains this by point-ing out that weak regimes have limited material resources and low levels of political institutionalization and that these conditions constrain the policy op-tions of elites who are threatened. Furthermore, Gurr contends that ruling elites who themselves have secured and maintained their positions by violent means are likely to choose violent responses to future challengers.

Following from this latter point, it is likely that the military coups promoted and engineered by international superpowers contribute to further state vio-lence in these client states as they go on to be more likely to use violence against those who challenge their rule. Gurr says that "the successful situational uses of state terror in polarized societies are likely to lead to institutionalized terror and to the preemptive use of terror to maintain political control. . . . Once rulers find terror to be effective in suppressing challenges, they are likely to regard it as an acceptable tactic in future challenges . . .[and] they are likely to regard it as an acceptable tactic in future conflicts" (Gurr, 1986, 55). Gurr finds that this so-cial learning of the effectiveness of state violence does not necessarily have to be from the elites own actions but can be learned from the modeling of others in *their* successful use of state violence, similar to how many forms of violence are learned at the interpersonal level. Gurr believes that the majority of episodes of state violence in this century have been patterned either on the historical use of state terrorism in the society in question or on the concurrent use of terror-ism by other rulers, especially those of ideologically similar regimes.

Other features of societies that relate to the levels of state violence, according to Gurr, are the democratic nature of the state and the levels of social hetero-geneity and inequality in the society. Regarding the first feature, Gurr contends that the patterns of state violence in the world today support the generalization that democratic principles and institutions inhibit political elites from using state violence. Thus he states that "state violence is generally less in democratic than authoritarian regimes, and state terror has seldom been used by elites within countries with a democratic political tradition. . . . Democratic political norms emphasize compromise in conflict and participation and responsiveness in re-lations between rules and ruled, traits that are inconsistent with reliance on vio-lence as an instrument of rule or opposition" (Gurr, 1986, 57–58). This finding is consistent with Sivard's (1986) analysis of state violence in the modern world. Sivard finds that the association between institutionalized political violence and military controlled governments is particularly strong. She writes that of those governments most prone to use torture there are almost three times as many among the military controlled as in other Third World countries (5).

In regard to the relationship between inequality and state violence, Gurr (1986) finds that the greater the heterogeneity and stratification in a society, the greater the likelihood that a regime will use violence as a principal means of social control. He explains this pattern by first demonstrating that in ethni-cally and religiously diverse societies, social cohesion tends to be low. There-fore, challenges to the regimes are more common, and elites are more likely to respond violently. As far as stratification is concerned, ruling classes in highly stratified societies are ruthless in their use of violence to suppress threats to their domination.

As we discussed earlier with regard to the relationship between stratification and violence, when it comes to being socialized in societies that are greatly stratified we learn to accept some people as being worth less than others. This idea contributes to a general acceptance of violence directed at those categorized as being of less worth. Thus, Legum (1966), in describing the factors that led to the 1966 massacres of 6,000 to 8,000 Ibos in northern Nigeria, finds that the danger signal is when government officials talk about a minority in nonhuman terms. Wolf (1976) has found that the Guaran-speaking Paraguayans who hunt the Ache use terminology like rabid rats to describe the native population. In a public speech made in Denver not long before the Sand Creek Massacre that occurred on November 28, 1864, U.S. Army Colonel Chivinton advocated the killing and scalping of Indians, even infants. "Nits make lice!" he declared. At the Sand Creek Massacre there was indiscriminant killing of 105 Indian women and children and twenty-eight men who were unarmed and standing around a white flag of surrender when the slaughter began (Brown, 1970).

Gurr (1986) concludes that minority elites (i.e., elites drawn from an ethnic population that is a numerical minority) in a highly stratified society are likely to use terror routinely as an instrument of rule. South Africa, Rwanda, and Burundi are excellent examples of this pattern. As Gurr argues, when the potential for internal challenges is intrinsically high and the social distance between advantaged rulers and ethnically or religiously distinct subjects is particularly great, violence is likely to be used for social control.

Gurr also focuses on characteristics of the international environment that contribute to state violence. He concludes that "regimes facing external threats are likely to use violence against domestic opponents. . . . In heterogeneous and politically divided societies, elites facing external enemies have strong incentives to suppress internal opposition" (Gurr, 1986, 60). Furthermore, regimes involved in proxy superpower conflicts (i.e., where satellite regimes aligned with super-power nations commit violence in the latter's political interests) are likely to use the most extreme forms of violence against challengers. When internal conflicts become polarized, as along lines of East-West (Communist and Capitalist regimes) and increasingly North-South (developed and developing countries) conflict, for example, external sponsors are likely to encourage the use of warfare and to provide their proxies with the advisers, technology, and even troops to do so, as in Afghanistan and Vietnam, and the internal conflicts with Guatemala, El Salvador, Nicaragua, Brazil, and Haiti. Sivard's (1986) analysis of 114 developing countries confirms this pattern. She notes that with respect to institutionalized political violence, the worst offenders are clients of one or the other superpower.

Gurr (1986) also points out that the highest levels of state violence occur in the periphery of the world system: Uganda and Equatorial Guinea, Ethiopia, the

Central African Republic, Burundi and Rwanda, and Kampuchea, to name a few. He reasons that executioners of state violence in such places have not been significantly dependent, politically or economically, on the world system. Thus they have not been deterred by the prospect of economic sanctions or embargoes because they have been largely self-sufficient or because their trade and aid partners have simply not cared enough to apply economic pressures.

Nevertheless, the cases Gurr raises as examples of the rule may actually be exceptions. For when we look at the levels of state violence in Latin America in particular, we see that the United States has played an important role in supporting and assisting state violence to suppress dissent and maintain stability, one of the central goals of U.S. foreign policy in its sphere of influence which is now the entire world. Furthermore, in all the cases cited (and in many others), the colonial history of domination created the peripheral status of the nation and may have contributed to the economic and political climate that increased the likelihood of the use of state violence. Thus historical ties may be more significant than the current context in which the state violence occurs.

Furthermore, Gurr assumes that the international community has had an impact on deterring state violence. Unfortunately, when we look at the incidences of state violence today, the superpowers have either ignored or supported instances of state violence conducted by their allies, and international bodies such as the United Nations and the World Court have had minimal impact on stopping or deterring elites from conducting campaigns of state violence in their countries.

State violence ultimately is used to maintain the order defined in terms of ranking people within nations and ranking nation-states within the international order. This order is defined ultimately in terms of a pattern of a distribution of power, a distribution, moreover, in which the framework is defined in terms of systems of stratification within the nation-state and between nation-states in the world system. We have seen that in nations where there are high levels of inequality, state violence is more pronounced. Furthermore, in regard to the nature of the world system, as the position of states in terms of a power hierarchy becomes more unequal and as the relationships between states within the system are defined by relationships of domination or imperialism, there is an increasing likelihood of the occurrence of state violence sponsored both nationally and internationally. Thus, nations that are themselves highly stratified internally and positioned in dominated or exploited locations in the world system are more likely to suffer from higher levels of state violence than nations that have lower levels of inequality and are positioned at the higher end of the world system. The state violence throughout Africa and Central and South America confirm this pattern. The exceptions to this pattern, of course, are those dominant powers that, although they may not have high levels of state violence within their own societies, nevertheless sponsor it internationally in order to maintain stability in terms of the distribution of power within those systems and internationally. State violence, in other words, has a two-tiered (i.e., center versus peripheral) existence in which the center nations internally show lower levels of state violence but sponsor it rampantly externally in the periphery in order to maintain their positions of dominance in the world.

Chomsky and Herman (1979) recognize that U.S. economic interests in the Third World have dictated a policy of containing revolution, preserving an open door for U.S. economic interests and assuring favorable conditions of investment. Thus the aim of the violence is pacification, discouraging popular movements or radical and even social democratic governments that could threaten patterns of property ownership, wage and tax structures affecting investments. This is the goal of U.S. foreign policy as well as the policies of other advanced capitalist governments.

Since the nineteenth century the United States, in its own hemisphere and throughout the rest of the world, has played a dominant role (if not the dominant role) in maintaining order through its use of state violence: in wars, in its involvement in covert forms of state violence through the activities of the CIA or through the training, arming, and directing of surrogate forces in the international periphery to carry out state violence. The United States past involvement in all these arenas of state violence is well documented in various countries of Latin America. Its role today is truly worldwide, with more than 300 military bases around the world, serving as the major arms supplier to developing countries, and providing funds to train and equip military and police forces (Klare, 1981; McClintock, 1985; Pierce, 1970; *New Internationalist*, 1994; Wheat, 1995). Through this web of sponsored repression, the United States alone does more to maintain and extend systems of stratification around the world, which again leads to an increase in levels of violence at all levels, from interpersonal to institutional, and to the last level that we discuss: structural violence.

CONCLUSION—STATE VIOLENCE AND INEQUALITY

State violence is about the exercise of power over those who threaten its distribution. As we have discussed, it takes many forms. But one pattern seems to be persistent. Those who are the most powerless in the society are easy victims when they act in ways that threaten the state or possess resources that the state or those who have the most power to influence the state wish to possess or control. They may be children, members of minority groups, workers, or members of dissident political parties. In country after country, where state violence is present, the pattern of victimization is repeated. Infrequently do you hear of members of the elite being victims of a massacre or extralegal executions, unless they too threaten the power of the state.

There is no databank on state violence. We would expect that societies in the world that have the lowest levels of inequality would have the lowest levels of state violence, while those that have the highest levels would have the highest levels of state violence. Furthermore, following from this, we would expect that as societies in the world and the world itself are increasingly unequal in the distribution of wealth and power, state violence is increasingly likely to be used to maintain and extend those patterns of inequality as defined nationally and internationally.

It makes little difference if we are looking at the state's legitimate use of violence (e.g. when it carries out executions of those who commit capital crimes) or illegitimate use of violence (e.g., sponsored death squad activities), the victims are in the vast majority of cases those who have the least. The violence of the state is one more piece of the puzzle in describing the nature of violence. And now to the last piece which is the centerpiece of the puzzle of violence.

REFERENCES

Amnesty International. 1977. *Amnesty International's Report on Torture, 1975–1976.* New York: Amnesty International.

———. 1983. *Political Killings by Government.* London: Amnesty International.

———. 1984. *Torture in the Eighties.* New York: Amnesty International.

———. 1992. *Amnesty International Report 1992.* New York: Amnesty International.

———. 1993. "Amnesty Action 1992: A Year of Trial and Triumph." *Amnesty Action.*

———. 1994a. *Amnesty International Report 1994.* New York: Amnesty International.

———. 1994b, Summer. "Colombia: Is U.S. Drug War Aid Financing Murder?" *Amnesty Action.*

———. 1998. *Rights for All—Amnesty International's Report on Human Rights in the United States of America.* New York: Amnesty International.

———. 1999, December 1. "Israel High Court should end the shame of torture." *AI-index:* MDE 15/005/1999.

———. 2001a. "China: Extensive use of torture—from police to tax collectors to birth control officials." *AI Index ASA* 17/003/2001, News Service Nr. 10. http://web.amnesty.org/ai.nsf/Index/ASA170032001?OpenDocument&of=COUNTRIES%5CCHINA

———. 2001b. *Amnesty International Report 2001.* New York: Amnesty International. www.amnestyusa.org/scripts/exit.cgi?www.amnesty.org/ailib/index.html

———. 2001c. *Racism and the Administration of Justice.* New York: Amnesty International. http://web.amnesty.org/ai.nsf/Index/ACT400202001?OpenDocument&of=THEMES\RACISM

———. 2002a. *Death Penalty Facts: Juveniles.* www.amnestyusa.org/abolish/juveniles.html

———. 2002b. *Amnesty International Website against the Death Penalty.* www.amnestyusa.org/scripts/exit.cgi?www.amnesty.org/ailib/index.html

———. 2002c, September 4. *Worldwide executions doubled in 2001.* AI-index: ACT 50/005/2002.

———. 2002d. *Red Hands to Stop the Use of Child Soldiers.* AI Index: ACT 76/001/2002. www.amnesty-usa.org/news/2002/world02122002.html

———. 2002e. *Guatemala's Lethal Legacy: Past Impunity and Renewed Human Rights Violations.* London: UK. www.amnestyusa.org/countries/guatemala/lethal_legacy.rtf

——. 2002f. *USA: A Safe Haven for Torturers.* New York: Amnesty International.

Associated Press. 1995, March 12. "Argentine Officer Admits Military Killed Prisoners." *(Fort Wayne, Ind.) Journal Gazette.*

——. 1994, March 20. "S. Africa Official Questions Validity of Violence Claims." *(Fort Wayne, Ind.) Journal Gazette,* 2A.

Ball, Patrick, Paul Kobrak, and Herbert F. Spirer. 1999. *State Violence in Guatemala, 1960–1996: A Quantitative Reflection.* Annapolis Junction, Md.: American Association for the Advancement of Science.

Berma, Paige. 1994, July. "Torture behind Bars." *The Progressive* 58: 21–27.

Betancur, Belisario. 1993. *From Madness to Hope: the 12-year war in El Salvador: Report of the Commission on the Truth for El Salvador: The Commission on the Truth for El Salvador.* United Nations: UN Doc. S/25500/Annex.

Bierne, Piers, and James Messerschmidt. 1991. *Criminology.* New York: Harcourt Brace Jovanovich.

Bissio, Roberto Remo. 1990. "A Creeping Bhopal." In *Third World Guide 91/92,* ed. R. R. Bissio. Montevideo, Uruguay: Garamond Press.

Blum, William. 1988. *The CIA, A Forgotten History: U. S. Global Interventions since World War 2.* London: Zed Books.

——. 1995. *Killing Hope: U.S. Military and CIA Interventions since World War II.* Monroe, Maine: Common Courage Press.

——. 2000. *Rogue State: A Guide to the World's Only Superpower.* Monroe, Maine: Common Courage Press.

Bodley, John H. 1982. *Victims of Progress.* Menlo Park, Calif.: Benjamin Cummings Publishing.

Booth, John A. 1991. "Socioeconomic and Political Roots of National Revolts in Central America." *Latin America Research Review* 26: 33.

Bowers, William. 1974. *Executions in America.* Lexington, Mass.: D. C. Heath.

Brown, Dee. 1970. *Bury My Heart at Wounded Knee.* New York: Henry Holt Company.

Bulletin of the Atomic Scientist. 1998, July/August. "U.S. Nuclear Weapons Stockpile." *NRDC Nuclear Notebook* 54, no. 4. www.bullatomsci.org/issues/nukenotes/ja98nukenote.html

Chambliss, William J. 1989. "State-Organized Crime—The American Society of Criminology, 1988 Presidential Address." *Criminology* 27: 183–208.

Chomsky, Noam. 1993. *Year 501: The Conquest Continues.* Boston: South End Press.

Chomsky, Noam, and Edward S. Herman. 1979. *The Washington Connection and Third World Fascism.* Boston: South End Press.

Church Committee. 1975. *Alleged Assassination Plots Involving Foreign Leaders.* Ed. by U.S. Senate Select Committee to Study Governmental Operations with Respect to Intelligence Activities. Washington, D.C.: Government Printing Office.

Churchill, Ward, and Jim Vander Wall. 1990. *Agents of Repression.* Boston: South End Press.

Coleman, James S. 1989. *The Criminal Elite.* New York: St. Martin's Press.

Colhoun, Jack. 1992, April 22. "Census Fails to Quash Report on Iraqi Deaths." *Guardian* 44, 39: 5.

Columbia Support Network. 2002, May 2. "Tito Libio Hernandez, Presente! (Colombian union leader assassinated)." www.colombiasupport.net/

Eisenberg, Daniel. 2002, May 13. "We're Taking Him Out." *Newsweek* 159, no. 19: 36–38.

Emerson, Steven. 1988. *Secret Warriors: Inside the Covert Military Operations of the Reagan Era*. New York: G. P. Putnam's Sons.

Ensign, Todd, and Glenn Alcalay. 1994, Summer. "Duck and Cover(up): U.S. Radiation Testing on Humans." *Covert Action Quarterly*: 28–35.

Frankel, Mark, Joshua Hammer, Joseph Contreras, Ron Moreau, and Christopher Dickey. 1995, August 14. "Boy Soldiers." *Newsweek*: 44–6.

Frappier, Jon. 1983. "Above the Law: Violations of International Law by the U.S. Government from Truman to Reagan." *Crime and Social Justice* 21–22: 1–36.

Fyfe, James. 1988. "Police Use of Deadly Force: Research and Reform." *Justice Quarterly* 5: 165–205.

General Accounting Office. 1990. *Death Penalty Sentencing: Research Indicates a Pattern of Racial Disparity*. GGD 90-57. http://161.203.16.4/t2pbat11/140845.pdf

———. 1993, November. *Nuclear Health and Safety: Examples of Post World War II Radiation Releases at U.S. Nuclear Sites*. RCED 94-51FS.

Guatemalan Historical Clarification Commission. 1999. *Guatemala: Memory of Silence*. http://hrdata.aaas.org/ceh/report/english/

Guest, Iain. 1983, February 1. "Report to U.N. Panel Cites 2 Million Executions." *International Herald Tribune* 7, 3.

Gurr, Ted Robert. 1986. "The Political Origins of State Violence and Terror: A Theoretical Analysis." In *Government Violence and Repression: An Agenda for Research*, edited by M. Stohl and G. A. Lopez. New York: Greenwood Press.

Harff, Barbara. 1986. "Genocide as State Violence." In *Government Violence and Repression: An Agenda for Research*, ed. by M. Stohl and G. A. Lopez, 45–71. New York: Greenwood Press.

Harris, Emily G. 1994, May/June. "Human Radiation Tests: An Old Story Finally Makes the Front Page." *Extra*, 8.

Haugaard, Lisa. 1997, September. "Textbook Repression: US Training Manuals Declassified." *Covert Action Quarterly*, no. 1: 29–39.

Haviland, William A. 1987. *Cultural Anthropology*. 5th ed. New York: Holt, Reinhart and Winston, 421–423.

Herman, Edward. 1982. *The Real Terror Network*. Boston: South End Press.

———. 1987. "U.S. Sponsorship of International Terrorism: An Overview." *Crime and Social Justice* 27–28: 1–29.

Herman, Edward, and Gerry O'Sullivan. 1989. *The Terrorism Industry*. New York: Pantheon.

Hinckle, Warren, and William Turner. 1981. *The Fish is Red*. New York: Harper and Row.

Hougan, Jim. 1978. *Spooks: The Haunting of America—The Private Use of Secret Agents*. New York: Morrow.

Human Rights Watch. 1999. *Leave None to Tell the Story: Genocide in Rwanda*. New York: Human Rights Watch.

Imerman, Vicky A. 1994, Spring. "The US Army School of the Americas—School of Assassins." *Witness for Peace Newsletter* 11:13–14.

Jenkins, Brian. 1984, November. "The Who, What, When, Where, How, and Why of Terrorism." Paper presented at the Detroit Police Department Conference on Urban Terrorism: Planning or Chaos.

Johnson, Chalmers. 2000. *Blowback: The Cost and Consequences of American Empire*. New York: Henry Holt and Company.

Jones, James H. 1987. *Bad Blood: The Tuskegee Syphilis Experiment*. New York: Free Press.

Karmen, Andrew. 1974. "Agent Provocateur in the Contemporary U.S. Leftist Movement." In *The Criminologist: Crime and the Criminal*, ed. by C. Reasons. Pacific Palisades, Calif.: Goodyear.

Kerr, Mary Lee, and Bob Hall. 1992, January. "Chickens Come Home to Roost." *The Progressive* 56: 1, 29.

Klare, Michael T. 1981. *Supplying Repression: U.S. Support for Authoritarian Regimes Abroad*. Washington, D.C.: Institute for Policy Studies.

Laqueur, Walter. 1987. *The Age of Terrorism*. Boston: Little Brown.

Lewis, Flora. 2002, May 6. "Israel Defiles Itself with These Assassinations of Palestinians." *International Herald Tribune*.

Legum, Colin. 1966, October. "The Massacre of the Proud Ibos." *Observer* 16.

Leyan, Brian. 2002, January 14. "Sharp Rise in Killings by Police, Says Report." *The Nation*.

Levinson, Arlene. 1995, September 24. "The Modern Face of Genocide" (Associated Press). *(Fort Wayne, Ind.) Journal Gazette*, C1.

Luft, Kerry. 1995, January 15. "For Bogota's Street Children, Death is Just Around the Corner." *Chicago Tribune*, 7.

Marx, Gary T. 1974. "Thoughts on a Neglected Category of Social Movement Participant: The Agent Provocateur and the Informant." *American Journal of Sociology* 80: 402–442.

Matthiessen, Peter. 1991. *In the Spirit of Crazy Horse*. New York: Viking Penguin.

McClintock, Michael. 1985. *The American Connection: State Terror and Popular Resistance in El Salvador*. London: Zed Books.

Michalowski, Raymond. 1985. *Order, Law, and Crime: An Introduction to Criminology*. New York: Random House.

Monthly Review. 2002, March. "U.S. Military Bases and Empire." 53, no. 10.

Moran, Michael. 1998, August 24. "Bin Laden comes home to roost: His CIA ties are only the beginning of a woeful story." MSNBC. www.msnbc.com/news/190144.asp

Nairn, Allan. 1984, May. "Behind the Death Squads." *The Progressive*, 19–29.

Ndiaye, Bacre Waly. 1996, 7 October. "Human Rights Questions: Human Rights Questions, Including Alternative Approaches for Improving The Effective Enjoyment Of Human Rights And Fundamental Freedoms. Report of the Special Rapporteur of the Commission on Human Rights on extrajudicial, summary or arbitrary executions." Agenda item 110 (b) Fifty-first session of the United Nations General Assembly. www.unhchr.ch/Huridocda/Huridoca.nsf/TestFrame/10729ea00b7c34b0802567080052b7e4?Opendocument

Neier, Aryeh. 1992, February 3. "Watching Rights." *The Nation*, 129.

New Internationalist. 1994, November. "That's the Way the Money Goes." *New Internationalist*, no. 261: 8–9.

New York Times. 1994, January 14. "Two Recall 1949 Radiation Tests on Them," A14. Cited in Todd Ensign and Glenn Alcalay, "Duck and Cover(up): U.S. Radiation Testing on Humans," *Covert Action Quarterly*, no. 49 (Summer 1994): 28–35.

Newsweek. 1993, December 27. "America's Nuclear Secrets." 15. Cited in Todd Ensign and Glenn Alcalay, "Duck and Cover(up): U.S. Radiation Testing on Humans," *Covert Action Quarterly*, no. 49 (Summer 1994): 31.

Pincus, Walter. 2001, October 21. "Silence of 4 Terror Probe Suspects Poses Dilemma." *Washington Post*, A06.

Parenti, Christian. 1994. "Urban Militarism." *Z Magazine* 7: 47–52.

Pearce, Jenny. 1982. *Under the Eagle*. Boston: South End Press.

Pierce, Chester M. 1970. "Violence and the National Character." In *Violence: Causes and Solutions*, ed. R. Hartogs and E. Artzt, 119–126. New York: Dell Books.

Project Ploughshares. 2001. *Armed Conflicts Report*. Waterloo, Canada: Institute of Peace and Conflict Studies, Conrad Grebel College. www.ploughshares.ca/CONTENT/ACR/ACR00/ACR00.html

Prouty, Fletcher L. 1992. *JFK: The CIA, Vietnam, and the Plot to Assassinate John F. Kennedy*. New York: Birch Lane Press.

Roebuck, Julian, and Stanley C. Weeber. 1978. *Political Crime in the United States*. New York: Praeger.

Rosenberg, Howard. 1981, September/October. "Informed Consent." *Mother Jones* 31–37, 44.

Russian Archives. 1995. "Revelations from the Russian Archives—Kirov Murder and Purges." Library of Congress exhibit displayed through Spring 1992. Translated excerpts displayed on *American Online*. Vienna, Va.: America Online, Education and Reference Department (Electronic Communication Network).

Schmetzer, Uli. 1994, August 29. "Transplant Coercion Charged." *Chicago Tribune*, 1–5.

Schneider, Keith. 1994, April 12. "Researchers are Accused of Forgeries." *New York Times*. Cited in Todd Ensign and Glenn Alcalay, "Duck and Cover(up): U.S. Radiation Testing on Humans," *Covert Action Quarterly*, no. 49 (Summer 1994): 28–35.

Sharkey, Jacqueline. 1990, May/June. "Nicaragua: Anatomy of an Election." *Common Cause Magazine*, 20–29.

Silverfarb, Daniel, and Majid Khadduri. 1997. *Britain's Informal Empire in the Middle East: A Case Study of Iraq 1929–1941*. New York: Oxford University Press.

Simon, David R., and D. Stanley Eitzen. 1993. *Elite Deviance*. Boston: Allyn and Bacon.

Sivard, Ruth Leger. 1982. *World Military and Social Expenditures*. Leesburg, Va.: World Priorities.

———. 1986. *World Military and Social Expenditures 1986*. Washington, D.C.: World Priorities.

Snyder, Howard N., and Melissa Sickmund. 1995. *Juvenile Offenders and Victims: A Focus on Violence*. Washington, D.C.: Office of Juvenile Justice and Delinquency.

SOA Watch. 2002. "School of the Americas: School of Assassins, USA." *Third World Traveler*. www.thirdworldtraveler.com/Terrorism/SOA.html

Sollenberg, Margareta, and Peter Wallensteen. 2001. "Patterns of major armed conflicts 1990–2000" *SIPRI Yearbook 2001*. Stockholm, Sweden: Stockholm International Peace Research Institute.

Stewart, Sarah. 1994, June. "No Pablo, No Story." *New Internationalist*, no. 256: 20–22.

Stockholm International Peace Research Institute. 1994. *SIPRI Yearbook 1994*. Oxford: Oxford University Press.

U.S. Council on Foreign Relations. 2002. *Assassination: Does It Work? Should America Try?* www.terrorismanswers.com/policy/assassination_print.html

U.S. Department of Justice, Bureau of Justice Statistics. 2000. *Sourcebook of Criminal Justice Statistics Online*. www.albany.edu/sourcebook/

Weber, Max. 1958. "Politics as a Vocation." In *From Max Weber: Essays in Sociology*, ed. H. H. Gerth and C. W. Mills, 77–128. New York: Oxford University Press.

Weiner, Tim. 1993, December 14. "In 1990, U.S. Was Still Training Salvador Civilians Tied to Killings." *New York Times*, A1.

Welsome, Eileen. 1993, November 15. "The Plutonium Experiment: Elmer Allen Loses His Leg—And All Hope." *Albuquerque Tribune*. Cited in Todd Ensign and Glenn

Alcalay, "Duck and Cover(up): U.S. Radiation Testing on Humans," *Covert Action Quarterly*, no. 49 (Summer 1994).

Wheat, Andrew. 1995, January/February. "Exporting Repression: Arms Profits vs. Human Rights." *Multinational Monitor* 16: 16–21.

Wolf, Eric. 1976. "Killing the Aches." In *Genocide in Paraguay*, ed. R. Arens, 47–57. Philadelphia: Temple University Press.

Chapter Eight

Structural Violence

According to official sources, there are 685,000 children in greater Buenos Aires alone who don't eat enough to stay alive, this plus another 385,000 children in the province of Buenos Aires, or a third of the children under fourteen in this province (George, 1988, 136).

Each day, 34,000 young children die from malnutrition and preventable infectious diseases (UN Development Programme, 1993).

About 17 million people die every year from preventable infectious and parasitic diseases, such as diarrhea, malaria, and tuberculosis (UN Development Programme, 1993).

Nearly 800 million people face persistent, everyday hunger in the world today (New Internationalist, 1995).

In the United States in 1985, black mothers died in childbirth at a rate four times that of white mothers. Infant mortality for whites is eight per 1,000 live births, but for blacks it is nineteen per 1,000 live births. Black infant mortality is higher than the rate in Poland and Cuba (UN Development Programme, 1993; Grant, 1994).

These are stories of structural violence. Maxine Waters, congresswoman from South Central Los Angeles, giving testimony before the U.S. Senate Banking Committee in the aftermath of the Los Angeles riots of 1992, quoted Robert Kennedy in a speech he made in 1968 after one of the most turbulent periods of urban rioting. "There is another kind of violence in America, slower but just as deadly, destructive as the shot or bomb in the night. . . . This is the violence of institutions; indifference and inaction and slow decay. This is the violence that afflicts the poor, that poisons relations between men and women because their skin is different colors. This is the slow destruction of a child by hunger, and schools without books and homes without heat in the winter" (Medoff and Sklar, 1994, 245). As we discussed in the introductory chapter, structural violence is violence that occurs in the context of establishing, maintaining, extending or reducing hierarchical relations between categories of people within a society. For example, violence can be an outcome of how we have organized a society in terms of access to basic necessities of survival. Or it can be an outcome of how we have organized a society in terms of access to a pollution free environment. Or it can be an outcome of how we have organized a society in terms of access to medical care and medicines to cure diseases. In short, it can be an outcome of how we have organized a society in terms of life chances. Life chances refer to the opportunities in life to realize one's potential—intellectual, physically, and spiritually. Differences in infant mortality rates among groups that occupy different positions in systems of stratification are a violent outcome of this arrangement of people. We know that in the United States, if you are born black you are more likely not to survive your first year of life than if you are born white. If you are born black you will have less access to health care and safe and nonpolluted communities. In short, if you are born black, you will on the average live six to seven years less than if you were born white.

These differences also manifest themselves in life expectancy differences between countries. If you are born in Afghanistan, you will live on average thirty-three fewer years than if born in the United States. These life expectancy differences are a result of the differences in the quality and opportunity for life available to people who occupy different positions in systems of stratification within one society and differences in the position of their society in the world system of stratification.

Structural violence can also be interpersonal or institutional violence. For example, the actions of individuals acting outside institutional roles to establish, maintain, extend, or reduce the hierarchical ordering of a category of people within a society would be both interpersonal and structural violence. In this chapter we discuss groups such as the Ku Klux Klan and Skinheads in this country and several other countries in Europe today, assaulting and killing members of minorities, in order to maintain or extend ethnic/racial hierarchical relations in a community. On the other hand, the Palestinian suicide bomber terrorist who is killing Israeli civilians to end the oppression and domination of Palestinians by the Israeli government is also violence that is interpersonal and structural. We also discuss the violence between religious groups within a society to maintain, extend, or reduce hierarchical relations between them. For example, the violence in India today between Muslim, Hindu, and Christian groups is an example of this type of violence.

The violence also may be a product of governmental or other institutional actions that serve to establish, maintain, extend or reduce the hierarchical ordering of categories of people within a society. Some examples of violence we have previously discussed in the family, religious, economic, and state violence chapters are also examples of structural violence.

HIERARCHICAL STRUCTURES WITHIN SOCIETIES

Before we begin discussing the violent outcomes or actions that stem from hierarchical relations in a society, it is important that we describe the nature of the hierarchies and how they are a fundamental structural feature of capitalist society and the world political economic system. Societies of the world today are organized in at least four fundamental hierarchical relations: class, gender, ethnic/racial identity, and age. All societies of the world today are either some type of capitalist society, in transition from a statist or state socialist system to a capitalist system, or are a state socialist society integrated into a world political economic system that is capitalist dominated. As you recall from our discussion of the mode of production in chapter 1, capitalism connotes a particular pattern of class stratification where there is an owning or capitalist class and a working class.

Other class positions are also present. These positions may be remnants of a subordinate mode of production in societies that are less advanced in terms of capitalist development or they may represent an emerging class position that develops because of changes in the nature of production in the society. For example, in many Latin American countries there exists a remnant of a class system that is rooted in a previous mode of production. The *latifundia* system of agriculture, which was based on a class of large landowners and a class of peasants or *campesinos* who worked the land for the landlords in order to have access to their own plots, represents a different class relationship then the dominant class relations in capitalist society between owner and wage workers.

Other class positions develop within advanced capitalist modes of productions that may or may not add stability to the system. For example, as capitalist systems develop a managerial class arises to control production for owners. As mentioned previously, these managers, like workers, do not own production, but unlike workers they do control it for those who own. This class becomes increasingly important as production becomes larger and the holdings of the capitalist class become more extensive, fluid, and distant.

An alternative to capitalist relations of production has also existed within many capitalist countries. The development of cooperatives where workers have joined together to own production is one case. The cooperatives in the Mondrigan region of Spain, the city of Sheffield in England as well in the Pacific Northwest of the United States with its plywood cooperatives are examples of these alternative class relations (Zwerdling, 1980; Morrison, 1991). However these alternatives are not promoted within capitalist society and generally are an exception to the relations of the production in advanced societies.

In capitalist political/economic systems, the fundamental relationship between those who own and control production and those who sell their labor is characterized by inequality, exploitation, and coercion. As a general pattern, capitalists have more power, income and wealth than workers do. The system itself is based on an unequal distribution of wealth and income that parallels the patterns of ownership and control of production.

The nature of the relationship between capitalists and workers is also characterized by exploitation. Exploitation simply refers to a pattern whereby workers produce more than is required for them to survive and the surplus resulting from their labor goes to those who own production as a right of ownership. In return for this surplus production, workers receive a wage, which allows them to acquire the necessities that is customary for members of this class within the society. Capitalists receive the surplus produced in production, for example, that which is not necessary to reproduce the production (workers, machinery, and raw materials). This surplus is the basis of profit and is realized in the marketplace.

Capitalists attempt to acquire larger and larger amounts of surplus in order to have more profits and attract more investment capital to grow in the marketplace. For capitalists, the law of survival in the marketplace is that you grow or you die. Growth depends on increasing the efficiency of production either by having workers produce more during the time that they work through speeding up the production process (this can be accomplished by means of the introduction of technology) and/or by cutting labor costs through de-skilling and wage cutting. Workers, on the other hand, are trying to acquire a larger and larger portion of the surplus that they produce by means of wage increases and to be able to have more control over their labor. These are the central points of conflict between owners and workers.

Workers are also in a coercive relationship with owners because they must sell their labor in order to acquire the necessities for survival. This coercion is often transparent in the transition to capitalist society. For example, British imperialists in many African countries placed a head tax on native populations that required the native population to sell their labor in the marketplace to acquire the currency to pay the taxes that were imposed on them. Similarly, missionaries played a role in coercing indigenous populations to produce a surplus for their new spiritual and political overlords. It occurred in the Southern United States prior to the civil war where most of the large-scale agricultural production (cotton and sugar cane) was accomplished by slave labor. It also occurs today in many South and Central American countries as small peasant landowners are forced off their plots of land as agricultural production undergoes a transition to cash crop production for export and are forced to sell their labor to capitalists to survive. In Peru and Guatemala 85 percent of rural workers are landless. In fact, a billion people living in villages in the developing world have no land of their own to farm (New Internationalist, 1995). As a rule, in the development of capitalism, as production becomes privately owned and there is less and less access to production either through common ownership or free land, workers are coerced to sell their labor to those who own and control production in order to have access to the means of survival. As ownership of production becomes more concentrated with the further development of capitalism, this process accelerates and the size of the working class increases dramatically as small owners become increasing displaced. The changes in farm ownership in the United States during the last century is an example of this concentration and displacement. Work under these circumstances is not a choice, it is forced on those displaced, who become the working class.

Not only are all societies ordered in terms of social class but they are also ordered in terms of gender. All societies today are patriarchal as it relates to the distribution of power along gender lines. Men rule all the institutions that make up today's societies. In every institutional arena, men systematically have more power than women do. Women are directed and controlled by men in the performance of roles within all societal institutions. This is the case no matter what institution we discuss: family, political system, educational institution, religious institution, or economy. Furthermore, the ultimate power of men is expressed in their ability to define women as significant principally in terms of their relationship to men. This is the case whether we are discussing the form of address used to distinguish between married and single women, Mrs. and Miss, or whether it is how women are portrayed in literature or mass media (as weaker than men and thus in need of protection from other men, as objects of love or lust by men, and as servers to men if wives and mothers).

Previously, we discussed gender hierarchy as it relates to the mode of reproduction. Patriarchy ultimately provides men with control over their progeny. In most stable societies patriarchy is integrated with capitalism so that each system of stratification reinforces the other. Women are traditionally a cheaper source of labor for capitalists. Discrimination directed at women in the workplace has served to divide the workforce. Furthermore, the unpaid labor of women in the home is a source of subsidy to owners. Wages are kept down as a result of the unpaid services provided by women. Last, patriarchy provides even poor, displaced men with a sense of power and control over others that is celebrated and promoted in hierarchical societies. It also provides a bridge across the division of social class for men. Thus men who are of very different economic positions can jointly celebrate their domination of women as they revel in their sexual exploits or conquests.

It is also important to note that the systems can become disarticulated where changes in one system of stratification may conflict with that of the other. We see this in the United States; as women's economic position has improved relative to men, there has been an erosion of the power of men in the home. Traditional divisions of labor that have justified women being entirely burdened with domestic and childrearing responsibilities together with work outside the home have increasingly been a point of contention in homes, leading to some change in the domestic division of labor.

The third crucial division within societies and the world in general is along ethnic/racial lines. Ethnic and racial conflict and hierarchies play an increasingly important role in the distribution of life chances within and between societies. The conflict and competition for scarcities often fall along racial and ethnic lines because these distinctions are important in defining position in the labor market and world economy as determined in terms of the political and economic positioning of nations. This positioning is a result of the heritage of imperialism that dominates the history of the relations between peoples around the globe. Ethnic disadvantage or advantage becomes institutionalized by racist and ethnocentric attitudes and institutional practices that justify, maintain, and extend the hierarchical ethnic relations.

Where these patterns of stratification are most evident is when populations are segregated within a society and this leads to the overt institutionalized denial of opportunities for development. The United States has had a history of segregation of ethnic minorities. The most overt case has been with the indigenous populations. Native Americans were conquered and driven out of their homelands and placed in remote areas of the country which were not of economic interests to the dominant white population. The history of treaty violations is a history whereby the lands that they were driven to were later deemed to be of value and thus taken away from them. This systematic denial of resources has led to the institutionalization of their impoverishment. The native populations on reservations in the United States have the highest rates of poverty, alcoholism, and mental illness than any other geographic locations. This same pattern is reproduced in other areas of white European conquest throughout Central and South America, Australia, Oceania, and Africa.

African American populations and Hispanic populations in the United States also experienced segregation and thus the denial of opportunities. Laws were established throughout many areas of the country that segregated populations. Legal changes began to occur in the early 1950s and have continued through executive orders and the passage of various civil rights acts beginning with the 1964 act. Only in the last half of the twentieth century have the white leadership within the United States begun to address the harms of this system of segregation. The patterns of distribution of income, wealth, education levels, mortality and morbidity differences still reflect these institutionalized patterns of segregation and racism. Today's ghettos in the largest cities in the United States still reflect this history of segregation. The populations who reside there are those ethnic populations who experienced legal segregation previously. The system of legal segregation and racism has resulted in a persistent pattern of de facto segregation and racism in many cities in the United States today.

Another dramatic example of this geographic pattern of ethnic stratification is the case of South Africa. Mukonoweshuro (1991) describes the establishment of the *bantustans*, native lands for black South Africans, as one of the bases of structural violence in South Africa. These ten white constructed areas of ethnic minority segregation or reserves were the poorest areas of South Africa. The population within these areas was totally dependent for energy, water, jobs, and consumer goods on white South Africa. The political leadership were generally puppet rulers installed by or with the consent of the white South Africa leadership. The *bantustans* were eliminated by the black majority government in 1994.

This is an excellent example of internal colonialism. The dominant white South African leadership established colonies within their own country with the hope that they would be recognized internationally as independent nations so that they would no longer be responsible for the black South African citizenship that resided there. It also provided the illusion that white South Africa was addressing its history of theft of the lands of the black African population by giving these tribal populations their own land and country. In reality, this institutionalized impoverished population would be a reserve of cheap labor that could be exploited to support the dominance of white South Africa. The land that was given was often barren of resources, and the black population had little capital for the technology to develop the land that was ceded to them. Thus the people of the *bantustans* were even more dependent on white South Africa, though they had lost the rights of citizenship in the process. Unfortunately for white South Africa, the international community could not embrace such a blatant racist strategy to solve their native population problem. Today there persists extensive problems of poverty and destitution, child malnutrition, shortage of medical personnel, and crime in the former *bantustans*, a legacy of this racist system.

The major division between countries of the north and countries of the south in the world economy is also characterized by ethnic/racial divisions. The countries of the north are populated by people of white European ancestry, while those of the south with a few exceptions are characterized by people of color who are of Asian, African, or Indo-American heritage. The average annual income of people of the north is $12,510, while the average income of people of the south is $710 (Bello, 1994).

These systems of stratification (class, gender, and race) intersect to create positions along a hierarchy of life chances and patterns of victimization for violence. We can think of the dominant positions in our own society and in the world in general as occupied by whites of European ancestry, males, capitalists who reside in countries referred to as the center of the world political economy (United States, Western Europe, Japan, Canada, and Australia). Those who occupy this position have the greatest power within societal institutions and have the greatest ability to fulfill their potentials as measured in terms of life expectancy, illness rates, educational level, control over resources, and so on. Those who occupy the most dominated positions in society and the world in general are female, ethnic minority group members (i.e., African, Hispanic, Asian or Native American), and members of the working class or another subservient position within a subordinate mode of production (peasantry). People who occupy this position have the least ability to fulfill their potential as measured in terms of life expectancy, illness rates, educational level, control over resources, and so on.

In a particular society, one dimension of stratification may have greater significance in defining one's position than another. For example, in South Africa until recently, race had greater significance in determining position than either class or gender. That is not to say that the other dimensions are insignificant, for life chances were certainly affected by class and gender position within racial categories. Thus, black or white South African males had more power than their female counterparts; however, black males generally had less power than white females in terms of life chances. The same applies to social class positions across the two racial or ethnic categories. These patterns are less clear in societies that have less rigid systems of stratification and where the distances between positions within a given dimension of stratification are less extreme.

Also, although we have described these dimensions of stratification as more or less distinguishable and independent of each other, they become intertwined as they define a particular position of an individual (African American, female worker, Hispanic male worker, White male manager, etc.). Mobility may occur between class positions, but most class mobility occurs within short ranges (within classes) and is principally intergenerational. The other two dimensions of stratification (ethnic and gender) are generally fixed; the positions you are born into are permanent. In this latter case, mobility occurs by moving out of the social system based on that stratification or changes occurring in the system of stratification as a whole in a society whereby positions change in relationship to each other. A women's movement can have an impact in changing the position of women as a whole relative to men. Or, as in Iran as a result of the Islamic fundamentalist revolution, women's position, as a whole, has declined significantly relative to men.

It is important to emphasize this last point. Societies are in a constant state of change. Systems of stratification within societies are also constantly changing. The changes can be dramatic, as the revolutionary change that occurred in Russia in 1917 and during the last decade, Cuba in 1952, China in 1949, or today's South Africa or Afghanistan. Or these changes can be more gradual and less fundamentally disruptive or shocking to the society, as are changes in systems of stratification in our own society. That is not to say that the levels of violence associated with the changes are any more or less in societies that experience quick, dramatic changes. For, as we see, the level of violence that occurs within a stable society as it relates to systems of stratification (class, gender, and ethnicity) may be far greater than what is found in societies that achieve quicker more dramatic changes in systems of stratification, although we may be more likely to recognize the violence in the latter.

HIERARCHICAL STRUCTURES BETWEEN SOCIETIES

Not only is it crucial for understanding the nature of structural violence to look at the nature of systems of inequality within societies, but equally if not more important as it relates to violence is to look at the structure of inequality between societies. Societies in the world are part of a larger hierarchical system that has an impact on the life chances of their populations as a whole and the

life chances of people who occupy different positions within systems of stratification within these societies.

Godrej (1995) notes that in Britain the richest ten people have as much
wealth as twenty-three poor countries with over 174 million people. Citizens of
the United States spent $30 billion dollars on jewelry and watches in 1991. This
sum is equivalent to the entire GNP of twenty low-income countries. The
wealthiest fifth of the world's population controls 85 percent of global income
while the poorest fifth lives off 1.4 percent of the income. The wealthiest countries of the world control most of the world's grain production, most of which
they use to feed livestock. At the same time almost a billion people in the world
do not have enough access to grain to fulfill minimum nutritional requirements
for a healthy life. Godrej notes that with money-economies firmly in place the
wealthy can pull markets in whichever direction they like. Something as basic
as food is completely skewed by the demands of the wealthy. Industrial countries contain 24 percent of the world's population, but they manage to use 48
percent of the world's grain and 61 percent of its meat. In fact they stuff quite
a lot of this grain into what will become the meat that they consume or in the
pets of their owners (Godrej, 1995, 9). While people in the poorest countries
die from disease of malnutrition, people in the wealthiest countries die, although on the average much later, from diseases of overconsumption and glut-
tony (i.e., heart disease and diabetes). How did this pattern of distribution, this
hierarchy of people of different nations come about?

Imperialism refers to the institutionalized pattern of domination of some
countries over others. Although imperialism precedes capitalism, it develops
further into a worldwide system as a product of capitalist development. In this
context, capitalism not only describes the nature of production in a given society but it is fundamentally an organizational framework for the world.

The study of capitalism as a world system is the study of imperialism, the
control and dominance of more developed over less developed societies.
Modern-day imperialism is rooted in the process whereby capitalists seek to
preserve and increase their capital through the extension of markets and production to locations outside their home societies. The driving force behind this
extension of capitalist relations is the competition between capitalists in the
marketplace. Competition between capitalists compels them to keep expanding capital in order to preserve it; thus progressive accumulation of surplus is
a necessity for the survival of individual capitalists. For the modern-day corporation, the rule still holds: you grow or you die in the marketplace. Owners
must seek ways of generating and realizing increasing levels of surplus and
must find additional outlets for the productive use of this increasing surplus to
keep extending the process. In the first case, owners search the globe for
cheaper costs of materials and labor, and for ways of making the process of
production more efficient by reducing the amount of time required to reproduce the labor power of the workers. In the second case, they search the
globe for new investment opportunities where their capital can produce more

surplus and more markets to realize this surplus or profits. Dowd (1993, 61) notes that expansion and exploitation are central to capitalist development.

> From its beginnings, capitalist economic expansion has depended upon intermittent and deepening waves of geographic expansion. Increasing access to exploitable cheap labor, natural resources, and broader markets has lifted the volumes of trade, investment, and production for the core (center or imperialist) national economies. This has allowed the maintenance or increase of profits and, in raising the level of socially defined subsistence, has helped to reduce social conflict in the core countries, but at the expense of external populations.

There are three broad stages of imperialism: plunder, trade, and finally direct investment (Edwards, Reich, and Weisskopf, 1978). In each stage, the societies that are dominated play a crucial role in the development of the dominating or imperialist societies. The plunder of the European explorers of the fifteenth, sixteenth, and seventeenth centuries serves as an important source of primitive accumulation.

Societies in African, Asia, Central and South America were divided up by the dominant European powers and later the United States to be sources for cheap resources and labor for the extraction of raw materials for the rapid expansion of the industries in the dominant countries. Populations were slaughtered and enslaved in order to enhance the riches of those who were dominant in these countries of the center of the world system. Agricultural systems and industries that existed and prospered in these dominated societies were destroyed in order to fit them into this new international system of exploitation. The economic and political systems of native peoples of India, South Africa, Mexico, North and South America (such as the Cherokee, Aztec, Mayan) were destroyed and reconstructed into a pattern of economic and political dependency on the colonizing power. Lord Lugard, one of the architects of British colonial rule in Africa, noted that "The partition of Africa was, as we all recognize, due primarily to the economic necessity of increasing the supplies of raw materials and food to meet the needs of industrialized nations of Europe" (Institute of Race Relations, 1982, 2). Racist belief systems were promoted to justify and extend the domination of people of color in these societies. Their history and their accomplishments were denied as they became defined as primitive, uncivilized, heathen, and savage. These beliefs of inherent inequality provided the justification for the violence and control of these populations. This is the same pattern of justification that we essentially see in most patterns of violence as noted in the third and fourth principles of violence outlined in chapter 1.

The second stage followed the industrialization of the capitalist nations of Western Europe. As industrialization ensued, the European owning class saw the lesser developed societies as not only a source of raw materials, disposing of surplus value (investment capital) and new markets to realize the surplus, but also a place to dispose of their surplus population (originally criminals, heretics and the poor became the first settlers of the colonies). Cecil Rhodes, British financier and colonial statesman, made this point most succinctly:

> I was in the East End of London yesterday and attended a meeting of the unemployed. I listened to the wild speeches, which were just a cry for bread, bread, bread, and on my way home I pondered over the scene and I became more than ever convinced of the importance of imperialism. . . . My cherished idea is a solution, i.e., in order to save the 40,000,000 inhabitants of the United Kingdom from a bloody civil war, we colonial statesman must acquire new lands to settle the surplus population, to provide new markets for the goods produced by them in the factories and mines. The empire, as I have always said, is a bread and butter question. If you want to avoid civil war, you must become imperialists. (Institute of Race Relations, 1982, 21)

With the rapid growth of world trade, capitalists in the dominant societies increasingly exported capital to the dominated societies to develop both the extraction of raw materials and eventually the markets for the disposal of finished goods. Sherman notes that "from 1890 to the Second World War was the peak period of colonialism, when all the world was divided among the West European and North American powers. In the late 1940s and 1950s a new era began with formal independence achieved by hundreds of millions of people throughout Asia and Africa as a result of struggles unleashed by the impact of two world wars, the Russian and Chinese revolutions, and the long pent-up pressures for liberation" (Sherman, 1987, 236). This period of imperialism during the nineteenth and early twentieth centuries is often referred to as the period of Pax Britannia. In short, the peace, or more accurately put the violence, of British Imperialism. Britain ruled the seas and the sun never set on the British Empire.

The last stage of imperialism has emerged in the second half of the twentieth century. The indigenous populations of the first stage of conquest and domination have either been destroyed or make up the most impoverished dominated sectors of the population of the societies that they occupy. Settlers exported from the dominant countries during the second stage have long assumed dominant positions within these societies. However, control or political domination from the center is still maintained by the economic and political ties that have long been established and institutionalized. The colonial structures of the preceding period have been replaced by neocolonial structures and capitalist penetration by multinational corporations. Overt, direct political domination by the imperialist powers is replaced by covert political domination. Sherman (1987) states, regarding the current hierarchy between nations of the world:

> On the one side are all the under-developed and newly "independent" countries, still under foreign economic domination, still facing all the old obstacles to development. On the other side are the advanced capitalist countries, still extracting vast profits from the dependent Third World. The imperialist group includes all those who extract profits by trade and investment. Thus, it includes most of West

Europe, Japan, and the United States. Most imperialist control now comes
through economic and monetary penetration, not direct occupation. The control
ranges from blatant forms such as subsidies and military supplies to highly complex monetary agreements. (236)

After World War II is the period of Pax Americana where the United States has
assumed dominance in the world system of imperialism. The United States is
the dominant military, economic, and political power in the world. Its responsibility and interests are in maintaining the world capitalist system with its
hierarchy between the societies of the center and the periphery for the benefit of its capitalist class.

The effect of imperialism on the development of the dominated societies has
varied with these different stages. Beginning with the second stage and advanc-
ing with the third stage, there is the implantation of capitalist development in
countries in the periphery, although this form of capitalist development is of a
dependent nature. This dependent economic development has three characteristics. The first is that of unequal trade. In the earliest stages it takes the form of
an exchange of raw materials by the dominated country for finished products
produced in the dominant countries. In the next stages it takes the form of the
importation of light manufactured component products in exchange for the end
product to be fully assembled in the dominant countries. Sherman notes that
most foreign capital invested in less developed countries still goes into raw materials extraction, in spite of the recent spread of some foreign investment to
manufacturing in certain countries. This pattern is more fully developed than earlier patterns of unequal trade like the case of West Africa during the first stage of
imperialism where slaves were shipped from West Africa to the West Indies and
the United States. Coffee, cotton, sugar and rum were then shipped from those
areas to Europe. Last, manufactured products including guns were shipped from
England to the West African slave traders to pay for the slaves (Gage, 1991).

The second characteristic of dependent development is that because the export trade in dominated countries is principally in agricultural products and
minerals, there is minimal industrial development in these countries. The
economy in the dominated country is geared principally to the needs of the
world market. Agricultural production that was for the local market of the consumer is transformed into cash crops for world export. In exchange for these
cash crops, there is the importation from the dominant countries of expensive
durable goods for the small class of well-off consumers, capital goods or machinery to increase the production for export, and processed foods of lesser
nutritional value to replace the fresh foods produced for export or displaced
by cash crop production. Sherman (1987), citing a UN Development report,
notes that through the first half of the 1980s, Third World countries had 79 percent of their exports in food, mineral fuels, and crude materials. The developed capitalist countries had 75 percent of their exports in machinery and
equipment, chemicals, and other manufactured goods.

The third characteristic of dependent development is that capital flows are on balance out of the dominated country to the dominant countries. This net surplus outflow restricts the development to that which is subservient to the interests of capitalists in the dominant countries. At any rate, in the present stage of mature imperialism, the situation is that the export of capital is exceeded by foreign earnings of the imperialist countries. "The profits (and interest payments) from the underdeveloped countries to the imperialist countries are greater than the flow of investments (and loans) going the other way. . . . Thus, for the entire period 1950–1975, the U.S. direct investment outflow was a total of 68.4 billion. In the very same period, investment income receipts flowing into the United States from direct investments were $110.6 billion. Hence, the U.S. economy gained $42.2 billion from abroad in that period in receipts minus costs" (U.S. Council on International Economic Policy, 1977; cited in Sherman, 1987, 240).

From 1950 to 1965, Sherman observes that in Latin America U.S. corporations invested $3.8 billion but extracted $11.3 billion, for a net flow of $7.5 billion from that area to the United States. Similarly, in Africa and Asia from 1950 through 1965 American corporations invested 5.2 billion, while transferring to the United States $14.3 billion in profits, for a net flow of $9.1 billion to the United States. Sherman also notes that in general the rates of return are much greater overseas; in 1974 the rate of return on investment (income/average capital invested) was 21 percent in the underdeveloped countries and only 10.5 percent in the developed countries; in 1980 the rate of return was 13.3 from the developed; but 52.2 from the underdeveloped, and in 1984, the rate of return was 9 percent from the developed, but 13 percent from the underdeveloped (Sherman, 1987, 240–41).

Production in the dominated countries is increasingly controlled by foreign capital. Initially this production was land. As dependent capitalist development continues it increasingly becomes factories, banks, and sales and distribution networks. In today's world economy the largest companies are owned by foreigners or, if there are restrictions on majority ownership by the government, foreigners will generally have a controlling interest. For example, in the 1970s and early 1980s in Brazil more than half of total manufacturing sales were accounted for by foreign owned companies (Bello, 1994). Today, almost 48 percent of the largest companies in the world are U.S. corporations, another 30 percent are from Europe and another 10 percent are Japanese (Petras, 2002). That's 98 percent of the largest corporations in the world that dominate world markets are headquartered in the dominant capitalist countries of the world. Petras notes that the world's markets are divided among 238 leading U.S. and 153 European companies and banks. This concentration and control according to Petras "defines the imperial nature of the world economy, together with the markets they control, the raw materials they pillage (80 percent of the leading oil and gas companies are U.S. and EU owned), and the labor they exploit" (Petras, 2002, 5). As Petras notes, this corporate penetration cuts across broad areas of the economies of the world and the United States and its corporations controlled by the its capitalist class are in a dominant position. "Within the imperial system, U.S. economic power is still dominant. Five of the top ten banks are U.S., six of the top ten pharmaceutical-biotech companies, four of the top ten telecommunications companies, seven of the top information technology companies, four of the top ten gas and oil companies, nine out of the top ten software companies, four of the top ten insurance companies, and nine of the top ten general retail companies" (Petras, 2002, 5).

One result of dependent capitalist development is that the economic cycles in the dominated countries are rooted in the supply and demand of the few raw materials exported. In countries like Algeria, Bangladesh, Burundi, Gabon, Ghana, Guinea-Bissau, Iran, Libya, Mauritius, Nigeria, Uganda, and Zambia more than 75 percent of their income is derived from one product (Institute for Race Relations, 1982). Sherman (1987) concludes that the colonial era left the economies of the underdeveloped countries very dependent on foreign demand and consequently very sensitive to the capitalist world economy's business cycle of expansion and depression.

In addition to this dependence on a narrow export market, the dominated countries are very dependent on foreign investment. Both factors make the economies of dependent capitalist nations subject to enormous fluctuations as a result of forces beyond their control. Sherman mentions the case of Ceylon where 80 percent of the population are employed directly or indirectly in the production and handling of raw material exports (tea, rubber, and coconuts). As the market for these products changes with demand in the world market, the economy of Ceylon is subject to change as well. Countries whose economies have been developed to fulfill the needs for a few raw materials used in production in dominant countries have also become increasingly vulnerable as a result of import substitution and increasing competition from other depressed dominated producers.

Not only do capitalists from the dominating countries in the world extract more capital than they invest in the dominated countries, but capitalists within these dominated countries also export their investment capital to banks and investment houses in the center for safety and high returns in the currency of the dominating nations. George (1988) observes that these dominated countries fall deeper into debt to subsidize the imperialist relationships by the funding of economic development strategies that are export oriented (production of raw materials for export to the center). The debt is also a product of the corruption of political elites and to pay for an increasing supply of weaponry to control a population that is increasingly displaced. Finance capitalists in the dominant counties of the world (especially those within the United States) extract increasing amounts of capital from the dominated countries to pay interest payments. For Latin America alone, new capital inflows (both aid and investment) came to under $38 billion between 1982 and 1985, while it paid back $144 billion in debt service. Net transfer from poor to rich: $106 billion (George, 1988,

63). This occurs during a time when per capita GNP had declined, and poverty and unemployment had increased. Thus the dominated countries becomes increasingly impoverished relative to those countries that are dominant, and those who do not own and control production continue to lose position relative to capitalists in their own society and capitalists in the dominating countries. Thus levels of inequality within dominated countries and between dominated and dominating countries increase as a product of imperialism. The 1993 UN Human Development Report notes that the global income disparity has doubled during the past three decades. The richest 20 percent of the world's population now receive more than 150 times the income of the poorest 20 percent. Almost one-third of the total world population, or 1.3 billion people, are in absolute poverty (UN Development Programme, 1993).

George analyzes the impact of dependent capitalist development throughout Africa and finds that the results are extremes in income and wealth inequality, increasing levels of poverty and malnutrition as the economy is less and less responsive to the needs of the majority of the population, economic displacement of the peasant population which in these countries is the majority as cultivable land becomes used for cash crop production for export, proletarianization of the population at very low wages and unsafe and hazardous working conditions, and increasing despoilization of the environment.

In regard to dependent development in Latin America, George (1988, 120) notes that

> the [South American] continent is the world's record-breaker for unequal income distribution. Brazilian, Mexican or Venezuelan elites need no lessons from the upper classes of New York, London or Milan in the fine art of money-flaunting. Latin American upper classes are, if anything, more opulent, more flamboyant in their conspicuous consumption. They can also draw on a larger pool of miserable and unprotected, unemployed people for servants than can their counterparts in the North. It is their elites that have made capital flight a national sport and a bonanza for the banking industry.

Gage (1991) notes that Brazil is the fourth largest food-exporter in the world, yet is the sixth hungriest country in the world. The 2001 United Nations Development report indicates that in Brazil the bottom 20 percent received 2.6 percent of the income and the top 10 percent received approximately 47 percent.

The principle vehicle for economic penetration and imperialist relations is the multinational corporation, beginning with the British East India Company and the British and Dutch Banking houses of the sixteenth and seventeenth centuries to Chase Manhattan, General Motors, Nestlé, and Coca-Cola today. Jalee (1965, 22) states that "through the multinational corporations, American capital directly owns a large chunk of West European industry, and the capitalists of all the imperialist countries together own the major industrial enterprises of the underdeveloped countries. There are no reliable figures for the Third World as a whole which measure the extent of foreign economic intervention, but it is certain that many, perhaps even most of the industrial undertakings of the underdeveloped countries are foreign-owned or controlled." Godrej (1995) reports that in 1989 transnational corporations controlled 70 percent of international trade and 80 percent of all land growing export crops. At the same time, transnational corporations only employed 3 percent of the world's paid labor. The UN Development Program (UNDP) notes in its Human Development Report (1999) that many global corporations now wield more economic power than nation-states. Fifty of the largest 100 economies in the world are run by multinationals, not by countries. For example, Mitsubishi is bigger than Saudi Arabia, General Motors is larger than either Thailand, Greece, Norway, or South Africa, and Wal-Mart is bigger than Malaysia, Israel or Colombia. The report notes that the combined annual revenues of the biggest 200 corporations are greater than those of 182 nation-states that contain 80 percent of the world's population. Ellwood notes that these corporate actors act in their short-term economic interests and not in the interests of the countries that they have invested capital. "Giant private companies have become the driving force behind economic globalization, wielding more power than many nation-states. Business values of efficiency and competition at all costs now dominate the debate on social policy, the public interest and the role of government. The tendency to monopoly combined with decreasing rates of profit drives and structures corporate decision-making—without regard for the social, environmental and economic consequences of those decisions" (Ellwood, 2001, 53).

Sherman (1987) notes that on the one side are all the underdeveloped and newly "independent" countries, still under foreign economic domination, still facing all the old obstacles to development. On the other side are the advanced capitalist countries, still extracting vast profits from the dependent Third World. The imperialist group includes all those who extract their profits by trade and investment. Thus, it includes most of Western Europe, Japan, and the United States. Most imperialist control now comes through economic and monetary penetration, not direct occupation. The control ranges from blatant forms such as subsidies and military supplies to highly complex monetary agreements including loans and direct and indirect investments. When all else fails, however, there is still the control that comes from direct military violence either by the military of the dominated countries that are trained and armed by the dominant capitalist countries (particularly the U.S.) or by the military of the dominant powers themselves. With military bases in more than sixty countries, fleets in strategic locations and rapid deployment forces that can respond in less than twenty-four hours to areas of instability of strategic interest, the United States is positioned to maintain its dominance in the world economy.

Economic dependency leads to political dependency. In the dominated countries there is often a weak internal ruling class, but the military grows in importance to deal with civil unrest resulting from investment strategies that displace and impoverish peasants. The United States as the dominant country in the imperialist system since World War II has increasingly played an important role in (1) policing (overtly by the U.S. military and covertly by the

Central Intelligence Agency) the world to maintain the security of market relations and foreign investment, (2) subsidizing military control and policing in the dominated country through training programs and the sale of weaponry, (3) subsidizing increasing investment by the dominant capitalist class through aid programs, and the operation of the World Bank, International Monetary Fund, and World Trade Organization which it controls and (4) subsidizing and influencing elections in developing countries to legitimate and maintain regimes that serve the interest of those who are dominant in the world system.

The role of violence should not be underestimated in maintaining the relations of domination in the imperialist system. In regard to Central America, the United States throughout the twentieth century has regularly used force to maintain its relationship of dominance. In 1927, Undersecretary of State Robert Olds stated: "We do control the destinies of Central America and we do so for the simple reason that the national interest absolutely dictates such a course. . . . Until now Central America has always understood that governments which we recognize and support stay in power, while those we do not recognize and support fail" (Barry, Wood, and Preusch, 1982, 5). President Taft was quite clear as to the imperialist goals of the United States capitalist class when in 1912 he stated: "The day is not far distant when three Stars and Stripes at three equidistant points will mark our territory: one at the North Pole, another at the Panama Canal, and the third at the South Pole" (Pearce, 1982, 17).

The Monroe Doctrine clearly defined the early U.S. Empire, and the Evart Doctrine developed under President Coolidge further justified intervention in the internal affairs of Latin American countries to protect the foreign holdings of U.S. nationals, later to become multinational corporations. Since the 1898 invasion of Cuba, the United States has dispatched troops to protect American interests, or the interests of the capitalist class, in Central America and the Caribbean twenty times, the invasions of Panama and Grenada being the most recent. But covert operations are more frequent and less costly, like the recent U.S. involvement in Nicaragua illustrate. The U.S. government, beginning in 1981, organized, funded (weapons and supplies), and directed the *contra* invasion and campaign of terrorism against the Nicaraguan population in order to force a second election in which the U.S. funded, pro–free market candidate could win the election (Mathews, 1986). Sharkley (1990) notes that by 1989, 30,000 Nicaraguans had been killed, the United States spent between $4 to $6 billion in training and arming the contras, and spent an additional $12.5 million or $7.00 per voter for the promotion of democracy. Most of this money was directly or indirectly funneled into the election campaign of the U.S. supported candidate Chamorro who won this second election.

General Smedley D. Butler, who headed many of the American interventions in the region during the early part of the twentieth century provided a frank accounting of his achievements:

> I spent thirty-three years and four months in active service as a member of our country's agile military force—the Marine corps. I served in all commissioned

ranks from a second lieutenant to major-general. And during that period I spent most of my time being a high-class muscle man for Big Business, for Wall Street, and for the bankers. In short, I was a racketeer for capitalism. . . . Thus, I helped make Mexico and especially Tampico safe for American oil interests in 1914. I helped make Haiti and Cuba a decent place for the National City Bank to collect revenues in. . . . I helped purify Nicaragua for the international banking house of Brown Brothers in 1909–1912. I brought light to the Dominican Republic for American sugar interests in 1916. I helped make Honduras right for American fruit companies in 1903. (Pearce, 1982, 20)

Although our military and political leaders would not be as blatant today in describing our role in maintaining and benefiting from a system of imperialism, the pattern continues. We are involved overtly and covertly around the world, maintaining stability and protecting and furthering our national interests as they are rooted in maintaining open markets and the rights of private property, both of which are in the interests of the dominant capitalist class in the world, those principally in the United States, Western Europe, and Japan. Table 8.1 summarizes imperialist forms of economic and political domination in the world today.

Table 8.1. Imperialist Forms of Economic and Political Domination

Economic Domination

1. *Control of production*—Direct or indirect ownership in dominated countries is by outsiders (multinational corporations, finance capital, foreign entrepreneurs).
2. *Debt to finance capital* (World Bank and IMF)—Structural Adjustment Programs— Debt established to move development in the direction of dependency on dominant actors in world economy or market.
3. *Direction of capital flows*—Capital flows principally from dominated countries to dominant countries. This is in terms of profit repatriation, debt payments, and investment capital from capitalists in dominated countries.
4. *Maldevelopment*—Stress on extraction industries—development is for the export market—principally for dominating countries of the world economy. Production geared to world market controlled by wealthiest consumers. Importation in dominated countries principally caters to top 20 percent of the population.
5. *Economic displacement of peasant populations* as a result of transformation of agricultural production for cash crops to outside markets. Increasing problems of poverty and inequality.
6. *Increasing economic concentration and inequality* as a result of the penetration of multinational corporations and the increasing capital intensive nature of production.
7. *Economic development decision making dominated by foreign interests*—The World Trade Organization is the principal coordinating agency of the world economy.
8. *Economic stabilization and destabilization efforts* as a means of foreign control— CIA, World Bank, IMF, WTO, AID programs function to maintain and extend dependent capitalist relations.
9. *AID programs also function to maintain and increase dependency*—Most aid tied to purchase of U.S. goods and services; also, aid is geared to development model that is export-oriented economy. Aid is also used as a form of international welfare that creates dependency.
10. *Imbalance of trade*—Protectionism in the center (dominating countries) and open access in the periphery (dominated countries).

Political Domination

1. *Control over selection of leaders*—Foundation for democracy/CIA-U.S. public and private funding and assisting in the election of pro-U.S. candidates.
2. *Political stabilization and destabilization efforts*—State terrorism to counter groups that threaten the stability of a client state and to destabilize a regime that threatens dominant capitalist interests.
3. *Foreign military bases*—U.S. has more than 300 bases around the world in sixty different countries, and a naval force in every major international body of water.
4. *Arming and training of domestic military and police forces*—Military and police dependent on dominating countries (particularly the U.S.) for hardware and training.
5. *Propaganda activities*—U.S. Central Intelligence Agency has established direct (ownership) and indirect (establishing friendly sources for disinformation) control of foreign media. Electronic and print mass media is increasingly controlled by multinational corporations throughout the world.
6. *Military interventions*—U.S. police actions to stabilize countries that have unrest because of the impact of developmental strategy on majority of countries' population. Military interventions against "renegade" countries whose actions threaten imperialist market relations.
7. *Establishment of military alliances for stabilization*—OAS, SEATO, NATO, etc.— Legitimate intervention by the dominant capitalist country and as a means of establishing informal controls through the linkage between client states.
8. *Educational/cultural exchanges* to promote modernization as defined in terms of dependent capitalist development.
9. *Political advisers* from dominant capitalist countries to promote "capitalist" forms of democratic government structures.
10. *Importance of imperialism* for domestic political stability in the dominant countries. Importation of cheap products reduces wage pressure from workers in dominant countries. Nationalism sentiments are generated by wars against dominated countries.

STRUCTURAL VIOLENCE AS INHIBITING HUMAN DEVELOPMENT

What are the violent outcomes of these patterns of inequality that occur within a society and between societies in the world system? One outcome is the inability of the vast majority of the world's people to develop their human potential. In this context the hierarchical relations in a society and the world inhibit people from living in health as many years as possible, and developing their intellectual and physical capabilities to their fullest potential. The UN Development Programme (2001) has developed an index (HDI) of human development that measures people's ability to live a long and healthy life, to communicate and participate in the life of the community and to have sufficient resources to obtain a decent living. The measure combines indicators of real purchasing power, education, and health. From the perspective of the Human Development Programme, human development is a process of enlarging people's choices.

The index is composed of the following indicators: health (longevity at birth), education (literacy weighted two-thirds, years of schooling one-third), and income (based on law of diminishing returns and GDP per capita relative to the poverty line). A score of 1 on the index indicates that the country is highest on all measures of human development, a score lower than 1 indicates that the country is lower on one or more of the indicators of human development compared to the country that has achieved the highest. It is important to realize that since we are principally focusing on averages within a given country on the measures of life expectancy and education, the measure is not sensitive to inequality within the country on these dimensions. Separate HDIs are calculated for different ethnic groups, by gender and income groups to determine the level of inequality in human development within a given country.

Two other indices have been developed to measure a country's development. The Human Poverty Index or HPI concentrates on the three essential elements of human life already reflected in the HDI: longevity (percentage of people expected to die before age forty), knowledge (percentage of adults who are illiterate) and a decent living standard (the percentage of people with access to health services and to safe water, and the percentage of malnourished children under five). The Gender Development Index or GDI measures achievement in the same basic capabilities as the HDI does, but takes note of inequality in achievement between women and men. The GDI is simply the HDI discounted, or adjusted downwards, for gender inequality.

Table 8.2 illustrates the distribution of selected countries in terms of human development. The disparity in human development across the two classification of high and low developed countries is dramatic. For example, the Human Development Index for Norway, which received the highest rating of development was .939, while for Sierra Leone, which received the lowest score, it was .258.

Looking at the differences in the separate components of the Human Development Index reveal the human costs of this disparity in HDI scores. For example, the life expectancy in Japan is 80.8 years, while for Sierra Leone it is more than forty-one years less at 38.3 years of life. The Swedes expect less than 2 percent of their population to die before the age of forty, while in Rwanda almost 52 percent of its population dies before the age of forty. Stolnitz (1983, 415) notes that international differences in expectations of life at birth twenty years ago were at historically high orders of magnitude—thirty-five years or more—with unprecedented convergence among developed countries, equally unprecedented disparities in the less developed countries, and vast consequent interregional variations in causes of death, quality of life, and socioeconomic arrangements.

Differences are also large when we look at education and income differences. The rate of adult illiteracy in the most advanced countries of the world is negligible. While the rate of adult illiteracy is very high in the least developed nations of the world where the majority of these populations are illiterate. Income disparities are also very great and the gap between the income between the most and least developed countries has grown dramatically since the 1960s. In 1999, the GDP per capita for the United States was $31,872, for Sierra Leone it was $448.

In general the level of income and wealth inequality internationally is growing within nations and between peoples of the world. According to a World Bank Development Report (2001), in 1960, per capita GDP in the richest twenty

Table 8.2. Human Development Indicators—1999

Country	Human Development Index	Gender Related Development Index	Life Expectancy at Birth	% of People Expected to Die Before 40	Adult Illiteracy Rate	% Under-Weight Children Under 5	Mortality Rate/1000 Under 5	Access to Essential Drugs	% Using Improved Water Source
Ten Most Developed									
Norway	.939	.937	78.4	2.4	—	0	4	100	100
Australia	.936	.935	78.8	3.0	—	0	5	100	100
Canada	.936	.934	78.7	2.7	—	0	6	100	100
Sweden	.936	.931	79.6	1.9	—	0	4	99	100
Belgium	.935	.928	78.2	2.9	—	0	6	99	
United States	.934	.932	76.8	3.9	—	1*	8	99	100
Iceland	.932	.930	79.1	2.3	—	0	5	100	
Netherlands	.931	.926	78.0	2.2	—	0	5	100	100
Japan	.928	.921	80.8	2.1	—	0	4	100	100
Finland	.928	.923	77.4	2.8	—	0	5	98	100
Twenty Least Developed									
Zambia	.427	.420	41.0	53.6	22.8	24.0	202	66	64
Côte d'Ivoire	.426	.409	47.8	40.2	54.3	24.0*	171	80	77
Senegal	.423	.413	52.9	28.5	63.6	22.0	118	66	78

(continued)

Table 8.2. Continued

Country	Human Development Index	Gender Related Development Index	Life Expectancy at Birth	% of People Expected to Die Before 40	Adult Illiteracy Rate	% Under-Weight Children Under 5	Mortality Rate/1000 Under 5	Access to Essential Drugs	% Using Improved Water Source
Angola	.422	—	45.0	41.6	—	42.0	295	20	38
Benin	.420	.402	53.6	29.7	61.0	29.0	156	77	63
Eritrea	.416	.403	51.8	31.7	47.3	44.0	105	57	46
Gambia	.398	.390	45.9	40.5	64.3	26.0	75	90	62
Guinea	.397	—	47.1	38.3	—	—	181	93	48
Malawi	.397	.386	40.3	50.4	40.8	30.0	211	44	57
Rwanda	.395	.391	39.9	51.9	34.2	27.0	180	44	41
Mali	.378	.370	51.2	38.5	60.2	40.0	235	60	65
Cent African Rep	.372	.361	44.3	45.3	54.6	27.0	172	50	60
Chad	.359	.346	45.5	41.0	59.0	39.0	198	46	27
Guinea-Bissau	.339	.308	44.5	42.2	62.3	23.0*	200	44	49
Mozambique	.323	.309	39.8	49.2	56.8	26.0	203	50	60
Ethiopia	.321	.308	44.1	43.6	62.6	47.0	176	66	24
Burkina Faso	.320	.306	46.1	43.0	77.0	36.0	199	60	—
Burundi	.309	.302	40.6	50.1	53.1	37.0*	176	20	—
Niger	.274	.260	44.8	41.4	84.7	50.0	275	66	59
Sierra Leone	.258	—	38.3	51.6	—	29.0*	316	44	28

* Data refer to a year or period other than that specified, differ from the standard definition or refer to only part of a country.

** Data from the Human Development Report (2001).

countries was eighteen times that in the poorest twenty countries. By 1995, this gap had widened to thirty-seven times, that is the gap doubled in thirty-five years. Milanovic (1999) calculates that world inequality has increased significantly from 1988 to 1993. The Human Development Report (1994) indicates that the richest fifth of the world's population consumes more of the world's wealth than the remaining four-fifths taken together. The richest fifth of the world's population receives 82.7 percent of the income, while the poorest fifth receives 1.4 percent. The *New Internationalist* (1994) notes that between 1987 and 1993 the number of billionaire families and individuals more than doubled, from ninety-eight to 233. A more recent estimate in 1999 has this figure more than double to 514, approximately, two out of every three are from the United States (Merrill Lynch/Gemini Consulting, 2001). The United Nations Human Development Report (2001), notes that in 1960 the richest one-fifth of the world's people were thirty times richer than the poorest fifth, by 1997 the ratio was 70 to 1. The worlds richest 101 individuals and families now control wealth valued at some $452 billion, more than the total yearly income of the entire population of India, Pakistan, Bangladesh, Nigeria, and Indonesia put together: 1.5 billion people in all.

MORBIDITY AND MORTALITY DIFFERENCES

One indicator of structural violence not included in the Human Development Index that nevertheless illustrates the differences in the life chances of people around the world is the mortality rate for children under five years of age. In Norway, four out of every 1,000 children die before they reach the age of five. In Senegal, the rate is almost twenty-nine times greater: 118 out of every 1,000 Senegalese children die before they reach the age of five. The rate is almost seventy-nine times greater in Sierra Leone, where 316 out of every 1,000 die before the age of five (Human Development Report, 2001).

A similar pattern of results is found when we look at infant and maternal mortality rate differences. What this means is that as a result of the location of one's birth, being born in Norway as opposed to Sierra Leone, you would have a greater chance for life. Similarly, when we look at death rates of mothers giving birth, we find significant differences that are a result of countries' locations in the world system of stratification. In Norway the average rate for the period 1980 to 1999 is six deaths per 100,000 live births, while for the Central African Republic and Mozambique the rate is 1100 deaths per 100,000 live births.

Although the differences are great between countries, great differences may also be found within countries. For example, the rate of infant mortality in many poor neighborhoods in American central cities such as Detroit, Washington, D.C., New York, or Chicago is equivalent to the average rates in many poorer developing countries. Similar disparities are found in countries throughout Africa and Latin America between urban and rural areas. Thus the structures of inequality within a society compound the disparities in mortality and morbidity that we find between countries.

There are three major reasons why people die in any society. They either degenerate as a result of cancer and circulatory ailments, they are killed by communicable diseases, or they are killed by the products of the social and economic environment. These three factors may be intertwined so that for many in the world today their economic and social environment increases the likelihood that their bodies will degenerate at a more rapid rate or are more vulnerable to communicable diseases. When we look at patterns of disease and mortality, human beings' positions via systems of stratification form a crucial factor in accounting for who, when, and why people die. In all societies, those in dominated positions, especially as defined in terms of class and ethnicity, experience higher rates of morbidity and mortality than those who are in dominant positions experience. Furthermore, in terms of the stratification system that rank countries in the world system, those countries that are in dominated positions as defined in terms of the world political economic order generally have higher rates of mortality and morbidity than those who are in dominant positions do. Much of these differences in patterns are accounted for by differences in availability of survival needs (diet, shelter, clean water and air) and differences in access to medical services during times of need.

Each day, approximately 30,000 young children die from malnutrition and disease (UN Development Programme, 2001). The vast majority of these children reside in the countries of the Southern Hemisphere and the periphery of the world political economic system. This tragedy of child death is a result of the structure of inequality that exists within and between nations of the world. In Bolivia 51 percent of children between the ages of two and five are stunted in their development as a result of malnutrition. In Guatemala the percentage of children jumps to 68 percent of those two to five years of age. Many African and Asian countries that are listed as low human development countries also have more than 50 percent of their children between the ages of two and five stunted in their development as a result of malnutrition (UN Development Programme, 1993).

Access to safe water, sanitation, and health care is also a serious problem in many areas around the world. This also relates to the presence of disease and high mortality levels in these countries. These three factors directly relate to the socioeconomic conditions of people. For example, in Senegal 78 percent of the population does not have access to safe water. In Rwanda 8 percent of the population is using adequate sanitation facilities. In Sierra Leone 28 percent of the population has access to safe water and adequate sanitation (UN Development Programme, 2001). In regard to access to health care as measured by access to essential drugs, throughout most of the sub-Saharan region of Africa more than half of the population is deprived of access. This together with the problems of sanitation and access to safe water creates a serious assault on the quality and quantity of life as measured by mortality and morbidity rates.

To what degree can we talk of these problems as acts of structural violence? Of course in looking at what segments of the population are most likely to be denied access to these essential services and resources, it is uniformly the poorer segments of the society. Among the poor those who are most vulnerable are children and women, or in other words, those with the least amounts of power as defined in terms of systems of stratification. In the extremely poor countries noted, only the wealthiest segments of the society are shielded from these dangers.

Furthermore, decisions by the elite in many of these countries to purchase weaponry to maintain their positions of dominance, to provide for access to luxury goods, to provide for investment credits to encourage investments that will benefit elite segments of the society, as well as the high cost of corruption among governing elites, constitutes violence because it denies resources to the poorest segments to provide for access to safe water, sanitation and health care to prevent disease and shortened life spans. But, it is not just the decisions of the national elites that result in acts of structural violence. It may be the case that the actions of the international elite have a far greater impact as it relates to the occurrence of structural violence in the countries on the periphery of the world economy.

Let's look at the AIDS epidemic and ask to what degree can we consider the death from this disease an example of structural violence. The AIDS epidemic claimed 3 million lives in 2001. This is a disease that since its discovery approximately twenty years ago has infected 60 million persons. Forty million persons are currently infected. There were 5 million new infections in 2001. The epidemic has not peaked yet. Is there a pattern to this rate of infection and death? Yes, those who reside in the poorest nations are those with the highest concentrations of the disease. Ninety-eight percent of the deaths occur in the Southern Hemisphere of the world. More than 80 percent of the deaths have occurred in the sub-Saharan region of Africa, that region of the world that is the poorest. Those who live in the poorest regions and who are often the poorest (who live for the most part on less than one dollar a day) and with the least access to healthcare, sanitation, and safe water are most vulnerable. They are also least likely to afford the cost of the current drug treatment therapy the antiretroviral combination cocktail that sells for $10,000 to $15,000 a year in the U.S.

For years the United States threatened countries that attempted to manufacture their own version of the drug therapy in violation of copyright laws. U.S. pharmaceutical companies that manufactured the products expressed concern about the reduction in profits that they would experience if they lowered the prices to give greater access to those in developing countries. Millions of people died and the rate of death has continued to climb for each and every year. In May 2001, President Clinton stated that the U.S. would not challenge laws in African countries that seek to improve access to AIDS drugs. UNAIDS (the Joint United Nations program on HIV/AIDS) has pressured the major manufacturers of effective drug treatment to set lower prices for developing countries. Finally, five major pharmaceuticals joined an "Accelerated Access" program to negotiate 60 percent to 80 percent reductions in AIDS drug prices for poor nations. In accordance with this program, each country must negotiate the price of each AIDS cocktail component with each company. McGeary (2001) notes that there has been barely any impact noted thus far in the sub-Saharan region. She notes that while Senegal might haggle prices down the cost by 75 percent or 80 percent, the therapy is still too costly at $1,200 a year for people who earn $510 a year, Senegal's per capita income. Thus, death occurs from the disease and as a result of the structural position of the victim in the world system of stratification.

Farmer (1999) draws the parallel between the AIDS and the tuberculosis (TB) pandemics and raises doubts as to whether the medication to effectively treat AIDS will ever reach the vast majority of the world's victims. He notes that TB, like infectious diseases in general, disproportionately kill the poor. Throughout history this has been the case and it is the case today. He notes that by the 1960s TB had disappeared from the public's view. However, it had never disappeared from the life of the poor in poor countries around the world and in the shelters and among the poorest populations within the United States. Recently there has been a significant increase in tuberculosis among minority populations in the United States. This is despite the fact that there has been low-cost effective treatment available for more than fifty years. However, the vast majority of victims will be within the poorest populations of the poorest countries throughout the world. "Fifty years after the introduction of almost 100 percent effective combination therapy, tuberculosis remains the world's leading infectious cause of preventable deaths. If the World Health Organization is correct, tuberculosis killed some three million people in 1996—more than died from complications of HIV infection, and more than have died of tuberculosis in any one year since 1900. If we've done such a poor job delivering effective and inexpensive cures to people in the prime of their lives, what are our chances with medications that are less effective and hundreds of times as costly?" (Farmer, 1999, 266). Farmer claims that "it is difficult to document any impact of the new treatment regimens on worldwide tuberculosis incidence: in the current decade, an estimated 300 million people will become infected with tubercle bacilli; 90 million will develop active tuberculosis; and, if access to care does not become a global priority, 30 million will die" (1999, 212). Farmer claims that inequality itself constitutes our modern plague. The linkage between inequality and national mortality rates in countries in North America, Europe, and Asian was documented in an analysis of ten separate sets of data from eight different groups of researchers (Wilkinson, 1996). Wilkinson writes that "it is now clear that the scale of income differences in a society is one of the most powerful determinants of health standards in different countries, and that it influences health through its impact on social cohesion" (Wilkinson, 1996, ix).

IMPERIALIST RELATIONS AND WORLD DEBT

One recent area where the actions of policymakers and the world's financial elite have clearly resulted in increasing the levels of death, especially among the most helpless, is in the resolution of the world debt crisis. How this works is that the governing elites (usually, the military and the landed oligarchy) are persuaded by bankers from the dominating countries that a development strategy based on the classic model of dependent capitalist development (cash crop production for the world market, capital-intensive, single-crop agricultural production, heavy investment in infrastructural development to encourage investment by multinational corporations) will provide a greater investment return on their investments and the most efficient path for the economic development of the country.

Ellwood (2001) notes that the debt of the non–oil producing Third World increased fivefold between 1973 and 1982, reaching a staggering $612 billion. He notes that the foreign debts of developing countries are more than 2 trillion (i.e, 2 million million) U.S. dollars and still growing. He notes that this translates to a debt of over $400 for every man, women and child in the developing world where the average income in the very poorest countries is less than a dollar a day. In 1999 debt had reached $3,000 billion and an ever increasing portion of this new debt was to service interest payments on the old debt, to keep money circulating and to keep the system up-and-running (Ellwood, 2001).

Another feature of the debt crisis is the high level of corruption that occurs as leaders are persuaded through financial payoffs to follow this path of development. There are also many wasted projects (roadways to nowhere, airports in remote locations, production facilities that are extravagant and costly) for the benefit of generating graft and paybacks for the economic and political elite of the country. Corruption has historically been an important means to provide access by corporations from the dominant capitalist nations to the resources of poorer countries. "The largest single debt of the Philippines is the Bataan nuclear power station. Completed in the mid-1980s at a cost of $2.3 billion, it was built on an earthquake fault at the foot of a volcano, and has never been used. The nuclear power station was built by the U.S. multinational Westinghouse, in spite of a much lower bid from General Electric. The then president of Philippines, Ferdinand Marcos, overruled the choice of General Electric. Westinghouse admitted it paid a commission to a Marcos associate, and the New York Times estimates Marcos was given $80 million by Westinghouse" (Hanlon and Pettifor, 2000). Hanlon and Pettifor note that the World Bank's own evaluation of project performance in the 1990s showed that in the poorest countries, and in South Asia and Africa, between 60 percent and 70 percent of projects failed. Another example noted by Hanlon and Pettifor is the case of Nigeria where according to government commission at least sixty-one development projects financed by more than $5 billion in foreign loans have either failed or never completed. Hanlon and Pettifor note that Nigeria estimates that former military governments have stolen billions of dollars, and deposited these in British, U.S., and Swiss banks. Nigeria's foreign debt is now $34 billion.

Hanlon and Pettifor also cite the case of Bolivia where a lead and platinum refinery was built using untested technology and requiring more ore than could be produced by local mines. They note that the project doubled in cost to $250 million and was built with $100 million in Belgian and German export credits plus German bank loans. The project has never functioned but the loan is still being repaid. Peru also is still paying a $70 million loan for boats worth $18 million and which never worked properly, and for aircraft engines that were never delivered. In regard to the billions of dollars loaned to Russia by the IMF, the U.S. Central Intelligence Agency reported as long ago as 1995 that money from International Monetary Fund loans was going to Swiss banks, but nothing was done except to approve the second largest loan in IMF history to Russia. It is estimated that at least $20 billion has gone astray (Hanlon and Pettifor, 2001). And the list goes on about the corruption and ill-conceived projects that were more designed to facilitate access to markets and resources by multinational corporations of the dominant countries in the world and to provide for the graft for a corrupted elite who are ruling many of these countries.

Another feature of the dependent capitalist development strategy that is accelerated by the loans given by the IMF and World Bank is that there is increasing displacement of the peasant populations as their land is usurped by large landowners who are producing for the export market. Export oriented production is more concentrated and in most areas of production controlled by a relatively few transnational corporations. Kneen (1995) points out that about twenty large transnational corporations control most of the world's agriculture. Seven of the twelve largest agribusinesses are based in the United States.

Local food prices in these dependent capitalist countries climb dramatically as the level of production for the local market shrinks, and there is increasing importation of foodstuffs from the dominating capitalist countries. As mentioned earlier, the food that is imported from the dominant countries is most often processed. The processing results in lowering the nutritional value of the product, yet increasing the cost (corn flakes instead of corn or worse yet, powdered baby formula for mothers' milk). The size of the working class increases dramatically, lowering the price of wages as displaced peasants flood into the cities looking for work or sell their labor to large landowners. This displacement and concentration of land also may lead to serious problems of famine that we will discuss later in this chapter.

As the debt accumulates, and the economy of the dominated country is more vulnerable to swings in the world economy, especially as it relates to the cyclical swings of the few cash crops they are exporting, this makes it more and more difficult for the country to reduce the debt. More money is spent to encourage more investment to produce for the world market, attracting the investment of multinational corporations through tax incentive and infrastructure development projects, and more money is spent on the ever increasing military and police forces to maintain control of the growing poor and displaced population within the country. What results is an increasing cycle of debt, dependent development, and violence.

As the debt problem reaches a crisis, there is a serious possibility of default. After Mexico defaulted on it's loans in the early 1980s, there was greater pressure placed on debtor countries to speed up the access to their markets and resources. As the debt crisis increases bankers from the World Bank and the International Monetary Fund, financial agencies of the dominant capitalist countries (principally the United States, the country with the largest debt, more than several times greater than the debt of all dominated countries combined), step in to impose a solution referred to as structural adjustment, which places the burden of repayment increasingly on the poorest segment of the populations in these countries The United States principally in control of the IMF and World Bank applied this pressure beginning in the mid 1980s with the Baker plan during the Reagan administration on indebted countries to continue to (in the language of the bank) "structurally adjust" their economies. More money was made available by the World Bank and IMF to avoid the debt crisis and in exchange the countries had to open themselves up for a greater level of access for multinational corporations. This financial leverage pushed the developing countries of the Third World further down the road to development that was dependent upon the dominant capitalist nations for their markets and for their investment capital to compete in the world market. The multinational corporations, the largest based in the U.S., received more access to cheaper labor as currencies were devalued and unemployment increased as a result of the reduction in government employment and subsidies to the poor.

As part of the structural adjustment, these indebted countries are required to reduce the size of their state budgets, principally in the areas of welfare, employment, and health care. State security sections of the budget, military and police forces, are usually increased, as well as infrastructure development costs to increase further investment for world market production. Increasing levels of social control (military and police) are required in these countries to control the majority of the populations of these countries as they become increasingly impoverished. The United States is the nation that provides the majority of aid to finance increases in military and police to maintain stability in these countries. More money is also loaned in order to provide for these increases in social control. The civil wars that are occurring around the globe— Philippines, throughout the sub-Saharan region of Africa, throughout Latin America—increasingly stem from this development strategy.

The world's largest banks and leading finance capitalists also received tremendous returns on Third World debt as they were loaning money for the transformations of these societies along a dependent capitalist development path. "More conditions were extended to countries to acquire new loan money to help pay off the debts that were due. They included 'privatizing' state-owned enterprises, reducing the size and cost of government through massive public sector layoffs; cutting basic social services and subsidies on basic foodstuffs; and reducing barriers to trade" (Ellwood, 2001, 48). According to Ellwood, this restructuring was highly successful from the point of view of the private banks who siphoned off more than $178 billion from the South between 1984 and 1990.

Currencies are also usually devalued as part of the structural adjustment strategy in order to cheapen the cost of the resources acquired by foreign investors and reduce the cost of the exports to the world market. This also directly affects the costs of the increasing amounts of imported foods in the marketplace that are difficult for the working population to purchase as a result of the reduction of wages and increases in the number of unemployed. This is all part of the structural adjustment strategy to encourage investment by foreign corporations. Countries are also strongly encouraged to remove restrictions on foreign investment in industry and financial services, to institute a system of incentives for producing for export markets, and to remove market restrictions on imports in order to make their local industry more efficient in response to the increased competition from multinational corporations. Last, as mentioned, governments in these countries are required to privatize state enterprises as rapidly as possible and engage in deregulation of the marketplace in order to encourage foreign investment. The pattern is reproduced in Africa, Central America, South America, and Asia, in short throughout the Southern Hemisphere (Bolles, 1983; Korten, 1993; Ahmad, 1992; Dewitt and Petras, 1981; McAfee, 1991; Bello, 1994).

Bello (1994, 31) states that "with over 70 Third World countries submitting to IMF and World Bank programs in the 1980s, stabilization, structural adjustment, and shock therapy managed from distant Washington became the common condition of the South in that decade." Using panel analysis and a data set containing inequality measures for sixty-five nations at two points in time, Beer and Boswell (2001) find that high within-nation inequality is due in large part to greater dependence on foreign investment. Beer and Boswell contend that a shift in capital/labor relations brought about by globalization is responsible for increases in income inequality within countries of the developing world. This inequality has violent consequences of disease, impoverishment, and death.

According to Bello, Chile is the country with the longest-running structural adjustment program, beginning with the CIA planned overthrown of President Allende in 1973. During this period, more than 600 state enterprises were sold off. Trade barriers and tariffs were significantly reduced or eliminated. Foreign investment increased dramatically, and the Chilean economy was more integrated into the international economy than ever in its history. Foreign trade accounted for 57.4 percent of GDP in 1990, whereas in 1970 it accounted for only 35 percent. Financial markets were also deregulated and total debt throughout the 1970s and 1980s increased dramatically as the IMF and World Bank continued to loan money to the government to stabilize the economy and to continue its development along a path of dependent capitalist development. Deindustrialization and increasing dependence on the exportation of raw materials and processed goods were major forces in the transformation of the Chilean economy. In general, the economy experienced a slower economic growth rate per year during the period of structural adjustment than in the years prior to it. While the government continued to safeguard and subsidize the wealthy, it cut government services and welfare to the working class.

The impact of these policies by the government and imposed by the World Bank and International Monetary Fund was that the proportion of families living below the line of destitution rose from 12 to 15 percent between 1980 and 1990, and the percentage living below the poverty line (but above the line of destitution) rose from 24 to 26 percent. This meant that at the end of the Pinochet period some 40 percent, or 5.2 million, of a population of 13 million people were defined as poor in a country that had once boasted of having a large middle class. Poverty translated into hunger and malnutrition; for 40 percent of the population the daily calorie intake dropped to 1,629 in 1990, from 2,019 in 1970 and 1,751 in 1980 (Bello, 1994, 45). Bello further notes that during this same period the share of the national income going to the poorest 50 percent declined from 20.4 percent to 16.8 percent, while the share going to the richest 10 percent rose from 36.5 percent to 46.8 percent. At the same time that these measures were being imposed on the population, the level of state violence accelerated rapidly as the government terrorized the population in order to maintain control and preserve the system of inequality, and the level of economic violence increased as unions were outlawed and the industrial accident rate climbed dramatically.

Jamaica is another country that has experienced dramatic intervention by the U.S. government and multilateral lending agencies. In response to the structural adjustment program implemented in Jamaica to pay off its debt during the ten-year period from 1975 to 1985 (1) real expenditures on social services were cut by 41 percent; (2) government expenditures for debt service increased from 21 percent to 44 percent from 1981 to 1985; (3) real spending on education was cut by 40 percent between 1981 and 1985, which had an impact on the rate of passage of high school exit exams falling from 62 percent to 34 percent during the same period; (4) real spending on health was cut by 35 percent between 1982 and 1985, capital spending on housing dropped in 1985, falling to 11 percent of the level of 1982; and (5) the cost of purchasing the least-cost basket of minimum food requirements for a five-person household increased by 429 percent from 1979 to 1985 (McAfee, 1991).

A similar pattern of cutbacks directed at the poorest elements of the society to pay for the cost of the dependent development strategy can be found in the Dominican Republic. According to the Working Group on Debt of the Association of Caribbean Economists, the result has been that the rate of infant malnutrition, grade III, in one of the principal hospitals in Santo Domingo increased from 14 percent to 30.8 percent for admitted infants between 1977 and 1986; and from 3.9 percent to 10 percent for infant outpatients. Maternal mortality in a major maternal hospital in Santo Domingo grew from 15 to 22 per 100,000 between 1981 and 1985 (McAfee, 1991,17). McAfee notes that in regard to the impact of debt and structural adjustment programs on Caribbean countries, per capita food production for domestic use had declined in the vast majority of countries in the region and that 44 percent of the region's population consumed less than the minimum dietary requirement for protein and 56 percent had an insufficient caloric intake (McAfee, 1991).

Susan George notes in *A Fate Worse Than Debt* that nutritional studies of Peru between 1972 and 1983 show a steady increase in malnutrition for children under age six. "In the poorest neighborhoods of Lima and the shanty towns around it the percentage of undernourished children climbed from 24 percent in 1972 to 28 percent in 1978 to 36 percent in 1983 (George, 1988, 135). She goes on to note that in Lima, as a result of the increasing impoverishment of the population, the restaurants have developed the practice of selling to the poor a plate of food at the back door that is called *siete sabores*, or "seven tastes," made up of the leavings and leftover scraps of all the dishes on the menu. The poor in Lima buy this when they have enough money. When they do not, they often eat *nicovita*, a fishmeal flour used for fattening chickens and manufactured under unsanitary conditions. George notes that the former governor of the Peruvian Central Bank, Manuel Moreyra, had to admit that the "social costs of this (IMF adjustment) policy are tragic. It means the death of some 500,000 children." World Bank statistics cited by a Swiss author are said to have placed Peruvian IMRs (infant mortality rates) at seventy per 1,000 in the 1970s but over eighty per 1,000 in the 1980s. Still other sources placed the overall IMR in Peru at more than 100, and some said that in the worst shanty towns half the newborns were dying before the age of one" (George, 1988, 135).

In Argentina and Brazil the pattern is repeated. Citing from official sources, George notes that 685,000 children in greater Buenos Aires alone do not eat enough to stay alive—a government minister said this plus another 385,000 children in the province of Buenos Aires. Thus, one-third of the children under fourteen in Buenos Aires province are starving. The tragedy is worse in poorer provinces in the northern part of the country where it is 40 to 50 percent of the children under fourteen are starving. In Brazil, the problem of malnutrition is believed to be the worst on the continent. The government in 1985 estimated that two-thirds of the population was suffering from malnutrition. The problem is worst in the northeastern sections of the country where the children's growth is so stunted as a result of nutritional deficiencies that nutritionists in Brazil have discovered an epidemic of dwarfism. The *nordeste* children are found to be 16 percent shorter and 20 percent lighter than children of similar ages in other sections of Brazil (George, 1988).

George quotes Cardinal Paulo Evaristo Arns, archbishop of Sao Paulo, a diocese of over 15 million people, regarding the impact of the debt crisis in Brazil:

The huge effort of the past two years resulted in an export surplus of a billion dollars a month. Yet this money served only to pay the interest on the debt. It's impossible to go on this way; we have already taken everything the people had to eat, even though two-thirds of them are already going hungry. When we borrowed, interest rates were 4 percent; they're 8 percent now and at one point they went as high as 21 percent. Even worse, these loans were contracted by the military, mostly for military ends—$40 billion were swallowed by six nuclear plants, none of which is working today. The people are now expected to pay off these debts in low salaries and hunger. But we have already reimbursed the debt, once or twice over, considering the interest paid. We must stop giving the blood and the misery of our people to pay the First World (George 1988, 138).

The problem of debt and the result of the structural adjustment programs imposed on countries as a strategy to repay the debt has had a pervasive effect on infant mortality rates throughout the dominated countries. Research by Sell and Kunitz (1989) found that the greater a country's participation in world markets, as measured by the degree of indebtedness, the slower life expectancy increased. Based on this analysis, George estimated that for each additional $10 a year in interest payments per capita, there was an associated decline in life expectancy improvement of approximately four months from 1970 to 1980 (George, 1988). Although we have focused our examples on Latin America, Bello (1994) reports that sub-Saharan Africa has been even more devastated. Total debt for the sub-Saharan region climbed dramatically to where it is now 100 percent of GNP, compared to 35 percent of GNP for other developing countries. One result of the structural adjustment program was that by the end of the 1980s some 200 million of the region's 690 million people were classified as poor; the World Bank estimated that by the year 2000 that number is sure to reach 300 million, 40 percent of the world's poverty population. Malnutrition among the population has grown. Bello cites one study of families in Zambia where the impact of the adjustment programs has been to reduce the number of meals per day from two to one in many families. Public health services have been collapsing as governments cut public expenditures per the guidelines of the structural adjustment program. This has resulted in the rapid spread of cholera. Furthermore, the spread of AIDS is having a devastating effect on the population. Bello cites statistics that indicate that 50 percent of the armed forces in Zimbabwe and 25 percent of women seen in maternity clinics in Kampala, Uganda, are infected with the virus.

Ellwood notes that "in Africa, external debt has ballooned by 400 percent since the Bank and the IMF began managing national economies, through structural adjustment. Today in Ethiopia, a hundred thousand children die annually from easily preventable diseases, while debt repayments are four times more than public spending on healthcare. In Tanzania, where 40 percent of people die before the age of thirty-five, debt payments are six times greater than spending on healthcare. From the whole of Africa where one in every two children of primary-school age is not in school, the government transfers four times more to Northern creditors in debt payments than they spend on the health and education of their citizens" (2001, 51)

George places the debt of the dominated countries as part of the larger strategy of imperialism, whereby the Northern Hemisphere countries control the resources and development of the Southern Hemisphere dominated countries. She describes the strategy as consistent with the transition to the use of low-intensity military conflict to maintain control.

> Highly visible, debilitating and exhaustively reported interventions like Vietnam have given way to Low-intensity Conflict (LIC). LIC has become the officially sanctioned and widely practiced strategy against movements popular in the Third World and governments unpopular in Washington. LIC is also LCC, or Low-cost Conflict— for the perpetrator. It costs little in money and in manpower; above all, it costs little in political opposition and turmoil at home because it is so hard to focus on. . . . Now let me take the LIC concept a step further. I'll call it FLIC, or Financial Low-intensity Conflict. FLIC is, aptly enough, the French slang word for police, the equivalent of 'cop' or 'fuzz'. Third World debt is now, perhaps, less a 'crisis' than an ongoing, dialectical FLIC waged against the South, a permanent global struggle exactly like LIC but played out on another terrain. As with LIC, FLIC does not seek to win because total victory—complete payback—would also mean bankruptcy for the debtors and the consequent collapse of the international financial system. The war would be over, and everyone would have lost. FLIC does, however, help to prevent the Third World from posing a threat, from dictating its terms, from changing the political balance of forces in the world. When creditor nations and institutions wage FLIC, they are not engaged in 'linear activity' comparable with traditional war in which debts are contracted, mature and are paid off. They are, rather, carrying out a process without any foreseeable end, one that allows the North to keep a check upon any pretensions to real independence on the part of the South and to ensure privileged access to the South's resources, and to its industrial capacity, on the cheapest possible terms (George 1988, 233–34).

George contends that the third world war has already started, but it is a silent war, a war whose victims are children and the unemployed in the dominated countries principally in the southern hemispheres of the world.

The impact of debt and the structural adjustment programs of the World Bank and the International Monetary Fund are just the most recent strategies in a war that has been going on since the fifteenth century. According to Chomsky the New World Order is a continuation of the pattern of domination that has been ongoing for the last five hundred years. "In the South, in contrast, the New World Order imposed by the powerful is perceived, not unrealistically, as a bitter international class war, with the advanced state capitalist economies and their transnational corporations monopolizing the means of violence and controlling investment, capital, technology, and planning and management decisions, at the expense of the huge mass of the population. Local elites in the southern dependencies can share in the spoils" (Chomsky, 1993, 45).

It is important also to recognize that structural violence, as it manifests itself in differences in infant mortality rates and problems of hunger, is not restricted to countries dominated by the most powerful countries economically and militarily, but also occur in countries that are in positions of dominance. Bello (1994) observes that the structural adjustment programs implemented in the southern hemispheric countries were one part of a Reagan administration strategy to roll back the position of working people in the United States as well. Cutbacks in welfare programs, deregulation, tax policies that favored the wealthy, tight fiscal policy by the Federal Reserve Board, and policies that facilitated the flight of investment capital overseas all had a significant impact in decreasing the standard of living of the bottom 60 percent of the working population, increasing the levels of wealth and income inequality and poverty in the nation. At the same time, the government conducted a war on drugs that was fought in the poorest communities and increased the percentage of the population in prison to the highest it has been in history (almost 400%; Sing, 1980). Furthermore, military spending skyrocketed and national debt climbed to the highest level, far exceeding the deficits accrued by the spending policies of all previous U.S. presidential administrations combined. By the end of the 1980s, the United States was the world's leading debtor nation, the country with the largest percentage of its population in prisons, and spent the most on weaponry for maintaining order nationally and internationally.

Sivard (1991) found that in the United States 5.5 million children under age twelve suffer from hunger. Altogether, in 1991 an estimated 30 million people were hungry in the United States. In 1985, black mothers died in childbirth at a rate four times that of white mothers (U.S. Bureau of Census, 1988). Infant mortality for whites is eight per 1,000 live births, but for blacks it is nineteen per 1,000 live births (UN Development Programme, 1993). The United States ranks twenty-eighth among nations in infant mortality rates, the same ranking as Poland, with eighteen infants dying for every 1,000 live births (Hurst, 1992).

FAMINE

Famine is the most extreme case of malnutrition and hunger. To what degree can we talk about the occurrence of famine and widespread patterns of hunger as cases of structural violence? Spitz (1978, 868) states that "the crisis created by a famine reveals the workings of the economic and social system and affords an insight into the structural violence which has the effect of denying the poorest members of society the right to feed themselves in order to stay alive." The problem of famine is a human-made problem. It is not the product of environmental disasters independent of human action, nor is it a result of overpopulation. George (1988, 1990) and others point out that environmental disasters may serve as a catalyst to preexisting situations of extreme poverty that in turn result in widespread death due to starvation. Furthermore, population size relative to size of the arable land in a country is not important when we consider countries with greater populations relative to available arable land that have never experienced famine in their modern histories.

Fundamentally, famine is a result of the extreme inequality in ownership and control over food production in a given society and in the world as a whole. For George (1982), famines are caused by people having no power over land and income. When people in rural agrarian economies have too little or no land or there is little or no income from other economic sources, it leads to hunger and a threat to physical existence. When this condition hits large segments of the population, we label this a famine (George, 1982, 98). When hunger is more dispersed and exists over long periods of time, we accept this as a condition of humanity or an artifact of underdevelopment.

A number of factors have been specifically identified as central to the problem of famine and extreme cases of malnutrition. We have already discussed the problems of debt, dependent capitalist development, and the structural adjustment programs imposed on dominated countries. All these factors point to the fact that famine in the modern world is ultimately an outcome of imperialism in the world economy. Spitz (1978) indicates how the legacy of classical colonialism of the European powers from the eighteenth to the first half of the twentieth century had a significant impact on land-tenure customs, land rights and farming systems, all of which contributed to making the colonized people less capable of producing enough food for themselves and inhibited them from building up the excess production needed to be used during emergency situations. Two studies on the problem of famine in the Sahelian region of Africa trace this legacy of colonialism and its impact on the problem of famine today in this region (Franke and Chasin, 1980; Watts, 1983). Tinker (1993) points to the impact of missionaries on forcing economic changes on the indigenous populations in North America, which at times resulted in hunger and famine, problems they did not experience in the past. There is an old African saying— When they first came they had the bible. We had the land. We now have the bible. They have our land (Institute of Race Relations, 1982, 3).

George (1982, 1990) sees hunger as a direct product of the hierarchical political economic ordering in the world. For George, hunger means the Third World. George maintains that because of tariff barriers that the dominant capitalist countries establish against the underdeveloped or dominated countries, their industrial development is held back and their dependent status is maintained. Bello (1994) argues that the Reagan administration targeted the newly industrial countries (NICs) for differential trade policies in order to reduce the U.S. trade deficit with the NICs. These countries were targeted to reduce their government's involvement with the economy, reduce the restrictions on foreign ownership, and reduce import tariffs. The Omnibus Trade and Competitive Act of 1988 and the General Agreement on Tariffs and Trade (GATT) were established mechanisms for U.S. overt retaliatory action against those deemed to be unfair traders. South Korea, Taiwan, and Singapore became targets of U.S. action. Universalism and the GATT, in short, are two faces of the same process of resubordination directed at those countries that threaten to make the breakthrough to developed status. In much the same way that structural adjustment programs seek to contain the poorer countries of the South, the GATT and aggressive unilateral trade policy aim to roll back the NICs and aspiring NICs (Bello, 1994, 85).

Moreover, industries in dependent capitalist countries do not create enough jobs to fulfill the needs of the millions of new workers displaced from land as a result of the transformations in agricultural production (cash crop production, large-scale mechanized farming, etc.). Jobless people with no money are hungry people. The economies in these poor countries are dominated by the interests of multinational corporations, finance capital, and the interests of governments of the dominant capitalist countries.

> Today, political colonialism is nearly dead. Either the mother countries granted independence or national liberation movements fought for it and won. But economic colonialism lives on. Its effects on peoples' diets are still disastrous. In many former colonies, the new leaders, usually educated in and by the mother countries, have made no efforts to change colonial crop patterns. Thus Senegal still devotes over half its arable land to peanuts and the Philippines grows coconut oil-palms and sugar on over half their cropland. What happens when a still-dominated country depends on just one or two cash crops for most of its income in hard currency? Sugar-cane, coffee, tea, cocoa, etc. are grown in poor countries, but the prices these crops fetch are set on rich country commodities markets. Individual producing countries have no control over world prices which are vulnerable to speculation. (George, 1982, 54)

The domination is reinforced because the processing of food occurs principally in the industrialized countries, and the processed foods are shipped back to the dominated country, which then pays more for them than the raw materials exported. Furthermore, the cost of manufactured goods is higher than the cost of raw materials. The overall result is unequal exchange in trade, whereby the dominated country continually falls behind economically relative to the dominated country.

Another factor is the concentration of land ownership in the countries where famine occurs. The very structure of the society as defined in terms of ownership of production, in particular agricultural production, leads to a limitation on food production and thus problems of famine. Four percent of the world's big landowners control half the world's cropland (just 0.23 percent of owners' control over half of all land worldwide). Fifty-eight percent of the world's landholders, small producers, must make do with 8 percent of the world's cropland. George notes that in eighty-three poor countries, 3 percent of the landholders own or control four-fifths of the land. In Java, Egypt, Bangladesh, Venezuela, Mexico, and parts of India, a third to a half of the rural population has no land at all (George, 1982,76–77). In Guatemala 22 percent of the country is made up of 482 huge plantations. At the same time, 54 percent of all farms are less than 1.4 hectares (Gage, 1991). In Brazil, where there is widespread problems of malnutrition in the population, eighteen large landowners control an area six times the size of Belgium (Shankland, 1995). Unequal distribution is not reserved for the Third World. In the United States, 5 percent of the farmers control over half the cropland. This is so despite the fact that small farmers produce more food per acre than large ones (George, 1982).

This concentration of ownership is related to the history of colonialism and the current position of the country in the world economy. The dependent capitalist development model promoted and fostered by the dominant capitalist countries and the leading banking institutions in the world is based on large-scale cash crop production. Furthermore, many of the largest farms in dominated countries are owned by multinational corporations or their subsidiaries. Small farmers and peasants are forced off their land by means of increases in taxes or forcibly by police, military, or thugs hired by the large landowners. The rural peasant population becomes marginalized economically and politically, increasing their vulnerability to famine. The agricultural production for the local market becomes reduced as more and more production is for the export market. Increasingly, foodstuffs are imported from the dominant capitalist countries at higher prices than could be produced locally and more often than not with less nutritional content.

Another important factor that leads to the problem of famine is, ironically, foreign aid by the dominant capitalist countries. Most foreign aid by dominant capitalist countries serves to maintain the relations of domination in the world economy. This is accomplished in three ways. First, foreign aid is a vehicle for disposing of excess agricultural production of farmers in the dominant capitalist countries. In this way it is a means of maintaining an agrarian producer class in the dominant countries by a system of subsidies. Those who are most likely to benefit from this subsidy system are the largest producers, corporate owners. Many of these same corporations are involved in agrarian production in the same dominated countries of the world to which the surplus is being shipped. Thus these large corporate producers receive a subsidy in the dominant country to ship foodstuffs to the same dominated countries that were increasingly impoverished, in part, as a result of these corporate owners' control of land in these countries producing food stuffs for exportation. As small producers in the dominated countries are not able to keep up with the cost of subsidized food aid, they lose their production (the land often being absorbed by the largest landholders in the country—contributing to further land concentration) and join the swelling ranks of the displaced working class. These same corporations also often receive subsidies from both the dominant and dominated countries for this production for exportation from the dominated country.

The system of subsidies also allows for the continued technical development of agriculture in the dominant countries, giving them an increasing market advantage relative to small producers. Another function of most aid is to further the economic dependency of the dominated countries as the aid economically displaces the local producers of foodstuffs in the dominated country, thus destroying any chance of economic self-sufficiency. As mentioned earlier food aid from the center is many times given away or sold at such low prices that it destroys the local producing sector. As a result, the country becomes increasingly dependent on the importation of foodstuffs from the dominant countries, and there is further integration of their own agricultural production (cash crop production) into the world market. This pattern of agricultural development that is promoted by foreign aid furthers the pattern of inequality as it relates to power and land ownership.

> Aid from the rich countries has made it possible to promote, not the development of the poor countries, but a certain type of industrial and agricultural growth, the unequally distributed benefits of which have enabled the dominant social classes in the poor countries to strengthen their domination. This increase in the wealth concentrated in the hands of a few aggravates structural violence in the poor countries. The rich in the poor countries then need to strengthen their military and police forces in order to maintain their domination. The rich countries are thus afforded fresh opportunities to make further profits, as is shown by the substantial growth of arms sales throughout the world (Spitz 1978, 889).

Aid also serves as a form of welfare that maintains the political stability of client regimes in the dominated country by keeping the poorest populations dependent on the government for survival. This dependency also keeps the poorest populations from rioting as they continue to receive the bare minimum nutritional requirements for their existence.

Last, technical aid serves to further the penetration of the dominated country by multinational corporations and furthers the dependent relationship as the production is geared increasingly to the export market and dependent on the importation of agricultural chemicals and equipment to maintain the production. One example of this technical aid is the green revolution, a program of agricultural development created by the Ford and Rockefeller foundations and pushed by American Universities and USAID. This program of technical aid was based on the distribution of genetically engineered seed that produced high-yielding plants (usually wheat or rice) that required lots of fertilizer, chemical protection, herbicides, and controlled irrigation and drainage. The increased need for chemical fertilizers and herbicides and tractors created new markets for U.S. multinational corporations.

The Green Revolution was promoted by the United States as an alternative to land reform, which would change the structural relations in these societies. George (1982) reports that from 1966 onward, the U.S. government made its food aid to poor countries conditional on their adoption of green revolution techniques. By means of the Green Revolution, peasant farmers would be able to produce more on their small plots, thus not requiring more access to the large concentrations of land held by a small segment, oftentimes the ruling oligarchy, of the population. Instead, according to Spitz (1978), this program increased the disparities between rich and poor and between regions well endowed with natural resources and less fortunate regions. Furthermore, it replaced the poor's direct dependence for food

supplies with a more insidious form of dependence consisting of the need to acquire fertilizers, pesticides, agricultural machinery and sources of energy, thus providing transnational corporations with ample opportunity to step in. Spitz contends
that the green revolution by magnifying inequalities and aggravating the effects of
the process of dispossession on the lives of the poorest, helps to exacerbate structural violence (884). The aid that was part of the Green Revolution served to increase the concentration of land ownership by large producers as they were able
to produce more, which required larger amounts of capital for equipment and
chemicals. Poor farmers who could not keep up with the cost of the technological
inputs increasingly required to maintain the higher level of crop yields were forced
off their land and became vulnerable to famine.

> Rich countries and international agencies with their "aid" programmes and "de-
> velopment solutions" contribute to making an already calamitous situation even
> worse. They push "population control" (and dump unsafe contraceptives in Third
> World countries) instead of trying to change the conditions that make people need
> children. They encourage cash-crop production and refuse most other Third World
> goods through trade barriers. They consistently give economic, political, and mil-
> itary support to regimes that have no intention of improving the lot of their own
> poor people. And they do everything to wreck the efforts of those who do strive
> for agrarian reform and fairer distribution. . . . Essentially, rich countries are trying
> to make Third World food systems resemble or serve their own. If they could man-
> age it (which they can't, entirely, yet), the most powerful countries would set up a
> single world food-system which they controlled. (George 1982, 103)

According to George, the Green Revolution increased both production and
hunger. Countries such as India, Bangladesh, the Philippines, parts of Africa,
and Indonesia, big recipients of the Green Revolution are testaments to the impact of this development strategy. In these countries more than half the population is living below the poverty line. At the same time, that the wealthy
landowning class dramatically increased its holdings, there has been increasing
agricultural production for the export market and increasing levels of imports of
agricultural chemicals and equipment, along with food aid from the dominant
capitalist countries, which promoted the revolution. George notes that these
outcomes of the Green Revolution were foreseen. She cites testimony to Congress in 1969, where experts said there would be further markets for industrial
products in these countries, the peasant land tenants would become a diminishing breed, and the rich may get richer from this "revolution" (George, 1982).

The end result of this pattern of domination internationally and nationally
in countries around the world is a level of violence that surpasses all other
forms of violence. For example, it results in an estimated 10 million people
who died in India in 1769–1770, or in more modern day examples, more than
250,000 dead in the Sahelian region of Africa in 1972 and 100,000 dead in
Bangladesh in 1974, all from famine created by the structural relations within
and between countries. Today, hundreds of millions of people around the

globe are struggling to get enough nutrition to fulfill one day of life, a result of a legacy of systems of inequality within and between nations. In 1996 the United Nations sponsored the first global gathering at the highest political level to focus solely on food security. At that time the United Nations esti- mated that 800 million persons (of which 300 million were children) around the world were not receiving the minimum nutrition to sustain life. The meet- ing established a goal of reducing the number of starving people by one half by 2015. In a recent review of progress, United Nations officials say the world is falling short of targets to reduce hunger and chronic malnutrition, but it is reported by food security experts that the situation is far worse and that the number of hungry people in many developing nations is rising (Knight, 2001).

The last point to note regarding patterns of hunger throughout the world is that we can look at how the problem is distributed along a hierarchy of countries in the world system from richest to poorest. The problem of hunger is distributed from richest to poorest within countries. Those who are in most dominated po- sitions via systems of stratification within countries around the globe are most vulnerable to the violence of hunger. Women and children of workers and peas- ants of ethnic minority populations are the most vulnerable. For example in Southeast Asia 64 percent of pregnant women are anemic, passing along a legacy of malnutrition to the infants they bear (Del Nevo, 1995, 21).

INTERPERSONAL AND INSTITUTIONAL STRUCTURAL VIOLENCE

Hate Crimes

As mentioned earlier, structural violence intersects with interpersonal and in- stitutional violence. Violence that stems from hate crimes is an example of structural violence that is also interpersonal. An FBI report noted that racial bias prompted 60 percent of the 4,558 reported hate crimes in 1991. In Brooklyn, New York, on March 15, 1990, Henry Kwok Kin Lau, a recent immigrant from Hong Kong, was stabbed to death on a train in Bay Ridge by a man who yelled anti-Asian slurs. In the previous year, on July 4, more than thirty white youths attacked a black family with baseball bats as they watched a fireworks display in Queens, New York. In Mount Clemens, Michigan, Charles Gibson, a nine- teen-year-old black man, was beaten to death by white teenagers while driving through a suburb. Mulugeta Seraw, an Ethiopian student, was murdered one night in Portland, Oregon, by skinheads who beat him to death with a baseball bat. In a major case in which the United Klans of Alabama was successfully sued in civil court, requiring them to sell off most of their assets, Michael Don- ald was killed by members of an Alabama chapter of the Ku Klux Klan.

For Bennie Hays, the 25 policemen gathering around Michael Donald's body rep- resented the happy conclusion to an extremely unhappy development. That week, a jury had been struggling to reach a verdict in the case of a black man accused of murdering a white policeman. . . . To Hays—the second highest Klan official in Alabama—and his fellow members of Unit 900 of the United Klans, the presence of blacks on the jury meant that a guilty man would go free. According to Klansmen who attended the unit's weekly meeting, Hays had said that Wednesday, "If a black man can get away with killing a white man, we ought to be able to get away with killing a black man." On Friday night, after the jurors announced they couldn't reach a verdict, the Klansmen got together in a house Bennie Hays owned on Herndon Avenue. According to later testimony from James (Tiger) Knowles, then 17 years old, Tiger produced a borrowed pistol. Henry Frances Hays, Bennie's 26 year old son, took out a rope. Then the two got in Henry's car and went hunting for a black man. Michael Donald (19 years old) was alone, walking home, when Knowles and Hays spotted him. They pulled over, asked him for directions to a night club, then pointed the gun at him and ordered him to get in. . . . When they stopped, Michael begged them not to kill him, then tried to escape. Henry Hays and Knowles chased him, caught him, hit him with a tree limb more than a hundred times, and when he was no longer moving, wrapped the rope around his neck. Henry Hays shoved his boot in Michael's face and pulled on the rope. For good measure, they cut his throat. . . . They then looped the rope over a camphor tree, raised Michael's body just high enough so it would swing (Bullard, 1991, 31).

The Southern Poverty Law Center's Intelligence Project counted 676 active hate groups in the United States in 2001. The Federal Bureau of Investigation reports that there were 9,430 hate crimes committed in 2000. Of those, 6,130 were crimes against the person, while 3,241 were crimes against property. Of the crimes against person there were nineteen murders, four rapes, and 1,184 aggravated assaults. The Southern Poverty Law Center and the Justice Department's own research indicates that there is significant problem of underreporting hate crimes (McDevitt et al., 2000; Southern Poverty Law Center, 2001). The Southern Poverty Law Center estimates that the occurrence of hate crimes is five times greater than what is reported in the government's statistics. The current government figures are the highest since the government has collected statistics on hate crimes. Given the increased concern regarding terrorism and the targeting of ethnic minorities, especially of Middle Eastern descent in retaliation, the problem is expected to increase in this most recent period. But the peak activity of hate crimes probably occurred much earlier in our history, lynchings of African Americans reached its peak in the South in the late nineteenth century and declined sharply after 1935. Beginning with the Reconstruction era in the United States and up to the mid-1930s, an estimated 3,402 lynchings of African Americans occurred (New Grolier Multimedia Encyclopedia, 1993). Between 1882 (when reliable statistics were first collected) and 1968 (when the classic forms of lynching had disappeared), 4,743 persons died of lynching. Dray (2002) points out that from 1882 to 1944, the number of people of color lynched averaged more than one a week. Silberman (1978) notes that between 1882 and 1903, no fewer than 1,985 blacks were killed by southern lynch mobs.

The United States is not alone with a problem of interpersonal violence directed at maintaining ethnic hierarchy. In Germany there are numerous cases of neo-Nazi extremists targeting immigrant populations (Lee, 1993). In a recent case, five members of a Turkish family, two young women and three girls, were burned to death when their home was set afire by a group of neo-Nazis (Whitney, 1993). On November 25, 1990, fifteen masked youths, identified as members of an organization of skinheads, in the town of Eberswalde attacked Amadeu Antonio Kiowa, a guest worker from Angola, outside a disco, beating him to death. In Dresden on April 18, 1991, Jorge Gomondai of Mozambique was killed as a result of being thrown from a moving streetcar by a group of skinheads. In another Dresden case in 1991 masked skinheads knocked down the door to the apartment of a pregnant Vietnamese women and brutally beat her. One of the most widely publicized cases in Germany occurred in August 1992 in Rostock. A large number of skinheads gathered in front of a hostel housing Rumanian Gypsy asylum seekers and Vietnamese guest workers. While local police and federal border guards stood by, the skinheads set fire to one of the buildings, trapping 140 Vietnamese inside. Most escaped with minimal harm (Neier, 1992).

Rape is another example of interpersonal violence that is also structural. As noted earlier, since the vast majority of rape victims are female, the structural position of women relative to men is reinforced and extended because of this pattern of victimization. Women's freedom is limited by the occurrence of rape. Their ability to develop their human potential is reduced because certain opportunities are not available to them because of the occurrence of rape. Rape is a form of power, a power that men have over women. It is used as a means of control and domination. Thus the motivation for rape is to maintain and extend the patriarchal structure that is the root cause of the violence. All unequal power relationships must, in the end, rely on the threat or reality of violence to maintain themselves (Clark and Lewis, 1977, 176). Rape is one form of violence that serves to maintain the institutionalized dominance of men over women.

Institutional Structural Violence

In regard to structural violence that is also institutional, we have in previous chapters discussed examples of state violence directed at minority populations, peasant and union movements, and politically dissident groups. In all cases, the goal of the violence is to maintain or change the structures of dominance in that society. Similarly, military interventions by the dominant capitalist powers throughout history with very few exceptions have been designed to maintain the imperialist relations (often times defined in terms of preserving a free market and defending the right of private property) threatened by political movements within the dominated country. With economic violence, again, those who are more likely to be victims are workers or peasants. Whether we are talking about product, production, or environmental violence, it is those who are in dominated positions in the society who are the victims. Thus, we can look at economic violence as structural in that the outcome of the violence is the maintenance or extension of the dominance as victims are placed at a disadvantage relative to those who are victimizing them. In family violence, again the pattern is repeated as it relates to age and gender. Women and the young are more likely to be victimized relative to adult men. Thus the pattern of victimization extends the hierarchical structure rooted in patriarchy. Last, as we discussed religious violence, its role conquest and the establishment of imperialist relations are key. Those who are most likely to be victimized by missionaries are those who have least power.

THE WEB OF STRUCTURAL VIOLENCE: THE CASE OF GUATEMALA

Hierarchical Structures within Guatemala

Let us illustrate how the many forms of structural violence can be interwoven by focusing on Guatemala. Guatemalan society contains two modes of production: a dependent capitalist mode of production and a remnant of what approximates a tributary mode of production (Amin, 1980). The capitalist mode of production is clearly the dominant mode: The capitalist class structure is composed of a small, dependent bourgeoisie (*ladino* agricultural export, traditional landowning class, and merchant bourgeoisie), medium size agricultural entrepreneurs, and what is referred to as a puppet bourgeoisie composed of those who occupy positions in public and private institutions that make them instruments of exploitation, that is leaders in the military and high-level government bureaucrats (Jonas and Tobias, 1981; Black, 1983b). Since the economic changes of the 1960s determined by the shift in U.S. investments, the capitalist class has become increasingly segmented into agrarian, industrial, financial, and commercial. The nature of their development has become dictated by the needs of transnational capital.

More important than this fragmentation, however, has been the increasing power of the military and their inclusion into the capitalist class as a separate element. Beginning in the 1970s with the Arana regime, the military developed its own economic interests. Initially brought into the government as a coercive protector of the established order, senior officers have increasingly used state power as a basis for owning production; agro-exporting, industrial, financial, and real estate enterprises. In the process they have become Guatemala's strongest political and economic force, which has at times threatened the traditional national owning class (Black, 1983a). This development in the capitalist class has created some interesting fragmentation and political alignment. Black contends that what may be more worrisome than this wealth of the military is the machinery created for its acquisition and protection. According to Black (1983b) an array of institutions fuse the armed forces with the state. This merging of economic and state interests, together with the monopoly of force and violence that the military holds, is a formula for extreme violence and repression of those who threaten this distribution of power. The estimated size of the bourgeoisie is 3 percent of the population.

The petty bourgeoisie includes members of the bureaucracies, small merchants, owners of family-sized artisan establishments, and owners of family-sized farms (14.88 hectares on the average). The petty bourgeoisie is estimated to be 20 percent of the population. The working class and peasantry are the remaining 77 percent of the population. This includes 21 percent who are industrial/service workers and 56 percent agricultural (including 30 percent semiproletariat and 6 to 10 percent seasonal workers). The semiproletariat is growing rapidly as the Indian population becomes increasingly displaced in the countryside.

There is also a tributary mode of production in Guatemala. A tributary mode of production is one where the surplus produced is not appropriated by an exploiting class. Instead, according to Amin (1980), it is centralized by a ruling group for the collective use and redistributed according to the needs of the population. This mode of production, although distinct from the capitalist mode of production, has become intertwined with it. Because communal land ownership has been severely limited, and most of the fertile land in the country has been stripped from the indigenous peasants, they cannot survive without participating in the dominant capitalist mode of production. These Indian or *Indios* populations become a convenient pool of cheap seasonal workers for the large landowners and the multinational corporations who own the plantations. This tributary mode of production is increasingly eliminated as there is further encroachment of their lands by the government and the large landowners, a further redivision of land in the form of inheritance to their children that creates problems of efficient use of the land and a need to export an increasingly large portion of their young to urban areas because the system cannot provide for all its members, and an increase in the amount of time the Indians need to participate in the capitalist mode of production in order to make up for what the tributary mode of production cannot provide. At the same time, mechanization of production on the large plantations and the switch to raising beef and other livestock, both of which require less labor, drives the Indian or Indios population into the cities to find work.

The society is also stratified in terms of ethnicity and gender. The society is divided ethnically in terms of three general ethnic strata: *criollos* (native-born Spaniards, a very small percentage of the population), *ladinos* (the product of intermarriage between Spaniards and natives, approximately 40 to 45 percent of the population), and *Indios* (or what the native population refers to as *naturales*, a little more than half of the population) (Jonas and Tobias, 1981). This last group is divided into at least three major ethnic groupings with twenty-two dialects and cultural groups with distinguishable dress and customs. Almost all the wealthy are *criollos* or *ladinos*; petty bourgeoisie are principally ladino, with a small segment of *Indios* in rural areas; and 45 percent of the working class (industrial and agrarian, including semiproletariat and seasonal workers) are *ladinos* and 55 percent *Indios*. In general, the poor are disproportionately *Indios* and the wealthy disproportionately *ladinos*.

Most women in Guatemala work for poor wages under hazardous conditions in the textile and food processing industries, as well as working as domestics in the cities. Middle- and upper-class women, on the other hand, are entering traditionally female professional jobs (Chinchilla, 1978). One indication of the condition of women in a country is the maternal mortality rate. Guatemala has the highest maternal mortality rate in Central America, a rate more than twice that in Nicaragua, Honduras, and Costa Rica (Bissio, 1990).

Impact of Dependent Capitalist Development

The Guatemalan economy, like others in the periphery of the world capitalist system, is plagued by problems of instability because of its dependence on export trade. This dependence on the world market has been worsened by the problems of inflation and the debt crisis. As an open economy whose external trade equals half of its Gross Domestic Product, Guatemala is tied to swings in the world market. Thirty percent of its trade is with the United States. In 1979 and 1980 the U.S. recession hit Guatemala hard, pulling down GDP growth rates, which had been running around a vigorous 5 percent, and pushing inflation, which had been running a rate lower than that of the U.S., above 15 percent (Nairn, 1983,100).

Guatemala's economy is highly concentrated. Over 80 percent of the land is held by 2 percent of farm families, 83 percent of farm families live on land too small to maintain a family, 87 percent of landowners own 19 percent of arable land (Jonas and Tobias, 1981). There has been and continues to be increasing problems of displacement of the peasantry resulting from the stealing of their land by the military and plantation owners who are increasing the size of their holdings. Over the 1970s, peasants lost 26 percent of their acreage, while the area devoted to export crops swelled 45 percent. The average size of a highland Indians farm was cut in half in the twenty-year period between 1955 and 1975; this pattern has continued to the present. In the industrial sector, monopoly patterns are found principally in oil refining and distribution, bonded paper production, steel tubing, tires, chemicals, and a large portion of food processing.

The pattern of market concentration is a direct product of U.S. multinational corporate penetration. The major shift from agriculture to manufacturing investments by U.S. corporations after the U.S-sponsored coup in 1954 took three forms. First, U.S. corporations purchased local companies. Twenty out of forty-six of the Fortune 500 corporations that have investments in Guatemala acquired Guatemalan companies as a means to enter the marketplace. The second form of penetration involves joint ventures with Guatemalan businessmen, with controlling interest residing with U.S. capital. The third method is production arrangements with competing firms, including product-licensing agreements. Aside from these direct methods of U.S. penetration, the influx of foreign capital has the effect of driving out of business local companies not tied to transnationals. The access of transnationals to credit and higher technology, as well as their ability to withstand temporary losses, contributes to increasing concentration and foreign domination of the Guatemalan economy. Companies that employ 100 or more employees are foreign owned or controlled, the majority U.S. owned. There are two sectors to the economy, one of which is labor intensive and the other capital intensive. Labor-intensive industries are generally referred to as offshore industries or runaway shops. Guatemala has become a haven for this type of investment, where the products are produced by Guatemalans to be sold in the United States. Textile and electronic assembly industries have utilized this resource. Although there has been a growth of jobs in these areas, the mechanization in agriculture has led to an increasing surplus population, which holds down wages.

As with all other countries in the Western Hemisphere, this pattern of dependent capitalist development is directed principally by the United States. After the 1954 coup and the installation of the Armas government, and through the 1970s, the United States spent $45 million in creating one of the most effective military machines in Central America. President Kennedy's Alliance for Progress and the formation of the Agency for International Development (AID), formed after the Cuban revolution to prevent the need for future communist revolutions, have been major pipelines for U.S. influence on Guatemalan society. Millions of dollars of AID money has been spent to strengthen the free enterprise system through providing seed money for the development of new businesses and loans for the purchase of U.S. capital goods and services (85 percent of bilateral aid is tied so that the money would be spent on U.S. capital goods and services) (Tobis, 1983). The first administrative provision of the Foreign Assistance Act of 1961 states: "It is declared to be the policy of the United States to encourage the efforts of other countries to increase the flow of international trade, to foster private initiative and competition . . . and to encourage the contribution of United States enterprise toward the economic strength of less developed friendly countries through private trade and investment abroad (and) private participation in programs carried under this act" (Barry et al., 1982, 83). Another large part of AID has been its efforts in counterinsurgency, through a civilian pacification campaign. After the guerrilla-based movement was neutralized in the late 1960s, AID continued its involvement in counterinsurgency through its Office for Public Safety (OPS). OPS trained over 30,000 Guatemalan police personnel between 1961 and 1970 in methods of policing and the control of dissidents.

The OPS program predates the Kennedy administration. The program was established under the Eisenhower administration to train Latin American police. This program expanded dramatically under Kennedy. A part of the program was the creation of the International Police Academy in Washington as well as training schools in several locations in the United States established to train Latin American police and military personnel. In the early 1960s public safety advisers were in forty-five foreign countries. U.S. money was available for local policing agencies for the purchase of equipment, training in the United States, and providing training at the local site by U.S. police trainers. The result in these countries was the strengthening of counter-insurgency warfare at the local police level and more repressive control of the population. As mentioned previously in the chapter on state violence, several authors tie the expansion of these programs in several Latin American countries with the creation of death squads coming out of local police forces (Herman and O'Sullivan, 1989; Nairn, 1984).

The OPS program ended in 1975. By this time $200 million worth of arms and equipment had been disbursed to local policing agencies, over 7,500 senior police officers had been trained in the United States, and more than a million rank-and-file police had been trained by U.S. personnel at local academies in the home country (Klare, 1981). A new program performing the same function (training police personnel in counterinsurgency warfare and riot control) is the International Narcotics Control Program that operates out of the State Department and works directly with the CIA. Much of the same personnel as under the OPS were initially used. Under this program the amount of money expanded rapidly, especially during the Reagan and Bush administrations. State violence in Colombia is in part funded by the United States under the guise of fighting the drug war.

New economic aid packages have the same intent in promoting capitalist relations of production within the dependent capitalist framework through providing investment opportunities for U.S. based corporations. Landes and Flynn (1984) state that the new economic programs promote export led development and nontraditional industries, such as tourism, new agricultural exports, and light assembly industries, thus increasing the pattern of dependency. Since the late 1970s, the resources of every aid program have been marshaled in an effort to bolster the status quo as defined in terms of dependent capitalist development. This was and is still the case in Guatemala.

Structural Violence in Guatemala

What has been the outcome of this pattern of dependent capitalist development as it relates to structural violence? Since the Spanish conquest the plight of the indigenous population has become worse as measured in terms of nutritional levels. The life expectancy in Guatemala is 63.4 years, the lowest in Central America. According to UNICEF, Guatemala has a higher level of child malnutrition than Haiti. Chomsky (1993) reports that a Health Ministry found that 40 percent of students suffer from chronic malnutrition. Two hundred fifty thousand children have been orphaned by political violence; 87 percent of the population live below the poverty line; 72 percent cannot afford a minimum diet; 3.6 million lack drinking water; and 6 million people have no access to health services. The purchasing power of the population dropped substantially throughout the 1970s and 1980s. In 1989, purchasing power was 22 percent of the 1972 level.

Furthermore, Guatemala has the worst human rights record in the Western Hemisphere. Beginning with the 8,000 peasants (many union organizers and

Indian village leaders) murdered in two months after the U.S.-sponsored military coup in 1954, approximately 200,000 unarmed civilians have been killed or have disappeared. Chomsky (1993) cites a recent report of the archbishop's office of human rights for the first half of 1992. The report identifies at least 399 assassinations, many of them extrajudicial executions conducted by the state security forces. The CIA had called its 1954 covert action against Guatemala "Operation Success." The year following the coup land reform stopped and any land distributed to poor peasants was returned to large landowners, 533 unions were banned, strikes outlawed—punishable by execution—and political parties were outlawed (Gage, 1991). Military dictators ruled the country for thirty years after the coup and the United States has been the major supplier of armaments and training to the military that has waged a war on the poorest sectors of the population for almost forty years (Jonas and Tobias, 1981; Moyers, 1988).

The activity of right-wing death squads connected to the military and state security officers is very significant in creating a level of violence and fear among the poorest populations in Guatemala (Amnesty International, 1983). Herman and O'Sullivan (1989, 18) write that

> Death squads made their appearance in ten different Latin American countries in the 1960s and 1970s, all of them recipients of U.S. military and police aid and training, which stressed counterinsurgency and unconventional warfare against subversion from the Kennedy era onward. Guatemala was the largest recipient of this aid and training in Central America throughout the 1960s and 1970s. This was an insurance policy provided by the United States to protect U.S. investments and the oligarchy in Guatemala. For example, the U.S. intervention in Guatemala in 1954, followed by military-police aid and training and political support for the regime, provided a safety net to the Guatemalan elite, giving it assured control of the state and ending any need for reform or nonviolent response to mass demands and needs. . . . The insurance policy thus encouraged and stimulated an institutionalization of state terrorism as an ongoing and permanent policy response to popular demands. (Herman and O'Sullivan, 1989, 18–19)

As part of the 1996 peace accords ending the civil war in Guatemala an investigation was to be conducted on the scope of the political violence that occurred in Guatemala. Bishop Gerardi of Guatemala was the driving force behind the project for the Recovery of Historical Memory (REMHI). The report concluded that 150,000 people died, 50,000 "disappeared," 1 million became refugees, 200,000 children were orphaned and 40,000 women became widows. The Guatemalan army was involved in most of the atrocities committed, and was blamed for at least 85 percent of all massacres, tortures, disappearances, and killings during the civil war. It carried out 626 massacres during a scorched-earth counter-insurgency campaign in the early 1980s. Four hundred forty Mayan villages were eliminated by the government during the civil war.

Two days after the bishop delivered a speech marking the end of their investigation, he was assassinated. He was bludgeoned to death in his garage. He was struck seventeen times to the face and head with a chunk of concrete. According to autopsy findings it took fifteen to thirty minutes for the elderly bishop to die, drowning on his own blood. Nothing of value was stolen. The case remains unresolved. The death squad, the Jaguar Avengers, a group that has been linked to the military, claimed responsibility. According to a recent Amnesty International report six years after the signing of the United Nations–brokered Peace Accords that ended thirty-six years of civil war in Guatemala, the country is once again descending into lawlessness and terror (Amnesty International, 2002). The report cites a UN Human Rights Verification Mission (MINUGUA) report that listed 390 lynchings that occurred between 1996 and 2001. In 97 percent of the cases, no one has been brought to justice.

Aside from military- and police-sponsored death squads, there is ethnographic evidence of *ladino* landowners organizing death squads to remove peasants from the land they have occupied for hundreds of years (Carmack, 1988). In many cases, the ancestral Indian land is merely taken away because the occupants do not have a legal title.

[T]he ancestral farming rights of the Kekchi of Alta Verapaz were abused more than most. As the Emibal Nickel mine began operations, Indians on the banks of the Rio Polochic were forcibly relocated to make way for strip mining. Plans for a new highway through the Franja made matters worse. Attracted by soaring land values, coffee-grower Ricardo Sapper Cordua ravaged long-settled Kekchi lands. In July 1976, Sapper claimed ownership of 3,375 acres of farmland embracing the Kekchi villages of Secuachil, Semocaoch and Yalicoc. Without formal deeds to the land, the Indians were simply expelled. Disputes escalated into the massacre of May 29, 1978 when peaceful Kekchi protesters marched into the town of Panzos to discuss land grievances at the government's invitation, they were met with a hail of bullets from the troops called in by a local landowner, 119 Kekchi dead. (Black, 1983a, 14)

Even where there is legal title, this does not assure people of their rights. The Indian relocation program, part of the strategic hamlet strategy to fight the guerrillas (a U.S. military strategy directly adopted from the Vietnam War and in some respect the conquest of indigenous populations on the North American continent), has resulted in the trading of better-quality Indian land for poor-quality farmland. Under this program, whole villages of peasant landholders are forcefully removed and relocated to another part of the country that is a distance from guerrilla activity. This strategy is intended to eliminate all local support and resources to guerrillas and supposedly to protect the peasants from becoming war casualties. Large landowners eventually acquire the land for production for export after the Indians are relocated.

In general, estimates are that over one-half of Central America's agricultural land is devoted to export crops. The result is that agricultural production increases at the same time that there is less food available for internal consumption, and the region's import food bill has increased dramatically. This is the pattern of dependent capitalist development. In Guatemala, peasants work land that once was theirs, now owned by large plantations and agribusiness corporations, producing inexpensive food and cotton fibers for the North American and European consumer. At the same time, the size of their subsistence plots have become smaller and smaller and increasingly of poor quality, and the prices of imported foods are further from their reach.

Economic violence directed at workers is widespread in Guatemala. Agricultural workers suffer from severe problems of pesticide poisonings. According to Murawski (1993, 6), it is common practice for landowners to spray fields with dangerous pesticides as they are being worked. According to the Central American Research Institute for Industry, the average DDT content in human blood in Guatemala's cotton areas is 520.6 parts per billion, in contrast to 46.4 parts per billion of the residents in Dade County, Florida. A study conducted by the Central American Nutritional Institute concluded that the amounts of DDT in mothers' milk in Guatemala were the highest in the Western world, over 185 times higher than the established safety limit (Barry et al., 1982). The average wage for agricultural workers who cut cane and pick cotton is between $1 and $2 dollars a day, far below the $56 a month necessary for the average family to stay out of poverty. Union organizers are regular victims of harassment and violence by death squads and the security forces. Croats (1991) notes that in the Guatemala *maquiladoras* workers are paid between $1 and $2 a day for long work days that may stretch to sixteen hours. Most factories require workers to work on Saturdays. Only 5 percent of the country's work force is organized. Croats notes that the figure in the *maquila* sector is close to zero. Today a small minority of the workers in U.S. owned *maquiladoras* that are scattered throughout Mexico, Central America and the Caribbean have been unionized, a testament to this strategy of intimidation.

Chomsky (1993, 174) describes this interconnection between state, economic, and structural violence:

> As terror improved the investment climate, export oriented economic programs led to rapid growth in production in agricultural commodities and beef for export, destruction of forests and traditional agriculture, sharp increases in hunger and general misery, the world championship for DDT in mothers' milk (185 times World Health Organization limits), and gratifying balance sheets for US agribusiness and local affiliates. The new maquiladoras are having a similar impact. Current economic plans, under the guidance of US advisers, are intensifying this range of effects.

Finally, rates of homicide are very high as levels of interpersonal violence are in general high in response to the impact of the displacement and impoverishment on the lives of the poorest segments of the population. Alcoholism and drug abuse is also high especially among the young. Gangs of displaced youth live on the streets of the capital, Guatemala City.

CONCLUSION

This chapter has discussed how violence emanates from systems of stratification. They manifest themselves in higher rates of disease and death for populations that are in the most dominated positions within societies. In more general terms, they manifest themselves in fewer life chances, chances to develop ones physical, spiritual, and intellectual potential, for populations who are most dominated. We have discussed the different dimensions of stratification that manifest themselves in terms of structural violence.

We have also discussed how systems of stratification are within societies and between societies. The nature of imperialism as a force serves to maintain and expand hierarchical relations within and between countries. When we compare countries throughout the world in terms of differential disease, death rates, and life chances, we clearly see the impact of the hierarchical relations that exist between countries. The exploitative relationships that deny populations a chance to live to their fullest potential are reproduced on an international scale when we examine the relationship between countries that are part of the capitalist core and countries that are part of the periphery of the world system.

We have discussed how the system of international debt is used as a means to further the goals of the dominant capitalist countries, the U.S. in particular, as it accelerates the pattern of dependent capitalist development in countries forced to enroll in structural adjustment programs supposedly to pay off debt. We have discussed the structural violence that follows from the imposition of the structural adjustment program, violence that manifests itself in higher infant mortality rates and malnutrition among the poor populations in Latin America and Africa. We also discussed how famine, a form of structural violence, is a direct outcome of stratification within and between countries. Last, we discussed how structural violence overlaps with institutional violence, as in the cases of much of state and economic violence in particular, and interpersonal violence, as in the case of hate crimes.

So far, we have discussed the many forms of violence in the world today. We began our discussion with acts of interpersonal violence: murder and rape. We then discussed the different forms of institutional violence such as family, religious, economic, and state. Finally, we discussed structural violence, violence that is an outcome of the very systems of stratification that organizes societies and the world. Is there a single thread that runs through all the forms of violence we have discussed? Is there a root cause to most of the violence that exists in the world today? In the concluding chapter we discuss the threads that tie all these forms of violence together. And we ask, how, then, do we begin to reduce the levels of violence in the world today?

REFERENCES

Ahmad, Nilufar. 1992. "Battling the World Bank." *Multinational Monitor* 13: 20–23.

Amin, Samir. 1980. *Class and Nation: Historically and in the Current Crisis.* New York: Monthly Review Press.

Amnesty International. 1983. *Political Killings by Government.* London: Amnesty International.

———. 2002. *Guatemala's Lethal Legacy: Past Impunity and Renewed Human Rights Violations.* London: Amnesty International. www.amnestyusa.org/countries/guatemala/lethal_legacy.rtf

Barry, Tom, Beth Wood, and Deb Preusch. 1982. *Dollars and Dictators.* Albuquerque, N.M.: Resource Center.

Bello, Walden. 1994. *Dark Victory: The United States, Structural Adjustment, and Global Poverty,* London: Pluto Press.

Bissio, Roberto Remo. 1990. *Third World Guide 91/92.* Montevideo, Uruguay: Garamond Press.

Black, George. 1983a. "Garrison Guatemala." *North American Congress on Latin America* 17: 1.

———. 1983b. "Guatemala: The War is Not Over." *North American Congress on Latin America* 17: 2.

Bolles, Lynn. 1983. "Kitchens Hit by Priorities: Employed Working-Class Women Confront the IMF." In *Women, Men, and the International Division of Labor,* ed. by J. Nash and M. P. Fernandez-Kelly. Albany: State University of New York Press.

Bullard, Sara. 1991. *The Ku Klux Klan: A History of Racism and Violence.* 4th ed. Atlanta, Ga.: Klanwatch, a project of the Southern Poverty Law Center.

Carmack, Robert M. 1988. *Harvest of Violence.* Norman: University of Oklahoma Press.

Chinchilla, Norma Stoltz. 1978. "Industrialization, Monopoly Capitalism, and Women's Work in Guatemala." *Signs: Journal of Women in Culture and Society* 3: 38–56.

Chomsky, Noam. 1993. *Year 501: The Conquest Continues.* Boston: South End Press.

Clark, L., and D. Lewis. 1977. *Rape: The Price of Coercive Sexuality.* Toronto: Women's Press.

Coats, Stephen 1991. "Made in Guatemala: Union Busting in the Maquiladoras." *Multinational Monitor* 12, no. 11.

del Nevo, Maria. 1995, May. "The Cost of Living." *New Internationalist* 267: 20–21.

Dewitt, Peter, and James Petras. 1981. "The Political Economy of Debt." In *Class, State, and Power in the Third World,* ed. J. Petras, 96–117. Montclair, N.J.: Allanheld, Osmun.

Dowd, Douglas. 1993. *U.S. Capitalist Development Since 1776.* Armonk, N.Y.: M. E. Sharpe.

Dray, Philip. 2002. *At the Hands of Persons Unknown: The Lynching of Black America.* New York: Random House.

Ellwood, Wayne. 2001. *The No-Nonsense Guide to Globalization.* Toronto: New Internationalist Publications.

Farmer, Paul. 1999. *Infections and Inequalities: The Modern Plagues.* Berkeley: University of California Press.

"Filthy Rich." 1994, September. *New Internationalist,* 259: 17–20.

Franke, Richard W., and Barbara H. Chasin. 1980. *Seeds of Famine: Ecological Destruction and the Development Dilemma in the West African Sahel.* Montclair, N.J.: Allanheld, Osmun.

Gage, Susan. 1991. *Colonialism in the Americas*. Victoria, British Columbia: Victoria International Development Education Association.

George, Susan. 1982. *Food for Beginners*. New York: Writers and Readers Publishing.

———. 1988. *A Fate Worse than Debt*. New York: Grove Press.

———. 1990. *Ill Fares the Land*. London: Penguin Books.

Godrej, Dinyar, May. 1995. "Hunger in a World of Plenty." *New Internationalist* 267: 7–10.

Grant, James. 1994. *The State of the World's Children 1994*. Oxford: Oxford University Press.

Hanlon, Joseph, and Ann Pettifor. 2000. *Kicking the Habit: Finding a lasting solution to addictive lending and borrowing—and its corrupting side-effects*. London: Jubilee Research. www.jubileeplus.org/analysis/reports/habitfull.htm

Herman, Edward, and Gerry O'Sullivan. 1989. *The Terrorism Industry*. New York: Pantheon Books.

Hurst, Charles. 1992. *Social Inequality: Forms, Causes, and Consequences*. Needham Heights, Mass.: Allyn and Bacon.

Institute of Race Relations. 1982. *Patterns of Racism*. London: Institute for Race Relations.

Jalee, Pierre. 1965. *The Pillage of the Third World*. New York: Monthly Review Press.

Jonas, Suzanne, and David Tobias. 1981. *Guatemala*. Berkeley, Calif.: North American Congress on Latin America.

Klare, Michael T. 1981. *Supplying Repression: U.S. Support for Authoritarian Regimes Abroad*. Washington, D.C.: Institute for Policy Studies.

Kneen, Brewster. 1995, May. "Captured by the Company." *The New Internationalist* 267: 23–5.

Knight, Danielle. 2001, May 29. "DEVELOPMENT: Food Security Worse, Outlook Dim—Experts." Inter Press Service News Agency. www.ipsnews.net/interna.asp?idnews= 10008

Korten, Alicia. 1993. "Cultivating Disaster." *Multinational Monitor* 14: 20–22.

Landes, David, and Patricia Flynn. 1984. "Dollars for Dictators: U.S. Aid in Central America and the Caribbean." In *The Politics of Intervention: The United States in Central America*, ed. by R. Burbach and P. Flynn. New York: Monthly Review Press.

Lee, Martin A. 1993. "Hitler's Offspring." *The Progressive* 57: 28–31.

Mathews, Robert. 1986. "Sowing the Dragon's Teeth: The U.S. War against Nicaragua." *North American Congress on Latin America* 20: 13–40.

McAfee, Kathy. 1991. *Storm Signals: Structural Adjustment and Development Alternatives in the Caribbean*. Boston: South End Press.

McDevitt, Jack, Jennifer M. Balboni, Susan Bennett, and Justice Research and Statistics Association. 2000. *Improving the Quality and Accuracy of Bias Crime Statistics Nationally: An Assessment of the First Ten Years of Bias Crime Data Collection*. Washington, D.C.: Bureau of Justice Statistics. www.dac.neu.edu/cj

McGeary, Johanna. 2001, February 12. "Paying for AIDS Cocktails; Who should pick up the tab for the Third World?" *Time Magazine*.

Medoff, Peter, and Holly Sklar. 1994. *Streets of Hope: The Fall and Rise of an Urban Neighborhood*. Boston: South End Press.

Merrill Lynch/Gemini Consulting. 2001. *World Wealth Report 2000*. www.foxexchange. com/public/fox/news/industry_trends/world_wealth_report_2000.pdf

Milanovic. 1999. "True World Income Distribution, 1988 and 1993." *Policy Research Working Paper* 2244. World Bank, Washington D.C.

Morrison, Roy. 1991. *We Build the Road as We Travel*. Philadelphia: New Society Publishers.

Moyers, Bill. 1988. *The Secret Government*. Washington, D.C.: Seven Locks Press.

Mukonoweshuro, Eliphas G. 1991. "Between Verwoerd and the ANC: Profiles of Contemporary Repression, Deprivation, and Poverty in South Africas Bantustans." *Social Justice* 18: 171–185.

Murawski, Anthony. 1993. "Challenging Guatamala's Labor Abuses." *Multinational Monitor* 14: 6–7.

Nairn, Allan. 1983. "Guatemala: Central America's Blue Chip Investment." In *Guatemala in Rebellion: Unfinished History*, ed. G. Fried and Peckenham. New York: Grove Press.

———. 1984, May. "Behind the Death Squads." *The Progressive*, 19–29.

Neier, Aryeh. 1992, February 3. "Watching Rights." *The Nation*, 533.

New Grolier Multimedia Encyclopedia. 1993. "Black Americans." Novato, Calif.: The Software Toolworks.

New Internationalist. 1995, May. "Hunger—The Facts." *The New Internationalist* 267: 18–9.

Pearce, Jenny. 1982. *Under the Eagle*. Boston: South End Press.

Petras, James. 2002, June. "Who Rules the World?" *Z Magazine* 15, no. 6: 5–6.

Reiman, Jeffrey. 1990. *The Rich Get Richer and the Poor Get Prison*. New York: Macmillan.

Sell, Ralph R., and Stephen J. Kunitz. 1987, Winter. "The Debt Crisis and the End of an Era in Mortality Decline." *Studies in Comparative International Development*: 3–30.

Sharkey, Jacqueline. 1990, May/June. "Nicaragua: Anatomy of an Election." *Common Cause*, 20–29.

Sherman, Howard J. 1987. *Foundations of Radical Political Economy*. Armonk, N.Y.: M. E. Sharpe.

Silberman, Charles E. 1978. *Criminal Violence, Criminal Justice*. New York: Random House

Sivard, Ruth Leger. 1991. *World Military and Social Expenditures 1991*. Washington, D.C: World Priorities.

Southern Poverty Law Center. 2001, Winter. "Discounting Hate." *Intelligence Report, a publication of the Southern Poverty Law Center.*

Spitz, Pierre. 1978. "Silent Violence: Famine and Inequality." *International Social Science Journal* 30: 867–91.

Stolnitz, George J. 1983. "Three to Five Main Challenges to Demographic Research." *Demography* 20: 415–32.

Tinker, George E. 1993. *Missionary Conquest*. Minneapolis, Minn.: Fortress Press.

Tobis, David. 1983. "The Alliance for Progress: Development Program for the United States." In *Guatemala in Rebellion: Unfinished History*, ed. Fried, Gettleman, and Levenson. New York: Grove Press.

U.S. Bureau of Census. 1988. *Statistical Abstract of the United States*. 108 ed. Washington, D.C.: Government Printing Office.

United Nations Development Programme. 1993. *Human Development Report*. New York: Oxford University Press.

———. 1994. *Human Development Report*. New York: Oxford University Press.

———. 2001. *Human Development Report: Making New Technologies Work for Human Development*. New York: Oxford University Press.

Watts, Michael. 1983. *Silent Violence: Food, Famine and Peasantry in Northern Nigeria.* Berkeley: University of California Press.

Whitney, Craig R. 1993. "Bonn Suspects Neo-Nazi Arson as 5 Turks Die." *New York Times*, 1–1.

Wilkinson, R. G. 1996. *Unhealthy Societies: The Afflictions of Inequality.* London: Routledge.

World Bank. 2001. *World Development Report 2000/2001: Attacking Poverty.* Oxford: Oxford University Press.

Zwerdling, Daniel. 1980. *Workplace Democracy.* New York: Harper Colophon.

Chapter Nine

Conclusion: Violence, Inequality, and Human Freedom

VIOLENCE AND INEQUALITY

Throughout this work a major focus has been the relationship between violence and inequality. We have discussed how inequality itself may be a cause of violence as offenders learn to define others as of less worth than they, and as they themselves have been defined by others. The structures of inequality that we experience, that we learn to accept, and that we maintain and extend through our everyday interpersonal interactions and in role performances within institutions contribute to our ability to separate ourselves from others and define others as in need of control, punishment, or subjugation.

Inequality → Violence

We have discussed how violence is caused by inequality. Beginning with our discussion of culture, we noted how culture itself is a product of the structures of inequality. In particular, our cultural understanding of violence is constructed for us by those who have more power in defining our understandings of the reality we experience. This is via the media, by our political leaders, our educators, our religious leaders, our leaders in the economic arena, and others who are in leadership positions in social institutions. The forms of violence that are least damaging in scope (e.g., stranger rape and murder) are defined for us as posing the greatest threats. Those forms of violence that are most damaging in scope (for example, forms of institutional and structural violence) are defined for us as posing the least threats or are defined as not violent in the deviant context or as necessary or justified. Thus inequality is related to the occurrence of violence by first establishing the relationships that give those who are in dominant positions the power to define forms of violence that are most destructive, and by which they benefit, as not violence to be addressed by agents of social control or even to be recognized by those who are victims. In

371

this way, structures of inequality contribute to the further occurrence of the forms of violence that are greatest in scope.

For example, when we think of rape what comes to mind is the stranger lurking in the shadows waiting to attack the innocent women walking home in the evening. We do not think of the husband or boyfriend who, by means of threats of violence, forces himself sexually on his wife or girlfriend, although these forms of rape are more frequent. They are precluded from our concern by the system of inequality, patriarchy, which questions whether these acts are to be considered rape, and the ideologies that legitimate this system of structured inequality and that form the basis of the law and its enforcement.

Another example would be production violence. Again, when we think of violence, we think of interpersonal violence where approximately 24,000 people are murdered each year in the United States. We do not think of the more than 100,000 people who die of work-related illnesses or injuries. We do not think of Bhopal, India, as a case of violence or mass murder, nor do we think of the large number of people whose lives are cut short from brown lung or black lung disease as victims of violence. The class relations we take for granted in our society preclude us from considering that these are acts of violence; after all, didn't these people volunteer to work under these conditions? The inequality and coercion that affects the bargaining position of workers relative to owners is not even recognized because we have internalized the dominant ideology that defines this system as normal, just, and appropriate. On the other hand, when we discover pesticide poisoning in child farm workers in Peru who are sent into the fields to assist in the spraying of DDT and Chlordane, pesticides that have been banned in this country because of their carcinogenic effects, we may see the coercion rooted in the inequality of social relations between the poor peasants and their children and the wealthy landowners. This is in part because it takes place outside our own societal context. Nevertheless, in both cases, violence has taken place. This is violence that is larger in scope than the interpersonal violence that we read about daily in our newspapers, that we are entertained by in our movies and television programs, that we think is the principle threat to people throughout the world and to the very existence of order. In general, the cultural understandings we have learned from those who are dominant allow us only to recognize forms of violence that are least in scope and to recognize these forms of violence as more threatening than forms which they commit that are larger in scope and more threatening.

There is one more step. As our understanding of violence is mediated by the ideologies that are a product of systems of inequality and how they serve to legitimate these systems of inequality, they contribute to the maintenance and extension of these systems through acts of violence. Those who are victims of the more devastating forms of violence that are not defined as violent are disempowered to address the causes of them. In this way, our understandings regarding violence and our resultant acceptance of violence leads to furthering the systems of structural inequality that are ultimately their cause. Thus the woman who is raped by her husband may not even recognize the act as rape or violence, thus furthering the pattern of male privilege as rooted in patriarchy. The worker who is victimized by production violence, or the consumer, who is victimized by product violence, may not recognize the act as violence; thus furthering the pattern of class privilege as rooted in the class system. The U.S. citizen who supports his troops (disproportionately composed of working-class and minority members) in battle during the recent wars with Iraq and Panama may not see these acts as forms of illegitimate violence or violence itself, thus furthering the pattern of the stratification internationally and the system of imperialism in the world.

Another way that systems of inequality can cause violence is through the effect it has on the social conditions of the actors involved. Beginning with interpersonal violence, to what degree do the conditions of one's life, as they are a product of systems of stratification, lead to acts of homicide and rape? In looking at patterns of homicide and rape, we see that those who are most likely to be victims and offenders are concentrated among the poorer segments of the society. Could we not say that if we removed young children who were born in East Los Angeles, Brownsville in Brooklyn, or the south side of Chicago and transplanted or adopted them at birth into families who reside in wealthy suburbs of these same cities, the probability that they will be involved either as a victim or offender or a witness to a violent crime would severely then be reduced? Thus, is violence an attribute of the child or is it an attribute of the social environment? The following is based on an interview of a sixteen-year-old boy who lives in the inner-city section of Indianapolis. Violence is an integral part of this boy's environment.

> Big Daddy, 16, Indianapolis. In my neighborhood, people are getting shot, getting killed, running around. People selling dope every day. They say average life span for a young black male is twenty-one years. Violence is definitely on the rise cause ain't nothing getting better. . . . But maybe a world without violence would be stupid cause people need something to talk about. I ain't saying its right to have violence and talk about it, but you never know. Sometimes you need violence to get your point across. I mean, violence was probably here for a reason. . . . We ain't got no relations with the police or nothing like that. Just as long as they go home, they don't care who they hurt or what they do. I mean, look at our little kids growing up, my nieces and nephews, how can they call the officer Mr. Friendly when they got guns all over? If you just go around popping each other, I don't think it'll never change cause that's all kids see nowadays. Just that (Goodwillie, 1993, 161–62).

Thus, is it not the condition of one's existence as defined in terms of systems of class and ethnic inequality that in part causes violence? Can we not say that in these cases class and ethnic stratification caused violence?

Another example of how systems of inequality can cause violence is the case of patriarchy. Most violence is the violence of men. If we socialize males to view themselves as superior to females, train them to view themselves as in control of women, and train them to believe that aggression and violence are signs of masculinity, are we not contributing to the occurrence of male violence? If our male gender role models on the playing fields, cinema, and public life teach the expediency of violence to address problems and to assert power and control, again signs of masculinity, are we not contributing to the occurrence of male violence? If we teach our male population to exercise this aggression in recreation and in work, at times to reward it, especially when it is most violent as in the case of a war hero or president who takes military action, are we not contributing to the occurrence of male violence? If toy weapons are given to male children and toy babies are given to female children to play and simulate adult behavior, are we not contributing to this male dominated pattern of violence? The socialization of males to be masculine in patriarchal, capitalist society is one of the causes of the violence between men and women, and between men in pursuit of ownership and control of women and other valued possessions.

On another level, because of the position of men in the society they are more likely to have access to weapons and to be empowered to use them in acts of violence. In this way the positions that men occupy in patriarchal society provide them with greater opportunities to be violent. When we looked at motives for interpersonal violence, the overwhelming reasons were controlling women, acquiring access to material wealth, or asserting power to gain position. In all cases, the relevance of the action exists only in the context of systems of inequality, where conditions of scarcity are created.

Systems of inequality also cause institutional and structural violence. When we address each form of institutional violence, we see a repeated pattern whereby those who are most likely to be victims tend to be those who are in dominated positions. Alternately, those who are perpetrators of violence are those who are in dominant position or are acting as agents of those who are dominant. Systems of inequality cause the occurrence of institutional violence in that the function of institutional violence is to maintain or extend those systems of domination that a society is based on. This is true whether we are discussing spousal assault and the system of male privilege rooted in patriarchy, production violence and private property rights rooted in the class system, or state-sponsored genocide and the concern for national security, or, more accurately put, the maintenance of power relations in a nation state or internationally as defined in terms of a system of imperialism.

Last, in structural violence, systems of inequality play a direct role. Structural violence is the form of violence that is most invisible. For it is by means of the dominant ideologies that by definition legitimate the basic structures of the society that we are rendered blind, or at least myopic, to the recognition of this form of violence. Because of such blinders, we are most likely to recognize the existence of this form of violence in other societies but not our own. Thus, we are more likely to see the violence of a system of apartheid in

South Africa, but not see the violence of racial stratification in our own society. As we discussed in the chapter on structural violence, this is the form of violence most directly linked to the hierarchical relations that exist within a society, and the hierarchical relations that exist between societies. Structural violence is the relatively high occurrence of infant mortality among lower-income and minority populations throughout the world. It is also the high rate of abortions of female fetuses in rural health clinics in rural areas in India. It is the life expectancy differences between positions within a society. It also is the difference in mortality and life expectancy between minority and majority people within a society and between countries positioned as dominant and dominated in the world system.

These differences in the quality and extent of life are direct products of the systems of stratification that are part of a nation-state system and an international system of imperialist relations. How long and what quality of life an individual will experience are significantly caused by the ranking of positions nationally and internationally and one's place within that rank. Whether we view the rankings as legitimate or not is irrelevant to our discussion of violence.

Violence → Inequality

We have discussed how violence can be caused by the structures of inequality that exist in a society and the world system. But there is reciprocity of reinforcement. Violence can cause inequality as well. By this we mean that the consequences of acts of violence may serve to maintain and extend levels of inequality. In interpersonal violence, the pattern of victimization of both rape and homicide leads to increasing levels of inequality in our society. As the poorer and less powerful segments of our society experience higher rates of victimization compared to those in positions that are dominant in the society, these forms of violence serve to further the distance between the positions. For instance, as women are victimized by rape, the occurrence and fear of the occurrence reduces the power of women relative to men. As poorer and minority working class populations experience a higher rate of homicide relative to the owning class and majority populations, their power is reduced relative to these higher positions.

Not only does the occurrence of acts of interpersonal violence serve to maintain and extend systems of inequality, but how we respond to this victimization does so as well. Formal state agents of social control are increasingly part of our everyday life. There is an increasing presence of armed authority and social control in our lives, more than at any other period in human history. In the United States, the proportion of the population that is performing an official role of social control as police officer, security guard, military personnel, prison guard, and the like is far greater than any other country in the world and far greater than any other moment in our history. Along with this pattern, the proportion of the population placed under intensive surveillance either by means of incarceration or probation is far greater in this society than any other society in the world and far greater than any other moment in our history. The number of state and federal prisoners in the United States has more than tripled since 1980 (U.S. Bureau of Justice, 2001). In 1980, 1,842,100 persons were under correctional personnel supervision, for the year 2000 that number had climbed to 6,467,200, more than a 350 percent increase. When we look at those who are in jail and prison during the same period, the increase is even greater at more than 380 percent. This translates into a prisonization rate of 472 prison inmates per 100,000 U.S. residents. In South Africa during the system of apartheid, another leading country in prison rates, 311 out of every 100,000 South Africans was in prison during the tumultuous early 1990s (Sniffen, 1994). The United States composes approximately 5 percent of the world's population, yet the U.S. prison population is one-fourth of the total world's prison population. This is all the product of what the dominant ideology, education and media outlets refer to as a free society.

Yet the presence of these agents in monitoring and surveying our activities and our geographic space is not uniform throughout the population. Those subpopulations that are in dominated positions, especially as defined in terms of class, gender, and ethnicity, are more likely to experience their presence. The inequality of power that the layperson experiences in the presence of agents of social control becomes magnified when the layperson is in a dominated social position. The experience of lower-income, minority, and female populations is often one of intimidation, humiliation, and subservience, if not victims of violence, in interaction with representatives of the state. Furthermore, the operation of policing agencies in general in addressing problems of interpersonal violence does not result in empowering the victims and other residents with the means to address the problem. Instead, it functions to remove the solution to the problem from the victim and community and to create greater dependence on the power of the state to address these problems in the future. This does not serve to reduce power inequalities in public life among these populations but does just the opposite.

As to how institutional and structural violence maintains and extends structures of inequality, we only have to look at the differences in patterns of victimization. Again, as with interpersonal violence, the distribution of victimization is not uniform throughout the population. As noted earlier, with few exceptions, those populations that are in dominated positions experience higher rates of institutional violence compared to those populations that are in dominant positions. This differential experience of victimization serves to maintain and extend the structures of inequality. Furthermore, the intent of institutional violence is the maintenance or extension of patterns of structured inequality. The husband who beats his wife, the activities of a death squad, the occurrence of production violence: all maintain and extend the patterns of structured inequality in the society.

The same pattern applies even more to structural violence. Populations in dominated positions experience higher levels of disease, shorter life spans, and in general less opportunity to develop their human capacities than those who are in dominant positions in the society. On another level, as poorer countries throughout the world are devastated by civil war, overt and covert military interventions, and famine their positions are reduced relative to the positions of those countries dominant in the world system. In general, as these structures of inequality are maintained and extended within and between nations, the more violence there is throughout the world, and the result is the extension of these very structures of inequality.

Of course, not all violence serves to maintain and extend inequality; violence may also reduce levels of inequality. The organized and unorganized violence of those who are dominated or in the interest of those who are dominated may cause a reduction in levels of inequality. Riots and rebellions throughout history have often resulted in a response by the elite to reduce the harshness of living conditions that are a product of systems of inequality. In our own society, whether we are talking about Shay's Rebellion during the eighteenth century, the rioting of the poor and unemployed throughout periods of economic crisis, slave rebellions sporadically in the South during the nineteenth century, the rioting that occurred around the country during the 1930s, the race and class riots of the 1960s, or the riots in the Miami and Los Angeles during the 1980s and 1990s, the result has often been the establishment or extension of economic or political rights that have reduced levels of inequality in the society (Cloward and Piven, 1977; Zinn, 1980).

VIOLENCE AND HUMAN FREEDOM

Violence → Freedom

Violence ultimately refers to a denial of human freedom. In societies and more specifically in geographic and social space where there are high levels of violence, there is less freedom than in societies and geographic and social space where violence is at lower levels. Violence as an act is often intended to lessen human freedom. The outcome of violence is always to lessen human freedom for those who have been successfully victimized. Whether we are discussing interpersonal violence, institutional violence, or structural violence, the outcome is less freedom for those who are victimized. But, as with all hierarchical interactions, those who are victims, in most cases those who are in dominated positions have less freedom in the society to begin with and experience less freedom as a result of the violence. Those who are the perpetrators or beneficiaries of the actions of the perpetrators, in most cases those who are in dominant positions, experience greater freedom as a result of the violence.

The husband, friend, acquaintance, or stranger who rapes the wife, friend, acquaintance, or stranger experiences a sense of control and power over his victim. He feels a sense of freedom of action, while his victim experiences the denial of that freedom. The murderer experiences a sense of control and power over his victim, and the victim experiences the ultimate denial of freedom, death.

Similarly, in acts of institutional violence, those who are the agents of institutions who commit the acts and those who are in dominant positions who are more or less the beneficiaries of the institutional actions experience a greater freedom, and those who are the victims of the institutional violence experience less freedom. Thus, whether we are talking about the violence of missionaries in their attempt to control indigenous populations, the actions of employers to generate more surplus in production by forcing workers to engage in unsafe production methods or work or live in unsafe environments, the husband who uses violence as a means to control his wife, or the military or police who use violence to control dominated populations that threaten the power of the state and the interests of those who have most power in directing the actions of the state, the result is to deny freedom to those who are victimized.

Last, the occurrence of structural violence as it manifests itself in mortality and morbidity differentials lessens the freedom of victims and increases the freedom of those who are the beneficiaries of the resources that allow them to maximize their human potential. The differences in access to health care, safe drinking water, shelter, and an adequate diet all manifest themselves in differences in the quality of one's existence and greater or lesser freedom in living. For example, the freedom that we have because of the availability of food in every variety and form results in less freedom for the billion people who struggle to achieve the minimum caloric requirement for daily survival.

Freedom → Violence

Not only does violence cause a loss of freedom, but a lessening of freedom causes violence as well. As some people are less free relative to others, they are prone to victimization. This is not only true in institutional and structural violence, but also by means of interpersonal violence by those who are also in oppressive conditions and who are attempting to assert freedom through exerting power and control over others in similar or poorer circumstances. Those who are less free experience this higher level of victimization because they have less of an ability to respond to their victimization. The pattern is present in all forms of violence. This relationship between freedom and violence is also evident globally. As Gurr, Sivard, and others have pointed out, societies where there is less freedom are prone to higher levels of violence.

The exception to the pattern whereby violence reduces human freedom is the case where violence is used to extend human freedom. Organized or unorganized violence by the oppressed or in the interest of the oppressed can serve to extend freedom. Liberation movements and revolutions around the world have at times resulted in the granting of greater freedoms to people in dominated positions. Nevertheless, as these movements have been successful in reducing levels of exploitation, they have reduced the freedom of those who have been the exploiters. Thus, if we can think for a moment of the Civil War in the United States as a war that had a liberation thrust (although this was not the principal motive behind the war), the result was in granting more freedom to those who were former slaves. At the same time, it granted less freedom to those who lost the right to this form of exploitation.

CYCLE OF VIOLENCE, INEQUALITY, AND FREEDOM

What we have been describing thus far is a cycle of violence, inequality and freedom. As violence increases, freedom is reduced in a society. There is a greater level of fear, which inhibits one's action, and as violence occurs those who are victimized lose their freedom as an outcome. Conversely, as the level of violence is reduced in a society, the level of freedom experienced by the population increases. This is especially the case for those who are most victimized with violence, those who have less freedom, and those who are in the most dominated positions in the society.

The level of freedom in a society also serves as a causal agent in its relationship with violence. As the level of freedom in a society declines, the level of violence increases. The population becomes more vulnerable to levels of repression as they have less freedom to respond to it. The wife whose every action is controlled by her husband is more vulnerable to violence than the wife who is less controlled and dominated. The workers who are more desperate to find work, who are less free in this sense, are more vulnerable to violence than the workers who have many choices. The citizens of a repressive government where there is little political freedom are more vulnerable to violence than the citizens of a liberal government where there are extensive rights for citizens.

As to the link between violence and inequality, as violence increases so do the levels of inequality in a society. Those who are most vulnerable to violence in any society are those who are in the most dominated positions. As violence increases in a society, they are the ones who experience the highest victimization, and this serves to reduce their position relative to those who are most dominant, which results in an increase in the levels of inequality. Conversely, as inequality increases, the level of violence increases. This was noted in the above discussion regarding freedom and its relationship to violence. As inequality increases, those whose position declines have less freedom which leads to an increased likelihood in their victimization. Furthermore, those who decline in position have less of an ability to respond to violence, thus again making them more vulnerable to victimization.

The last connection in the cycle is that between inequality and freedom. As inequality increases, freedom is reduced in a society for those in dominated positions. This is in part self-evident. The least free in any society and in the world are those who are in the most dominated positions. As levels of inequality increase there is less freedom. Another way this relationship manifests itself is that increases in inequality in a society result in more coercion and control as dominated populations become economically and politically desperate and are perceived to be more threatening to those who are in dominant positions. Historically concern about crime is connected not to recent upsurges in its occurrence but rather in the restlessness or perceived threat of dominated populations (Michalowski, 1985). The calls for law and order in our society often means a call for control of those populations who are in the most dominated positions. When we look at the composition of our jails and prison populations this is obvious. The vast majority of those imprisoned come from the lowest income and most dominated ethnic positions.

Another way that increases in inequality lead to a lessening of freedom is through their impact on time and space freedom. Those who decline in their position spend more of their time and energy meeting their basic needs as defined by the society that they reside in. There is less free time to enjoy life and develop talents and abilities.

Conversely, as freedom declines, the level of inequality increases. One loses freedom relative to those who are in control. Those who are in control are in a better position to realize their interest relative to those who are controlled. Thus, increases in inequality are a logical outcome of increases in repression and a lessening of human freedom in a society (see figure 9.1).

In conclusion, violence, freedom and inequality are linked to each other in a cycle. As violence in a society increases, freedom is increasingly denied for those who are most dominated and systems of inequality are extended. As violence in a society decreases, freedom increases and systems of inequality are reduced. As in the case of all cycles, the starting or end point may be at any of three points. One may start with changes in the levels of freedom and its impact on inequality and violence, or start with the changes in patterns of inequality and its impact on violence and freedom, or start with changes in the level of violence and how it impacts levels of freedom and inequality.

What are the policy implications of the cycle of violence, inequality, and freedom? The first implication relates to how we attempt to solve problems of

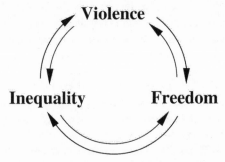

Violence

Inequality   **Freedom**

Figure 9.1.   The Cycle of Violence, Inequality, and Freedom

violence in our society. Attempts to combat the problem of violence by means of violence or repression are likely to lead in the long run to increasing the levels of violence in the society. This is evident from the nature of the cycle described above. Violence ultimately lessens the level of freedom in the society, especially for the dominated in the society, which is likely in turn to lead to higher levels of inequality and consequently more violence. Thus, as we use increasing amounts of repression to control criminal violence, these populations who are criminalized when eventually released will have greater problems of inequality and freedom as a result of the stigmatization of their ex-convict status. The result is that there is a greater chance that they will commit acts of violence in response to their social position. Strategies to reduce gang violence in today's inner cities by increasing levels of law enforcement, or repression, are likely to lead to increasing levels of violence via the impact on freedom and inequality of these groups.

A second implication relates to the impact of changing social policies on systems of inequality and its impact on levels of violence and freedom. For example, as economic policies that result in increasing the levels of inequality are implemented in a society, as was the case of the economic and tax policies of the Reagan administration (Philips, 1990), there is likely to be an increase in the levels of violence and a reduction in freedom in the society. During Reagan's first term, the tax burden of the richest 1 percent of the population fell by 14 percent, while the bottom 10 percent of the population increased their tax share by 28 percent. Under the pretense of balancing the federal budget, deep cuts were leveled against programs that provided a safety net for the working class and safeguarded the environment, working conditions, and product quality. By 1985, nondefense procurement was down $16 billion from 1981, and funds for entitlement programs were cut by close to $30 billion. At the same time, defense spending increased by over $35 billion. Under the pretext of the development of a missile defense program, the military-industrial complex received a tremendous dose of corporate socialism to increase profit levels to stratospheric levels throughout the 1980s. Another major area of growth in spending was in crime control. Expenditures on policing and prisons more than doubled in the wake of these economic reforms. These expenditures have continued to increase through the 1990s such that federal spending on the criminal justice system increased more than 400 percent during the last twenty years (U.S. Bureau of Justice, 2001). With the dramatic increase in defense spending after the terrorist attack on the United States in 2001 and the dramatic tax cuts for the wealthiest segments of the population and corporations there appears to be a repeat of the Reagan years under the current administration of George W. Bush with increases in inequality and the use of violence internally and externally to maintain order.

These policies have led to an increasingly two-tiered society: the working class and middle-income sector lost position as the spread of income and wealth inequality grew in the society. A report of the Economic Policy Institute entitled the *State of Working America 1992–1993* notes that by the end of the conservative

Republican era, the top 20 percent of the population had the highest share of income and the bottom 60 percent of the population had the lowest share of income ever recorded in U.S. history (Mishel and Bernstein, 1993). This trend has also continued through the 1990s. After tax income levels increased 14 percent for the bottom 80 percent of the population between 1977 and 1999, while they increased 43 percent for the top 20 percent and within that group the income of the top 1 percent of the population increased 115 percent during the same period (Shapiro and Greenstein, 2000). Levels of income and wealth inequality in the United States are at historic highs. The United States also has the highest rate of poverty among children compared to other advanced industrial countries in the world and two-thirds of the adult poor are women.

This growth of inequality and poverty was complemented by a growth in the proportion of the population in prison. Today, the United States has the highest proportion of its population incarcerated in its history and the highest or next to the highest (Russia may have the highest) in the world. Last, there is increasing fear of violence throughout the country. Communities throughout the nation have formed task forces to address the problem of violence, particularly youth violence that has increased in the aftermath of these policy changes. This ultimately impacts one's personal freedom in the society. As we become more fearful of the violence that is occurring in our society we are less free, and as we are victimized by the violence we experience less freedom. Furthermore, as our positions are reduced in the society in terms of systems of stratification it lessens our freedom. Today there is less freedom for working people as they spend increasing amounts of time working and holding onto their jobs in order to maintain their economic position, looking for one because they have recently become unemployed, or are attempting to be employed for the first time (Schor, 1993). Another example is the impact of structural adjustment programs on levels of inequality, violence, and freedom. Throughout the world the imposition of conditions of lending that lead to further increases in the levels of inequality in the society and the world have lead to increasing levels of violence and increasing loss of freedom.

A third implication relates to the cost of policies that result in reducing levels of freedom in the society and its impact on violence and inequality. As freedom is reduced in a society, it is likely to lead to increases in the levels of inequality and violence in the society. This may relate to the creation of laws that limit freedom of lifestyles that are not violent in themselves; for example, gay lifestyles or drug use as a part of one's lifestyle may result in violence. In the first case, the denial of the freedom of gay lifestyles may result in increasing levels of violence via hate crimes and the state's response to those who violate the moral codes safeguarding heterosexuality and patriarchy. This violence impacts levels of inequality as that population is marginalized by the loss of freedom and violence. In the case of drug use, violence increases as a result of the government's violent tactics to control the behavior, and the violence that stems from black market conditions. Levels of inequality are affected by the marginalization and criminalization of the population of those who use drugs as part of their lifestyle. The recent strategies of employers to conduct drug testing and firing of employees that fail the test impacts the economic position of those who use drugs as part of their lifestyle. Another case of how the lessening of freedom impacts violence and inequality is South Africa and its system of apartheid. The government regulations on travel and work of black South Africans led to the extension of levels of inequality and violence in that society.

Let's illustrate the cycle of violence, inequality, and freedom with the case of juvenile violence. There is a growing concern about youthful violence in our society. The response of governments at all levels has been increasing punitive measures to offenders and increasing restrictions on youths in general. As these responses lead to increasing the dependence of youth on adults and reducing their position relative to adults, it is likely to lead to increasing levels of violence as youth respond to the increase in forced dependency and status deprivation. Furthermore, dependency and status deprivation may make youths increasingly vulnerable to victimization by the adults in their lives. This may result from the fact that youths would have less ability to respond to their victimization in a way to deter future actions, or it may result from the increased strain placed on adults as a result of the increasing dependency and deprivation of youths.

As economic policies lead to reducing the opportunities for youth employment in the society and to increasing their impoverishment, there is likely to be a decline in the freedom of youth in the society and a resultant increase in the level of violence. This occurs as youths become increasingly rebellious in response to their condition, and it occurs as they become vulnerable to acts of violence by adults and other youth acting to exert power and control.

Last, as more and more laws and criminal justice and therapeutic strategies are implemented that reduce the freedom of youth, it is likely to lead to higher levels of violence and inequality for youth. Thus, as youth violence has increased in the society, the economic condition of youth has declined as measured by youth poverty and unemployment rates, and their freedom has lessened as a larger proportion of children are under treatment or incarceration for what is defined as abnormal or deviant behavior.

The impact of these policy interventions is higher levels of violence, inequality, and a loss of freedom for the youth population to the point that a crisis is reached where new strategies may be stumbled on that may reverse the cycle. These new strategies must reduce levels of inequality by integrating youths more into the adult world by giving them opportunities to develop their potential through participation in the society. This integration and reduction in status deprivation will increase levels of freedom as they achieve the rights of adulthood that have been denied to them. Last, as the levels of deprivation are reduced and levels of freedom are increased, there is a reduction in the levels of violence.

Another level is how parents' strategies for controlling their children's misbehavior have had an impact on their violence, inequality, and freedom. Think about how some parents respond to children with increasing restrictions or loss of freedom to control their behavior, how this leads to the levels of inequality between the child and the adult, creating a greater level of separation between them, all of which leads to increasing the probability of violence in their relationship. Rigoli and Hewitt (1994), in their theory of differential oppression, discuss how parental and adult oppression leads to youth adaptive responses such as the exercise of illegitimate coercive power and retaliation resulting in violence. Instead of parental strategies that restrict freedom, we should explore strategies that give our children more freedom. Instead of strategies that create further levels of inequality and separation, we should explore strategies that reduce levels of inequality and separation between parent and child. The impact of these strategies that create more freedom and less inequality will be less violence in the home.

What about the violence between men and women? Does the cycle of violence, inequality, and freedom provide any insight into explaining this violence? What about the violence directed at workers as in the case of production violence? Does the cycle of violence, inequality, and freedom provide any insight into explaining this violence? What about acts of state violence, as in Guatemala, Argentina, or Uganda? Does the cycle of violence, inequality, and freedom provide any insight into explaining this violence? What about the nature of structural violence, as illustrated by the tremendous disparities in life expectancies between Norway and Sierra Leone, or Germany and Ghana, or Sweden and Zambia? Does the cycle of violence, inequality, and freedom provide any insight into explaining this violence? In each case, as levels of inequality increase and levels of freedom decline, levels of violence increase. Conversely, as levels of inequality decrease, as levels of freedom increase, there are decreasing levels of violence. In countries around the world where would you likely experience higher levels of violence within all spheres (interpersonal, institutional, and structural) in Zambia or Sweden, in Norway or Sierra Leone, or Germany or Ghana? As indicated by the cycle of violence, inequality, and freedom, countries where there is more freedom and less inequality are places where there is less violence. Countries where there is less freedom and more inequality are places where there is more violence.

CHAIN OF VIOLENCE

Throughout this work we have described the different forms of violence in terms of three spheres: interpersonal, institutional, and structural. Although we can view these forms and spheres as distinct, they often overlap and are linked to each other in a causal sequence. One of the principles of violence described in chapter 1 was the chain of violence. The basic idea is that spheres of violence are linked in a hierarchical manner, going from the more macro forms of structural violence to the micro level of violence at the interpersonal level (see figure 9.2).

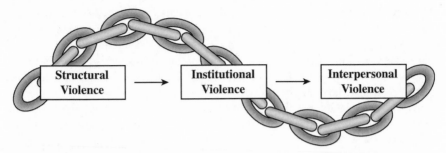

Figure 9.2.   Chain of Violence.

Violence begins at the structural level. What allows us to victimize others is our ability to think less of those we victimize, and our ability to separate ourselves from those we victimize. In an act of violence we think of our victim as less because we are conditioned to view others in our society differently, based on our perception of human value or quality. These differences of perception in the evaluation of others are rooted in the structural divisions that form the basis of the social order: class, gender, and ethnic systems of stratification. Inequalities of all kinds are fundamentally social constructions. Differences exist between people on a whole range of attributes. The transformation of these differences into inequalities is a social transformation based on systems of inequality within the society. The differences we perceive as hierarchies justify our violent behavior in terms of needing to control and punish those perceived to be less competent and forced to be our dependents. This is true whether we are victimizing children, women, ethnic minorities, or poor members of the displaced working class.

The violence that begins at the structural level (i.e., differences in illness rates, in infant mortality rates, in life expectancy rates, and in life chances to develop human potential) is the first link in the chain of violence. This violence is then linked to institutional violence. Those victimized at the structural level, at birth, are more likely to be victimized at the institutional level in schools, by religious organizations, in the family, in the economy, and in the political system. Last, the violence manifests itself at the interpersonal level, in some cases directed at those perceived as victimizers at the higher levels, in most cases at those who experience similar victimization.

The dominant pattern of interpersonal violence, whether we are talking about murder, assault, or rape, is that those who participate in violence at this level were more likely previously victimized at higher levels. Thus the causal chain of violence in any society begins with structural violence and ends with interpersonal violence. We noted earlier that it is at this point in the chain that the violence is officially recognized and defined as violence. The earlier links are made invisible. Thus, in searching for the causes of violence in a society, it is crucial to begin in assessing the society first in terms of patterns of structural violence and institutional violence and then to look at the patterns of interpersonal violence and how they are linked to the other two. Unfortunately, because we have been traditionally blinded from understanding violence as anything but interpersonal, we often look only at the causes of this violence at the interpersonal level, and our focus ends in blaming the victim in explaining the violence in our midst.

A corollary to this principle is that societies with high levels of structural violence will also have high levels of institutional and interpersonal violence. Conversely, societies that have low levels of structural violence will have low levels of institutional and interpersonal violence. Thus, to assess the level of violence in a society, it is crucial that we begin by measuring the violence at the highest levels.

How do we assess the United States in terms of levels of structural and institutional violence? As we noted previously, the levels of structural violence in our own society as measured by mortality and morbidity differentials are very significant. Those who are poor and of ethnic minority status (of African, Mexican, Hawaiian, or Native American ancestry) become ill and die at six to ten years earlier than those in dominant positions via systems of stratification. Furthermore, the occurrence of interpersonal/structural violence and institutional/structural violence is also high relative to countries of a similar level of development. Hate crimes and economic and state violence have been and continue to be part of the American landscape. The result is that the ghetto for our poor minorities in cities across the nation are racked by high levels of violence at all levels.

This structural violence then affects the institutional violence in our society. The same populations who are victims of structural violence are primed for institutional violence victimization. As noted in our discussion of inequality and institutional violence, populations who are the most dominated in our society experience the highest rates of institutional violence. They experience the most hazardous employment, consume the unsafe products, and live in the most environmentally unsafe areas. They suffer from the greatest levels of violence from policing agencies, and their political movements have historically been the targets of state terrorism. Women and children from these positions disproportionately populate shelters for child and spouse abuse.

The last link in the chain is interpersonal violence. When we look at the pattern of homicide and rape, again, it is those populations that have experienced the greatest amounts of victimization at the higher two levels that with few exceptions have the highest rates of rape and murder victimization and perpetration. As we noted in the fourth principle, we generally learn that violence can be expressive in that it is learned to be an "appropriate" response to anger or frustration. Our ability to enact violence on those who have less power than ourselves allows us to experience the illusion that we have power and control over others and thus over our own lives when in most cases it is because of its absence that violence occurs. The learning provides the linkages between the levels of violence noted earlier. Violence that we are accustomed to at the structural level becomes a matter of policy at the institutional level and a mode of personal behavior at the interpersonal level. As we learn the cultural and ideological justifications for the structural violence, and learn the legitimacy of the violent policy actions at the institutional level, the violence we enact in our personal lives becomes "natural" or "normal."

INTERNATIONAL CHAIN OF VIOLENCE

The chain of violence is not only contained within a given nation-state, as the chain is international in nature. In order to comprehend the patterns of interpersonal violence in our own society, we must first recognize how it is a part of an international chain. This chain of violence begins at the highest levels of international systems of stratification within a world political economic system. The world system defined in terms of a hierarchy of nation-states is all part of a system of imperialist relations whereby those who have historically dominated others militarily, politically, culturally, and economically begin the process of structural violence. Those who experience the highest levels of structural violence are those who experience the greatest levels of economic, political, cultural, and military domination from the center. Countries in the Southern Hemisphere, which have been dominated historically by one imperialist power after another, have the highest levels of structural violence (see figure 9.3). We highlighted Guatemala in a previous chapter. Its history of domination by one empire after another continues to have a devastating impact on the levels of violence. Guatemala is not unique. We could have inserted a number of countries in Central and South America, Africa, and Asia to illustrate this pattern of the link between structural, institutional, and interpersonal violence.

The cause of the structural violence that begins the chain is a country's structural position in the world economy and the enforcement of the maintenance of this position by imperialist relations. Countries at the center experience the violence that results from the displacement of working-class populations because of the superexploitative relationships the multinational corporations are able to create with workers in less developed countries in the periphery. Workers in peripheral countries experience the deprivations that are a product of dependent capitalist development, deprivations in part caused by the increasing surplus populations as rural populations are displaced as the agrarian economy

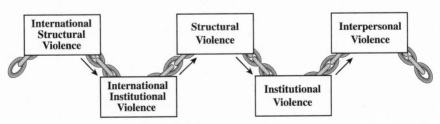

Figure 9.3.   International Chain of Violence.

makes a transition to cash crop production. The impoverishment of peripheral nations and their people leads to international institutional violence. International institutional violence reproduces, maintains, and extends the hierarchy in social relations between nation-states and sectors of the world system. International structural violence is also linked to the structural violence within a given social system that is in part a product of world structural position and to the institutional violence that reproduces, maintains, and extends the hierarchy within nation-states.

Again in Guatemala, we see how the United States has played and continues to play an important role in international institutional violence. This occurs through the economic violence by U.S.-based multinational corporations, which have dumped unsafe products and utilized unsafe working conditions. It is also evident in the actions of the World Bank and International Monetary Fund, both largely controlled by the United States as the major contributor to both agencies, in instituting structural adjustment programs that have led to the further impoverishment and displacement of the poorest populations. The U.S. government policy of funding, arming, and training the military and police who have been linked to coups, death squads, and state terrorism against the poorest populations in Guatemala is another example. And last, there is the role of U.S.-based missionaries in the cultural genocide of indigenous populations converting them religiously and ideologically so that their thinking no longer poses a threat to the maintenance of dependent capitalist relations and the hierarchical relations within Guatemala. The international structural violence also leads to high levels of structural violence within Guatemala as evidenced by high levels of differences in mortality and morbidity between class positions and ethnic positions in systems of stratification within the society.

Finally, we arrive at the interpersonal violence between those who are acting in response to the social conditions and social relations that are a product of their positions in the social system. Here we must recognize that the interpersonal violence concentrated in the most dominated positions within a society is linked to the higher levels. It may take the form of violence that is rebellious against the very organization of the society. Here the violence may be *interpersonal, institutional* or *interpersonal, structural* or *interpersonal, institutional* or *structural*. Guerrilla bands develop and begin a strategy of violence directed at the state and the classes that the state supports. Guatemala has had guerrilla activity that for the most part has been supported by the poorest segments of the society.

The recent rebellion in Chiapas, Mexico, is another example of this violence. Chiapas, with a population of 3.5 million, is one of the poorest regions in Mexico. One-third of the homes are not electrified, 40 percent of the dwellings have no running water, a third of the population is illiterate. Chiapas has the highest tuberculosis rate in the nation, and Reavis (1994) reports that in 1994 15,000 residents died of malnutrition and curable diseases. The revolt that started on January 1, 1994, was in response to the economic dislocation experienced by residents of the region. These economic dislocations were in part a product of changes in economic agreements (NAFTA) between nation-states linked via imperialist relations in the world system and the structural adjustment program imposed by world lending agencies. Whether the end result will be more inequality and repression or less inequality and more freedom is yet to be determined (Reavis, 1994).

The interpersonal violence may be adaptive and instrumental as a means to achieve power and control over others and one's own life. The responses may be an act of violence to achieve an end that the structural arrangement may block from achieving. In this way, violence is an instrumental adaptive response to the structures. Violence connected to theft or black markets is an example of this form of violence.

Last, the violence may be expressive. In this case, the violence is an emotional expression of frustration in response to the social conditions stemming from the structures. Here the violence may appear to be the most vicious and the most dangerous because there does not seem to be any rationale for it. The explosion of anger and violence of young minority males against innocent victims happens often in the drama of the inner city today.

If we focus only on the lowest levels, we see the trees but we miss the forest of which they are a part. And we fail to understand the forces that are beyond the individual actors who are in their own personal drama of violence. This is true of interpersonal violence in the ghettos of the United States. If we do not understand how this violence is part of a larger web of violence that is national and international in scope beginning at the highest levels of violence, structural, then we lose the ability to address its causes.

WHAT LESSON CAN BE LEARNED?

What forms of violence do we begin with and at what level (national or international) and with what strategies do we address violence? All forms of violence are ultimately linked. The violence that we experience in our inner cities is linked to the international structural violence and institutional violence experienced in remote areas of the world. As people are victimized in countries on the periphery of the world system, they create an economic and political disadvantage for those dominated in the center countries. Populations in Brazil, Guatemala, Bolivia, and Ghana become more desperate to acquire access to the means of survival. State violence in the periphery directed at union organizing efforts, the structural adjustment programs imposed on poor indebted countries which are following the path of dependent capitalist development, the international and state repression of political parties that attempt to represent the interest of the dominated sectors of peripheral societies, all serve to make this rapidly growing working class of displaced persons increasingly desperate for access to production in the center and the periphery.

Investments in jobs that once appeared to be secure for the working class in the center nations now become insecure as owners discover new opportunities for the generation of surplus as another population is more desperate for access to production so that they will work for cheaper wages and with less concern for safety and security of employment. As capital is exported to the periphery to these desperate and more oppressed working class populations, economic displacement occurs in the center, leading to increases in unemployment and increases in inequality between the classes in the center countries affected by the capital export.

As the displacement occurs there is an increase in the level of violence in response to the changes in the social environment. It manifests itself at the interpersonal level with an increase in the level of violent crime by populations that are most desperate, and there will be increasing opportunities for black market situations that circumvent the blocked opportunities that are a result of the capital export. Violence will manifest itself at the institutional level as more families experience strain resulting from the economic stress of unemployment and falling wages. Violence directed at children and spouses often occurs during these times. It will manifest itself in more economic violence as the economically displaced population within the center nation becomes increasingly desperate for access to jobs and are increasingly willing to trade safe working conditions and a healthy living environment for jobs. It will manifest itself in increased state violence as the state responds to actual or perceived threats to the systems of stratification as defined in terms of property, gender, and ethnic relations. Last, it will manifest itself in increases in structural violence within the center nations, as differences in life chances expand between those who are in dominated positions and those in dominant positions.

Ultimately the levels of violence are interwoven because they are rooted in the same social conditions—conditions characterized by inequality (exploitation) and a lack of freedom. All violence is ultimately a means to control another, to force him or her to act in ways that he or she has chosen not to. This other can be a child or a spouse or a neighbor or someone who threatens your pursuit of the scarcity created by the system of inequality.

How we respond to violence ultimately leads to either increasing or decreasing levels of violence. If we respond, as we have increasingly done in recent years, by increasing the levels of repression against those who are most powerless and engaging in violence, we increase the level of violence in the society as these populations experience less freedom and more inequality. If we recognize that people choose their actions, even violent actions, then we stand to reduce violence, but not by decreasing the choices available to people as occurs with increased government repression and control and increasing inequality. Rather we decrease violence by providing people with more choices of action, more freedom, and less inequality in opportunities to develop their potential.

The current policies of increasing police presence, levels of punishment, and levels of inequality through economic deregulation will in the long run increase the levels of violence and increase the perceived need for more repression. This has the potential of leading to a downward spiral of violence and repression that may eventually reach crisis proportions within the population. Thus, more resources should not be channeled into agencies of repression, but in creating opportunities for people to choose other paths of behavior.

More attention needs to be focused on patterns of structural and institutional violence in the society and internationally that are more destructive in themselves and eventually lead to problems of interpersonal violence. We need to intervene at the beginning of the chain, not at the end. The violence experienced at birth by those who are in the most dominated positions in the society and world and then occurs as a result of institutional action as the life cycle continues, in most cases manifests itself at the interpersonal level.

In conclusion, in order to comprehend the patterns of interpersonal violence in society, we must first recognize how it is a part of an interactive chain. This chain of violence begins at the highest levels of international systems of stratification within a world political economic system (international structural violence). It then leads to international institutional violence that reproduces, maintains, and extends the hierarchy in social relations between nation states and sectors of the world system. This then leads to the pattern of structural violence within a given social system stemming from the patterns of stratification that are in part a product of world structural position, to the institutional violence that reproduces, maintains, and extends the hierarchy within nation-states. Finally, we arrive at the interpersonal violence between those who are acting in response to social conditions and social relations that are a product of positions within social systems. If we focus only on the lowest levels, we fail to understand the forces that are beyond the individual actors in their personal drama of violence. And if we respond to violence by decreasing the range of choices to those who are in most dominated positions, we will eventually increase the levels of violence in the system.

As in ecological theory, a web of life connects us to each other across all living things, across and within species. This web of life connects each person to another across groups, structures, and systems. The web of violence is the antithesis to the web of life. It is not a social Darwinian cleansing mechanism that strengthens the vitality of the whole. For, unlike other species, humans grow and develop because of interaction with their own, creating and re-creating themselves and their social world in a developmental spiral that extends their life. Thus, as members are lost, opportunities are lost for growth and development for all. The loss of a member of your primary group (a family) is a loss of opportunity through social interaction for growth. Similarly, the loss of members of your community, state, nation, or world community is a loss of opportunity for growth for the individual and the species. Thus, from the smallest scale or level of interpersonal relations to the highest, the web of violence systematically leads to destruction and injury, beginning with the least powerful, but eventually affecting us all as it serves to destroy the entire system of interconnectedness which makes life possible.

REFERENCES

Cloward, Richard A., and Frances Fox Piven. 1977. *Poor People's Movements*. New York: Pantheon Books.

Goodwillie, Susan. 1993. *Voices from the Future*. New York: Crown.

Michalowski, Raymond. 1985. *Order, Law, and Crime: An Introduction to Criminology*. New York: Random House.

Mishel, Lawrence, and Jared Bernstein. 1993. *The State of Working America*. Armonk, N.Y: M. E. Sharpe.

Philips, Kevin. 1990. *The Politics of Rich and Poor*. New York: Harper Collins.

Reavis, Dick J. 1994, May. "Chiapas Is Mexico." *The Progressive* 58: 28–32.

Rigoli, Robert M., and John D. Hewitt. 1994. *Delinquency in Society: A Child-Centered Approach*. New York: McGraw-Hill.

Schor, Juliet. 1993. *The Overworked American*. New York: Basic Books.

Shapiro, Isaac, and Robert Greenstein. 2000. *The Widening Income Gulf*. Washington, D.C.: Center on Budget and Policy Priorities. www.cbpp.org/9-4-99tax-rep.htm#The%20CBO%20Data

Sniffen, Michael J. 1994, June 2. "Prison Population Triples since 1980." *(Fort Wayne, Ind.) Journal-Gazette*, 8A.

U. S. Bureau of Justice. 2001. "The number of adults in the correctional population has been increasing." *U.S. Bureau of Justice Statistics. Social Statistics Briefing Room.* www.ojp.usdoj.gov/bjs/glance/tables/corr2tab.htm

Zinn, Howard. 1980. *A People's History of the United States*. New York: Harper & Row.

Index

A.C. Lawrence Leather Company, 234
Afghan freedom fighters, 286
Afghanistan, 25, 39, 41, 175, 286
Africa, 24, 44; extrajudicial executions, 267; malnutrition, 338; world debt, 347
African Americans, 1, 12, 21, 31, 33, 102–103, 105, 130–131, 264; deadly force against, 265; environmental violence and, 238; experiments on, 299–302; genocide and, 293; hate crimes, 356; hierarchy and, 320; infant mortality, 2, 23, 316; patterns of violence and, 4; slavery and, 33, 318; state violence and, 272; youth, 111
African National Congress (ANO), 34, 279, 289, 296
agents provocateurs, 303–304
A.H. Robbins Company, 210
AIDS, 23, 339–340; Accelerated Access program, 340; pharmaceutical companies, 340; rape and, 126; Sub-Saharan Africa and, 339; UNAIDS, 339
Air America, 285–286
Allied Chemical, 245
Alpha 66, 285
Al Qaeda, 34, 175. *See also* Taliban
American Psycho (Ellis), 55
American Revolution, 25, 35
American Service Members Protection Act, 262
Amin, Idi, 279–280

Amnesty International, 125, 133, 262–236, 267, 280
apartheid, 13, 21,42, 277, 383. *See also* South Africa
Aquinas, Thomas, 75
Archbishop of Lima, 196
Archbishop Oscar Romero, 288
Argentina, 32, 43, 280, 346
Argonne National Laboratory, 301
arms suppliers, 290
Armstrong Tire Company, 248
asbestos, 224–225
Asia, 12, 44, 268
assassins, origin of name, 180
Atomic Energy Commission, 300–301
axis of evil, 43
Ayatollah Ruhollah Khomeini, 175, 178–179
Aztecs, 53, 66

baghouse dust, 239
Bailey, Abigail Abbot, 148–149
Baker Plan, 343
Ball Park hotdogs, 213
Bandura, Albert, 61–62
Bantustans, 320–321
Basel Convention on the Transboundary Movements of Hazardous Wastes and Their Disposal, 244
bear baiting, 52
Bill of Rights, 60

Billy the Kid, 59
bin Laden, Osama, 175, 286. *See also* Al
   Qaeda; Taliban
Bio-Test Labs, 221
Bishop Gerardi, 363–364
black lung, 227–228
Black Panthers, 272, 295–296, 302, 304
Branch Davidians, 183–184
Brazil, 124, 197, 276, 329
Bridgestone/Firestone Goodrich, 67, 220,
   225
British Tobacco Company, 217
Brookhaven National Laboratory, 236
brown lung, 228
Brown v. Board of Education, 12
Buckley, William, 77
Buffalo Mining Company, 252–253
Bureau of Indian Affairs, 270
Burke, Edmund, 75
Bush, George H. W., 164, 294–295
Bush, George W., 262, 265, 295, 381
byssinosis. *See* brown lung

Campbell Soup Company, 72
campesinos, 273, 285, 317
capitalism, 13, 19,102, 120, 318, 329, 331,
   348, 362; famine and, 352; hierarchy
   and, 317; homicide and, 119;
   imperialism and, 323–326; monopolies
   and, 15; patriarchy and, 319; society
   and, 35; world debt and, 328, 343
capital punishment, 25, 263; African
   Americans and, 263; countries
   abolishing death penalty, 264;
   countries with the most executions,
   264; ethnic minorities and, 264;
   Peoples Republic of China and, 265;
   populations, 264; youth and, 263–264
Carson, Kit (fictional character), 59
Castro, Fidel, 285, 294
Center for Disease Control and
   Prevention (CDC), 217
Central Intelligence Agency (CIA),
   362–363; assassinations and, 294;
   Congo and, 294; Meo tribe, 285–286;
   organized crime and, 285; state
   violence and, 282, 285–286
chain of violence, viii, 40– 41, *40,*
   384–387, *385*; international chain of

violence, 387–389, *387;* United States
   and, 386
Chemical Control Corporation, 235
Chevron, 248
Chiapas, Mexico, 388
child abuse, 36, 54, 150, 162–168; battered
   child syndrome, 150; Bobo doll, 61–62;
   causes of, 167–168; children's rights,
   150; culture and, 168; definition of,
   165; dynamics of, 167–168; England
   and, 163; hierarchy and, 163; history
   of, 150, 163–164; gender and, 168; laws
   against, 166; patriarchy and, 163, 165,
   168; Roman society and, 163; statistics,
   165–166; United States and, 163–164;
   women and, 154; worldwide, 169. *See
   also* domestic violence; family violence
children, viii, 3, 32; child labor, 163–164,
   229–231; learning and, 61–62;
   malnutrition and disease, 338, 346;
   media violence and, 55, 69; rape and,
   126; role models and, 55; sports for,
   56; state violence and, 276–278;
   victims, 66, 68; world debt and, 347.
   See also child abuse; family violence
Chile, 32, 297, 344–345
Chisso Chemical Plant, 249
chlordane/heptachlor, 210
Church of Jesus Christ of Latter-Day
   Saints. *See* religious violence
Civil Rights Act of 1964 and 1968, 13
Civil War, 33, 76, 108, 109, 150, 379
classical conditioning, 61
classical liberalism. *See* individualist
   conservatism
class oppression, 90, 93
Clean Water Act, 234
Clinton, William Jefferson, 184, 262, 265,
   339
COINTELPRO, 302
Colombia, 34, 39, 43; murder rate in,
   280–281; state violence and, 277,
   280–281
Columbine High School, 54
*A Comparison of the Metabolism of
   Plutonium in Man and the Rat*
   (classified scientific report), 301
conflict theory approach: capitalism and,
   11–14; class and, 11; competition and,

10; diversity and, 10, 12; gender and, 12; goal of, 18; institutions, 13–14, 19; Marxist theory and, 10–11, 14; materialism, 10; organismic analogy, 10; patriarchy and, 12; pluralist, 10; political orientation of, 16, 19; production and reproduction, 10– 12, *11*, 14–15; social order and, 19–20; structuralist conflict, 10; violence and, 16–17, *17*, 19–20, 22. *See also* violence, sociological approach
Contras, 43, 286, 331
cooperatives, 317
Council of Trent, 177
cross-cultural analysis, 20–21, 49
culture, 5, 49, 60, 70, 371
cyanide poisoning, 226
cycle of violence, 379–384; youth violence and, 383–384

Dalkon shield, 25, 210–211
DBCP pesticide, 208
DDT, 208–209, 364
death squads, 32, 34, 276, 284, 364; ANSESAL, 284; Askaris squads, 279; CIA and, 283–284; El Salvador and, 284–285; *Mano Blanco* (White Hand), 284; massacre at Rio Sumpul, 284–285; ORDEN, 284–285; state violence and, 275; United States and, 283–285, 363
Democratic National Convention, 303
Depo-Provera, 211
desensitization to violence, 54–55, 63, 66, 68, 70
Desert Storm, 39
Dickens, Charles, 164
dioxin, 232
domestic violence, 25–26, 35–36, 54, 62, 66, 123, 148–149, 154–155, 157; Act for the Prevention and Punishment of Aggravated Assaults on Women, 151; alcohol and, 160; battered husband syndrome, 157; child abuse and, 160; colonial America and, 3, 26, 148–149; cult of violence and, 156; dynamics of, 159–162; female initiated violence, 157, 161; feminism and, 158; gender stereotypes, 132, 159, 161; *A Godlie Forme of Householde Government*,

151; hierarchy and, 159, 161–162; historical laws against, 151–152; inequality and, 161, 169; intergenerational transfer hypothesis, 160–161; legitimization of, 151, 162; male foundations for, 159–160; medieval Europe and, 150; patriarchy and, 152, 156, 159, 161–162, 169; patterns of, 155–159; Roman law, 150; rule of thumb, 151; statistics, 155–159; United States and, 132; Wife Beaters Act, 151; women and, 157–158, 162; worldwide, 169. *See also* family violence; spousal abuse
Donald, Michael, 355–356
Dow Chemical Company, 208
Dresden, 54
drugs and violence, 19, 34, 51, 57, 382–383

Eastman Kodak, 248
economic violence, 71; definition of, 207. *See also* production violence
Eisenhower, Dwight, 294, 361
Elizabethan England, 52, 108
El Salvador, 32, 39, 273, 278, 288
environmental violence: Africa and, 240, 241; air pollution, 244–247; Amazon and, 221, 243, 251–252; and Bhopal, India, 246–247; capitalism and, 241; categories of, 231; definition of, 231; Department of Defense and, 236–237; Department of Energy and, 236, 238; Department of the Interior and, 250; dumping of waste and, 18, 41, 231–244, 252; Eastern Europe and, 241–241; Environmental Protection Agency (EPA) and, 236, 239, 244, 250; Japan and, 249; *Khian Sea* and, 240; mining and, 251–252; organized crime and, 235; oversees dumping, 236, 241; Philippines and, 236–237; Poland and, 241–242; rain forests, 250–251; resource depletion, 250–253; Subic Bay and, 236–237; United Nations and, 240, 244; United States and, 231–233, 237–238, 242–243, 245, 251; water pollution, 247–250; Yucca Mountain and, 238

Equal Rights Amendment, 86
ethnic minorities, 33; environmental
    violence and, 238; ethnic/racial
    hierarchy, 316; state violence and,
    270–273; status, 13, 386
Evart Doctrine, 331

Falun Gong, 268
family violence, 99, 123, 152; Biblical
    history and, 150, 151; biological view
    of, 154; Historicist/New-Marxist view
    of, 154; history of, 150–152; inequality
    and, 152–154. *See also* child abuse;
    domestic violence; spousal abuse
famine, 44, 348–355;colonialism and,
    352; foreign aid and, 352–354;
    inequality and, 350; land ownership
    and, 351–352; multinational
    corporations and, 352
Federal Bureau of Investigation (FBI),
    184, 270, 287, 302–303
Fernald School, 301
Film Recovery Systems, 226–227
food, 342, 346; additives, 213; famine
    and, 350; genetically engineered seed
    and, 353–354; pesticides and, 209;
    wealthiest countries and, 323 Food
    Lion, 213
Forbes (magazine), 81
Ford Motor Company, 67, 72, 218–220
Foreign Assistance Act of 1961, 361
Foreign Military Sales Program, 290
formaldehyde, 221
Formosa Plastics Corporation, 226, 241
Foster, Jodi, 34
Franklin, Benjamin, 108–109
freedom, viii, 377–380, *380*

Gandhi, Indira, 34, 179
Garcia, Romeo Lucas, 275–276
Gaston Cooper Recycling Corporation,
    239
gender, 4, 15, 20, 62, 373–374; capitalism
    and, 12; definition of, 12; enculturation
    of attitudes of, 152– 153; hierarchy
    and, 13, 319; homicide and, 100–101,
    111, 114; ideology, class and, 74;
    inequality, 138, 152; oppression, 90,

93; organic conservatism and, 76; rape
    and, 128–129, 136–138; roles, 152;
    socialization, 61, 374; state violence
    and, 319. *See also* African Americans;
    Hispanics; indigenous populations;
    Native Americans
Gender Development Index, 334
General Agreement on Tariffs and Trade,
    (GATT), 350–351
General Electric, 248, 234
General Motors, 219
General Pinochet, 297
genocide, 21, 42, 291–293; amount of
    people killed by, 293; Armenians and,
    293; cultural, 193, 197, 388; definition
    of, 291–292; indigenous populations,
    192–193; Turkey and, 293
Germany, 21; Buchenwald, 299;
    concentration camps, 299;
    experimentation, 299; genocide,
    293; hate crimes and, 356–357;
    Police Battalion 101, 64–65; Police
    Battalion 309, 63. *See also* Hitler,
    Adolph; Nazism
Grand Central Partnership, 277
Greenpeace, 239, 241, 296
Green Revolution, 353–354
Green River tests, 300
Guatemala, 32, 43: bourgeoisie, 358;
    capitalism and, 358, 365; class and,
    358–359; death squad lynchings, 276;
    dependent capitalist development,
    360–362; economic violence and, 364;
    food, 364–365; genocide, 275;
    hierarchy and, 358–360; human rights
    record, 362–363; La Matanza massacre
    and, 276; life expectancy in, 362;
    malnutrition and, 338; military, 358;
    multinational corporations, 360–361;
    poor and ethnic groups in, 359–360;
    state violence and, 274–275, 277;
    structural violence, 358–365; tributary
    mode of production in, 359; United
    States and, 360–362; women in, 360

Hare Krishnas. *See* religious violence
Hanford Nuclear Reservation, 300
Harpers (magazine), 86

hate crimes, 355–357, 382; Middle
Eastern descent and, 356; underrepresentation of, 356
hate groups, 33. *See also* Ku Klux Klan
Heritage Foundation, 77
hierarchy, 13, 22, 31, 41, 43, 49, 65, 121,
149, 317, 319, 322, 384–385, 387–388;
ethnic/racial hierarchy and conflict,
319–321; family violence and, 152–154,
169; famine and, 350; freedom and,
377; history of systems of stratification,
73; homicide and, 119; morbidity and
mortality and, 338; organizational
structure, 21, 31; rape and, 129;
religious violence and, 191; state
violence and, 307; structural violence
and, 333, 357–358; war and, 290
Hinckley, John, 34
Hinduism. *See* religious violence
Hiroshima, 54
Hispanics, 12, 30–31, 272, 320
Hitler, Adolph, 21, 51, 54, 181–182
Holocaust, 42, 63, 293
holy wars, 177–179
homeless, 26, 276–277
homicide. *See* murder
The Honeymooners (situation comedy), 3
Hooker Chemical and Plastics
Corporation, 232, 233
Human Development Program of the
United Nations, 28
human nature, 37–38, 48, 52, 60–61,
90–91
Human Poverty Index, 334
human sacrifice, 53, 66
Hussein, Saddam, 295
Hutu: genocide and, 292; rape and, 125;
state violence and, 273
Hy-tex Marketing Company, 239

ideologies, 65, 71–72, 74, 372; definition,
71; individual conservativism, 74,
74–75; organic conservativism, 74,
74–75; reform corporate
liberal/feminism, 74, 84–85;
socialism/feminism, 74, 84–85
imperialism, 322–324, 326, 332–333,
348, 387; definition of, 323; European,

324–325; famine and, 350;
industrialization and, 324; religion
and, 176–177; between societies,
322–323; trash, 239; United States
and, 326; world debt and, 341–349
Incas, 66, 196
Index of Human Development, 333–334
India, 37, 53, 118, 180–181; dowry deaths,
114, 169; Punjab, 38–39; *suttee* and, 53,
169; women in, 31, 53, 114
indigenous populations, 30–32, 41, 73,
192–197, 237–238, 243, 251, 270–273,
275, 292–293, 304, 318, 320, 324–325,
350, 359, 362–364, 388; Ache, 272,
306; Arawak, 270–271; Asai, 338;
Australia and, 31; Brazil and, 271–272;
Buid, 115; clergy and, 196; Columbus,
Christopher, and, 31, 270–271;
exploitation of, 195; Guatemala and,
31; Kaypo, 252; !Kung, 115–116;
Matsoi, 38; Mexico and, 31;
Minamata, 249; Peru and, 31; San, 24;
Tainos, 270–271. *See also* Native
Americans; Yanomamo
individualist conservatism, 80–84;
capitalism and, 80; central values of,
82; class and, 80; competition and, 80;
entrepreneurs and, 80; freedom and,
82; free market, 81, 83; hierarchy and,
82; history of, 80; human nature and,
81; industry and, 80; inequality and,
82; petty bourgeoisie, 81;
publications, 81; society and, 81–82;
state and, 81–82; violence and, 83.
See also ideologies
inequality, viii, 40, 57, 111, 121, 371–382
institutional violence: definitions of,
28–30; education and, 30; family and,
30; institutions and, 29
International Labor Organization (ILO),
28, 42, 164, 223, 230
International Monetary Fund (IMF),
342–345, 348, 388
interpersonal violence, 99; bias and,
385; criminals and, viii; definition of,
23, 28; institutional, 33–34;
international, 41; media and, 69. *See
also* murder; rape

Iran, 39, 42, 67, 178–179; religious violence and, 175, 185; state violence and, 283
Iran Contra scandal, 63
Iraq, 42, 294
Islam. *See* religious violence
Israel, vii, 43, 269, 297

Japan, 37, 59–60; and comfort women, 125–126
Jefferson, Thomas, 176
Jews, 21, 54, 63–65, 293
jihad, 179. *See also* holy wars
Johnson, Lyndon, 20, 86
Jones, Jim. *See* religious violence
Judaism. *See* religious violence

Kepone, 245
Khmer Rouge, 274
King, Rodney, 265
Klinefelters Syndrome, 18
Koresh, David. *See* Branch Davidians
Ku Klux Klan, 33, 76, 355–356
Kuwait, 42, 66–67

labeling theory, 22
Latifundia system, 317
Latinos. *See* Hispanics
Lebanon, 1, 176
LeBaron Brothers, 199
legitimate versus illegitimate, 28, 39, 66, 69
Lehi case, 68
Libertarians, 81
Libya, 39, 43
life expectancies, 31, 41, 44, 316
Life Sciences Company, 245
Limbaugh, Rush, 77
Lincoln, Abraham, 34, 109
Lorenz, Konrad, 61
Love Canal, 232–233

Maquiladora plants, 242–243, 364
Marvi Buti, 118–119
Marvi Chule, 118–119
mass media: interpersonal violence and, 70; media violence, 55; reporting of crime, vii, 68–69; social order and, 73
Mayans, 276
McMartin Case, 67–68

MER 29, 212
mercury ethyl, 249
meritocracy, 88
methyl isocyanate, 246
Milgram experiments, 62–63
missionaries, 73, 192–198, 388; environmental violence and, 251; hierarchy and, 318; imperialism and, 350. *See also* indigenous populations; Native Americans; religious violence
Moctezuma II, 53
Monroe Doctrine, 331
Monsanto Company, 233–234
Mormons. *See* religious violence
Mortal Kombat, 56
Ms. Magazine, 132
Mukhtaran, 38–39
murder: age and, 101–102, *109, 113;* alcohol and, 107–108, 121; Australia and, 122; confrontational, 123–124; cultural differences and, 111–112; definition of, 99; disputes and, 120; domestic quarrels and, 120, 122; ethnic status and, 102–104; female infanticide and, 18; female labor force and, 114, 138, *115;* gangs and, 35, 57, 105; guns and, 103, 106–107; historical trends in, 108–111; inequality and, 111–121; intimates and, 120, 122; intimates versus stranger and, 100, 104–106; masculinity and, 122; patterns of, 121; Philadelphia and, 122, *122;* poverty and, 113–114; property and, 118–121; social class and, 104; statistics and, 99–101, 105, 110, 11, *113;* victimization and, 111; war and, 110
My Lai massacre, 63

Nader, Ralph, 219, 231
Nagasaki, 54
National Advisory Commission on Civil Disorders, 20
National Center for Health Statistics, 4
National Center on Child Abuse and Neglect, 165–166
National Commission on Product Safety, 207
National Highway Traffic Administration, 67

National Institute of Health (NIH), 301
National Institute of Occupational Safety and Health, 222
National Organization for Women (NOW), 86
Native Americans, 12, 30–31, 73, 178, 194–195, 197, 237–238, 270–271, 293, 306, 320; Chippewas, 271; Colonel Chivington, 306; Custer, George Armstrong, 178; environmental violence and, 30, 237–238; education and, 30; Eskimo, 118; Ghost Dance, 178, 195; Great Sioux Uprising, 178; Hopi Snake Dance, 195; income of, 30; Indian schools, 30; Lakota, 271; life expectancy of, 30; Pequot, 293; religious violence and, 192–193; 195–196; reservations, 195, 320; Sand Creek Massacre, 306; Sitting Bull, 178; state violence and, 270–271; Sun Dance, 195; Wounded Knee, 195. *See also* indigenous populations
Nazism, 21, 42, 51, 54, 169, 181–182, 293, 299; neo-Nazism, 34, 357; Order Police, 63–64; propaganda, 51, 64. *See also* Hitler, Adolph
Nestlé Corporation, 214
Newsweek (magazine), 86
New York Times, 217
Nicaragua, 35, 39, 42–43, 286
Night Trap, 56
North, Oliver, 63
North American Free Trade Agreement (NAFTA), 217, 389

O&G Corporation, 238
Office for Public Safety, 361–362
Oliver Twist (Dickens), 164
OMEGA 7, 285
Omnibus Trade and Competitive Act of 1988, 350
operant conditioning, 61
Operation Condor, 283
Operation Enduring Freedom, 39
Operation Phoenix, 282, 285
Operation Success, 363
order theory approach: cultural systems and, 9; definition of, 7; organismic analogy, 7–9; roots of, 18; social change and, 9; social order, 19; violence and, 16–17, *17,* 19–20. *See also* violence, sociological approach
organic conservative ideology, 75–80; American royalists and, 76; capitalism and, 79; central values of, 78; Christian paternalism and, 75, 77–79; class and, 76–78; democracy and, 78–79; economy and, 76; family and, 78; feudalism and, 75–76, 78–79; freedom and, 78; hierarchy and, 77–78; history of, 75–77; inequality and, 77; law and order, 78; nature of humans and, 77; patriarchy and, 76; publications, 77; religious fundamentalism and, 76; slavery and, 76; society and, 77, 79; South and, 76–77; U.S. Constitution and, 77; variants of, 76–77; violence and, 79–80. *See also* ideologies

Palestine, 35, 43, 175, 269, 316
parathion, 229
parents, 35, 383–384. *See also* child abuse; family violence
partner violence. *See* domestic violence
Pascal, Blaise, 175
patriarchy, 20, 38, 72, 86, 90, 126, 373–374, 382; family violence and, 154; hierarchy and, 319; structural violence and, 358
PCBs, 233–234
Pentagon, 1, 34, 175, 235–236, 299
Peru, 53, 196, 346
pesticides. *See* production violence
Philip Morris, 216–217
Phillip the Fair, 187–188
Pittston Corporation, 252
plutonium, 301
Pope Innocent III, 186
Pope John Paul II, 192
Pope Urban II, 177
popular music, 56
positivism, 88–89
poverty, 31, 44, 68, 345, 388
production violence, 372: cotton and coal dust, 227–228; definition of, 22; mining accidents and, 228; occupational disease and, 223–224;

pesticides and, 208–209, 228–229, 364; statistics, 222–223, 229; textile mills and, 228; Third World and, 223–224, 228–229
product violence, 207–222; apples and, 210; automobile industry and, 218–221; bottled water and, 215; capitalism and, 214; chocolate and, 210; coffee beans and, 209; definition of, 207; food industry and, 212–215; herbicides and, 221; illegal aliens and, 227; infant formula and, 214; pharmaceutical industry and, 211–212; product dumping, 207–211; research industry and, 221–222; safety testing, 221; statistics, 207; Third World and, 207, 214; women and, 210–211, 214. *See also* tobacco
Protestantism. *See* religious violence

Qaddafi, Muammar, 294–295
Quaker Oats Company, 301

racism, 26, 31, 64, 270, 324, 355; institutionalized, 12–13, 26–27
radiation experiments, 202, 300–302
rape, 1, 26, 31–32, 35, 38–39, 41, 56, 65, 124–140, 148, 175, 372, 377–378; age and, 130; and Boston, Mass., 131; Cambodia and, 126; class and, 131; colleges and, 128, 130, 132; date, 135–136, 138–139; definition of, 126, 138; ethnic status and, 130–131; gender inequality and, 136–138; hate crimes and, 357; historical trends of, 125–127, 133–34; inequality and, 136–140; intimates and, 132; law enforcement and, 139; legal views of, in U.S., 127; marital, 127, 130–136, 138–139; media and, 124–125; military and, 125; motives and, 134–136; patriarchy and, 133, 135–139; pattern of, 134; Philadelphia and, 131; power and control and, 129; prostitution and, 126; psychopathology and, 134–136; racism and, 140; relationships and, 132–133; reporting of, 132–134; sexism and, 140; statutory, 126, 129; Thailand and, 126;

types of, 134; United States and, 127, 134, 138; World War II and, 125–126
Raymond of Aquilers, 177–178
Readers Digest, 77, 215
Reagan, Ronald, 34, 286, 294, 343, 349–350
reality shows, 69
recognition of forms of violence, 372–373
redlining, 26
reduccion system, 194–195
reform corporate liberal/feminism, 85–89; capitalism and, 85; class and, 85; economy and, 85; freedom and, 88; history of, 85–86; human nature and, 86; inequality and, 87; monopolies and, 85; political process and, 87–88; publications, 86; society and, 87–88; violence and, 88–89; women's movement, 86. *See also* ideologies
religious violence: anti-Semitism and, 64; Bahais, 175; in Christianity, Islam, and Judaism, 181, 186; Church of the First Born of the Fullness of Time and, 199; Church of Jesus Christ of Latter-Day Saints and, 68, 197, 199, 186; clergy and, 189–191; crusades, 177–178, 180; cults, 198–200; cultural genocide and, 193–196; deprogramming and, 200; economic vehicles of,194–195; and Eliot, John, 192, 194–195; fur trading companies and, 195; Hare Krishnas and, 199; Heaven's Gate and, 184; hierarchical versus congregational groups and, 191; Hinduism and, 179–180; inequality and, 176; Irish Catholic immigrants and, 185–186; Islam and, 179–180; Jewish congregations and, 190; Jones, Jim, 182; Knights Templer and, 187–188; messiahs and, 187; missionaries and, 41, 192–194, 197; Muslim fundamentalism, 175; Nation of Islam and, 200; Old Believers and, 182–183; Order of the Solar Temple and, 184; persecution of heretics and, 185–189; prophets and, 178; Protestantism and, 190, 195, 197; Puritans and, 185,

194–195; Quakers and, 185; religious zealots and, 181–183; Reorganized Church of Latter-Day Saints and, 199; Roman Catholic Church and, 189–190; Russian Orthodox Church and, 182; and Salem, Massachusetts, 188–189; Saracens and, 177; Satanism and, 187–189; and Serra, Junipero, 192–195; and Servants of the Paraclete at Jemez Springs, New Mexico, 190; Shakers and, 185; South Asia and, 179; Spanish Inquisition and, 186–187; theology and, 180–185; and Torquemada, Tomas de, 186; war and, 176–180; and The Way, 199; witches and, 187–188; youth and, 184, 190; zipper factor and, 190. *See also* missionaries

reporters and official views of crime, 68
Reserve Mining Company, 249–250
Richardson Merrell Company, 211–212
Richard the Lion-Hearted, 178
riots, 20, 33, 377: Cincinnati, 265; Liberty City, 265; Los Angeles, 265, 315; race, 32–33, 40
R. J. Reynolds, 216
roles and violence, 3–4, 49, 63, 65, 67–68
Roman Catholic Church. *See* religious violence
Roman Catholicism. *See* religious violence
Rousseau, Jean Jacques, 82
Rwanda, vii, 25, 267; genocide and, 292; state violence and, 273
Russia, 63, 269, 296

Sadat, Anwar, 34
Safe Drinking Water Act, 225
Safetyforum Research, 236–237
Sandinistas, 35, 286
sanitation, 338
Saturday Evening Post, 77
School of the Americas (SOA), 288, 299
school shootings, 30, 54. *See also* Columbine High School
September 11, 2001, vii, 25, 175, 286, 381
Serbia, 125, 269, 273
Shakespeare, William, 53
Shell Oil Company, 208
SIM-POC, 230

slavery. *See* African Americans
Smith, William Kennedy, 125
social control by police, 375–376
socialism, 89–90
socialist feminist ideology, 89–93; capitalism and, 91–92; hierarchy and, 91, 93; history, 89–90; human nature and, 90; inequality and, 91, 92; patriarchy and, 91–92; production and reproduction, 91–92; society and, 91–92; violence and, 92–93. *See also* ideologies
Society for the Prevention of Cruelty to Animals, 150
Society for the Prevention of Cruelty to Children, 150
solutions to problems of violence, 380–381
Son My village, 63
sorcerer killings, 116–118
South Africa, 15, 21, 27, 33–34, 42, 139, 273, 277–279, 320–322, 383; assassinations, 296; prison inmates, 376; private groups, 288–289. *See also* apartheid
spheres of violence, 28, *29, 33,* 384
sports violence, 56
spousal abuse, 154–162. *See also* domestic violence
Standard Fruit, 208
state violence, 21–22, 35; accidental killings and, 295; agents of, 278–289; Albanians and, 269, 273; assassination and, 280, 282–283, 294–297; black jacketing, 302–303; blowback, 286–287; Burma (Myanmar) and, 268; businesses and, 277; Chicago Police Department and, 298; children forced into military and, 277–278; Cocoran State prison and, 268; Columbus, Christopher, and, 292–293; conditions for, 304–308; creation of dissent and, 302–303; Cuba and, 285; defining the victim and, 65, 306; definition of, 261–262; dissident political groups and, 273–276; diversity and, 305; drug war in Colombia, 280; El Salvador and, 288; experimentation on populations

and, 299–302; extent of, 261, 265–270; extrajudicial executions and, 267, 269; Indonesia and, 268, 273–274; inequality and, 305; Kosovo and, 269; mass slaughter and, 54, 274–275; military and, 265, 280–281, 297, 305; Montana State Penitentiary and, 298; Nigeria and, 306; organ transplants and executions and, 265; patterns of, 304–308; Peoples Republic of China and, 268; police and, 265, 282–283, 290; private groups and, 283–289; purposes of, 263; Slacker and Palmer raids and; Sri Lanka and, 272; superpowers and, 290, 305, 307; terrorism and, 34–35, 42–43, 48, 262, 283, 287, 297–299, 305–306; Third World and, 267, 291; torture and, 298; Turkey and, 269; Tutsi and, 273; types of, 289–304; Uganda and, 279; Venezuela and, 268; Vietnam and, 63, 282, 285; Yugoslavia and, 269. *See also* capital punishment; death squads; genocide; radiation experiments; riots; world debt

Stepan Chemical, 243
stereotypes, 68–69
Stoller Chemical Corporation, 239
structural violence: definition of, 31, 316; dependent capitalist development, 326–328, 341–342; foreign investment and, 344; human development and, 333–337, *335–336;* income and, 334, 337; inequality and, 322, 374; institutional, 23, 32, 34, 357–358; international, 41–42; interpersonal structural violence, 32–33, 34; Latin America and, 317, 328, 331; life chances and, 316, 321–322, 337; malnutrition and, 323, 349; media and, 69; morbidity and mortality and, 31, 37, 41, 316, 337–340, 348, 375, 378; multinational corporations and, 317–318, 323, 327, 329–330; outcome of, 333; Pax Americana, 326; Pax Britannia, 325; poor and, 339; South and Central America and, 318; Sub–Saharan Africa and, 339, 347;

weaponry and, 328, 339. *See also* famine; hate crimes; imperialism
sulfur trioxide, 245
Summer Institute of Linguistics, 197
survivalist groups, 182
symbols and violence, 30, 50–51; art, 51; hand gestures, 50–51

Taliban, 175, 286. *See also* Al Qaeda
Tasaday, 48–49
taxes and income levels, 381–382
Texaco, 243
thalidomide, 212
Third World: capital flows and, 327; cause of rising conflict in, 290; dependent economic development, 326, 330; economic aid to, 291, 362; environmental violence and, 239, 242; industries seeking cheaper labor, 15–16; war violence and, 289–290; world debt, 291, 241, 343–344
Thuggee cult, 180
Tiananmen Square, 1, 25
thugs, origin of name, 180
Time Magazine, 86, 230
tobacco, 215–218; Africa and, 217; Eastern Europe and, 217; expansion oversees, 216; hazards, 215; industry, 215– 216; Joe Camel and, 216; Latin America and, 217; minority populations and, 216; People's Republic of China and, 217; Third World and, 217; United States as industry ally, 216; youth and, 216–217
Tommy the Traveler Tongyai, 304
tricholorophenol, 232
Tsar Nicolas II, 34
tuberculosis, 340
Tuskegee Syphilis Experiment, 299–300

Union Carbide, 246–247
United Mine Workers, 227
United Slaves Organization (USO), 302
United States, 39, 41–43, 108; arms supplier, 290; assassinations and, 294; chain of violence and, 386; colonies and religious violence, 185; corporations, 327–328; dependent

economic development and, 327, 330–331; extrajudicial executions, 265; family violence and, 169; famine and, 349, 353–354; fringe groups and, 198; frontier tradition of violence, 57–59; Guatemala and, 388; homicide and, 112; Japan and, 59–60; literature and violence, 58–59; mercenaries and, 286; police/terrorist training and, 283, 287–288, 361–362; prison population, 376, 382; segregation and, 320; state violence and, 276–277, 281– 282, 307–308; structural violence and, 331; Sub-Saharan Africa and, 39; torture and, 298–299; toxic dumping violations, 235–237; world debt and, 343, 349

U.S. Bureau of Alcohol, Tobacco, and Firearms, 183–184

U.S. Department of Health and Human Services, 165–166, 226

U.S. News and World Report, 81

Velsicol Chemical Company, 208

victimization and perpetrators, 61, 100–103, 376, 386

video games, 56

vinyl chloride, 225–226

violence: causes of, 2–5, 41, 60–61; chain of, 40–41, *40;* contexts of, 39–40; definition of, 21, 23–28; hierarchy and, 36–37; history of, 57–59; international causal chain, 43–44, *43;* internationalization and, 41–42; learning of, 37–38, 49, 61; motives for, 121–124; patterns of, 4–5, 7, 20, 71; power and, 35; reproduction and production, 15; social structures and, 35–39, 42–43; as unitary phenomenon, 5–7

violence, sociological approach to, ix, 2–5, 20–21, 45, 57; conflict theory, 7; order theory, 7. *See also individual headings*

Voting Rights Act of 1965, 13

Wall Street Journal, 81

war, 289–291

war on terrorism, 294

Washington Post, 233

Waste Tech Incorporated, 237

Wicca. *See* religious violence

Wild Bill Hickok, 59

witchcraft. *See* religious violence

women, 31, 62, 375; colonial Mexico, 119; fear of violence, 137; hierarchy and, 319; homicide and, 122–123; human development and, 337; intimate partner violence, 106; learning to be victim, 66; maternal mortality, 337, 345; media violence, 55; rape and, 128, 136, 139; witchhunts, 88; workforce, 16

women's movement, 15, 54, 65, 86

wife beating. *See* domestic violence

working class, 13, 31, 44, 73, 318, 321, 381; capitalism and, 72; environmental violence and, 234; workplace hazards, 32, 223

World Bank, 243, 331, 341–348, 388

World Court International Court of Justice, 28, 42, 286, 307

world debt, 341–349; corruption and, 341; default, 343, 345; Dominican Republic and, 345; infant mortality, 347; Jamaica and, 345; multinational corporations and, 343; Nigeria and, 341–342; Philippines and, 341; returns on, 343–344

World Health Assembly, 214–215

World Health Organization (WHO), 42, 112, 214–215, 217, 340,

World Trade Center, vii, 1, 34, 54, 175, 265, 286

Wyatt Earp, 59

Wyclife Bible Translators, 197

Yanomamo, 3, 18, 27, 51–52, 125

youth, 31, 101–102, 139; abuse and, 149; guns and, 106; inequality and, 383–384; murder and, 103; religious violence and, 188. *See also* family violence, child abuse, children

About the Authors

Peter Iadicola is professor of sociology at the joint campus of Indiana and Purdue Universities in Fort Wayne. He received his doctorate from the University of California, Riverside. His research specialties include the study of violence, crime and delinquency, political economy, and applied sociology. He is the author of two books, several research reports, and more than twenty articles. His current interest is in research on the effectiveness of interventions to reduce violence in the world.

Anson Shupe is professor of sociology at the joint campus of Indiana and Purdue Universities in Fort Wayne. He received his doctorate from Indiana University, Bloomington. His research specialties include the study of violence, deviance, religion, and social psychology. He is the author of more than two dozen monographs and edited volumes. He is currently researching clergy misconduct across a diverse array of religions, seeking to combine the sociology of religion and criminology.